THE INCREDIBLE
HULK
PLANET HULK

P9-CDO-980

HULK: PLANET HULK. Contains material originally published in magazine form as INCREDIBLE HULK #92-105, GIANT-SIZE HULK #1, AMAZING FANTASY #15 and PLANET HULK: GLADIATOR GUIDEBOOK. Ninth printing 2016. ISBN# 978-0-7851-2012-4. Published by MARVEL WORLDWIDE, INC., a subsidiary of MARVEL ENTERTAINMENT, LLC. OFFICE OF PUBLICATION: 135 West 50th Street, New York, NY 10020. Copyright © 2008 MARVEL No similarity between any of the names, characters, persons, and/or institutions in this magazine with those of any living or dead person or institution is intended, and any such similarity which may exist is purely coincidental. **Printed in Canada.** ALAN FINE, President, Marvel Entertainment; DAN BUCKLEY, President, TV, Publishing & Brand Management; JOE QUESADA, Chief Creative Officer; TOM BREVOORT, SVP of Publishing; DAVID BOGART, SVP of Business Affairs & Operations, Publishing & Partnership; C.B. CEBULSKI, VP of Brand Management & Development, Asia: DAVID GABRIEL, SVP of Sales & Marketing, Publishing; JEFF YOUNGQUIST, VP of Production & Special Projects; DAN CARR, Executive Director of Publishing Technology; ALEX MORALES, Director of Publishing Operations; SUSAN CRESPI, Production Manager; STAN LEE, Chairman Emeritus. For information regarding advertising in Marvel Comics or on Marvel.com, please contact Vit DeBellis, Integrated Sales Manager, at vdebellis@marvel.com. For Marvel subscription inquiries, please call 888-511-5480. **Manufactured between 2/24/2016 and 3/28/2016 by SOLISCO PRINTERS, SCOTT, QC, CANADA.**

PLANET HULK

WRITER: Greg Pak

EXILE

PENCILERS: Carlo Pagulayan with Michael Avon Oeming, Alex Niño & Marshall Rogers
INKERS: Jeffrey Huet with Mike Allred, Alex Niño & Tom Palmer

BANNER WAR

PENCILER: Aaron Lopresti
INKER: Danny Miki

ANARCHY

PENCILER: Aaron Lopresti
INKERS: Danny Miki & Sandu Florea

ALLEGIANCE

PENCILERS: Carlo Pagulayan & Aaron Lopresti with Gary Frank
INKERS: Jeffrey Huet & Sandu Florea with Jon Sibal

ARMAGEDDON

PENCILER: Carlo Pagulayan
INKER: Jeffrey Huet

COLORISTS: Chris Sotomayor with Laura Martin & Lovern Kindzierski
LETTERER: VC's Randy Gentile
COVER ARTISTS: Ladrönn, Bryan Hitch & Michael Turner
ASSISTANT EDITOR: Nathan Cosby
EDITOR: Mark Paniccia

MASTERMIND EXCELLO

WRITER: Greg Pak
ARTIST: Takeshi Miyazawa
COLORIST: Christina Strain
LETTERER: Artmonkeys' Dave Lanphear
ASSISTANT EDITOR: Nathan Cosby
EDITOR: Mark Paniccia

PLANET CHO

WRITER: Greg Pak
PENCILER: Gary Frank
INKER: Jon Sibal
COLORIST: Chris Sotomayor
LETTERER: VC's Randy Gentile
ASSISTANT EDITOR: Nathan Cosby
EDITOR: Mark Paniccia

Hulk created by Stan Lee & Jack Kirby

COLLECTION EDITOR: Mark D. Beazley
ASSOCIATE EDITOR: Sarah Brunstad
ASSOCIATE MANAGER, DIGITAL ASSETS: Joe Hochstein
ASSOCIATE MANAGING EDITOR: Alex Starbuck
EDITOR, SPECIAL PROJECTS: Jennifer Grünwald
VP, PRODUCTION & SPECIAL PROJECTS: Jeff Youngquist
SVP PRINT, SALES & MARKETING: David Gabriel
BOOK DESIGNER: Patrick McGrath

EDITOR IN CHIEF: Axel Alonso
CHIEF CREATIVE OFFICER: Joe Quesada
PUBLISHER: Dan Buckley
EXECUTIVE PRODUCER: Alan Fine

PREVIOUSLY...

Bruce Banner has long feared the potential of his alter ego, the Incredible Hulk, to become Earth's most dangerous monster. So when he saw the chance to put the Hulk's strength to positive use, Banner accepted a mission from S.H.I.E.L.D. to save the world by destroying an artificially intelligent satellite gone rogue. But when the mission was complete, the Hulk learned that a group of Marvel heroes including Reed Richards, Iron Man, Dr. Strange, and Black Bolt, had created a plan to extricate him from the Earth, sending him to an idyllic uninhabited planet where, Reed promised, "There will be no one there to hurt you. And no one you can hurt."

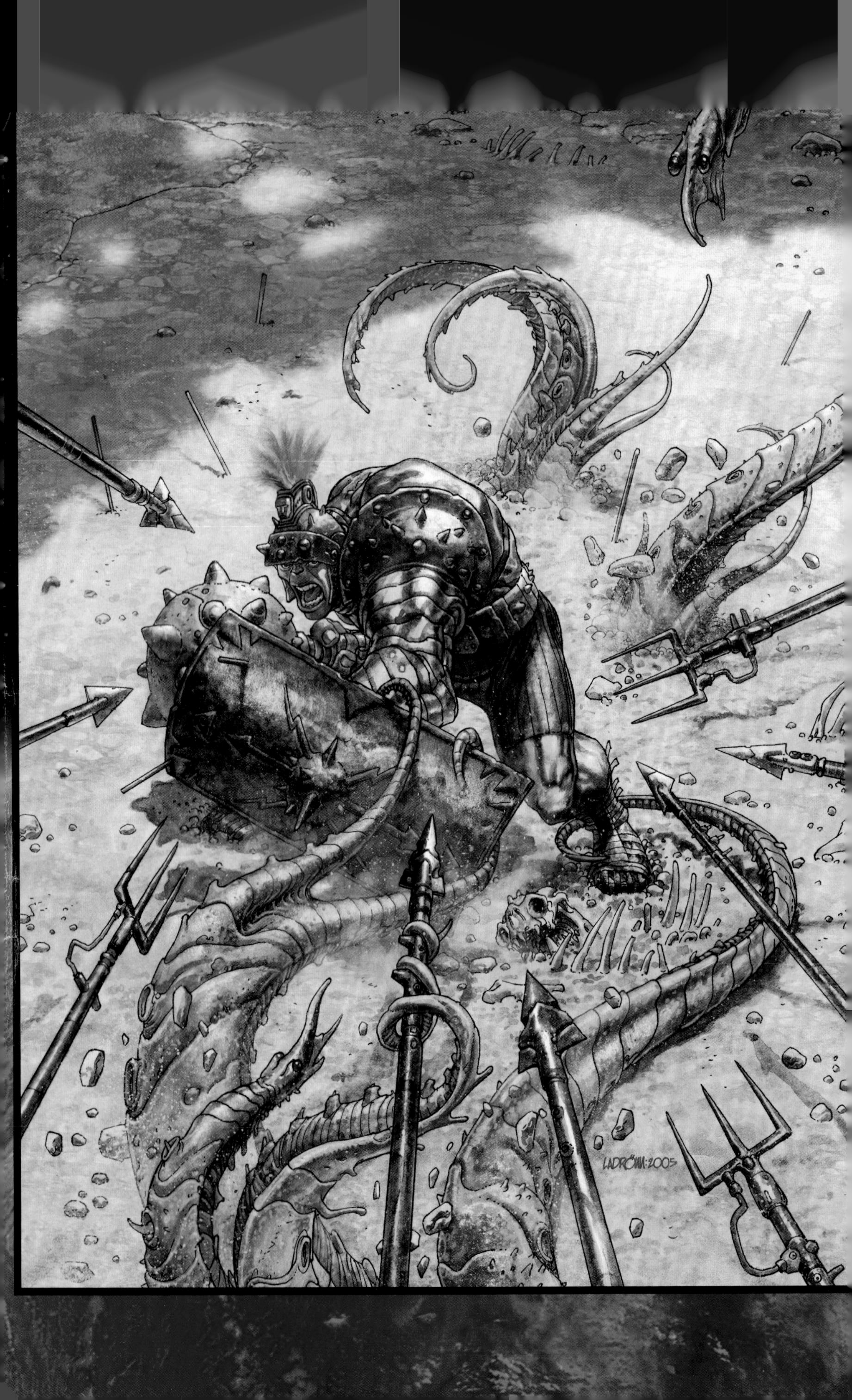
LADRÖNN:2005

92 VARIANT

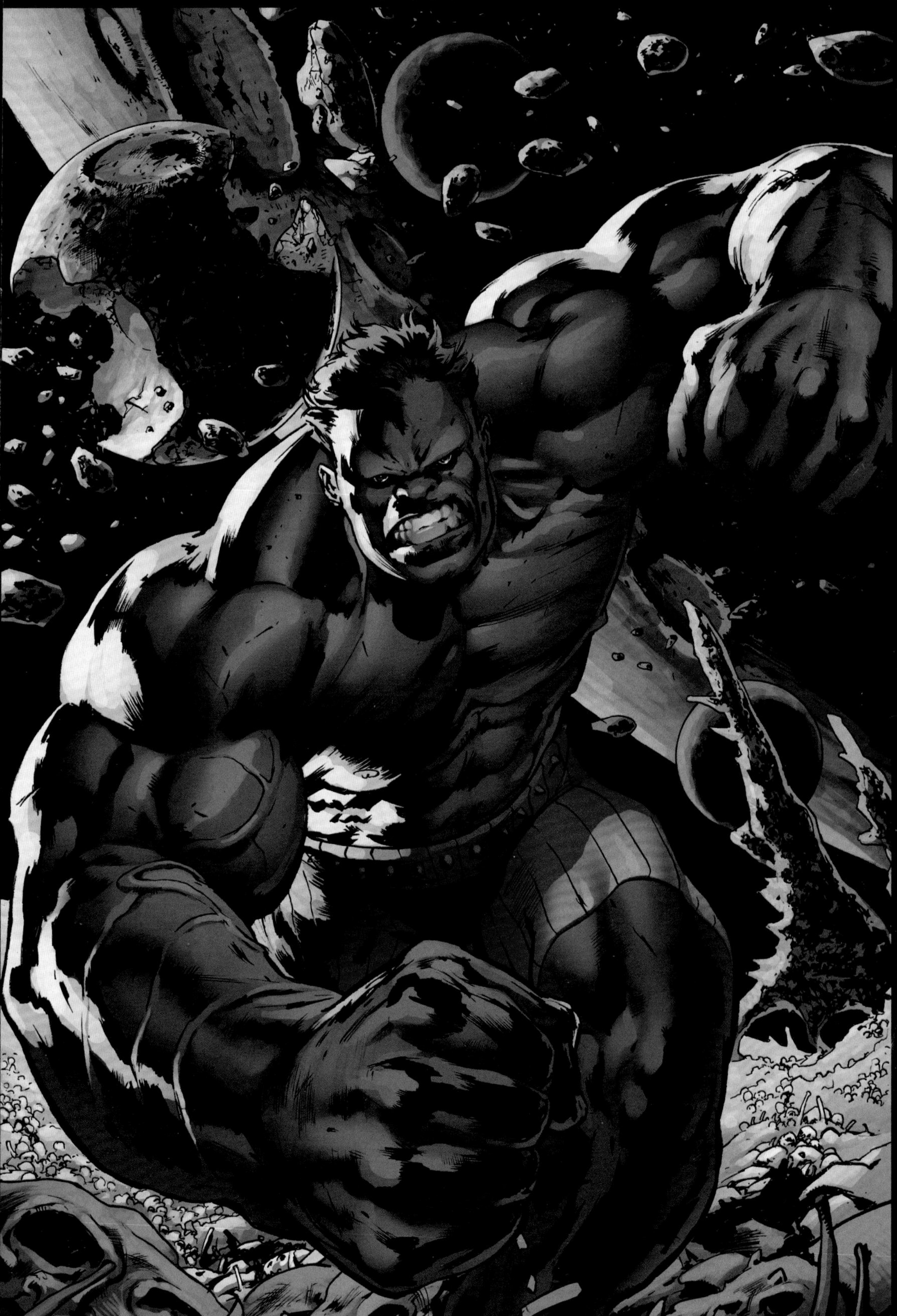

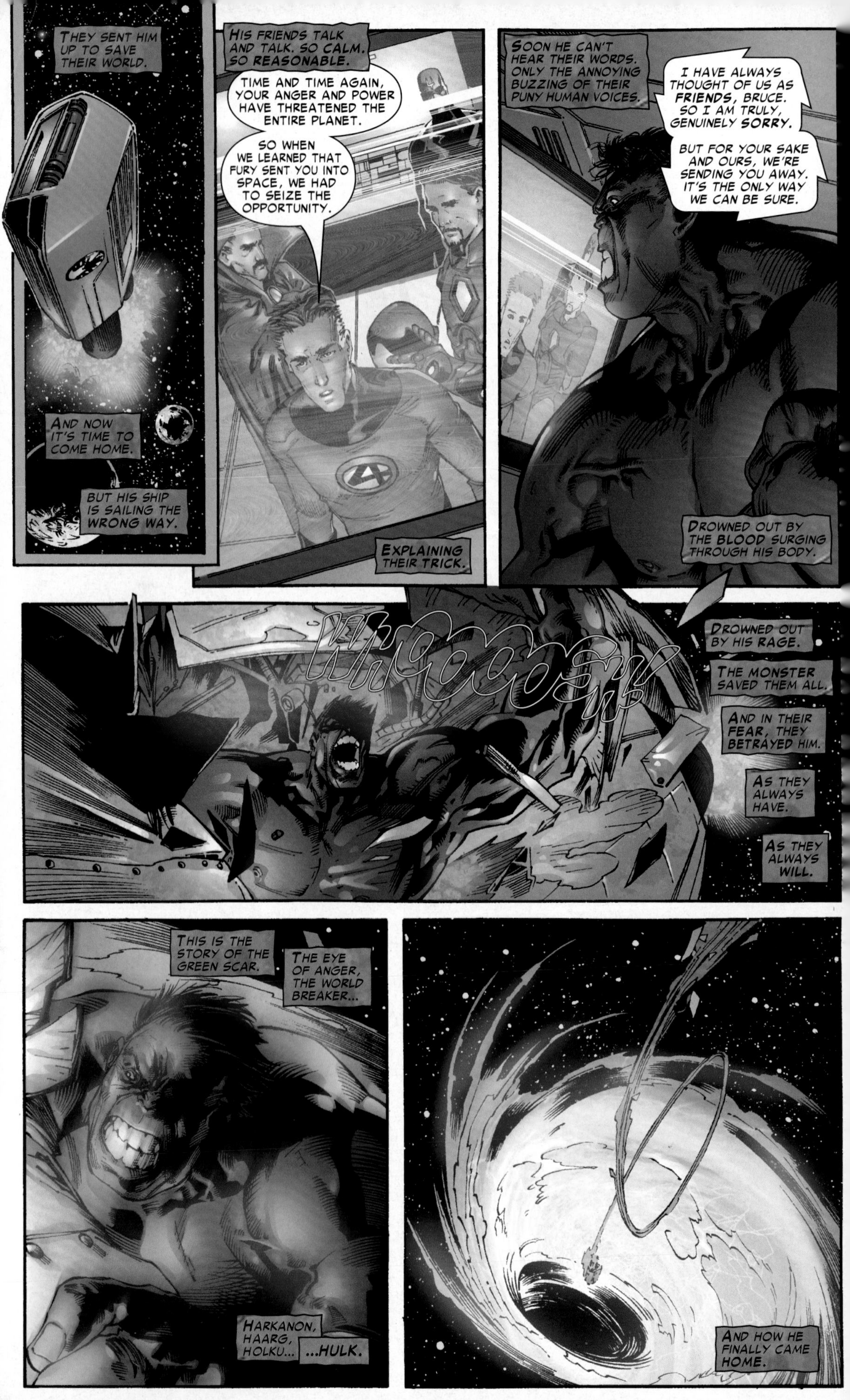

THEY SENT HIM UP TO SAVE THEIR WORLD.
AND NOW IT'S TIME TO COME HOME.
BUT HIS SHIP IS SAILING THE WRONG WAY.
HIS FRIENDS TALK AND TALK. SO CALM. SO REASONABLE.
TIME AND TIME AGAIN, YOUR ANGER AND POWER HAVE THREATENED THE ENTIRE PLANET.
SO WHEN WE LEARNED THAT FURY SENT YOU INTO SPACE, WE HAD TO SEIZE THE OPPORTUNITY.
EXPLAINING THEIR TRICK.
SOON HE CAN'T HEAR THEIR WORDS. ONLY THE ANNOYING BUZZING OF THEIR PUNY HUMAN VOICES.
I HAVE ALWAYS THOUGHT OF US AS FRIENDS, BRUCE. SO I AM TRULY, GENUINELY SORRY.
BUT FOR YOUR SAKE AND OURS, WE'RE SENDING YOU AWAY. IT'S THE ONLY WAY WE CAN BE SURE.
DROWNED OUT BY THE BLOOD SURGING THROUGH HIS BODY.
WHOOOOSH
DROWNED OUT BY HIS RAGE.
THE MONSTER SAVED THEM ALL.
AND IN THEIR FEAR, THEY BETRAYED HIM.
AS THEY ALWAYS HAVE.
AS THEY ALWAYS WILL.
THIS IS THE STORY OF THE GREEN SCAR.
THE EYE OF ANGER, THE WORLD BREAKER...
HARKANON, HAARG, HOLKU...
...HULK.
AND HOW HE FINALLY CAME HOME.

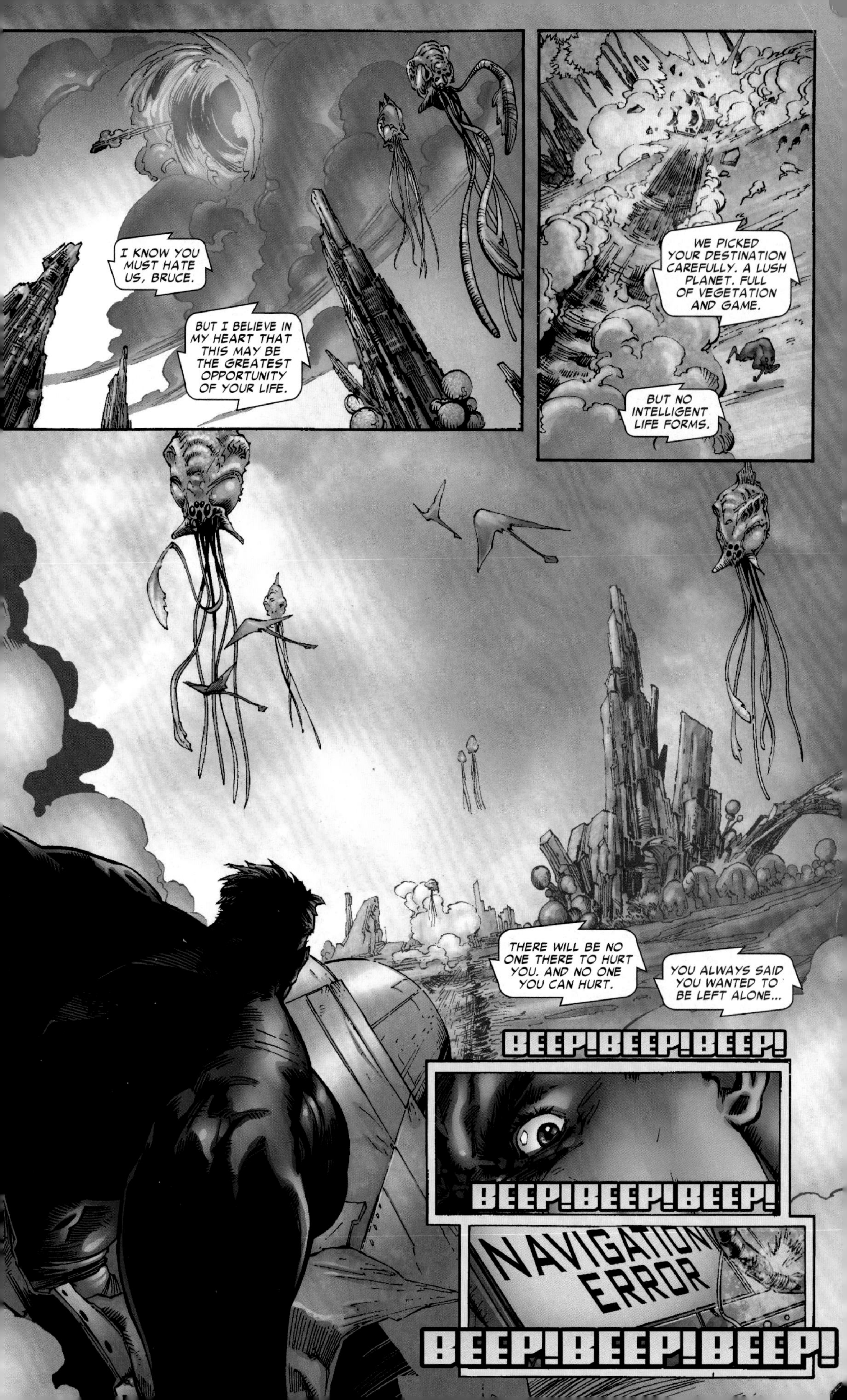
I KNOW YOU MUST HATE US, BRUCE.
BUT I BELIEVE IN MY HEART THAT THIS MAY BE THE GREATEST OPPORTUNITY OF YOUR LIFE.
WE PICKED YOUR DESTINATION CAREFULLY. A LUSH PLANET. FULL OF VEGETATION AND GAME.
BUT NO INTELLIGENT LIFE FORMS.
THERE WILL BE NO ONE THERE TO HURT YOU. AND NO ONE YOU CAN HURT.
YOU ALWAYS SAID YOU WANTED TO BE LEFT ALONE...
BEEP! BEEP! BEEP!
BEEP! BEEP! BEEP!
NAVIGATION ERROR
BEEP! BEEP! BEEP!

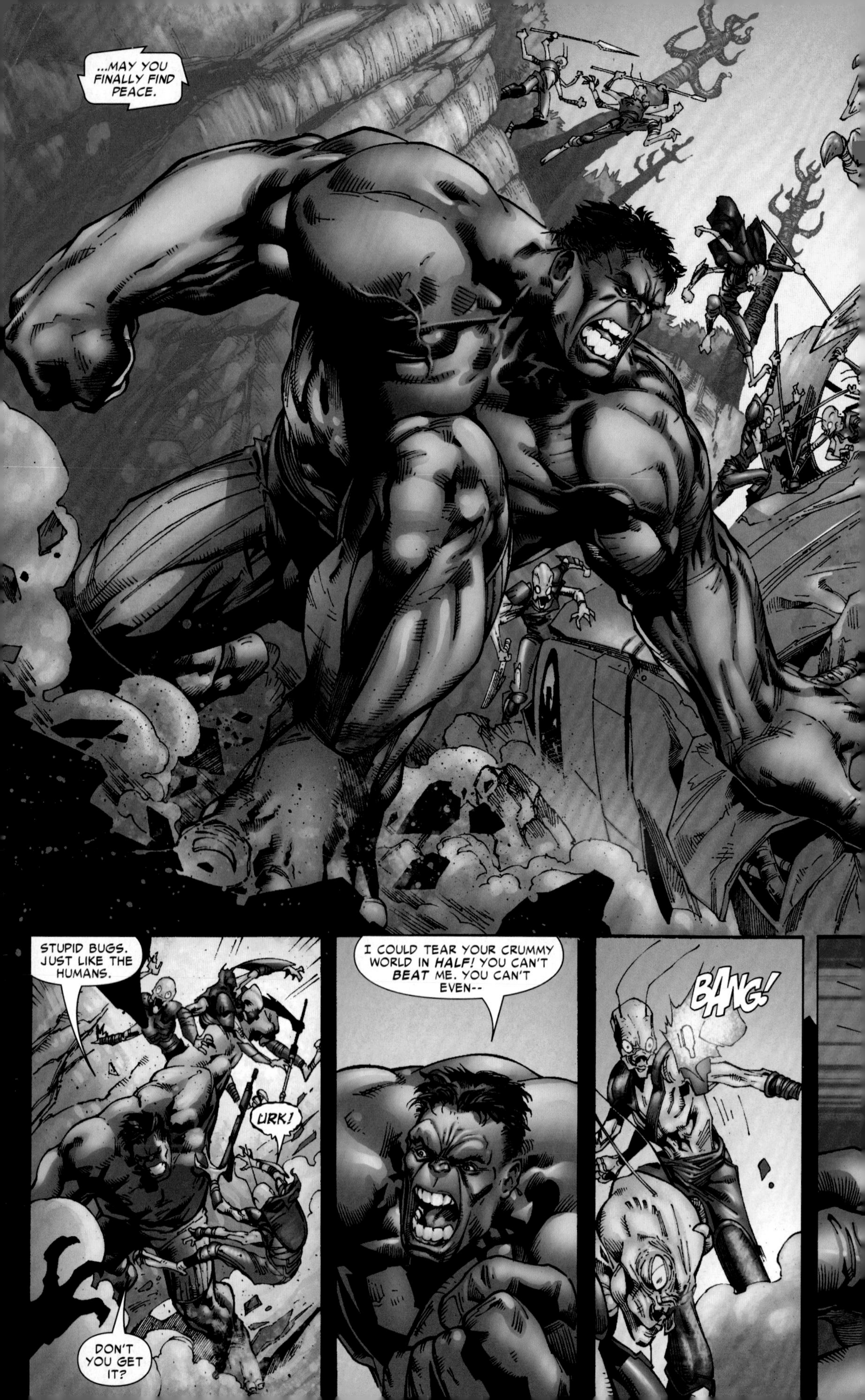
...MAY YOU FINALLY FIND PEACE.
STUPID BUGS. JUST LIKE THE HUMANS.
URK!
DON'T YOU GET IT?
I COULD TEAR YOUR CRUMMY WORLD IN HALF! YOU CAN'T BEAT ME. YOU CAN'T EVEN--
BANG!

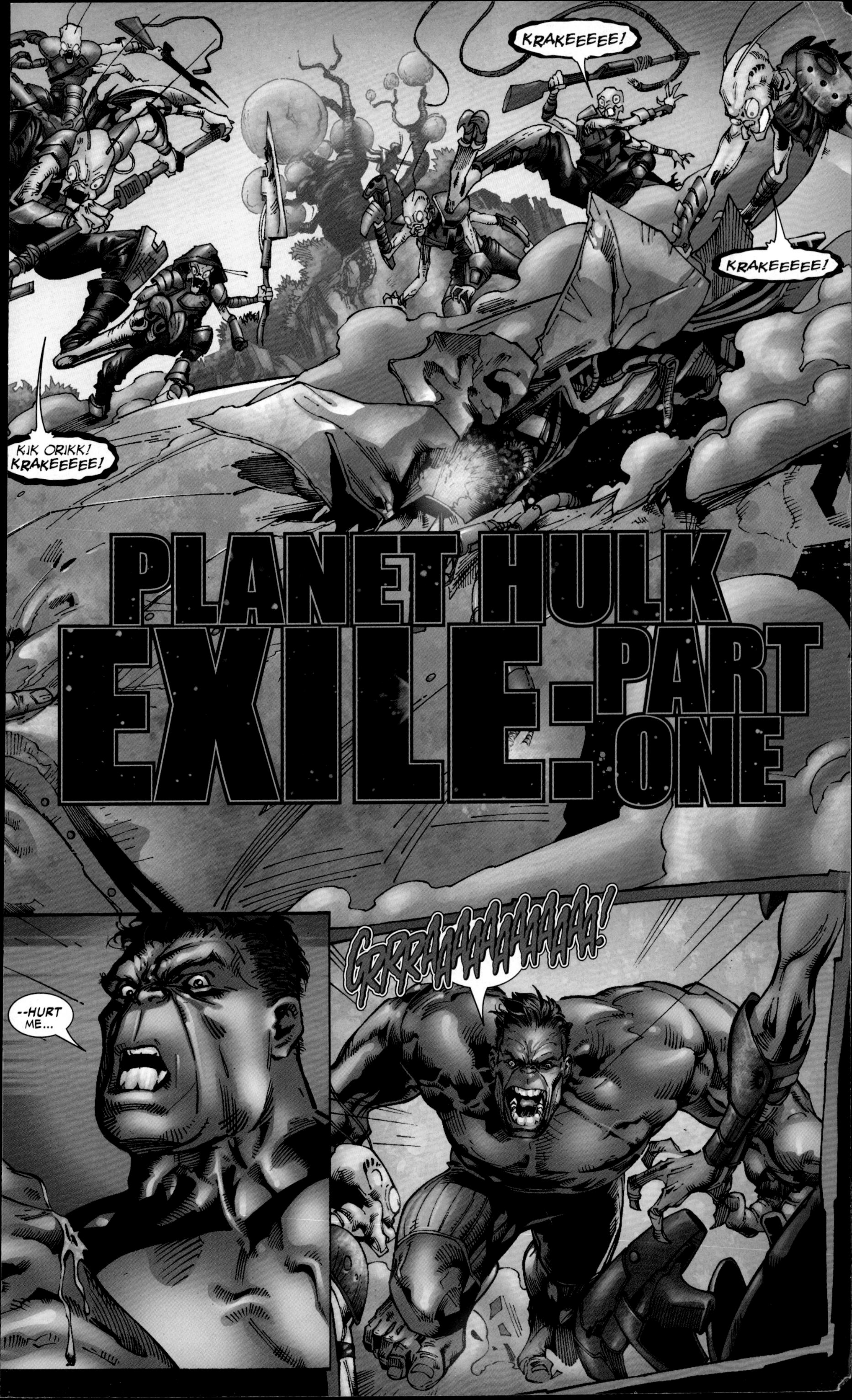

KRAKEEEEE!
KRAKEEEEE!
KIK ORIKK! KRAKEEEEE!
PLANET HULK
EXILE: PART ONE
--HURT ME...
GRRRAAAAAAAAAAA!

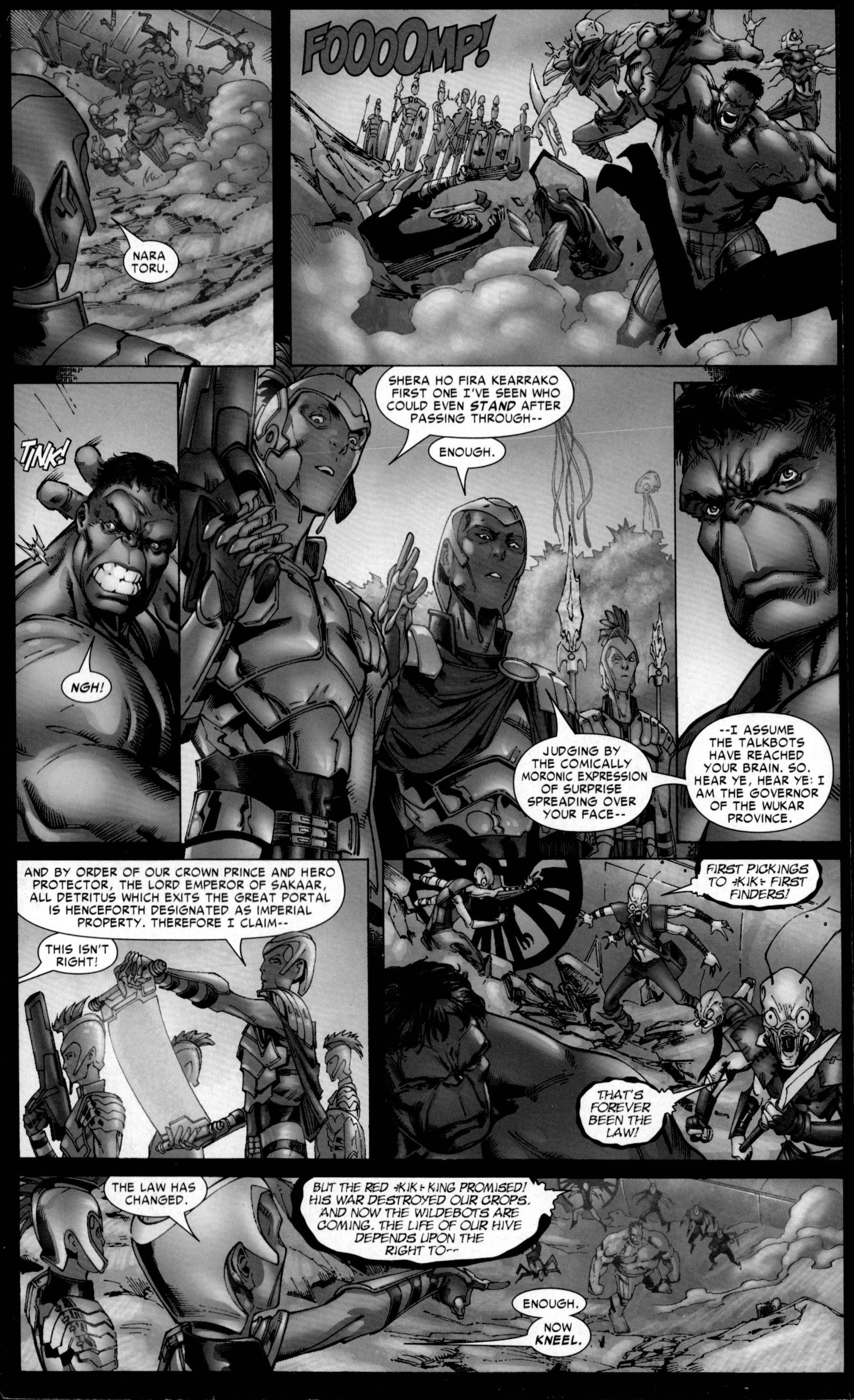
NARA TORU.
FOOOOMP!
SHERA HO FIRA KEARRAKO FIRST ONE I'VE SEEN WHO COULD EVEN STAND AFTER PASSING THROUGH--
ENOUGH.
TINK!
NGH!
JUDGING BY THE COMICALLY MORONIC EXPRESSION OF SURPRISE SPREADING OVER YOUR FACE--
--I ASSUME THE TALKBOTS HAVE REACHED YOUR BRAIN. SO. HEAR YE, HEAR YE: I AM THE GOVERNOR OF THE WUKAR PROVINCE.
AND BY ORDER OF OUR CROWN PRINCE AND HERO PROTECTOR, THE LORD EMPEROR OF SAKAAR, ALL DETRITUS WHICH EXITS THE GREAT PORTAL IS HENCEFORTH DESIGNATED AS IMPERIAL PROPERTY. THEREFORE I CLAIM--
THIS ISN'T RIGHT!
FIRST PICKINGS TO KIK FIRST FINDERS!
THAT'S FOREVER BEEN THE LAW!
THE LAW HAS CHANGED.
BUT THE RED KIK KING PROMISED! HIS WAR DESTROYED OUR CROPS. AND NOW THE WILDEBOTS ARE COMING. THE LIFE OF OUR HIVE DEPENDS UPON THE RIGHT TO--
ENOUGH.
NOW KNEEL.

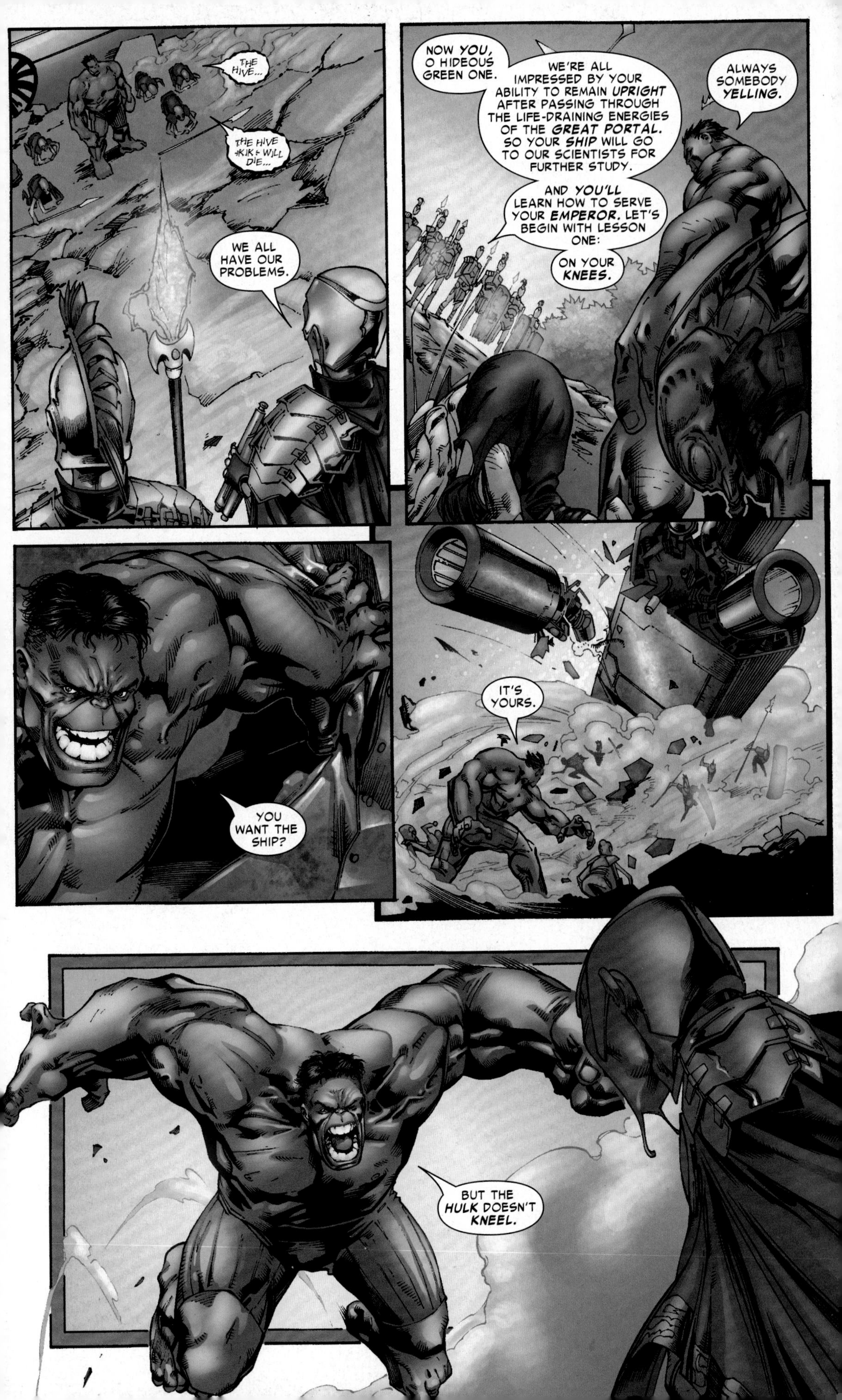
THE HIVE...
THE HIVE +KIK+ WILL DIE...
WE ALL HAVE OUR PROBLEMS.
NOW YOU, O HIDEOUS GREEN ONE.
WE'RE ALL IMPRESSED BY YOUR ABILITY TO REMAIN UPRIGHT AFTER PASSING THROUGH THE LIFE-DRAINING ENERGIES OF THE GREAT PORTAL. SO YOUR SHIP WILL GO TO OUR SCIENTISTS FOR FURTHER STUDY.
AND YOU'LL LEARN HOW TO SERVE YOUR EMPEROR. LET'S BEGIN WITH LESSON ONE:
ON YOUR KNEES.
ALWAYS SOMEBODY YELLING.
YOU WANT THE SHIP?
IT'S YOURS.
BUT THE HULK DOESN'T KNEEL.

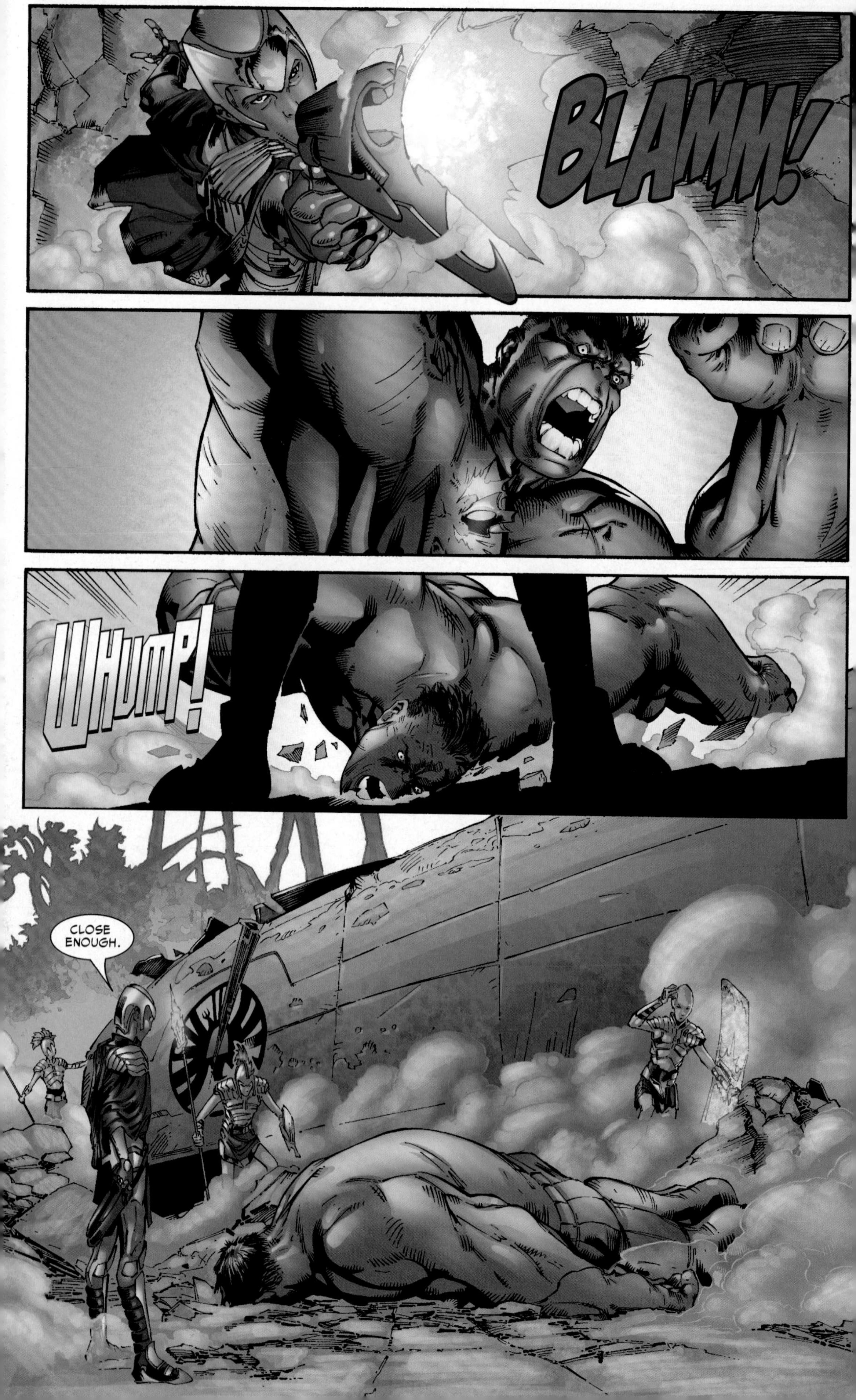

BLAMM!
WHUMP!
CLOSE ENOUGH.

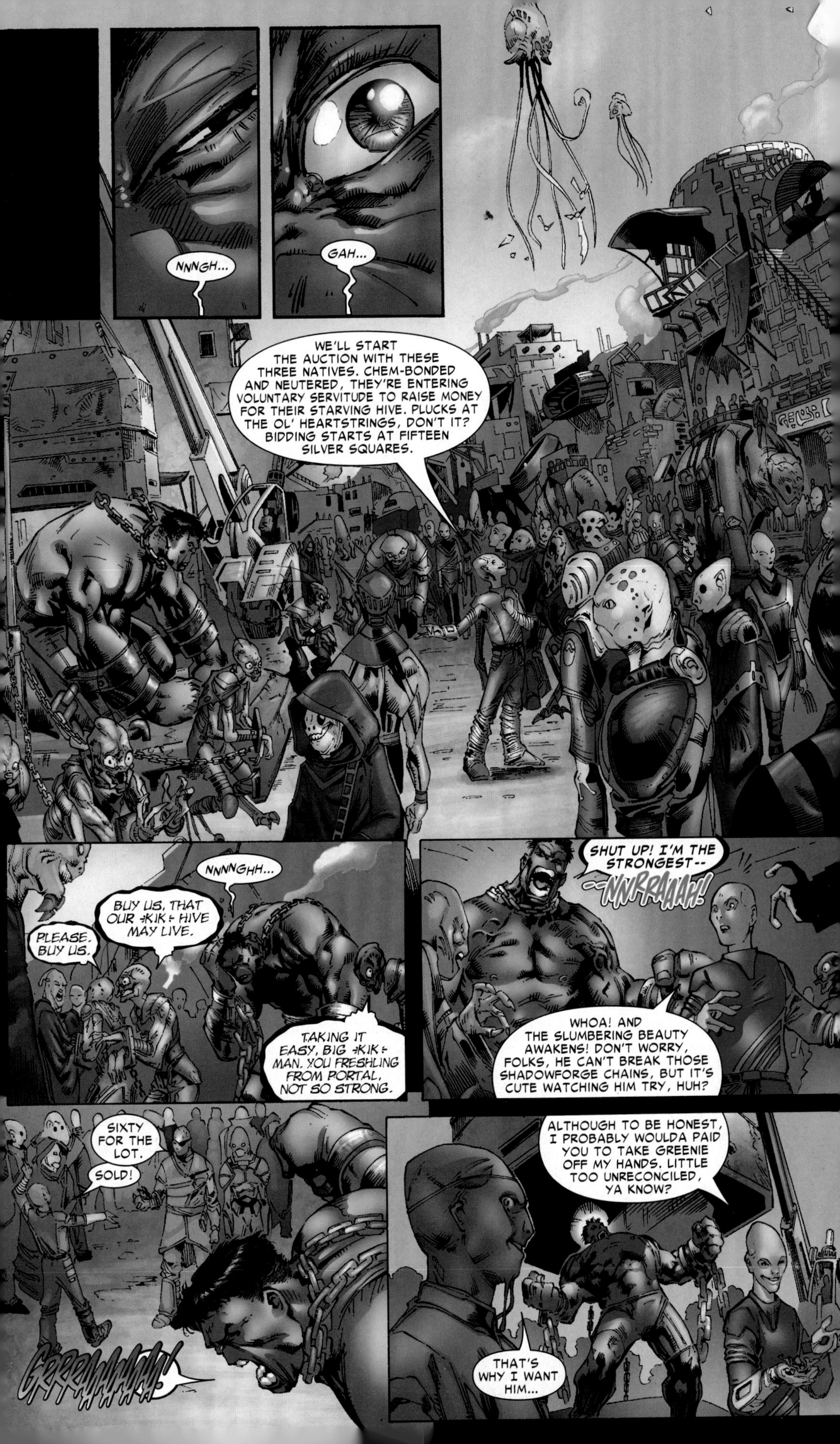
NNNGH...
GAH...
WE'LL START THE AUCTION WITH THESE THREE NATIVES. CHEM-BONDED AND NEUTERED, THEY'RE ENTERING VOLUNTARY SERVITUDE TO RAISE MONEY FOR THEIR STARVING HIVE. PLUCKS AT THE OL' HEARTSTRINGS, DON'T IT? BIDDING STARTS AT FIFTEEN SILVER SQUARES.
NNNNGHH...
BUY US, THAT OUR ≠KIK≠ HIVE MAY LIVE.
PLEASE. BUY US.
TAKING IT EASY, BIG ≠KIK≠ MAN. YOU FRESHLING FROM PORTAL, NOT SO STRONG.
SHUT UP! I'M THE STRONGEST--
--NNRRAAAH!
WHOA! AND THE SLUMBERING BEAUTY AWAKENS! DON'T WORRY, FOLKS, HE CAN'T BREAK THOSE SHADOWFORGE CHAINS, BUT IT'S CUTE WATCHING HIM TRY, HUH?
SIXTY FOR THE LOT.
SOLD!
GRRRAAAAH!
ALTHOUGH TO BE HONEST, I PROBABLY WOULDA PAID YOU TO TAKE GREENIE OFF MY HANDS. LITTLE TOO UNRECONCILED, YA KNOW?
THAT'S WHY I WANT HIM...

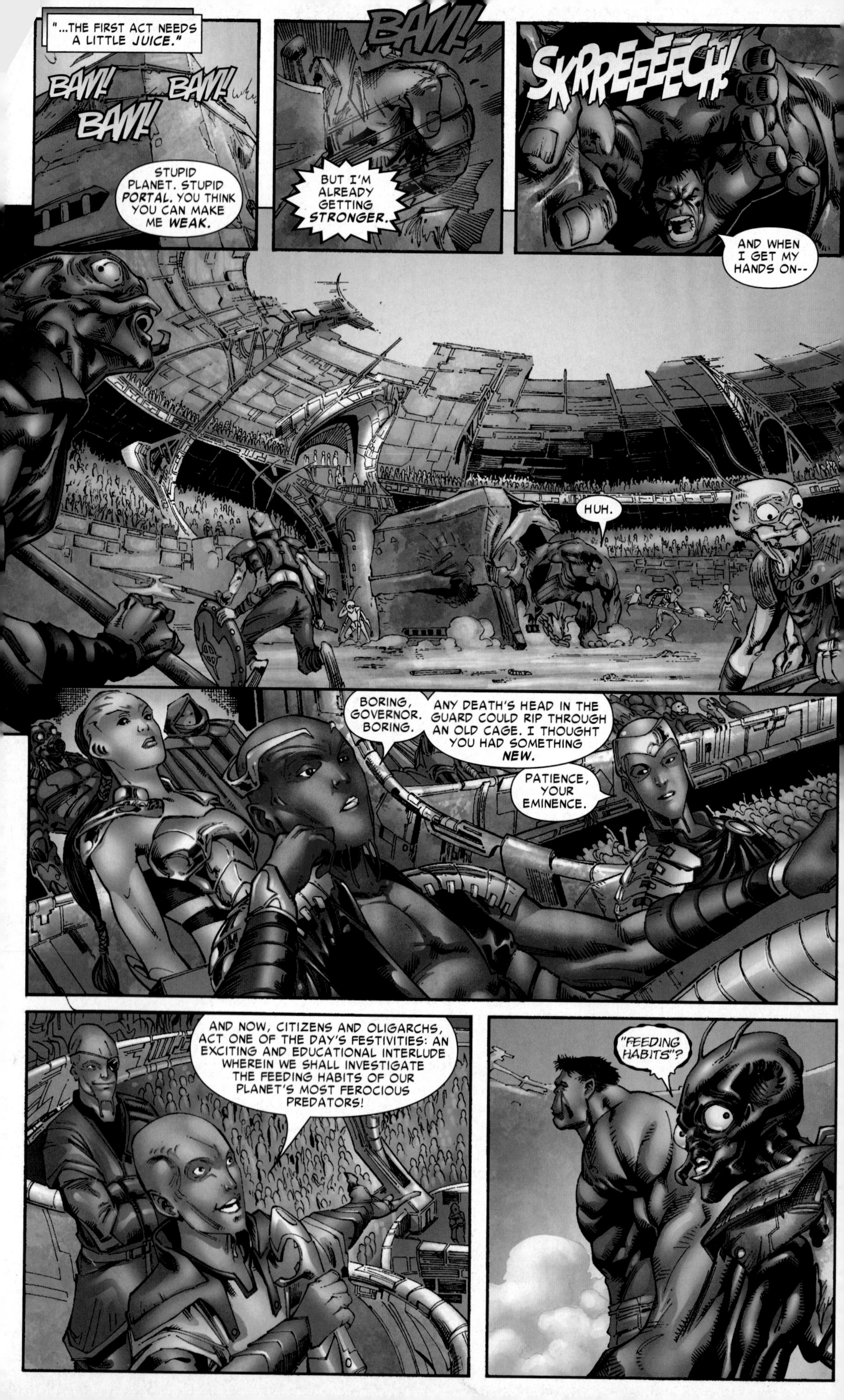
"...THE FIRST ACT NEEDS A LITTLE JUICE."
BAM! BAM! BAM!
STUPID PLANET. STUPID PORTAL. YOU THINK YOU CAN MAKE ME WEAK.
BAM!
BUT I'M ALREADY GETTING STRONGER.
SKRREEEEECH!
AND WHEN I GET MY HANDS ON--
HUH.
BORING, GOVERNOR. BORING.
ANY DEATH'S HEAD IN THE GUARD COULD RIP THROUGH AN OLD CAGE. I THOUGHT YOU HAD SOMETHING NEW.
PATIENCE, YOUR EMINENCE.
AND NOW, CITIZENS AND OLIGARCHS, ACT ONE OF THE DAY'S FESTIVITIES: AN EXCITING AND EDUCATIONAL INTERLUDE WHEREIN WE SHALL INVESTIGATE THE FEEDING HABITS OF OUR PLANET'S MOST FEROCIOUS PREDATORS!
"FEEDING HABITS"?

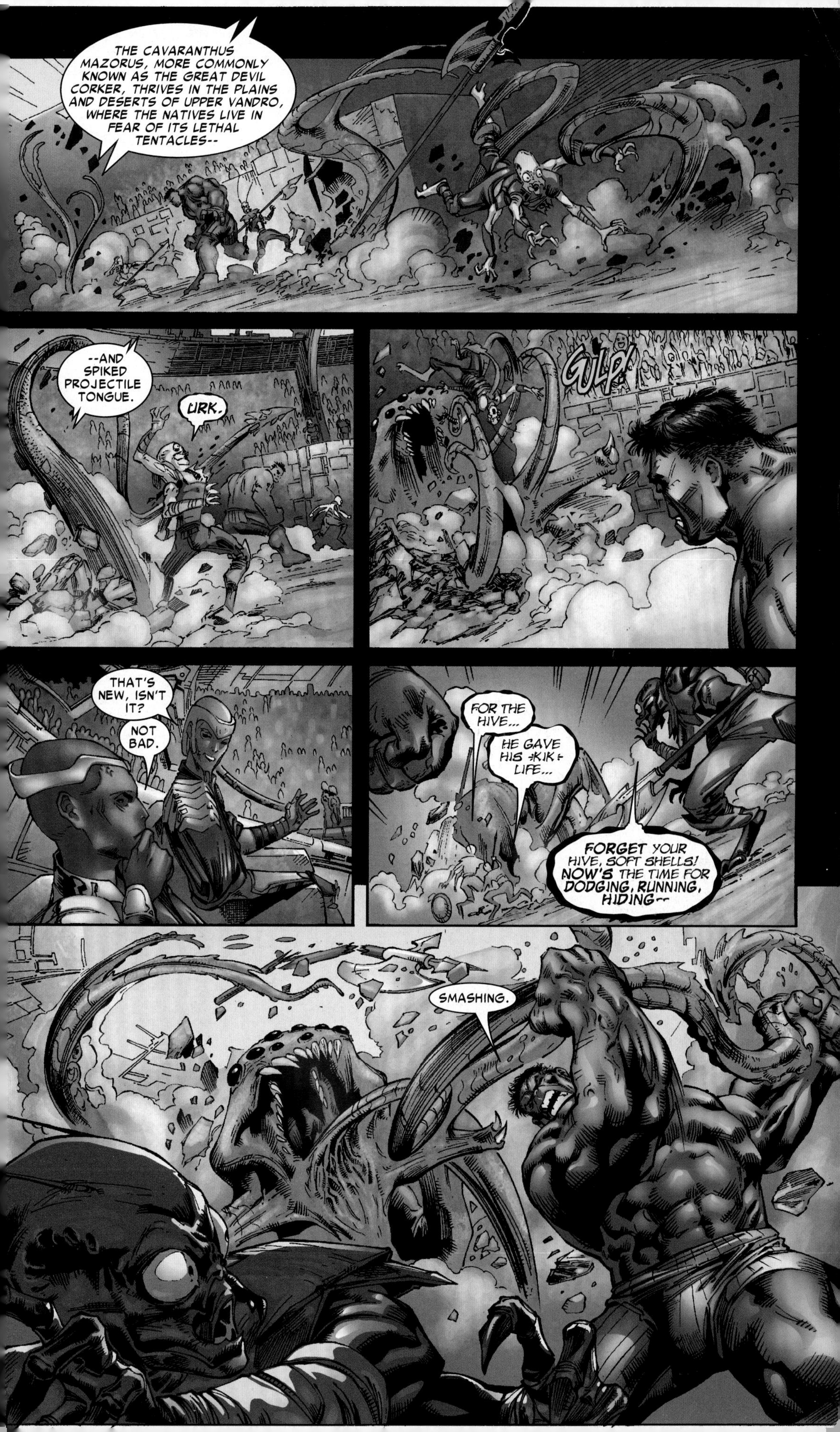
THE CAVARANTHUS MAZORUS, MORE COMMONLY KNOWN AS THE GREAT DEVIL CORKER, THRIVES IN THE PLAINS AND DESERTS OF UPPER VANDRO, WHERE THE NATIVES LIVE IN FEAR OF ITS LETHAL TENTACLES--
--AND SPIKED PROJECTILE TONGUE.
URK.
GULP!
THAT'S NEW, ISN'T IT?
NOT BAD.
FOR THE HIVE...
HE GAVE HIS ≠KIK≠ LIFE...
FORGET YOUR HIVE, SOFT SHELLS! NOW'S THE TIME FOR DODGING, RUNNING, HIDING--
SMASHING.

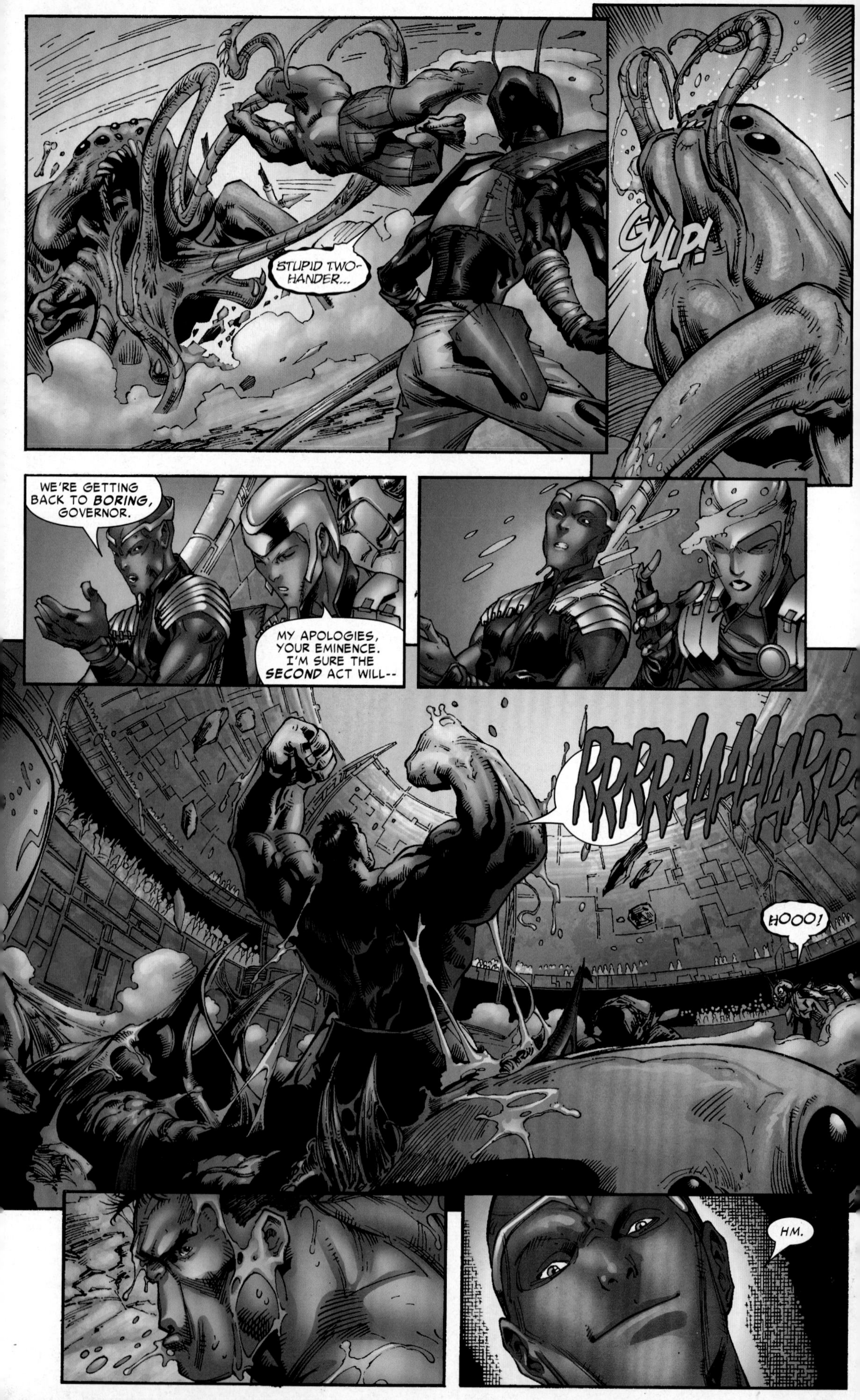
STUPID TWO-HANDER...
GULP!
WE'RE GETTING BACK TO BORING, GOVERNOR.
MY APOLOGIES, YOUR EMINENCE. I'M SURE THE SECOND ACT WILL--
RRRRAAAAARR-
HOOO!
HM.

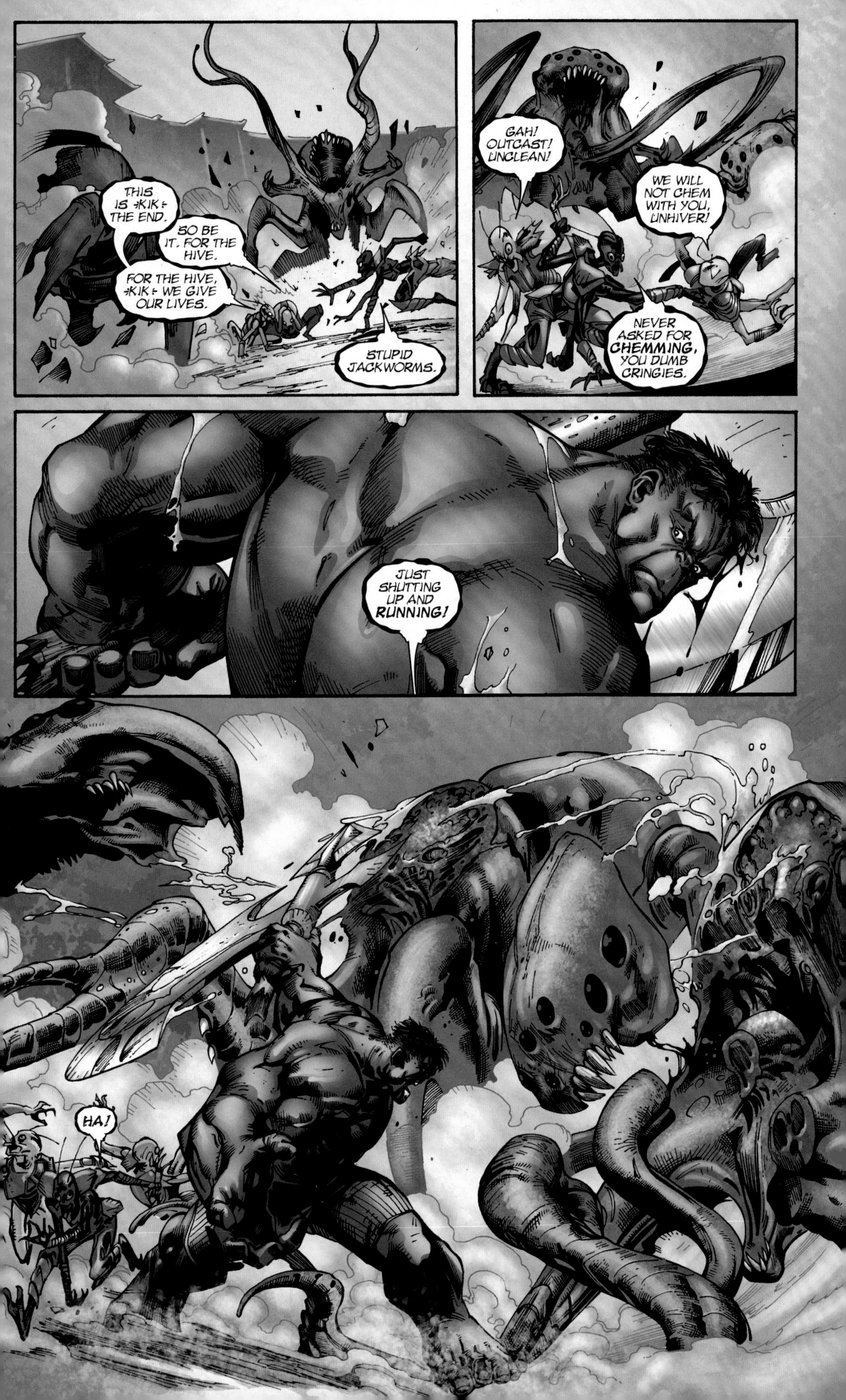
THIS IS ⸗KIK⸗ THE END.
SO BE IT. FOR THE HIVE.
FOR THE HIVE, ⸗KIK⸗ WE GIVE OUR LIVES.
STUPID JACKWORMS.
GAH! OUTCAST! UNCLEAN!
WE WILL NOT CHEM WITH YOU, UNHIVER!
NEVER ASKED FOR **CHEMMING,** YOU DUMB CRINGIES.
JUST SHUTTING UP AND **RUNNING!**
HA!

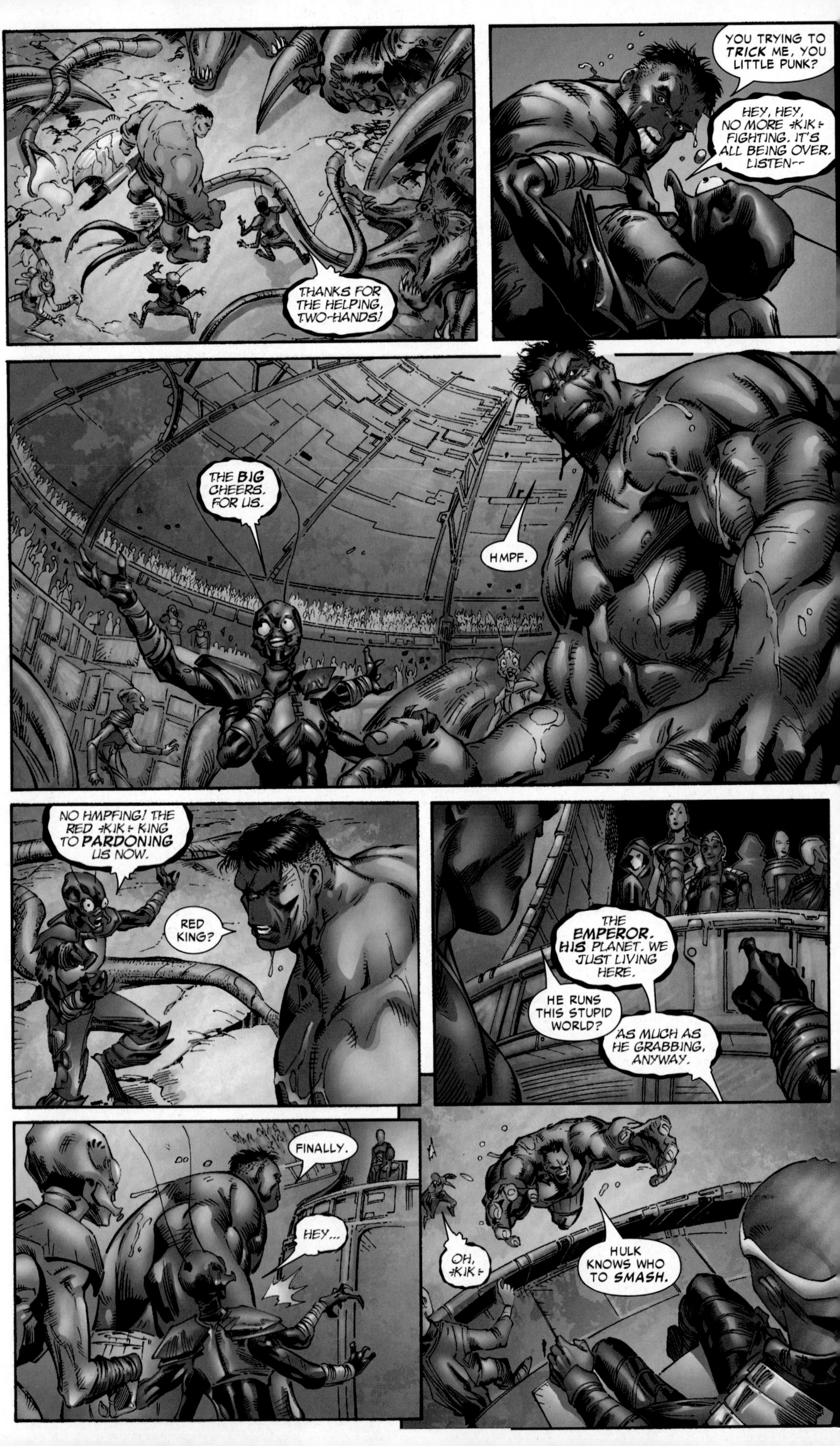
THANKS FOR THE HELPING, TWO-HANDS!
YOU TRYING TO TRICK ME, YOU LITTLE PUNK?
HEY, HEY, NO MORE -KIK- FIGHTING. IT'S ALL BEING OVER. LISTEN--
THE BIG CHEERS. FOR US.
HMPF.
NO HMPFING! THE RED -KIK- KING TO PARDONING US NOW.
RED KING?
THE EMPEROR. HIS PLANET. WE JUST LIVING HERE.
HE RUNS THIS STUPID WORLD?
AS MUCH AS HE GRABBING, ANYWAY.
FINALLY.
HEY...
OH, -KIK-
HULK KNOWS WHO TO SMASH.

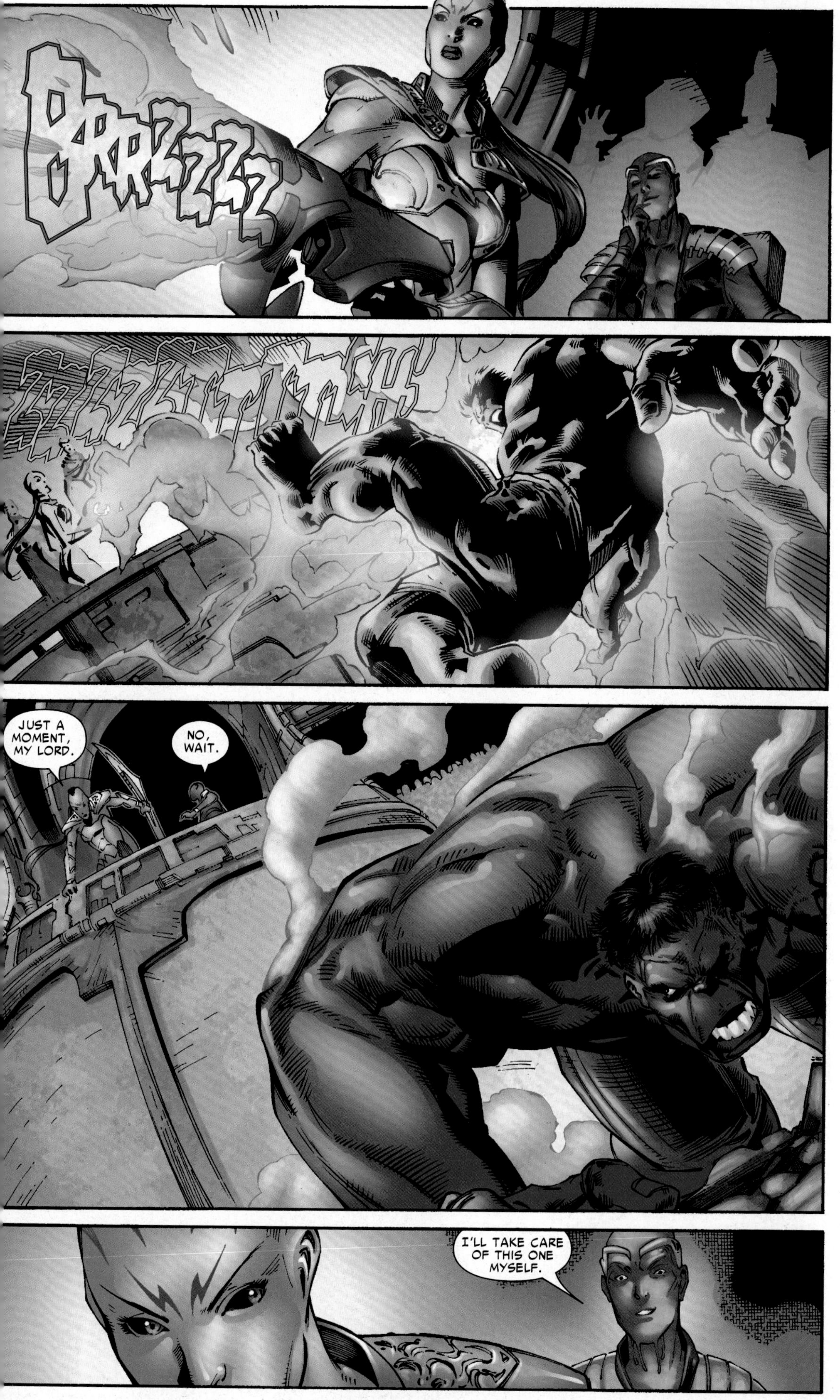
JUST A MOMENT, MY LORD.
NO, WAIT.
I'LL TAKE CARE OF THIS ONE MYSELF.

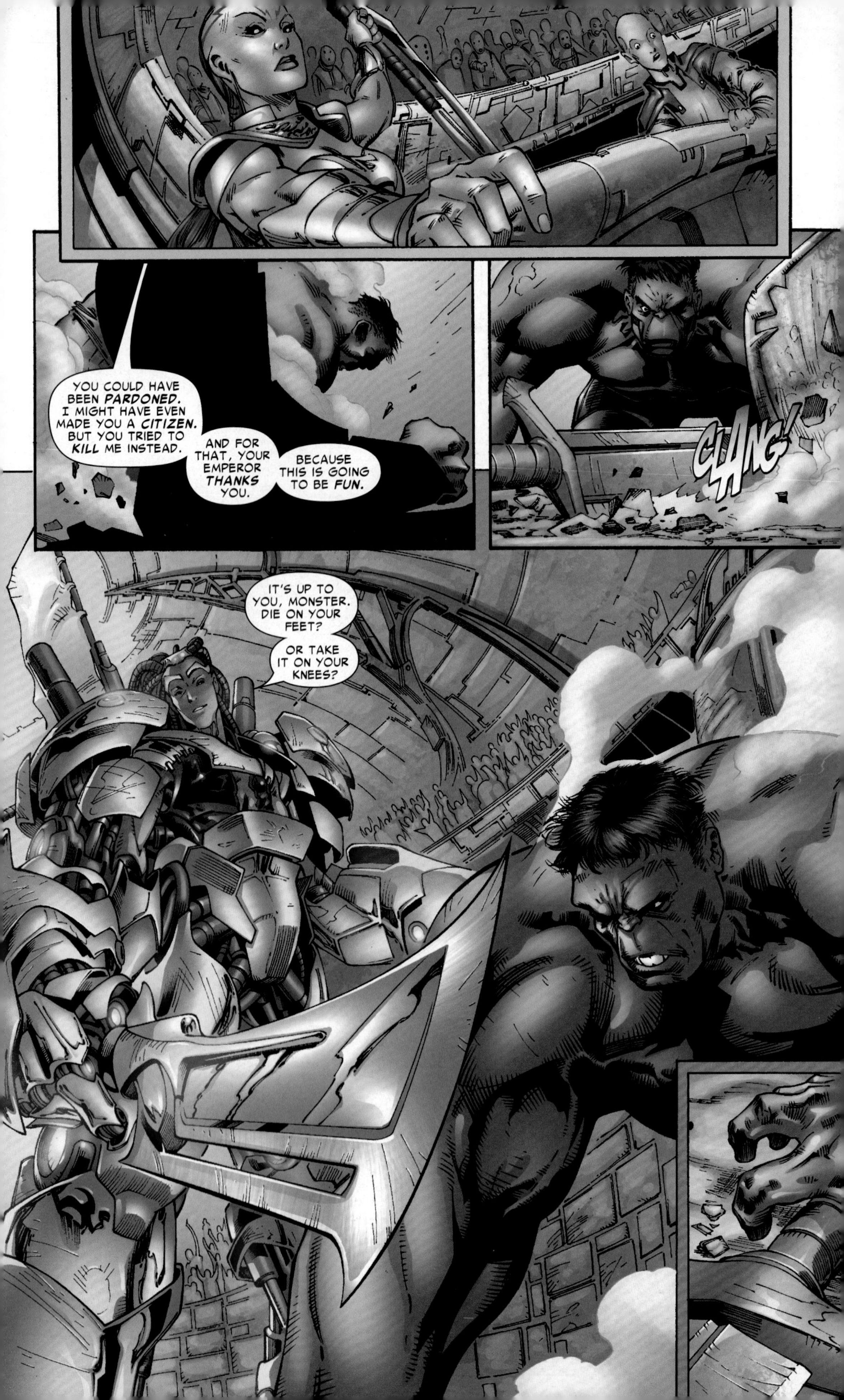
YOU COULD HAVE BEEN PARDONED. I MIGHT HAVE EVEN MADE YOU A CITIZEN. BUT YOU TRIED TO KILL ME INSTEAD.
AND FOR THAT, YOUR EMPEROR THANKS YOU.
BECAUSE THIS IS GOING TO BE FUN.
CLANG!
IT'S UP TO YOU, MONSTER. DIE ON YOUR FEET?
OR TAKE IT ON YOUR KNEES?

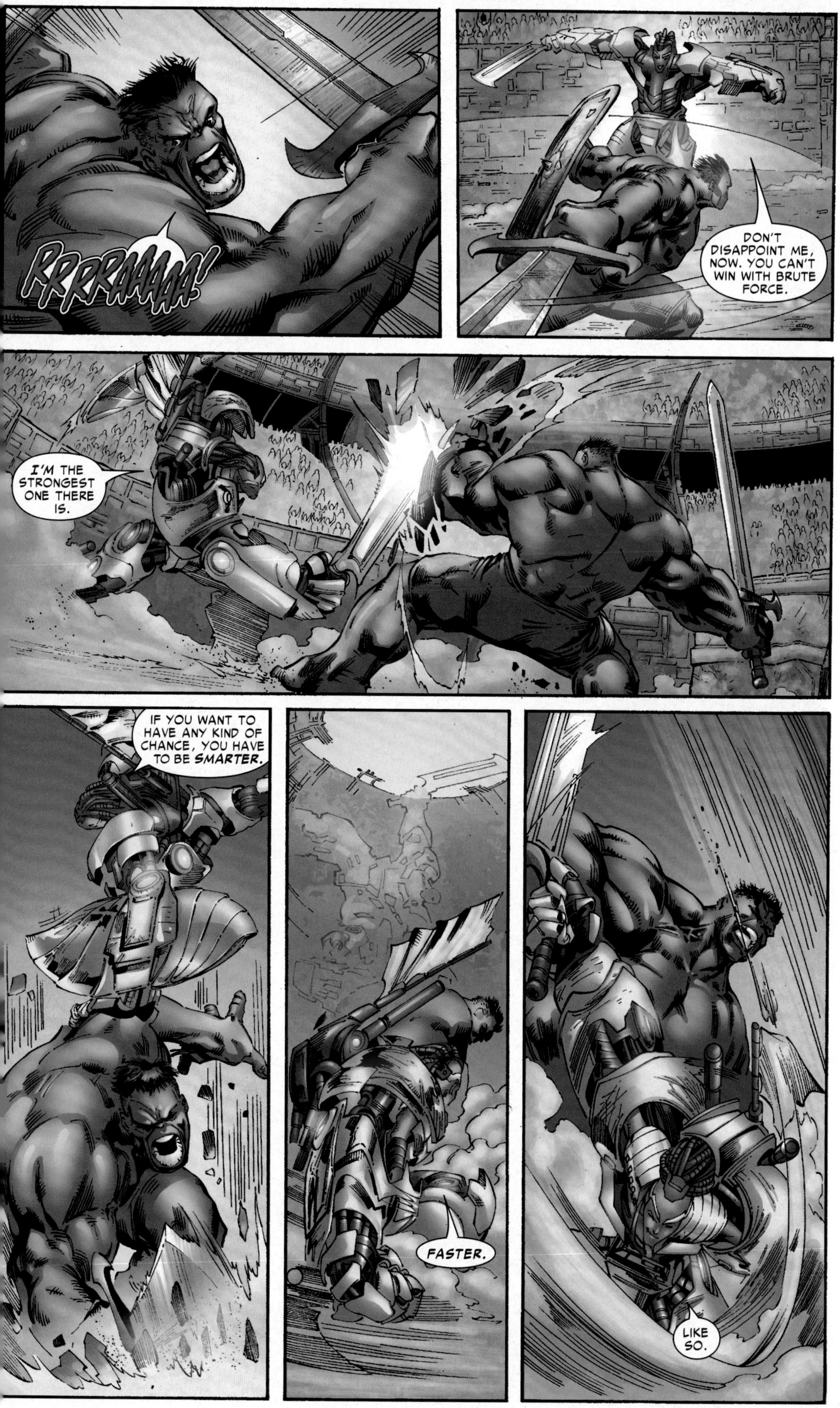
RRRRAAAAAA!
DON'T DISAPPOINT ME, NOW. YOU CAN'T WIN WITH BRUTE FORCE.
I'M THE STRONGEST ONE THERE IS.
IF YOU WANT TO HAVE ANY KIND OF CHANCE, YOU HAVE TO BE SMARTER.
FASTER.
LIKE SO.

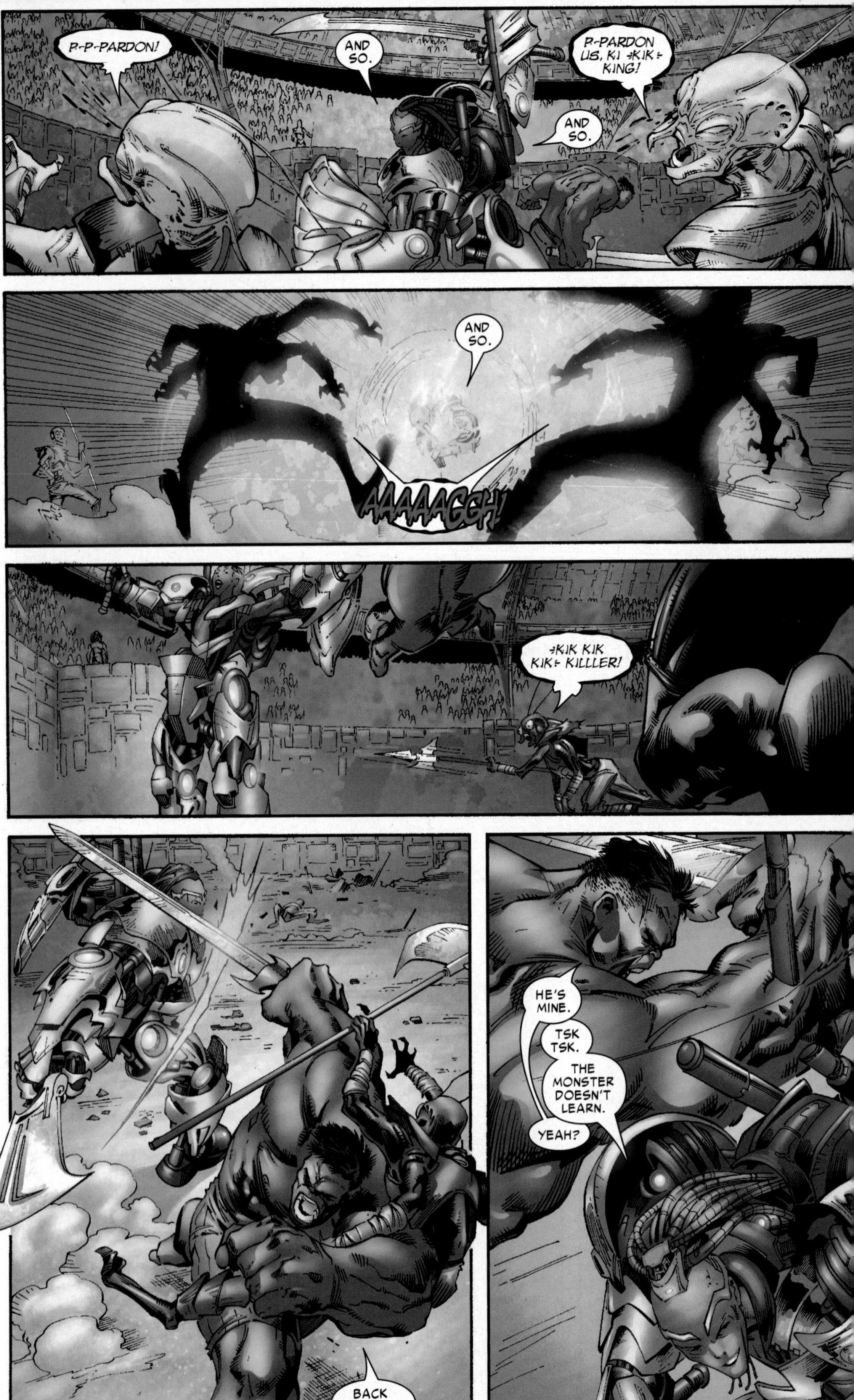
P-P-PARDON!
AND SO.
P-PARDON US, KI ≠KIK≠ KING!
AND SO.
AND SO.
AAAAAGGH!
≠KIK KIK KIK≠ KILLLER!
BACK OFF, BUG.
HE'S MINE.
TSK TSK.
THE MONSTER DOESN'T LEARN.
YEAH?

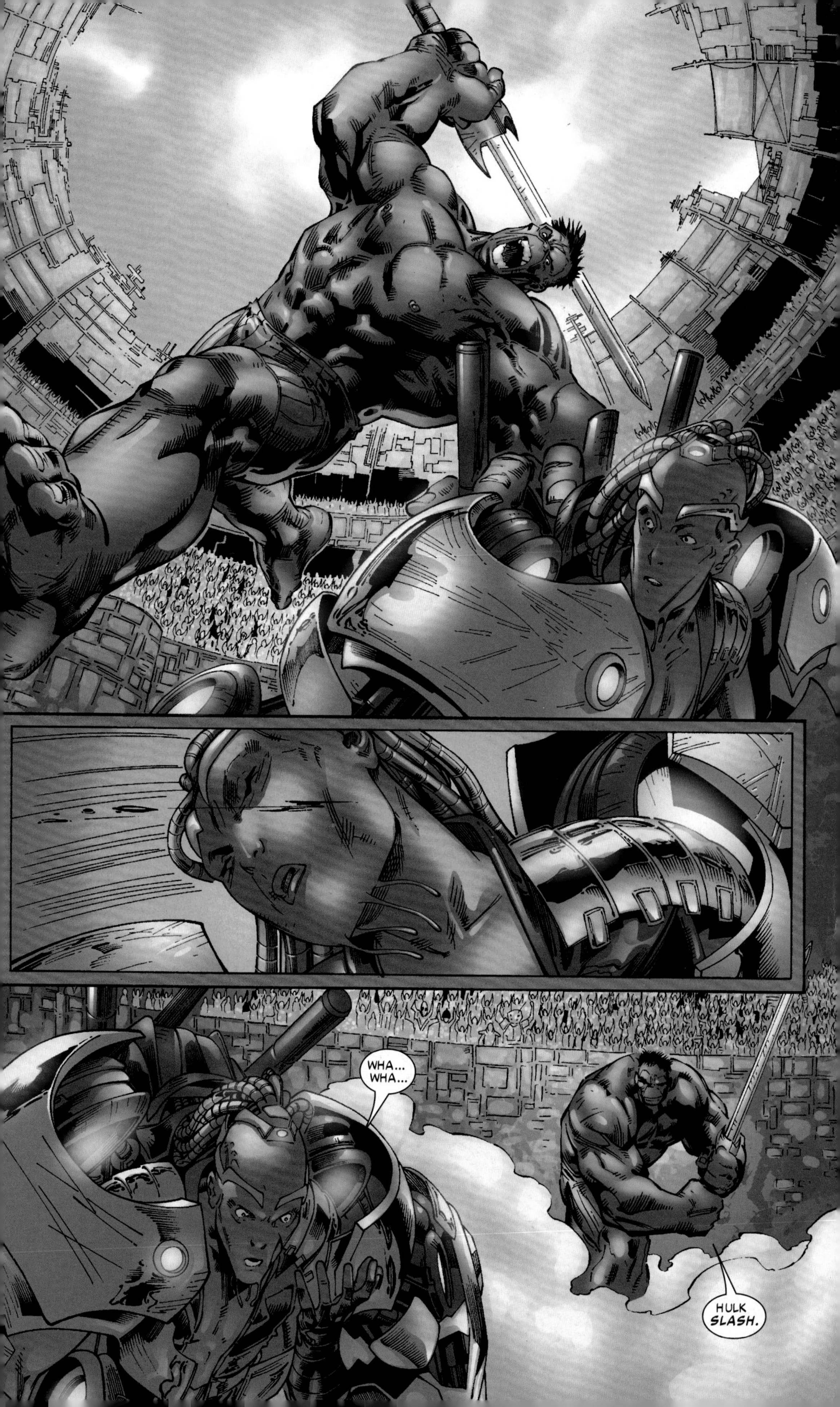
WHA...
WHA...
HULK
SLASH.

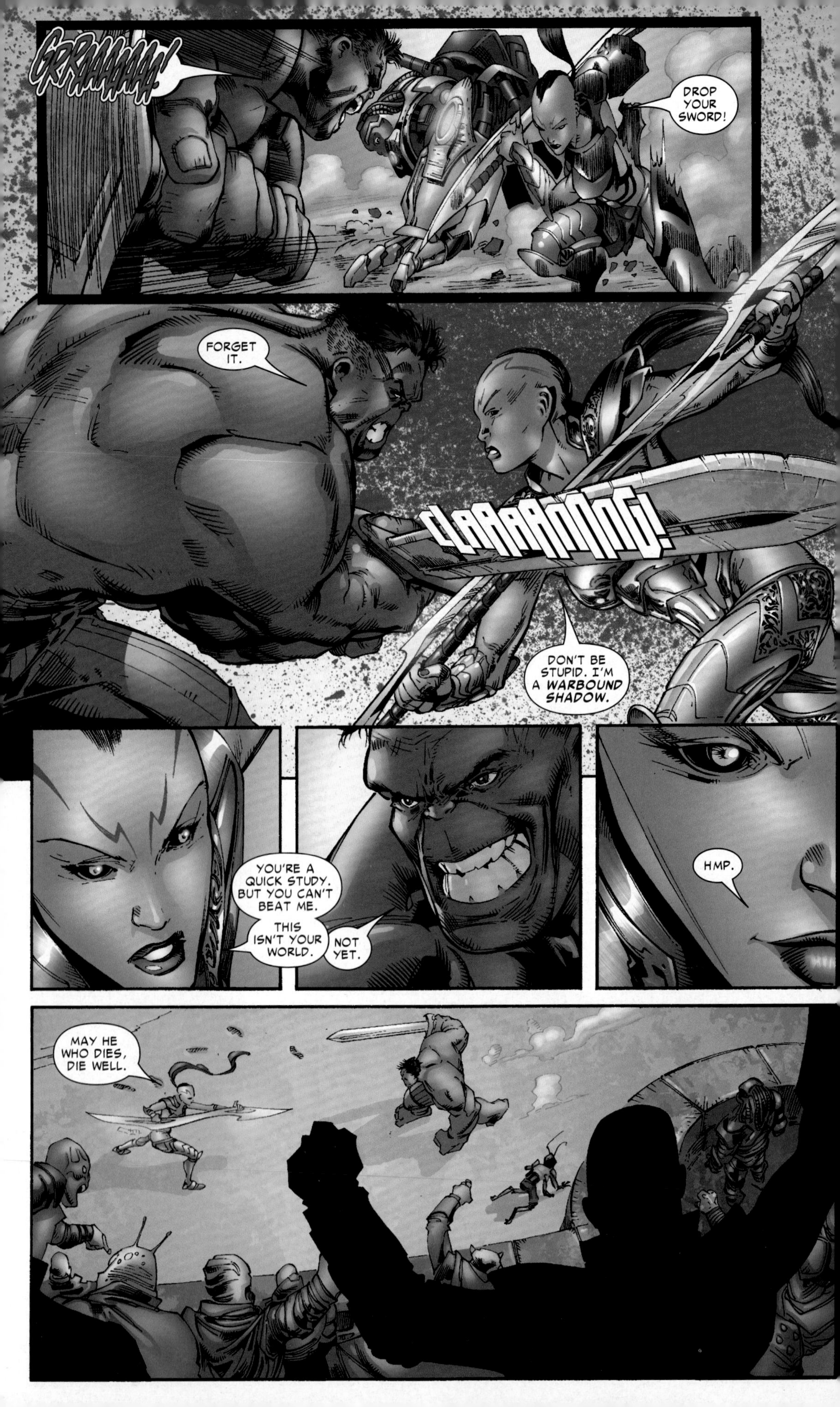
GRRAAAAAA!
DROP YOUR SWORD!
FORGET IT.
CLAAAANNNG!
DON'T BE STUPID. I'M A WARBOUND SHADOW.
YOU'RE A QUICK STUDY. BUT YOU CAN'T BEAT ME.
THIS ISN'T YOUR WORLD.
NOT YET.
HMP.
MAY HE WHO DIES, DIE WELL.

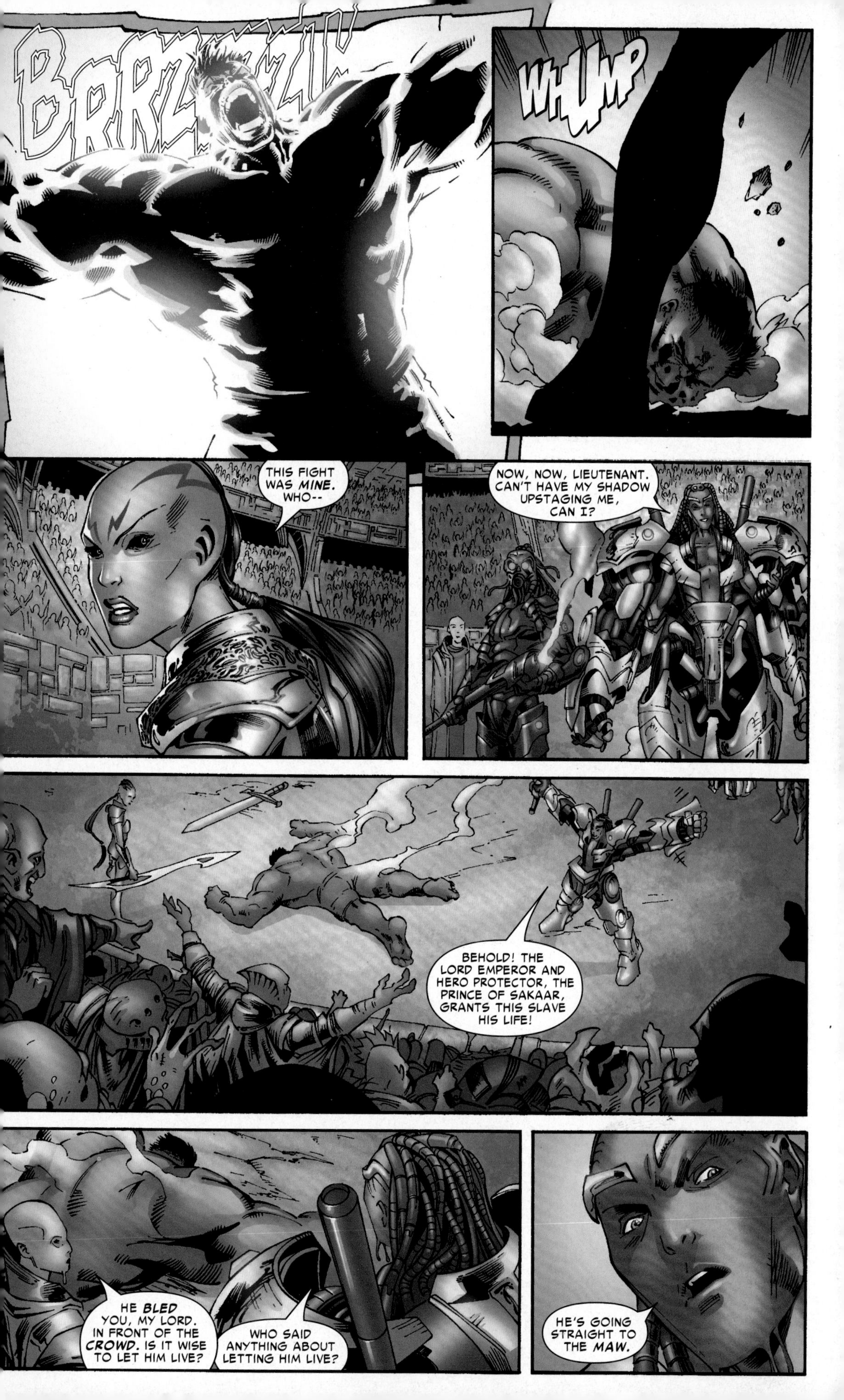
BRRZZZZT
WHUMP
THIS FIGHT WAS MINE. WHO--
NOW, NOW, LIEUTENANT. CAN'T HAVE MY SHADOW UPSTAGING ME, CAN I?
BEHOLD! THE LORD EMPEROR AND HERO PROTECTOR, THE PRINCE OF SAKAAR, GRANTS THIS SLAVE HIS LIFE!
HE BLED YOU, MY LORD. IN FRONT OF THE CROWD. IS IT WISE TO LET HIM LIVE?
WHO SAID ANYTHING ABOUT LETTING HIM LIVE?
HE'S GOING STRAIGHT TO THE MAW.

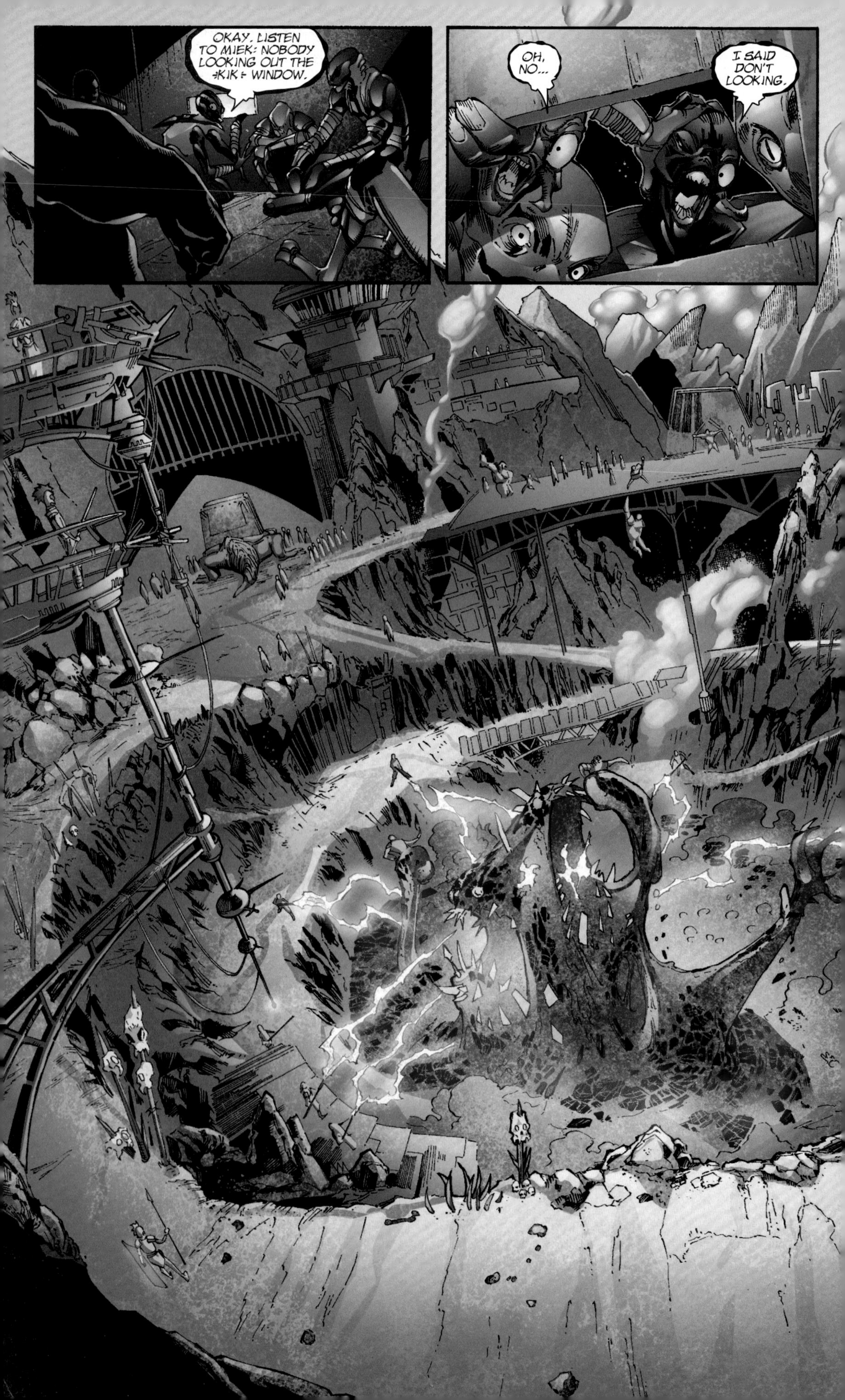
OKAY. LISTEN TO MIEK: NOBODY LOOKING OUT THE ≠KIK≠ WINDOW.
OH, NO...
I SAID DON'T LOOKING.

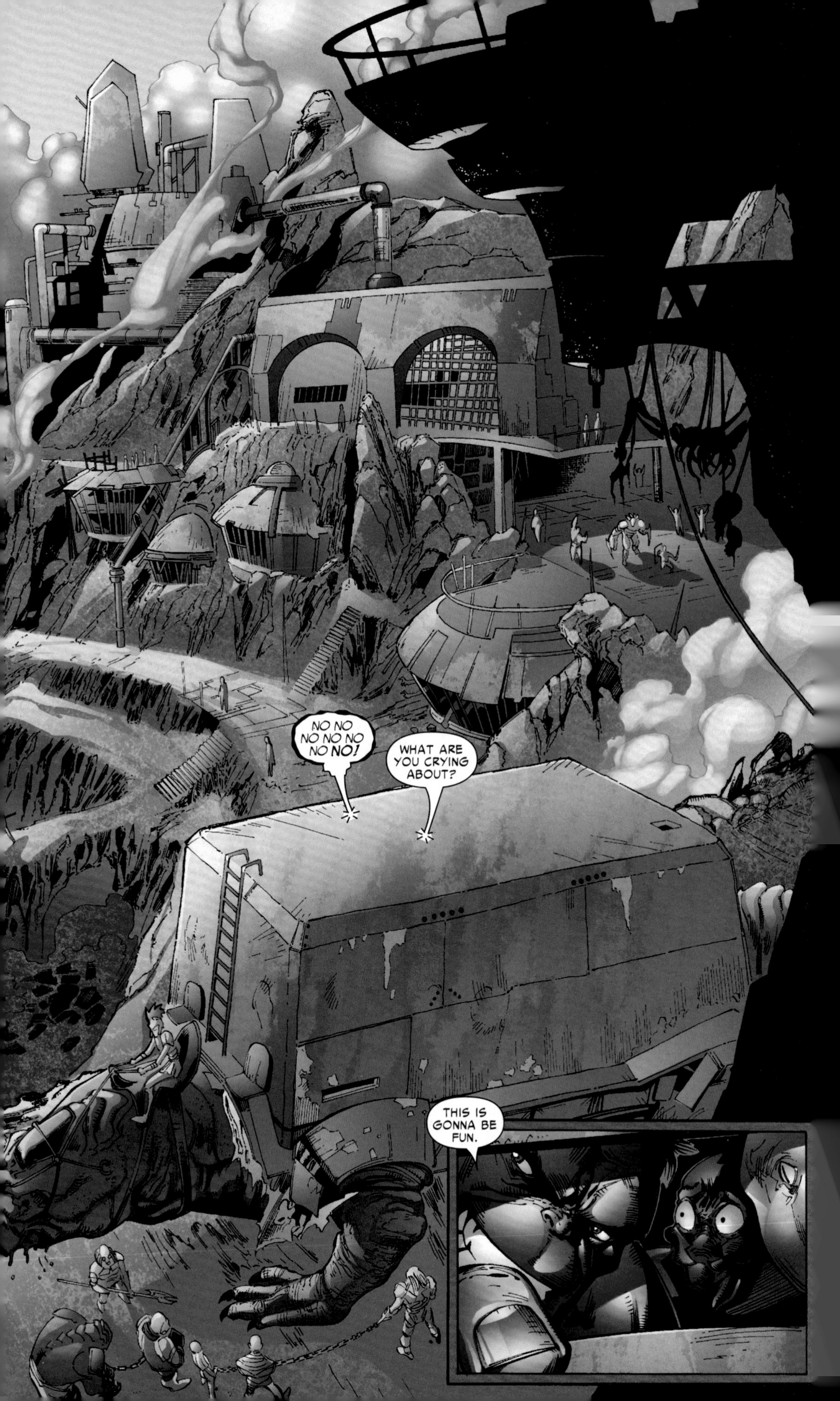
NO NO
NO NO NO
NO NO!
WHAT ARE
YOU CRYING
ABOUT?
THIS IS
GONNA BE
FUN.

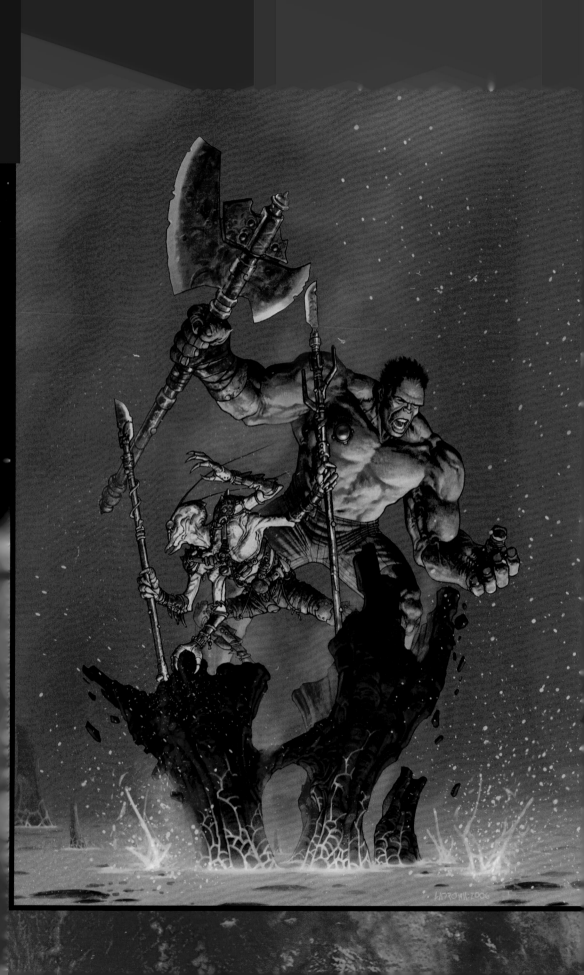

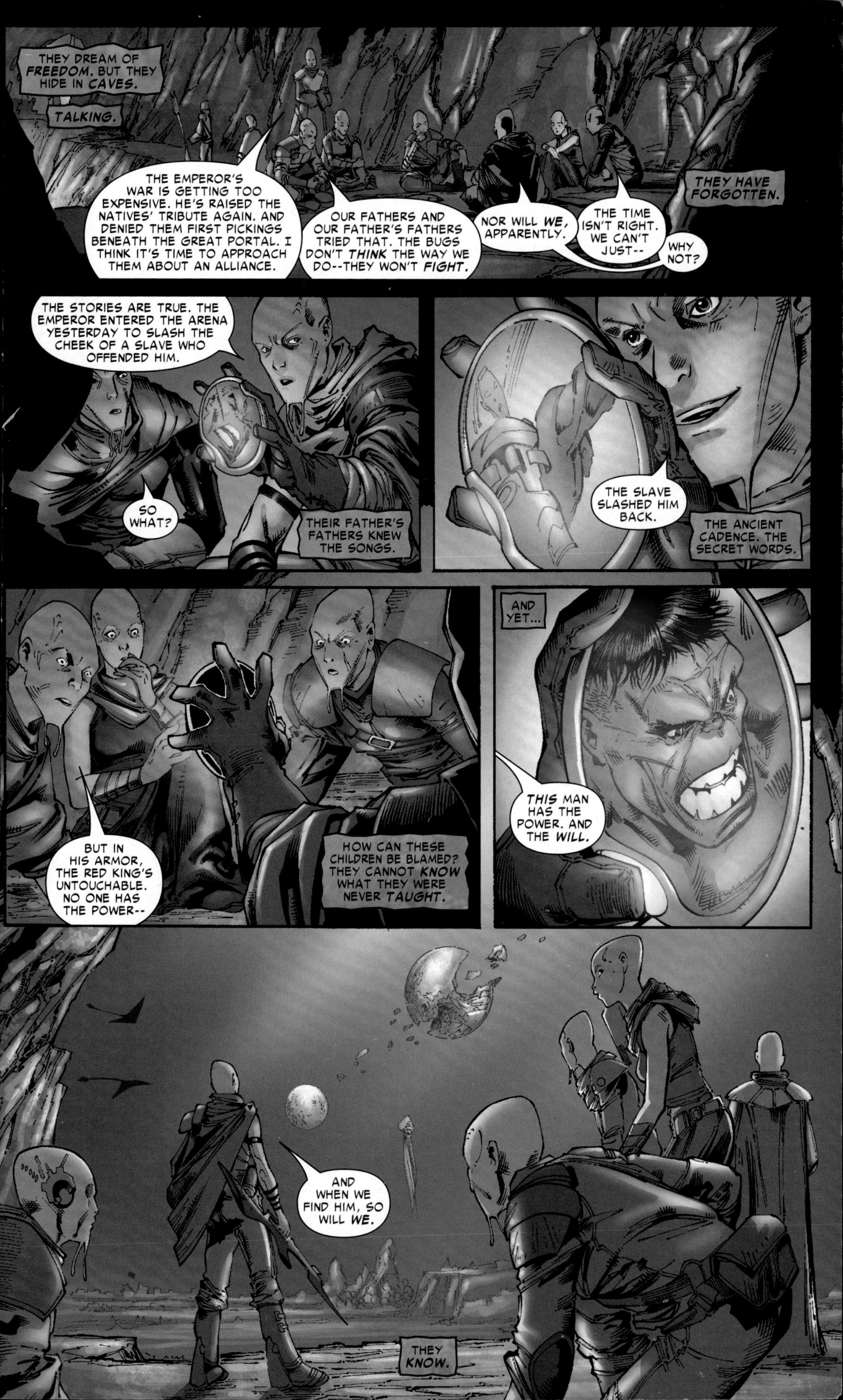
THEY DREAM OF FREEDOM. BUT THEY HIDE IN CAVES.
TALKING.
THE EMPEROR'S WAR IS GETTING TOO EXPENSIVE. HE'S RAISED THE NATIVES' TRIBUTE AGAIN. AND DENIED THEM FIRST PICKINGS BENEATH THE GREAT PORTAL. I THINK IT'S TIME TO APPROACH THEM ABOUT AN ALLIANCE.
OUR FATHERS AND OUR FATHER'S FATHERS TRIED THAT. THE BUGS DON'T THINK THE WAY WE DO--THEY WON'T FIGHT.
NOR WILL WE, APPARENTLY.
THE TIME ISN'T RIGHT. WE CAN'T JUST--
WHY NOT?
THEY HAVE FORGOTTEN.
THE STORIES ARE TRUE. THE EMPEROR ENTERED THE ARENA YESTERDAY TO SLASH THE CHEEK OF A SLAVE WHO OFFENDED HIM.
SO WHAT?
THEIR FATHER'S FATHERS KNEW THE SONGS.
THE SLAVE SLASHED HIM BACK.
THE ANCIENT CADENCE. THE SECRET WORDS.
BUT IN HIS ARMOR, THE RED KING'S UNTOUCHABLE. NO ONE HAS THE POWER--
HOW CAN THESE CHILDREN BE BLAMED? THEY CANNOT KNOW WHAT THEY WERE NEVER TAUGHT.
AND YET...
THIS MAN HAS THE POWER. AND THE WILL.
AND WHEN WE FIND HIM, SO WILL WE.
THEY KNOW.

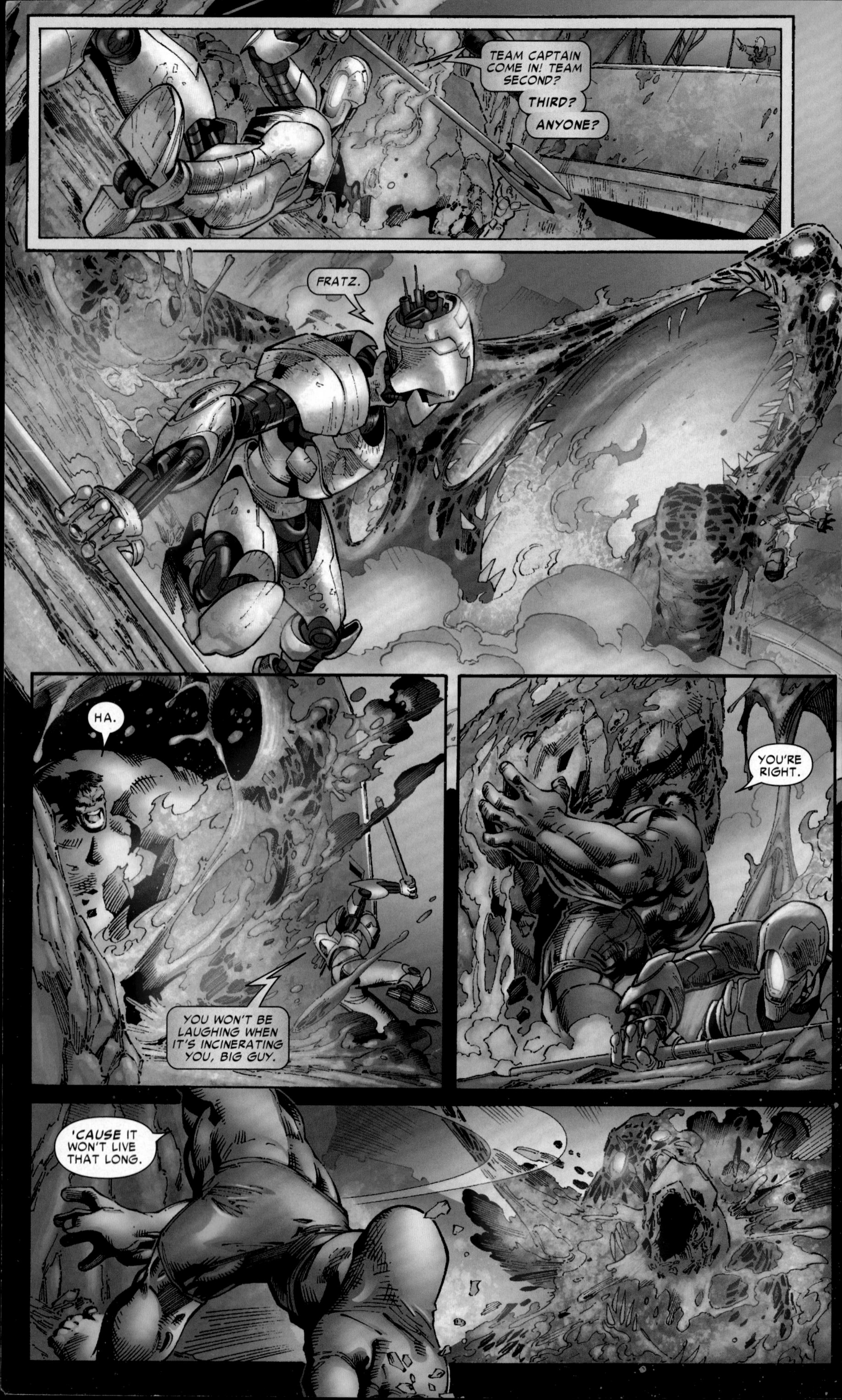
TEAM CAPTAIN COME IN! TEAM SECOND?
THIRD?
ANYONE?
FRATZ.
HA.
YOU WON'T BE LAUGHING WHEN IT'S INCINERATING YOU, BIG GUY.
YOU'RE RIGHT.
'CAUSE IT WON'T LIVE THAT LONG.

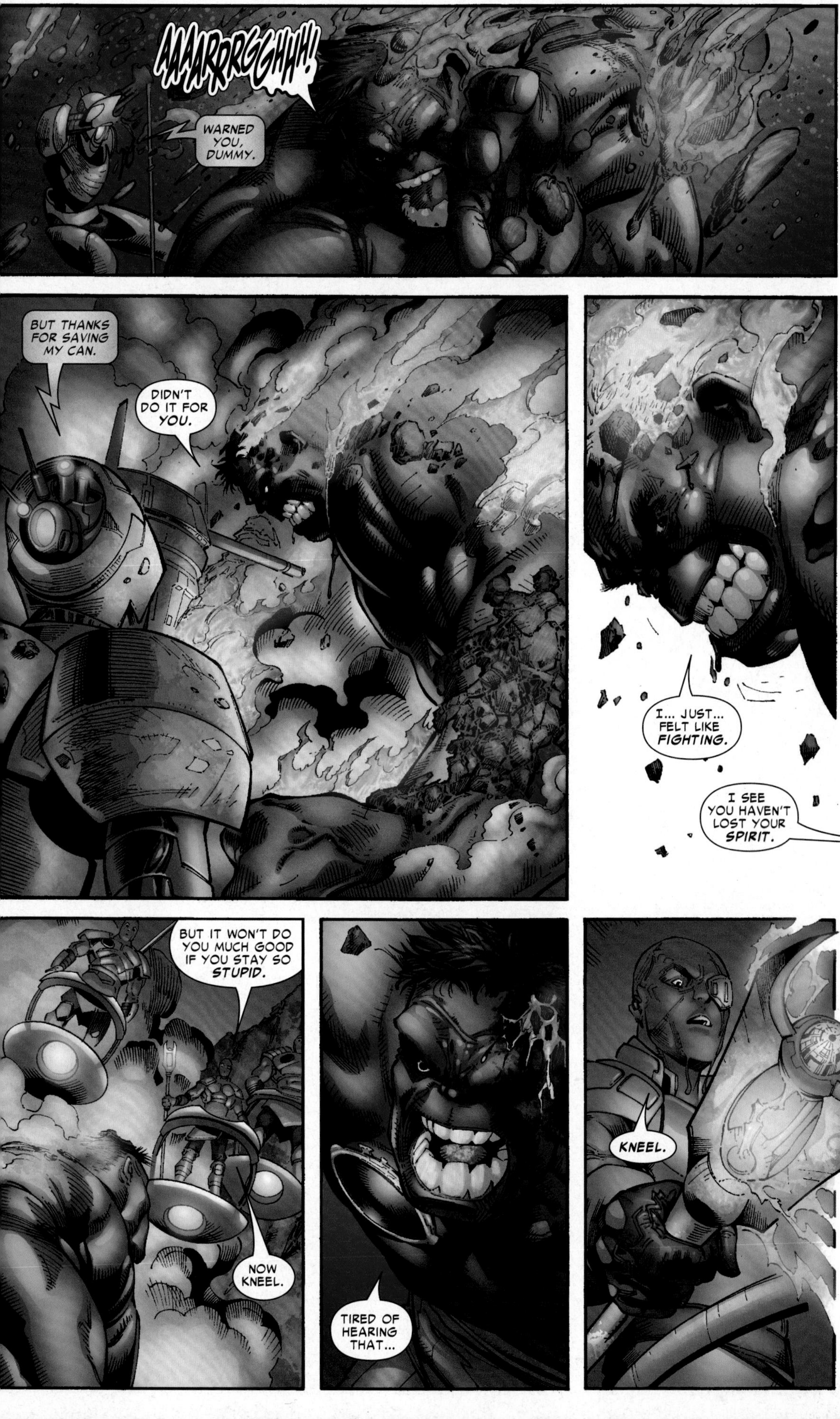
AAAARRRGGHHH!
WARNED YOU, DUMMY.
BUT THANKS FOR SAVING MY CAN.
DIDN'T DO IT FOR YOU.
I... JUST... FELT LIKE FIGHTING.
I SEE YOU HAVEN'T LOST YOUR SPIRIT.
BUT IT WON'T DO YOU MUCH GOOD IF YOU STAY SO STUPID.
NOW KNEEL.
TIRED OF HEARING THAT...
KNEEL.

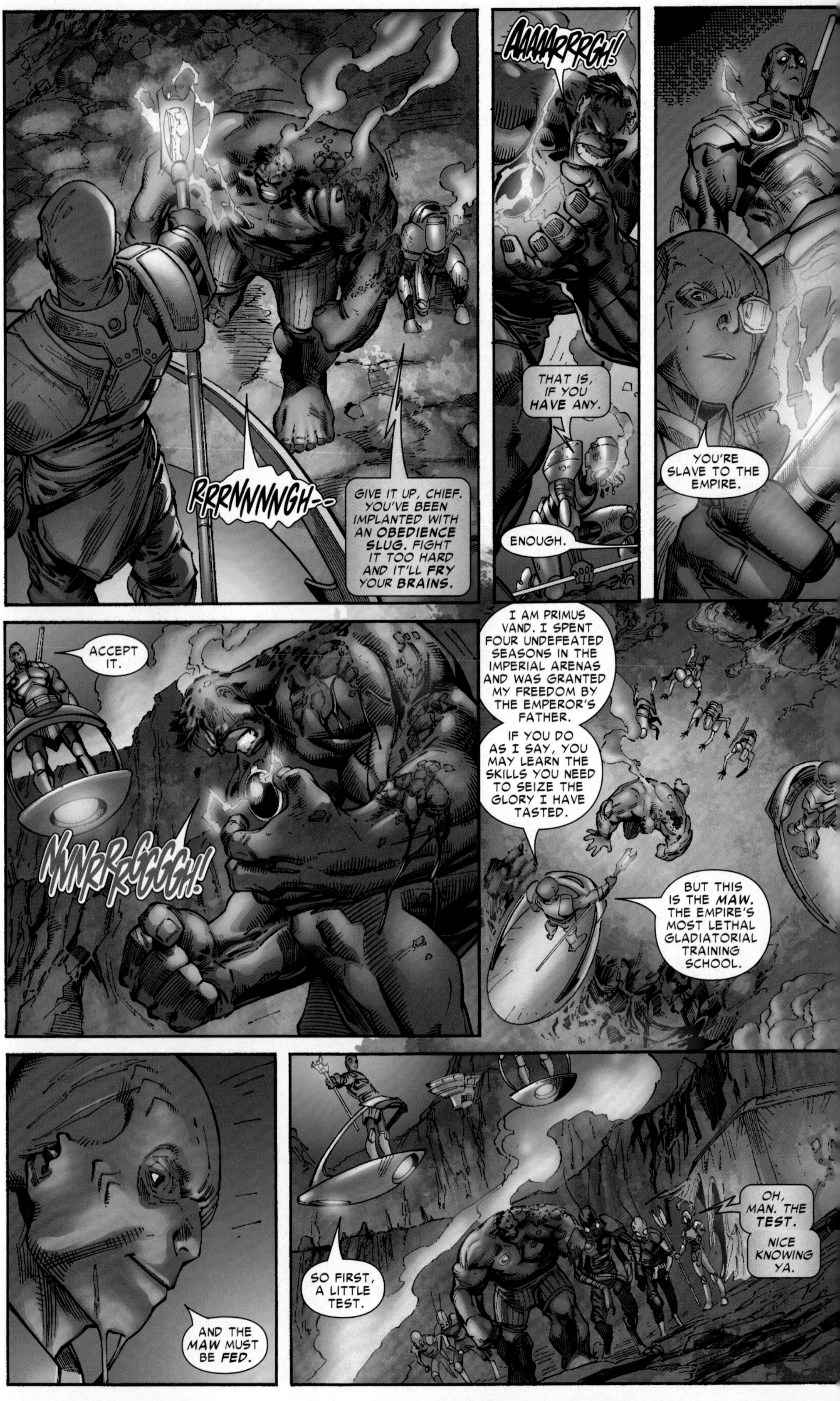
RRRNNNNGH--
GIVE IT UP, CHIEF. YOU'VE BEEN IMPLANTED WITH AN OBEDIENCE SLUG. FIGHT IT TOO HARD AND IT'LL FRY YOUR BRAINS.
AAAAARRRGH!
THAT IS, IF YOU HAVE ANY.
ENOUGH.
YOU'RE SLAVE TO THE EMPIRE.
ACCEPT IT.
NNNRRRGGGGH!
I AM PRIMUS VAND. I SPENT FOUR UNDEFEATED SEASONS IN THE IMPERIAL ARENAS AND WAS GRANTED MY FREEDOM BY THE EMPEROR'S FATHER.
IF YOU DO AS I SAY, YOU MAY LEARN THE SKILLS YOU NEED TO SEIZE THE GLORY I HAVE TASTED.
BUT THIS IS THE MAW. THE EMPIRE'S MOST LETHAL GLADIATORIAL TRAINING SCHOOL.
AND THE MAW MUST BE FED.
SO FIRST, A LITTLE TEST.
OH, MAN. THE TEST.
NICE KNOWING YA.

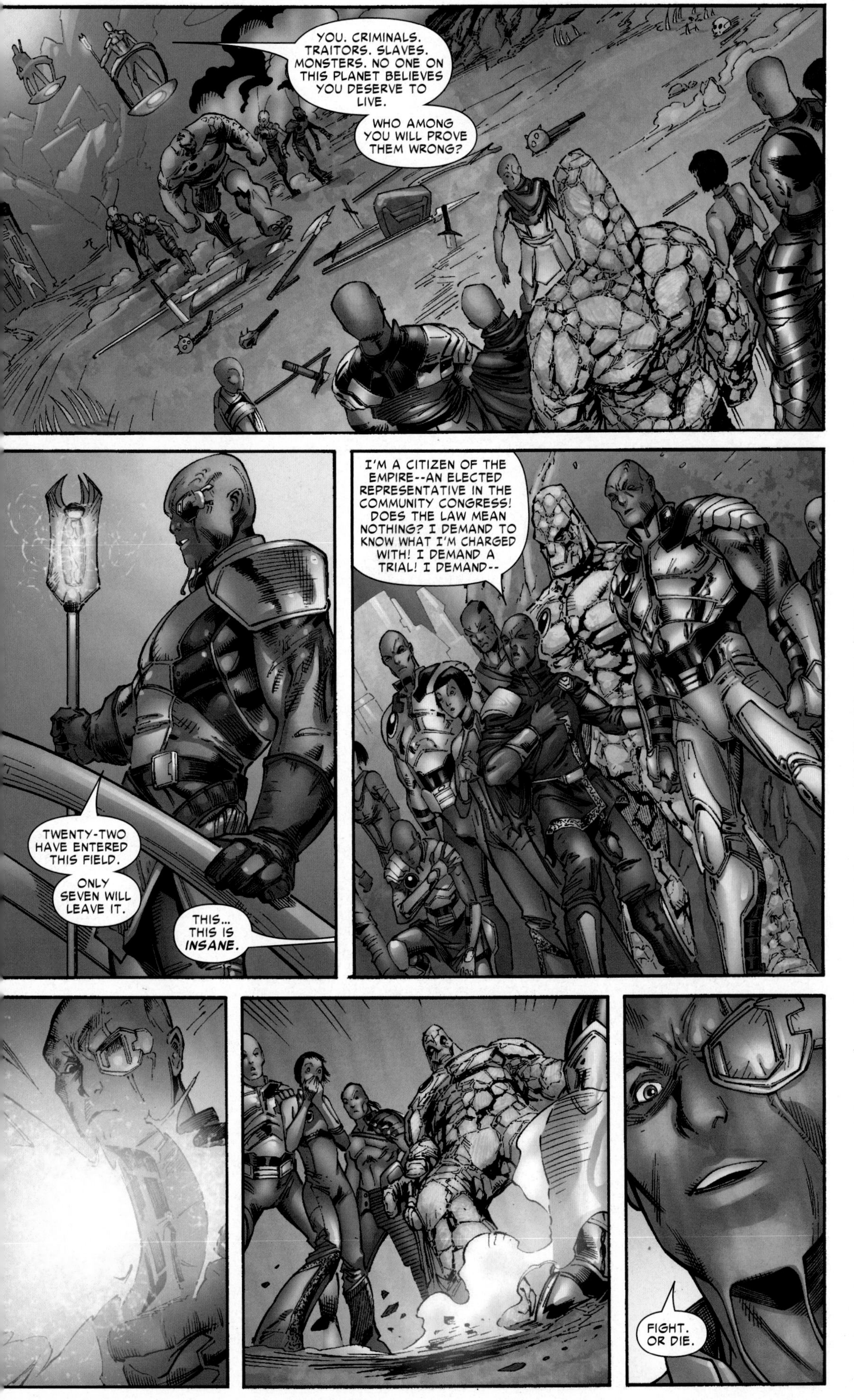
YOU. CRIMINALS. TRAITORS. SLAVES. MONSTERS. NO ONE ON THIS PLANET BELIEVES YOU DESERVE TO LIVE.
WHO AMONG YOU WILL PROVE THEM WRONG?
TWENTY-TWO HAVE ENTERED THIS FIELD.
ONLY SEVEN WILL LEAVE IT.
THIS... THIS IS *INSANE*.
I'M A CITIZEN OF THE EMPIRE--AN ELECTED REPRESENTATIVE IN THE COMMUNITY CONGRESS! DOES THE LAW MEAN NOTHING? I DEMAND TO KNOW WHAT I'M CHARGED WITH! I DEMAND A TRIAL! I DEMAND--
FIGHT. OR DIE.

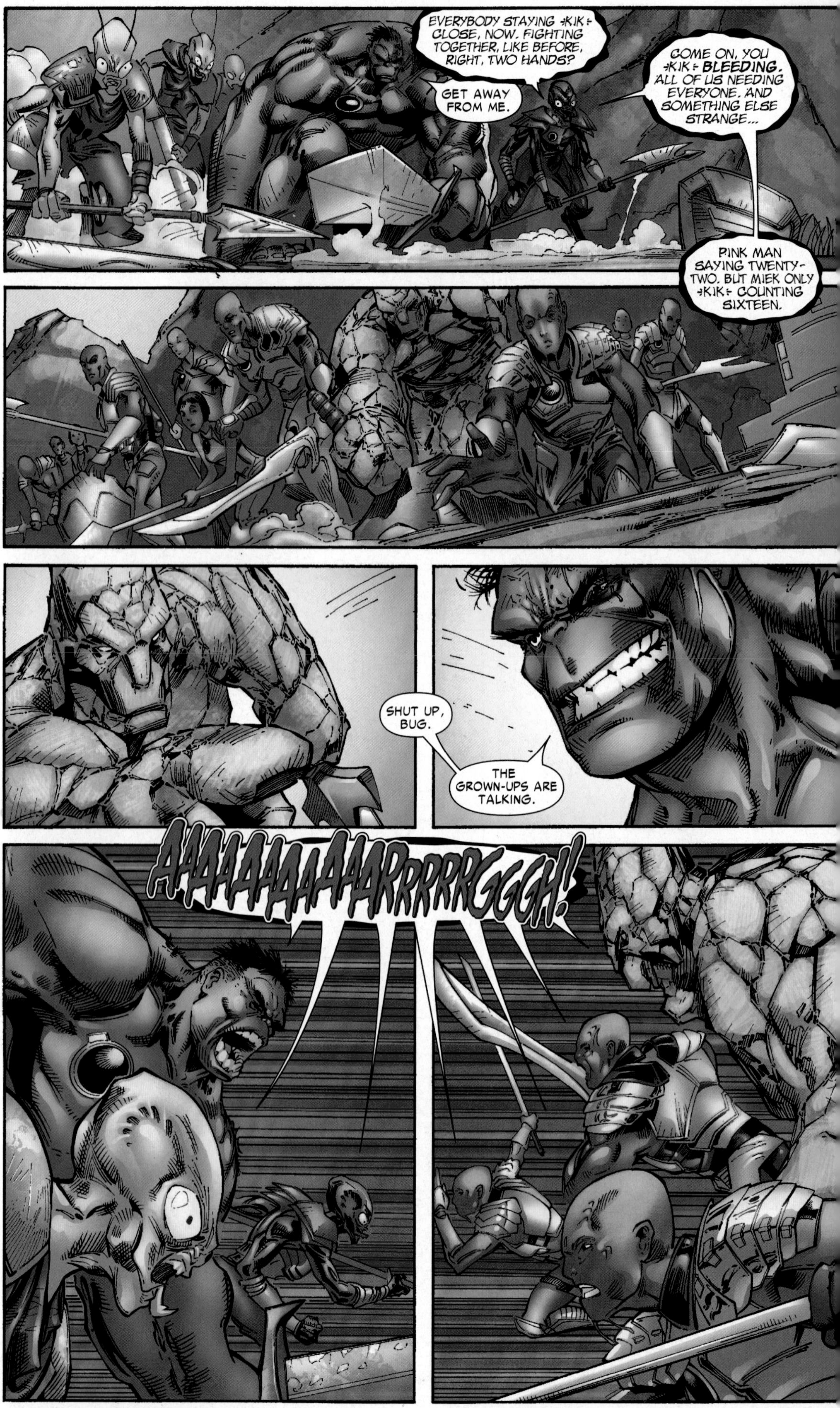
EVERYBODY STAYING ⁜KIK⁜ CLOSE, NOW. FIGHTING TOGETHER, LIKE BEFORE, RIGHT, TWO HANDS?
GET AWAY FROM ME.
COME ON, YOU ⁜KIK⁜ BLEEDING. ALL OF US NEEDING EVERYONE. AND SOMETHING ELSE STRANGE...
PINK MAN SAYING TWENTY-TWO. BUT MIEK ONLY ⁜KIK⁜ COUNTING SIXTEEN.
SHUT UP, BUG.
THE GROWN-UPS ARE TALKING.
AAAAAAAAAAARRRRRGGGH!

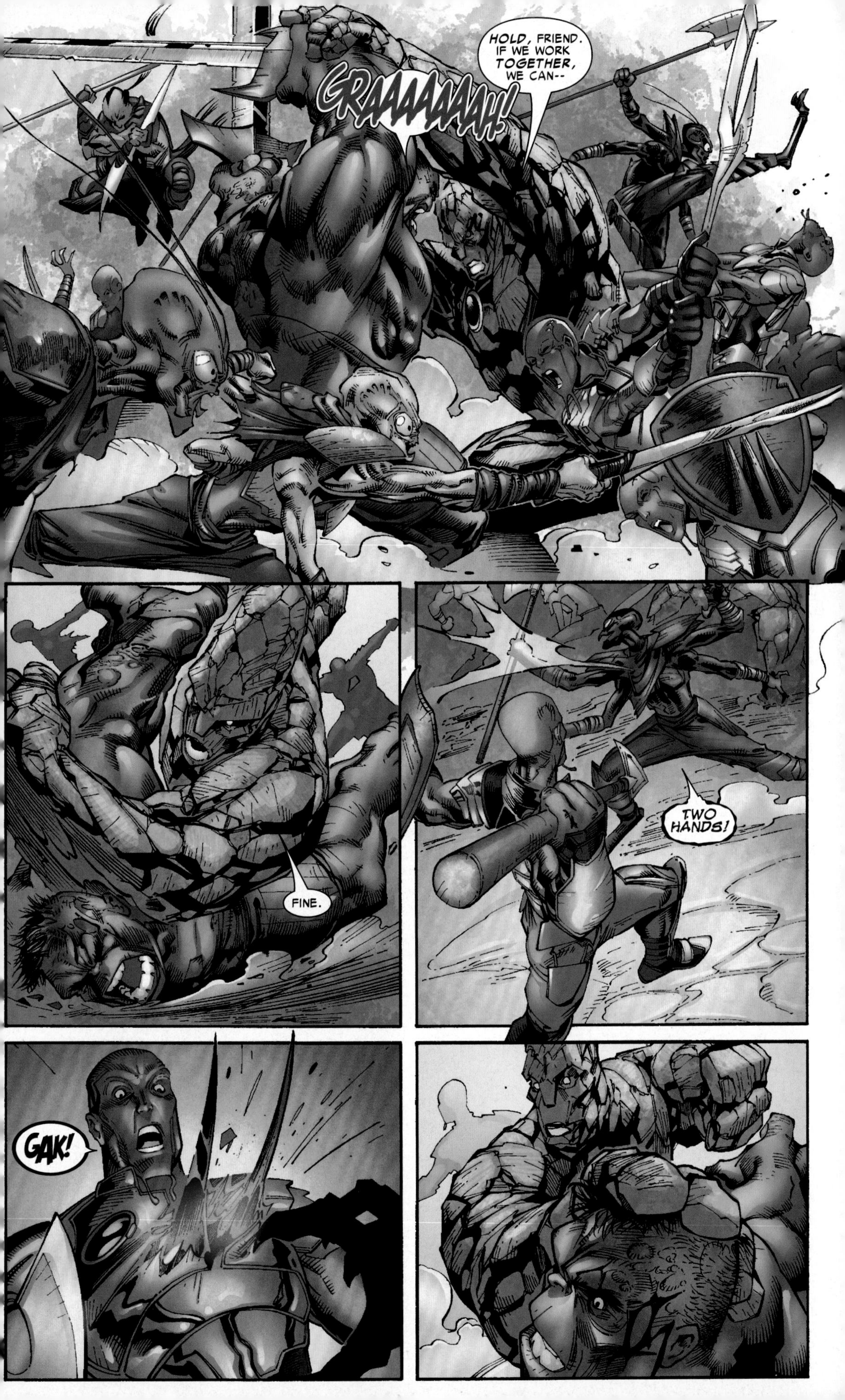
GRAAAAAAAH!
HOLD, FRIEND. IF WE WORK TOGETHER, WE CAN--
FINE.
TWO HANDS!
GAK!

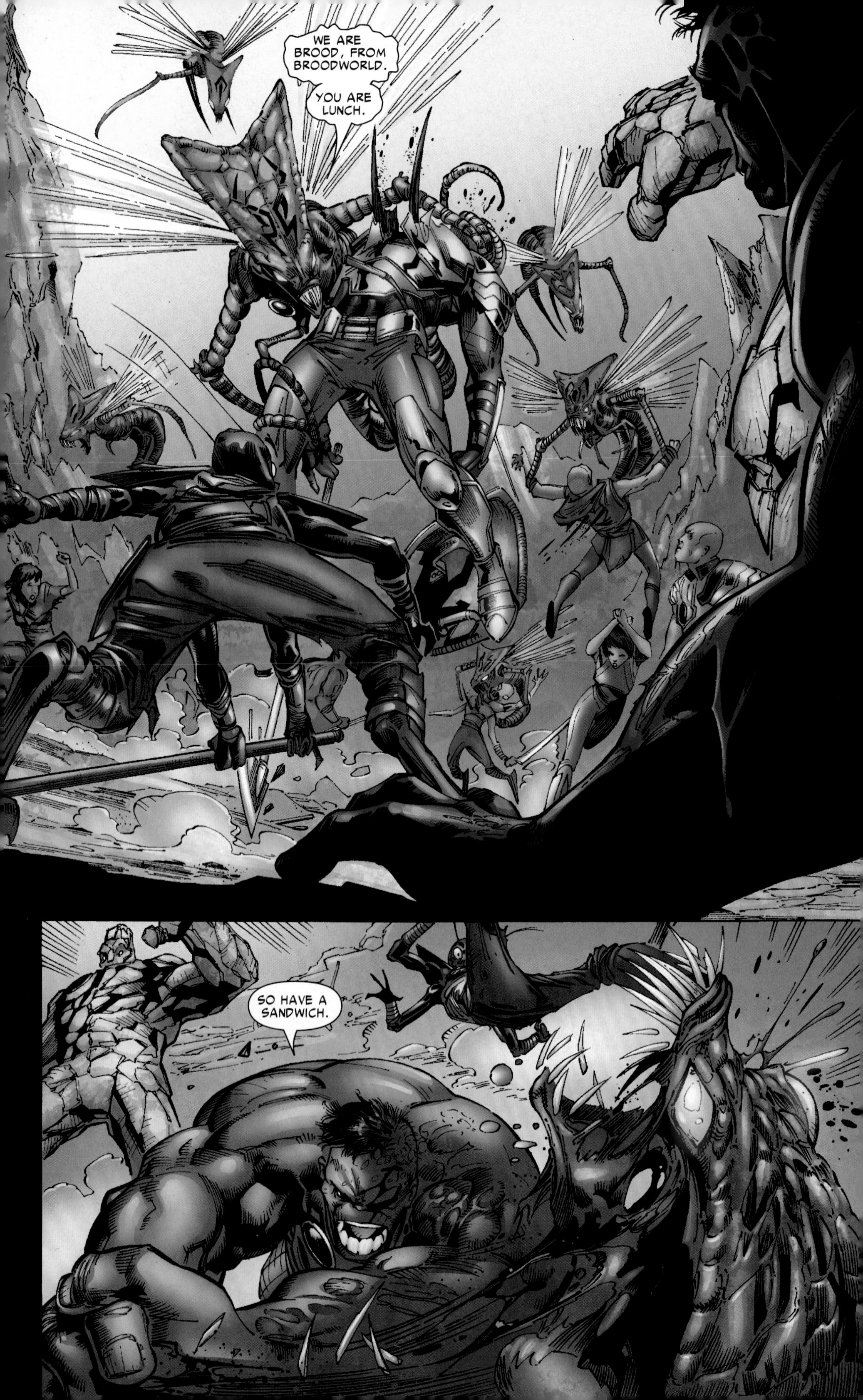
WE ARE BROOD, FROM BROODWORLD.
YOU ARE LUNCH.
SO HAVE A SANDWICH.

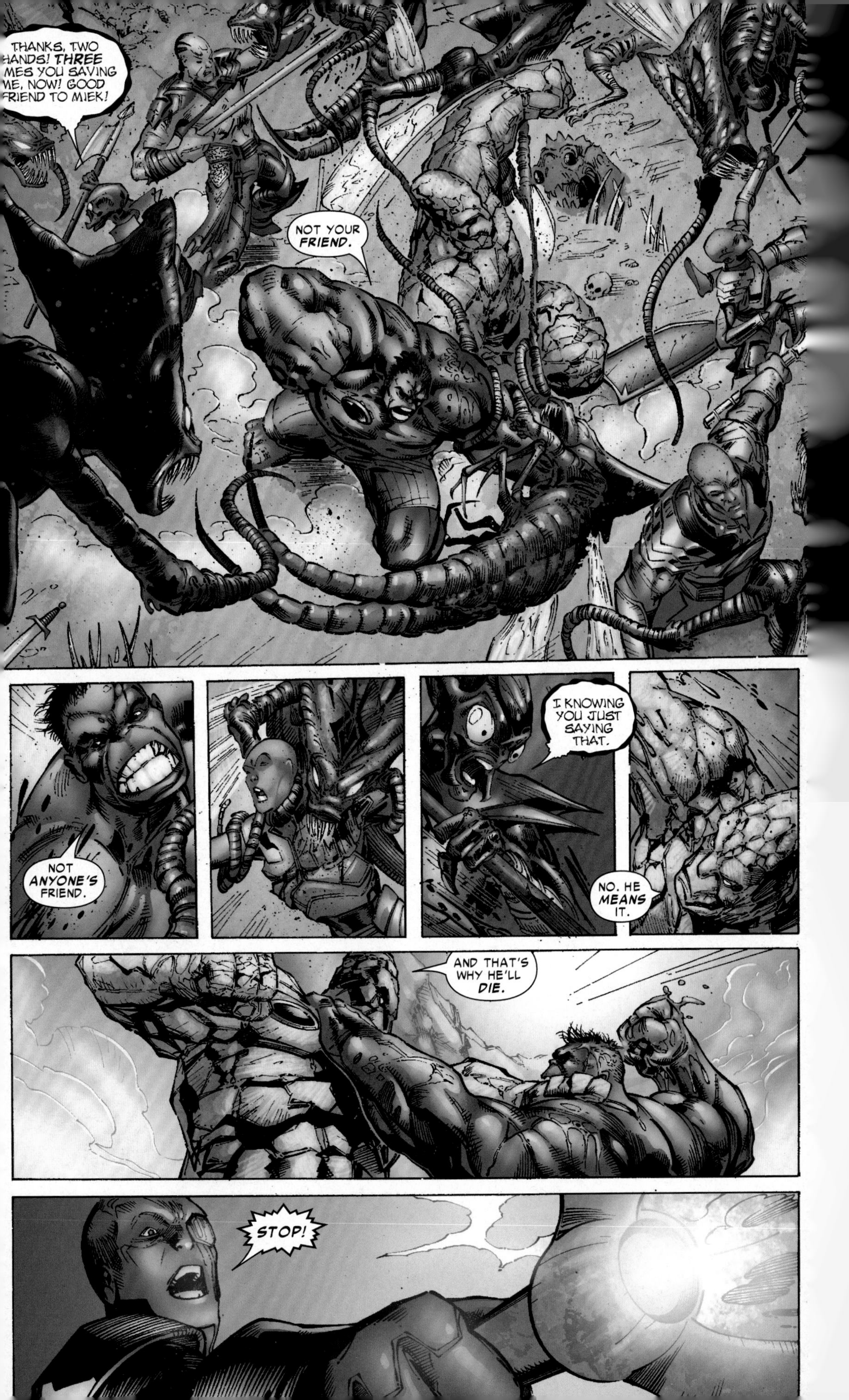
THANKS, TWO HANDS! THREE MES YOU SAVING ME, NOW! GOOD FRIEND TO MIEK!
NOT YOUR FRIEND.
NOT ANYONE'S FRIEND.
I KNOWING YOU JUST SAYING THAT.
NO. HE MEANS IT.
AND THAT'S WHY HE'LL DIE.
STOP!

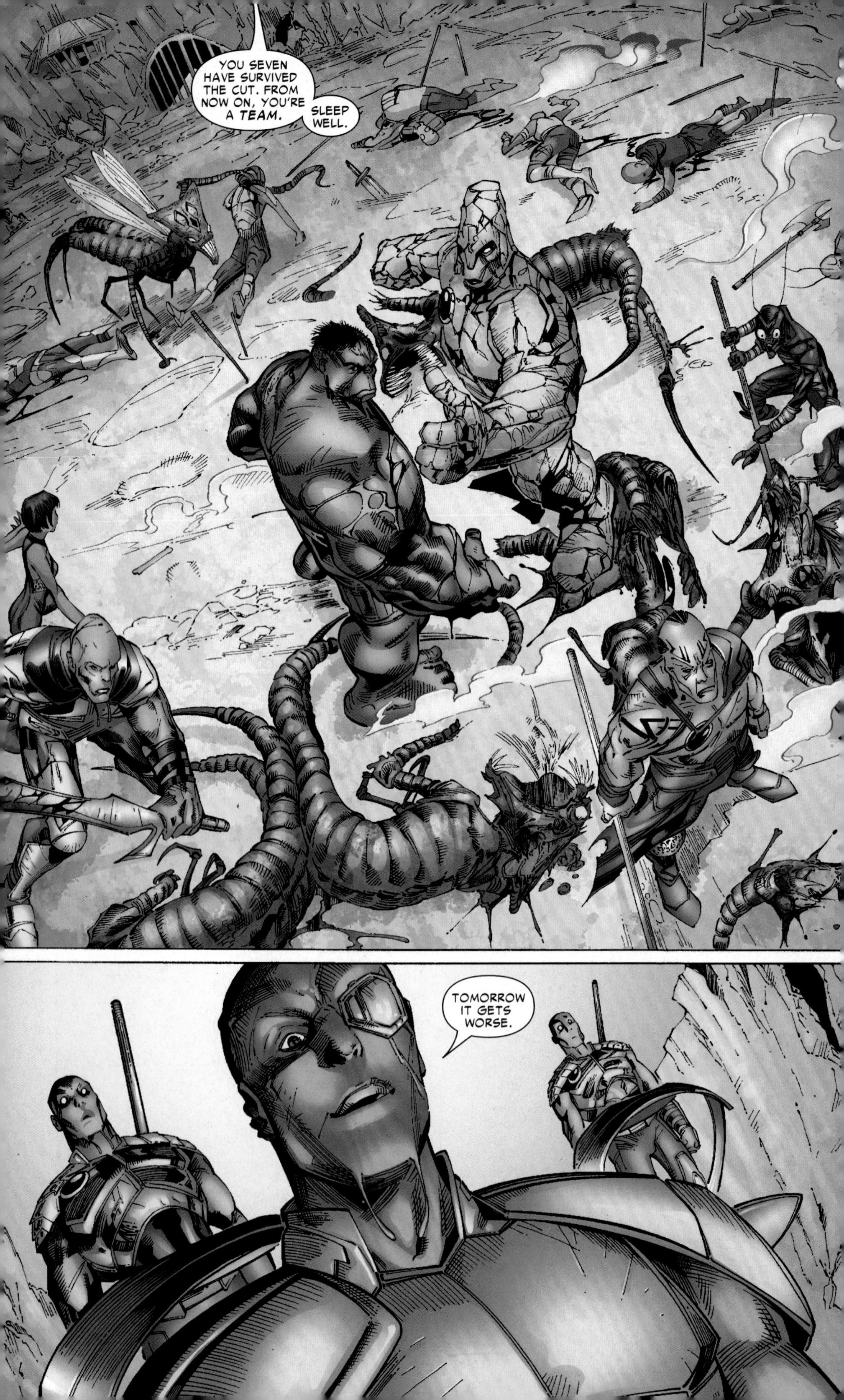
YOU SEVEN HAVE SURVIVED THE CUT. FROM NOW ON, YOU'RE A *TEAM*.
SLEEP WELL.
TOMORROW IT GETS WORSE.

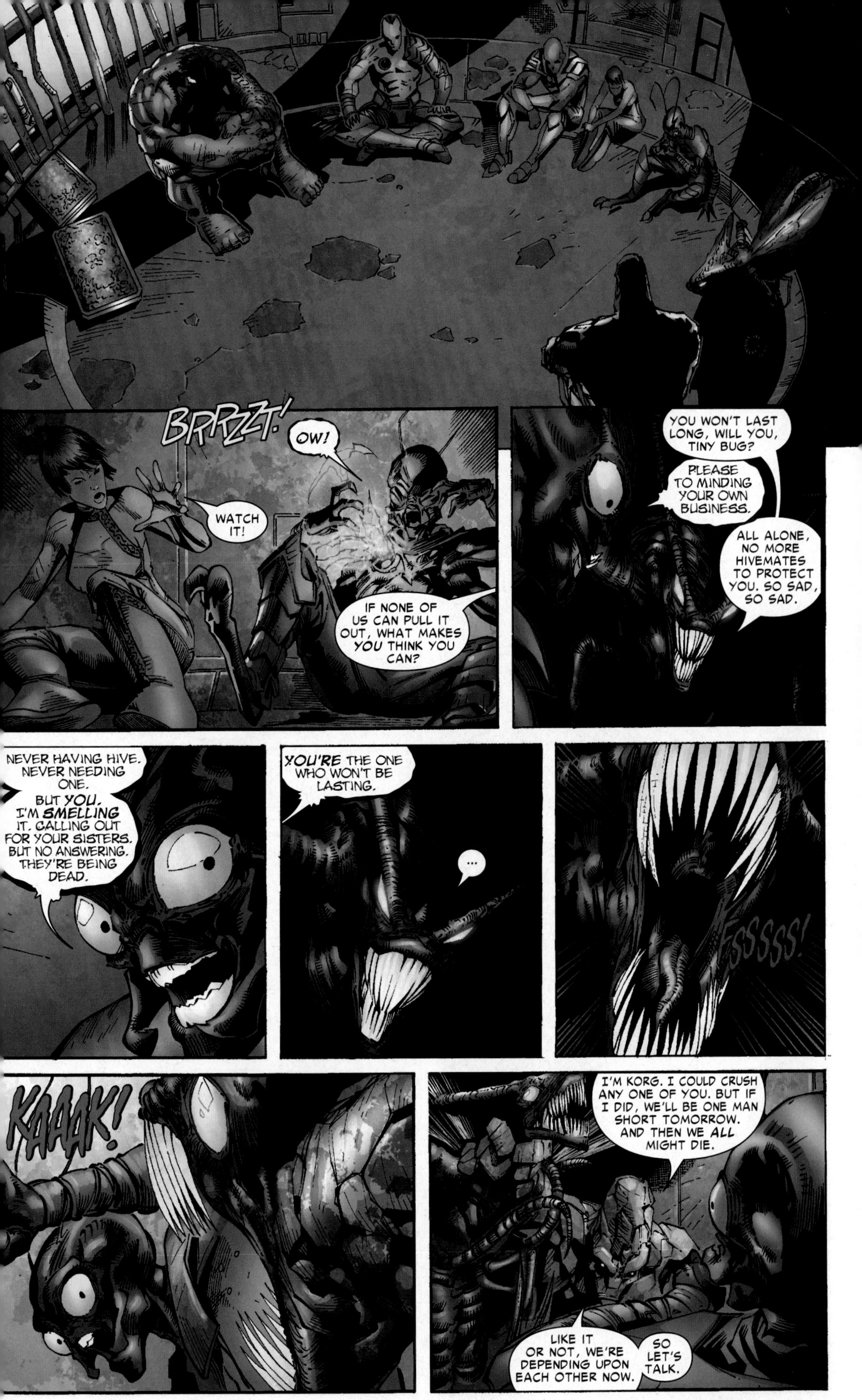

BRRZZT!
OW!
WATCH IT!
IF NONE OF US CAN PULL IT OUT, WHAT MAKES YOU THINK YOU CAN?
YOU WON'T LAST LONG, WILL YOU, TINY BUG?
PLEASE TO MINDING YOUR OWN BUSINESS.
ALL ALONE, NO MORE HIVEMATES TO PROTECT YOU. SO SAD, SO SAD.
NEVER HAVING HIVE. NEVER NEEDING ONE.
BUT YOU, I'M SMELLING IT. CALLING OUT FOR YOUR SISTERS. BUT NO ANSWERING. THEY'RE BEING DEAD.
YOU'RE THE ONE WHO WON'T BE LASTING.
...
FSSSSS!
KAAAK!
I'M KORG. I COULD CRUSH ANY ONE OF YOU. BUT IF I DID, WE'LL BE ONE MAN SHORT TOMORROW. AND THEN WE ALL MIGHT DIE.
LIKE IT OR NOT, WE'RE DEPENDING UPON EACH OTHER NOW.
SO LET'S TALK.

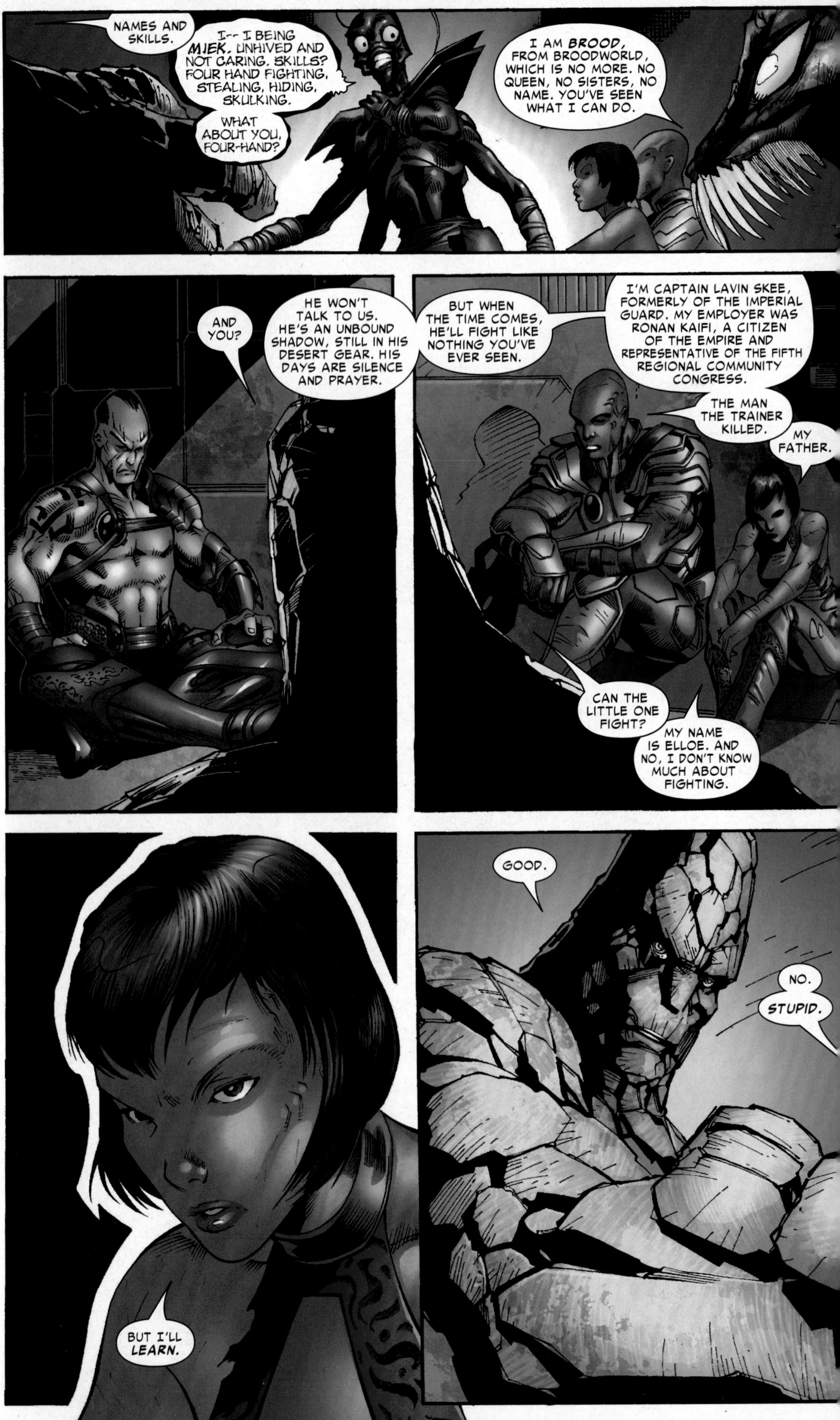
NAMES AND SKILLS.
I-- I BEING MIEK. UNHIVED AND NOT CARING. SKILLS? FOUR HAND FIGHTING, STEALING, HIDING, SKULKING.
WHAT ABOUT YOU, FOUR-HAND?
I AM BROOD, FROM BROODWORLD, WHICH IS NO MORE. NO QUEEN, NO SISTERS, NO NAME. YOU'VE SEEN WHAT I CAN DO.
AND YOU?
HE WON'T TALK TO US. HE'S AN UNBOUND SHADOW, STILL IN HIS DESERT GEAR. HIS DAYS ARE SILENCE AND PRAYER.
BUT WHEN THE TIME COMES, HE'LL FIGHT LIKE NOTHING YOU'VE EVER SEEN.
I'M CAPTAIN LAVIN SKEE, FORMERLY OF THE IMPERIAL GUARD. MY EMPLOYER WAS RONAN KAIFI, A CITIZEN OF THE EMPIRE AND REPRESENTATIVE OF THE FIFTH REGIONAL COMMUNITY CONGRESS.
THE MAN THE TRAINER KILLED.
MY FATHER.
CAN THE LITTLE ONE FIGHT?
MY NAME IS ELLOE. AND NO, I DON'T KNOW MUCH ABOUT FIGHTING.
BUT I'LL LEARN.
GOOD.
NO.
STUPID.

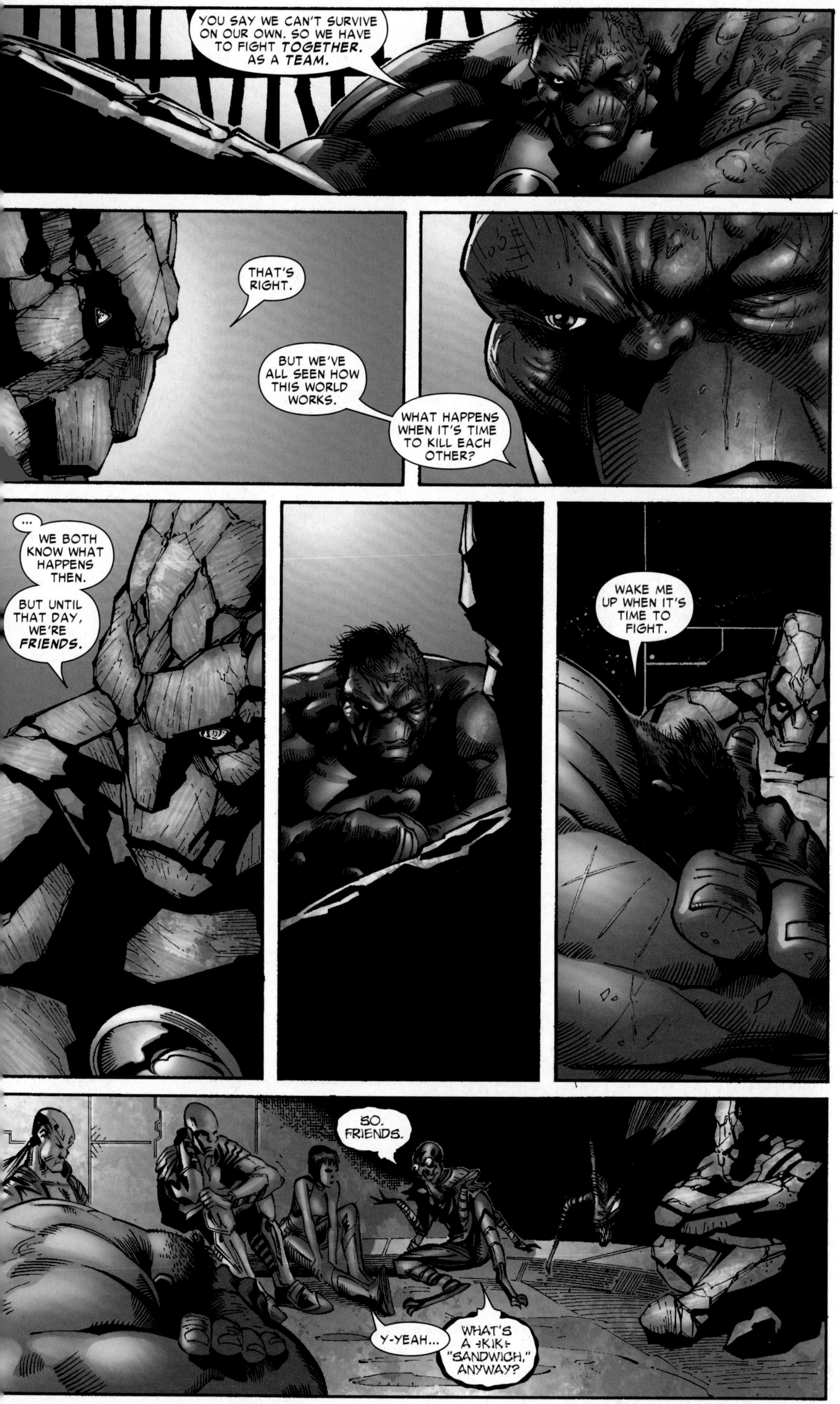
YOU SAY WE CAN'T SURVIVE ON OUR OWN. SO WE HAVE TO FIGHT *TOGETHER.* AS A *TEAM.*
THAT'S RIGHT.
BUT WE'VE ALL SEEN HOW THIS WORLD WORKS.
WHAT HAPPENS WHEN IT'S TIME TO KILL EACH OTHER?
...WE BOTH KNOW WHAT HAPPENS THEN.
BUT UNTIL THAT DAY, WE'RE *FRIENDS.*
WAKE ME UP WHEN IT'S TIME TO FIGHT.
SO. FRIENDS.
Y-YEAH...
WHAT'S A KIK "SANDWICH," ANYWAY?

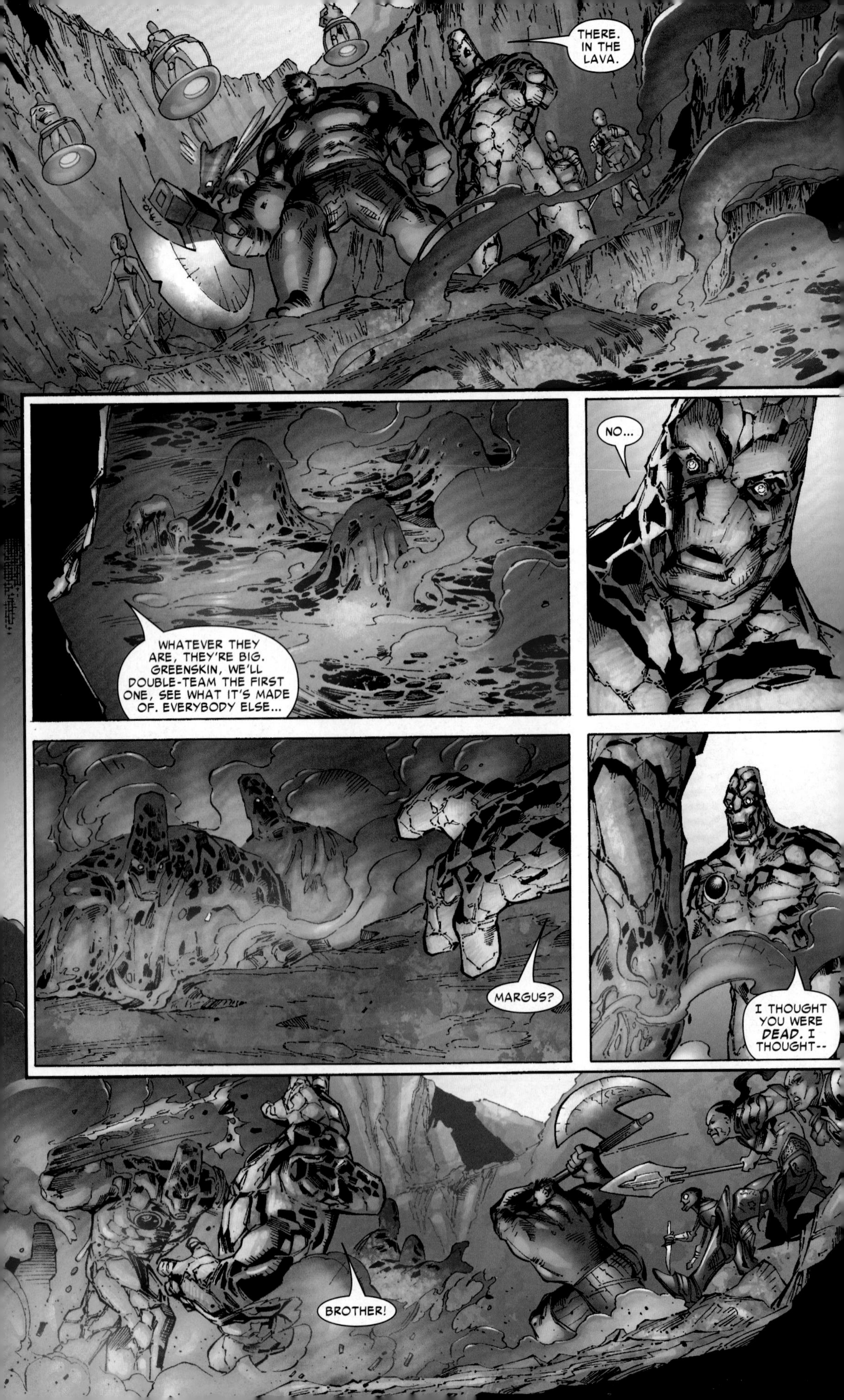
THERE. IN THE LAVA.
WHATEVER THEY ARE, THEY'RE BIG. GREENSKIN, WE'LL DOUBLE-TEAM THE FIRST ONE, SEE WHAT IT'S MADE OF. EVERYBODY ELSE...
NO...
MARGUS?
I THOUGHT YOU WERE *DEAD*. I THOUGHT--
BROTHER!

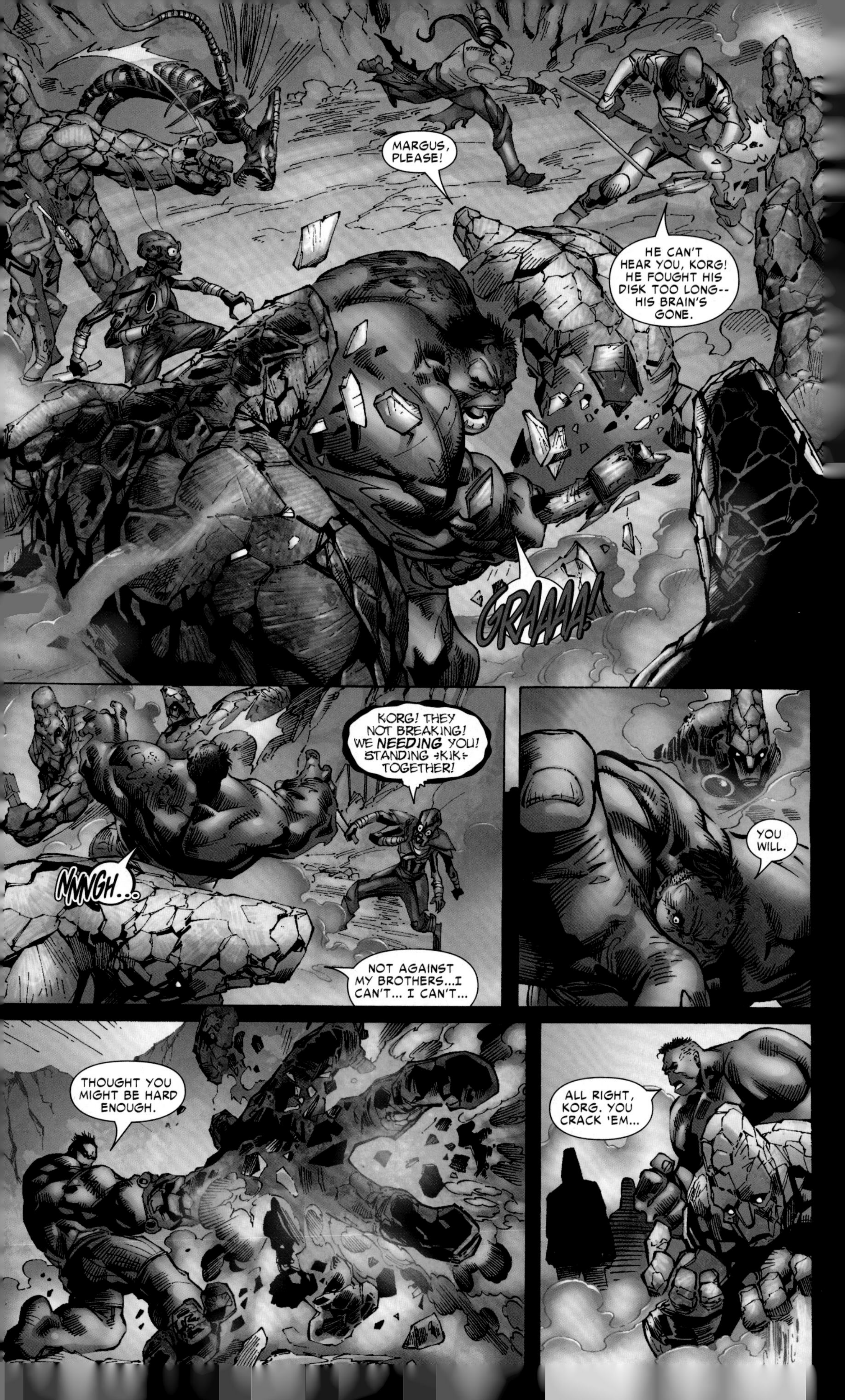
MARGUS, PLEASE!
HE CAN'T HEAR YOU, KORG! HE FOUGHT HIS DISK TOO LONG-- HIS BRAIN'S GONE.
GRAAAAA!
KORG! THEY NOT BREAKING! WE NEEDING YOU! STANDING -KIK- TOGETHER!
NNNGH...
NOT AGAINST MY BROTHERS...I CAN'T... I CAN'T...
YOU WILL.
THOUGHT YOU MIGHT BE HARD ENOUGH.
ALL RIGHT, KORG. YOU CRACK 'EM...

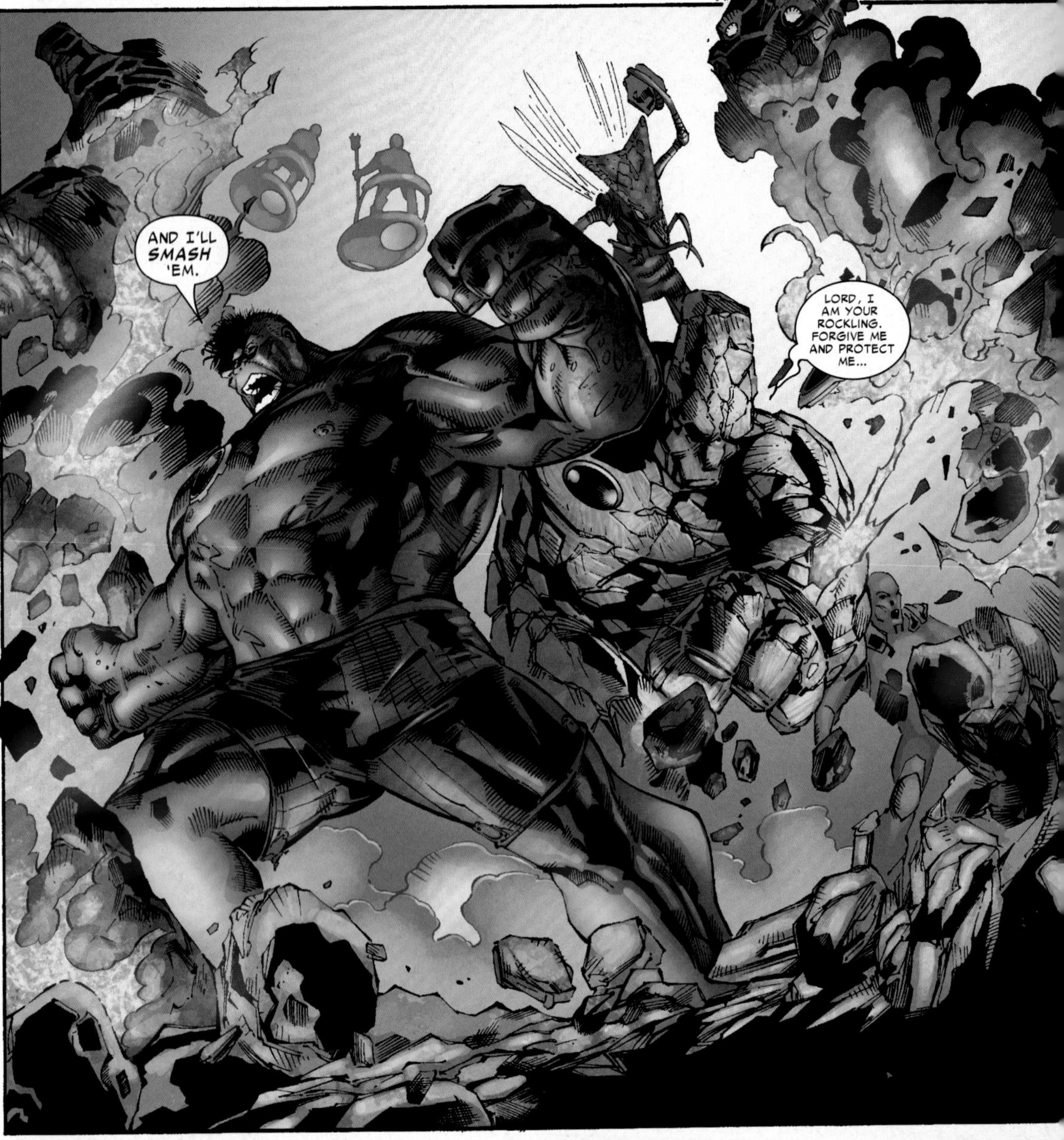
AND I'LL SMASH 'EM.
LORD, I AM YOUR ROCKLING. FORGIVE ME AND PROTECT ME...

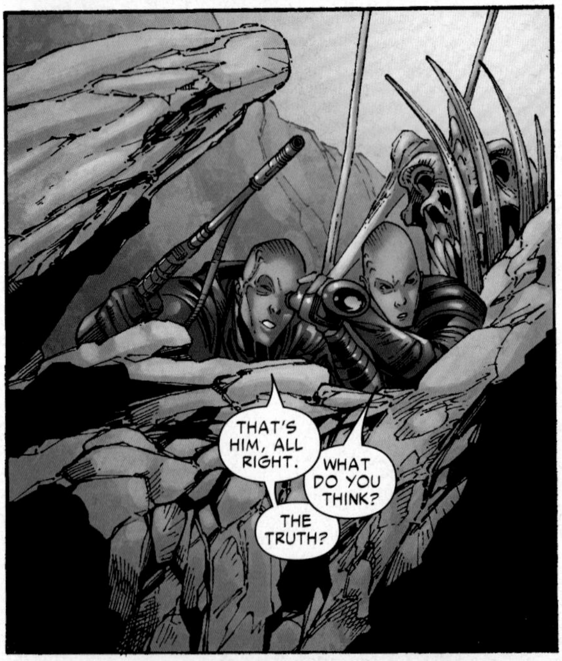
THAT'S HIM, ALL RIGHT.
WHAT DO YOU THINK?
THE TRUTH?

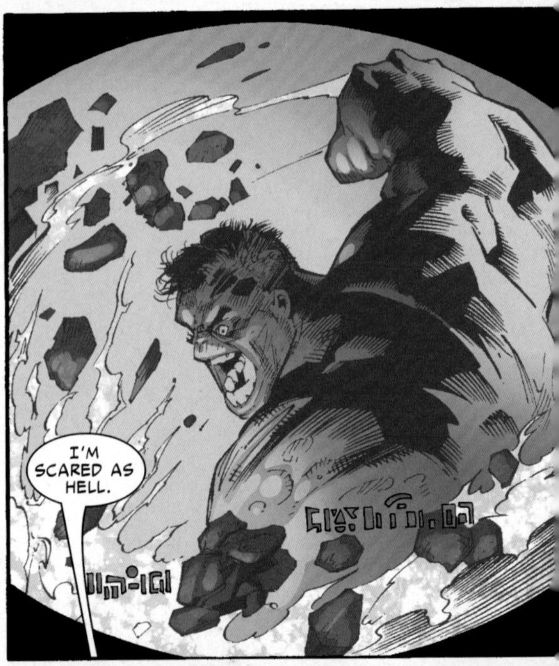
I'M SCARED AS HELL.

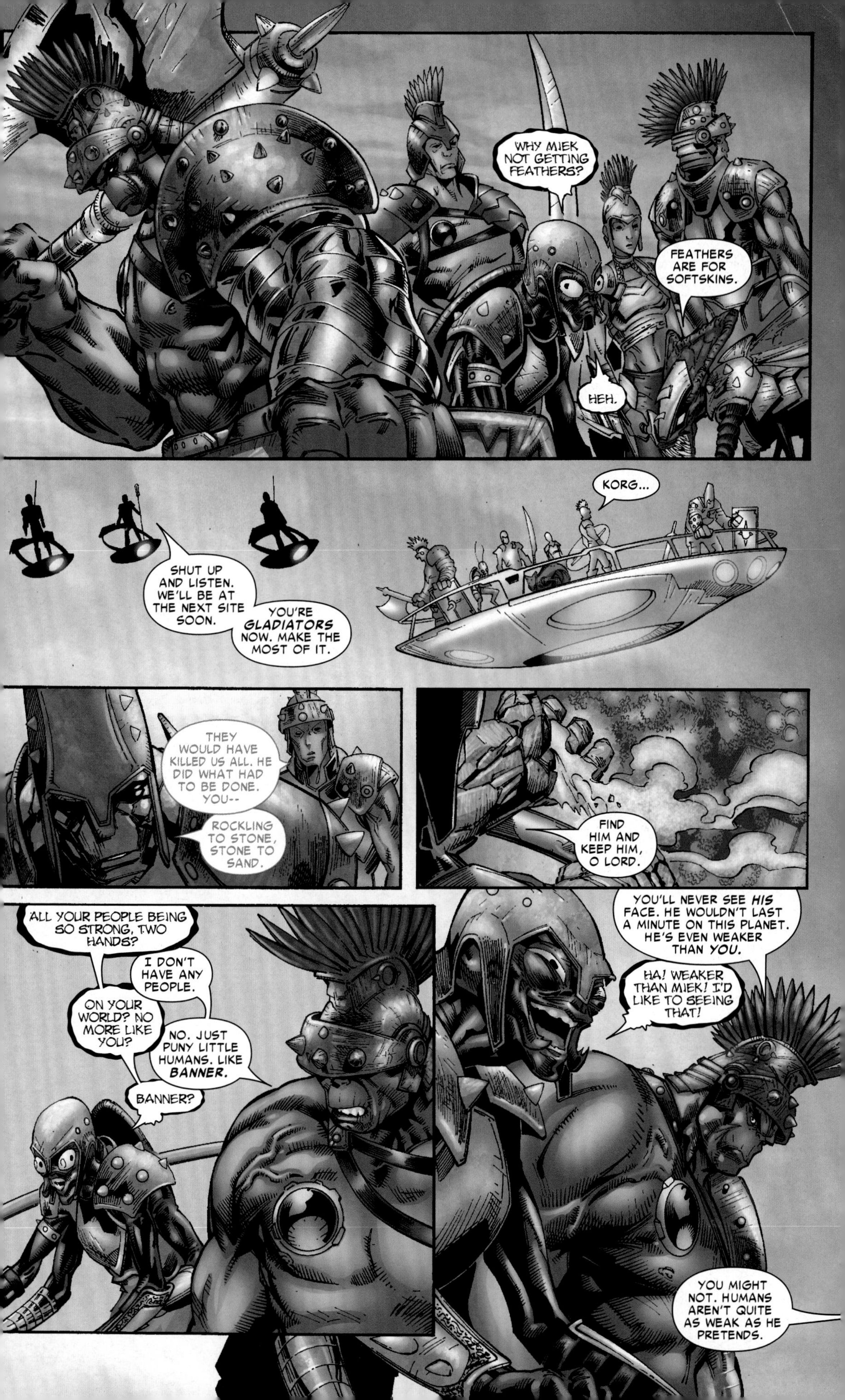
WHY MIEK NOT GETTING FEATHERS?
FEATHERS ARE FOR SOFTSKINS.
HEH.
KORG...
SHUT UP AND LISTEN. WE'LL BE AT THE NEXT SITE SOON.
YOU'RE GLADIATORS NOW. MAKE THE MOST OF IT.
THEY WOULD HAVE KILLED US ALL. HE DID WHAT HAD TO BE DONE. YOU--
ROCKLING TO STONE, STONE TO SAND.
FIND HIM AND KEEP HIM, O LORD.
ALL YOUR PEOPLE BEING SO STRONG, TWO HANDS?
I DON'T HAVE ANY PEOPLE.
ON YOUR WORLD? NO MORE LIKE YOU?
NO. JUST PUNY LITTLE HUMANS. LIKE BANNER.
BANNER?
YOU'LL NEVER SEE HIS FACE. HE WOULDN'T LAST A MINUTE ON THIS PLANET. HE'S EVEN WEAKER THAN YOU.
HA! WEAKER THAN MIEK! I'D LIKE TO SEEING THAT!
YOU MIGHT NOT. HUMANS AREN'T QUITE AS WEAK AS HE PRETENDS.

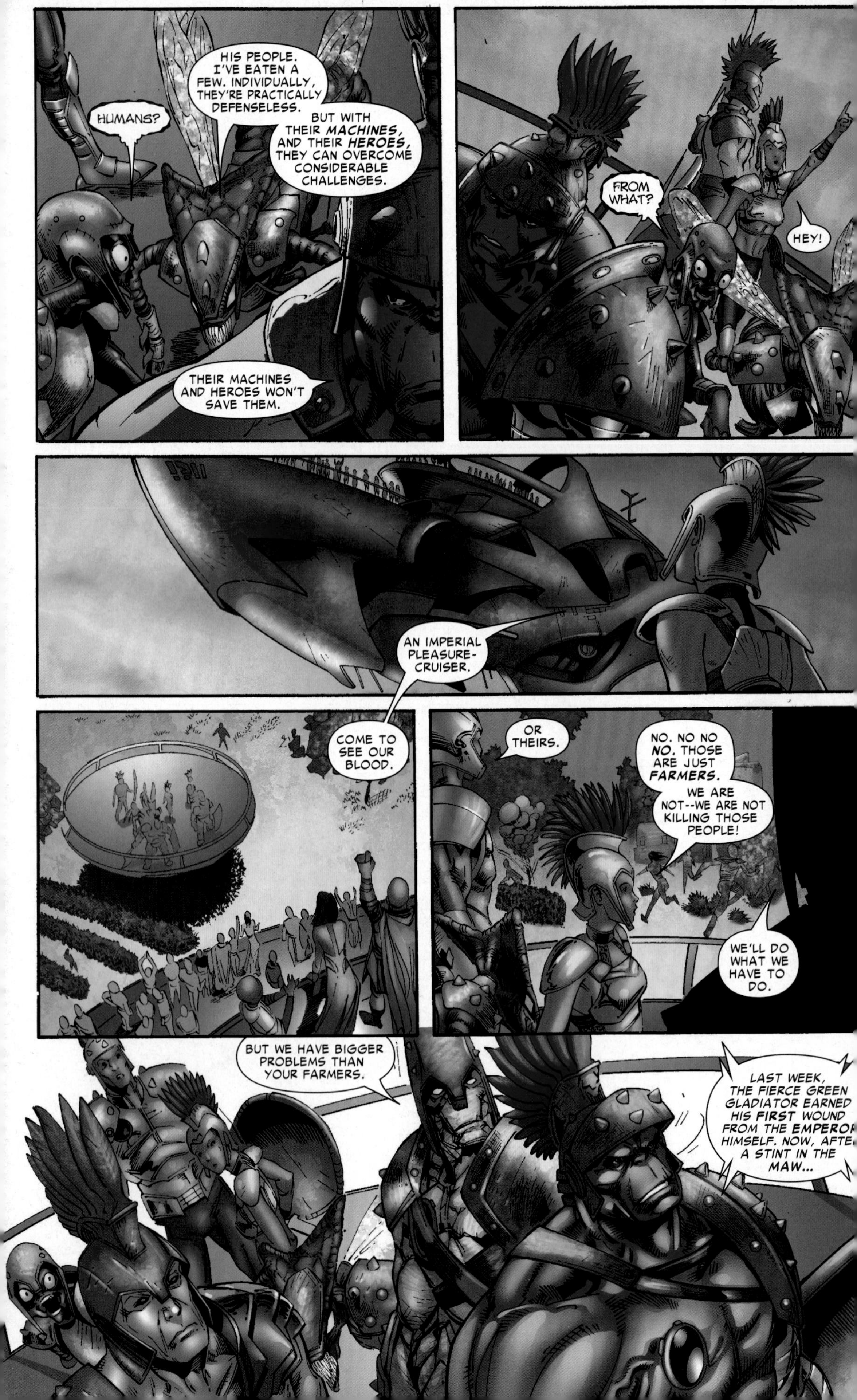
HUMANS?
HIS PEOPLE. I'VE EATEN A FEW. INDIVIDUALLY, THEY'RE PRACTICALLY DEFENSELESS.
BUT WITH THEIR MACHINES, AND THEIR HEROES, THEY CAN OVERCOME CONSIDERABLE CHALLENGES.
THEIR MACHINES AND HEROES WON'T SAVE THEM.
FROM WHAT?
HEY!
AN IMPERIAL PLEASURE-CRUISER.
COME TO SEE OUR BLOOD.
OR THEIRS.
NO. NO NO NO. THOSE ARE JUST FARMERS.
WE ARE NOT--WE ARE NOT KILLING THOSE PEOPLE!
WE'LL DO WHAT WE HAVE TO DO.
BUT WE HAVE BIGGER PROBLEMS THAN YOUR FARMERS.
LAST WEEK, THE FIERCE GREEN GLADIATOR EARNED HIS FIRST WOUND FROM THE EMPERO HIMSELF. NOW, AFTE A STINT IN THE MAW...

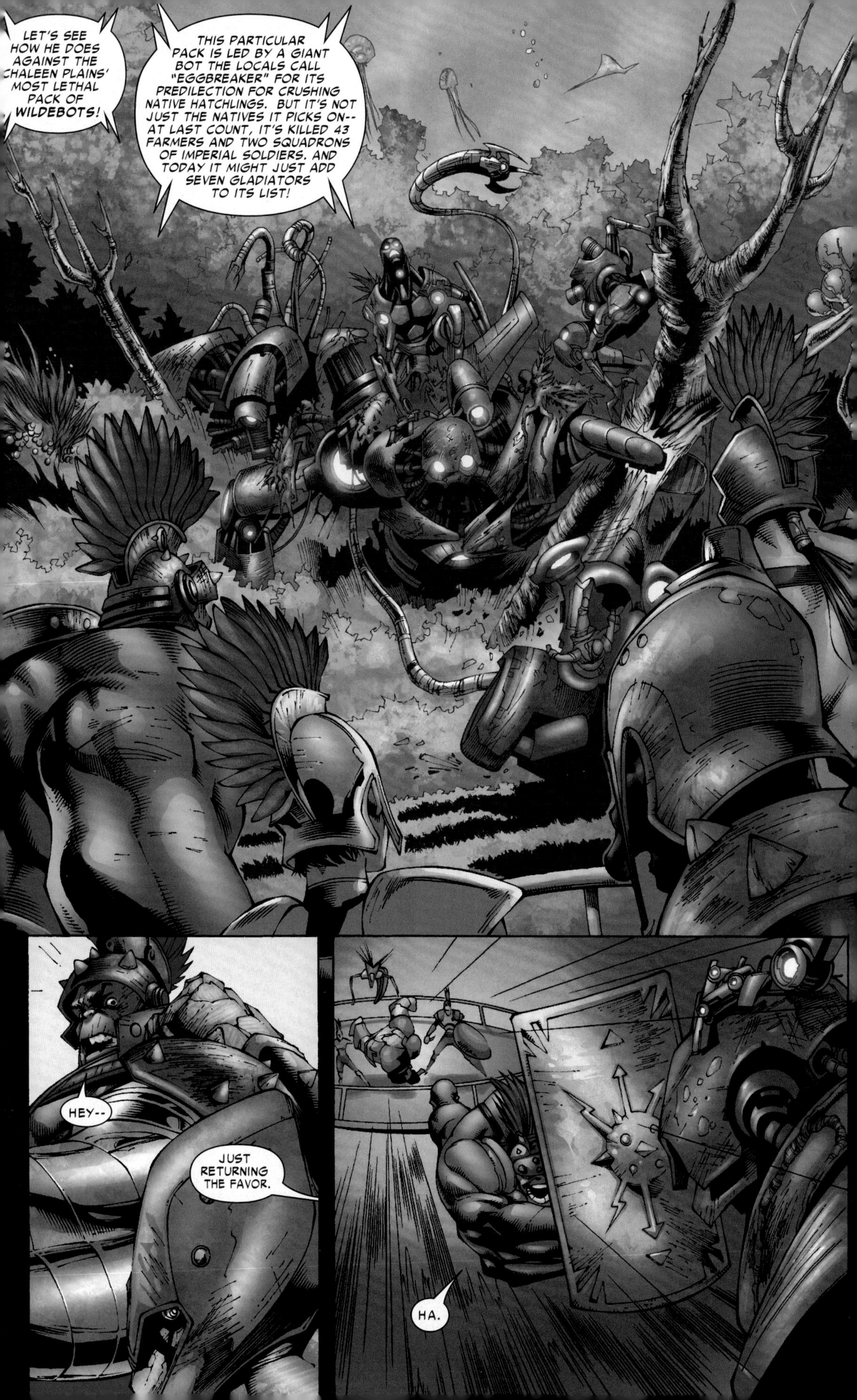

LET'S SEE HOW HE DOES AGAINST THE CHALEEN PLAINS' MOST LETHAL PACK OF WILDEBOTS!
THIS PARTICULAR PACK IS LED BY A GIANT BOT THE LOCALS CALL "EGGBREAKER" FOR ITS PREDILECTION FOR CRUSHING NATIVE HATCHLINGS. BUT IT'S NOT JUST THE NATIVES IT PICKS ON-- AT LAST COUNT, IT'S KILLED 43 FARMERS AND TWO SQUADRONS OF IMPERIAL SOLDIERS. AND TODAY IT MIGHT JUST ADD SEVEN GLADIATORS TO ITS LIST!
HEY--
JUST RETURNING THE FAVOR.
HA.

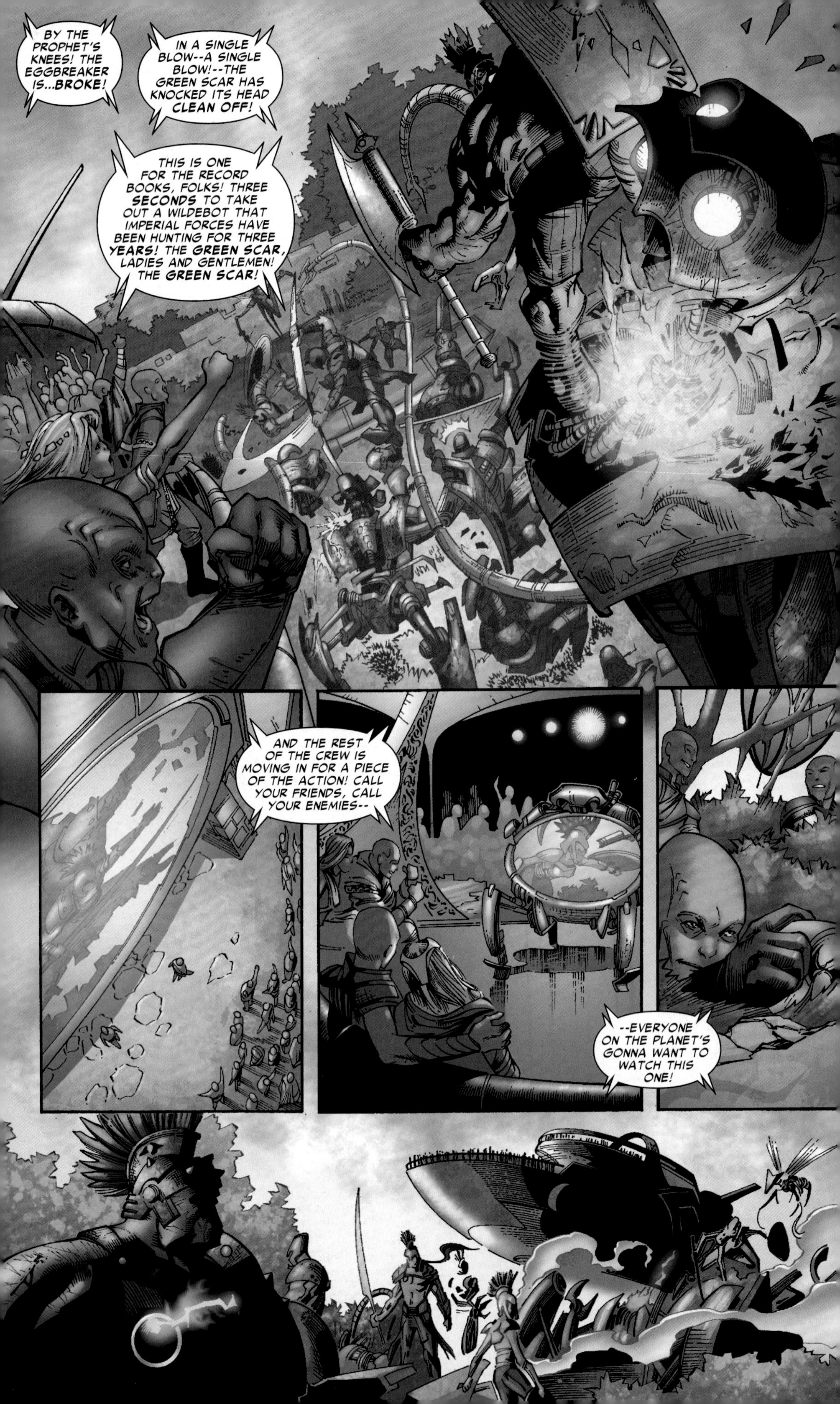

BY THE PROPHET'S KNEES! THE EGGBREAKER IS...BROKE!
IN A SINGLE BLOW--A SINGLE BLOW!--THE GREEN SCAR HAS KNOCKED ITS HEAD CLEAN OFF!
THIS IS ONE FOR THE RECORD BOOKS, FOLKS! THREE SECONDS TO TAKE OUT A WILDEBOT THAT IMPERIAL FORCES HAVE BEEN HUNTING FOR THREE YEARS! THE GREEN SCAR, LADIES AND GENTLEMEN! THE GREEN SCAR!
AND THE REST OF THE CREW IS MOVING IN FOR A PIECE OF THE ACTION! CALL YOUR FRIENDS, CALL YOUR ENEMIES--
--EVERYONE ON THE PLANET'S GONNA WANT TO WATCH THIS ONE!

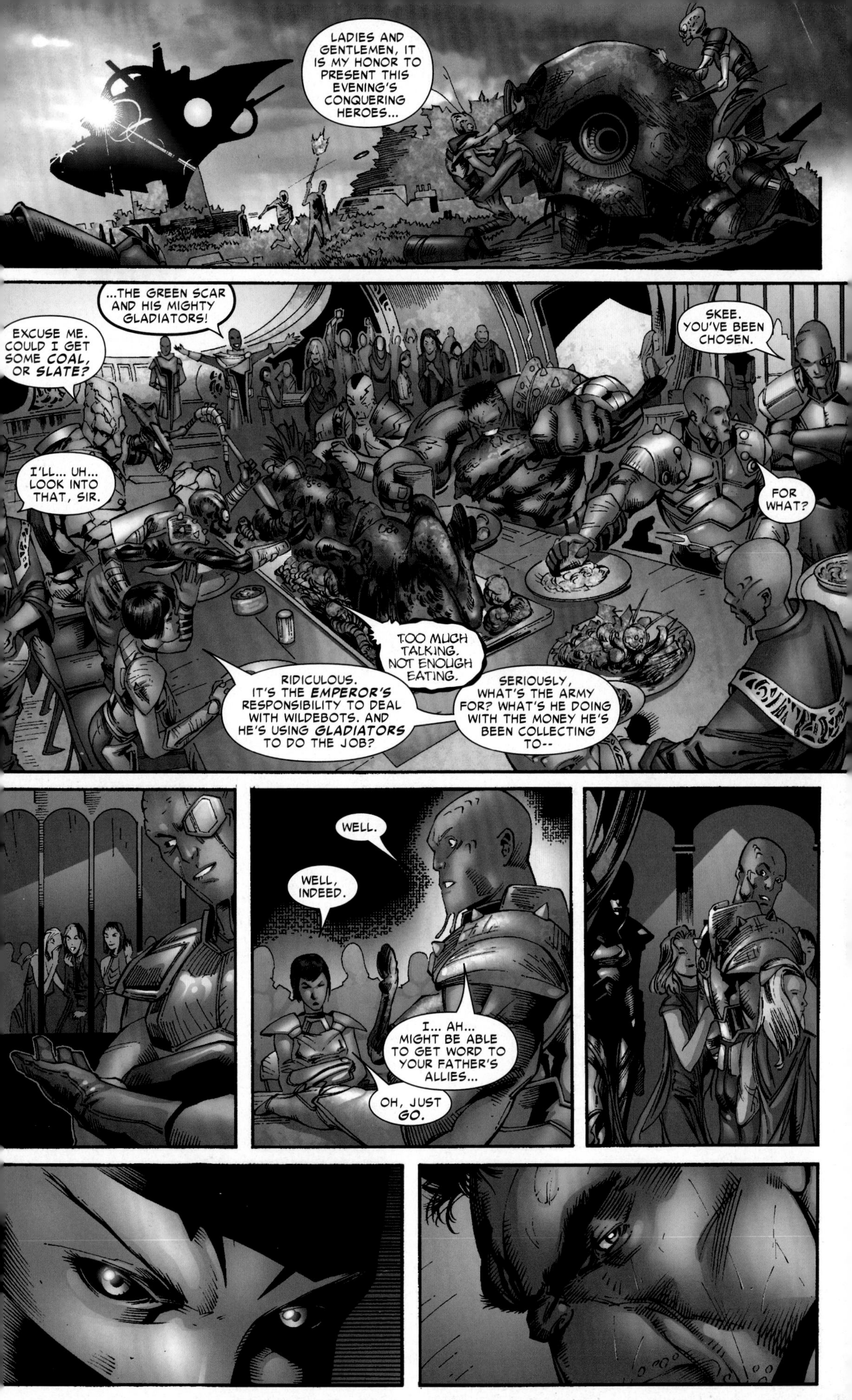
LADIES AND GENTLEMEN, IT IS MY HONOR TO PRESENT THIS EVENING'S CONQUERING HEROES...
...THE GREEN SCAR AND HIS MIGHTY GLADIATORS!
EXCUSE ME. COULD I GET SOME COAL, OR SLATE?
I'LL... UH... LOOK INTO THAT, SIR.
SKEE. YOU'VE BEEN CHOSEN.
FOR WHAT?
TOO MUCH TALKING. NOT ENOUGH EATING.
RIDICULOUS. IT'S THE EMPEROR'S RESPONSIBILITY TO DEAL WITH WILDEBOTS. AND HE'S USING GLADIATORS TO DO THE JOB?
SERIOUSLY, WHAT'S THE ARMY FOR? WHAT'S HE DOING WITH THE MONEY HE'S BEEN COLLECTING TO--
WELL.
WELL, INDEED.
I... AH... MIGHT BE ABLE TO GET WORD TO YOUR FATHER'S ALLIES...
OH, JUST GO.

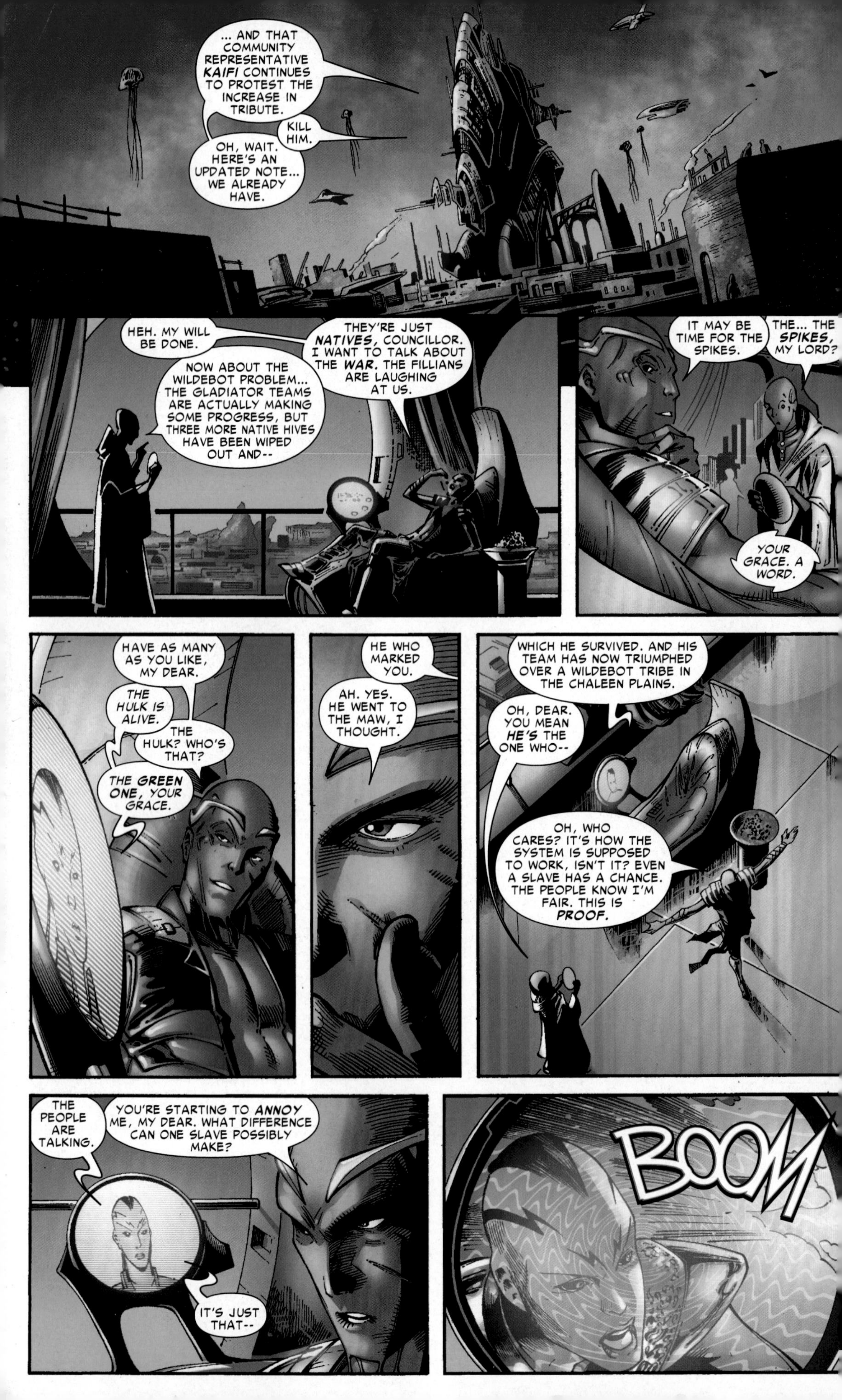
... AND THAT COMMUNITY REPRESENTATIVE KAIFI CONTINUES TO PROTEST THE INCREASE IN TRIBUTE.
KILL HIM.
OH, WAIT. HERE'S AN UPDATED NOTE... WE ALREADY HAVE.
HEH. MY WILL BE DONE.
NOW ABOUT THE WILDEBOT PROBLEM... THE GLADIATOR TEAMS ARE ACTUALLY MAKING SOME PROGRESS, BUT THREE MORE NATIVE HIVES HAVE BEEN WIPED OUT AND--
THEY'RE JUST NATIVES, COUNCILLOR. I WANT TO TALK ABOUT THE WAR. THE FILLIANS ARE LAUGHING AT US.
IT MAY BE TIME FOR THE SPIKES.
THE... THE SPIKES, MY LORD?
YOUR GRACE. A WORD.
HAVE AS MANY AS YOU LIKE, MY DEAR.
THE HULK IS ALIVE.
THE HULK? WHO'S THAT?
THE GREEN ONE, YOUR GRACE.
HE WHO MARKED YOU.
AH. YES. HE WENT TO THE MAW, I THOUGHT.
WHICH HE SURVIVED. AND HIS TEAM HAS NOW TRIUMPHED OVER A WILDEBOT TRIBE IN THE CHALEEN PLAINS.
OH, DEAR. YOU MEAN HE'S THE ONE WHO--
OH, WHO CARES? IT'S HOW THE SYSTEM IS SUPPOSED TO WORK, ISN'T IT? EVEN A SLAVE HAS A CHANCE. THE PEOPLE KNOW I'M FAIR. THIS IS PROOF.
THE PEOPLE ARE TALKING.
YOU'RE STARTING TO ANNOY ME, MY DEAR. WHAT DIFFERENCE CAN ONE SLAVE POSSIBLY MAKE?
IT'S JUST THAT--
BOOM

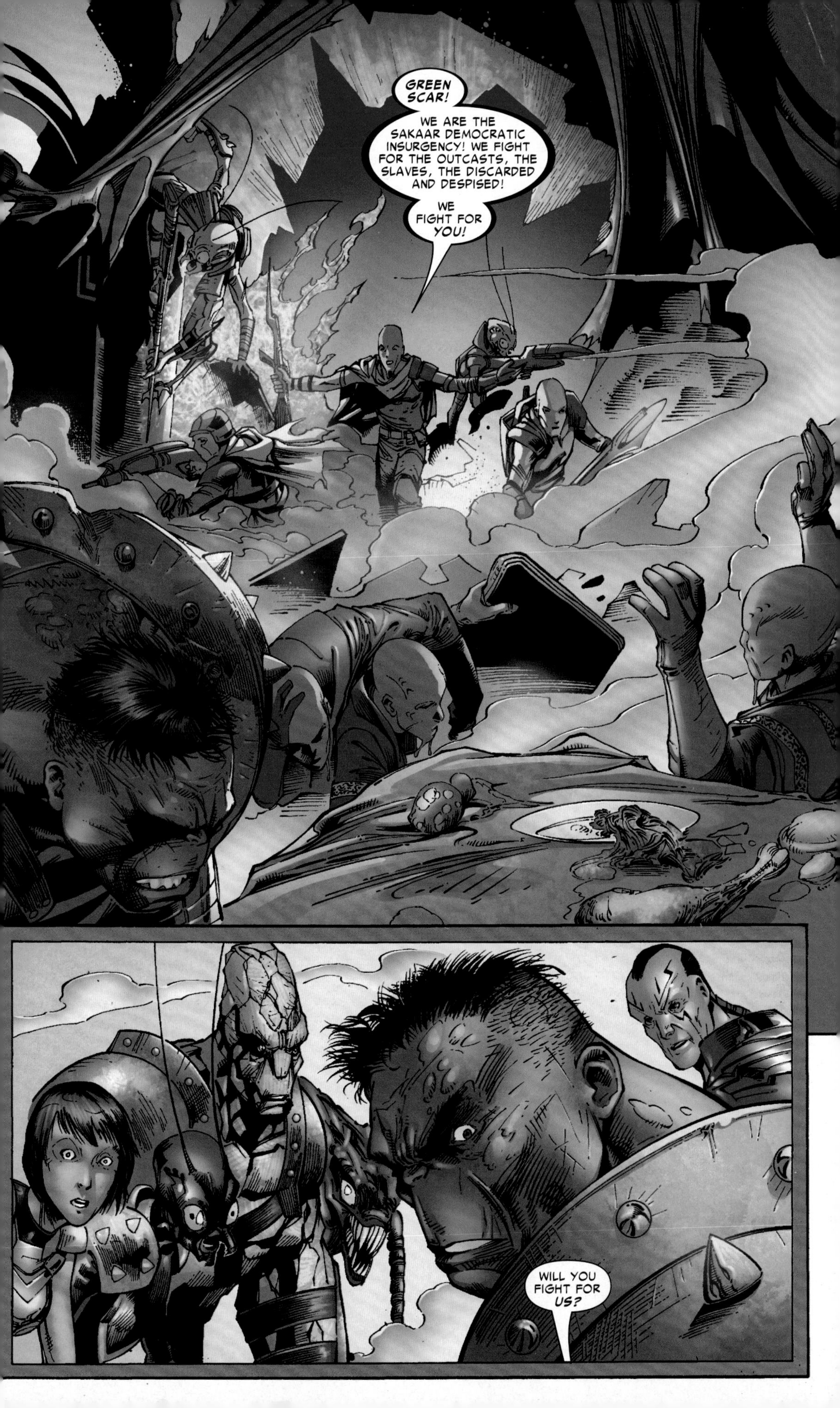
GREEN SCAR!
WE ARE THE SAKAAR DEMOCRATIC INSURGENCY! WE FIGHT FOR THE OUTCASTS, THE SLAVES, THE DISCARDED AND DESPISED!
WE FIGHT FOR YOU!
WILL YOU FIGHT FOR US?

#94

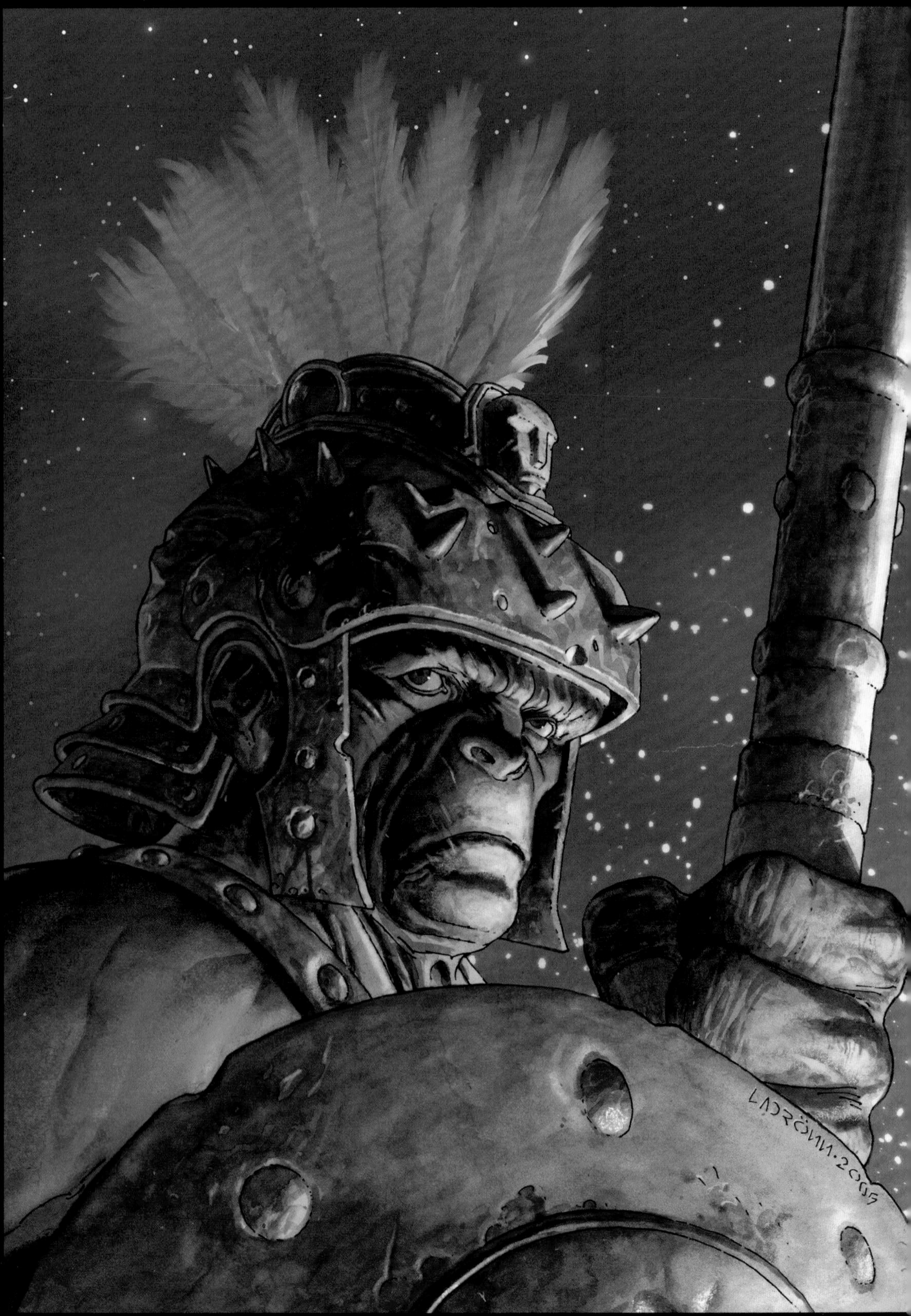
LADRÖNN·2005

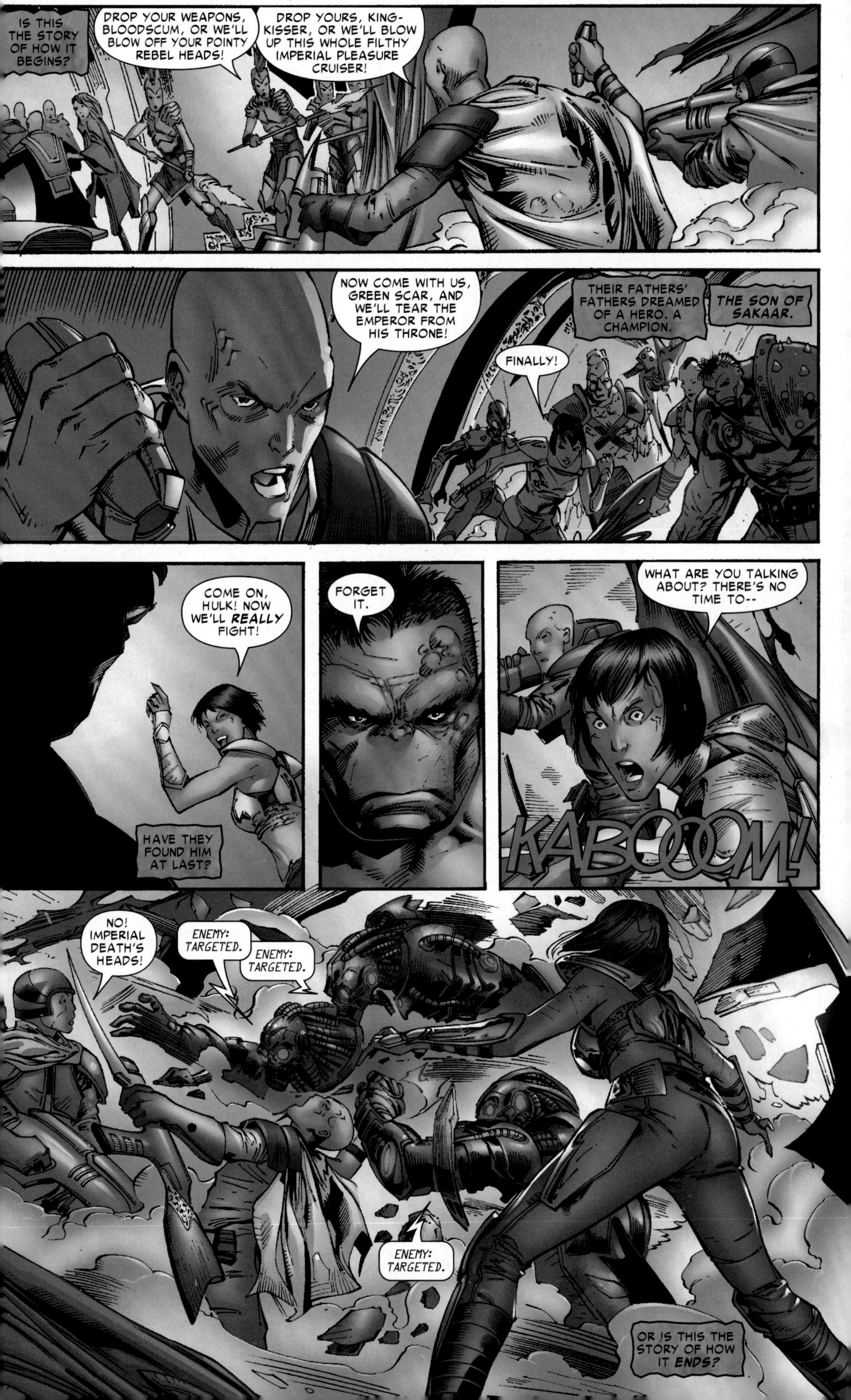

IS THIS THE STORY OF HOW IT BEGINS?
DROP YOUR WEAPONS, BLOODSCUM, OR WE'LL BLOW OFF YOUR POINTY REBEL HEADS!
DROP YOURS, KING-KISSER, OR WE'LL BLOW UP THIS WHOLE FILTHY IMPERIAL PLEASURE CRUISER!
NOW COME WITH US, GREEN SCAR, AND WE'LL TEAR THE EMPEROR FROM HIS THRONE!
THEIR FATHERS' FATHERS DREAMED OF A HERO. A CHAMPION.
THE SON OF SAKAAR.
FINALLY!
COME ON, HULK! NOW WE'LL REALLY FIGHT!
HAVE THEY FOUND HIM AT LAST?
FORGET IT.
WHAT ARE YOU TALKING ABOUT? THERE'S NO TIME TO--
KABOOOM!
NO! IMPERIAL DEATH'S HEADS!
ENEMY: TARGETED.
ENEMY: TARGETED.
ENEMY: TARGETED.
OR IS THIS THE STORY OF HOW IT ENDS?

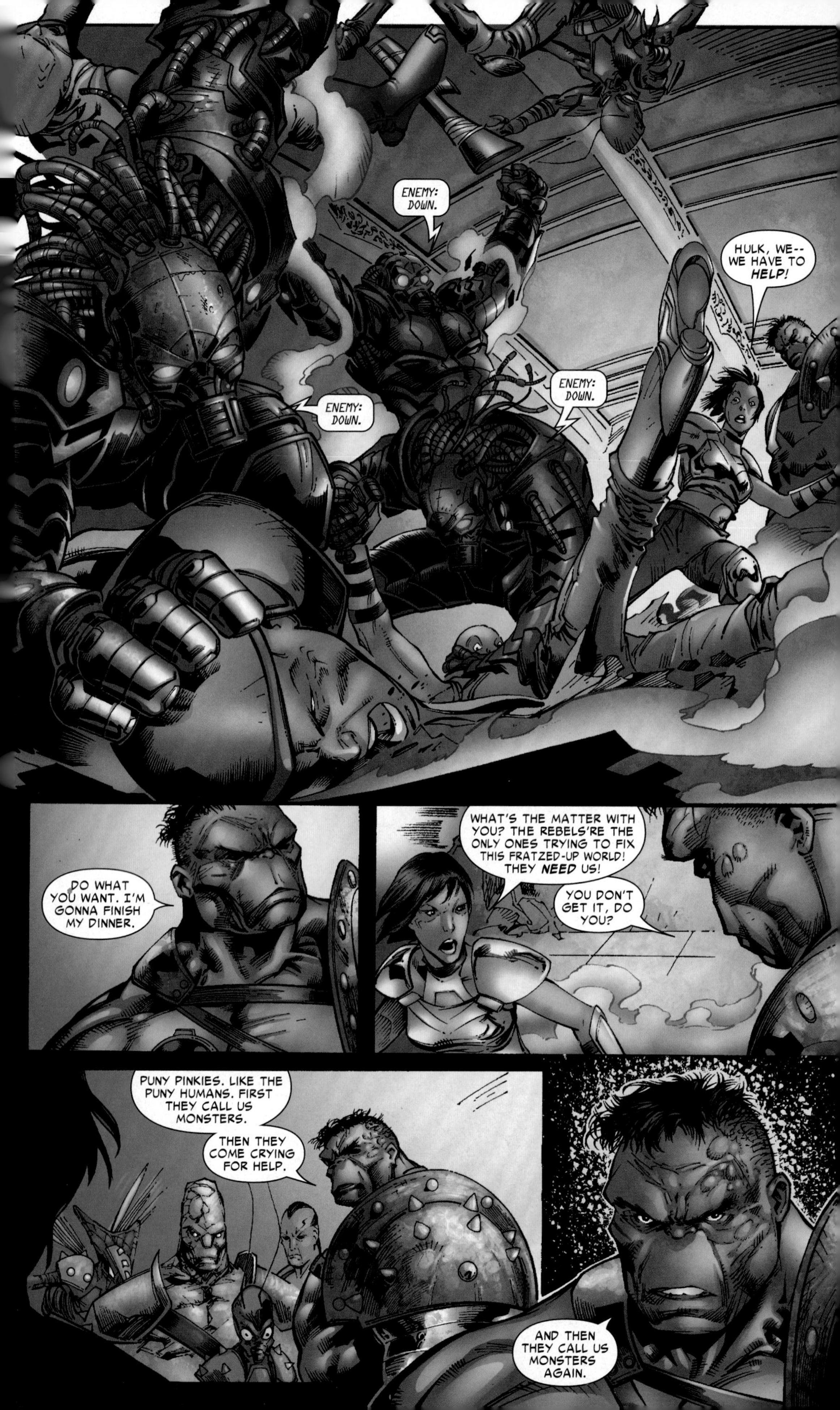
ENEMY: DOWN.
HULK, WE-- WE HAVE TO HELP!
ENEMY: DOWN.
ENEMY: DOWN.
DO WHAT YOU WANT. I'M GONNA FINISH MY DINNER.
WHAT'S THE MATTER WITH YOU? THE REBELS'RE THE ONLY ONES TRYING TO FIX THIS FRATZED-UP WORLD! THEY NEED US!
YOU DON'T GET IT, DO YOU?
PUNY PINKIES. LIKE THE PUNY HUMANS. FIRST THEY CALL US MONSTERS.
THEN THEY COME CRYING FOR HELP.
AND THEN THEY CALL US MONSTERS AGAIN.

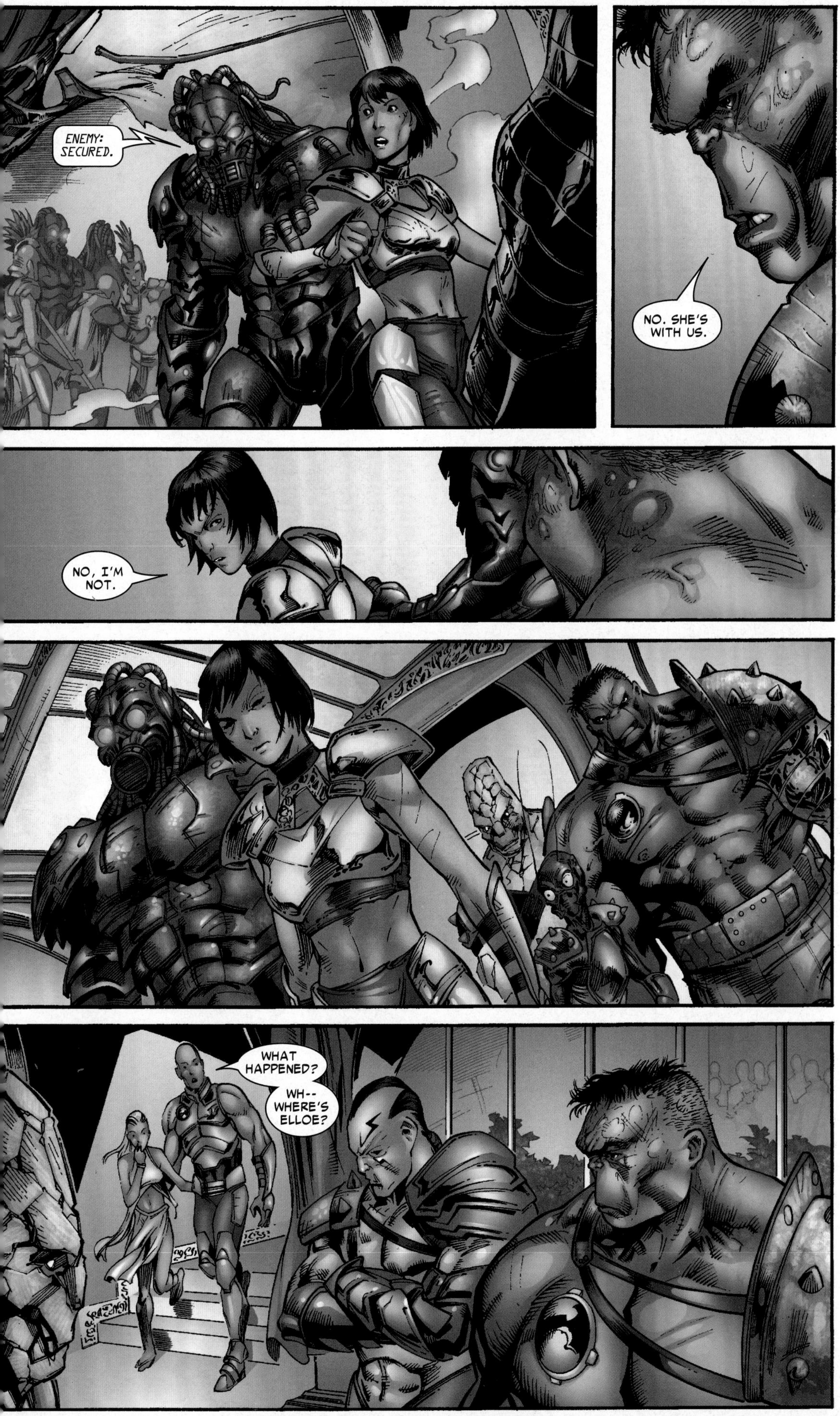

ENEMY: SECURED.
NO. SHE'S WITH US.
NO, I'M NOT.
WHAT HAPPENED?
WH-- WHERE'S ELLOE?

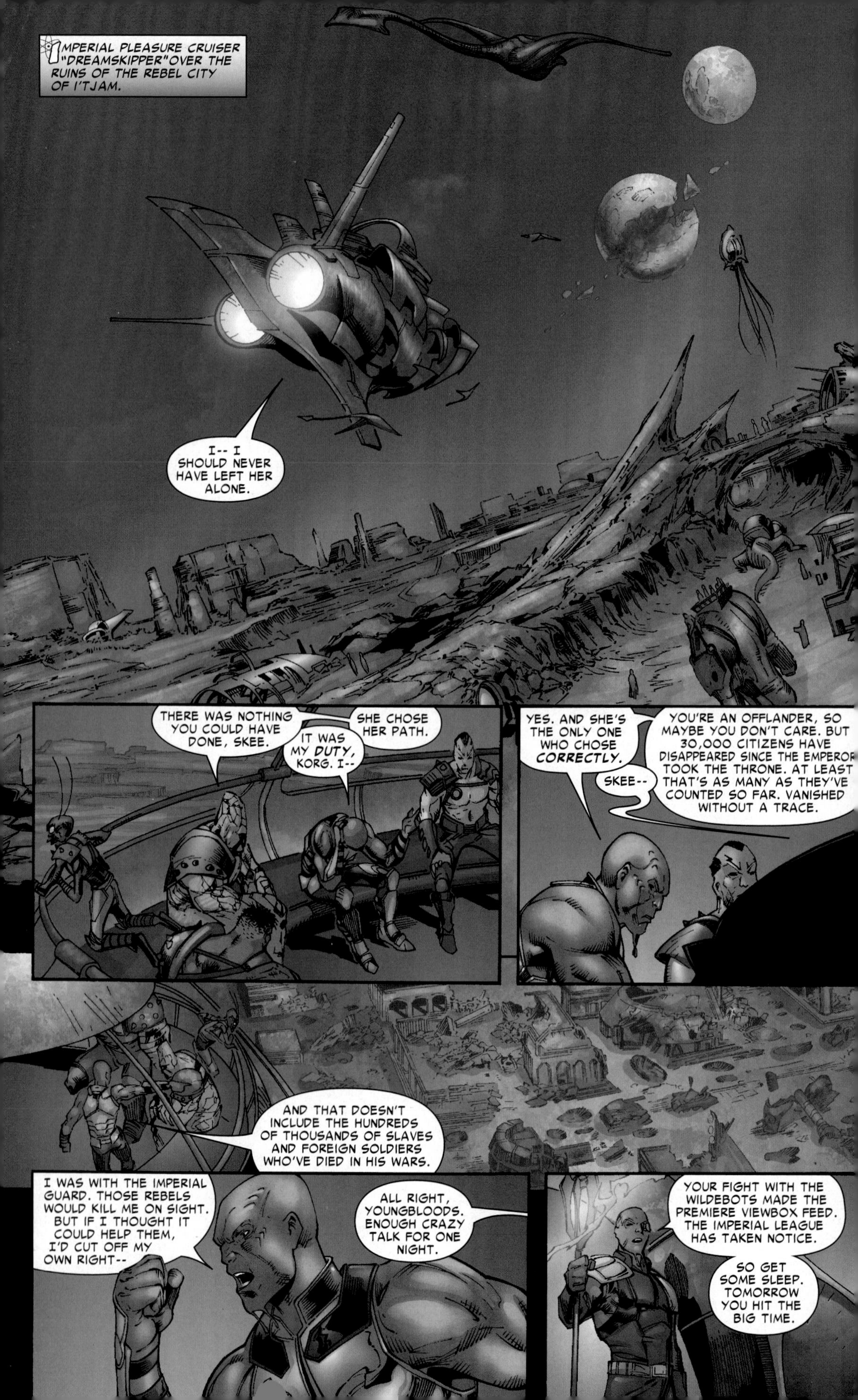
IMPERIAL PLEASURE CRUISER "DREAMSKIPPER" OVER THE RUINS OF THE REBEL CITY OF I'TJAM.
I-- I SHOULD NEVER HAVE LEFT HER ALONE.
THERE WAS NOTHING YOU COULD HAVE DONE, SKEE.
SHE CHOSE HER PATH.
IT WAS MY DUTY, KORG. I--
YES. AND SHE'S THE ONLY ONE WHO CHOSE CORRECTLY.
SKEE--
YOU'RE AN OFFLANDER, SO MAYBE YOU DON'T CARE. BUT 30,000 CITIZENS HAVE DISAPPEARED SINCE THE EMPEROR TOOK THE THRONE. AT LEAST THAT'S AS MANY AS THEY'VE COUNTED SO FAR. VANISHED WITHOUT A TRACE.
AND THAT DOESN'T INCLUDE THE HUNDREDS OF THOUSANDS OF SLAVES AND FOREIGN SOLDIERS WHO'VE DIED IN HIS WARS.
I WAS WITH THE IMPERIAL GUARD. THOSE REBELS WOULD KILL ME ON SIGHT. BUT IF I THOUGHT IT COULD HELP THEM, I'D CUT OFF MY OWN RIGHT--
ALL RIGHT, YOUNGBLOODS. ENOUGH CRAZY TALK FOR ONE NIGHT.
YOUR FIGHT WITH THE WILDEBOTS MADE THE PREMIERE VIEWBOX FEED. THE IMPERIAL LEAGUE HAS TAKEN NOTICE.
SO GET SOME SLEEP. TOMORROW YOU HIT THE BIG TIME.

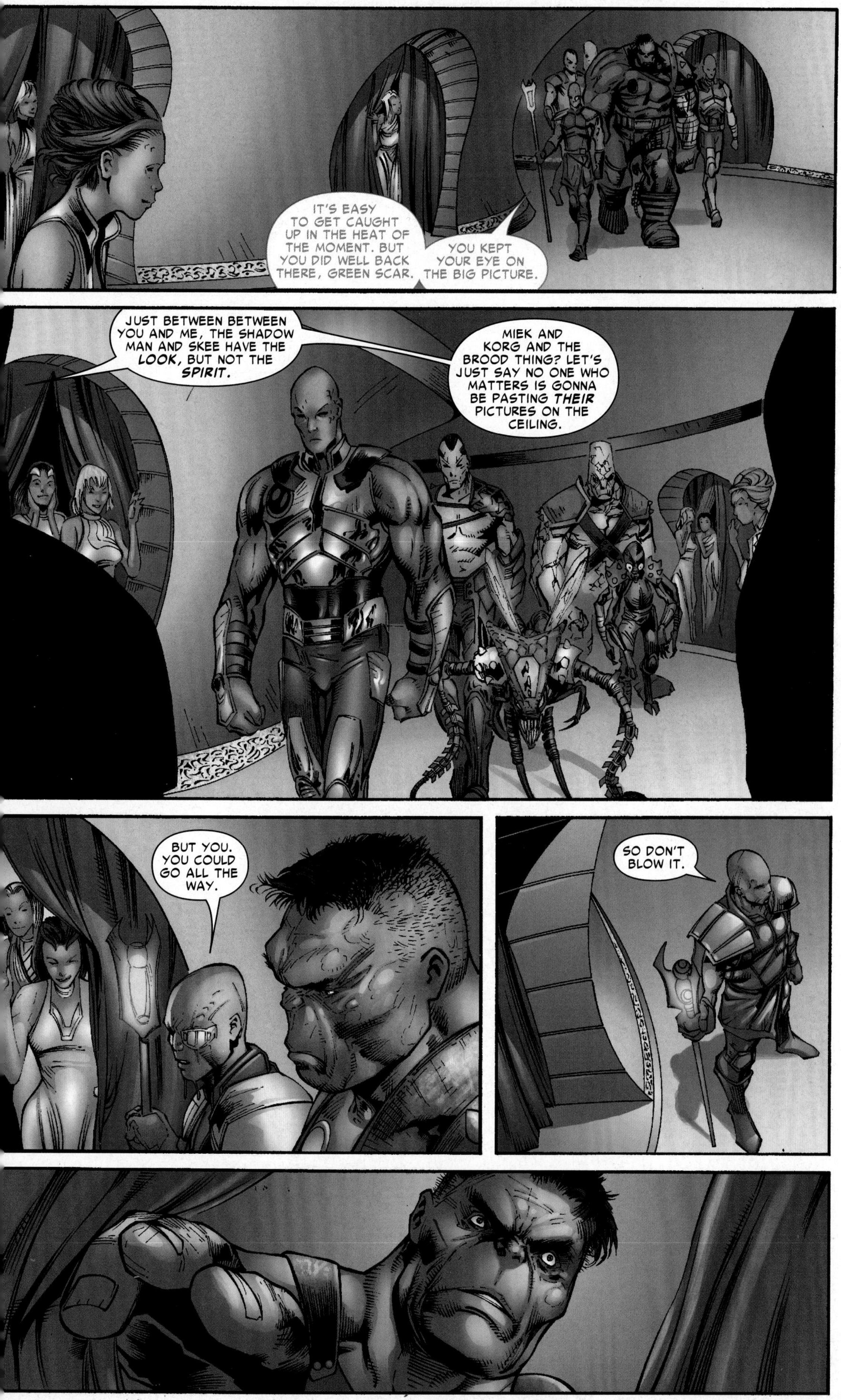

IT'S EASY TO GET CAUGHT UP IN THE HEAT OF THE MOMENT. BUT YOU DID WELL BACK THERE, GREEN SCAR.
YOU KEPT YOUR EYE ON THE BIG PICTURE.
JUST BETWEEN BETWEEN YOU AND ME, THE SHADOW MAN AND SKEE HAVE THE LOOK, BUT NOT THE SPIRIT.
MIEK AND KORG AND THE BROOD THING? LET'S JUST SAY NO ONE WHO MATTERS IS GONNA BE PASTING THEIR PICTURES ON THE CEILING.
BUT YOU. YOU COULD GO ALL THE WAY.
SO DON'T BLOW IT.

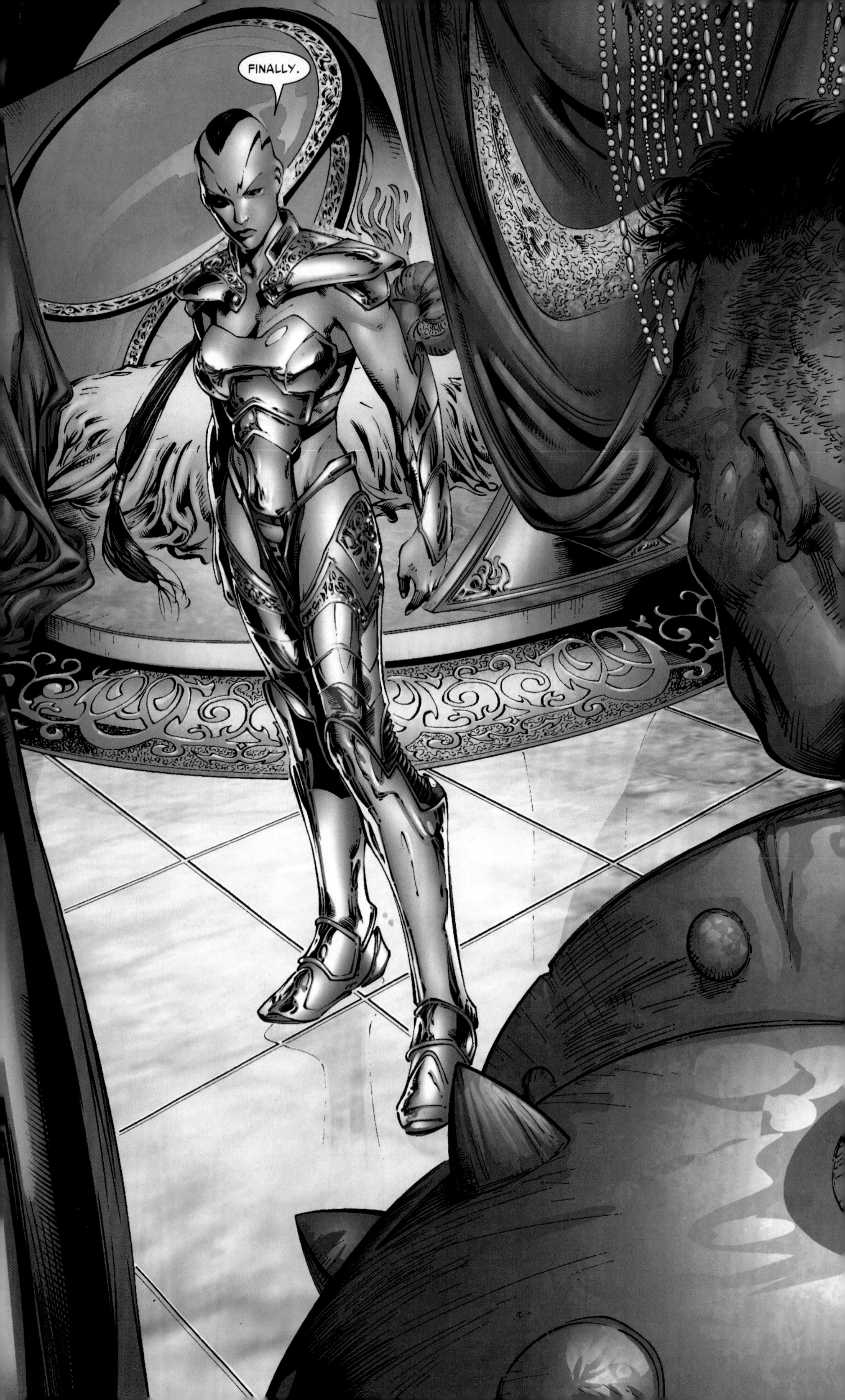
FINALLY.

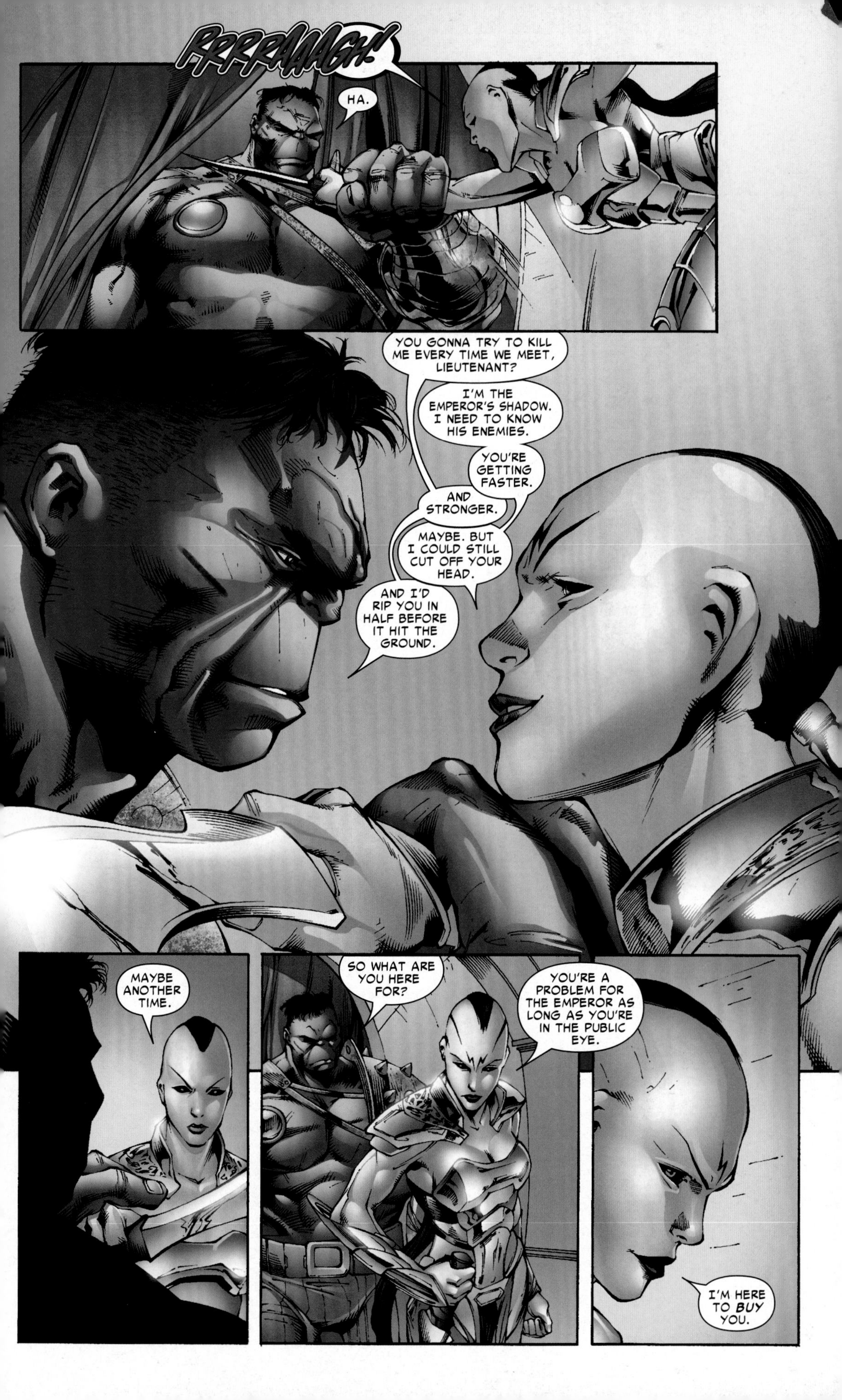
RRRRAAAAGH!
HA.
YOU GONNA TRY TO KILL ME EVERY TIME WE MEET, LIEUTENANT?
I'M THE EMPEROR'S SHADOW. I NEED TO KNOW HIS ENEMIES.
YOU'RE GETTING FASTER.
AND STRONGER.
MAYBE. BUT I COULD STILL CUT OFF YOUR HEAD.
AND I'D RIP YOU IN HALF BEFORE IT HIT THE GROUND.
MAYBE ANOTHER TIME.
SO WHAT ARE YOU HERE FOR?
YOU'RE A PROBLEM FOR THE EMPEROR AS LONG AS YOU'RE IN THE PUBLIC EYE.
I'M HERE TO *BUY* YOU.

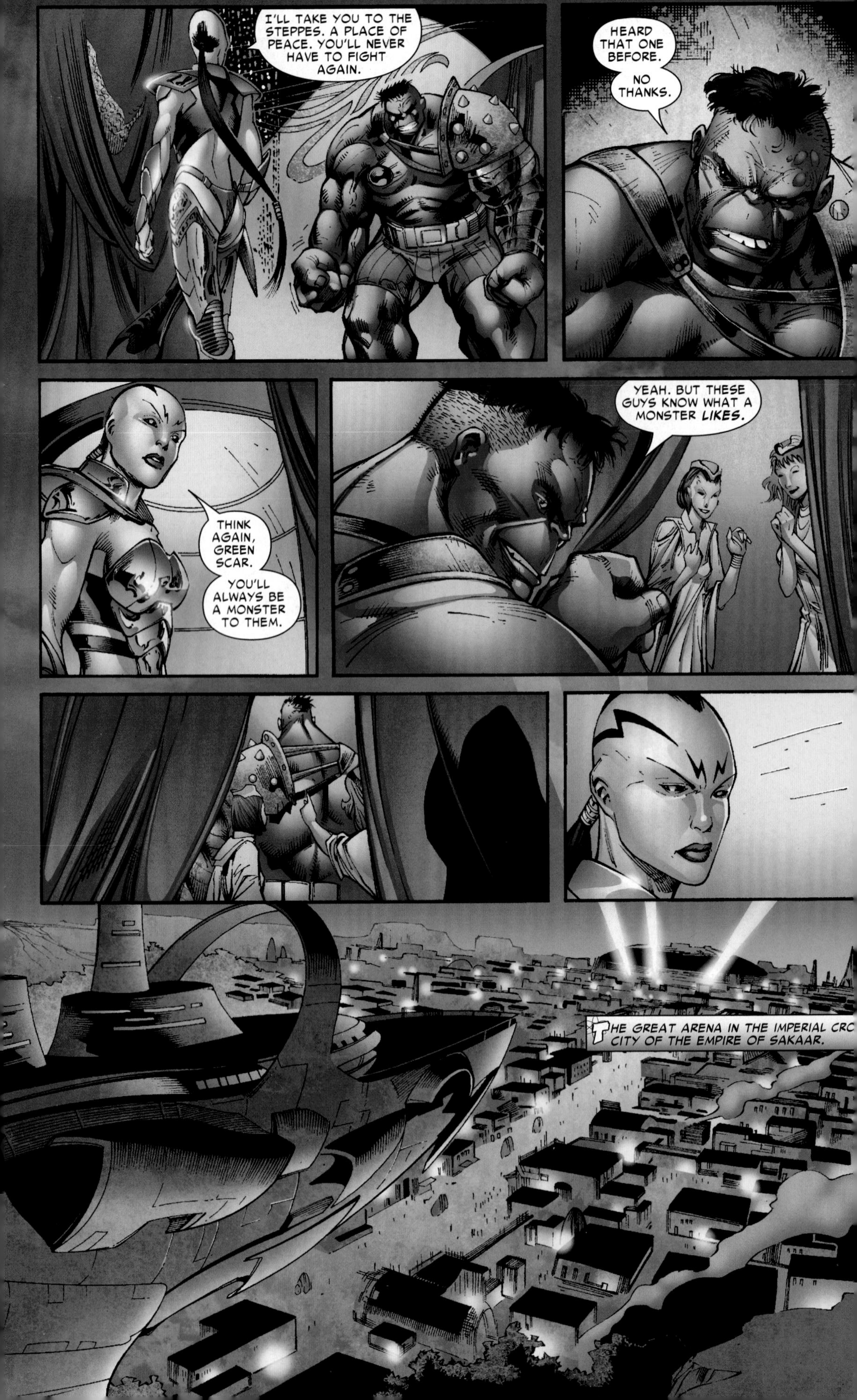
I'LL TAKE YOU TO THE STEPPES. A PLACE OF PEACE. YOU'LL NEVER HAVE TO FIGHT AGAIN.
HEARD THAT ONE BEFORE.
NO THANKS.
THINK AGAIN, GREEN SCAR.
YOU'LL ALWAYS BE A MONSTER TO THEM.
YEAH. BUT THESE GUYS KNOW WHAT A MONSTER LIKES.
THE GREAT ARENA IN THE IMPERIAL CRO
CITY OF THE EMPIRE OF SAKAAR.

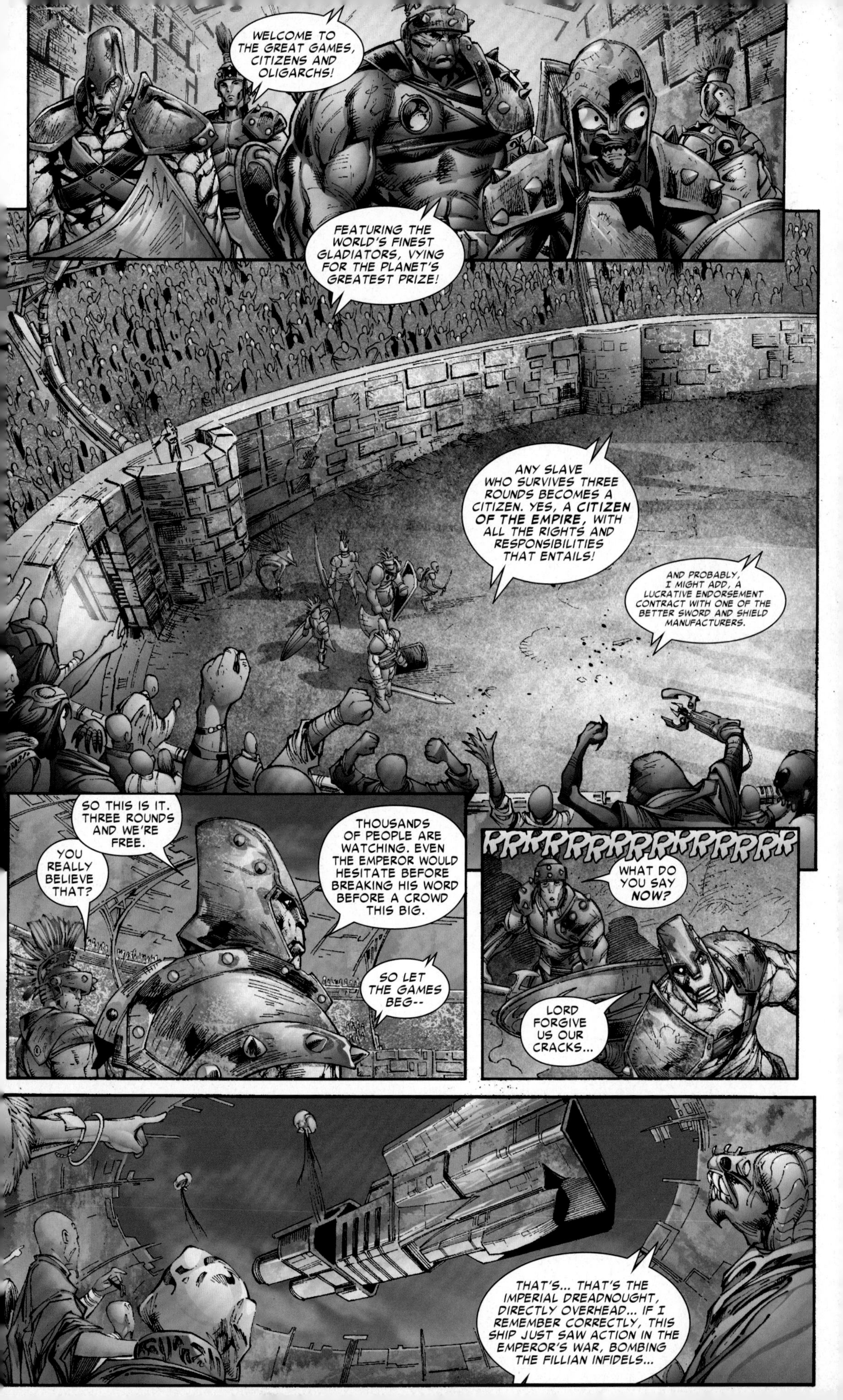
WELCOME TO THE GREAT GAMES, CITIZENS AND OLIGARCHS!
FEATURING THE WORLD'S FINEST GLADIATORS, VYING FOR THE PLANET'S GREATEST PRIZE!
ANY SLAVE WHO SURVIVES THREE ROUNDS BECOMES A CITIZEN. YES, A CITIZEN OF THE EMPIRE, WITH ALL THE RIGHTS AND RESPONSIBILITIES THAT ENTAILS!
AND PROBABLY, I MIGHT ADD, A LUCRATIVE ENDORSEMENT CONTRACT WITH ONE OF THE BETTER SWORD AND SHIELD MANUFACTURERS.
SO THIS IS IT. THREE ROUNDS AND WE'RE FREE.
YOU REALLY BELIEVE THAT?
THOUSANDS OF PEOPLE ARE WATCHING. EVEN THE EMPEROR WOULD HESITATE BEFORE BREAKING HIS WORD BEFORE A CROWD THIS BIG.
SO LET THE GAMES BEG--
RRKRRRRRRRRKRRRRRR
WHAT DO YOU SAY NOW?
LORD FORGIVE US OUR CRACKS...
THAT'S... THAT'S THE IMPERIAL DREADNOUGHT, DIRECTLY OVERHEAD... IF I REMEMBER CORRECTLY, THIS SHIP JUST SAW ACTION IN THE EMPEROR'S WAR, BOMBING THE FILLIAN INFIDELS...

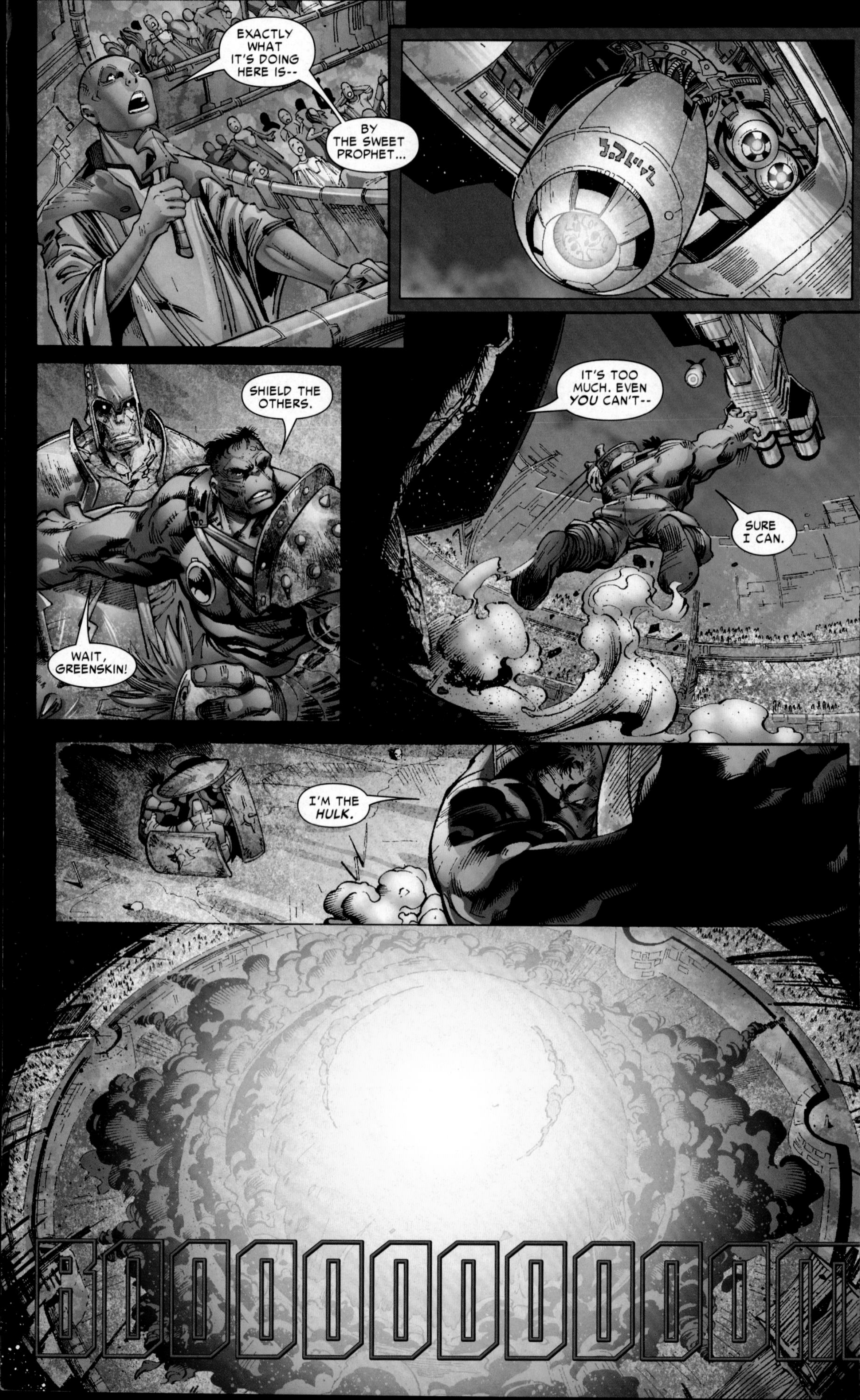
EXACTLY WHAT IT'S DOING HERE IS--
BY THE SWEET PROPHET...
SHIELD THE OTHERS.
WAIT, GREENSKIN!
IT'S TOO MUCH. EVEN *YOU* CAN'T--
SURE I CAN.
I'M THE *HULK.*
BOOOOOOOOOOM

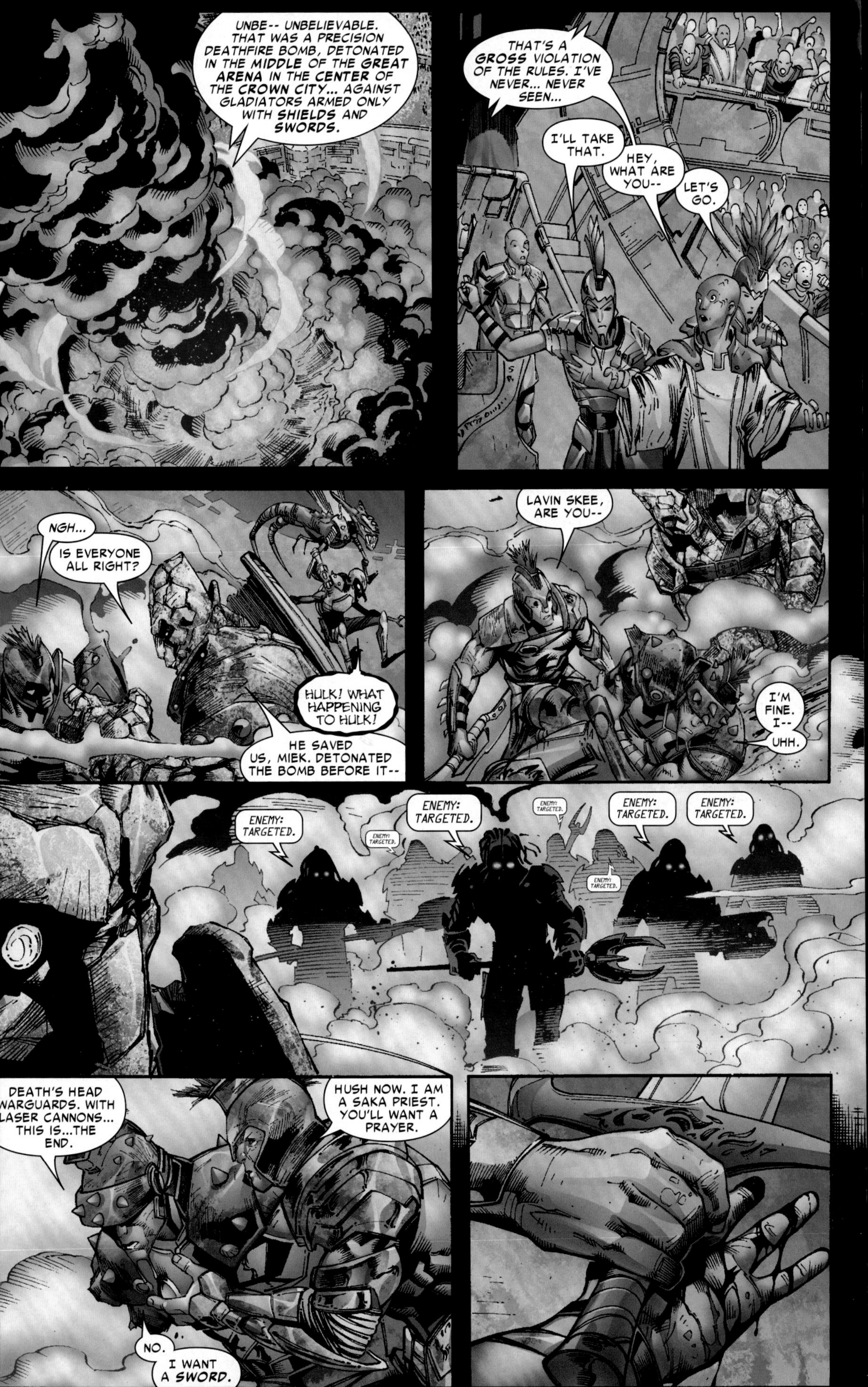
UNBE-- UNBELIEVABLE. THAT WAS A PRECISION DEATHFIRE BOMB, DETONATED IN THE MIDDLE OF THE GREAT ARENA IN THE CENTER OF THE CROWN CITY... AGAINST GLADIATORS ARMED ONLY WITH SHIELDS AND SWORDS.
THAT'S A GROSS VIOLATION OF THE RULES. I'VE NEVER... NEVER SEEN...
I'LL TAKE THAT.
HEY, WHAT ARE YOU--
LET'S GO.
NGH...
IS EVERYONE ALL RIGHT?
HULK! WHAT HAPPENING TO HULK!
HE SAVED US, MIEK. DETONATED THE BOMB BEFORE IT--
LAVIN SKEE, ARE YOU--
I'M FINE. I--
UHH.
ENEMY: TARGETED.
ENEMY: TARGETED.
ENEMY: TARGETED.
ENEMY: TARGETED.
ENEMY: TARGETED.
ENEMY: TARGETED.
ENEMY: TARGETED.
DEATH'S HEAD WARGUARDS. WITH LASER CANNONS... THIS IS...THE END.
HUSH NOW. I AM A SAKA PRIEST. YOU'LL WANT A PRAYER.
NO.
I WANT A SWORD.

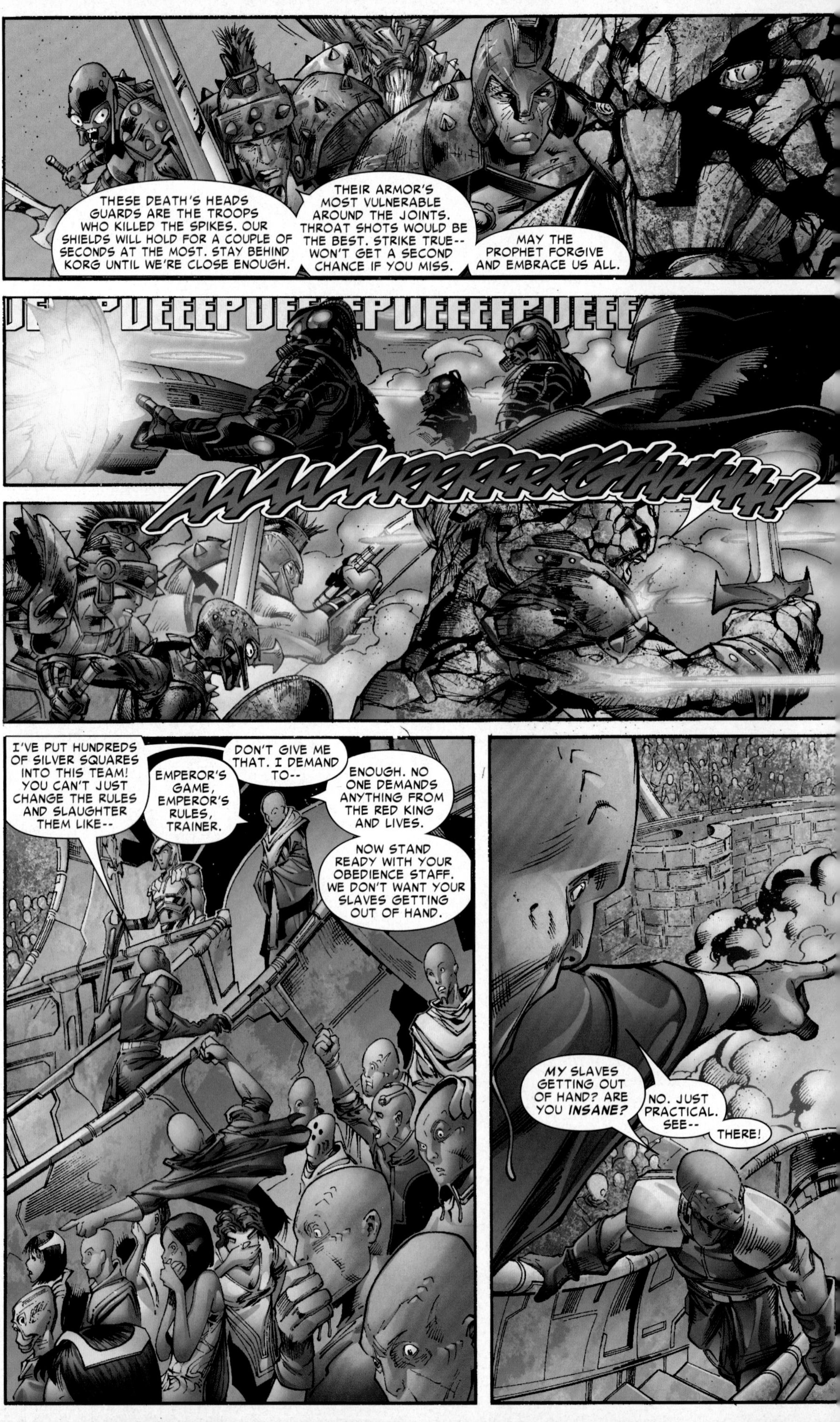
THESE DEATH'S HEADS GUARDS ARE THE TROOPS WHO KILLED THE SPIKES. OUR SHIELDS WILL HOLD FOR A COUPLE OF SECONDS AT THE MOST. STAY BEHIND KORG UNTIL WE'RE CLOSE ENOUGH.
THEIR ARMOR'S MOST VULNERABLE AROUND THE JOINTS. THROAT SHOTS WOULD BE THE BEST. STRIKE TRUE--WON'T GET A SECOND CHANCE IF YOU MISS.
MAY THE PROPHET FORGIVE AND EMBRACE US ALL.
PVEEEPVEEEEPVEEEEEPVEEE
AAAAAARRRRRRRRRGHHHHHHH!
I'VE PUT HUNDREDS OF SILVER SQUARES INTO THIS TEAM! YOU CAN'T JUST CHANGE THE RULES AND SLAUGHTER THEM LIKE--
EMPEROR'S GAME, EMPEROR'S RULES, TRAINER.
DON'T GIVE ME THAT. I DEMAND TO--
ENOUGH. NO ONE DEMANDS ANYTHING FROM THE RED KING AND LIVES.
NOW STAND READY WITH YOUR OBEDIENCE STAFF. WE DON'T WANT YOUR SLAVES GETTING OUT OF HAND.
MY SLAVES GETTING OUT OF HAND? ARE YOU INSANE?
NO. JUST PRACTICAL. SEE--
THERE!

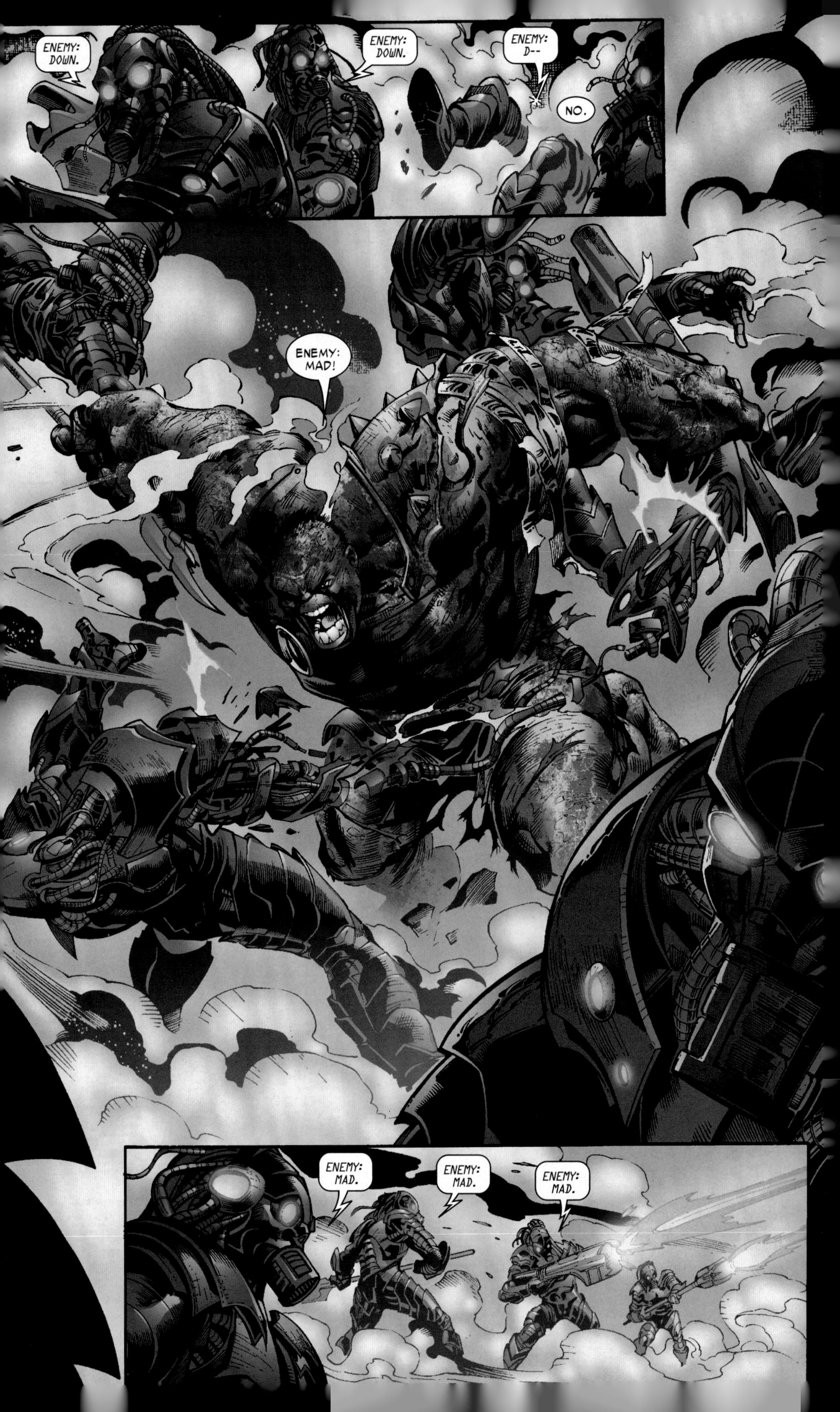
ENEMY: DOWN.
ENEMY: DOWN.
ENEMY: D--
NO.
ENEMY: MAD!
ENEMY: MAD.
ENEMY: MAD.
ENEMY: MAD.

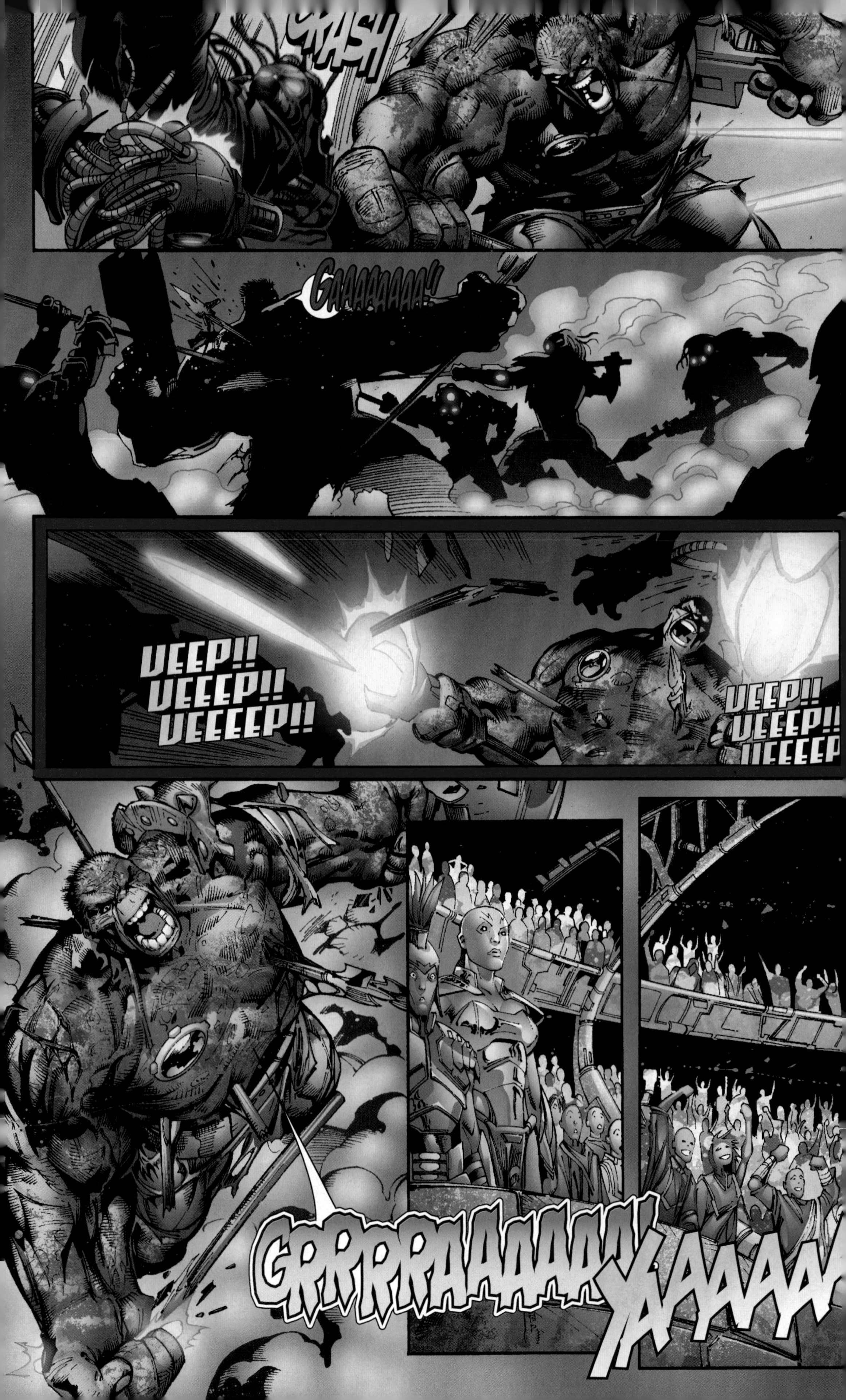
CRASH
GAAAAAAAA!!
VEEP!!
VEEEP!!
VEEEEP!!
VEEP!!
VEEEP!!
GRRRRAAAAAAAAAAAA

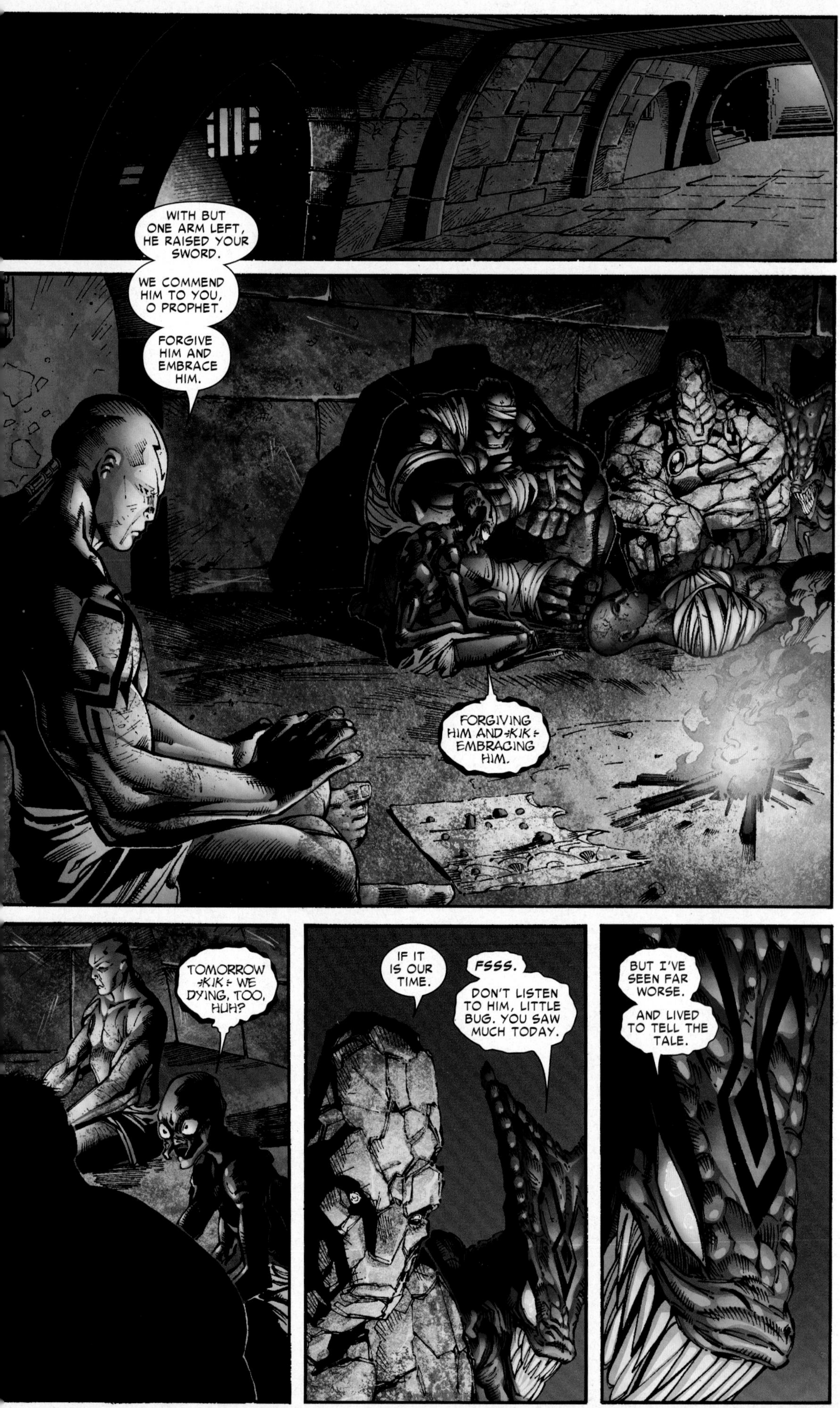
WITH BUT ONE ARM LEFT, HE RAISED YOUR SWORD.
WE COMMEND HIM TO YOU, O PROPHET.
FORGIVE HIM AND EMBRACE HIM.
FORGIVING HIM AND *KIK* EMBRACING HIM.
TOMORROW *KIK* WE DYING, TOO, HUH?
IF IT IS OUR TIME.
FSSS.
DON'T LISTEN TO HIM, LITTLE BUG. YOU SAW MUCH TODAY.
BUT I'VE SEEN FAR WORSE.
AND LIVED TO TELL THE TALE.

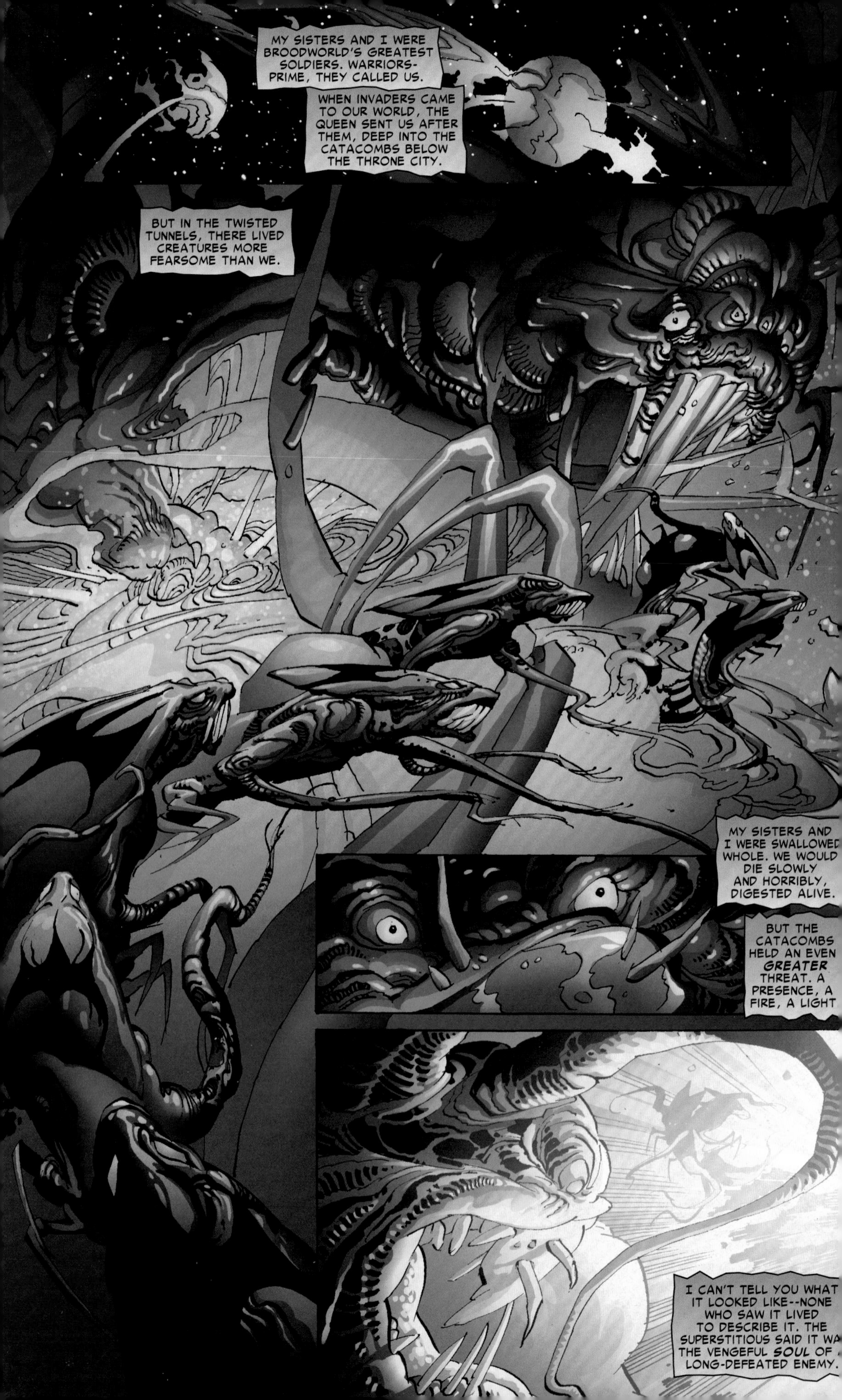

MY SISTERS AND I WERE BROODWORLD'S GREATEST SOLDIERS. WARRIORS-PRIME, THEY CALLED US.
WHEN INVADERS CAME TO OUR WORLD, THE QUEEN SENT US AFTER THEM, DEEP INTO THE CATACOMBS BELOW THE THRONE CITY.
BUT IN THE TWISTED TUNNELS, THERE LIVED CREATURES MORE FEARSOME THAN WE.
MY SISTERS AND I WERE SWALLOWED WHOLE. WE WOULD DIE SLOWLY AND HORRIBLY, DIGESTED ALIVE.
BUT THE CATACOMBS HELD AN EVEN GREATER THREAT. A PRESENCE, A FIRE, A LIGHT
I CAN'T TELL YOU WHAT IT LOOKED LIKE--NONE WHO SAW IT LIVED TO DESCRIBE IT. THE SUPERSTITIOUS SAID IT WA THE VENGEFUL SOUL OF LONG-DEFEATED ENEMY.

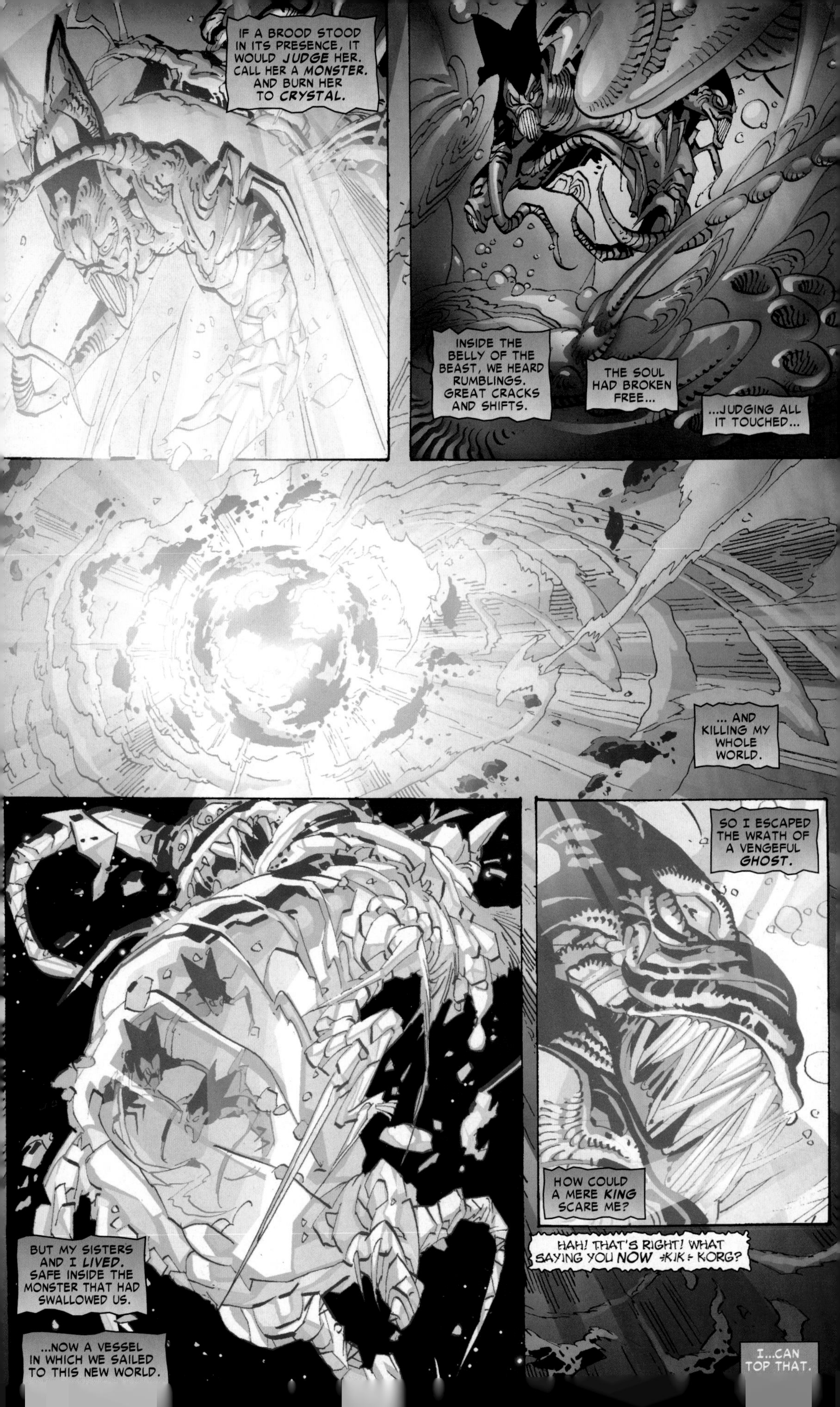
IF A BROOD STOOD IN ITS PRESENCE, IT WOULD JUDGE HER. CALL HER A MONSTER. AND BURN HER TO CRYSTAL.
INSIDE THE BELLY OF THE BEAST, WE HEARD RUMBLINGS. GREAT CRACKS AND SHIFTS.
THE SOUL HAD BROKEN FREE...
...JUDGING ALL IT TOUCHED...
... AND KILLING MY WHOLE WORLD.
BUT MY SISTERS AND I LIVED. SAFE INSIDE THE MONSTER THAT HAD SWALLOWED US.
...NOW A VESSEL IN WHICH WE SAILED TO THIS NEW WORLD.
SO I ESCAPED THE WRATH OF A VENGEFUL GHOST.
HOW COULD A MERE KING SCARE ME?
HAH! THAT'S RIGHT! WHAT SAYING YOU NOW ⱡKIK ⱡ KORG?
I...CAN TOP THAT.

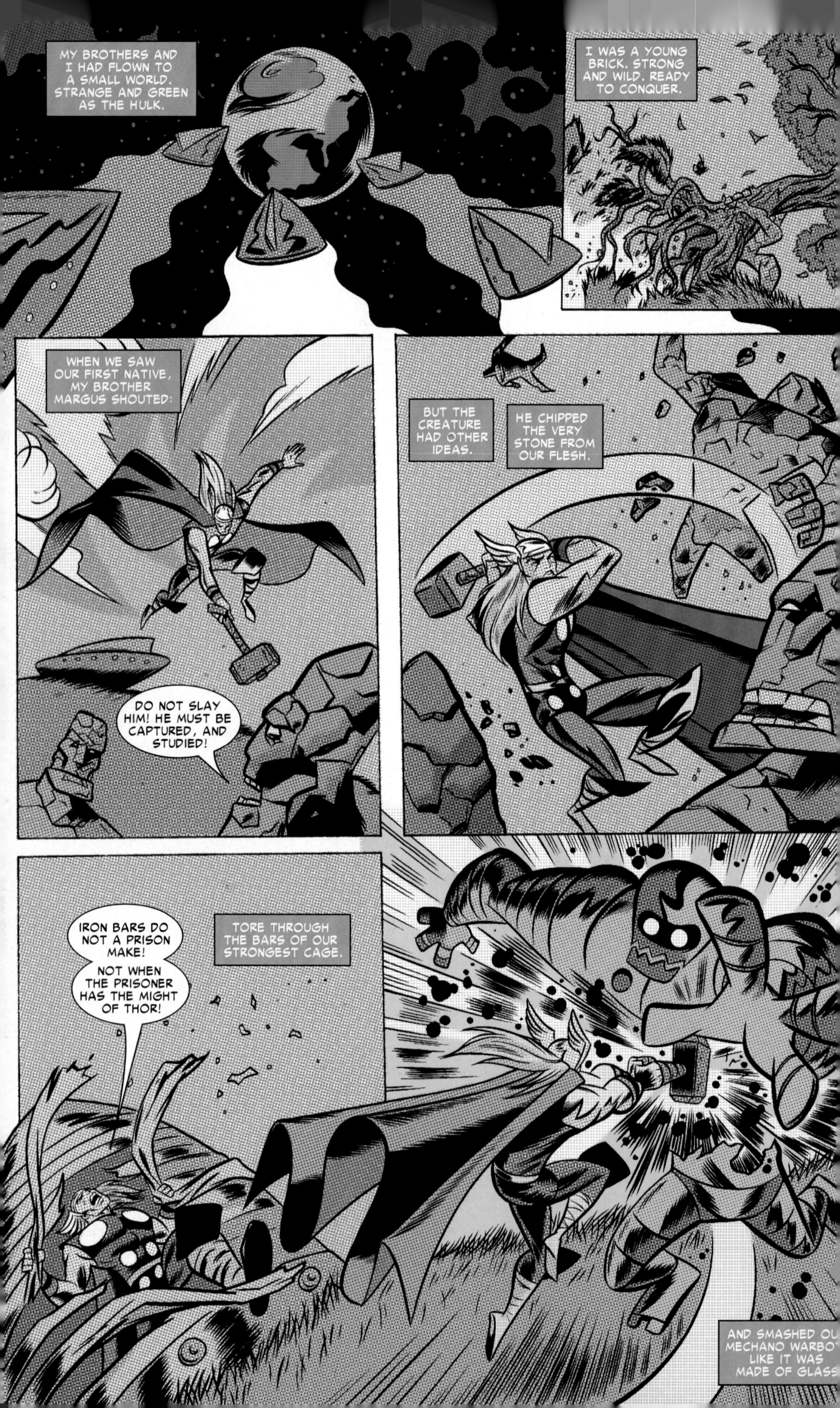
MY BROTHERS AND I HAD FLOWN TO A SMALL WORLD. STRANGE AND GREEN AS THE HULK.
I WAS A YOUNG BRICK. STRONG AND WILD. READY TO CONQUER.
WHEN WE SAW OUR FIRST NATIVE, MY BROTHER MARGUS SHOUTED:
DO NOT SLAY HIM! HE MUST BE CAPTURED, AND STUDIED!
BUT THE CREATURE HAD OTHER IDEAS.
HE CHIPPED THE VERY STONE FROM OUR FLESH.
IRON BARS DO NOT A PRISON MAKE!
NOT WHEN THE PRISONER HAS THE MIGHT OF THOR!
TORE THROUGH THE BARS OF OUR STRONGEST CAGE.

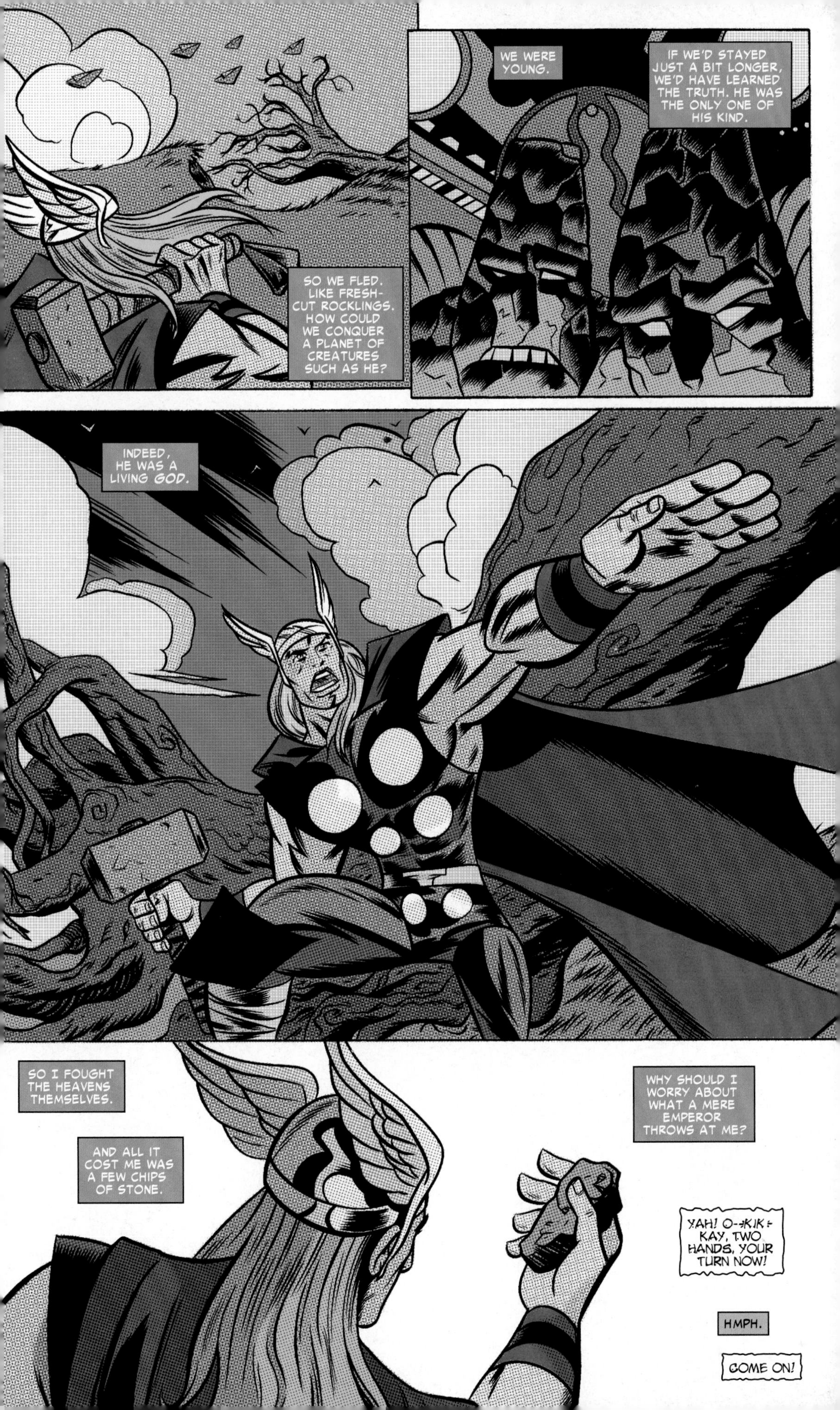
SO WE FLED. LIKE FRESH-CUT ROCKLINGS. HOW COULD WE CONQUER A PLANET OF CREATURES SUCH AS HE?
WE WERE YOUNG.
IF WE'D STAYED JUST A BIT LONGER, WE'D HAVE LEARNED THE TRUTH. HE WAS THE ONLY ONE OF HIS KIND.
INDEED, HE WAS A LIVING GOD.
SO I FOUGHT THE HEAVENS THEMSELVES.
AND ALL IT COST ME WAS A FEW CHIPS OF STONE.
WHY SHOULD I WORRY ABOUT WHAT A MERE EMPEROR THROWS AT ME?
YAH! O-KIK-KAY, TWO HANDS, YOUR TURN NOW!
HMPH.
COME ON!

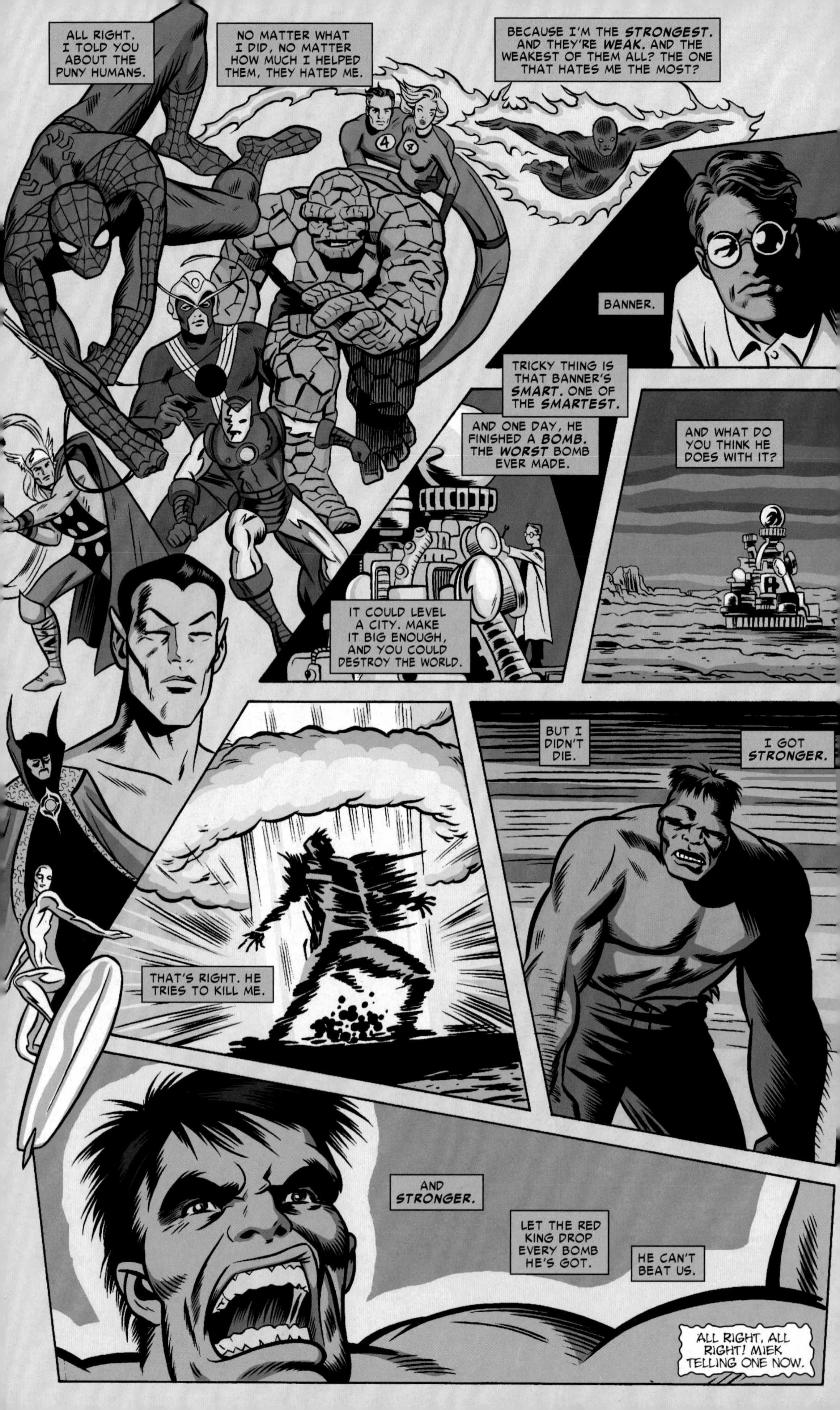
ALL RIGHT. I TOLD YOU ABOUT THE PUNY HUMANS.
NO MATTER WHAT I DID, NO MATTER HOW MUCH I HELPED THEM, THEY HATED ME.
BECAUSE I'M THE STRONGEST. AND THEY'RE WEAK. AND THE WEAKEST OF THEM ALL? THE ONE THAT HATES ME THE MOST?
BANNER.
TRICKY THING IS THAT BANNER'S SMART. ONE OF THE SMARTEST.
AND ONE DAY, HE FINISHED A BOMB. THE WORST BOMB EVER MADE.
IT COULD LEVEL A CITY. MAKE IT BIG ENOUGH, AND YOU COULD DESTROY THE WORLD.
AND WHAT DO YOU THINK HE DOES WITH IT?
THAT'S RIGHT. HE TRIES TO KILL ME.
BUT I DIDN'T DIE.
I GOT STRONGER.
AND STRONGER.
LET THE RED KING DROP EVERY BOMB HE'S GOT.
HE CAN'T BEAT US.
ALL RIGHT, ALL RIGHT! MIEK TELLING ONE NOW.

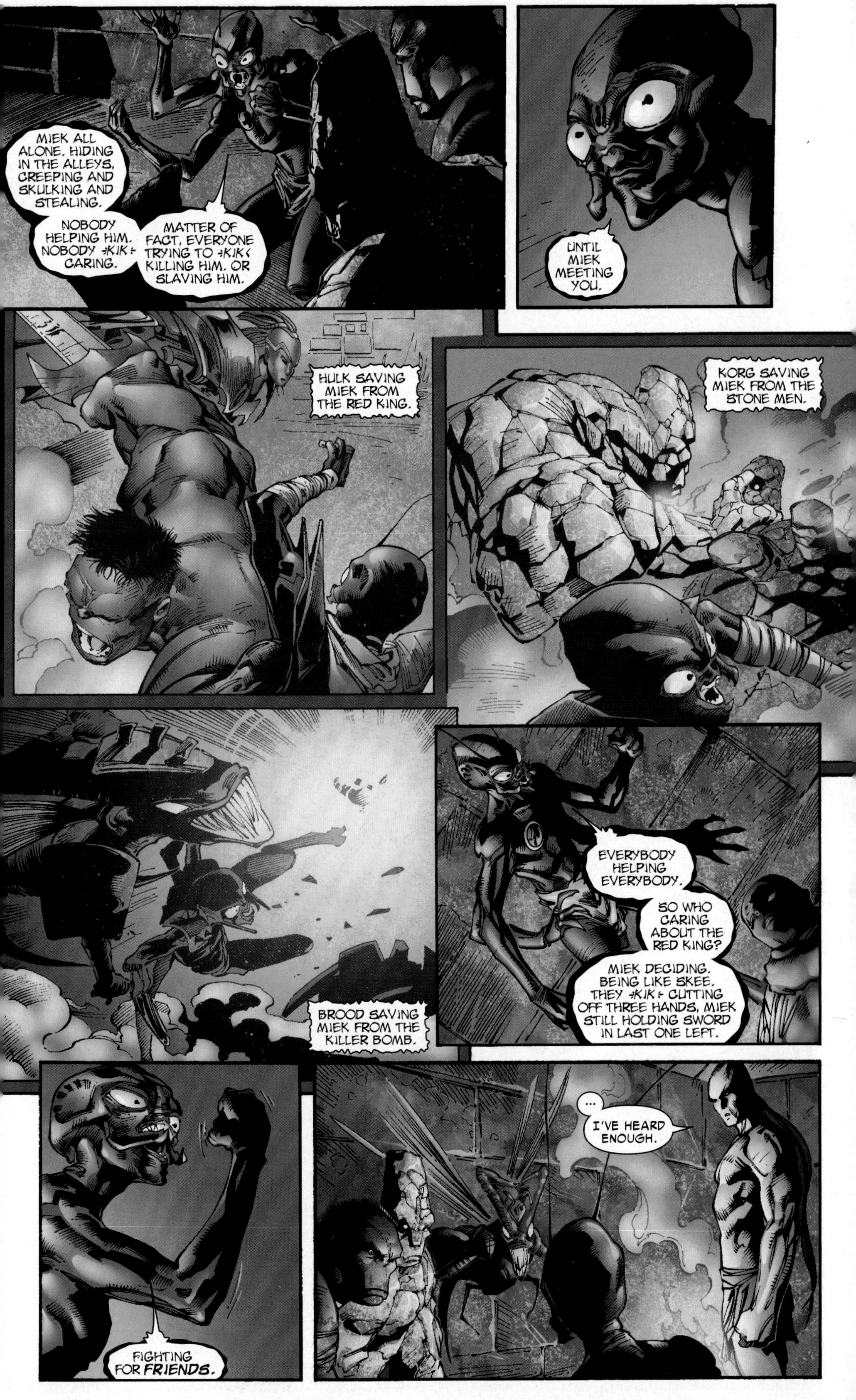
MIEK ALL ALONE. HIDING IN THE ALLEYS, CREEPING AND SKULKING AND STEALING.
NOBODY HELPING HIM. NOBODY ≠KIK≠ CARING.
MATTER OF FACT, EVERYONE TRYING TO ≠KIK≠ KILLING HIM. OR SLAVING HIM.
UNTIL MIEK MEETING YOU.
HULK SAVING MIEK FROM THE RED KING.
KORG SAVING MIEK FROM THE STONE MEN.
BROOD SAVING MIEK FROM THE KILLER BOMB.
EVERYBODY HELPING EVERYBODY.
SO WHO CARING ABOUT THE RED KING?
MIEK DECIDING. BEING LIKE SKEE. THEY ≠KIK≠ CUTTING OFF THREE HANDS, MIEK STILL HOLDING SWORD IN LAST ONE LEFT.
FIGHTING FOR **FRIENDS**.
...
I'VE HEARD ENOUGH.

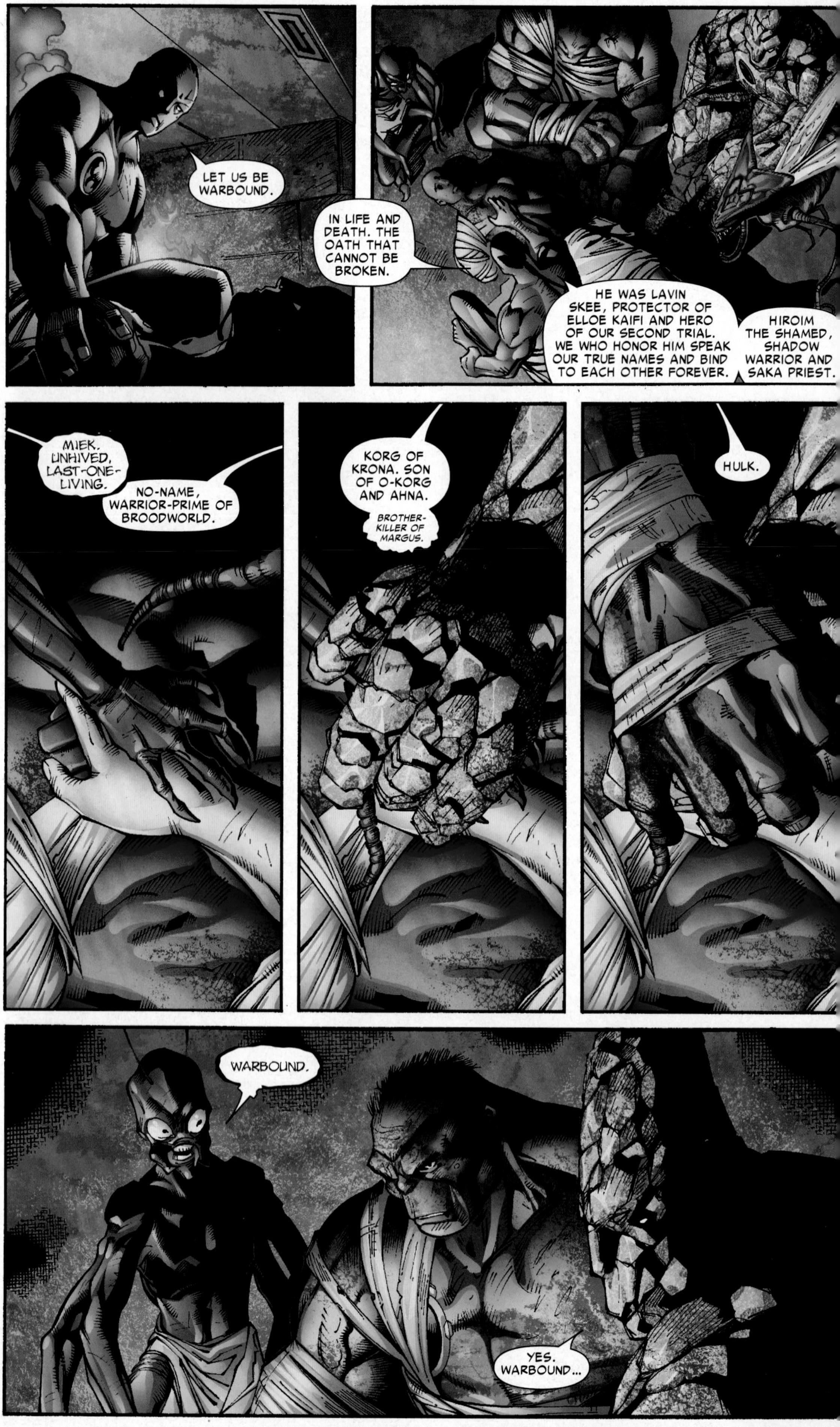

LET US BE WARBOUND.
IN LIFE AND DEATH. THE OATH THAT CANNOT BE BROKEN.
HE WAS LAVIN SKEE, PROTECTOR OF ELLOE KAIFI AND HERO OF OUR SECOND TRIAL. WE WHO HONOR HIM SPEAK OUR TRUE NAMES AND BIND TO EACH OTHER FOREVER.
HIROIM THE SHAMED, SHADOW WARRIOR AND SAKA PRIEST.
MIEK. UNHIVED, LAST-ONE-LIVING.
NO-NAME, WARRIOR-PRIME OF BROODWORLD.
KORG OF KRONA. SON OF O-KORG AND AHNA.
BROTHER-KILLER OF MARGUS.
HULK.
WARBOUND.
YES. WARBOUND...

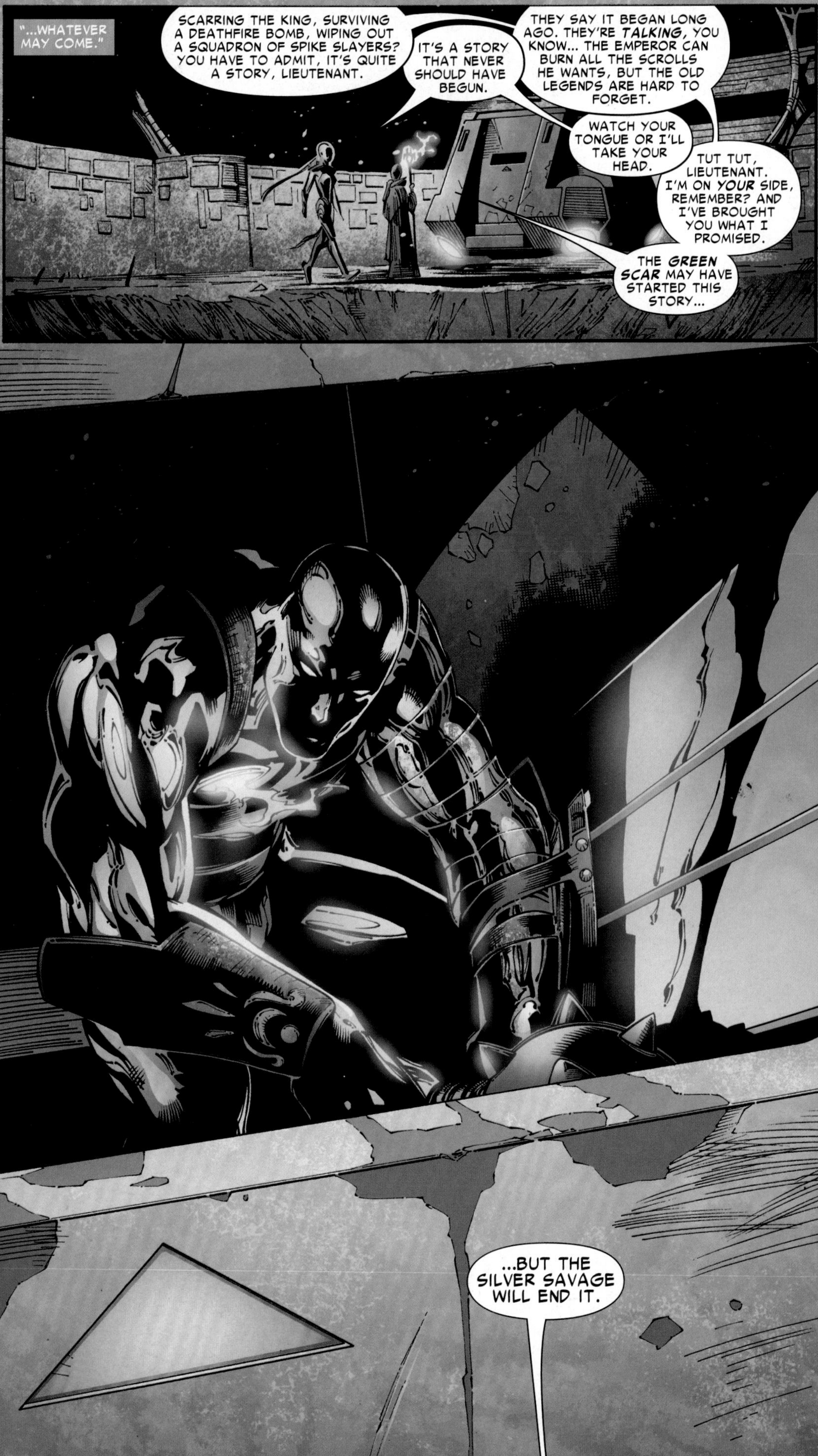
"...WHATEVER MAY COME."
SCARRING THE KING, SURVIVING A DEATHFIRE BOMB, WIPING OUT A SQUADRON OF SPIKE SLAYERS? YOU HAVE TO ADMIT, IT'S QUITE A STORY, LIEUTENANT.
IT'S A STORY THAT NEVER SHOULD HAVE BEGUN.
THEY SAY IT BEGAN LONG AGO. THEY'RE TALKING, YOU KNOW... THE EMPEROR CAN BURN ALL THE SCROLLS HE WANTS, BUT THE OLD LEGENDS ARE HARD TO FORGET.
WATCH YOUR TONGUE OR I'LL TAKE YOUR HEAD.
TUT TUT, LIEUTENANT. I'M ON YOUR SIDE, REMEMBER? AND I'VE BROUGHT YOU WHAT I PROMISED.
THE GREEN SCAR MAY HAVE STARTED THIS STORY...
...BUT THE SILVER SAVAGE WILL END IT.

#95

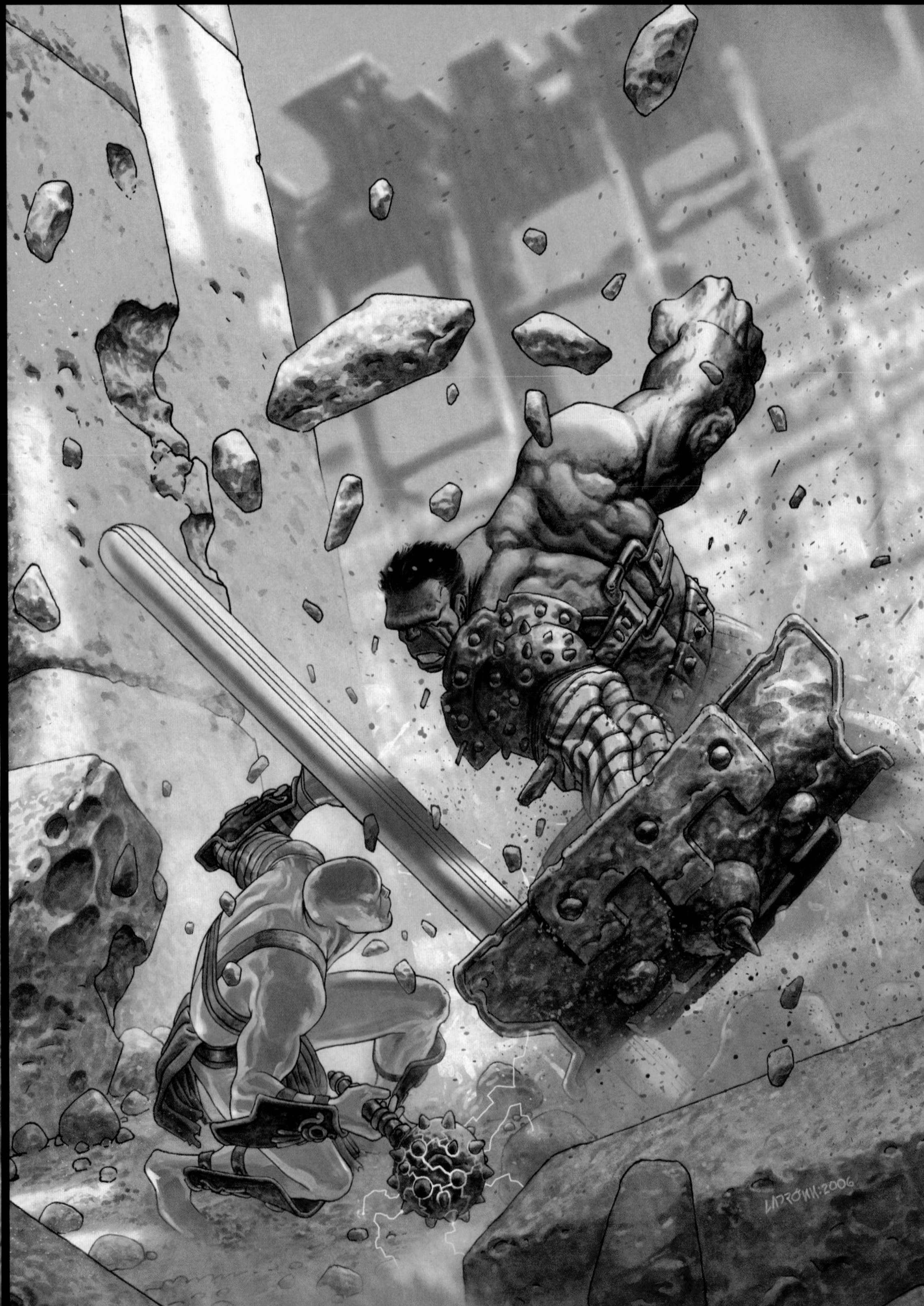
LADRÖNN·2006

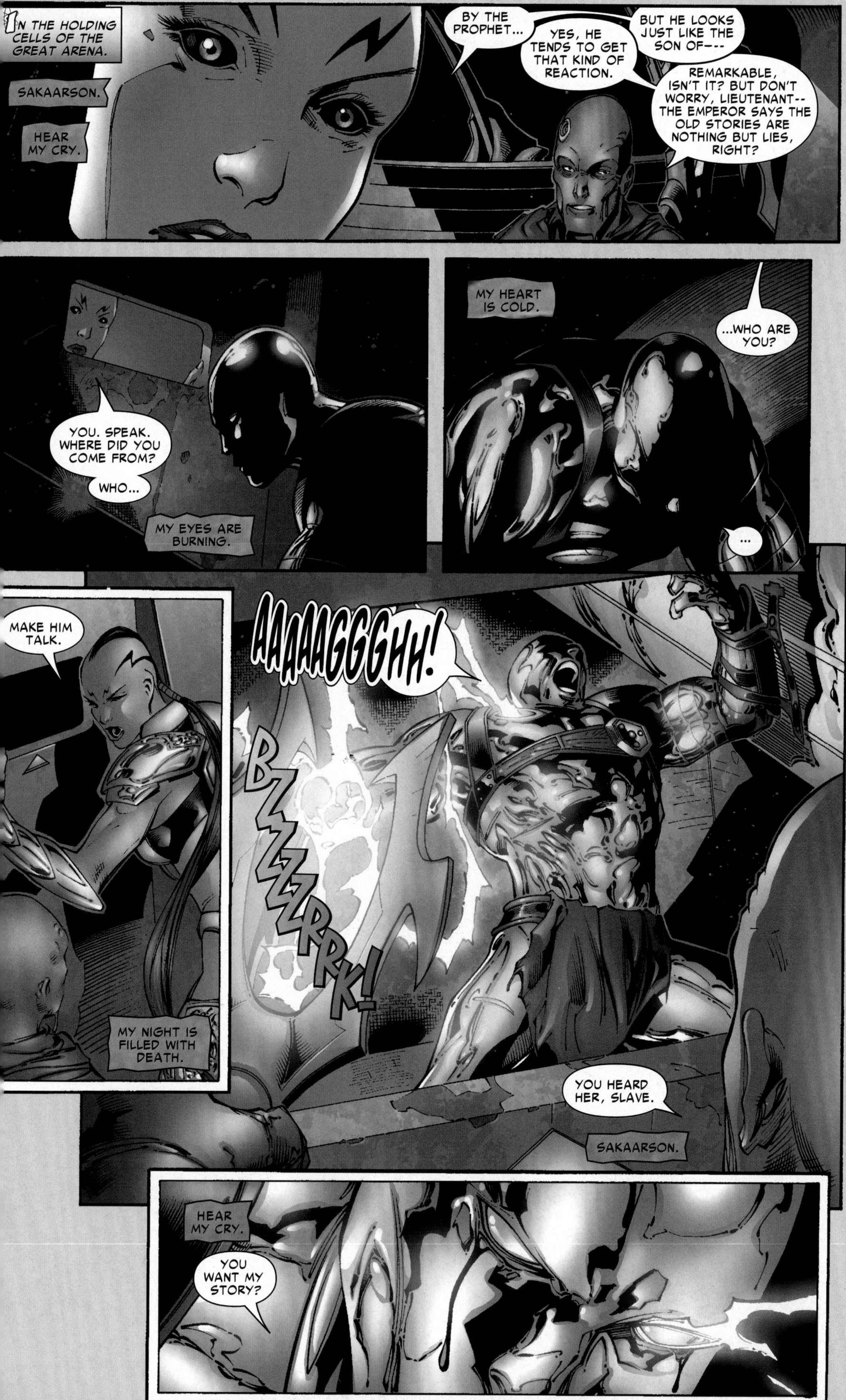
IN THE HOLDING CELLS OF THE GREAT ARENA.
SAKAARSON.
HEAR MY CRY.
BY THE PROPHET...
YES, HE TENDS TO GET THAT KIND OF REACTION.
BUT HE LOOKS JUST LIKE THE SON OF---
REMARKABLE, ISN'T IT? BUT DON'T WORRY, LIEUTENANT-- THE EMPEROR SAYS THE OLD STORIES ARE NOTHING BUT LIES, RIGHT?
YOU. SPEAK. WHERE DID YOU COME FROM?
WHO...
MY EYES ARE BURNING.
MY HEART IS COLD.
...WHO ARE YOU?
...
MAKE HIM TALK.
AAAAAGGGHH!
BZZZRRK!
MY NIGHT IS FILLED WITH DEATH.
YOU HEARD HER, SLAVE.
SAKAARSON.
HEAR MY CRY.
YOU WANT MY STORY?

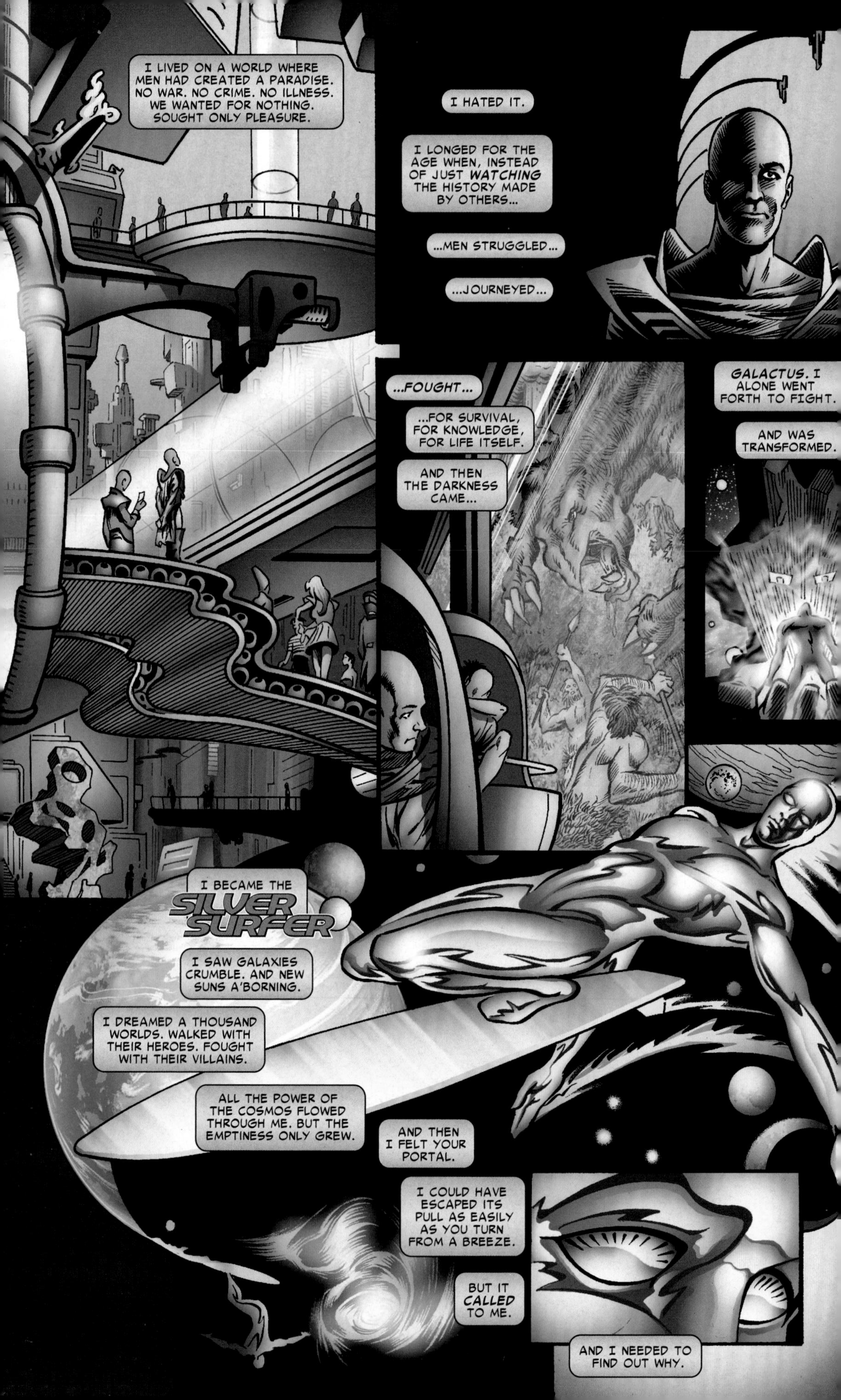
I LIVED ON A WORLD WHERE MEN HAD CREATED A PARADISE. NO WAR. NO CRIME. NO ILLNESS. WE WANTED FOR NOTHING. SOUGHT ONLY PLEASURE.
I HATED IT.
I LONGED FOR THE AGE WHEN, INSTEAD OF JUST WATCHING THE HISTORY MADE BY OTHERS...
...MEN STRUGGLED...
...JOURNEYED...
...FOUGHT...
...FOR SURVIVAL, FOR KNOWLEDGE, FOR LIFE ITSELF.
AND THEN THE DARKNESS CAME...
GALACTUS. I ALONE WENT FORTH TO FIGHT.
AND WAS TRANSFORMED.
I BECAME THE
SILVER SURFER
I SAW GALAXIES CRUMBLE. AND NEW SUNS A'BORNING.
I DREAMED A THOUSAND WORLDS. WALKED WITH THEIR HEROES. FOUGHT WITH THEIR VILLAINS.
ALL THE POWER OF THE COSMOS FLOWED THROUGH ME. BUT THE EMPTINESS ONLY GREW.
AND THEN I FELT YOUR PORTAL.
I COULD HAVE ESCAPED ITS PULL AS EASILY AS YOU TURN FROM A BREEZE.
BUT IT CALLED TO ME.
AND I NEEDED TO FIND OUT WHY.

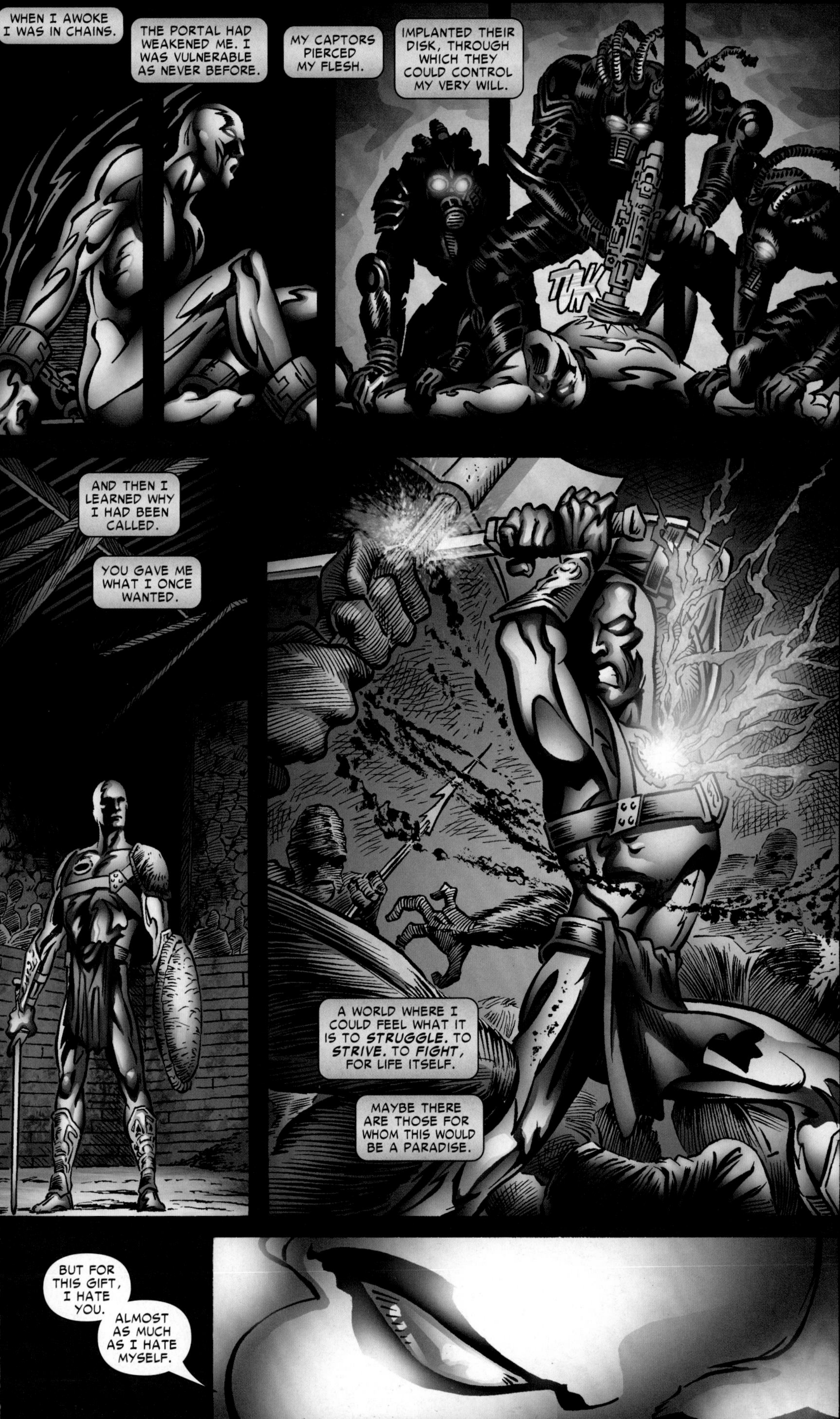
WHEN I AWOKE I WAS IN CHAINS.
THE PORTAL HAD WEAKENED ME. I WAS VULNERABLE AS NEVER BEFORE.
MY CAPTORS PIERCED MY FLESH.
IMPLANTED THEIR DISK, THROUGH WHICH THEY COULD CONTROL MY VERY WILL.
TUK
AND THEN I LEARNED WHY I HAD BEEN CALLED.
YOU GAVE ME WHAT I ONCE WANTED.
A WORLD WHERE I COULD FEEL WHAT IT IS TO STRUGGLE. TO STRIVE. TO FIGHT, FOR LIFE ITSELF.
MAYBE THERE ARE THOSE FOR WHOM THIS WOULD BE A PARADISE.
BUT FOR THIS GIFT, I HATE YOU.
ALMOST AS MUCH AS I HATE MYSELF.

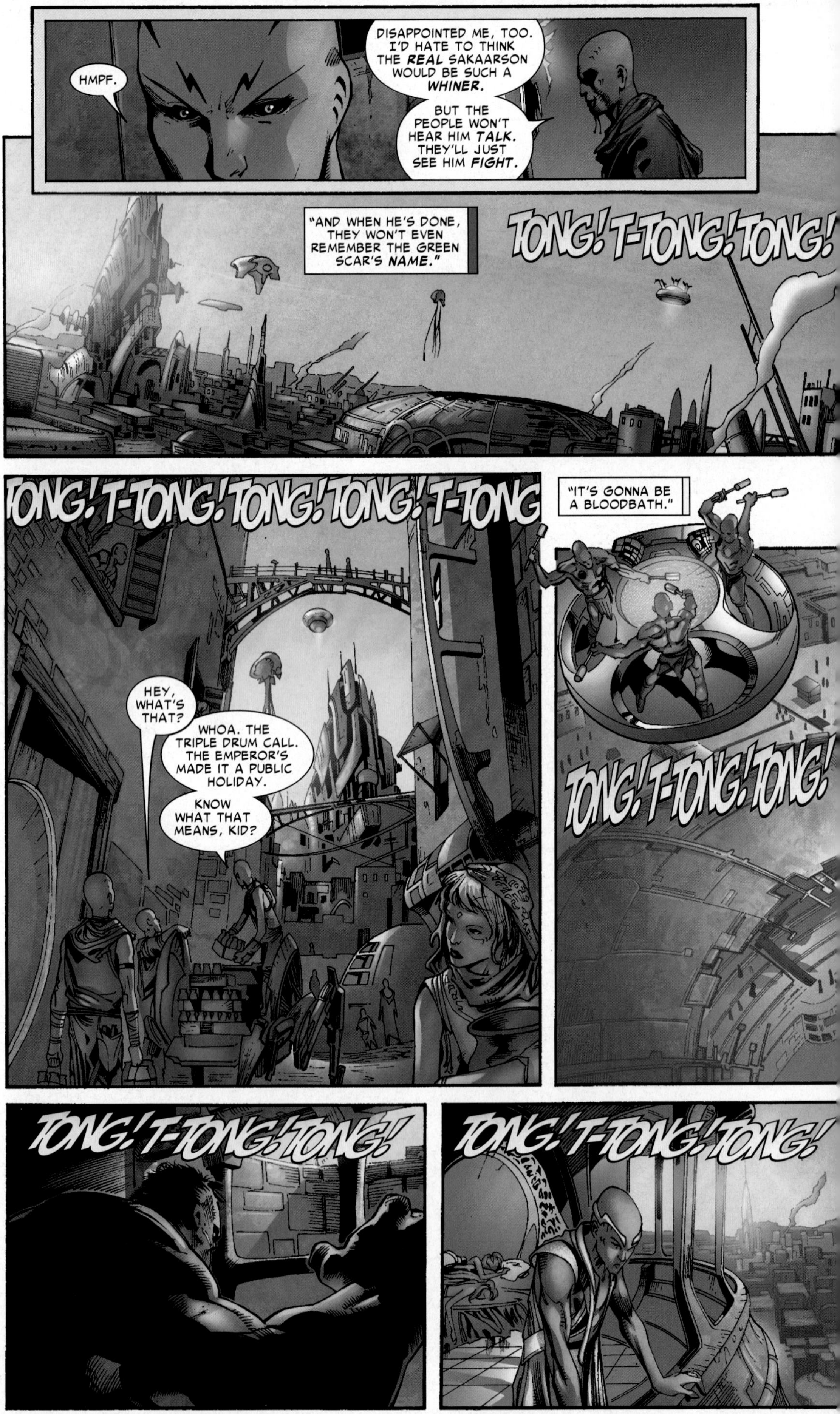
HMPF.
DISAPPOINTED ME, TOO. I'D HATE TO THINK THE *REAL* SAKAARSON WOULD BE SUCH A *WHINER*.
BUT THE PEOPLE WON'T HEAR HIM *TALK*. THEY'LL JUST SEE HIM *FIGHT*.
"AND WHEN HE'S DONE, THEY WON'T EVEN REMEMBER THE GREEN SCAR'S *NAME*."
TONG! T-TONG! TONG!
TONG! T-TONG! TONG! TONG! T-TONG
HEY, WHAT'S THAT?
WHOA. THE TRIPLE DRUM CALL. THE EMPEROR'S MADE IT A PUBLIC HOLIDAY.
KNOW WHAT THAT MEANS, KID?
"IT'S GONNA BE A BLOODBATH."
TONG! T-TONG! TONG!
TONG! T-TONG! TONG!
TONG! T-TONG! TONG!

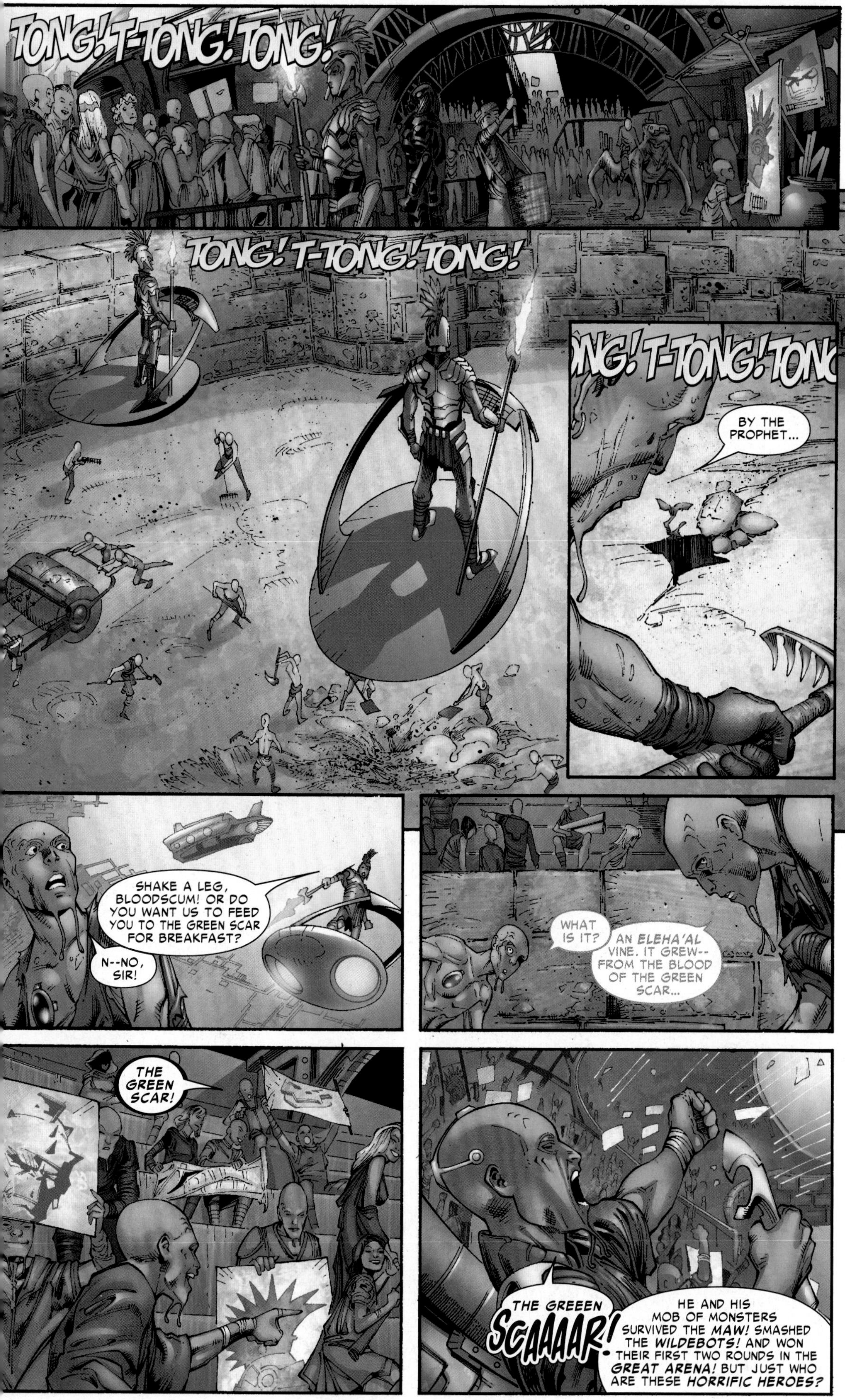

TONG! T-TONG! TONG!
TONG! T-TONG! TONG!
NG! T-TONG! TONG
BY THE PROPHET...
SHAKE A LEG, BLOODSCUM! OR DO YOU WANT US TO FEED YOU TO THE GREEN SCAR FOR BREAKFAST?
N--NO, SIR!
WHAT IS IT?
AN ELEHA'AL VINE. IT GREW-- FROM THE BLOOD OF THE GREEN SCAR...
THE GREEN SCAR!
THE GREEEN SCAAAAR!
HE AND HIS MOB OF MONSTERS SURVIVED THE MAW! SMASHED THE WILDEBOTS! AND WON THEIR FIRST TWO ROUNDS IN THE GREAT ARENA! BUT JUST WHO ARE THESE HORRIFIC HEROES?

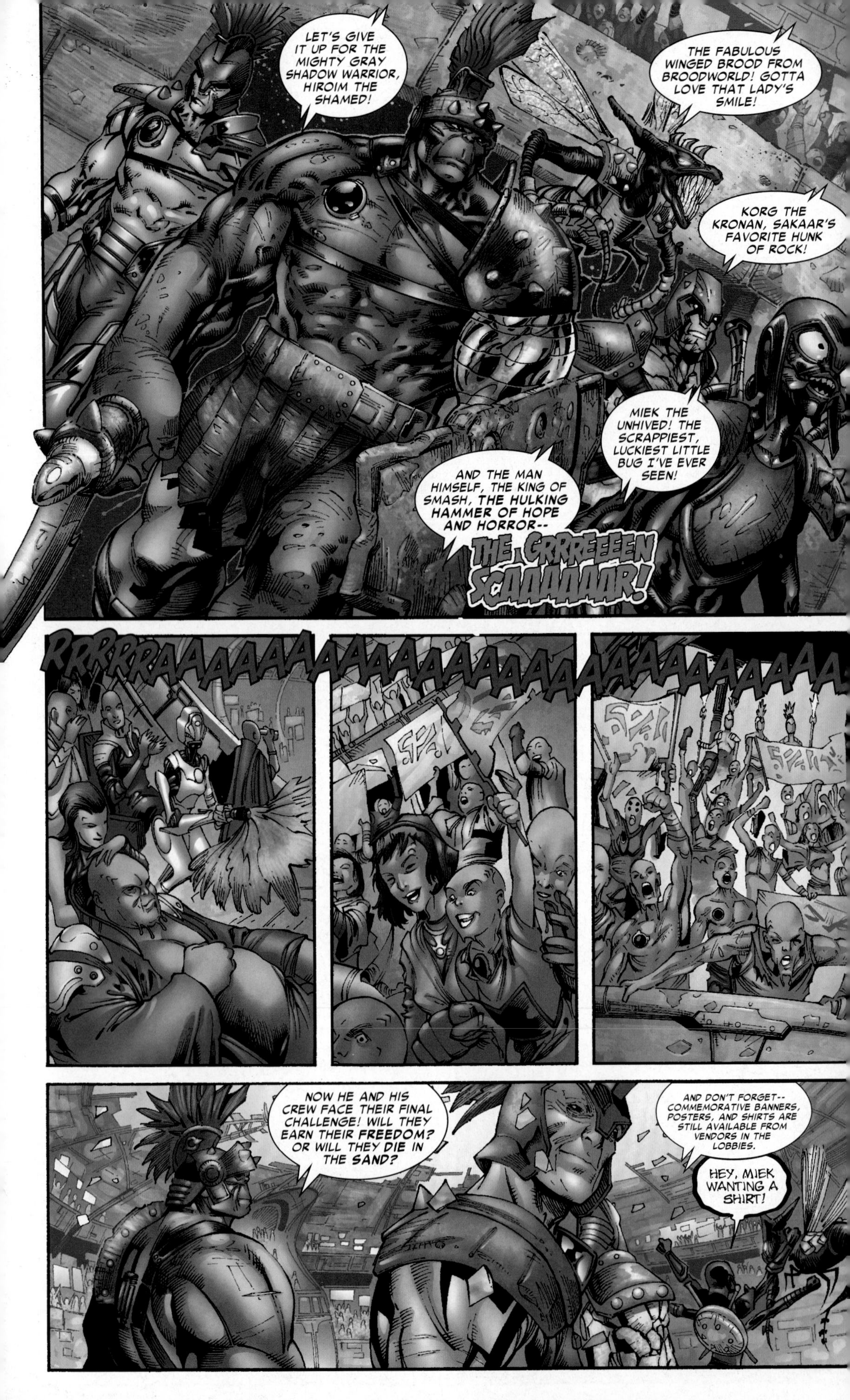
LET'S GIVE IT UP FOR THE MIGHTY GRAY SHADOW WARRIOR, HIROIM THE SHAMED!
THE FABULOUS WINGED BROOD FROM BROODWORLD! GOTTA LOVE THAT LADY'S SMILE!
KORG THE KRONAN, SAKAAR'S FAVORITE HUNK OF ROCK!
MIEK THE UNHIVED! THE SCRAPPIEST, LUCKIEST LITTLE BUG I'VE EVER SEEN!
AND THE MAN HIMSELF, THE KING OF SMASH, THE HULKING HAMMER OF HOPE AND HORROR--
THE GRRREEEEN SCAAAAAAR!
RRRRRAAAAAAAAAAAAAAAAAAAAAAAAAAAAA
NOW HE AND HIS CREW FACE THEIR FINAL CHALLENGE! WILL THEY EARN THEIR FREEDOM? OR WILL THEY DIE IN THE SAND?
AND DON'T FORGET-- COMMEMORATIVE BANNERS, POSTERS, AND SHIRTS ARE STILL AVAILABLE FROM VENDORS IN THE LOBBIES.
HEY, MIEK WANTING A SHIRT!

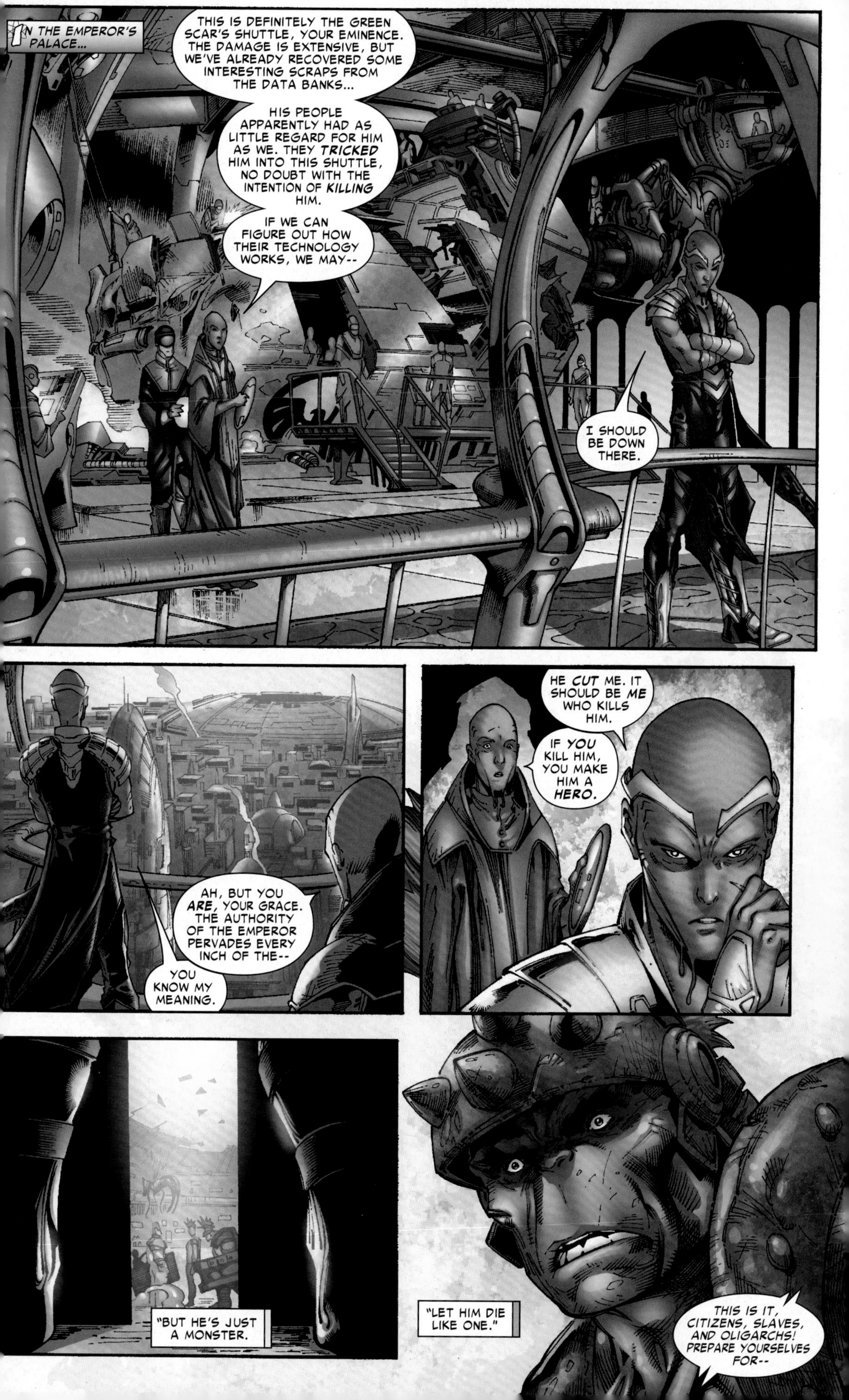
IN THE EMPEROR'S PALACE...
THIS IS DEFINITELY THE GREEN SCAR'S SHUTTLE, YOUR EMINENCE. THE DAMAGE IS EXTENSIVE, BUT WE'VE ALREADY RECOVERED SOME INTERESTING SCRAPS FROM THE DATA BANKS...
HIS PEOPLE APPARENTLY HAD AS LITTLE REGARD FOR HIM AS WE. THEY TRICKED HIM INTO THIS SHUTTLE, NO DOUBT WITH THE INTENTION OF KILLING HIM.
IF WE CAN FIGURE OUT HOW THEIR TECHNOLOGY WORKS, WE MAY--
I SHOULD BE DOWN THERE.
AH, BUT YOU ARE, YOUR GRACE. THE AUTHORITY OF THE EMPEROR PERVADES EVERY INCH OF THE--
YOU KNOW MY MEANING.
HE CUT ME. IT SHOULD BE ME WHO KILLS HIM.
IF YOU KILL HIM, YOU MAKE HIM A HERO.
"BUT HE'S JUST A MONSTER.
"LET HIM DIE LIKE ONE."
THIS IS IT, CITIZENS, SLAVES, AND OLIGARCHS! PREPARE YOURSELVES FOR--

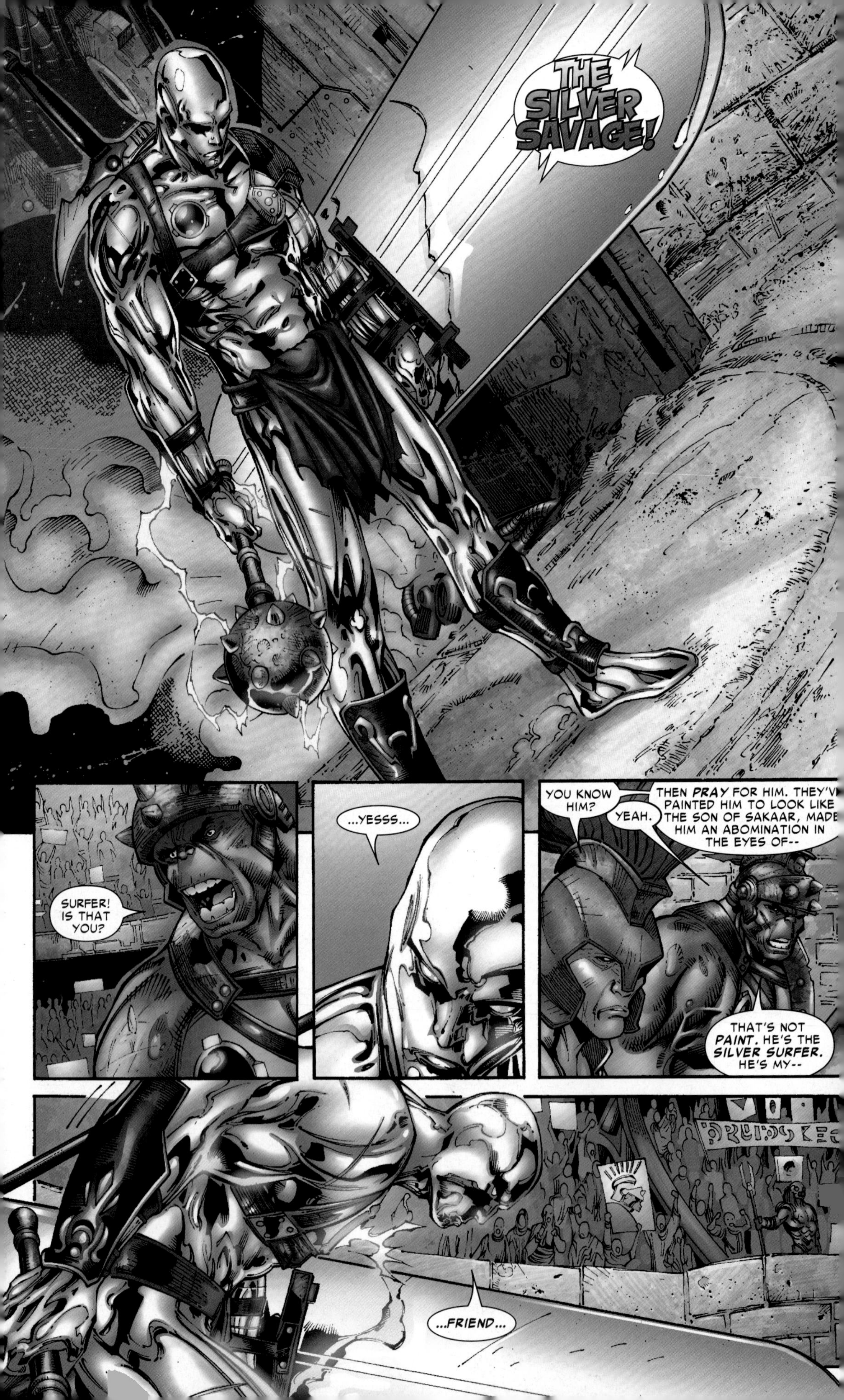
THE SILVER SAVAGE!
SURFER! IS THAT YOU?
...YESSS...
YOU KNOW HIM?
YEAH.
THEN PRAY FOR HIM. THEY'VE PAINTED HIM TO LOOK LIKE THE SON OF SAKAAR, MADE HIM AN ABOMINATION IN THE EYES OF--
THAT'S NOT PAINT. HE'S THE SILVER SURFER. HE'S MY--
...FRIEND...

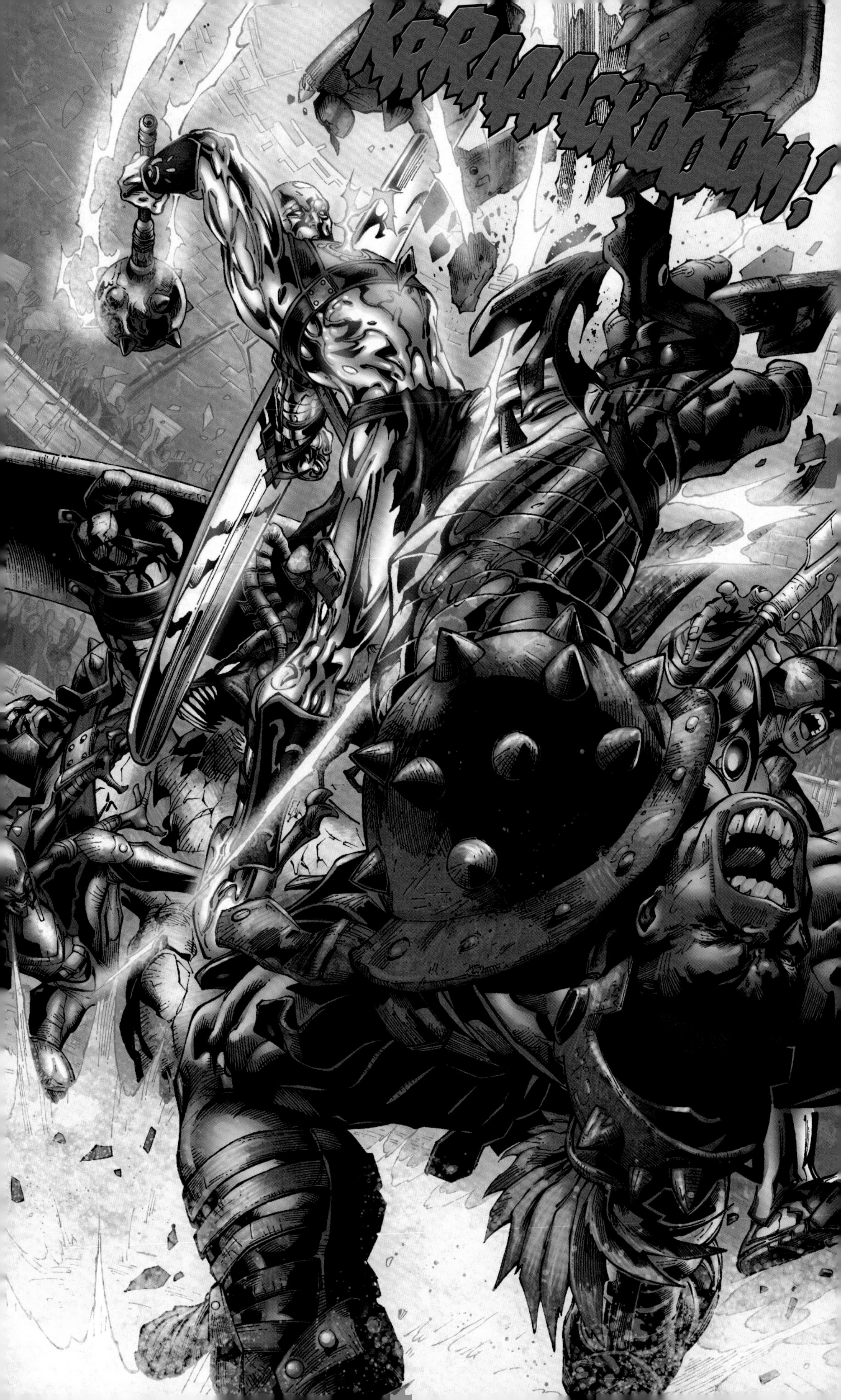
KRRAAAACKOOOM!!

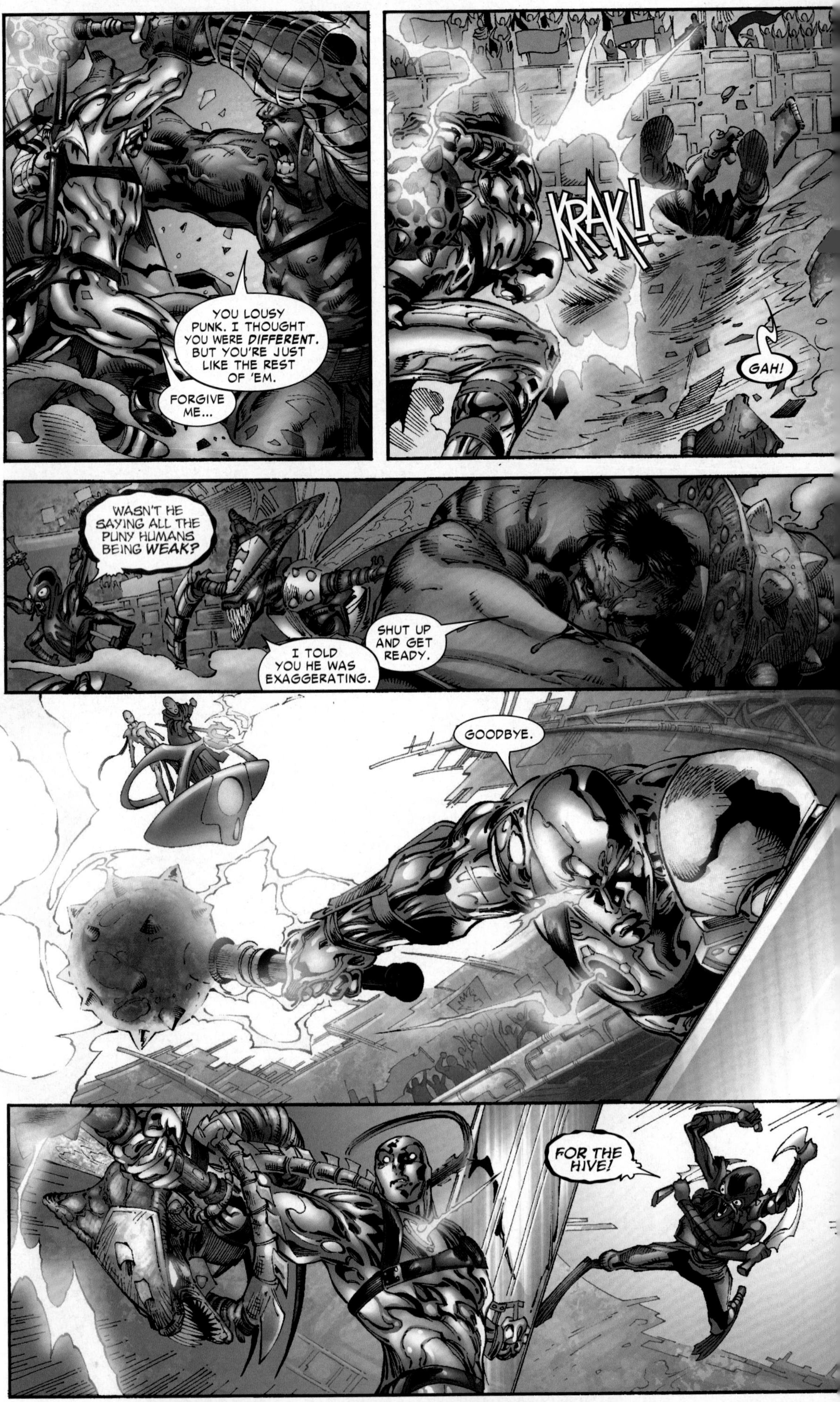
YOU LOUSY PUNK. I THOUGHT YOU WERE *DIFFERENT*. BUT YOU'RE JUST LIKE THE REST OF 'EM.
FORGIVE ME...
KRAK!
GAH!
WASN'T HE SAYING ALL THE PUNY HUMANS BEING *WEAK?*
I TOLD YOU HE WAS EXAGGERATING.
SHUT UP AND GET READY.
GOODBYE.
FOR THE HIVE!

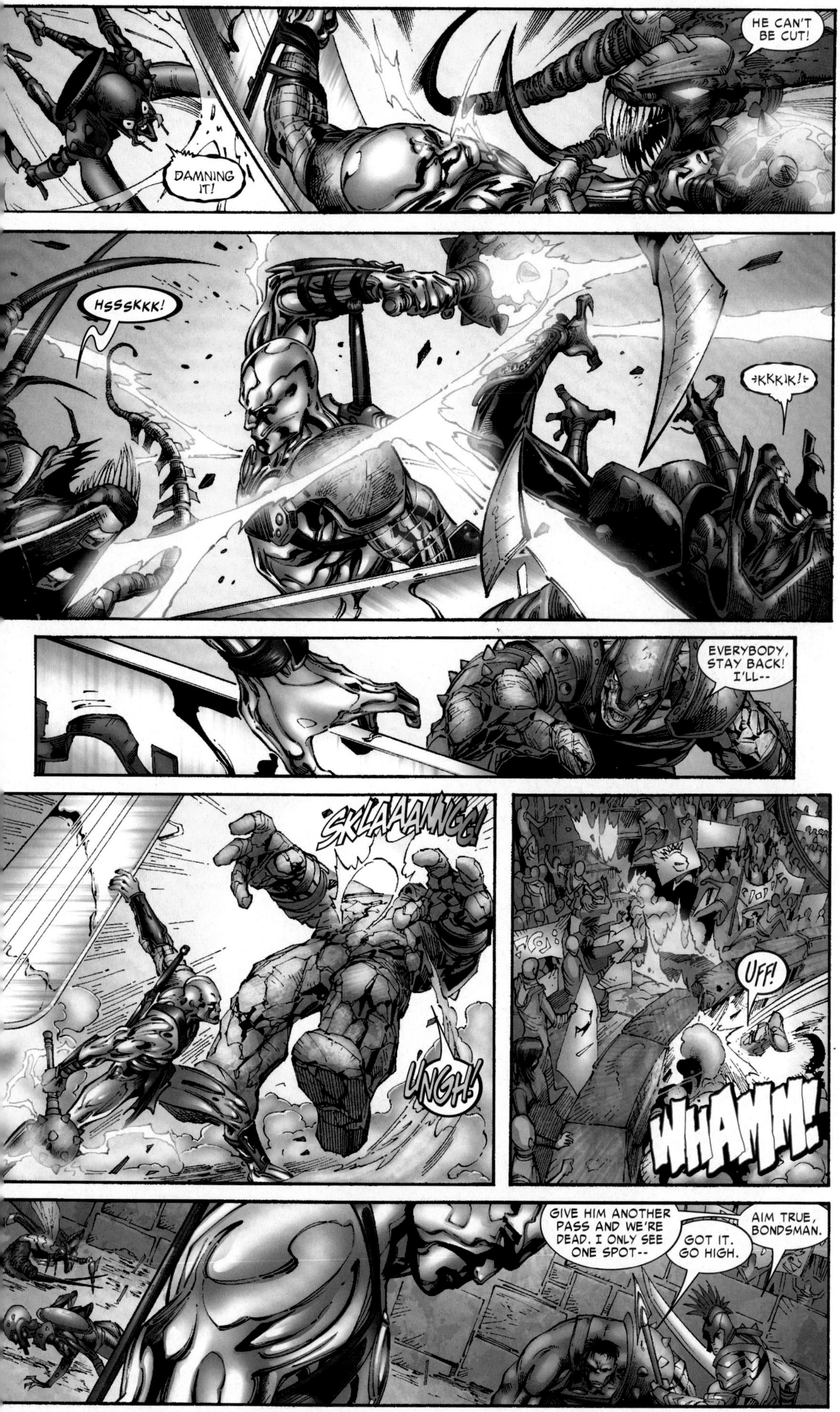
HE CAN'T BE CUT!
DAMNING IT!
HSSSKKK!
KKKIK!
EVERYBODY, STAY BACK! I'LL--
SKLAAANNGG!
UNGH!
UFF!
WHAMM!
GIVE HIM ANOTHER PASS AND WE'RE DEAD. I ONLY SEE ONE SPOT--
GOT IT. GO HIGH.
AIM TRUE, BONDSMAN.

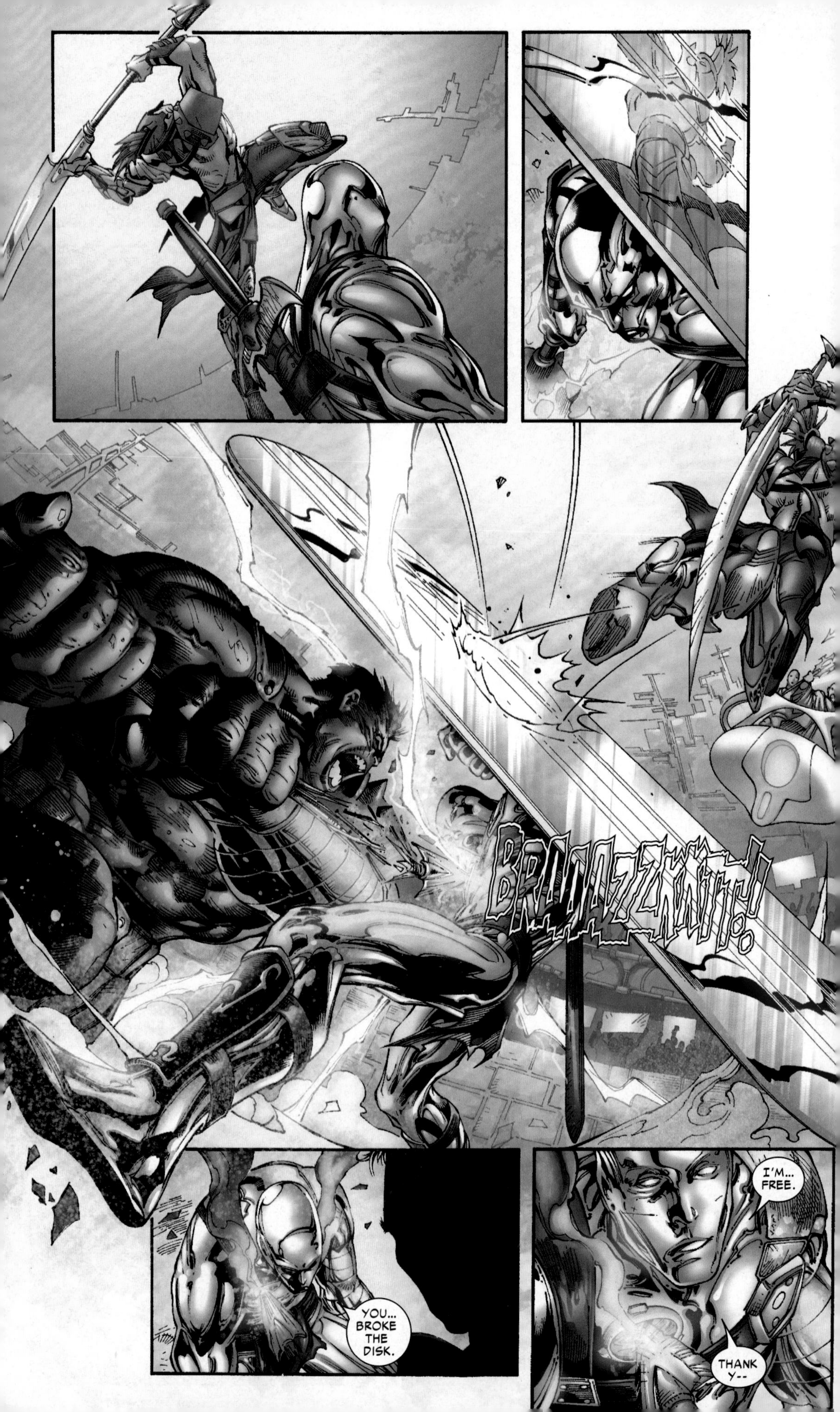
BRAAAZZKKTT!
YOU... BROKE THE DISK.
I'M... FREE.
THANK Y--

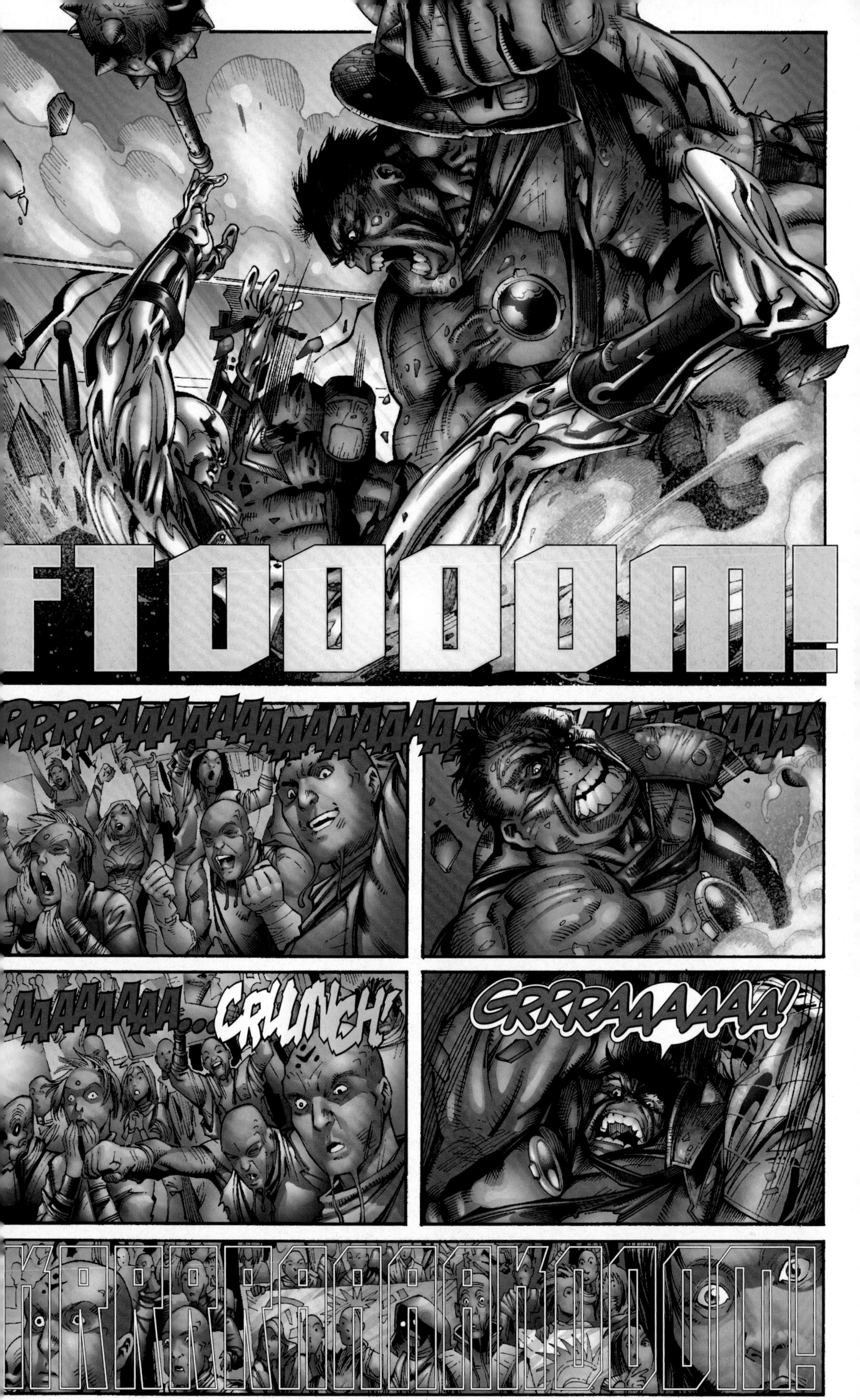
FTOOOM!
RRRRAAAAAAAAAAAAAA-AA-AAAAAA!
AAAAAAA...CRUNCH!
GRRRAAAAAAA!
KRRRRAAAAKOOOM!

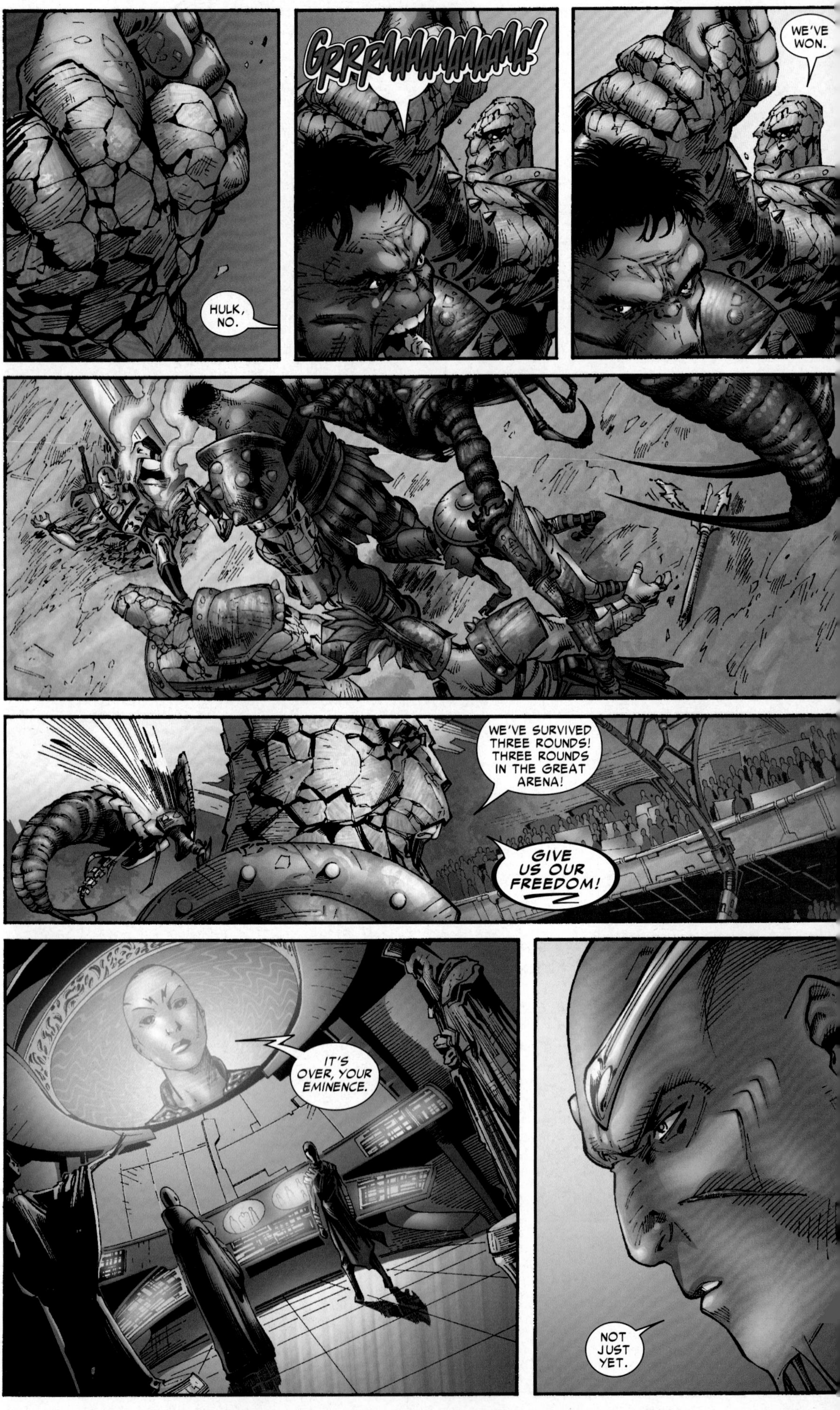
HULK, NO.
GRRRAAAAAAAAAA!
WE'VE WON.
WE'VE SURVIVED THREE ROUNDS! THREE ROUNDS IN THE GREAT ARENA!
GIVE US OUR FREEDOM!
IT'S OVER, YOUR EMINENCE.
NOT JUST YET.

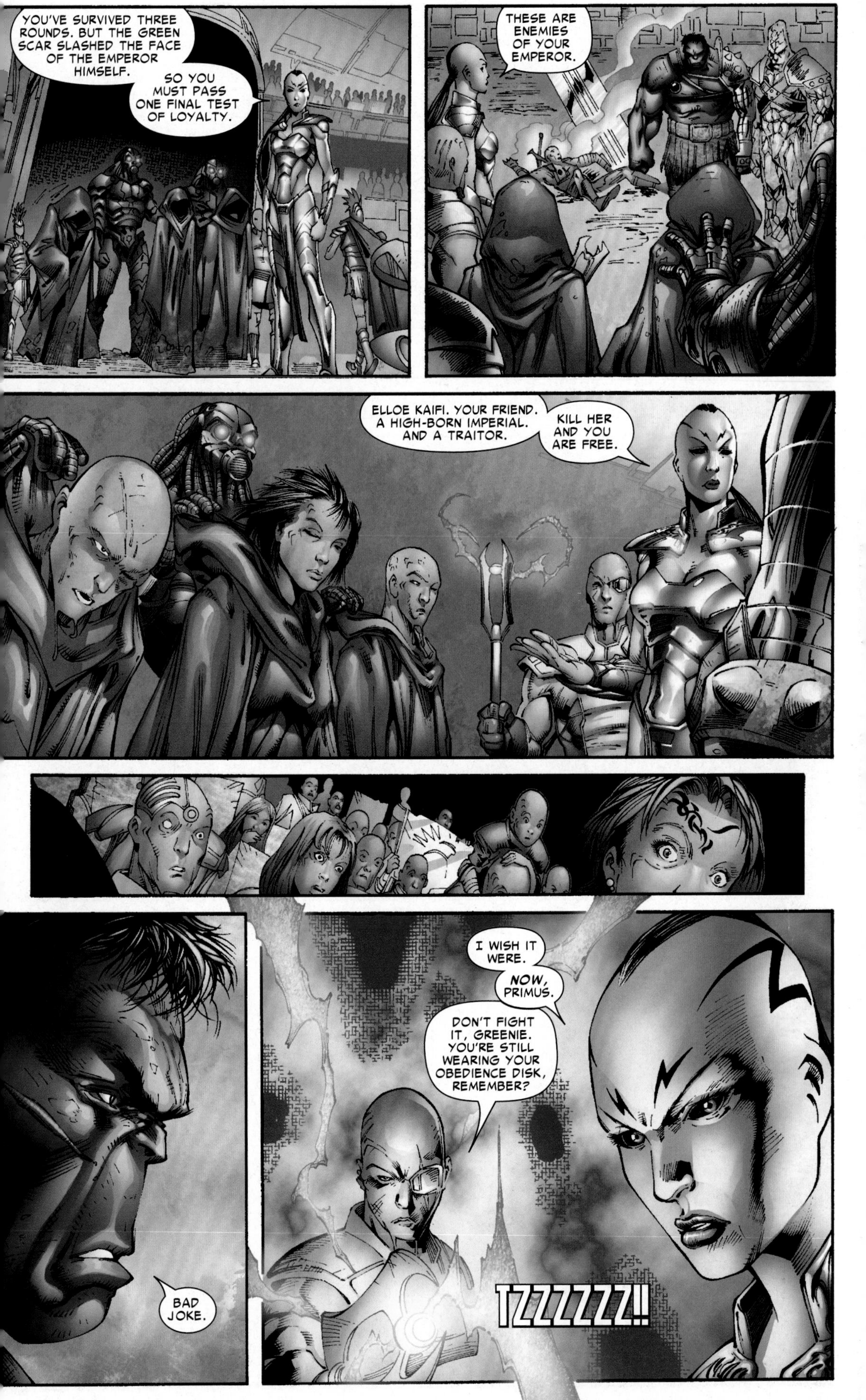
YOU'VE SURVIVED THREE ROUNDS. BUT THE GREEN SCAR SLASHED THE FACE OF THE EMPEROR HIMSELF.
SO YOU MUST PASS ONE FINAL TEST OF LOYALTY.
THESE ARE ENEMIES OF YOUR EMPEROR.
ELLOE KAIFI. YOUR FRIEND. A HIGH-BORN IMPERIAL. AND A TRAITOR.
KILL HER AND YOU ARE FREE.
BAD JOKE.
I WISH IT WERE.
NOW, PRIMUS.
DON'T FIGHT IT, GREENIE. YOU'RE STILL WEARING YOUR OBEDIENCE DISK, REMEMBER?
TZZZZZZ!!

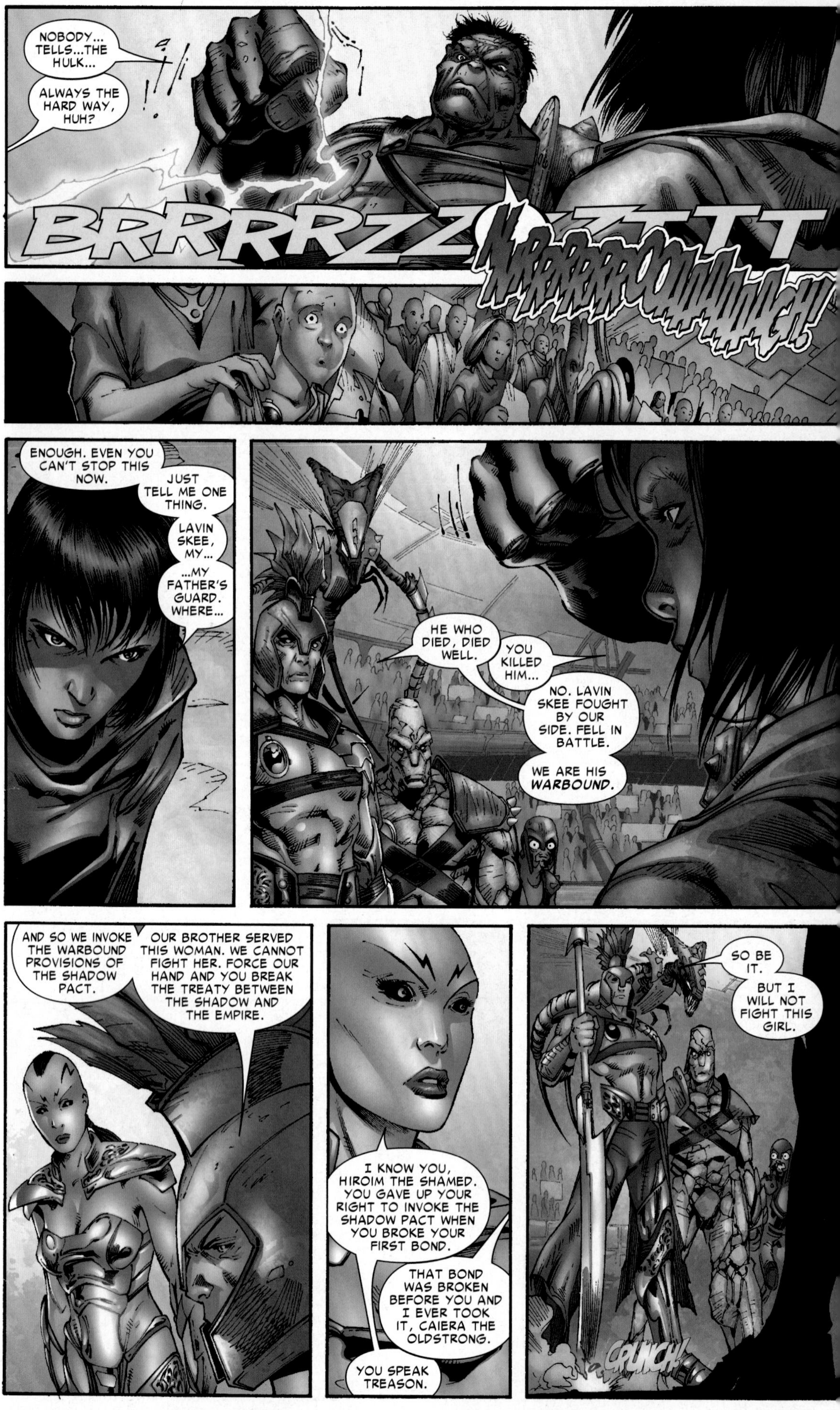
NOBODY... TELLS...THE HULK...
ALWAYS THE HARD WAY, HUH?
BRRRRZZZZTTT
NARRRRRRROOAAAAAAGH!
ENOUGH. EVEN YOU CAN'T STOP THIS NOW.
JUST TELL ME ONE THING.
LAVIN SKEE, MY...
...MY FATHER'S GUARD. WHERE...
HE WHO DIED, DIED WELL.
YOU KILLED HIM...
NO. LAVIN SKEE FOUGHT BY OUR SIDE. FELL IN BATTLE.
WE ARE HIS WARBOUND.
AND SO WE INVOKE THE WARBOUND PROVISIONS OF THE SHADOW PACT.
OUR BROTHER SERVED THIS WOMAN. WE CANNOT FIGHT HER. FORCE OUR HAND AND YOU BREAK THE TREATY BETWEEN THE SHADOW AND THE EMPIRE.
I KNOW YOU, HIROIM THE SHAMED. YOU GAVE UP YOUR RIGHT TO INVOKE THE SHADOW PACT WHEN YOU BROKE YOUR FIRST BOND.
THAT BOND WAS BROKEN BEFORE YOU AND I EVER TOOK IT, CAIERA THE OLDSTRONG.
YOU SPEAK TREASON.
SO BE IT.
BUT I WILL NOT FIGHT THIS GIRL.
CRUNCH!

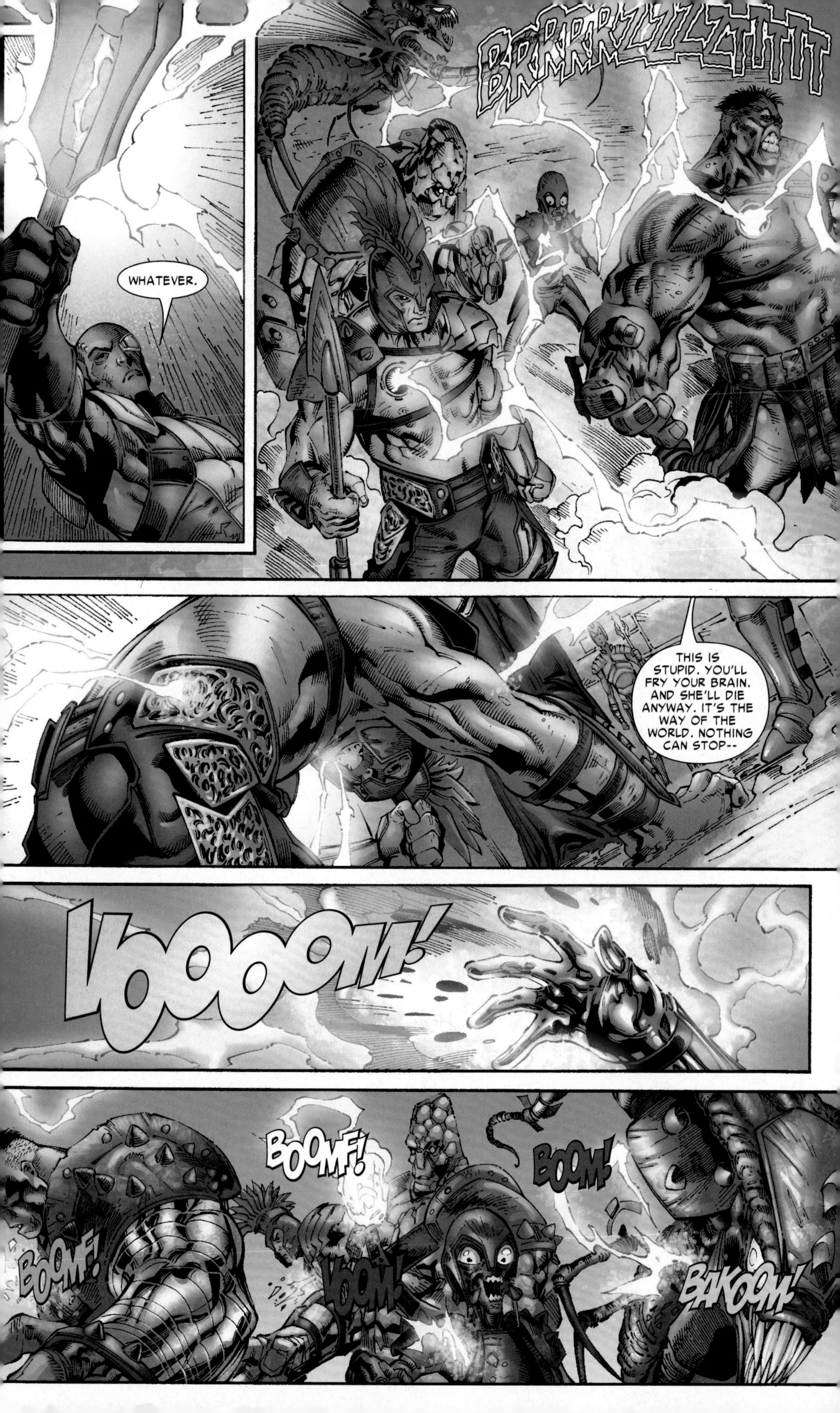
WHATEVER.
BRRRRZZZZTTTTT
THIS IS STUPID. YOU'LL FRY YOUR BRAIN. AND SHE'LL DIE ANYWAY. IT'S THE WAY OF THE WORLD. NOTHING CAN STOP--
VOOOOOM!
BOOMF!
BOOM!
BOOMF!
VOOM!
BAKOOM!

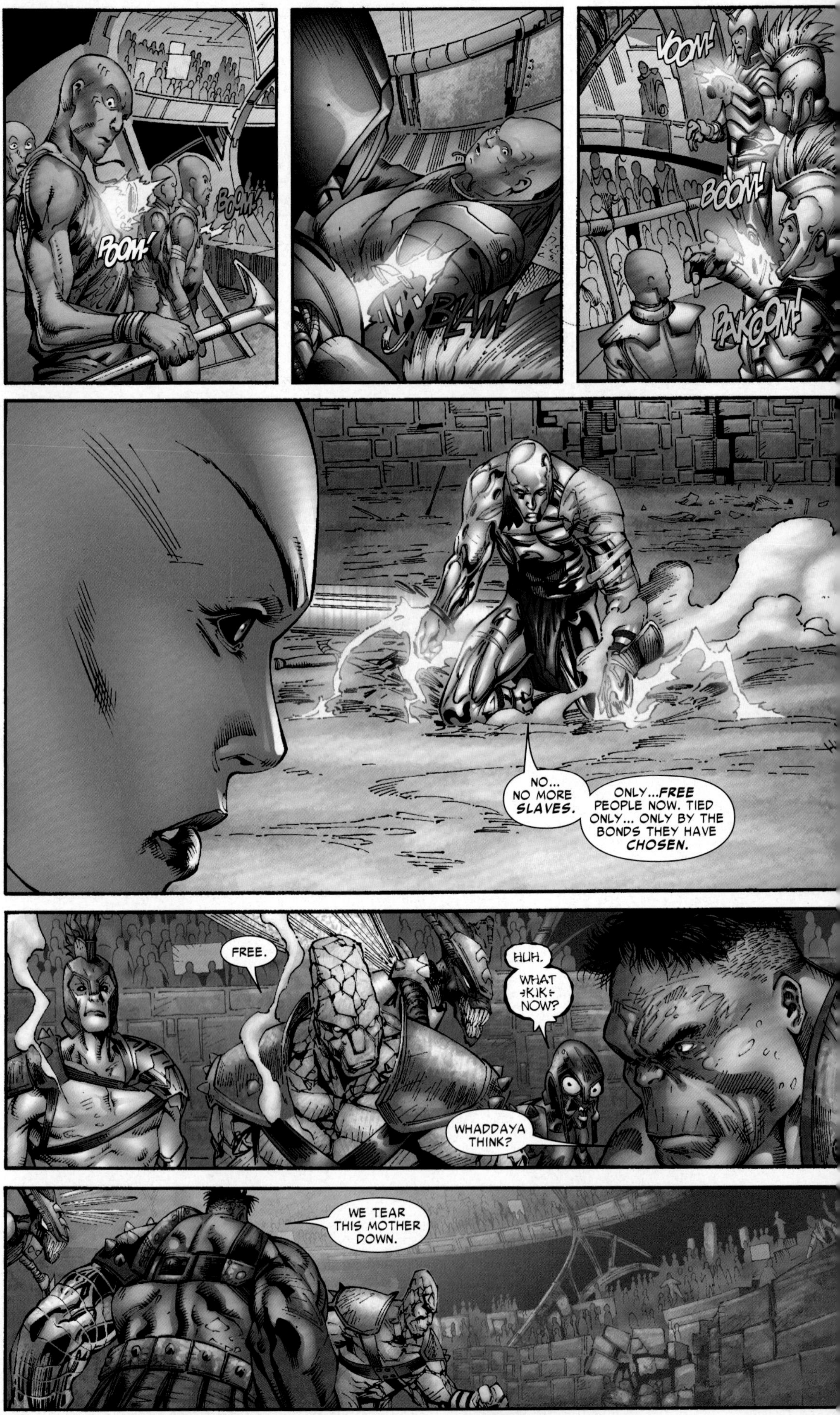
POOM!
BOOM!
BLAM!
VOOM!
BOOM!
PAKOOM!
NO... NO MORE SLAVES.
ONLY...FREE PEOPLE NOW. TIED ONLY... ONLY BY THE BONDS THEY HAVE CHOSEN.
FREE.
HUH.
WHAT ‡KIK‡ NOW?
WHADDAYA THINK?
WE TEAR THIS MOTHER DOWN.

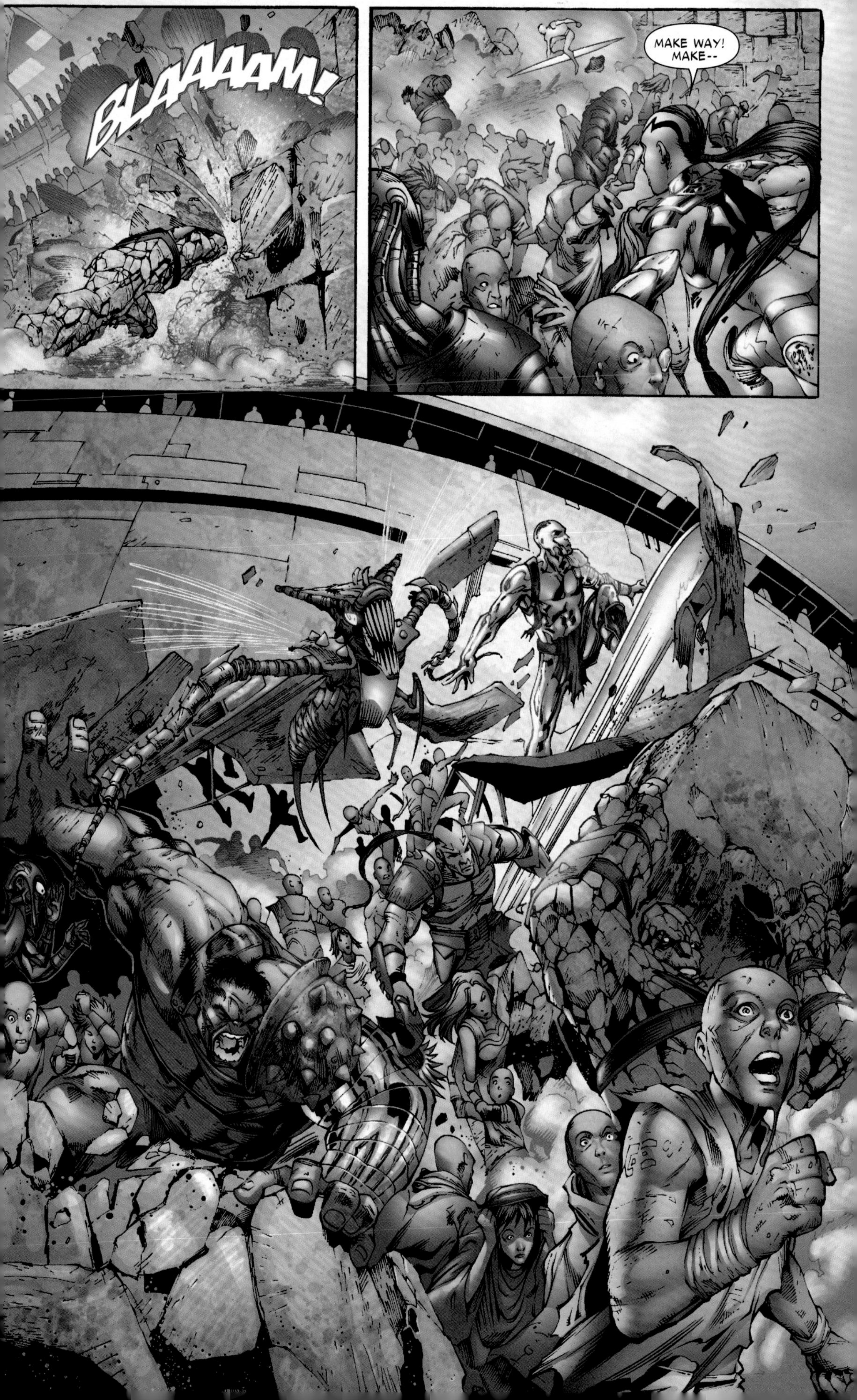
BLAAAAM!
MAKE WAY! MAKE--

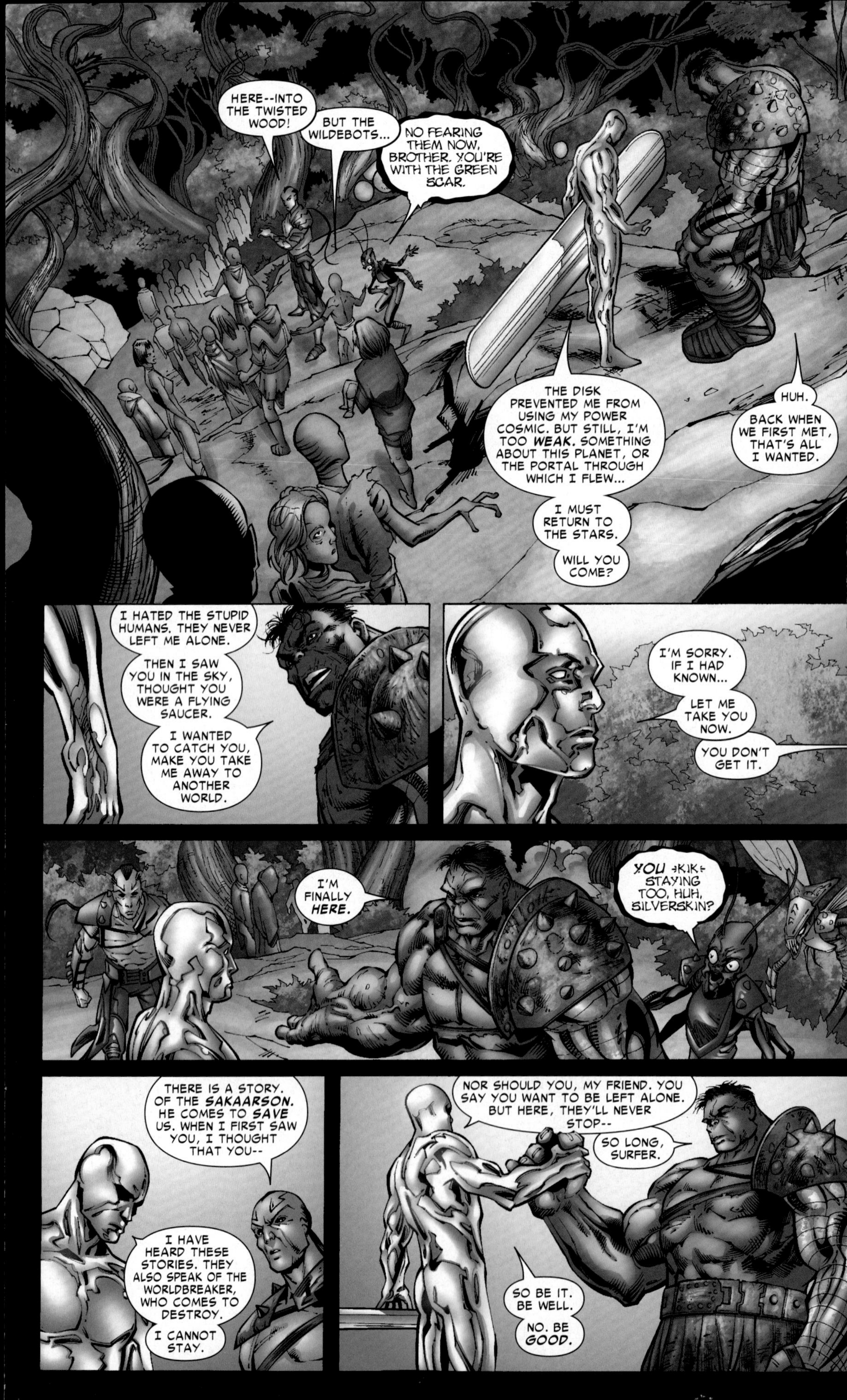
HERE--INTO THE TWISTED WOOD!
BUT THE WILDEBOTS...
NO FEARING THEM NOW, BROTHER. YOU'RE WITH THE GREEN SCAR.
THE DISK PREVENTED ME FROM USING MY POWER COSMIC. BUT STILL, I'M TOO WEAK. SOMETHING ABOUT THIS PLANET, OR THE PORTAL THROUGH WHICH I FLEW...
I MUST RETURN TO THE STARS.
WILL YOU COME?
HUH.
BACK WHEN WE FIRST MET, THAT'S ALL I WANTED.
I HATED THE STUPID HUMANS. THEY NEVER LEFT ME ALONE.
THEN I SAW YOU IN THE SKY, THOUGHT YOU WERE A FLYING SAUCER.
I WANTED TO CATCH YOU, MAKE YOU TAKE ME AWAY TO ANOTHER WORLD.
I'M SORRY. IF I HAD KNOWN...
LET ME TAKE YOU NOW.
YOU DON'T GET IT.
I'M FINALLY HERE.
YOU -KIK- STAYING TOO, HUH, SILVERSKIN?
THERE IS A STORY. OF THE SAKAARSON. HE COMES TO SAVE US. WHEN I FIRST SAW YOU, I THOUGHT THAT YOU--
I HAVE HEARD THESE STORIES. THEY ALSO SPEAK OF THE WORLDBREAKER, WHO COMES TO DESTROY.
I CANNOT STAY.
NOR SHOULD YOU, MY FRIEND. YOU SAY YOU WANT TO BE LEFT ALONE. BUT HERE, THEY'LL NEVER STOP--
SO LONG, SURFER.
SO BE IT. BE WELL.
NO. BE GOOD.

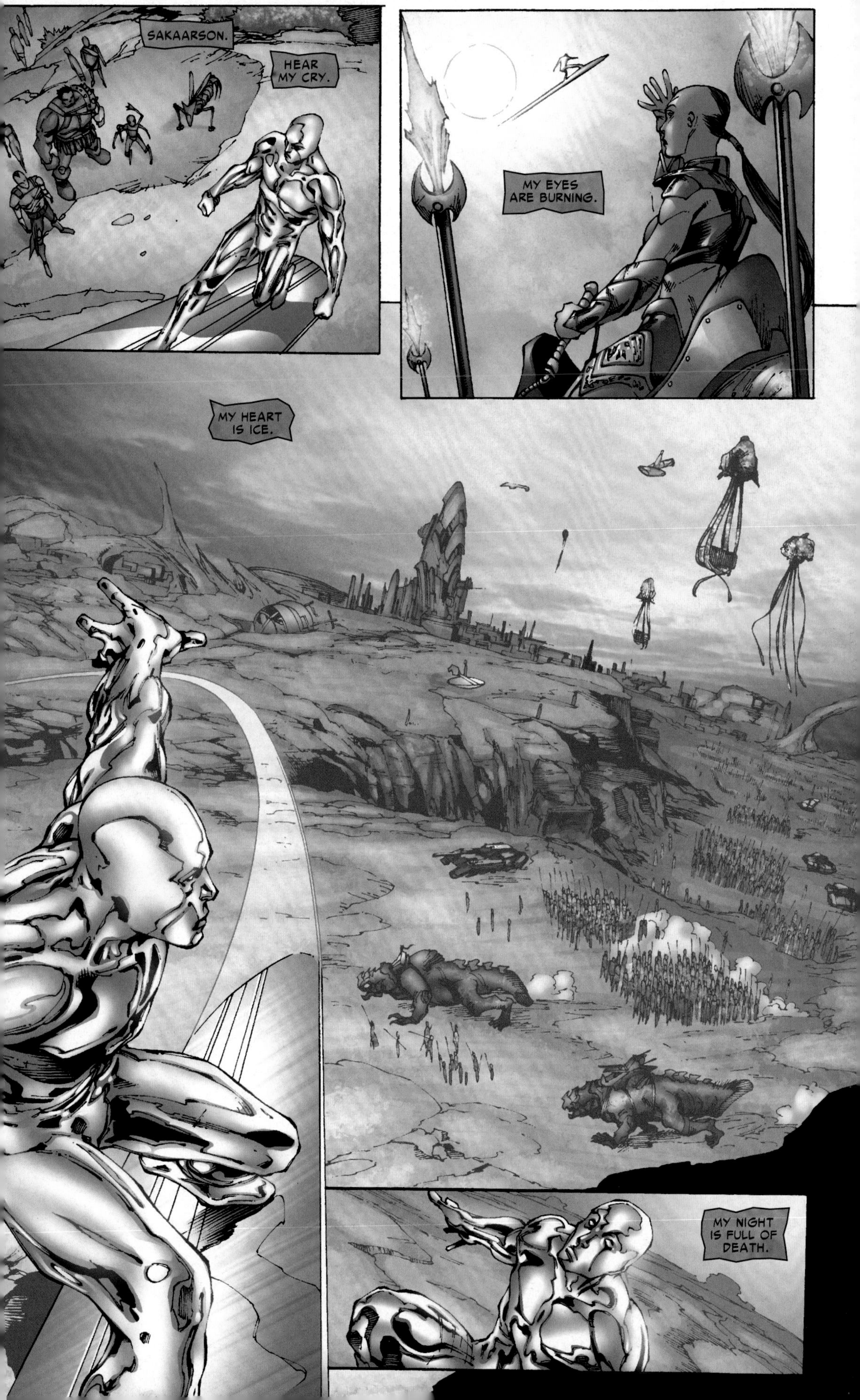
SAKAARSON.
HEAR MY CRY.
MY EYES ARE BURNING.
MY HEART IS ICE.
MY NIGHT IS FULL OF DEATH.

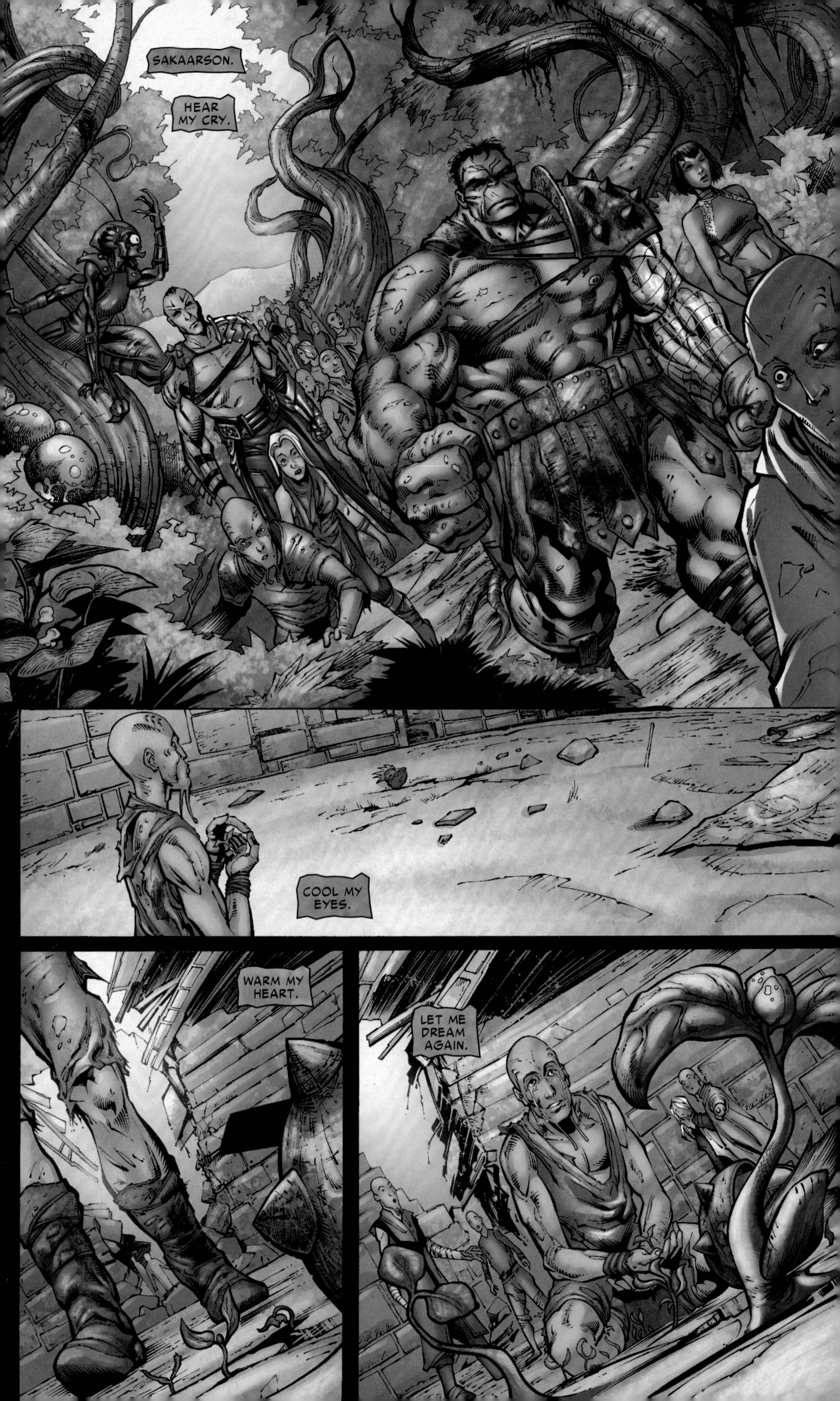
SAKAARSON.
HEAR MY CRY.
COOL MY EYES.
WARM MY HEART.
LET ME DREAM AGAIN.

GIANT-SIZE HULK #1

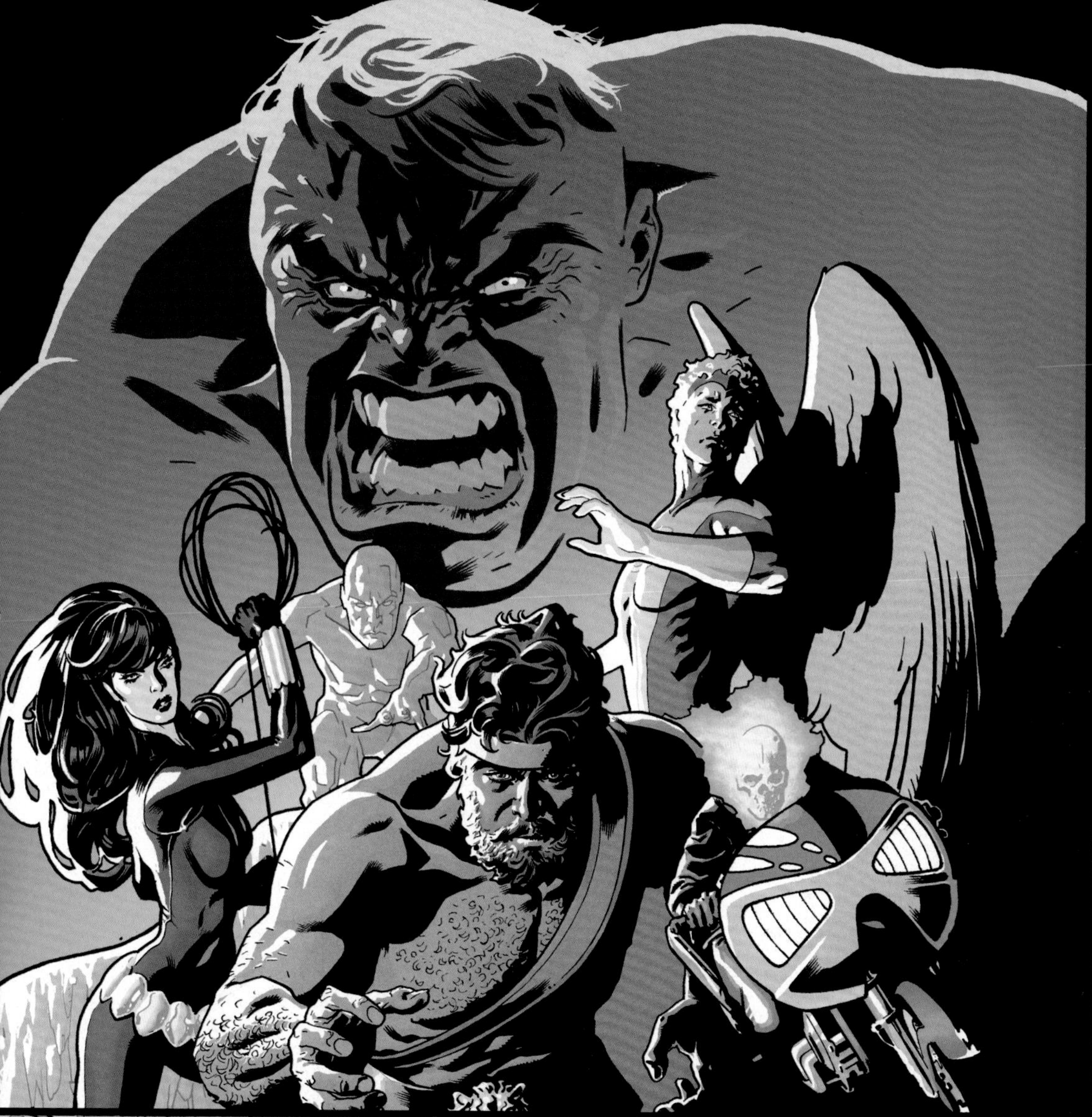

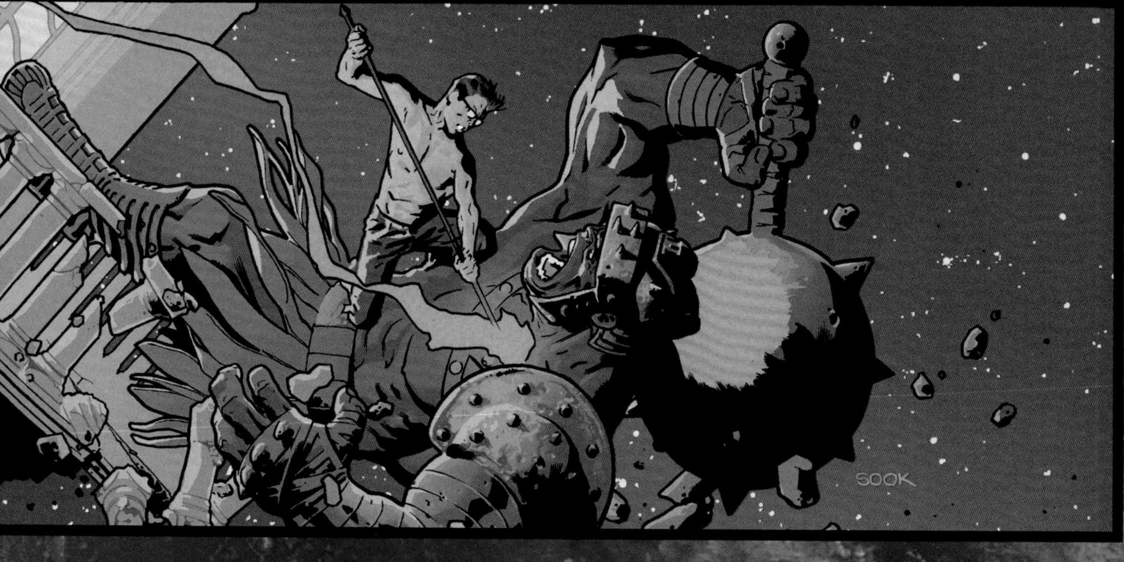
SOOK

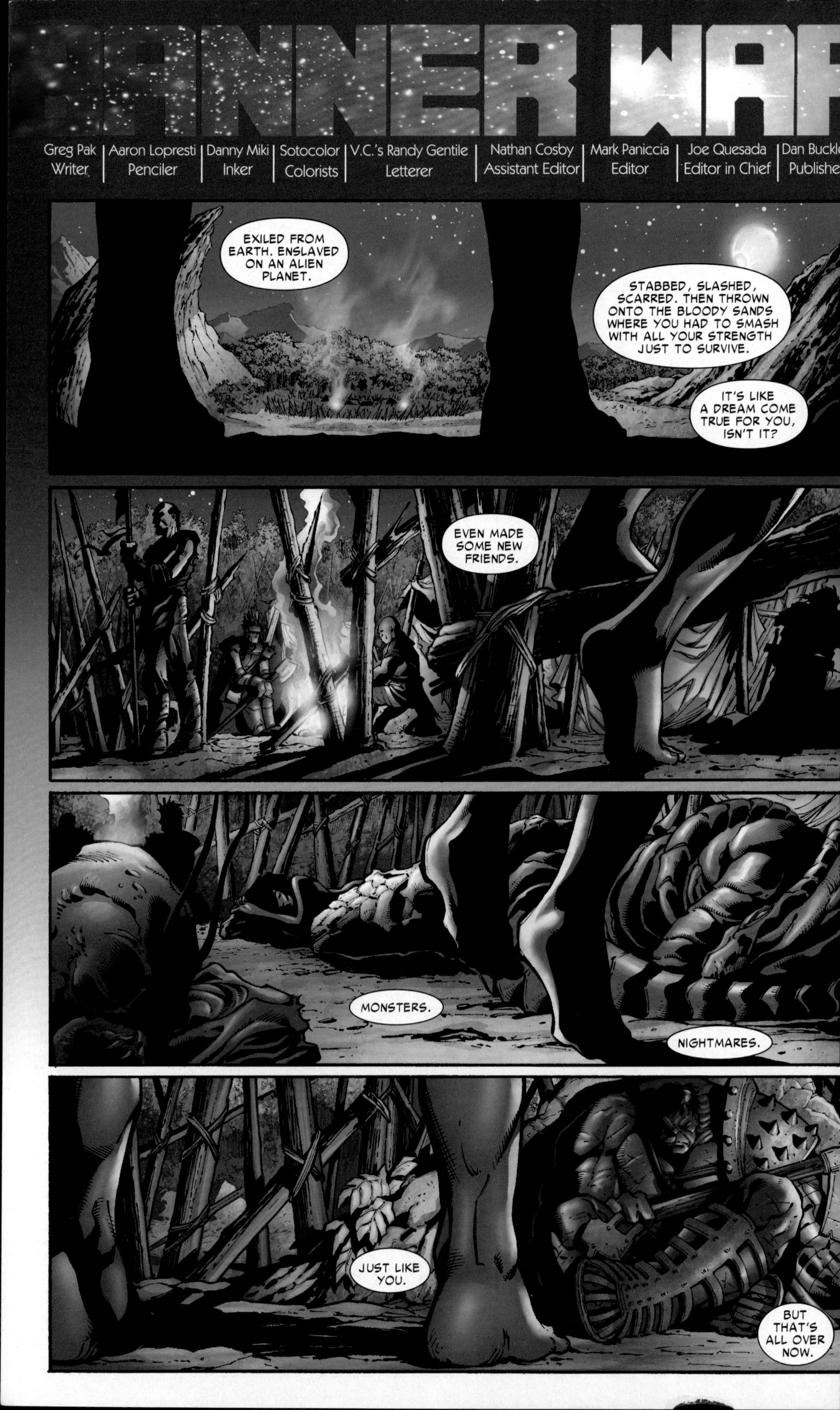

BANNER WAR
Greg Pak Writer
Aaron Lopresti Penciler
Danny Miki Inker
Sotocolor Colorists
V.C.'s Randy Gentile Letterer
Nathan Cosby Assistant Editor
Mark Paniccia Editor
Joe Quesada Editor in Chief
Dan Buckley Publisher
EXILED FROM EARTH. ENSLAVED ON AN ALIEN PLANET.
STABBED, SLASHED, SCARRED. THEN THROWN ONTO THE BLOODY SANDS WHERE YOU HAD TO SMASH WITH ALL YOUR STRENGTH JUST TO SURVIVE.
IT'S LIKE A DREAM COME TRUE FOR YOU, ISN'T IT?
EVEN MADE SOME NEW FRIENDS.
MONSTERS.
NIGHTMARES.
JUST LIKE YOU.
BUT THAT'S ALL OVER NOW.

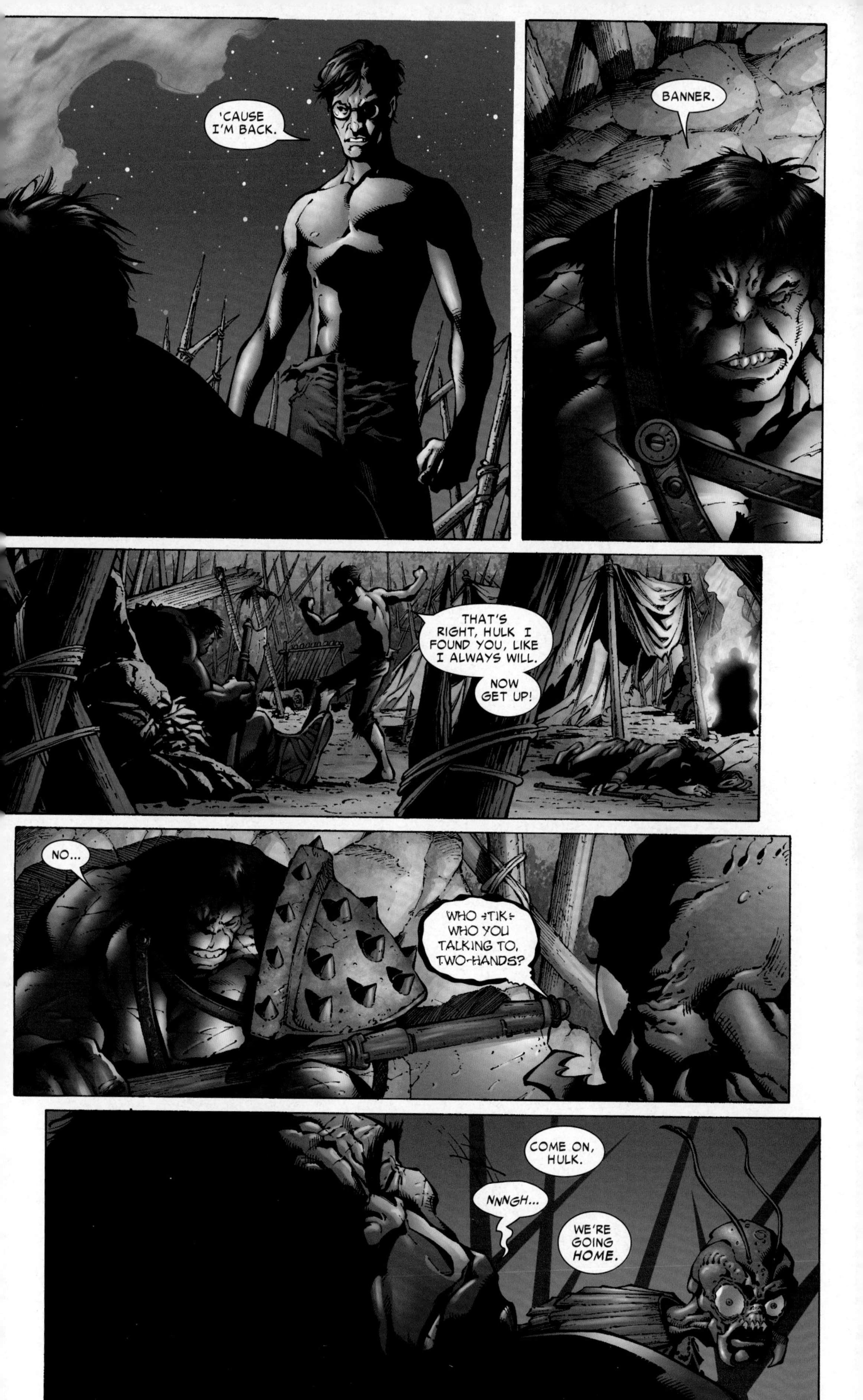
'CAUSE I'M BACK.
BANNER.
THAT'S RIGHT, HULK I FOUND YOU, LIKE I ALWAYS WILL.
NOW GET UP!
NO...
WHO =TIK= WHO YOU TALKING TO, TWO-HANDS?
COME ON, HULK.
NNNGH...
WE'RE GOING HOME.

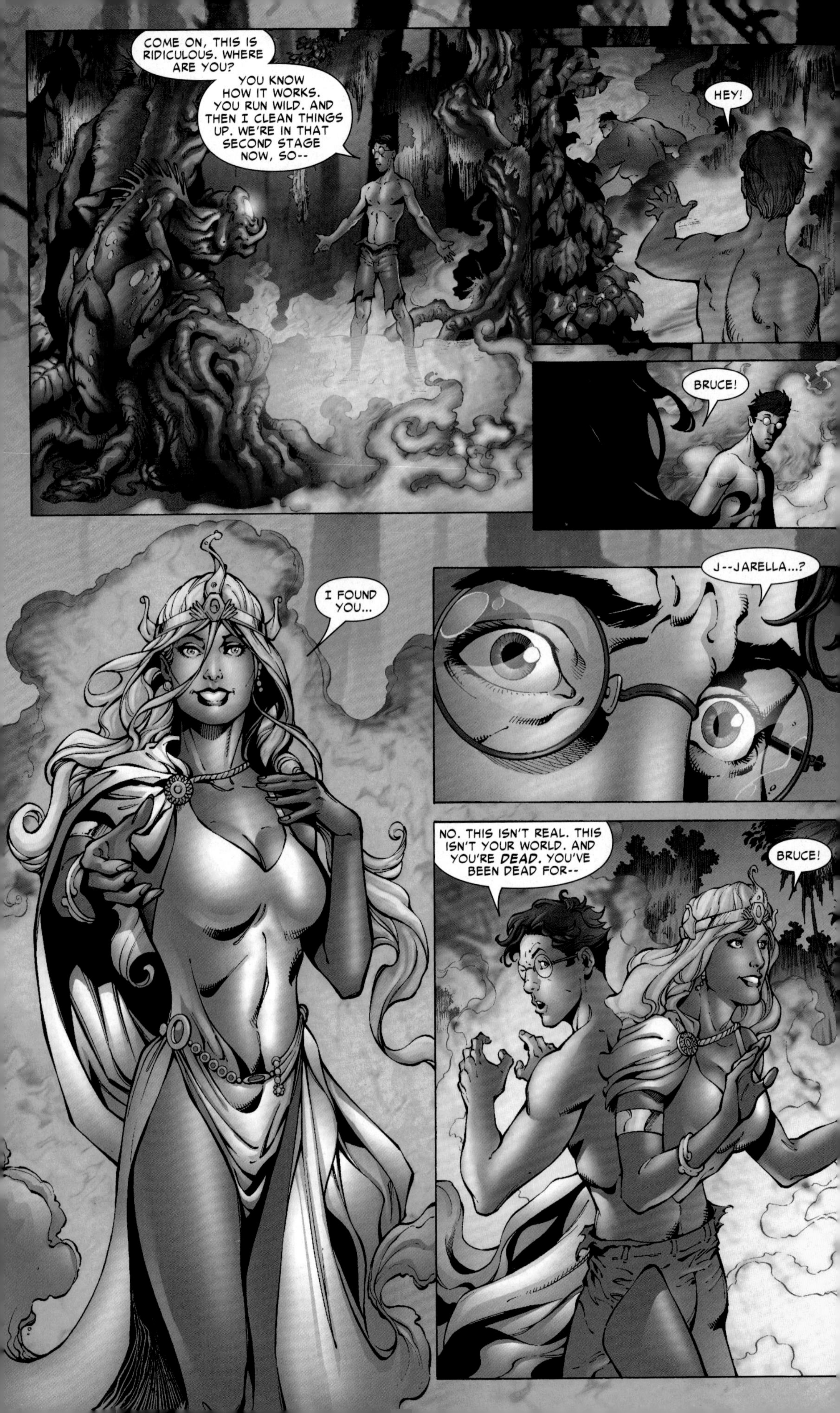
COME ON, THIS IS RIDICULOUS. WHERE ARE YOU?
YOU KNOW HOW IT WORKS. YOU RUN WILD. AND THEN I CLEAN THINGS UP. WE'RE IN THAT SECOND STAGE NOW, SO--
HEY!
BRUCE!
I FOUND YOU...
J--JARELLA...?
NO. THIS ISN'T REAL. THIS ISN'T YOUR WORLD. AND YOU'RE *DEAD*. YOU'VE BEEN DEAD FOR--
BRUCE!

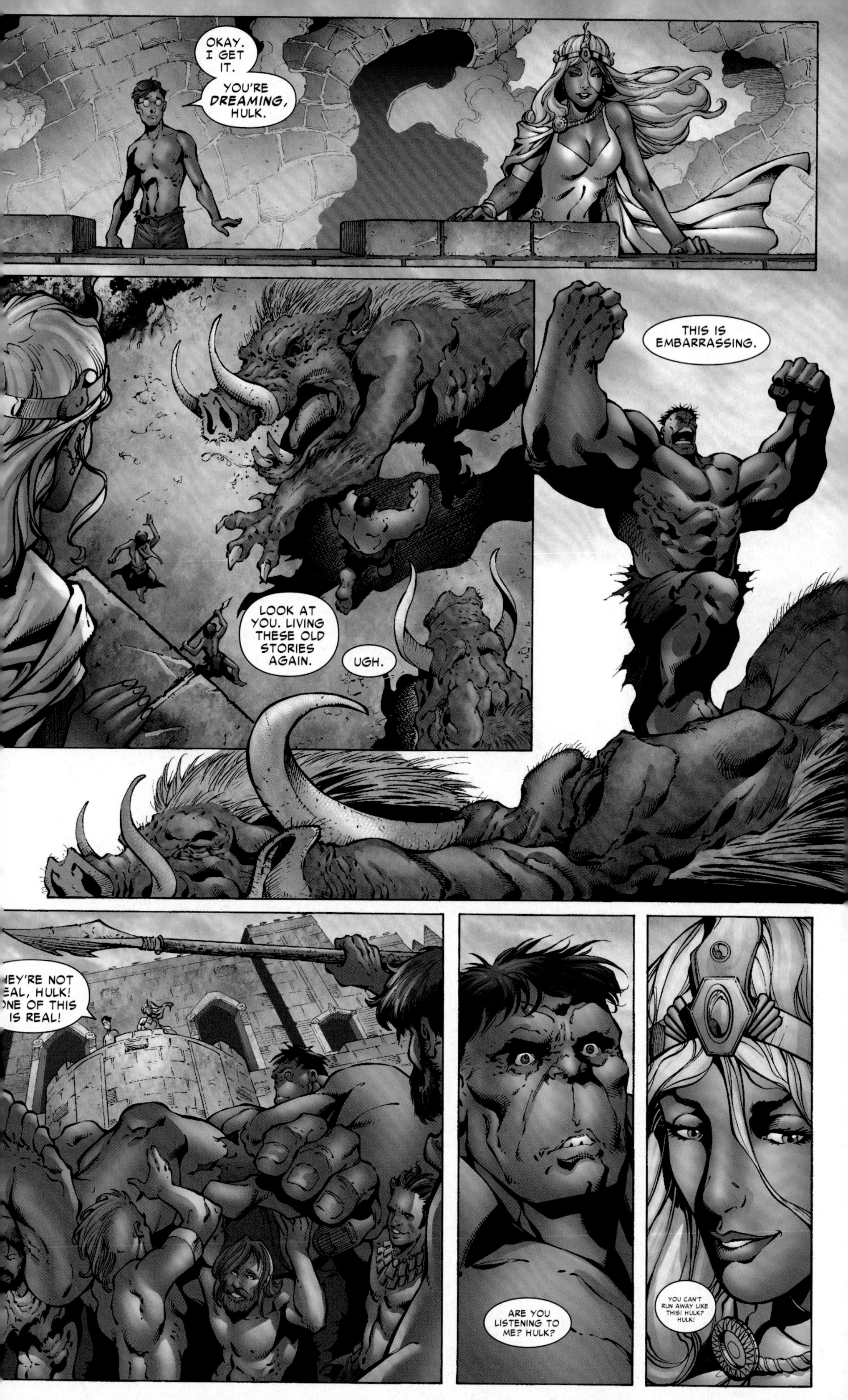
OKAY. I GET IT.
YOU'RE DREAMING, HULK.
THIS IS EMBARRASSING.
LOOK AT YOU. LIVING THESE OLD STORIES AGAIN.
UGH.
HEY'RE NOT EAL, HULK! ONE OF THIS IS REAL!
ARE YOU LISTENING TO ME? HULK?
YOU CAN'T RUN AWAY LIKE THIS! HULK? HULK!

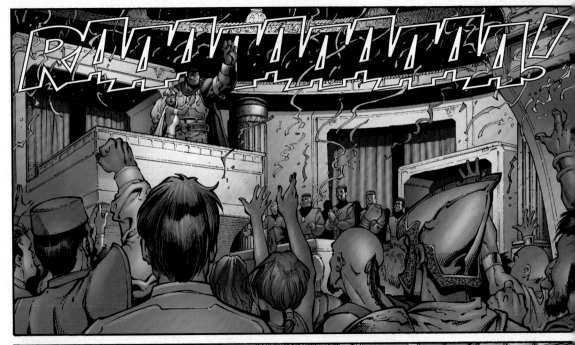

RATTTAAATTA!

"HULK JUST WANTS TO BE LEFT ALONE."

RIIIIGHT.

NO!

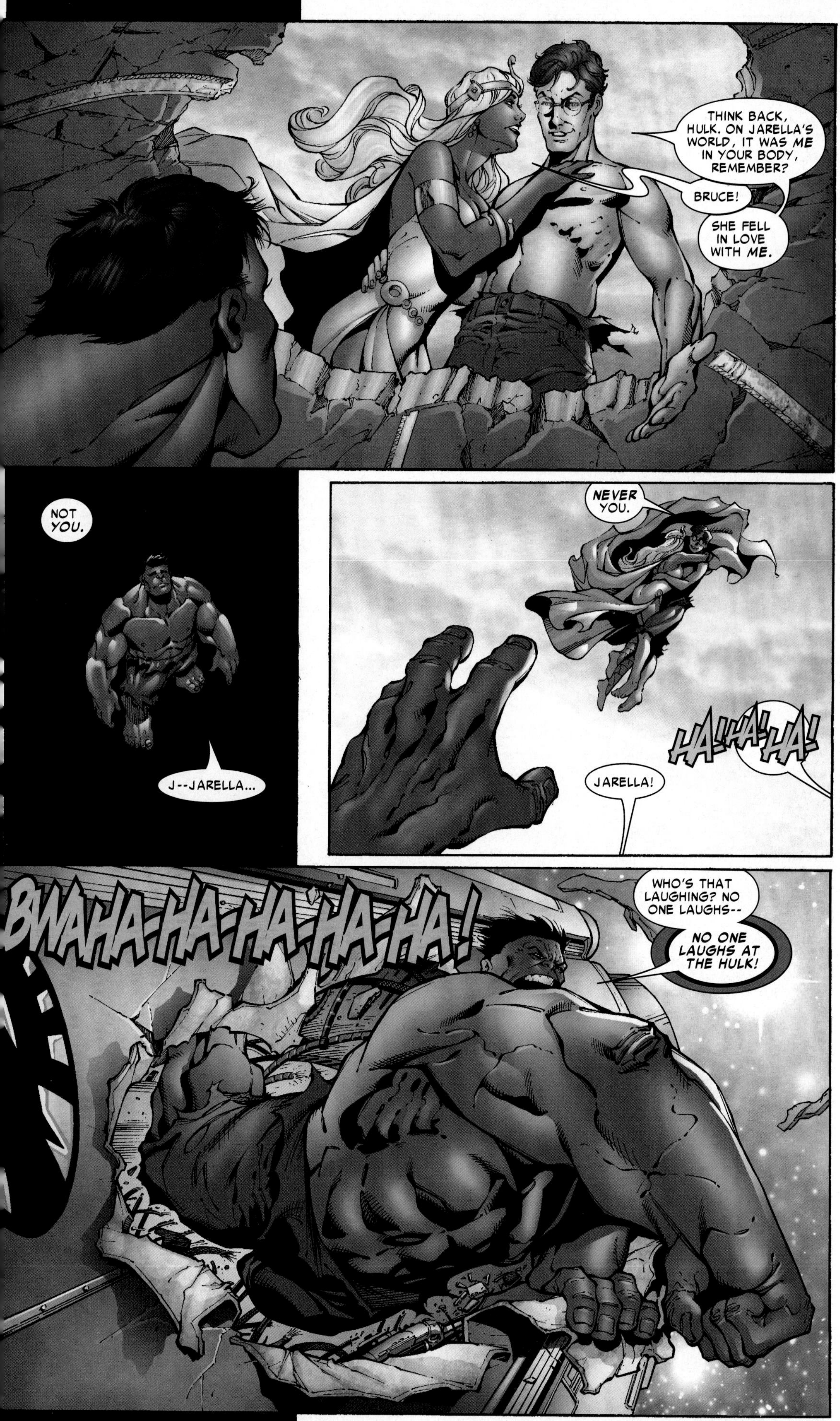
THINK BACK, HULK. ON JARELLA'S WORLD, IT WAS *ME* IN YOUR BODY, REMEMBER?
BRUCE!
SHE FELL IN LOVE WITH *ME*.
NOT YOU.
J--JARELLA...
NEVER YOU.
HA! HA! HA!
JARELLA!
BWAHA-HA-HA-HA-HA!
WHO'S THAT LAUGHING? NO ONE LAUGHS--
NO ONE LAUGHS AT THE HULK!

WHAT'RE YOU, KIDDIN'?

HEH.

HOOO BOY!

HEE HEE!

HA HA HA HA!

YOU POOR SAP. OF *COURSE* WE'RE LAUGHING AT YOU, ALL THE TIME!

HA *HA*! THE JEST MAY BE CRUEL, BUT 'TIS TRUE, GREEN BRUTE, 'TIS TRUE!

AAAAA HA HA HA!

BY THE HOARY HO-- HO-- AAAAWW, HA HA HA AAAH!

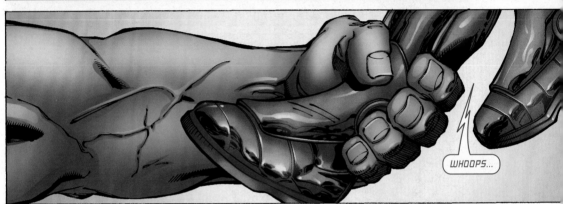

WHOOPS...

OUCH.

BETTER HIM THAN ME...

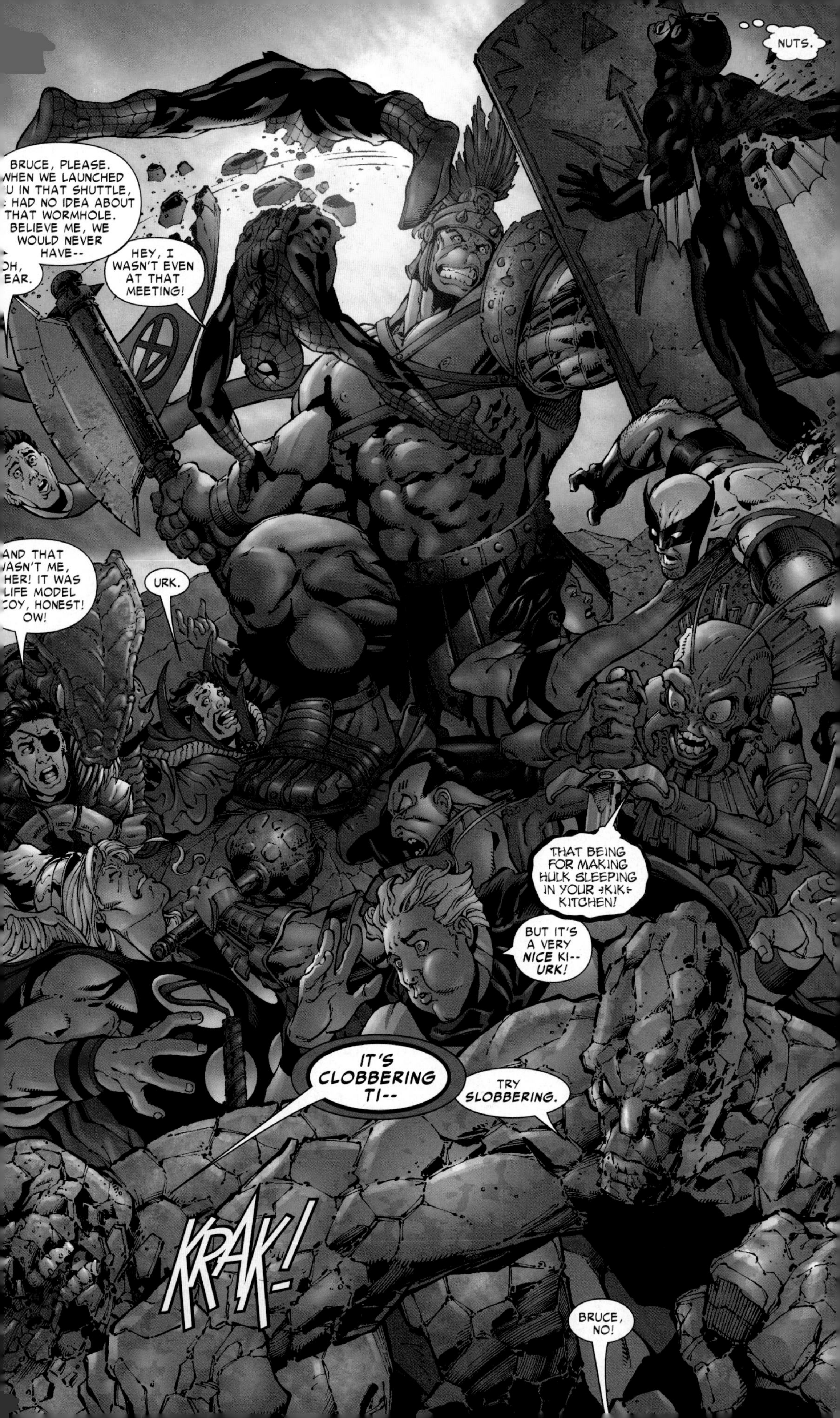

NUTS.
BRUCE, PLEASE. WHEN WE LAUNCHED U IN THAT SHUTTLE, : HAD NO IDEA ABOUT THAT WORMHOLE. BELIEVE ME, WE WOULD NEVER HAVE--
OH, EAR.
HEY, I WASN'T EVEN AT THAT MEETING!
AND THAT WASN'T ME, HER! IT WAS LIFE MODEL COY, HONEST! OW!
URK.
THAT BEING FOR MAKING HULK SLEEPING IN YOUR -KIK- KITCHEN!
BUT IT'S A VERY NICE KI-- URK!
IT'S CLOBBERING TI--
TRY SLOBBERING.
KRAK!
BRUCE, NO!

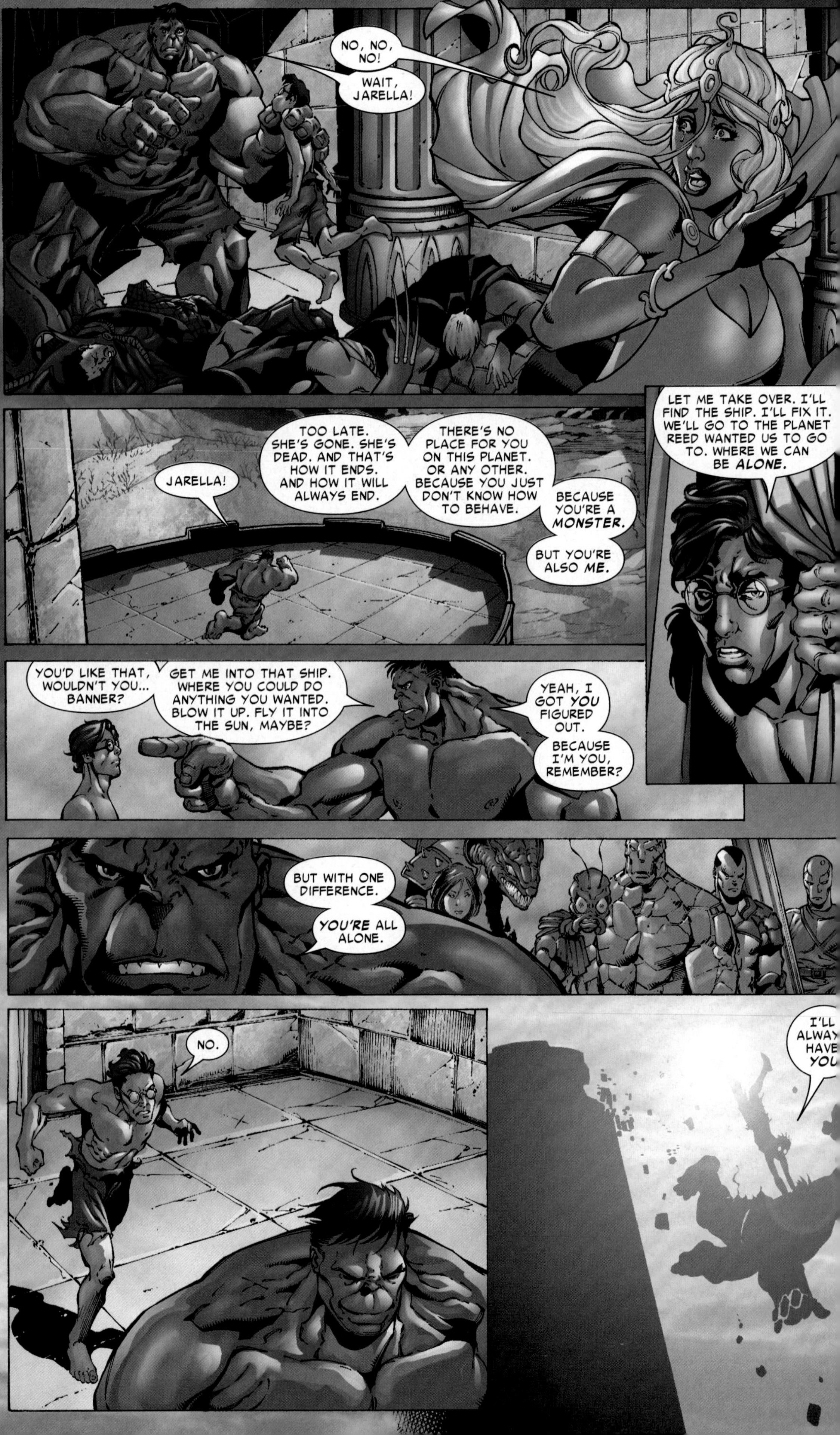
NO, NO, NO!
WAIT, JARELLA!
JARELLA!
TOO LATE. SHE'S GONE. SHE'S DEAD. AND THAT'S HOW IT ENDS. AND HOW IT WILL ALWAYS END.
THERE'S NO PLACE FOR YOU ON THIS PLANET. OR ANY OTHER. BECAUSE YOU JUST DON'T KNOW HOW TO BEHAVE.
BECAUSE YOU'RE A MONSTER.
BUT YOU'RE ALSO ME.
LET ME TAKE OVER. I'LL FIND THE SHIP. I'LL FIX IT. WE'LL GO TO THE PLANET REED WANTED US TO GO TO. WHERE WE CAN BE ALONE.
YOU'D LIKE THAT, WOULDN'T YOU... BANNER?
GET ME INTO THAT SHIP. WHERE YOU COULD DO ANYTHING YOU WANTED. BLOW IT UP. FLY IT INTO THE SUN, MAYBE?
YEAH, I GOT YOU FIGURED OUT.
BECAUSE I'M YOU, REMEMBER?
BUT WITH ONE DIFFERENCE.
YOU'RE ALL ALONE.
NO.
I'LL ALWAY HAVE YOU

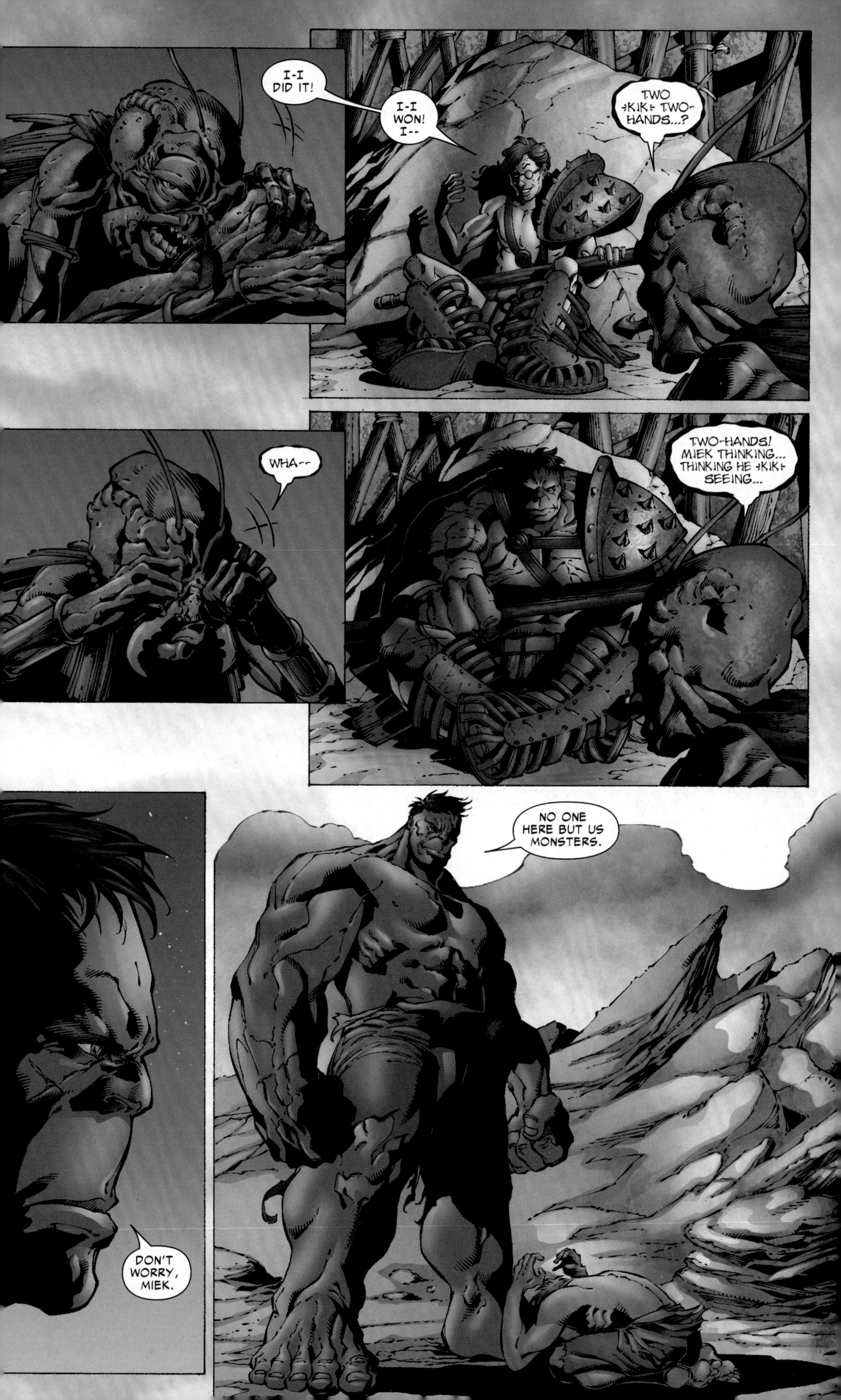
I-I DID IT!
I-I WON! I--
TWO ≠KIK≠ TWO-HANDS...?
WHA--
TWO-HANDS! MIEK THINKING... THINKING HE ≠KIK≠ SEEING...
DON'T WORRY, MIEK.
NO ONE HERE BUT US MONSTERS.

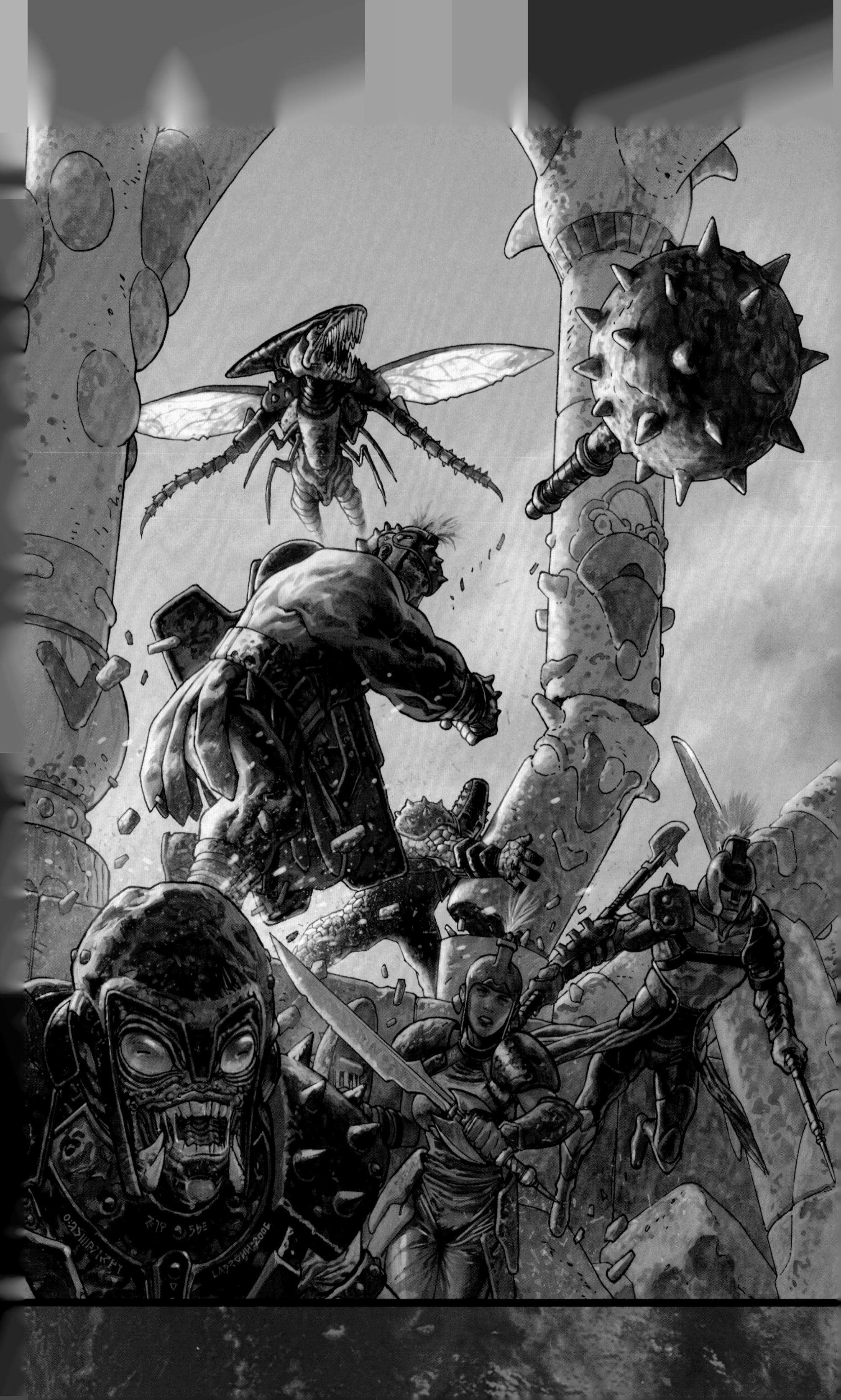

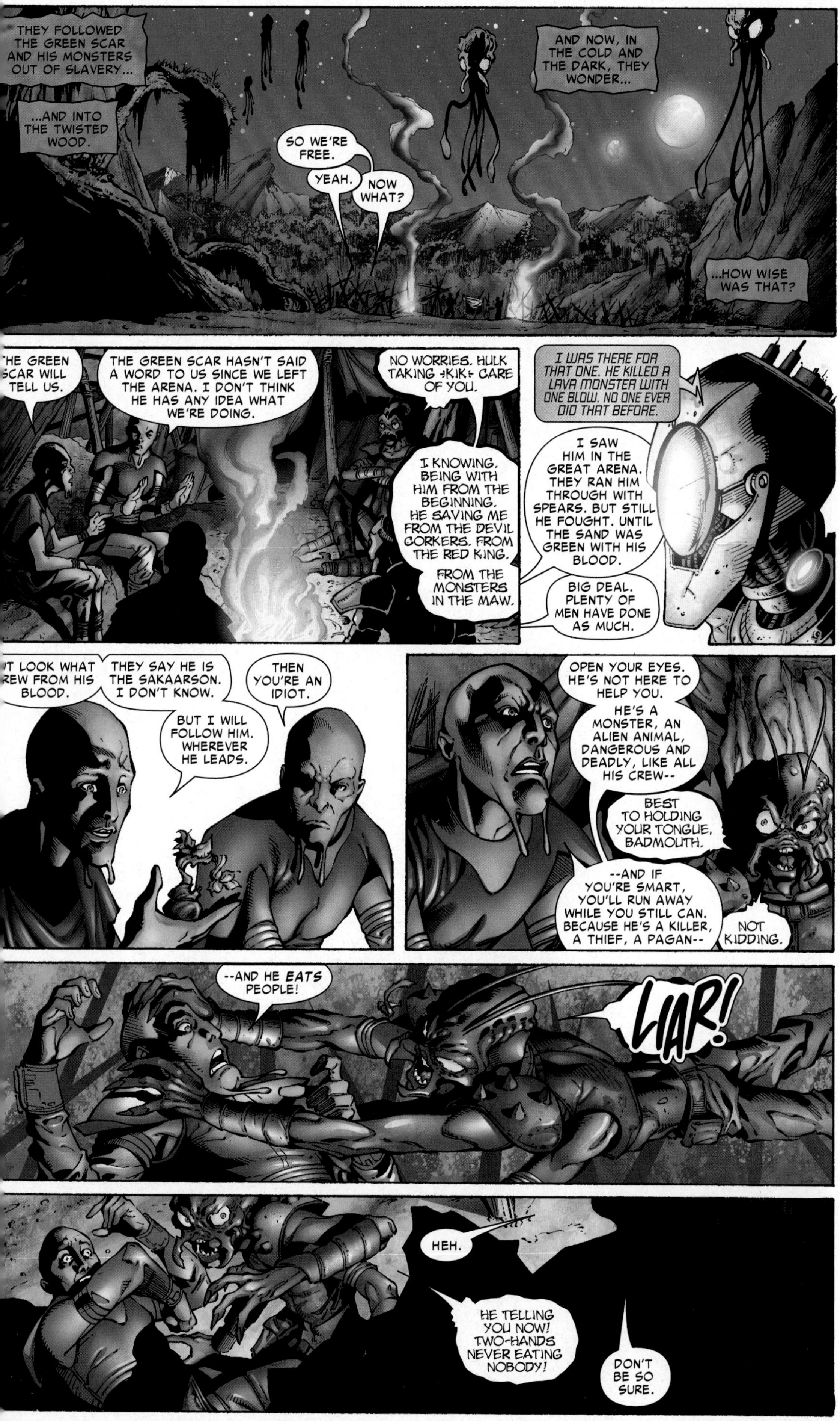
THEY FOLLOWED THE GREEN SCAR AND HIS MONSTERS OUT OF SLAVERY...
...AND INTO THE TWISTED WOOD.
SO WE'RE FREE.
YEAH.
NOW WHAT?
AND NOW, IN THE COLD AND THE DARK, THEY WONDER...
...HOW WISE WAS THAT?
THE GREEN SCAR WILL TELL US.
THE GREEN SCAR HASN'T SAID A WORD TO US SINCE WE LEFT THE ARENA. I DON'T THINK HE HAS ANY IDEA WHAT WE'RE DOING.
NO WORRIES. HULK TAKING -KIK- CARE OF YOU.
I KNOWING. BEING WITH HIM FROM THE BEGINNING. HE SAVING ME FROM THE DEVIL CORKERS. FROM THE RED KING.
FROM THE MONSTERS IN THE MAW.
I WAS THERE FOR THAT ONE. HE KILLED A LAVA MONSTER WITH ONE BLOW. NO ONE EVER DID THAT BEFORE.
I SAW HIM IN THE GREAT ARENA. THEY RAN HIM THROUGH WITH SPEARS. BUT STILL HE FOUGHT. UNTIL THE SAND WAS GREEN WITH HIS BLOOD.
BIG DEAL. PLENTY OF MEN HAVE DONE AS MUCH.
UT LOOK WHAT REW FROM HIS BLOOD.
THEY SAY HE IS THE SAKAARSON. I DON'T KNOW.
BUT I WILL FOLLOW HIM. WHEREVER HE LEADS.
THEN YOU'RE AN IDIOT.
OPEN YOUR EYES. HE'S NOT HERE TO HELP YOU.
HE'S A MONSTER, AN ALIEN ANIMAL, DANGEROUS AND DEADLY, LIKE ALL HIS CREW--
BEST TO HOLDING YOUR TONGUE, BADMOUTH.
--AND IF YOU'RE SMART, YOU'LL RUN AWAY WHILE YOU STILL CAN. BECAUSE HE'S A KILLER, A THIEF, A PAGAN--
NOT KIDDING.
--AND HE EATS PEOPLE!
LIAR!
HEH.
HE TELLING YOU NOW! TWO-HANDS NEVER EATING NOBODY!
DON'T BE SO SURE.

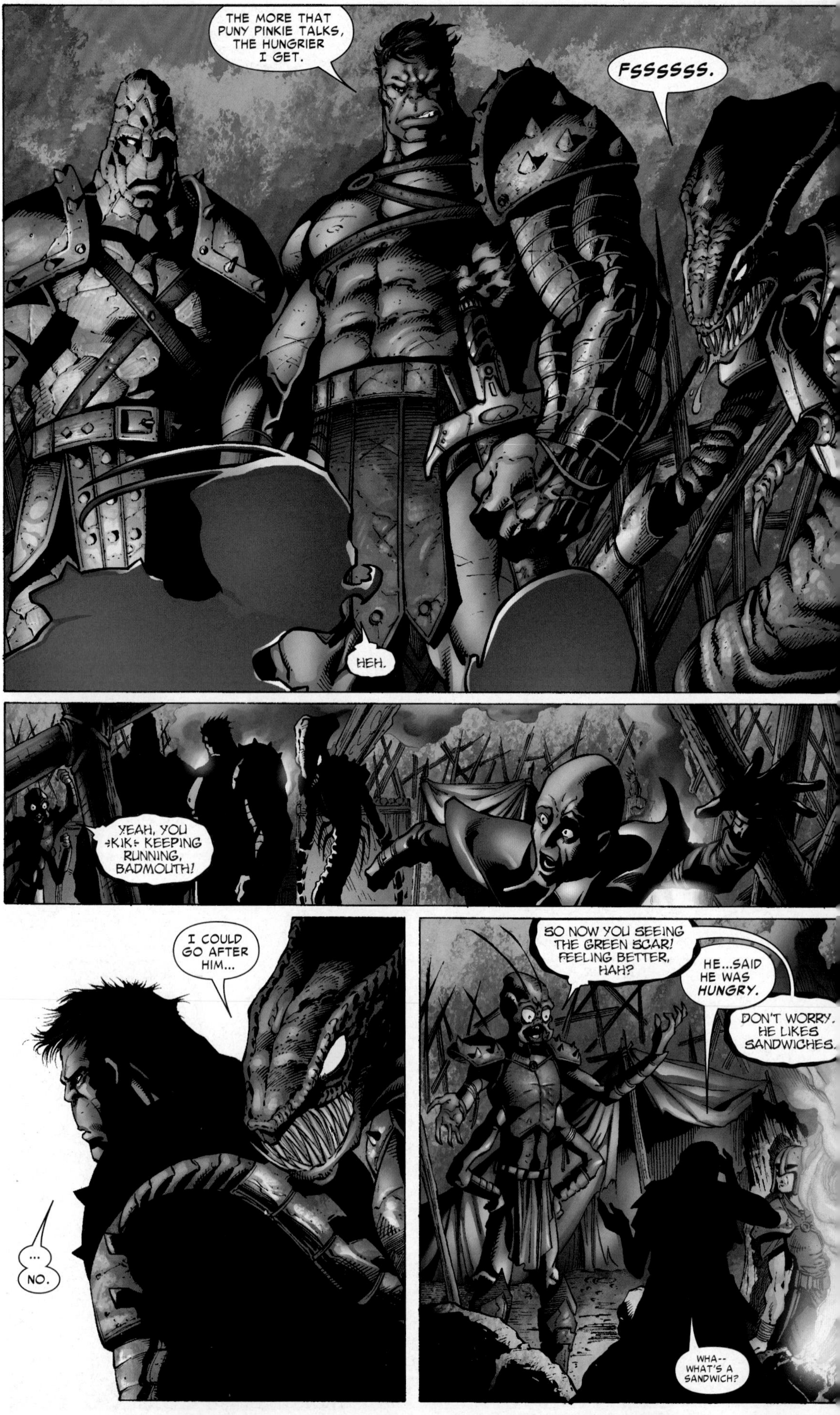
THE MORE THAT PUNY PINKIE TALKS, THE HUNGRIER I GET.
FSSSSSS.
HEH.
YEAH, YOU -KIK- KEEPING RUNNING, BADMOUTH!
I COULD GO AFTER HIM...
... NO.
SO NOW YOU SEEING THE GREEN SCAR! FEELING BETTER, HAH?
HE...SAID HE WAS HUNGRY.
DON'T WORRY. HE LIKES SANDWICHES.
WHA-- WHAT'S A SANDWICH?

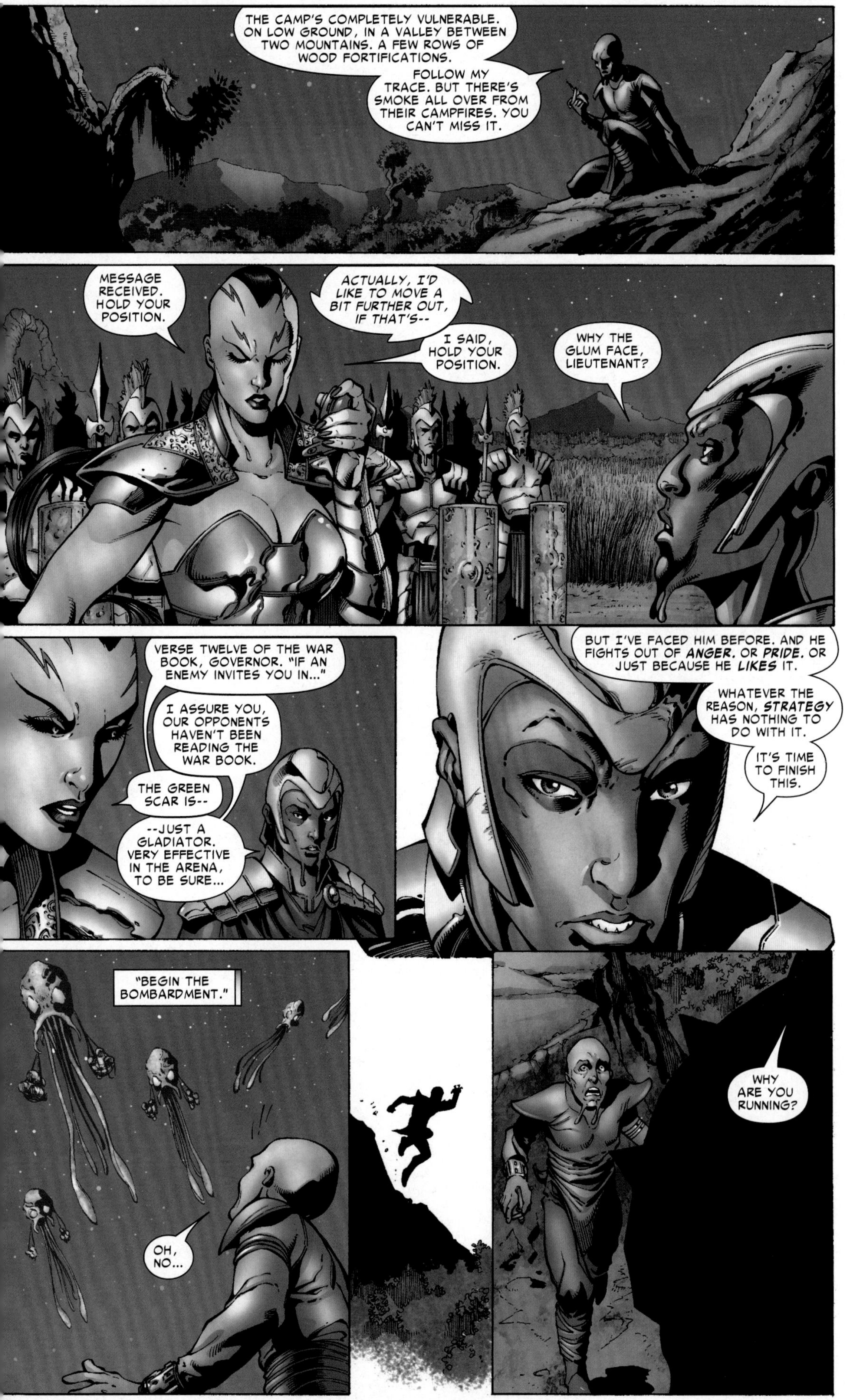
THE CAMP'S COMPLETELY VULNERABLE. ON LOW GROUND, IN A VALLEY BETWEEN TWO MOUNTAINS. A FEW ROWS OF WOOD FORTIFICATIONS.
FOLLOW MY TRACE. BUT THERE'S SMOKE ALL OVER FROM THEIR CAMPFIRES. YOU CAN'T MISS IT.
MESSAGE RECEIVED. HOLD YOUR POSITION.
ACTUALLY, I'D LIKE TO MOVE A BIT FURTHER OUT, IF THAT'S--
I SAID, HOLD YOUR POSITION.
WHY THE GLUM FACE, LIEUTENANT?
VERSE TWELVE OF THE WAR BOOK, GOVERNOR. "IF AN ENEMY INVITES YOU IN..."
I ASSURE YOU, OUR OPPONENTS HAVEN'T BEEN READING THE WAR BOOK.
THE GREEN SCAR IS--
--JUST A GLADIATOR. VERY EFFECTIVE IN THE ARENA, TO BE SURE...
BUT I'VE FACED HIM BEFORE. AND HE FIGHTS OUT OF ANGER. OR PRIDE. OR JUST BECAUSE HE LIKES IT.
WHATEVER THE REASON, STRATEGY HAS NOTHING TO DO WITH IT.
IT'S TIME TO FINISH THIS.
"BEGIN THE BOMBARDMENT."
OH, NO...
WHY ARE YOU RUNNING?

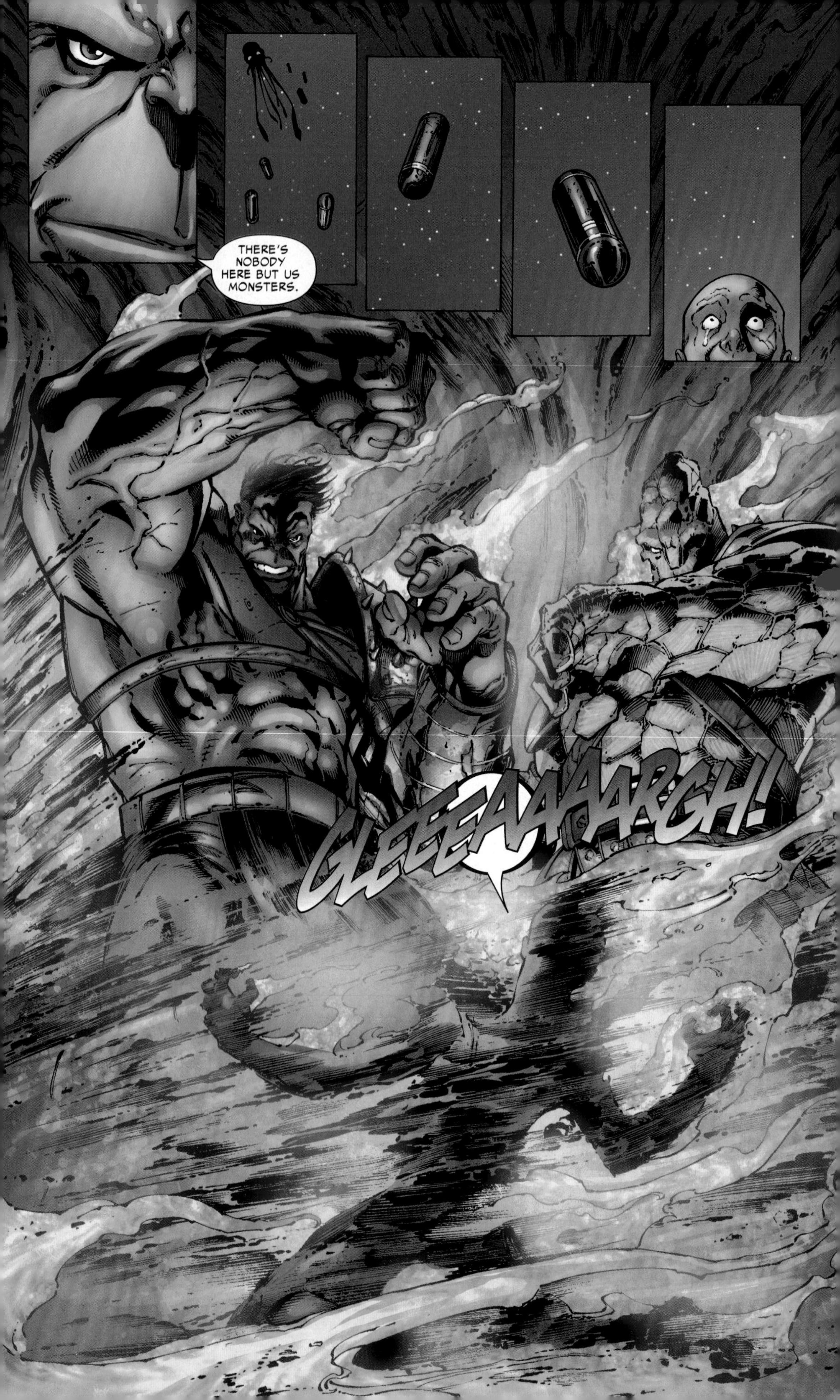
THERE'S NOBODY HERE BUT US MONSTERS.
GLEEEAAAARGH!

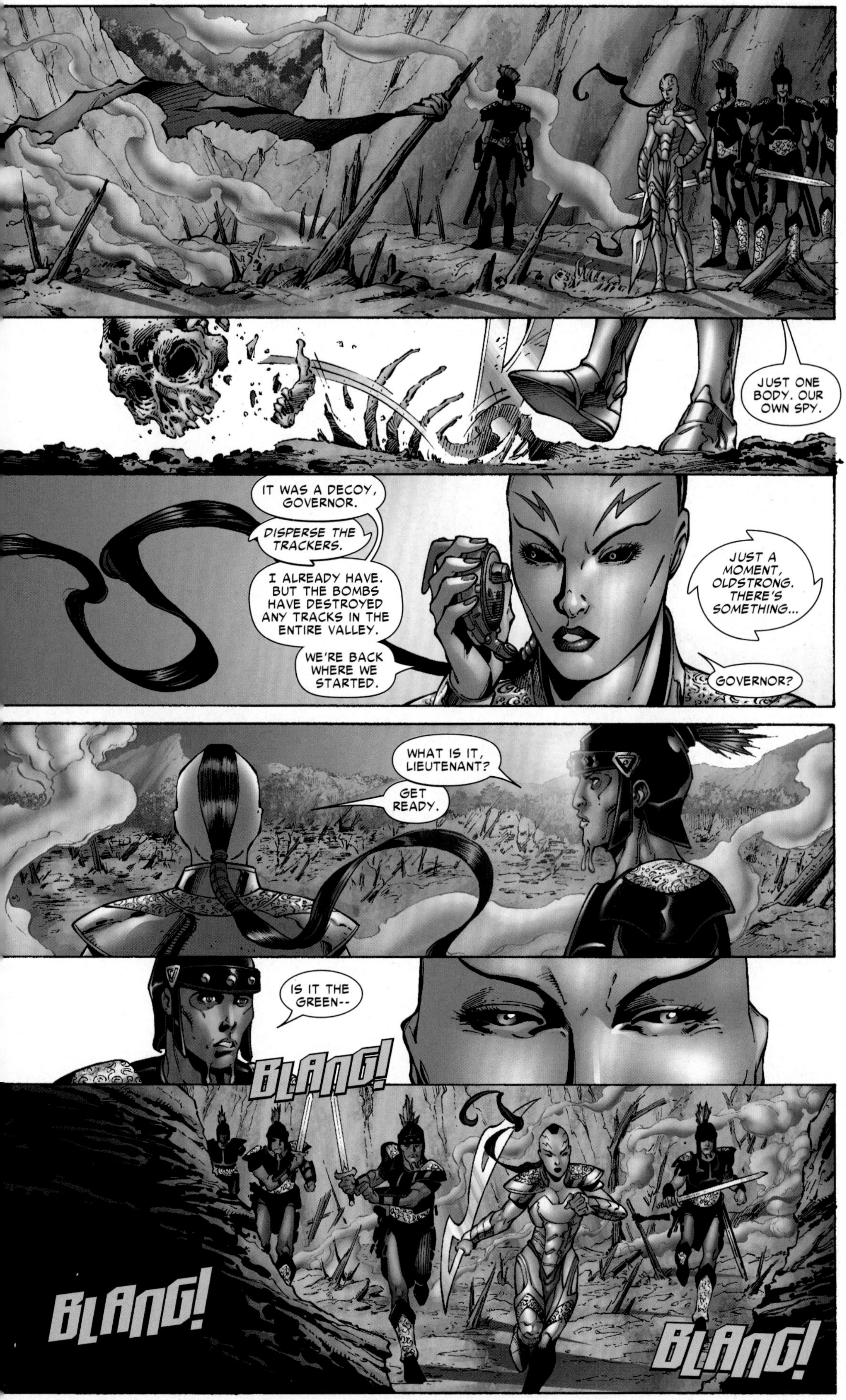

JUST ONE BODY. OUR OWN SPY.
IT WAS A DECOY, GOVERNOR.
DISPERSE THE TRACKERS.
I ALREADY HAVE. BUT THE BOMBS HAVE DESTROYED ANY TRACKS IN THE ENTIRE VALLEY.
WE'RE BACK WHERE WE STARTED.
JUST A MOMENT, OLDSTRONG. THERE'S SOMETHING...
GOVERNOR?
WHAT IS IT, LIEUTENANT?
GET READY.
IS IT THE GREEN--
BLANG!
BLANG!
BLANG!

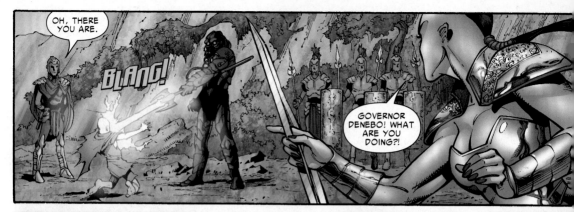

OH, THERE YOU ARE.

BLANG!

GOVERNOR DENEBO! WHAT ARE YOU DOING?!

OH, JUST DEALING WITH SOME LOCAL VILLAGERS. THEY WERE HIDING FOOD FROM THE ARMY. HAVE TO KEEP UP OUR STANDARDS.

AND I THOUGHT IT MIGHT ADD A LITTLE BAIT TO YOUR TRAP.

IN COLD-BLOOD... LAST TIME THEY'LL EVER HAVE THE CHANCE. THERE'S ONLY A DOZEN OF THEM.

LET'S GO, HULK.

WAIT.

IF YOUR ENEMY INVITES YOU IN...

WHAT?

LOOK TO THE FAR RIDGE, ELLOE.

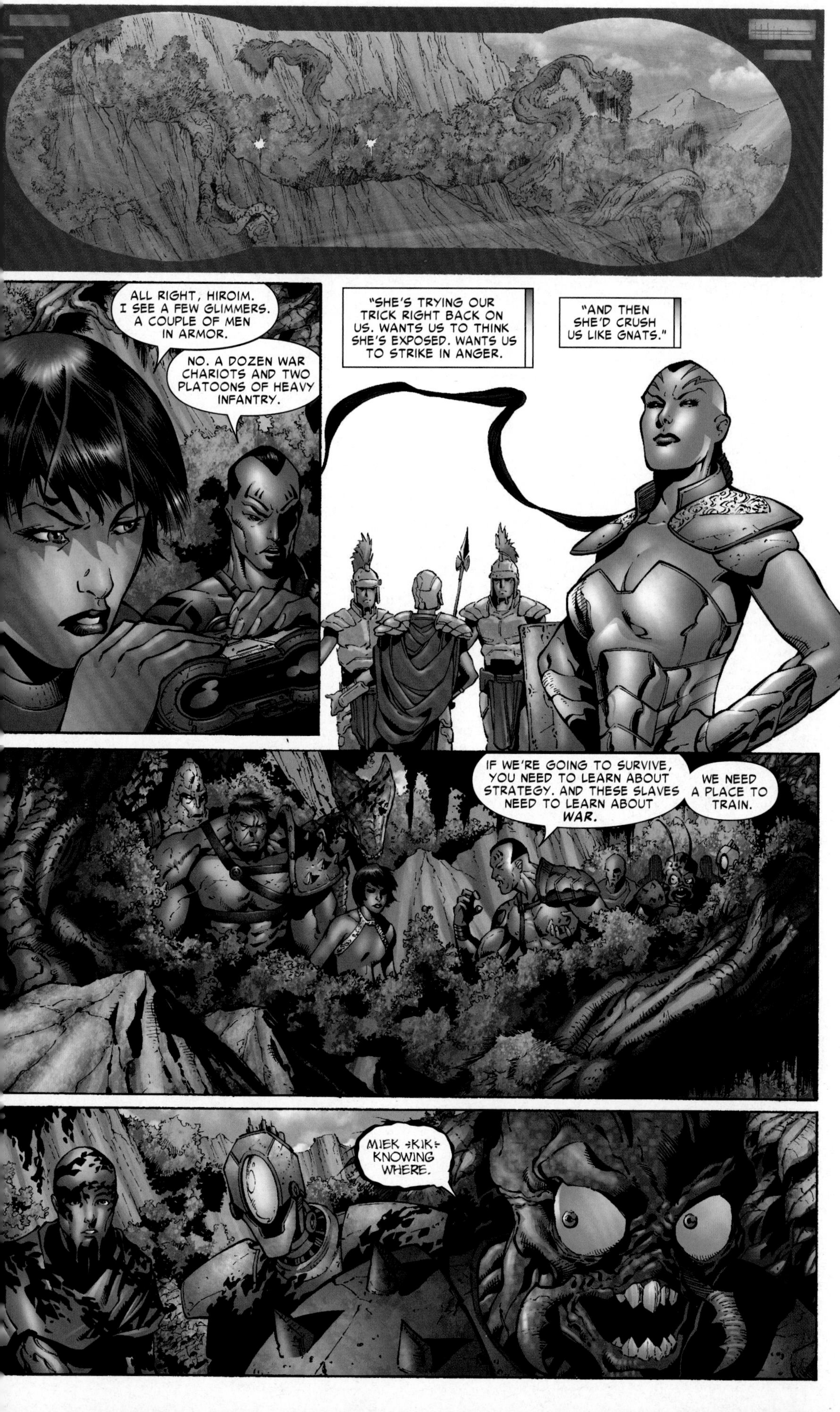
ALL RIGHT, HIROIM. I SEE A FEW GLIMMERS. A COUPLE OF MEN IN ARMOR.
NO. A DOZEN WAR CHARIOTS AND TWO PLATOONS OF HEAVY INFANTRY.
"SHE'S TRYING OUR TRICK RIGHT BACK ON US. WANTS US TO THINK SHE'S EXPOSED. WANTS US TO STRIKE IN ANGER.
"AND THEN SHE'D CRUSH US LIKE GNATS."
IF WE'RE GOING TO SURVIVE, YOU NEED TO LEARN ABOUT STRATEGY. AND THESE SLAVES NEED TO LEARN ABOUT **WAR.**
WE NEED A PLACE TO TRAIN.
MIEK ÷KIK÷ KNOWING WHERE.

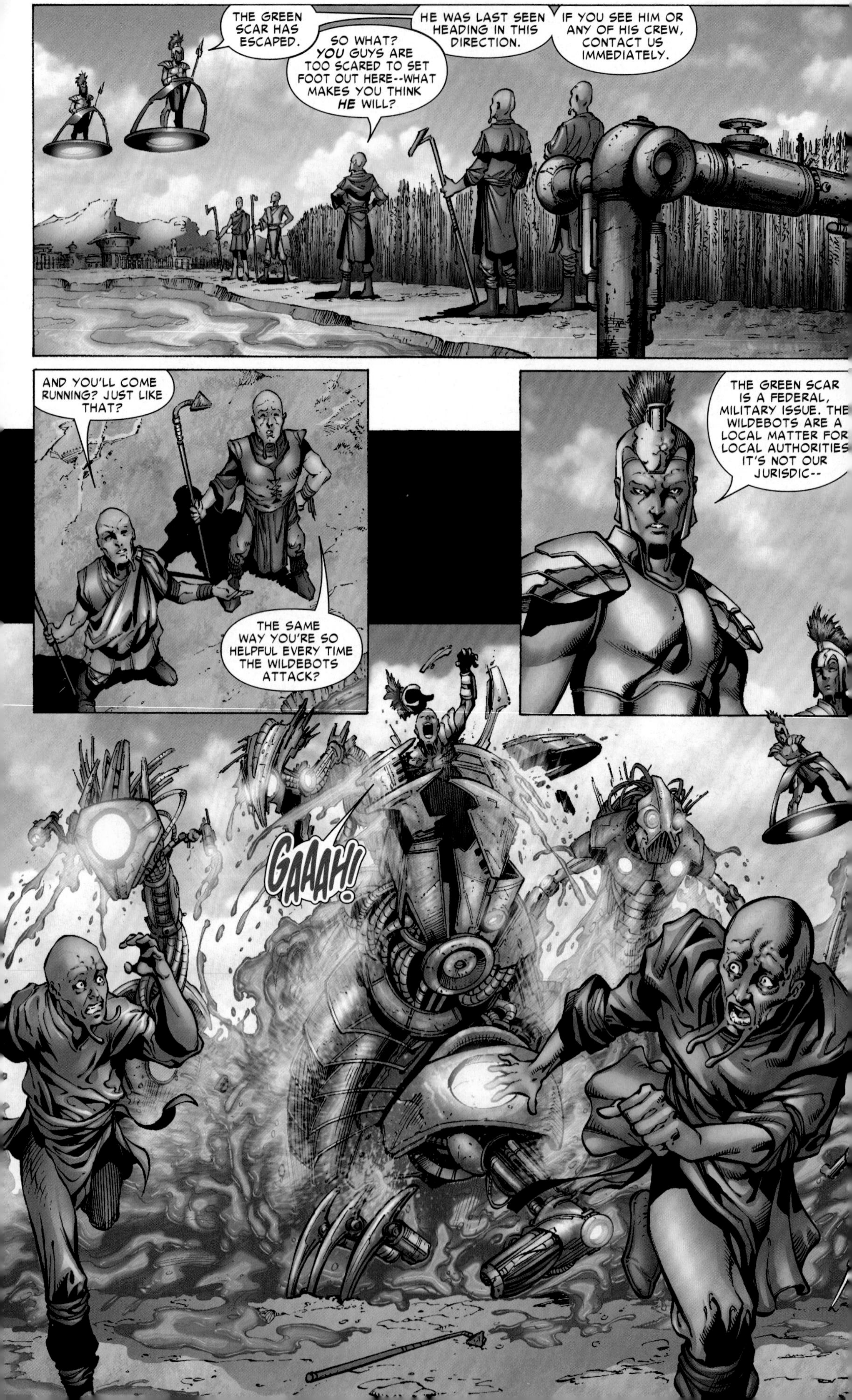

THE GREEN SCAR HAS ESCAPED.
HE WAS LAST SEEN HEADING IN THIS DIRECTION.
IF YOU SEE HIM OR ANY OF HIS CREW, CONTACT US IMMEDIATELY.
SO WHAT? YOU GUYS ARE TOO SCARED TO SET FOOT OUT HERE--WHAT MAKES YOU THINK HE WILL?
AND YOU'LL COME RUNNING? JUST LIKE THAT?
THE SAME WAY YOU'RE SO HELPFUL EVERY TIME THE WILDEBOTS ATTACK?
THE GREEN SCAR IS A FEDERAL, MILITARY ISSUE. THE WILDEBOTS ARE A LOCAL MATTER FOR LOCAL AUTHORITIES IT'S NOT OUR JURISDIC--
GAAAH!

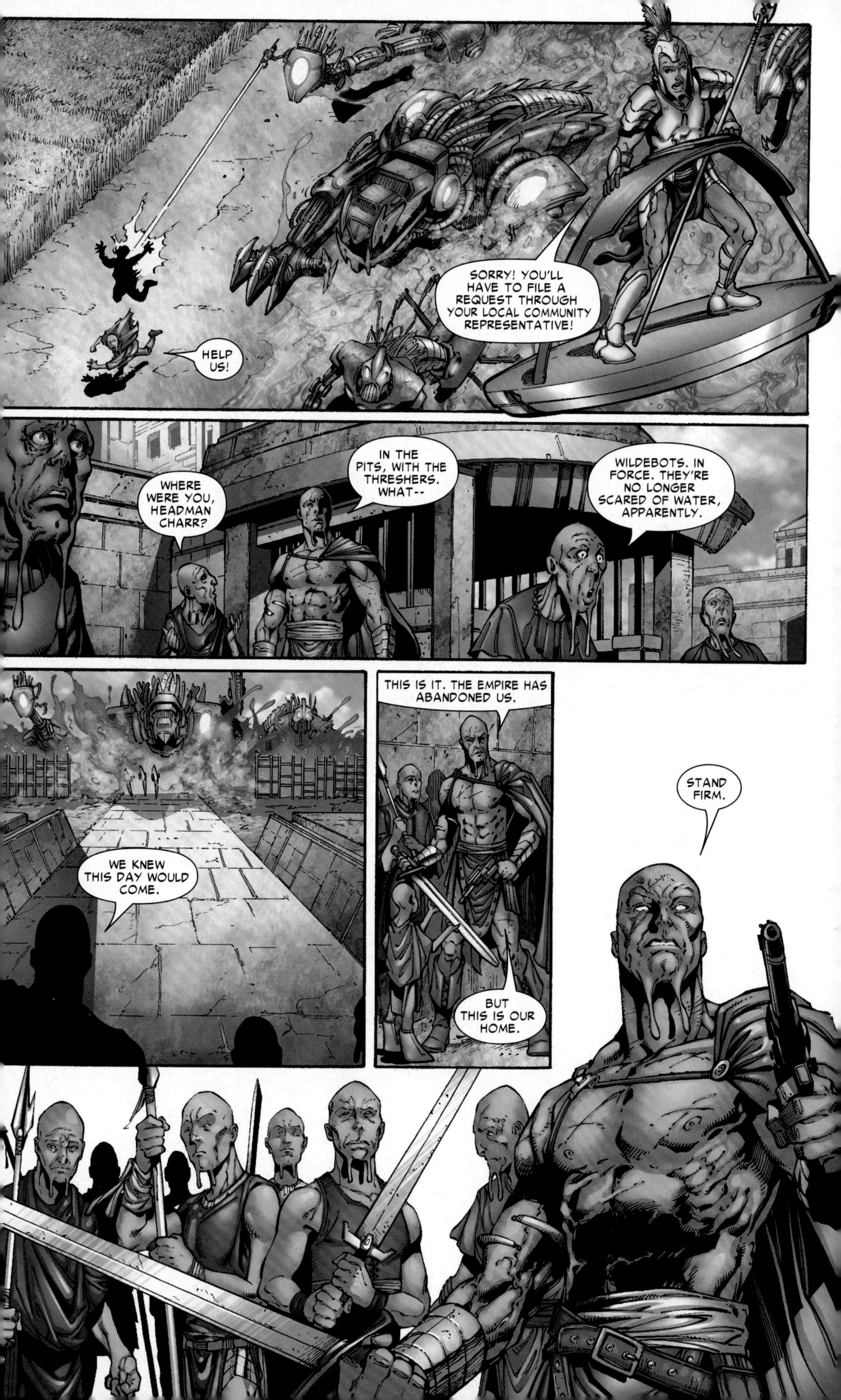
SORRY! YOU'LL HAVE TO FILE A REQUEST THROUGH YOUR LOCAL COMMUNITY REPRESENTATIVE!
HELP US!
WHERE WERE YOU, HEADMAN CHARR?
IN THE PITS, WITH THE THRESHERS. WHAT--
WILDEBOTS. IN FORCE. THEY'RE NO LONGER SCARED OF WATER, APPARENTLY.
WE KNEW THIS DAY WOULD COME.
THIS IS IT. THE EMPIRE HAS ABANDONED US.
BUT THIS IS OUR HOME.
STAND FIRM.

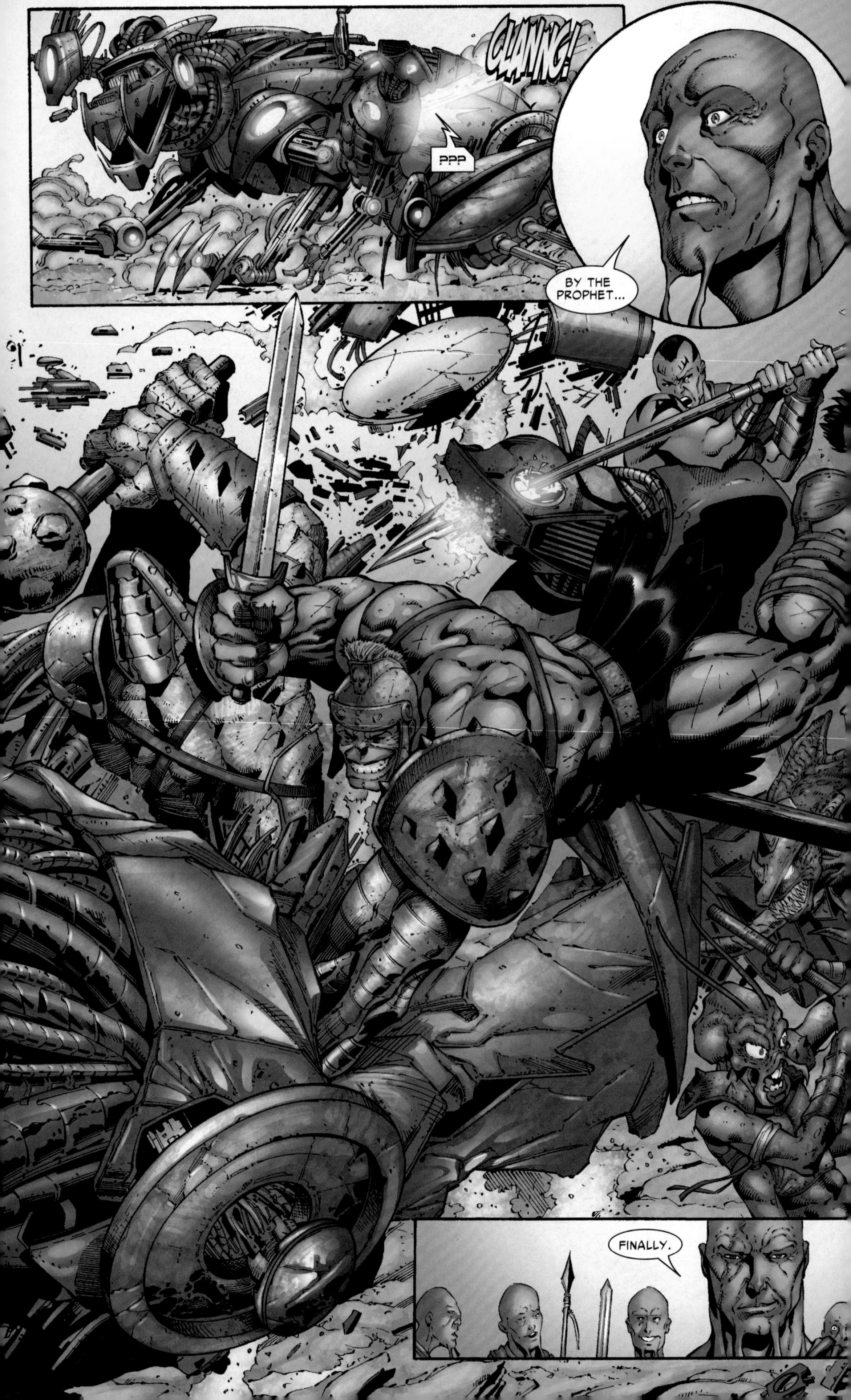
CLANNG!
PPP
BY THE PROPHET...
FINALLY.

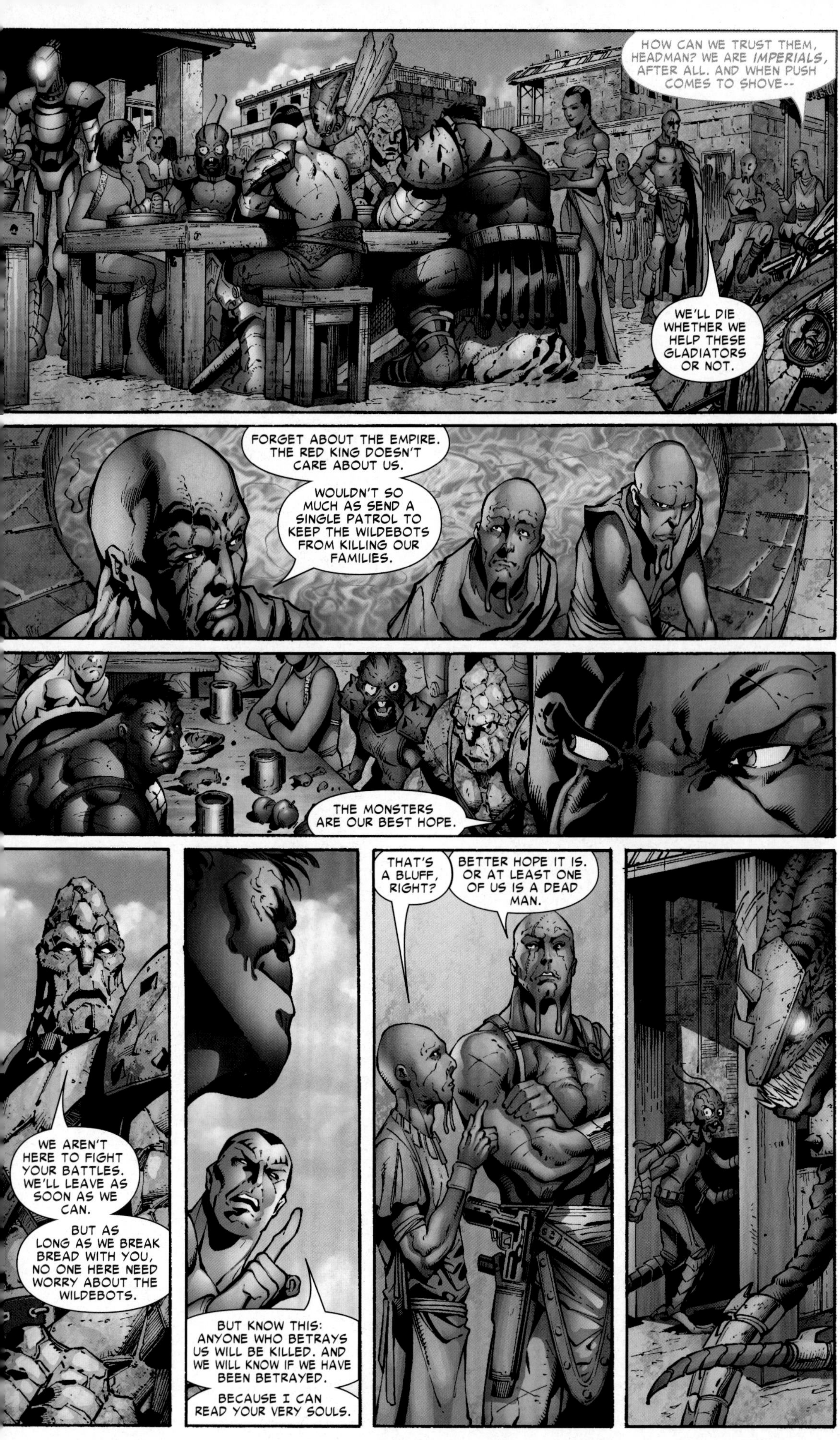

HOW CAN WE TRUST THEM, HEADMAN? WE ARE *IMPERIALS*, AFTER ALL. AND WHEN PUSH COMES TO SHOVE--
WE'LL DIE WHETHER WE HELP THESE GLADIATORS OR NOT.
FORGET ABOUT THE EMPIRE. THE RED KING DOESN'T CARE ABOUT US.
WOULDN'T SO MUCH AS SEND A SINGLE PATROL TO KEEP THE WILDEBOTS FROM KILLING OUR FAMILIES.
THE MONSTERS ARE OUR BEST HOPE.
WE AREN'T HERE TO FIGHT YOUR BATTLES. WE'LL LEAVE AS SOON AS WE CAN.
BUT AS LONG AS WE BREAK BREAD WITH YOU, NO ONE HERE NEED WORRY ABOUT THE WILDEBOTS.
BUT KNOW THIS: ANYONE WHO BETRAYS US WILL BE KILLED. AND WE WILL KNOW IF WE HAVE BEEN BETRAYED.
BECAUSE I CAN READ YOUR VERY SOULS.
THAT'S A BLUFF, RIGHT?
BETTER HOPE IT IS. OR AT LEAST ONE OF US IS A DEAD MAN.

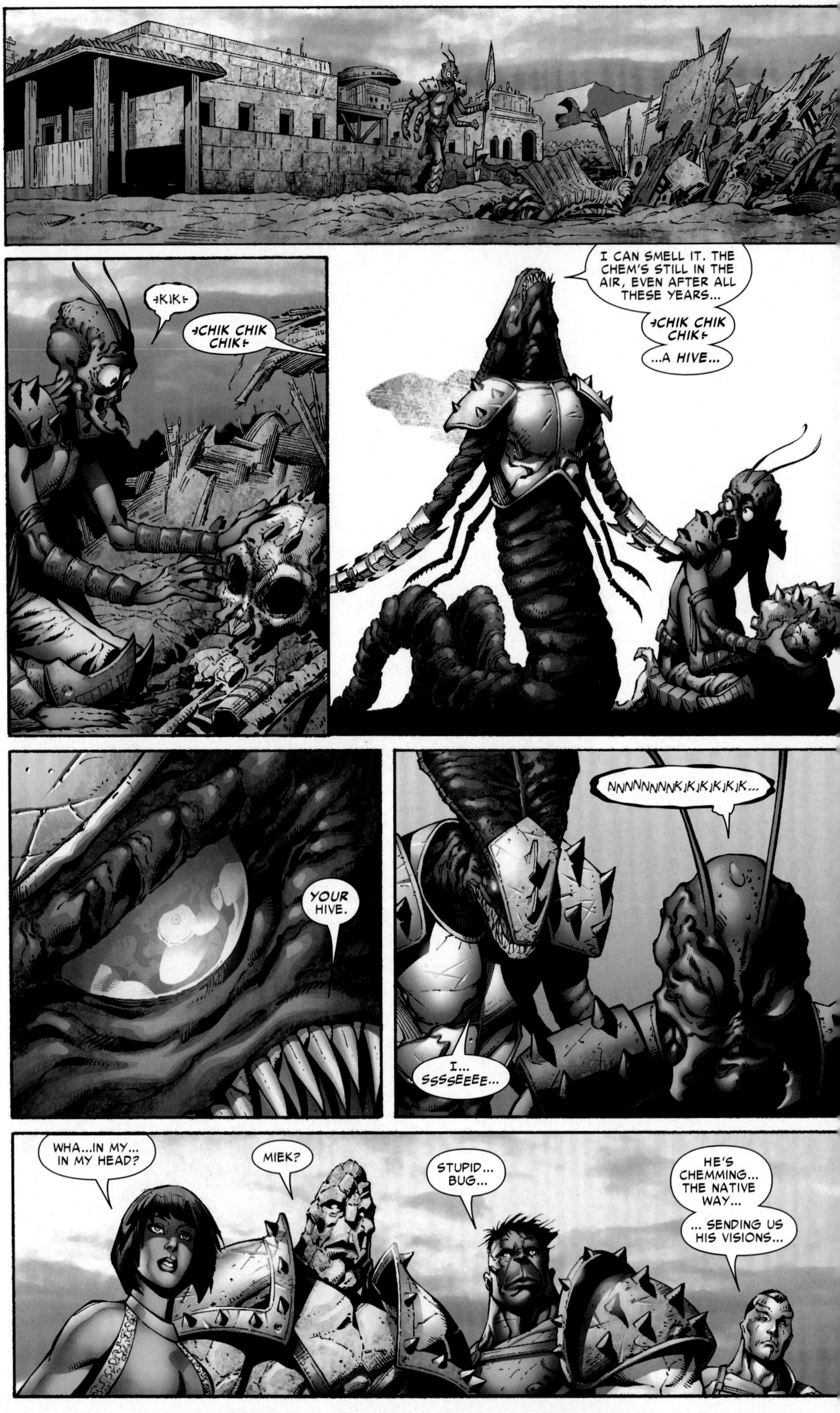

⊰KIK⊱
⊰CHIK CHIK CHIK⊱
I CAN SMELL IT. THE CHEM'S STILL IN THE AIR, EVEN AFTER ALL THESE YEARS...
⊰CHIK CHIK CHIK⊱
...A HIVE...
YOUR HIVE.
NNNNNNNNKIKIKIKIKIK...
I... SSSSEEEE...
WHA...IN MY... IN MY HEAD?
MIEK?
STUPID... BUG...
HE'S CHEMMING... THE NATIVE WAY...
... SENDING US HIS VISIONS...

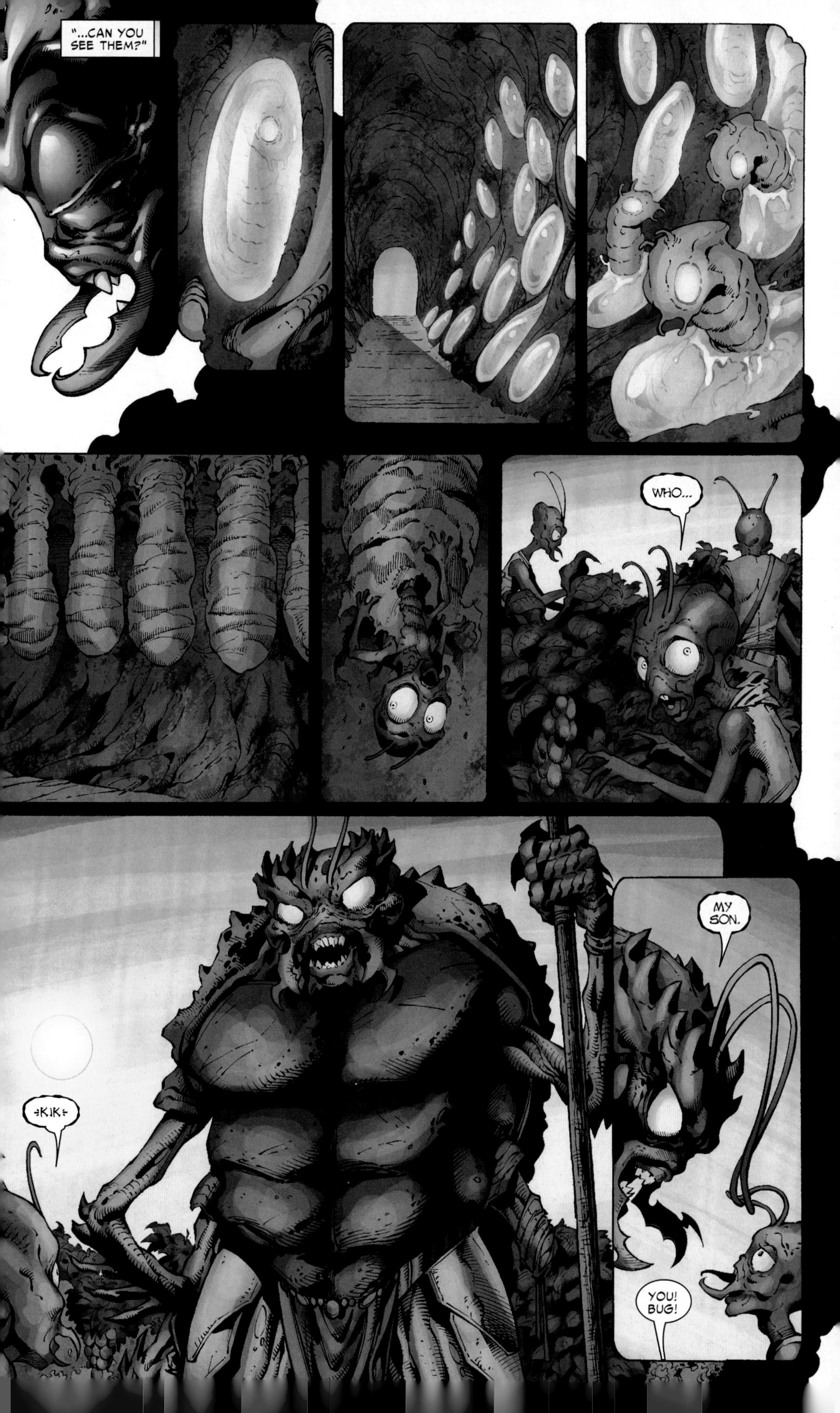
"...CAN YOU SEE THEM?"
WHO...
MY SON.
≈KIK≈
YOU! BUG!

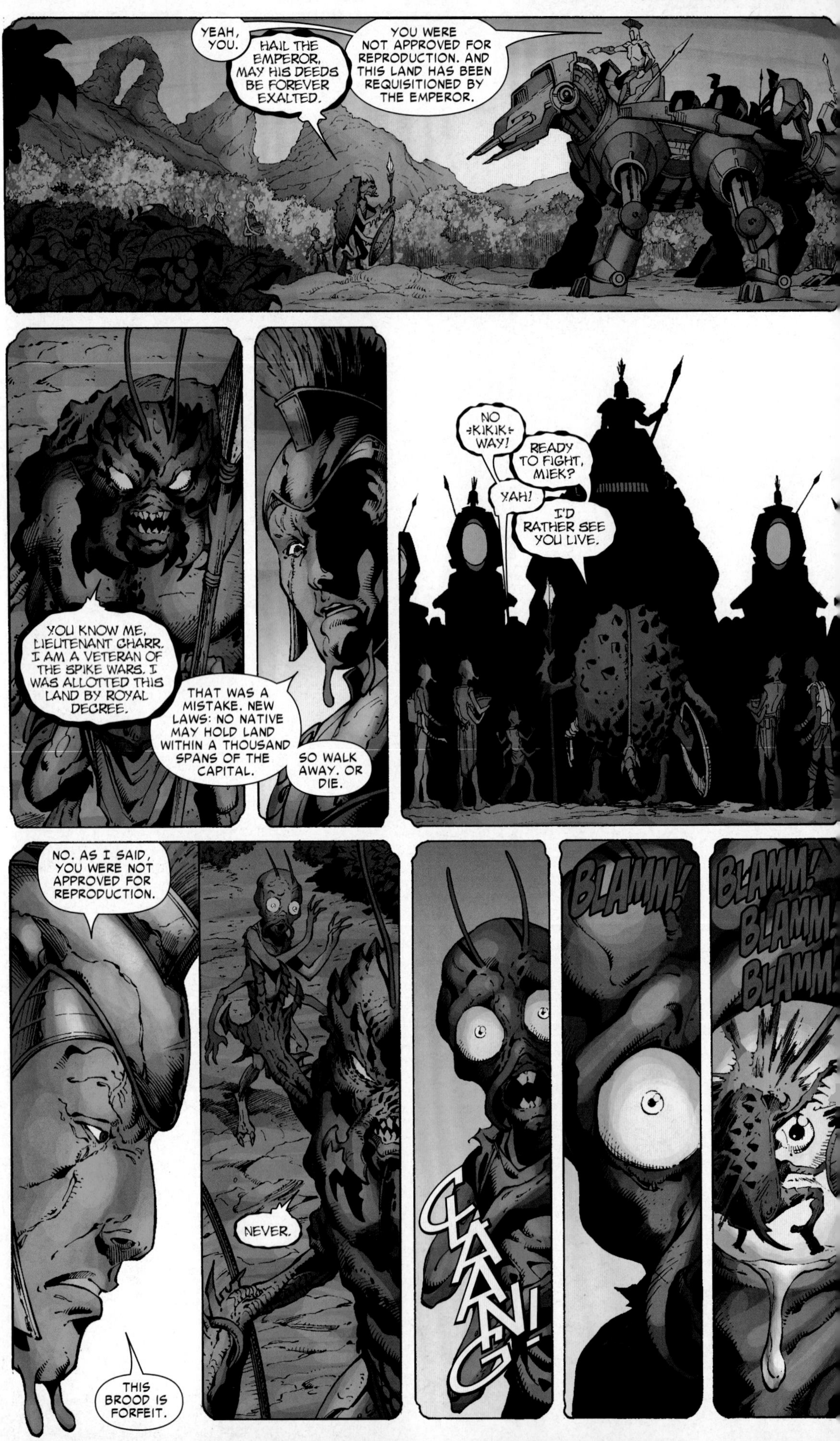
YEAH, YOU.
HAIL THE EMPEROR, MAY HIS DEEDS BE FOREVER EXALTED.
YOU WERE NOT APPROVED FOR REPRODUCTION. AND THIS LAND HAS BEEN REQUISITIONED BY THE EMPEROR.
YOU KNOW ME, LIEUTENANT CHARR. I AM A VETERAN OF THE SPIKE WARS. I WAS ALLOTTED THIS LAND BY ROYAL DECREE.
THAT WAS A MISTAKE. NEW LAWS: NO NATIVE MAY HOLD LAND WITHIN A THOUSAND SPANS OF THE CAPITAL.
SO WALK AWAY. OR DIE.
NO -KIKIK- WAY!
READY TO FIGHT, MIEK?
YAH!
I'D RATHER SEE YOU LIVE.
NO. AS I SAID, YOU WERE NOT APPROVED FOR REPRODUCTION.
THIS BROOD IS FORFEIT.
NEVER.
CLANG!
BLAMM!
BLAMM! BLAMM! BLAMM

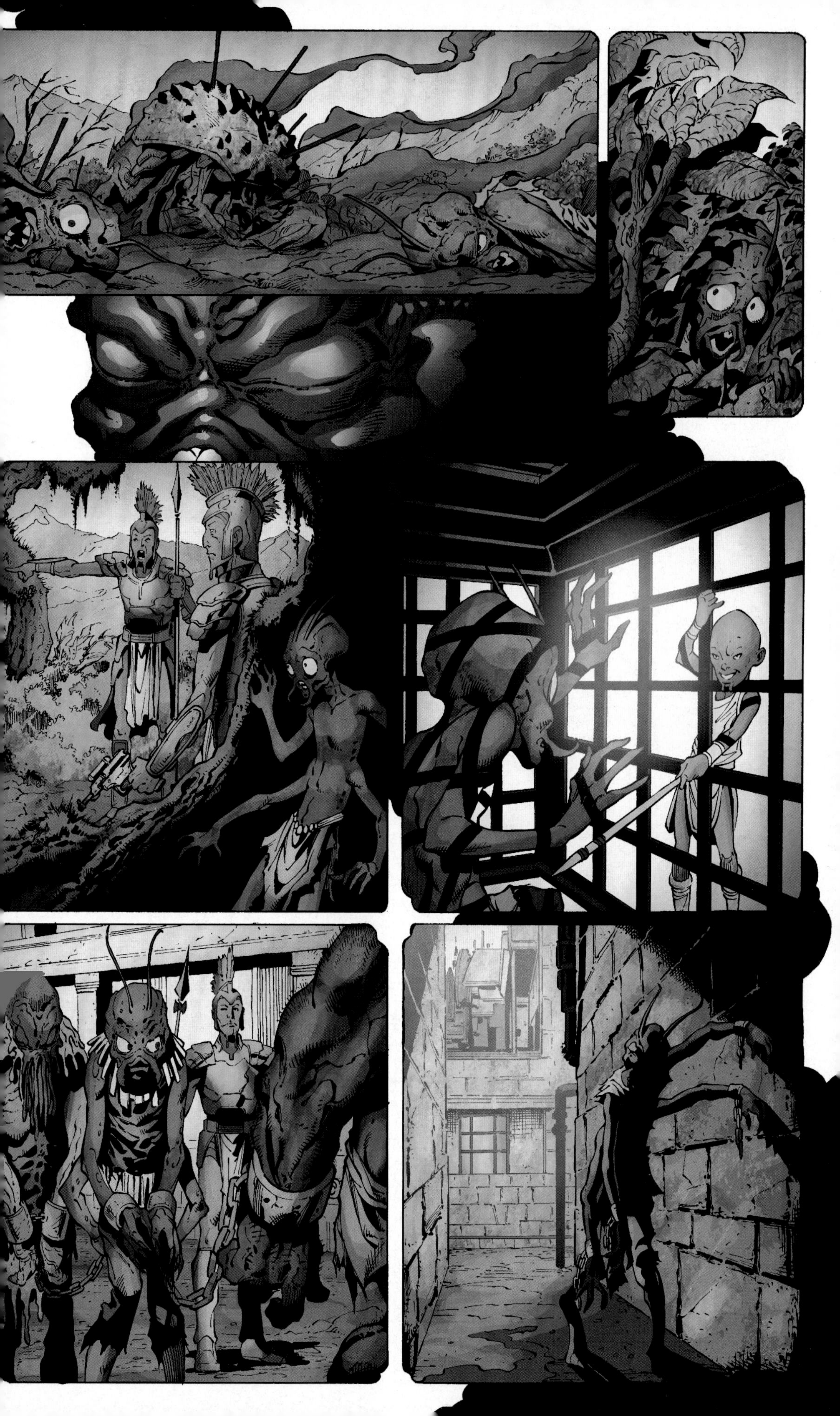

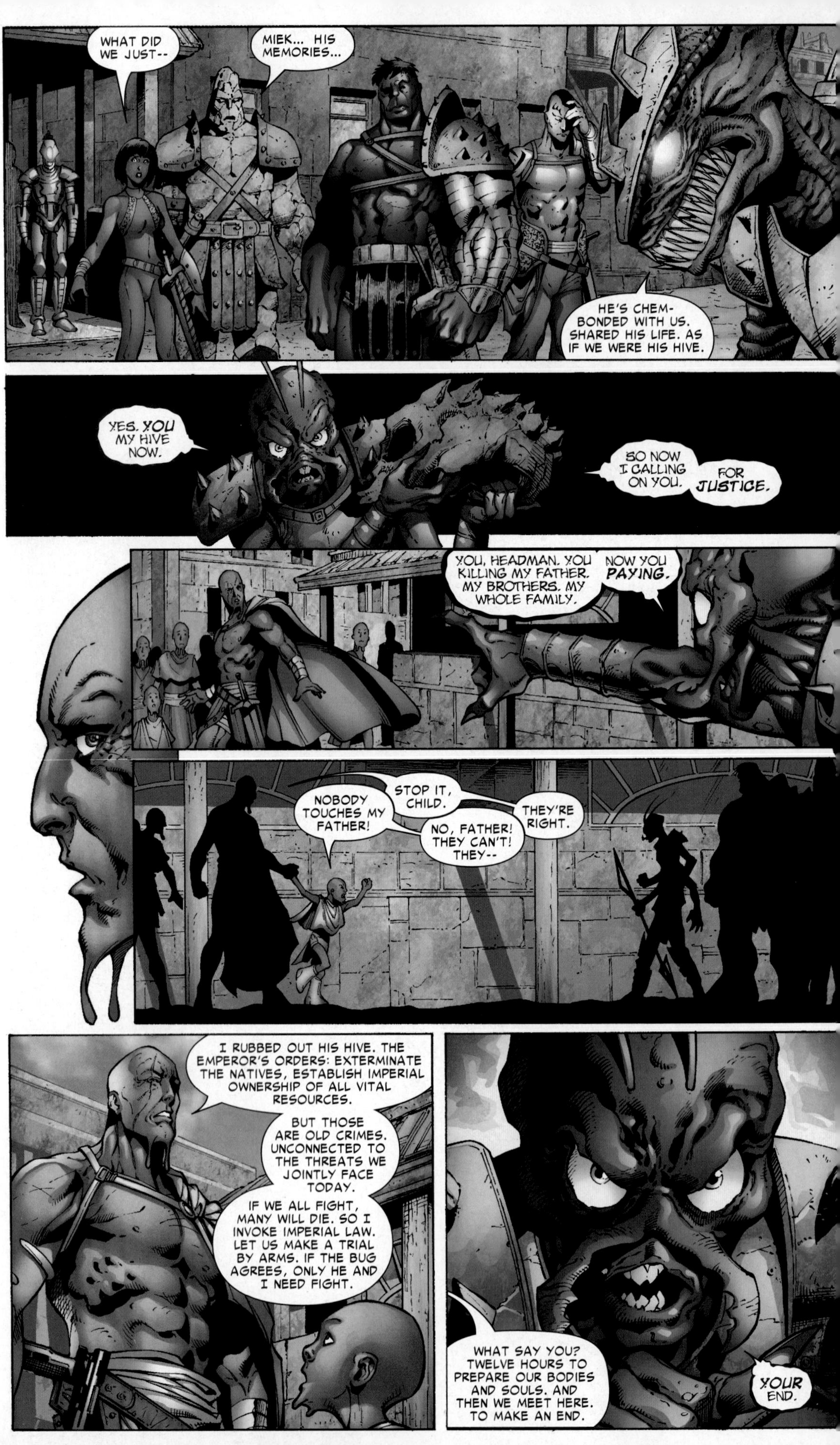
WHAT DID WE JUST--
MIEK... HIS MEMORIES...
HE'S CHEM-BONDED WITH US. SHARED HIS LIFE. AS IF WE WERE HIS HIVE.
YES. YOU MY HIVE NOW.
SO NOW I CALLING ON YOU.
FOR JUSTICE.
YOU, HEADMAN. YOU KILLING MY FATHER. MY BROTHERS. MY WHOLE FAMILY.
NOW YOU PAYING.
NOBODY TOUCHES MY FATHER!
STOP IT, CHILD.
NO, FATHER! THEY CAN'T! THEY--
THEY'RE RIGHT.
I RUBBED OUT HIS HIVE. THE EMPEROR'S ORDERS: EXTERMINATE THE NATIVES, ESTABLISH IMPERIAL OWNERSHIP OF ALL VITAL RESOURCES.
BUT THOSE ARE OLD CRIMES. UNCONNECTED TO THE THREATS WE JOINTLY FACE TODAY.
IF WE ALL FIGHT, MANY WILL DIE. SO I INVOKE IMPERIAL LAW. LET US MAKE A TRIAL BY ARMS. IF THE BUG AGREES, ONLY HE AND I NEED FIGHT.
WHAT SAY YOU? TWELVE HOURS TO PREPARE OUR BODIES AND SOULS. AND THEN WE MEET HERE. TO MAKE AN END.
YOUR END.

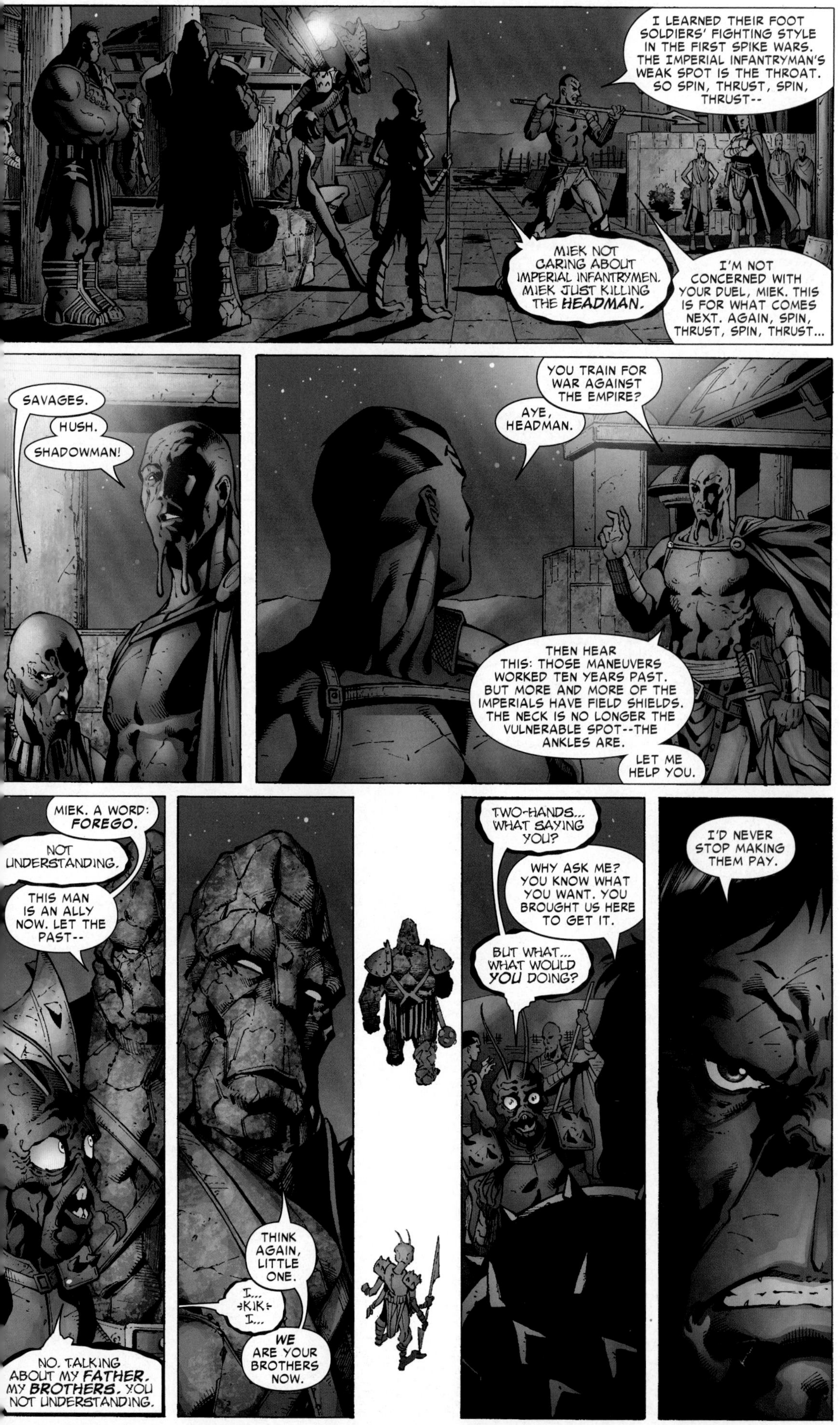
I LEARNED THEIR FOOT SOLDIERS' FIGHTING STYLE IN THE FIRST SPIKE WARS. THE IMPERIAL INFANTRYMAN'S WEAK SPOT IS THE THROAT. SO SPIN, THRUST, SPIN, THRUST--
MIEK NOT CARING ABOUT IMPERIAL INFANTRYMEN. MIEK JUST KILLING THE HEADMAN.
I'M NOT CONCERNED WITH YOUR DUEL, MIEK. THIS IS FOR WHAT COMES NEXT. AGAIN, SPIN, THRUST, SPIN, THRUST...
SAVAGES.
HUSH.
SHADOWMAN!
YOU TRAIN FOR WAR AGAINST THE EMPIRE?
AYE, HEADMAN.
THEN HEAR THIS: THOSE MANEUVERS WORKED TEN YEARS PAST. BUT MORE AND MORE OF THE IMPERIALS HAVE FIELD SHIELDS. THE NECK IS NO LONGER THE VULNERABLE SPOT--THE ANKLES ARE.
LET ME HELP YOU.
MIEK. A WORD: FOREGO.
NOT UNDERSTANDING.
THIS MAN IS AN ALLY NOW. LET THE PAST--
NO. TALKING ABOUT MY FATHER. MY BROTHERS. YOU NOT UNDERSTANDING.
THINK AGAIN, LITTLE ONE.
I... ‡KIK‡ I...
WE ARE YOUR BROTHERS NOW.
TWO-HANDS... WHAT SAYING YOU?
WHY ASK ME? YOU KNOW WHAT YOU WANT. YOU BROUGHT US HERE TO GET IT.
BUT WHAT... WHAT WOULD YOU DOING?
I'D NEVER STOP MAKING THEM PAY.

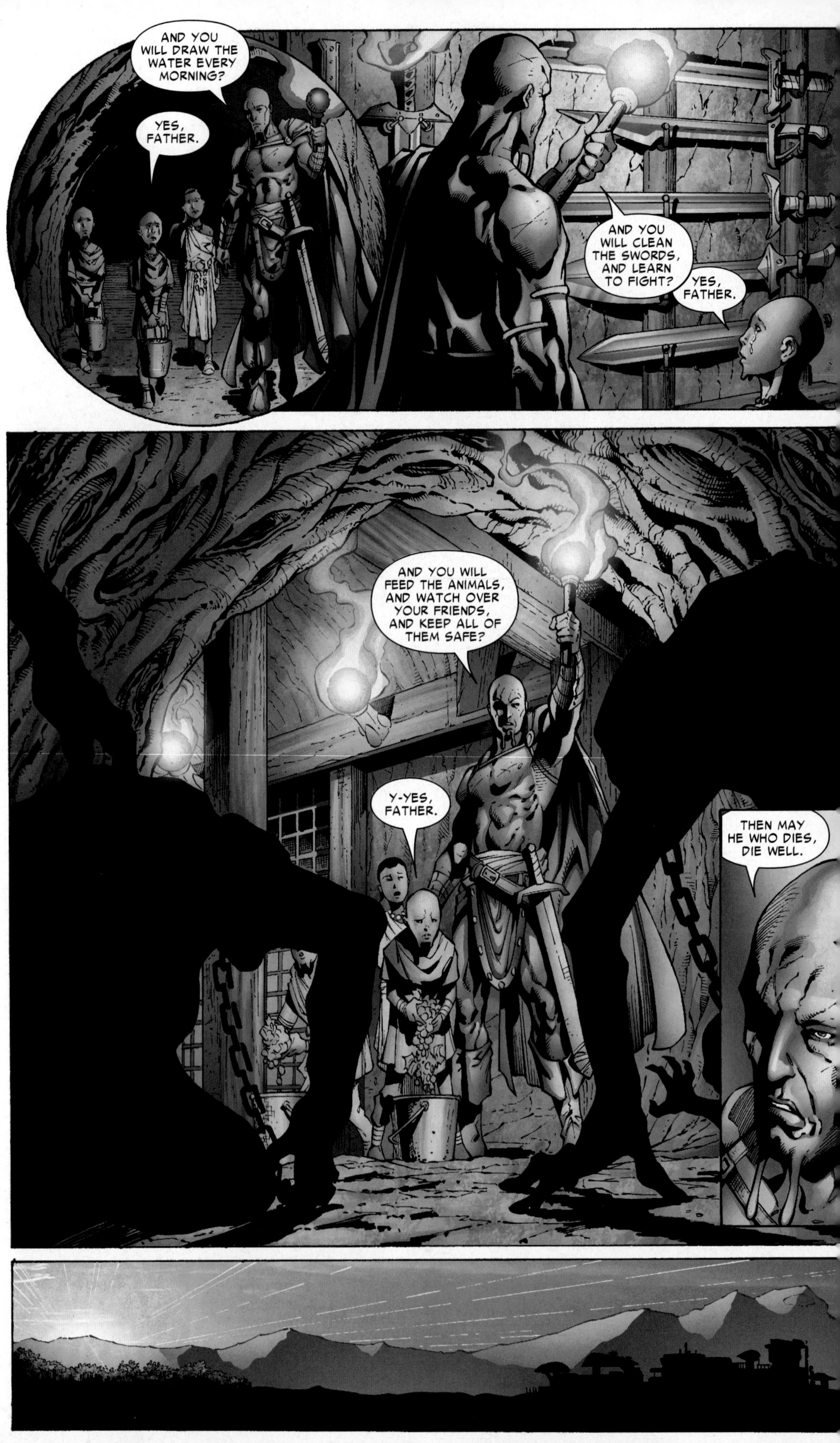
AND YOU WILL DRAW THE WATER EVERY MORNING?
YES, FATHER.
AND YOU WILL CLEAN THE SWORDS, AND LEARN TO FIGHT?
YES, FATHER.
AND YOU WILL FEED THE ANIMALS, AND WATCH OVER YOUR FRIENDS, AND KEEP ALL OF THEM SAFE?
Y-YES, FATHER.
THEN MAY HE WHO DIES, DIE WELL.

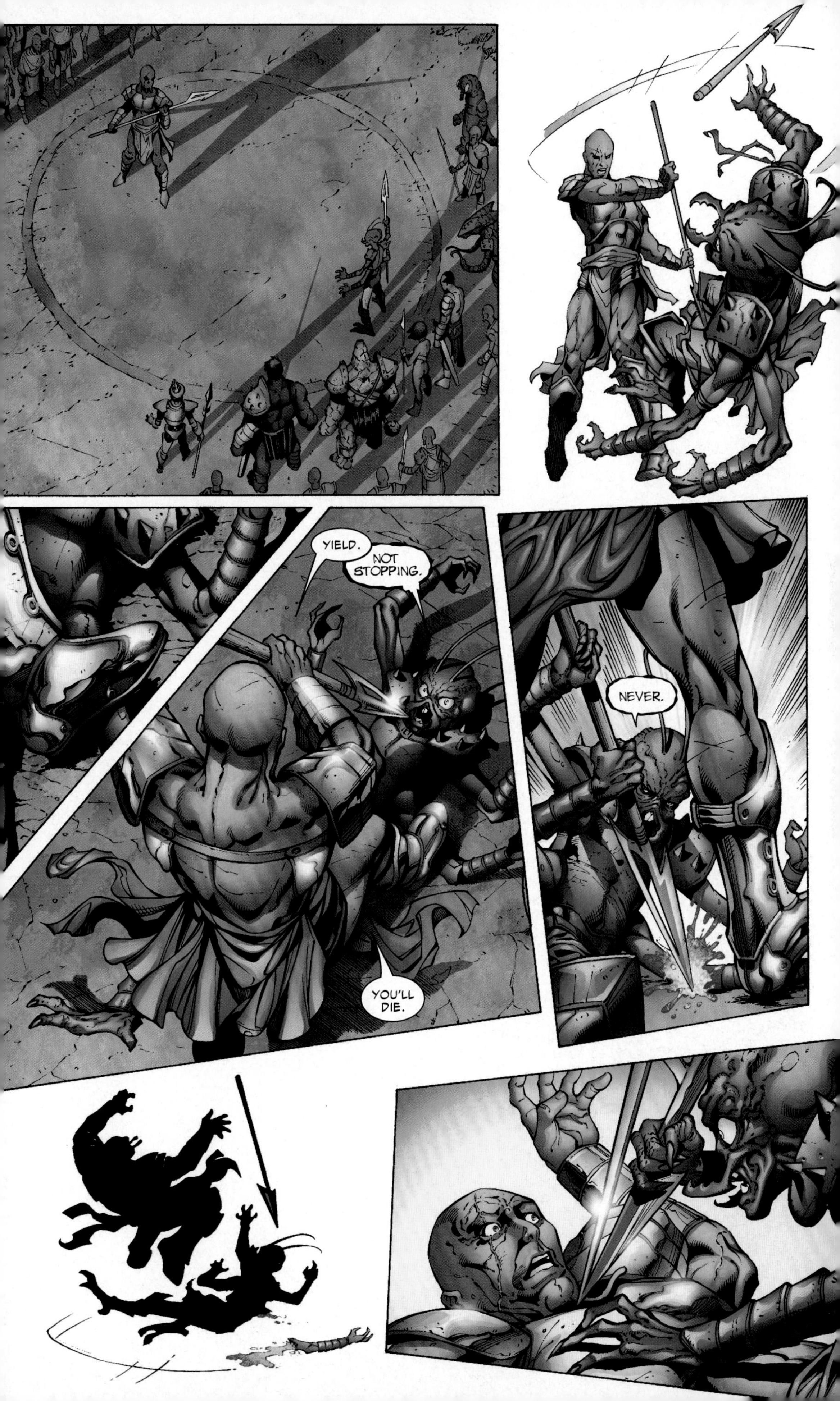
YIELD.
NOT STOPPING.
YOU'LL DIE.
NEVER.

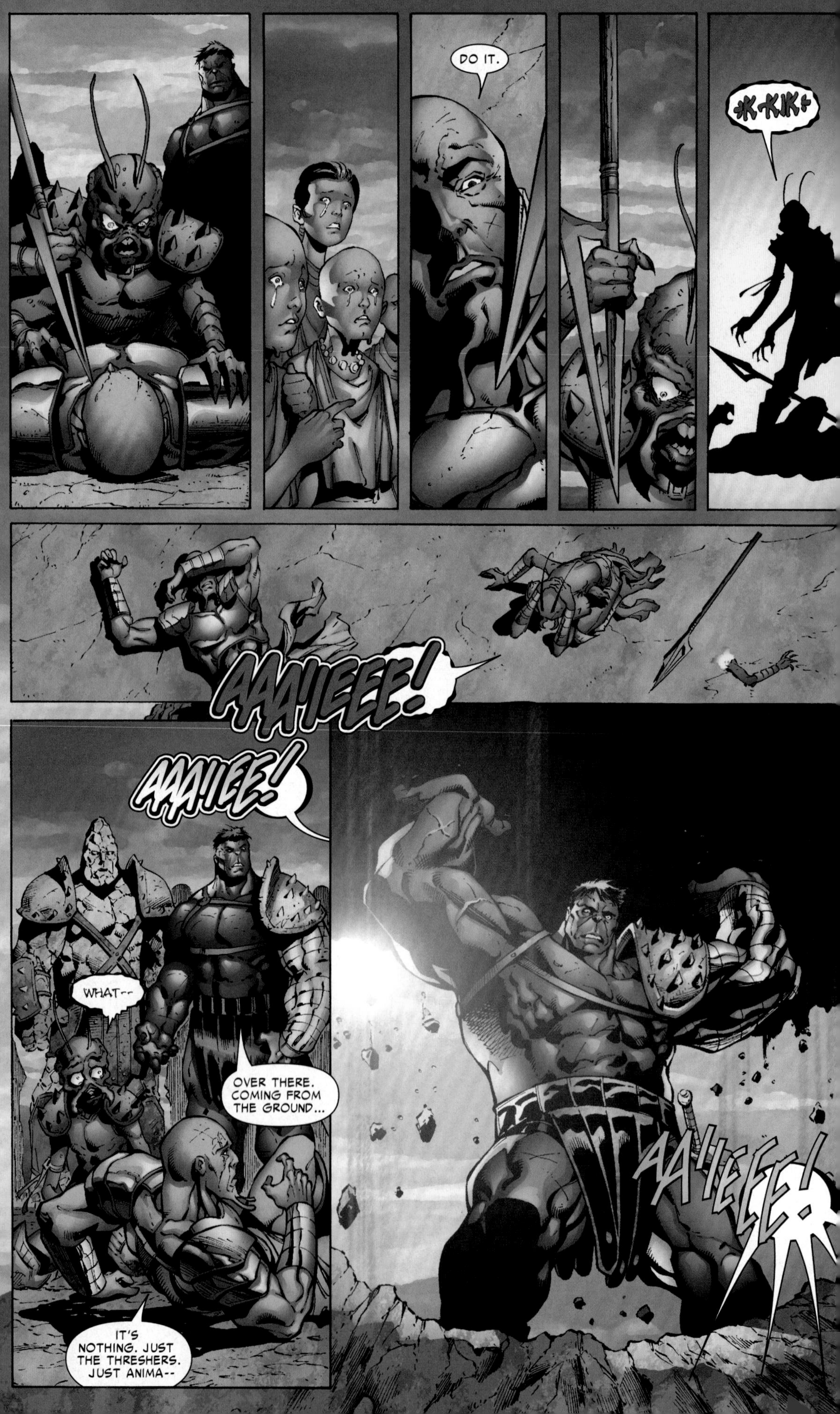
DO IT.
K-KIK
AAAIIEEE!
AAAIIEE!
WHAT--
OVER THERE. COMING FROM THE GROUND...
IT'S NOTHING. JUST THE THRESHERS. JUST ANIMA--
AAIIEEE!

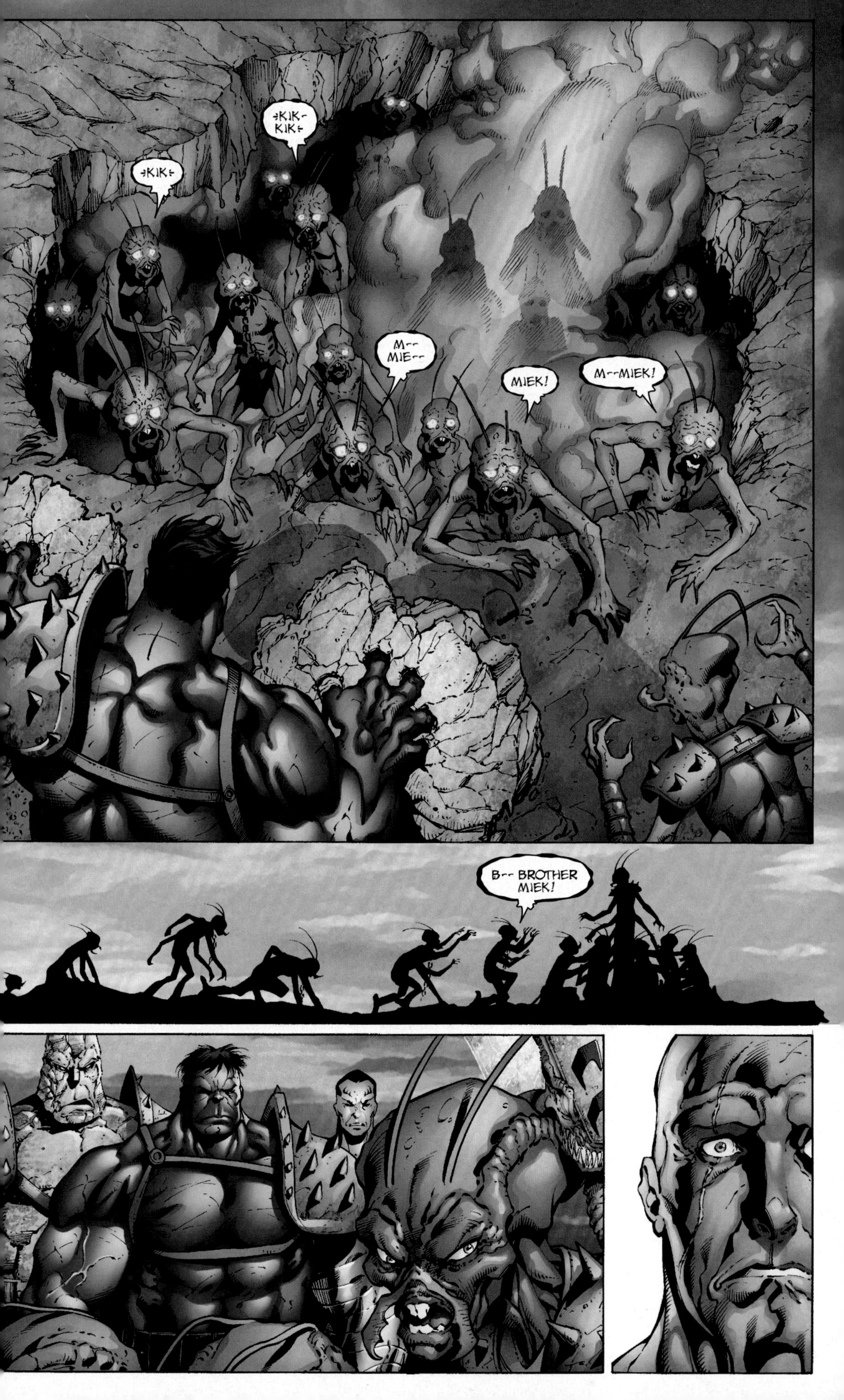

KIK
KIK-KIK
M-- MIE--
MIEK!
M--MIEK!
B-- BROTHER MIEK!

HE WAS THERE, OLDSTRONG! NO MORE THAN THREE HOURS AGO!

YOU, HEADMAN. HAVE YOU SEEN THE GREEN SCAR?

OR ANY OF HIS MONSTERS?

THE GREEN SCAR...

MONSTERS?

YES.

THAT'S ALL I SEE.

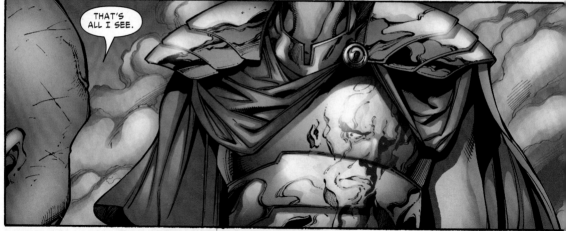

#97

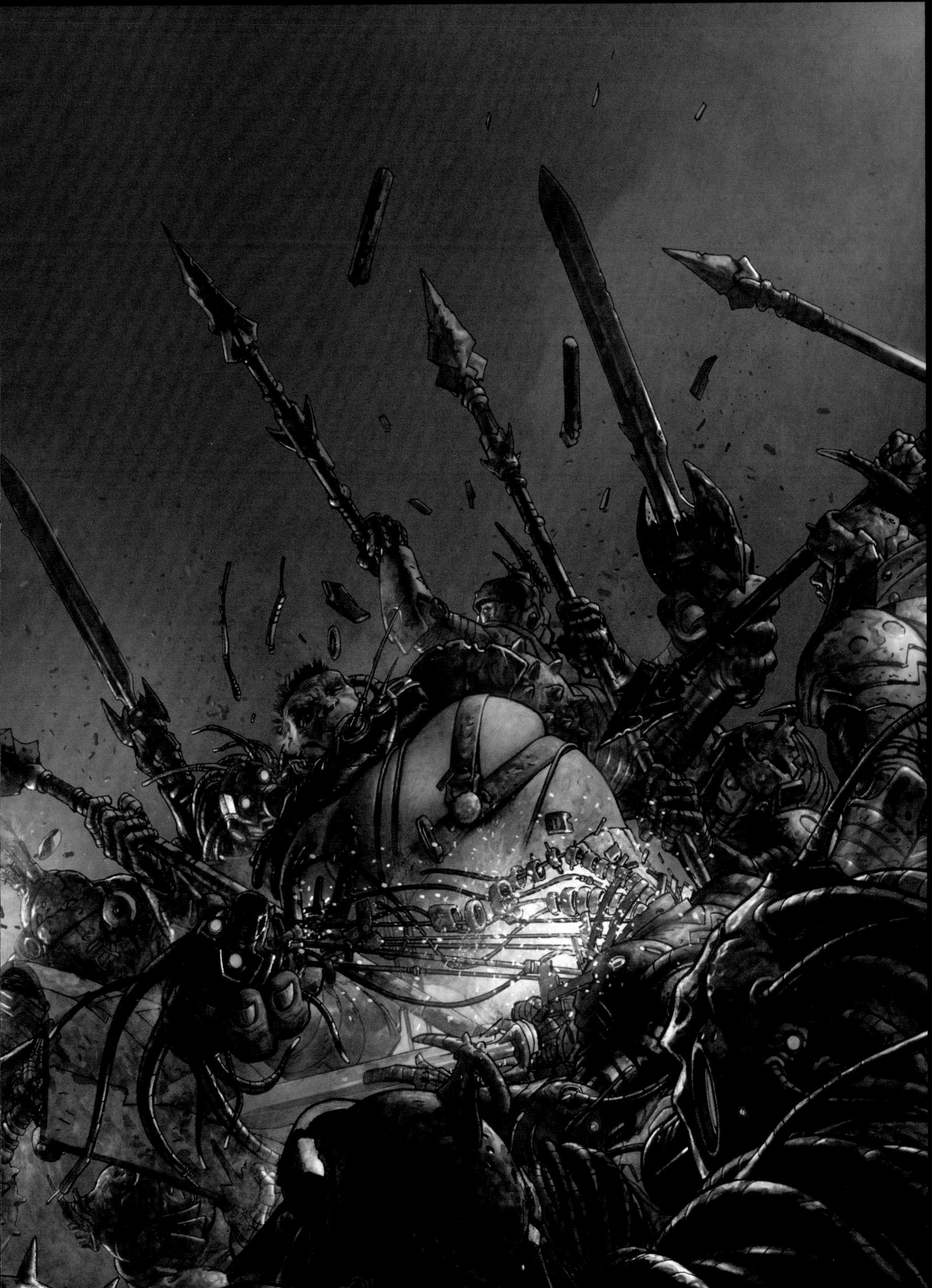

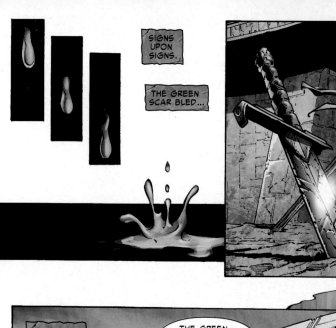

SIGNS UPON SIGNS.

THE GREEN SCAR BLED...

AND THE ELEHA'AL VINES GREW.

AND THE GREAT STONES CRUMBLED.

THE GREEN SCAR'S ON THE MOVE! SMASHED AN IMPERIAL VILLAGE, FREED THEIR NATIVE SLAVES!

YAAAA!

COME ON, BROTHERS-- TO THE PALACE!

MAY THE PROPHET PRESERVE US...

LOOOSH

THE PROPHET CAN'T HELP YOU, SLAVE.

AND FIRE FELL FROM THE SKIES.

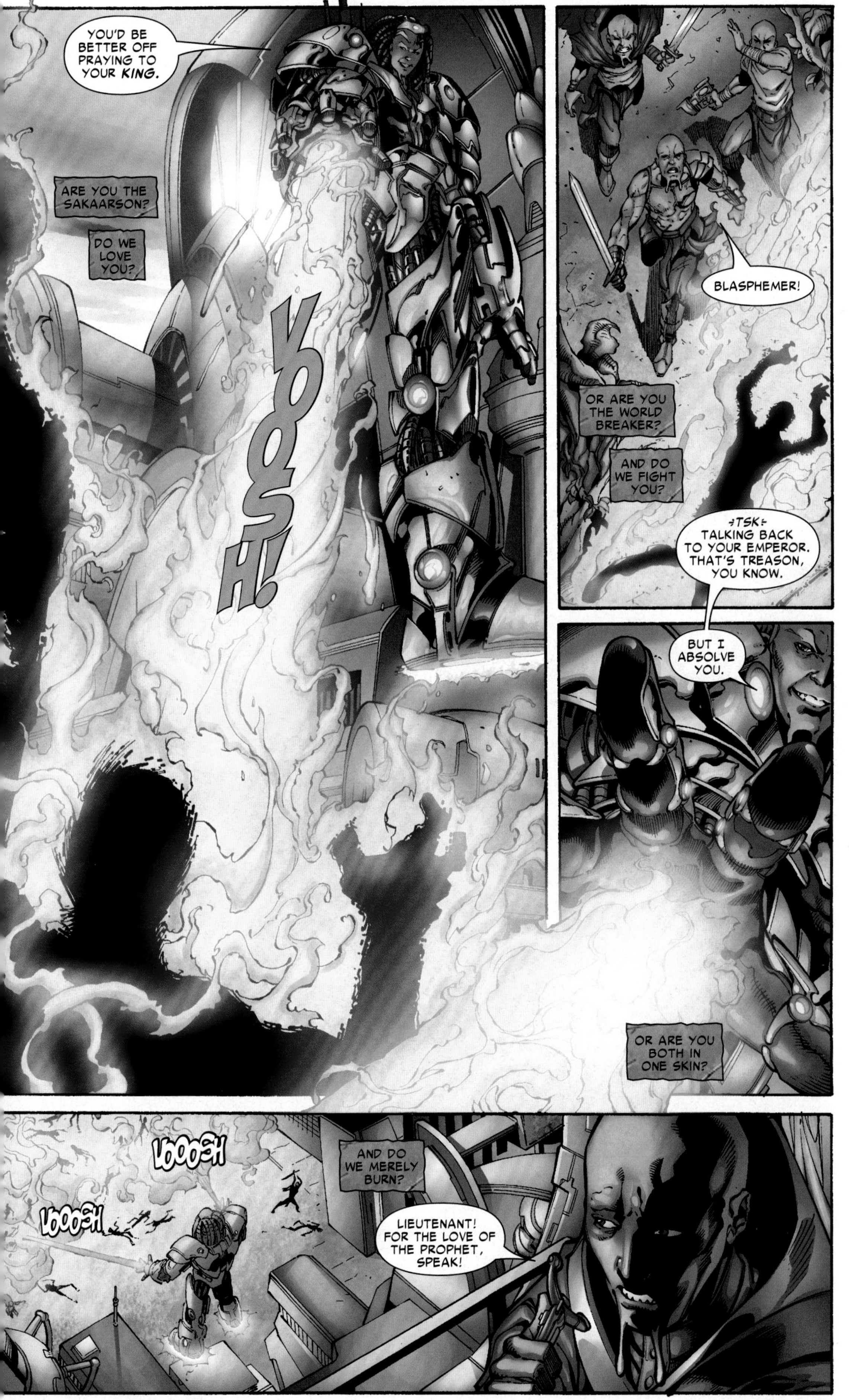
YOU'D BE BETTER OFF PRAYING TO YOUR KING.
ARE YOU THE SAKAARSON?
DO WE LOVE YOU?
VOOSH!
BLASPHEMER!
OR ARE YOU THE WORLD BREAKER?
AND DO WE FIGHT YOU?
TSK
TALKING BACK TO YOUR EMPEROR. THAT'S TREASON, YOU KNOW.
BUT I ABSOLVE YOU.
OR ARE YOU BOTH IN ONE SKIN?
VOOOSH
VOOOSH
AND DO WE MERELY BURN?
LIEUTENANT! FOR THE LOVE OF THE PROPHET, SPEAK!

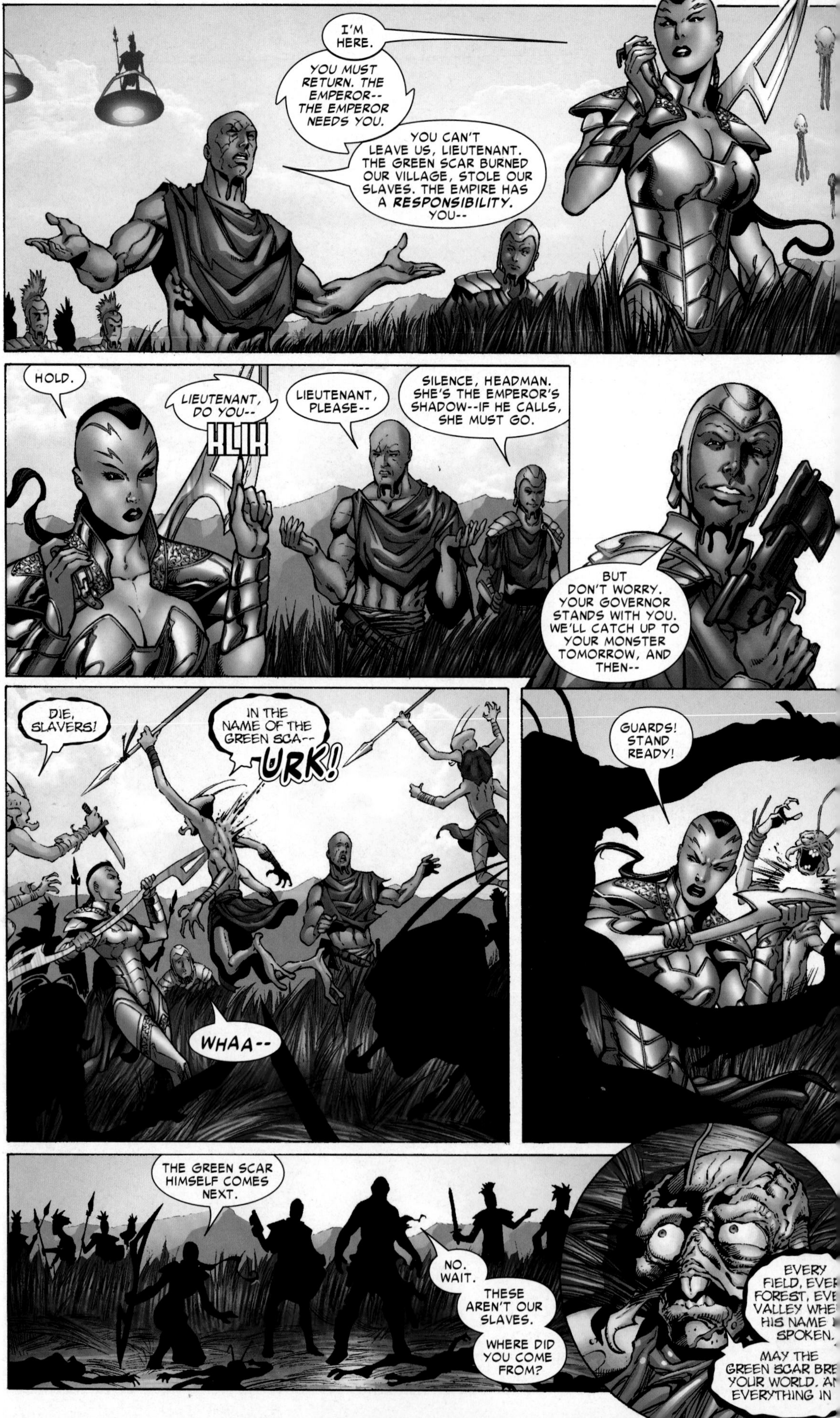

I'M HERE.
YOU MUST RETURN. THE EMPEROR-- THE EMPEROR NEEDS YOU.
YOU CAN'T LEAVE US, LIEUTENANT. THE GREEN SCAR BURNED OUR VILLAGE, STOLE OUR SLAVES. THE EMPIRE HAS A RESPONSIBILITY. YOU--
HOLD.
LIEUTENANT, DO YOU--
KLIK
LIEUTENANT, PLEASE--
SILENCE, HEADMAN. SHE'S THE EMPEROR'S SHADOW--IF HE CALLS, SHE MUST GO.
BUT DON'T WORRY. YOUR GOVERNOR STANDS WITH YOU. WE'LL CATCH UP TO YOUR MONSTER TOMORROW, AND THEN--
DIE, SLAVERS!
IN THE NAME OF THE GREEN SCA--
URK!
WHAA--
GUARDS! STAND READY!
THE GREEN SCAR HIMSELF COMES NEXT.
NO. WAIT.
THESE AREN'T OUR SLAVES.
WHERE DID YOU COME FROM?
EVERY FIELD, EVER FOREST, EVE VALLEY WHE HIS NAME SPOKEN.
MAY THE GREEN SCAR BRE YOUR WORLD. AN EVERYTHING IN

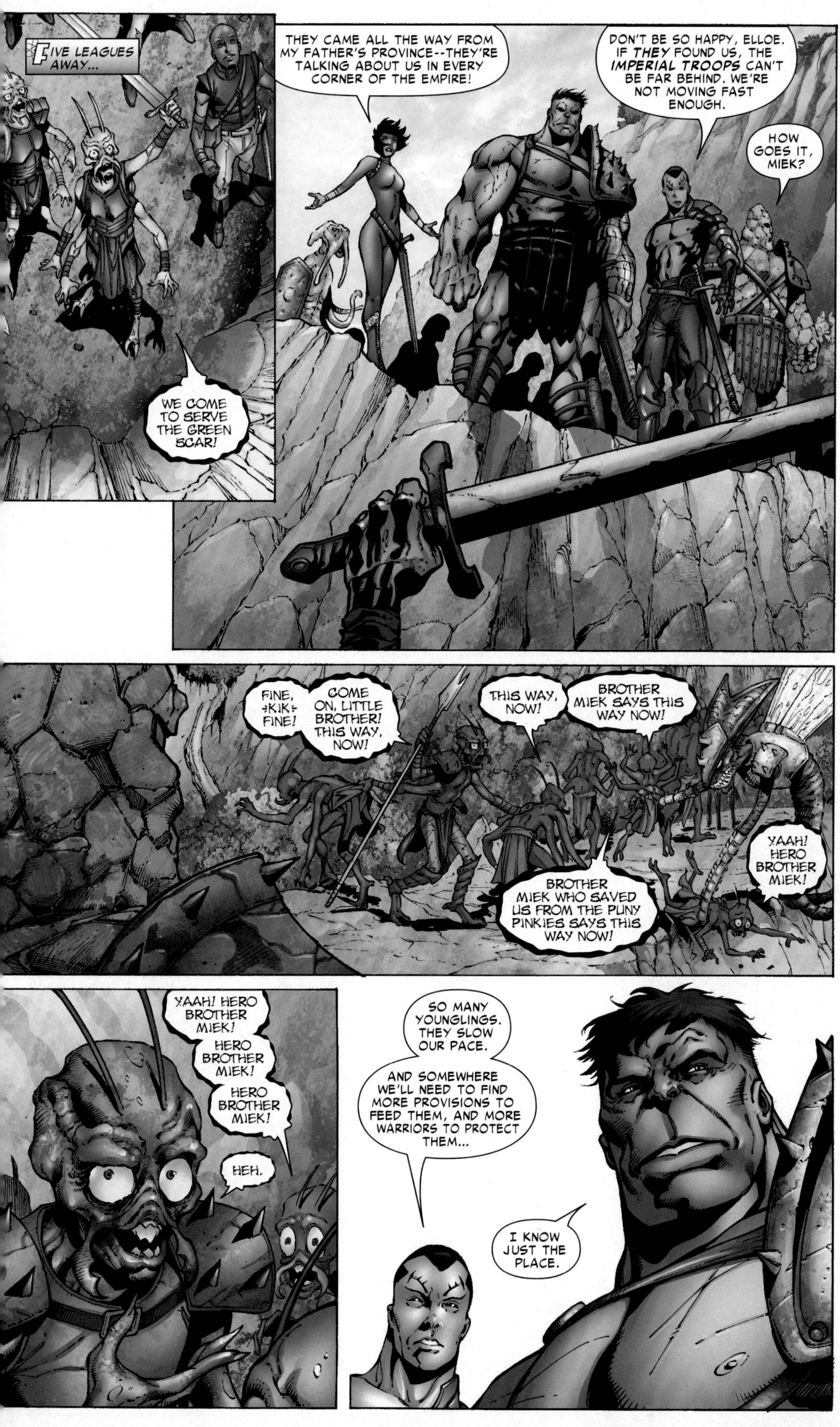

FIVE LEAGUES AWAY...
WE COME TO SERVE THE GREEN SCAR!
THEY CAME ALL THE WAY FROM MY FATHER'S PROVINCE--THEY'RE TALKING ABOUT US IN EVERY CORNER OF THE EMPIRE!
DON'T BE SO HAPPY, ELLOE. IF THEY FOUND US, THE IMPERIAL TROOPS CAN'T BE FAR BEHIND. WE'RE NOT MOVING FAST ENOUGH.
HOW GOES IT, MIEK?
FINE, -KIK- FINE!
COME ON, LITTLE BROTHER! THIS WAY, NOW!
THIS WAY, NOW!
BROTHER MIEK SAYS THIS WAY NOW!
BROTHER MIEK WHO SAVED US FROM THE PUNY PINKIES SAYS THIS WAY NOW!
YAAH! HERO BROTHER MIEK!
YAAH! HERO BROTHER MIEK!
HERO BROTHER MIEK!
HERO BROTHER MIEK!
HEH.
SO MANY YOUNGLINGS. THEY SLOW OUR PACE.
AND SOMEWHERE WE'LL NEED TO FIND MORE PROVISIONS TO FEED THEM, AND MORE WARRIORS TO PROTECT THEM...
I KNOW JUST THE PLACE.

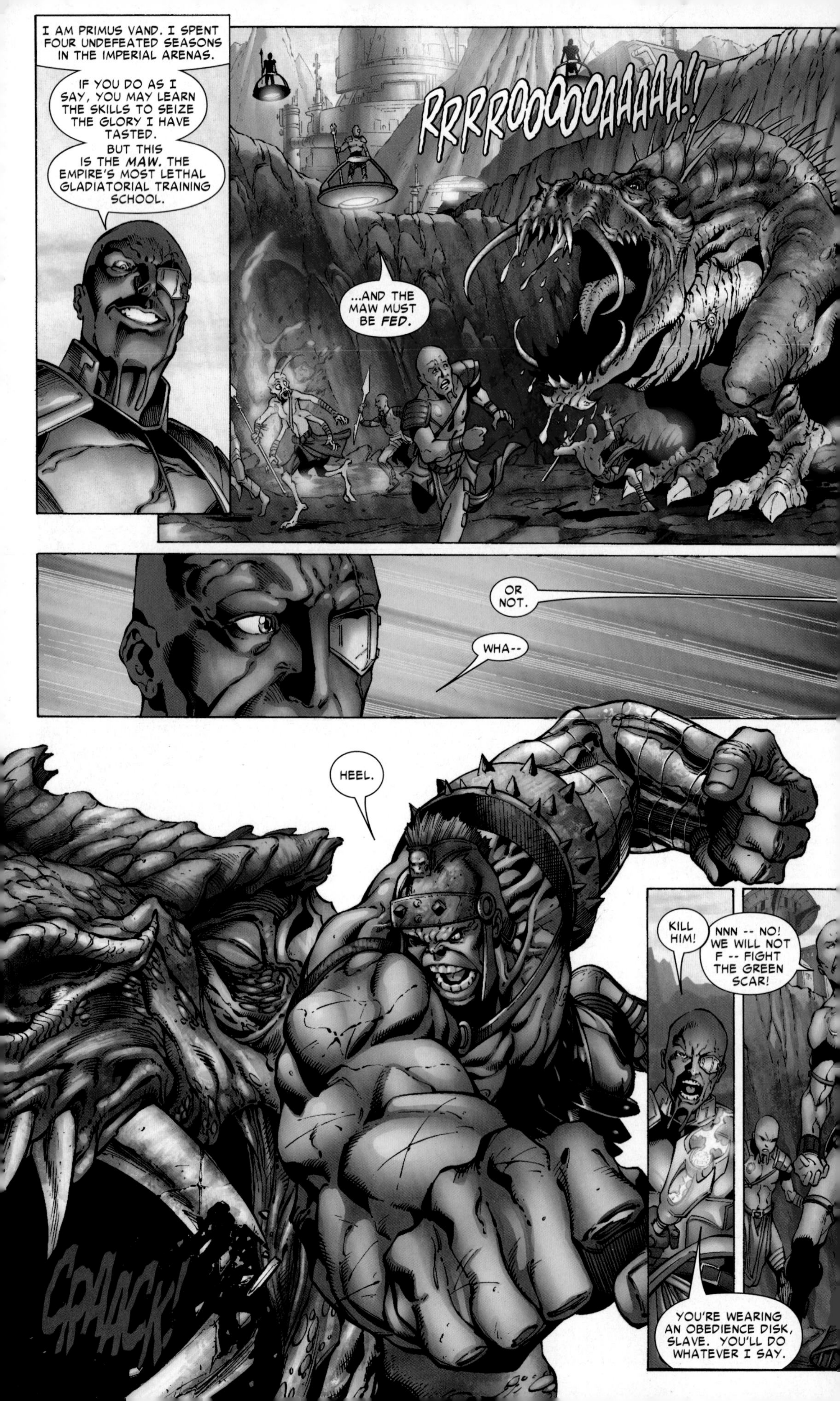

I AM PRIMUS VAND. I SPENT FOUR UNDEFEATED SEASONS IN THE IMPERIAL ARENAS.
IF YOU DO AS I SAY, YOU MAY LEARN THE SKILLS TO SEIZE THE GLORY I HAVE TASTED.
BUT THIS IS THE MAW. THE EMPIRE'S MOST LETHAL GLADIATORIAL TRAINING SCHOOL.
RRRROOOOOAAAAAA!!
...AND THE MAW MUST BE FED.
OR NOT.
WHA--
HEEL.
GRAACK!
KILL HIM!
NNN -- NO! WE WILL NOT F -- FIGHT THE GREEN SCAR!
YOU'RE WEARING AN OBEDIENCE DISK, SLAVE. YOU'LL DO WHATEVER I SAY.

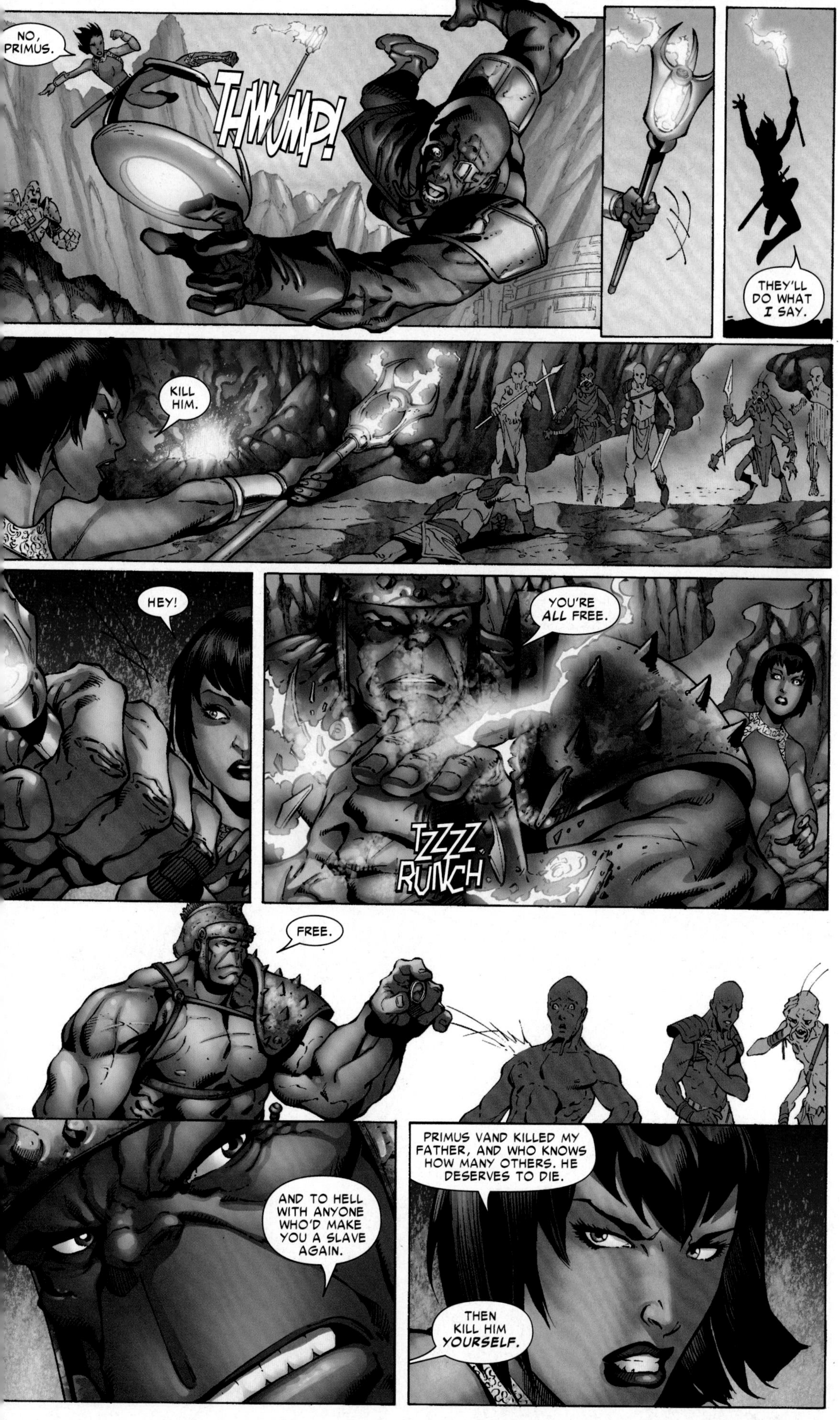

NO, PRIMUS.
THWUMP!
THEY'LL DO WHAT I SAY.
KILL HIM.
HEY!
YOU'RE ALL FREE.
TZZZZ RUNCH
FREE.
AND TO HELL WITH ANYONE WHO'D MAKE YOU A SLAVE AGAIN.
PRIMUS VAND KILLED MY FATHER, AND WHO KNOWS HOW MANY OTHERS. HE DESERVES TO DIE.
THEN KILL HIM YOURSELF.

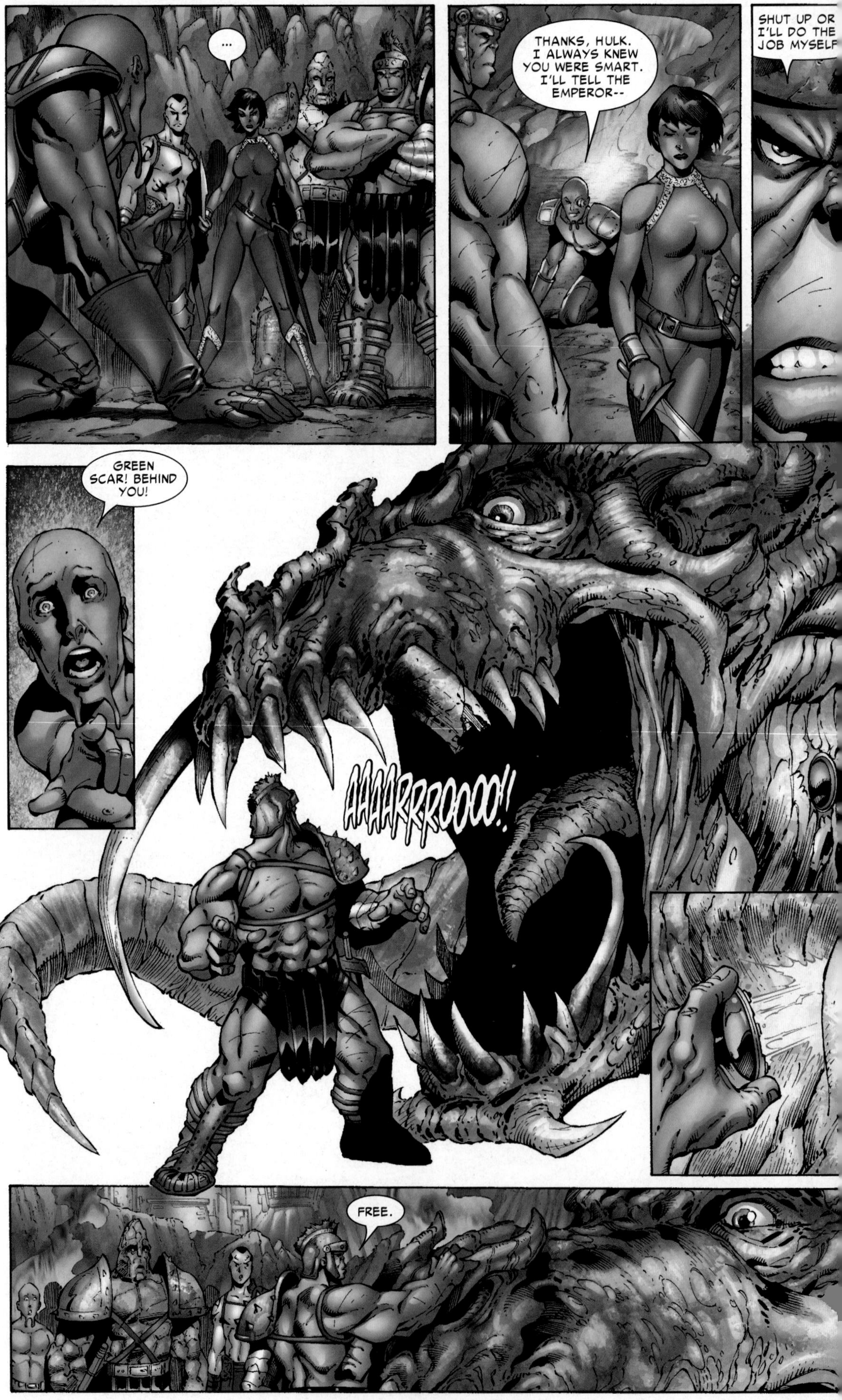

...
THANKS, HULK. I ALWAYS KNEW YOU WERE SMART. I'LL TELL THE EMPEROR--
SHUT UP OR I'LL DO THE JOB MYSELF
GREEN SCAR! BEHIND YOU!
AAAARRROOOO!!
FREE.

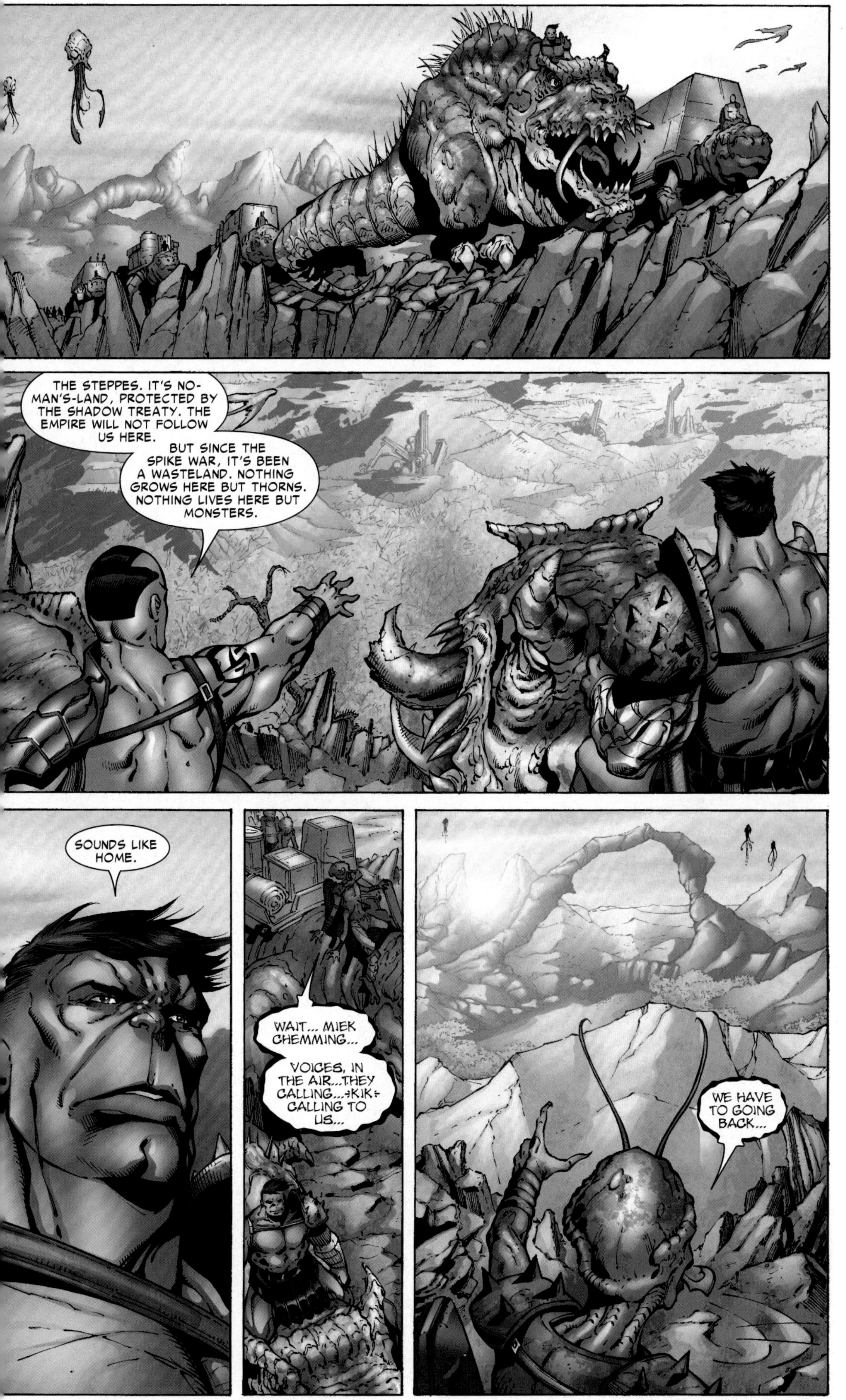

THE STEPPES. IT'S NO-MAN'S-LAND, PROTECTED BY THE SHADOW TREATY. THE EMPIRE WILL NOT FOLLOW US HERE.
BUT SINCE THE SPIKE WAR, IT'S BEEN A WASTELAND. NOTHING GROWS HERE BUT THORNS. NOTHING LIVES HERE BUT MONSTERS.
SOUNDS LIKE HOME.
WAIT... MIEK CHEMMING...
VOICES, IN THE AIR...THEY CALLING... ‡KIK‡ CALLING TO US...
WE HAVE TO GOING BACK...

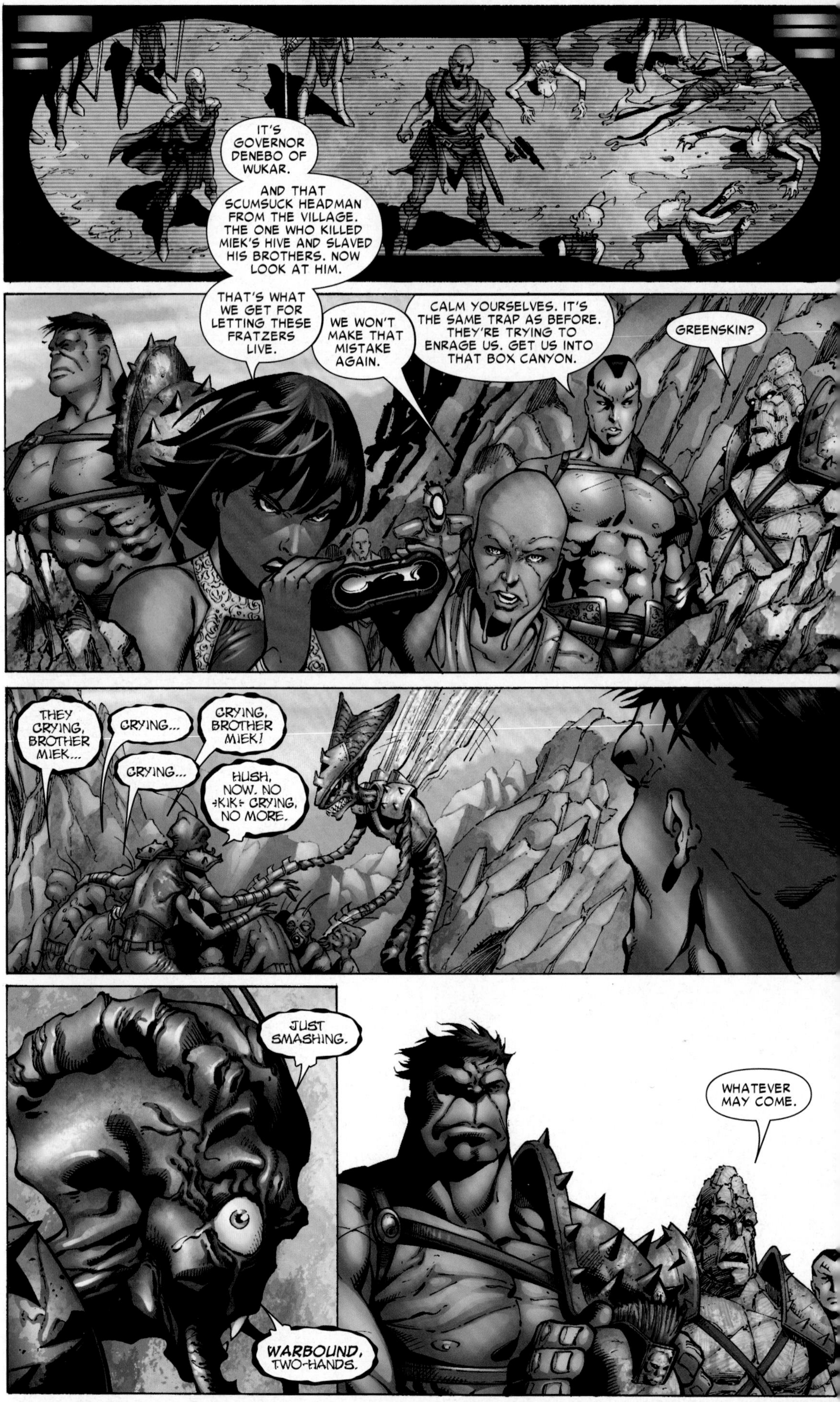
IT'S GOVERNOR DENEBO OF WUKAR.
AND THAT SCUMSUCK HEADMAN FROM THE VILLAGE. THE ONE WHO KILLED MIEK'S HIVE AND SLAVED HIS BROTHERS. NOW LOOK AT HIM.
THAT'S WHAT WE GET FOR LETTING THESE FRATZERS LIVE.
WE WON'T MAKE THAT MISTAKE AGAIN.
CALM YOURSELVES. IT'S THE SAME TRAP AS BEFORE. THEY'RE TRYING TO ENRAGE US. GET US INTO THAT BOX CANYON.
GREENSKIN?
THEY CRYING, BROTHER MIEK...
CRYING...
CRYING...
CRYING, BROTHER MIEK!
HUSH, NOW. NO ≠KIK≠ CRYING, NO MORE.
JUST SMASHING.
WHATEVER MAY COME.
WARBOUND, TWO-HANDS.

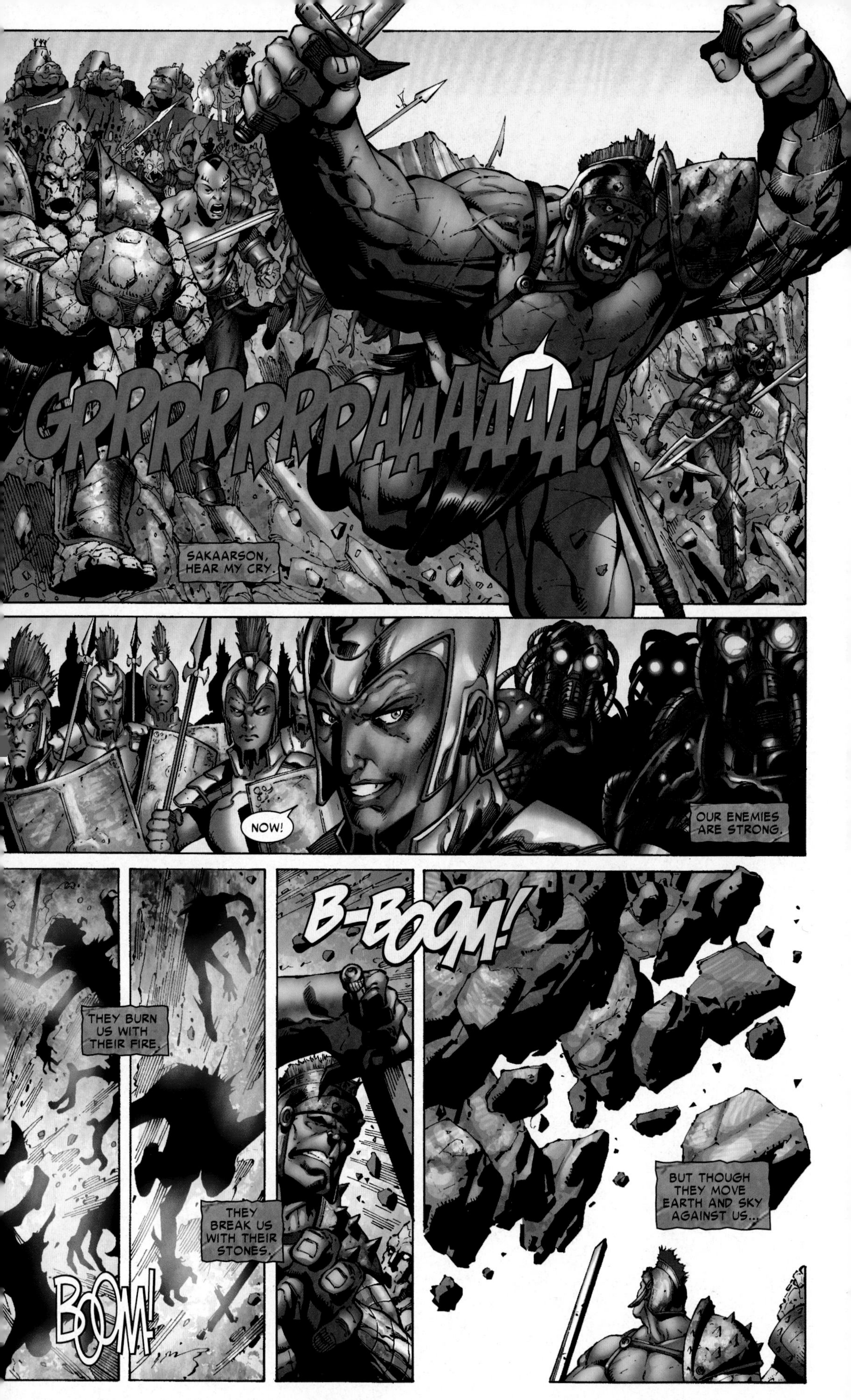
GRRRRRRRAAAAAA!!
SAKAARSON, HEAR MY CRY.
NOW!
OUR ENEMIES ARE STRONG.
THEY BURN US WITH THEIR FIRE.
BOOM!
THEY BREAK US WITH THEIR STONES.
B-BOOM!
BUT THOUGH THEY MOVE EARTH AND SKY AGAINST US...

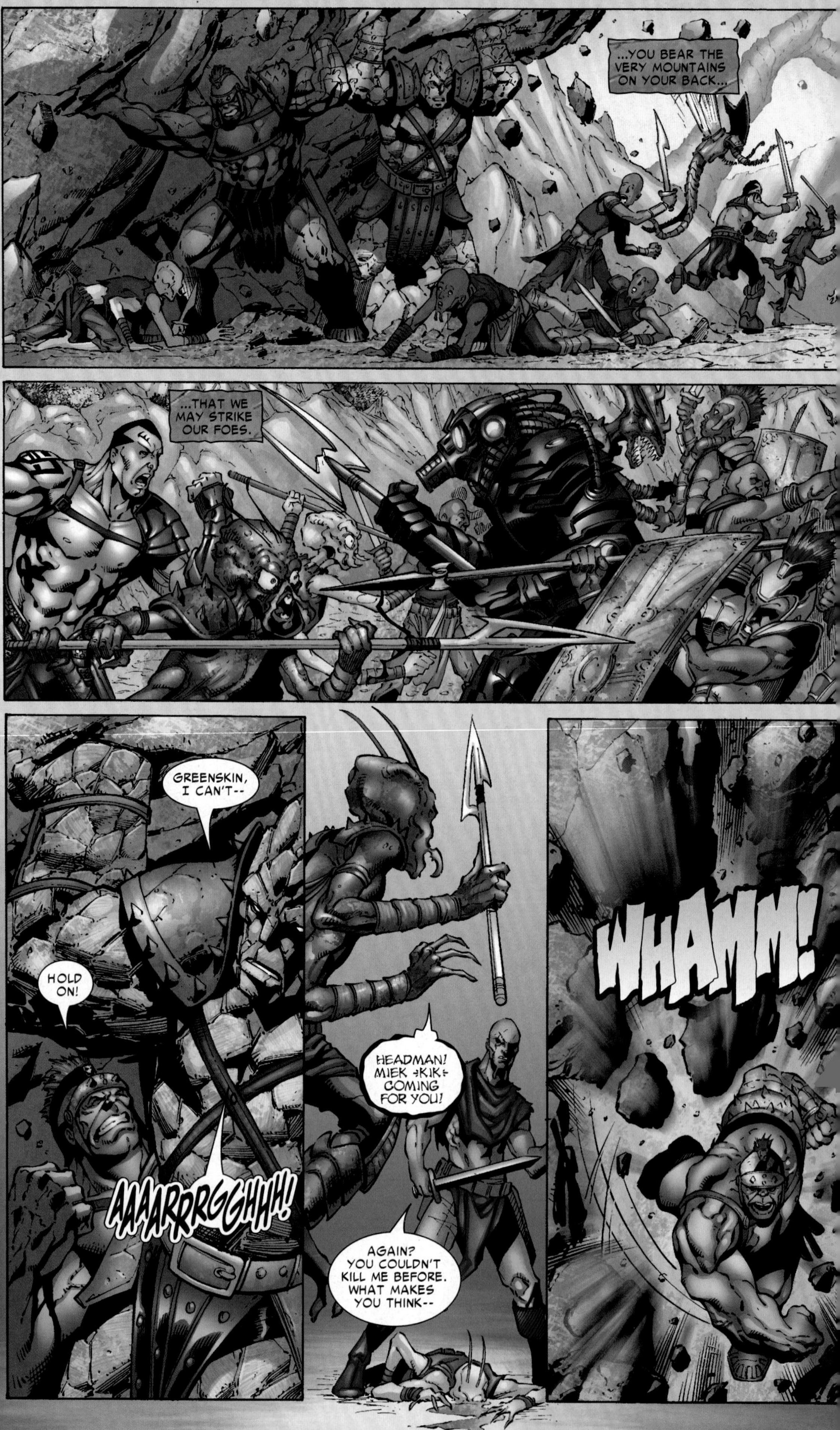

...YOU BEAR THE VERY MOUNTAINS ON YOUR BACK...
...THAT WE MAY STRIKE OUR FOES.
GREENSKIN, I CAN'T--
HOLD ON!
AAAARRRGGHHH!
HEADMAN! MIEK +KIK+ COMING FOR YOU!
AGAIN? YOU COULDN'T KILL ME BEFORE. WHAT MAKES YOU THINK--
WHAMM!

G--GOOD. NOW...YOU'RE JUST LIKE... ME.

GRRRAAAAAAA!

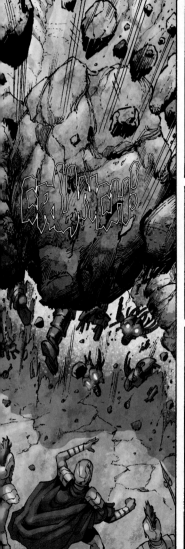

GCRUNCH

MIEK. IT'S OVER.

OVER?

MIEK JUST STARTING.

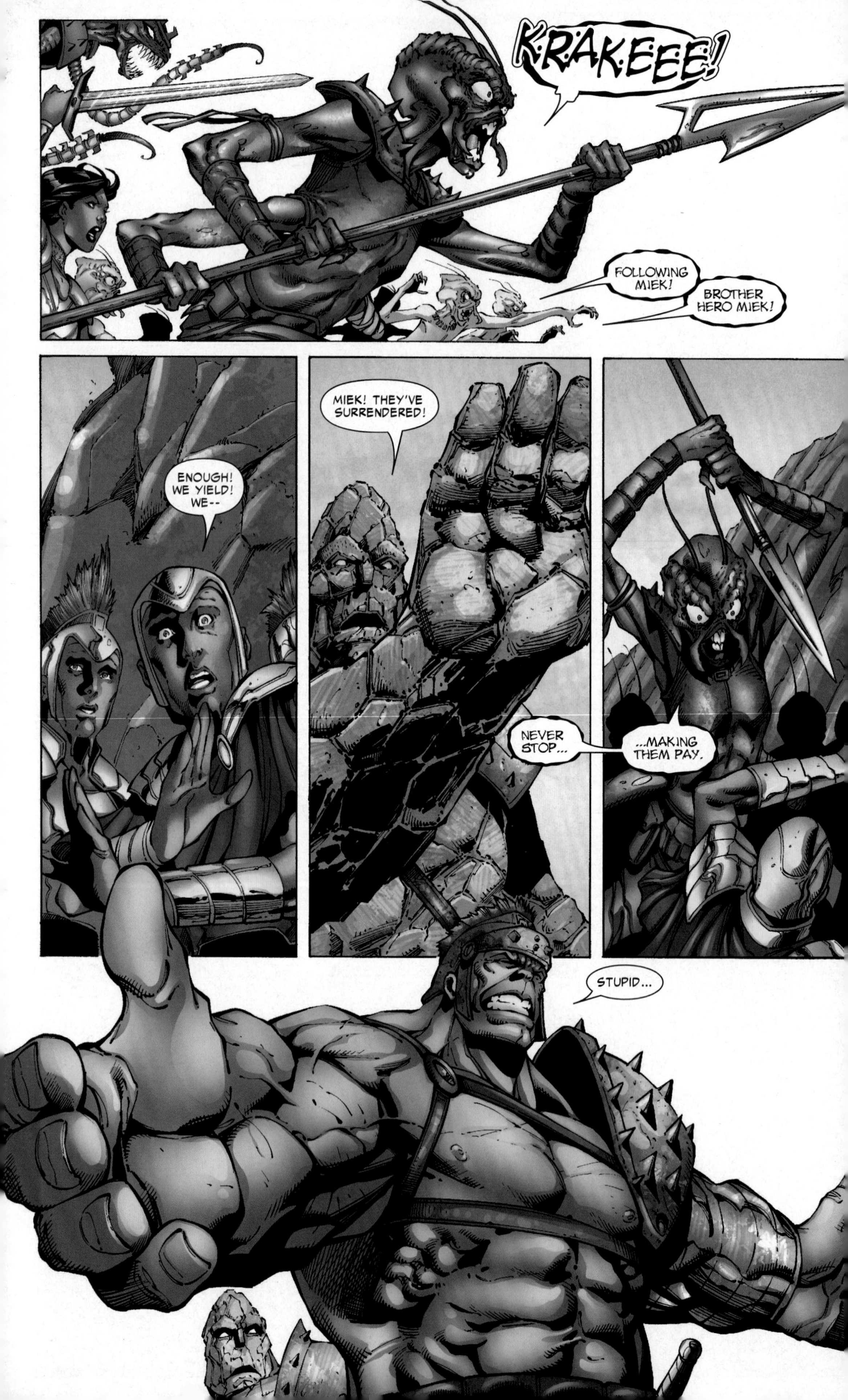
K-R-A-K-E-E-E!
FOLLOWING MIEK!
BROTHER HERO MIEK!
ENOUGH! WE YIELD! WE--
MIEK! THEY'VE SURRENDERED!
NEVER STOP...
...MAKING THEM PAY.
STUPID...

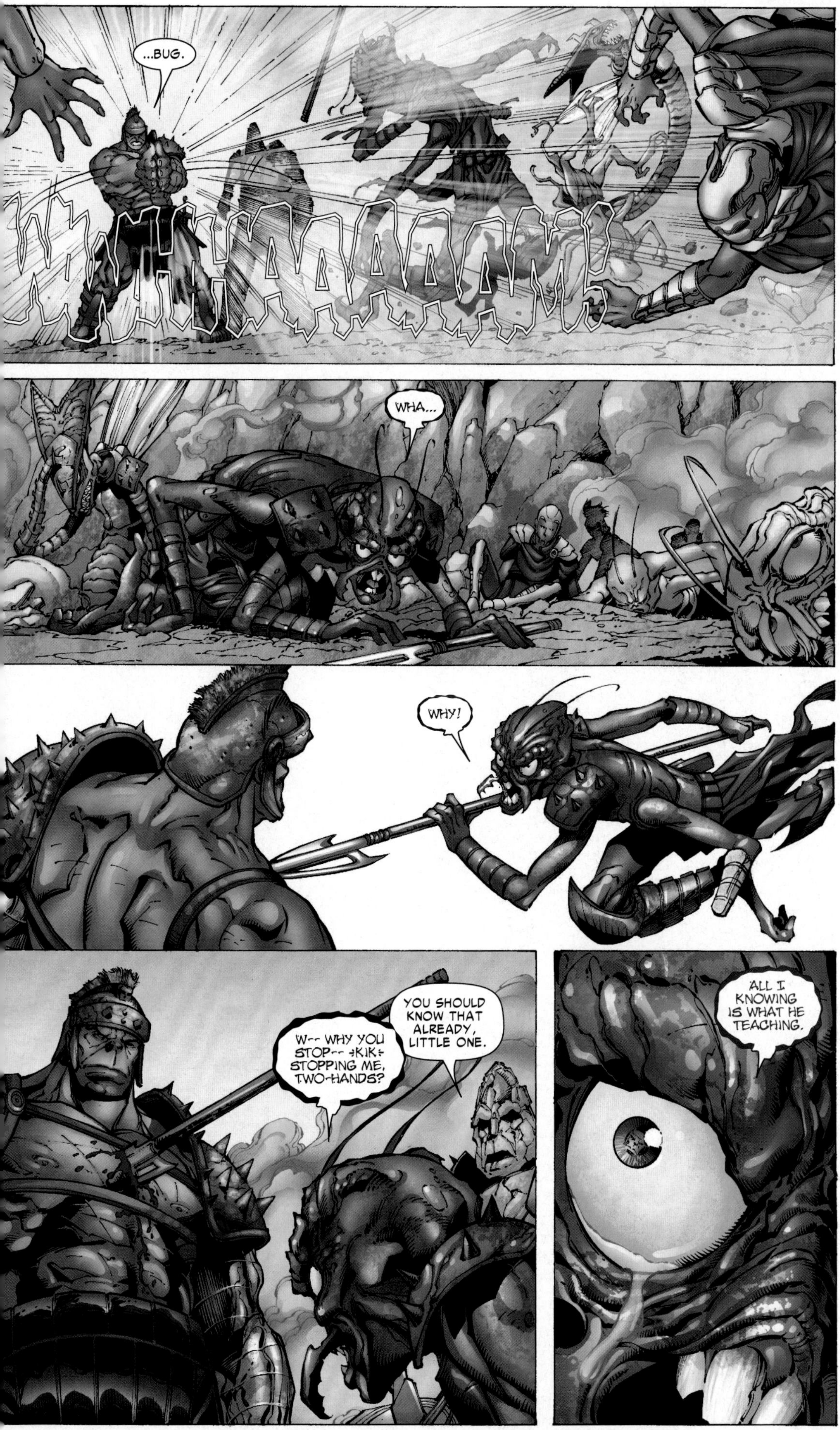
...BUG.
WHHHAAAAAAMB
WHA...
WHY!
W-- WHY YOU STOP-- +KIK+ STOPPING ME, TWO-HANDS?
YOU SHOULD KNOW THAT ALREADY, LITTLE ONE.
ALL I KNOWING IS WHAT HE TEACHING.

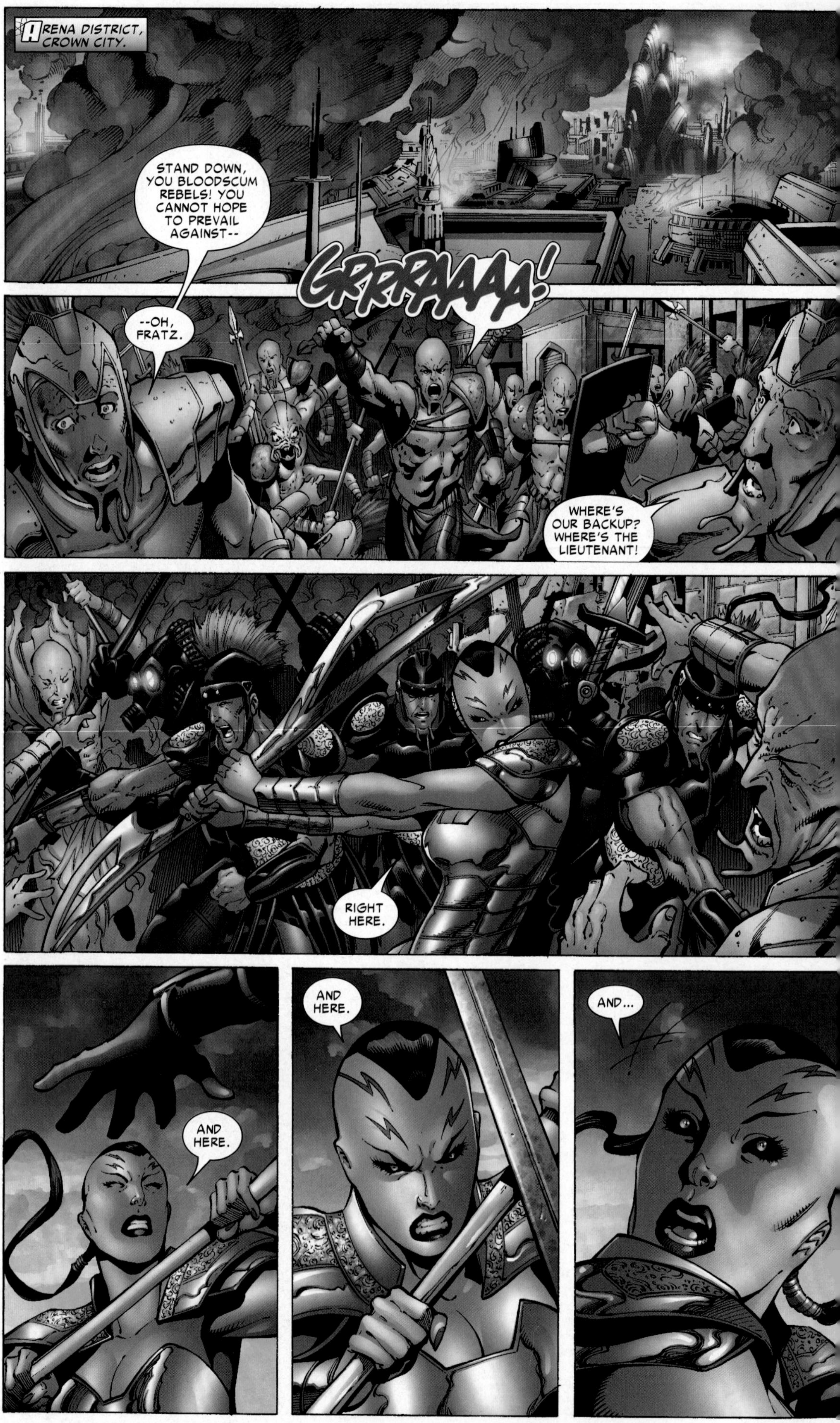
ARENA DISTRICT, CROWN CITY.
STAND DOWN, YOU BLOODSCUM REBELS! YOU CANNOT HOPE TO PREVAIL AGAINST--
GRRRAAAA!
--OH, FRATZ.
WHERE'S OUR BACKUP? WHERE'S THE LIEUTENANT!
RIGHT HERE.
AND HERE.
AND HERE.
AND...

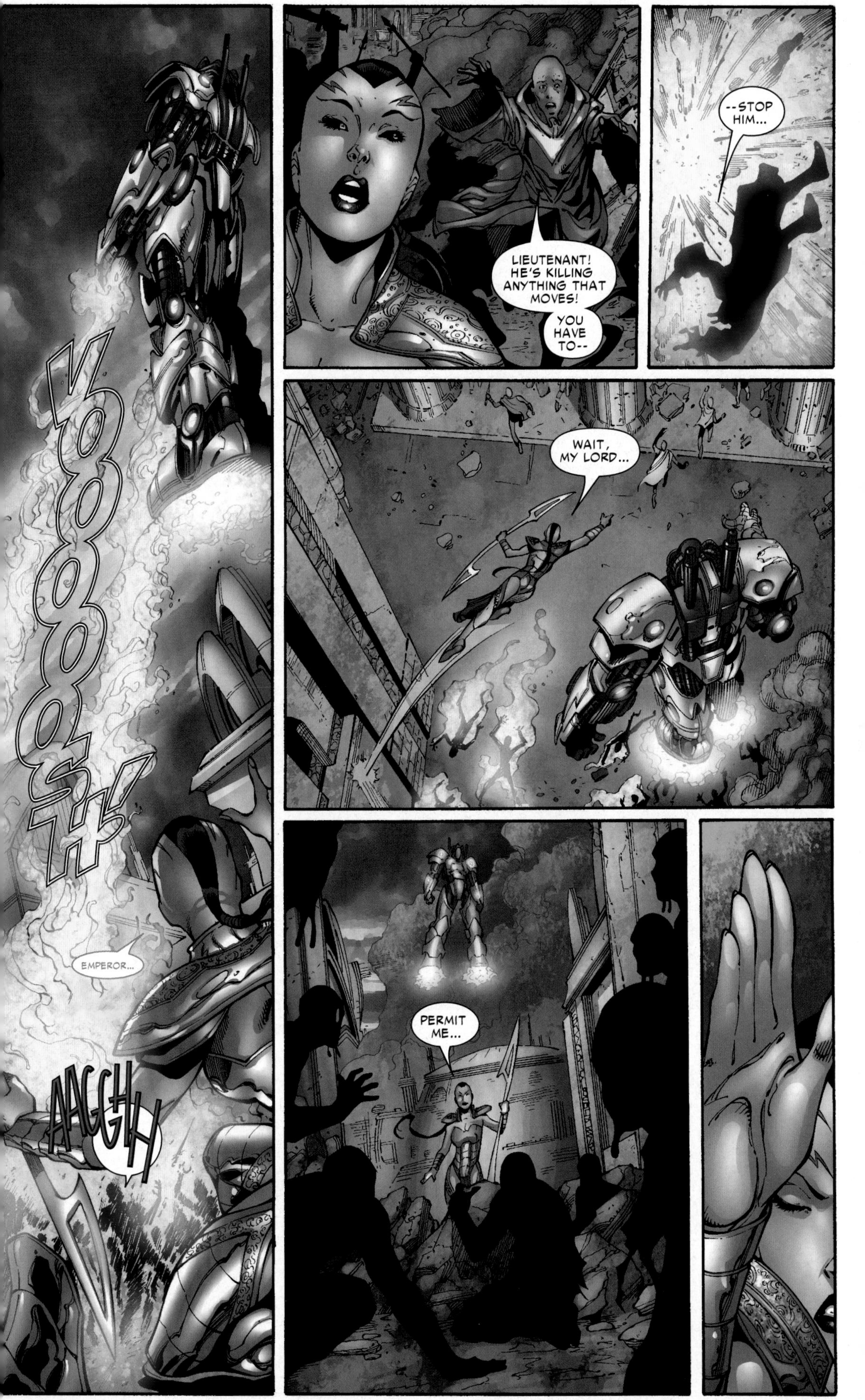
LIEUTENANT! HE'S KILLING ANYTHING THAT MOVES!
YOU HAVE TO--
--STOP HIM...
WAIT, MY LORD...
EMPEROR...
AAGGHH
PERMIT ME...

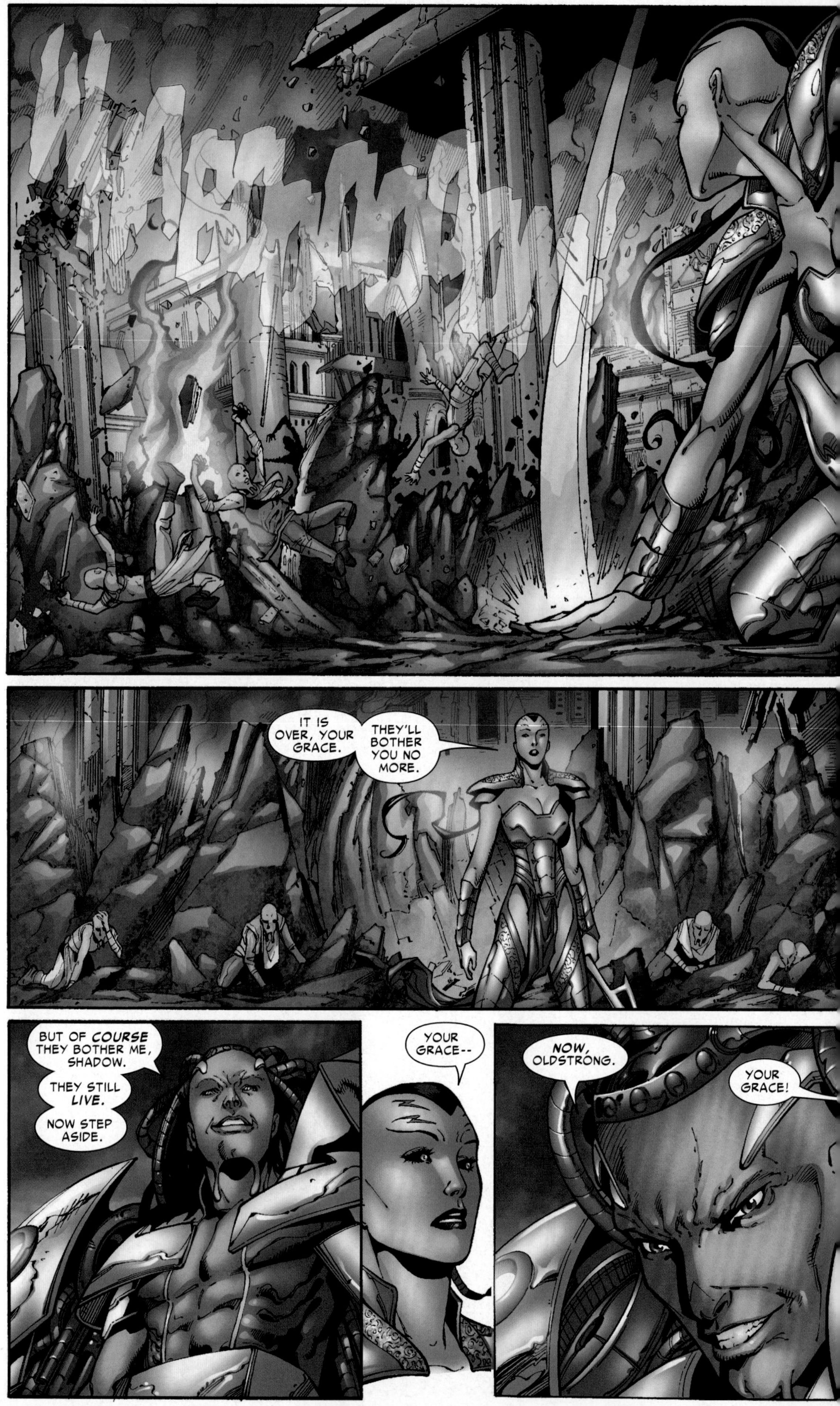
IT IS OVER, YOUR GRACE.
THEY'LL BOTHER YOU NO MORE.
BUT OF COURSE THEY BOTHER ME, SHADOW.
THEY STILL LIVE.
NOW STEP ASIDE.
YOUR GRACE--
NOW, OLDSTRONG.
YOUR GRACE!

G--GOVERNOR DENEBO RETURNS...

WHERE IS YOUR ARMOR, DENEBO?

WHERE IS YOUR ARMY?

LIKE THE OLD RHYMES SAID...

...HE BORE MOUNTAINS ON HIS BACK...

WHO, THE GREEN SCAR?

HE'S NOT THE GREEN SCAR...

...HE'S THE SAKAARSON.

WSSSHHH!

AAGHH!!

LET IT BE SAID, THROUGHOUT THE WORLD.

I AM HE. THE HERO PROTECTOR. THE DELIVERER OF THE PEOPLE. THE ONE TRUE SON OF SAKAAR.

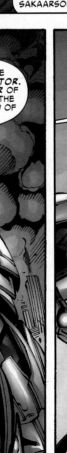

AND YOU, MY SHADOW.

YOU WILL DESTROY ALL PRETENDERS TO MY THRONE.

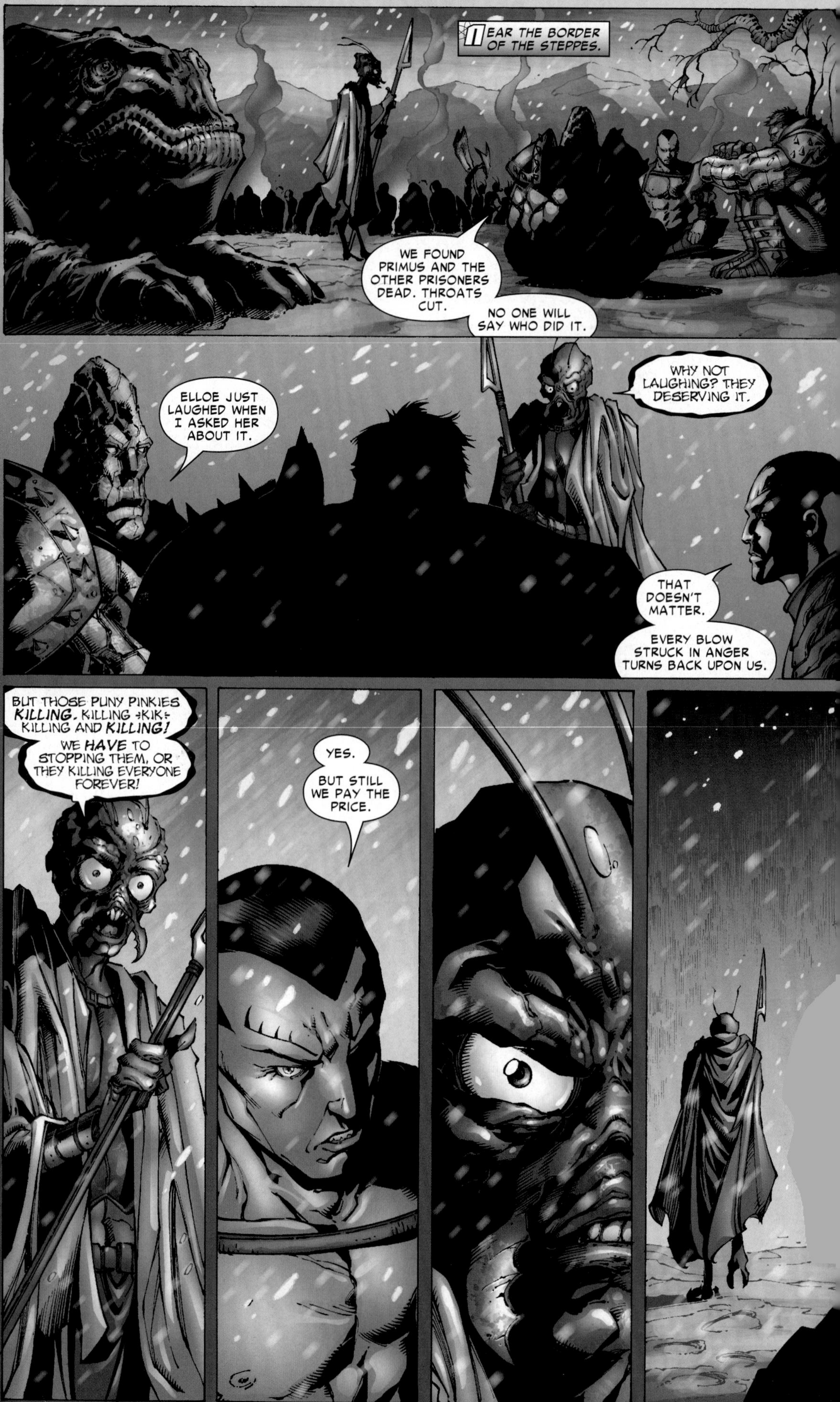
NEAR THE BORDER OF THE STEPPES.
WE FOUND PRIMUS AND THE OTHER PRISONERS DEAD. THROATS CUT.
NO ONE WILL SAY WHO DID IT.
ELLOE JUST LAUGHED WHEN I ASKED HER ABOUT IT.
WHY NOT LAUGHING? THEY DESERVING IT.
THAT DOESN'T MATTER.
EVERY BLOW STRUCK IN ANGER TURNS BACK UPON US.
BUT THOSE PUNY PINKIES KILLING. KILLING -KIK- KILLING AND KILLING!
WE HAVE TO STOPPING THEM, OR THEY KILLING EVERYONE FOREVER!
YES.
BUT STILL WE PAY THE PRICE.

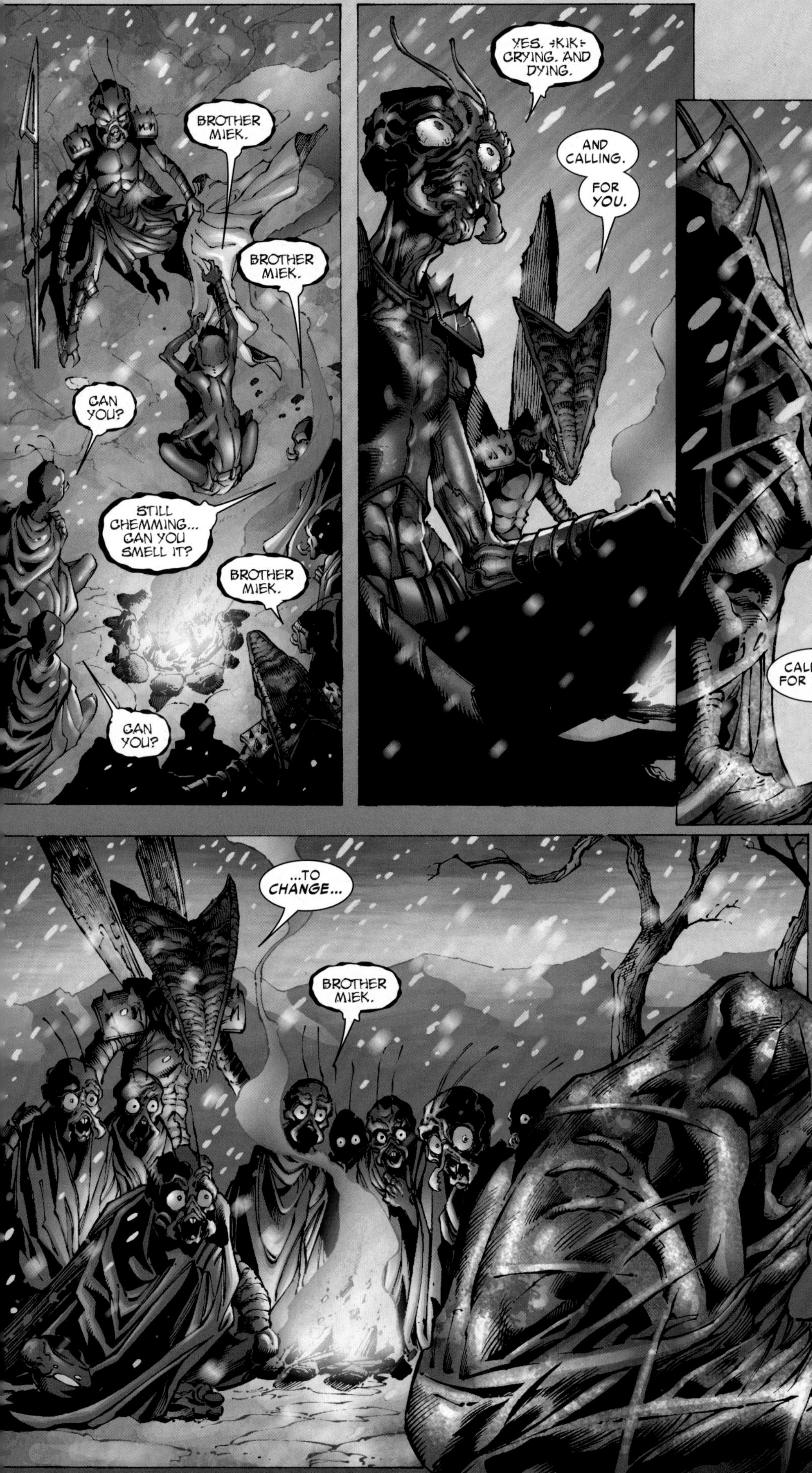
BROTHER MIEK.
BROTHER MIEK.
CAN YOU?
STILL CHEMMING... CAN YOU SMELL IT?
BROTHER MIEK.
CAN YOU?
YES. ‡KIK‡ CRYING. AND DYING.
AND CALLING.
FOR YOU.
CALLING FOR YOU...
...TO CHANGE...
BROTHER MIEK.

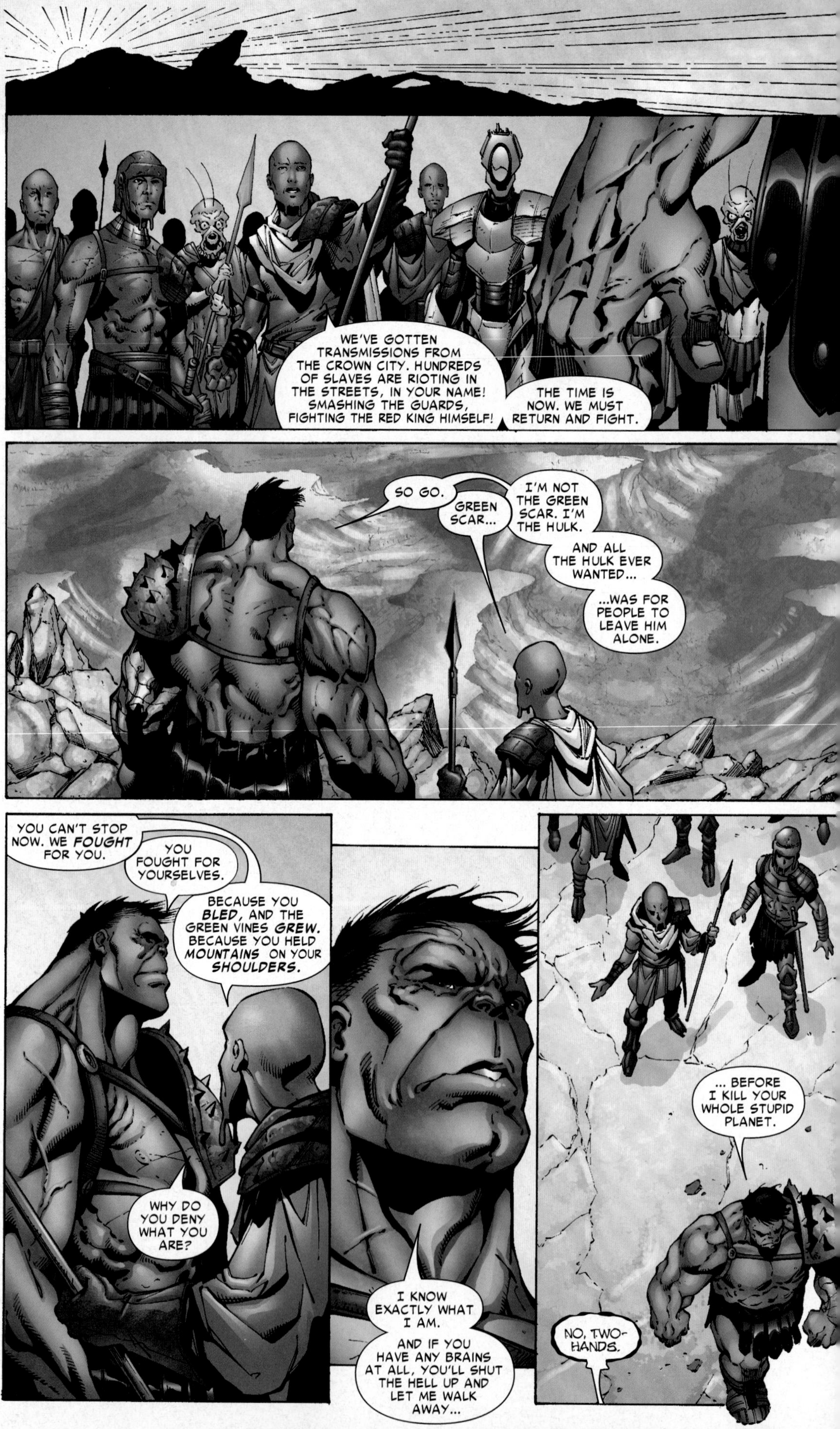
WE'VE GOTTEN TRANSMISSIONS FROM THE CROWN CITY. HUNDREDS OF SLAVES ARE RIOTING IN THE STREETS, IN YOUR NAME! SMASHING THE GUARDS, FIGHTING THE RED KING HIMSELF!
THE TIME IS NOW. WE MUST RETURN AND FIGHT.
SO GO.
GREEN SCAR...
I'M NOT THE GREEN SCAR. I'M THE HULK.
AND ALL THE HULK EVER WANTED...
...WAS FOR PEOPLE TO LEAVE HIM ALONE.
YOU CAN'T STOP NOW. WE *FOUGHT* FOR YOU.
YOU FOUGHT FOR YOURSELVES.
BECAUSE YOU *BLED*, AND THE GREEN VINES *GREW*. BECAUSE YOU HELD *MOUNTAINS* ON YOUR *SHOULDERS*.
WHY DO YOU DENY WHAT YOU ARE?
I KNOW EXACTLY WHAT I AM.
AND IF YOU HAVE ANY BRAINS AT ALL, YOU'LL SHUT THE HELL UP AND LET ME WALK AWAY...
... BEFORE I KILL YOUR WHOLE STUPID PLANET.
NO, TWO-HANDS.

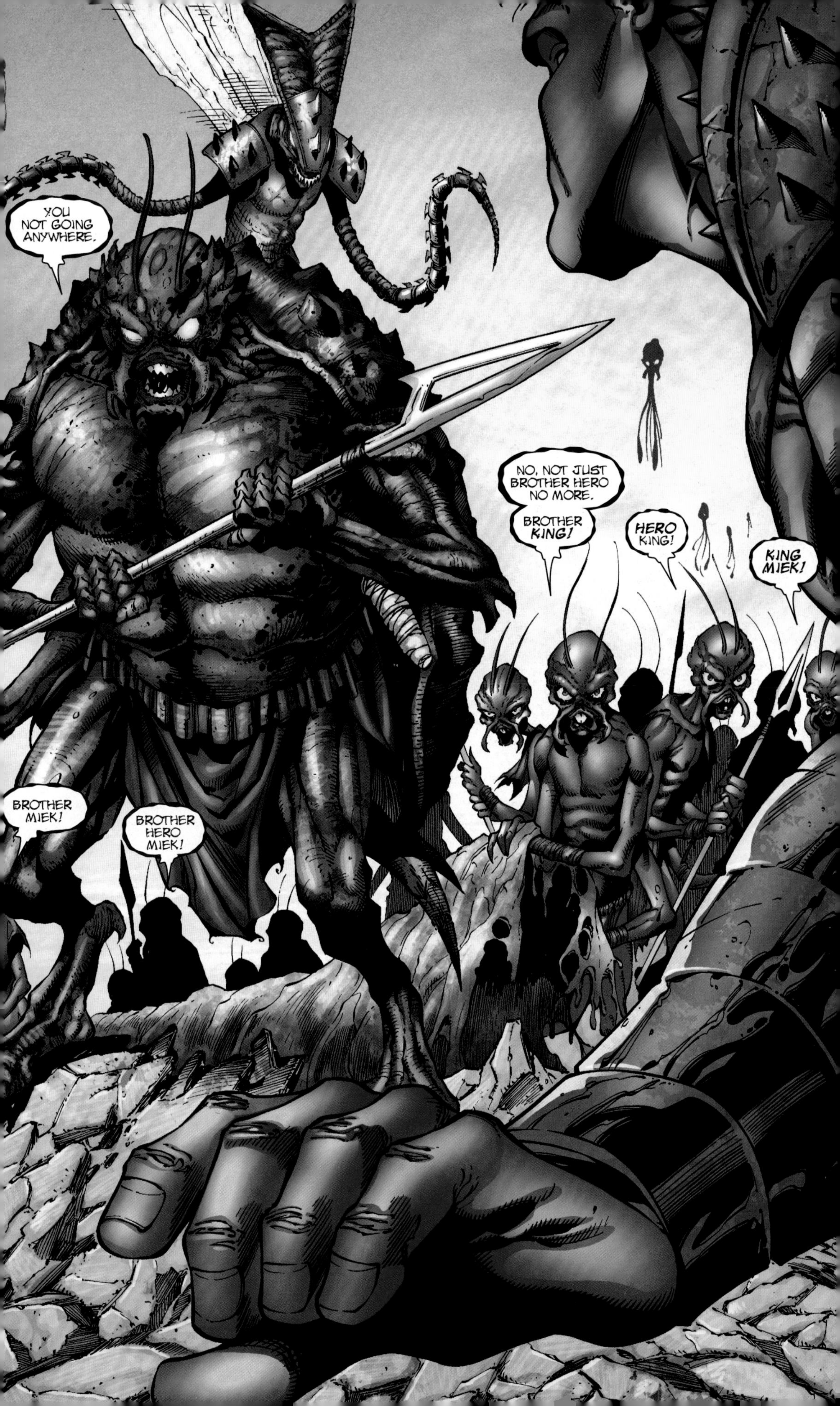
YOU NOT GOING ANYWHERE.
NO, NOT JUST BROTHER HERO NO MORE.
BROTHER KING!
HERO KING!
KING MIEK!
BROTHER MIEK!
BROTHER HERO MIEK!

#98

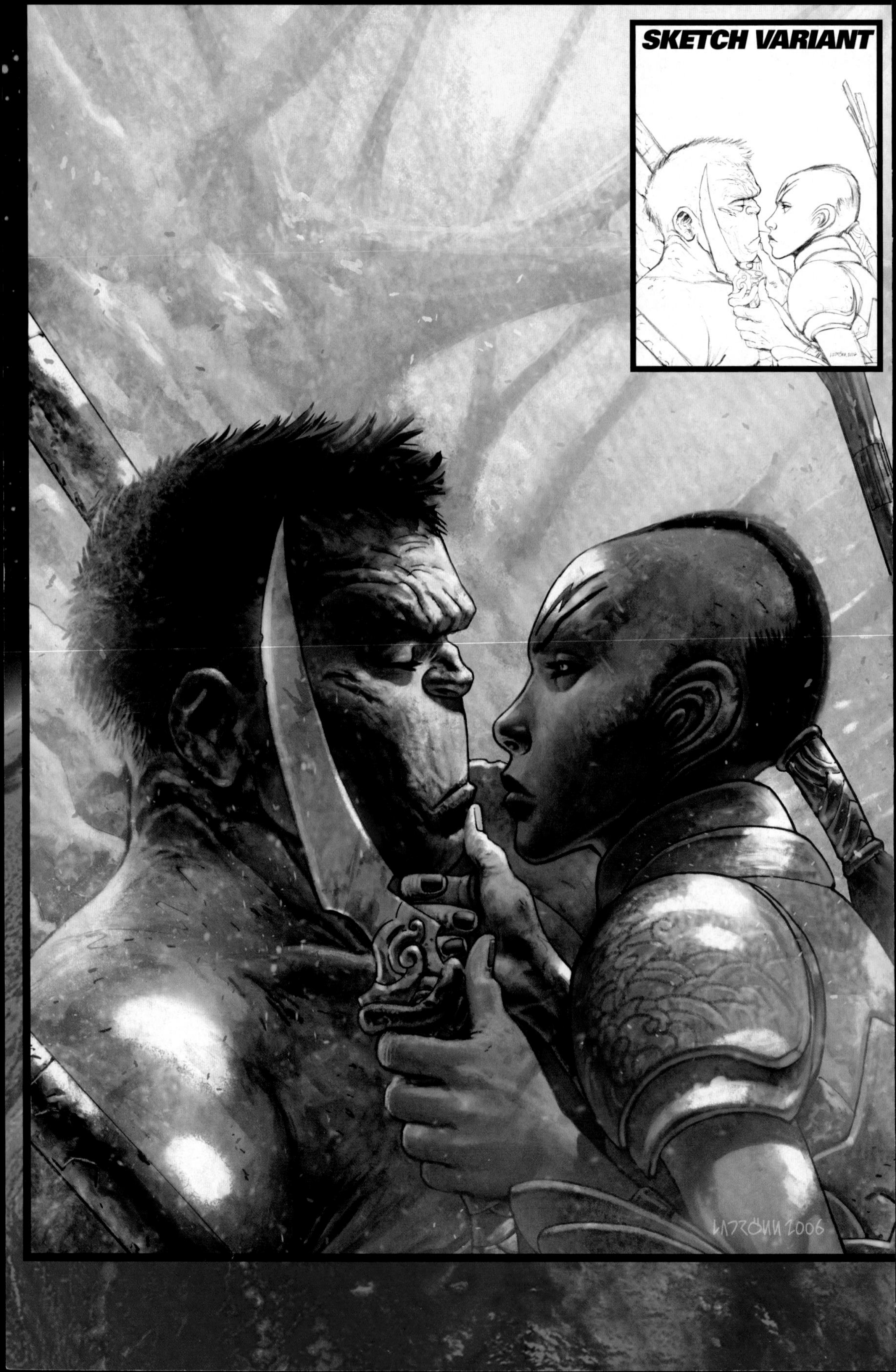
SKETCH VARIANT

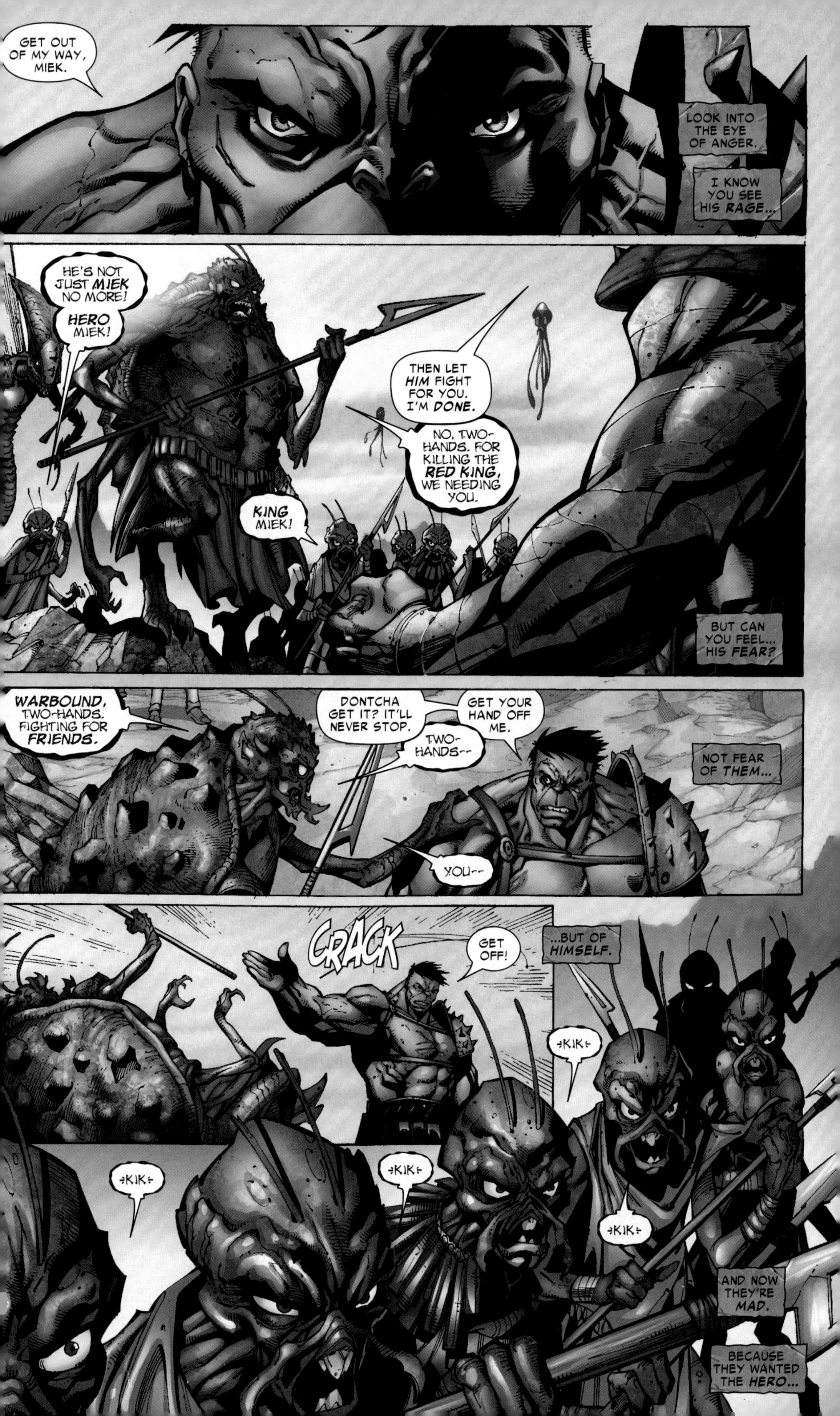
GET OUT OF MY WAY, MIEK.
LOOK INTO THE EYE OF ANGER.
I KNOW YOU SEE HIS RAGE...
HE'S NOT JUST MIEK NO MORE!
HERO MIEK!
THEN LET HIM FIGHT FOR YOU. I'M DONE.
NO, TWO-HANDS. FOR KILLING THE RED KING, WE NEEDING YOU.
KING MIEK!
BUT CAN YOU FEEL... HIS FEAR?
WARBOUND, TWO-HANDS. FIGHTING FOR FRIENDS.
DONTCHA GET IT? IT'LL NEVER STOP.
GET YOUR HAND OFF ME.
TWO-HANDS--
NOT FEAR OF THEM...
YOU--
CRACK
GET OFF!
...BUT OF HIMSELF.
KIK
KIK
KIK
KIK
AND NOW THEY'RE MAD.
BECAUSE THEY WANTED THE HERO...

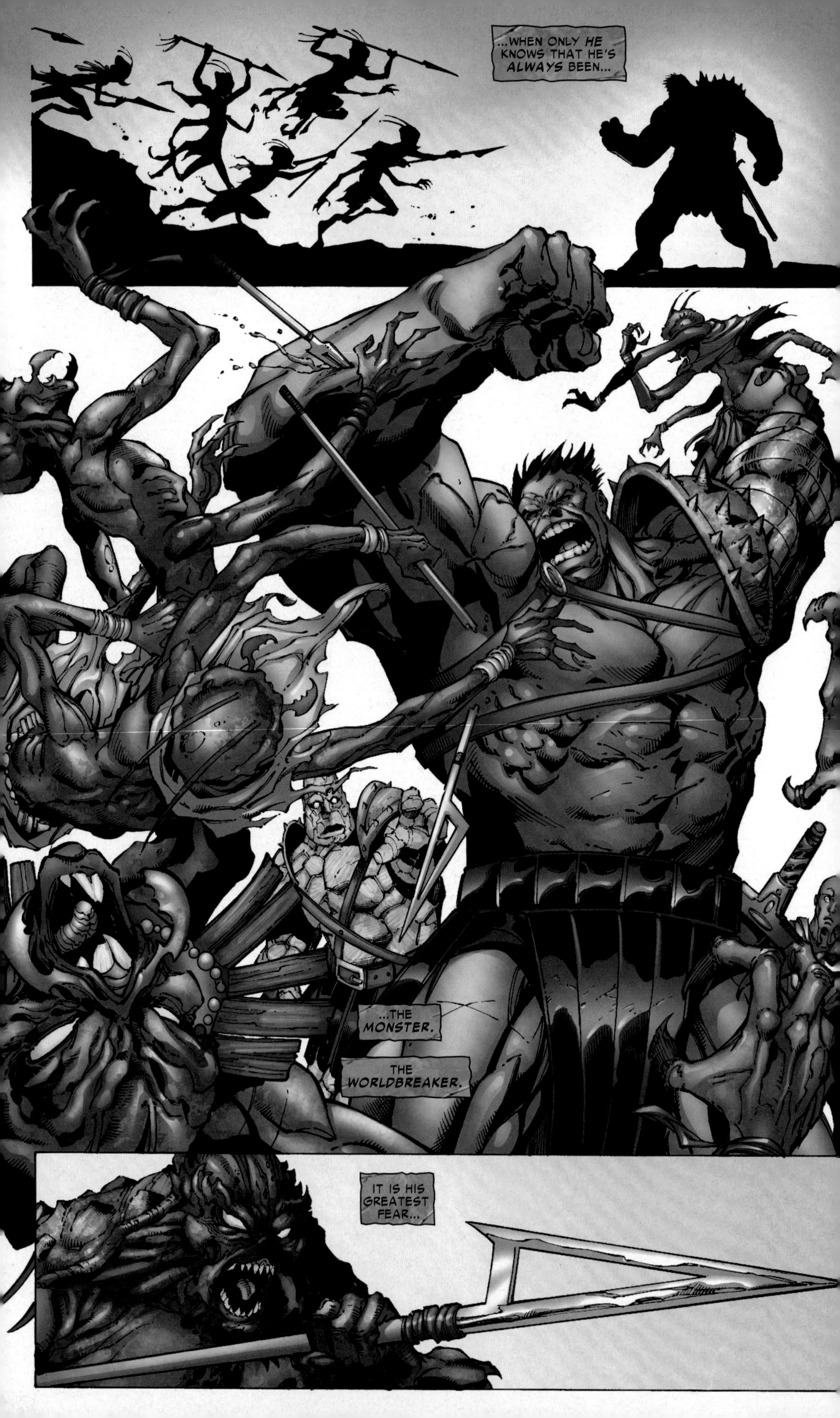
...WHEN ONLY *HE* KNOWS THAT HE'S *ALWAYS* BEEN...
...THE *MONSTER.*
THE *WORLDBREAKER.*
IT IS HIS GREATEST FEAR...

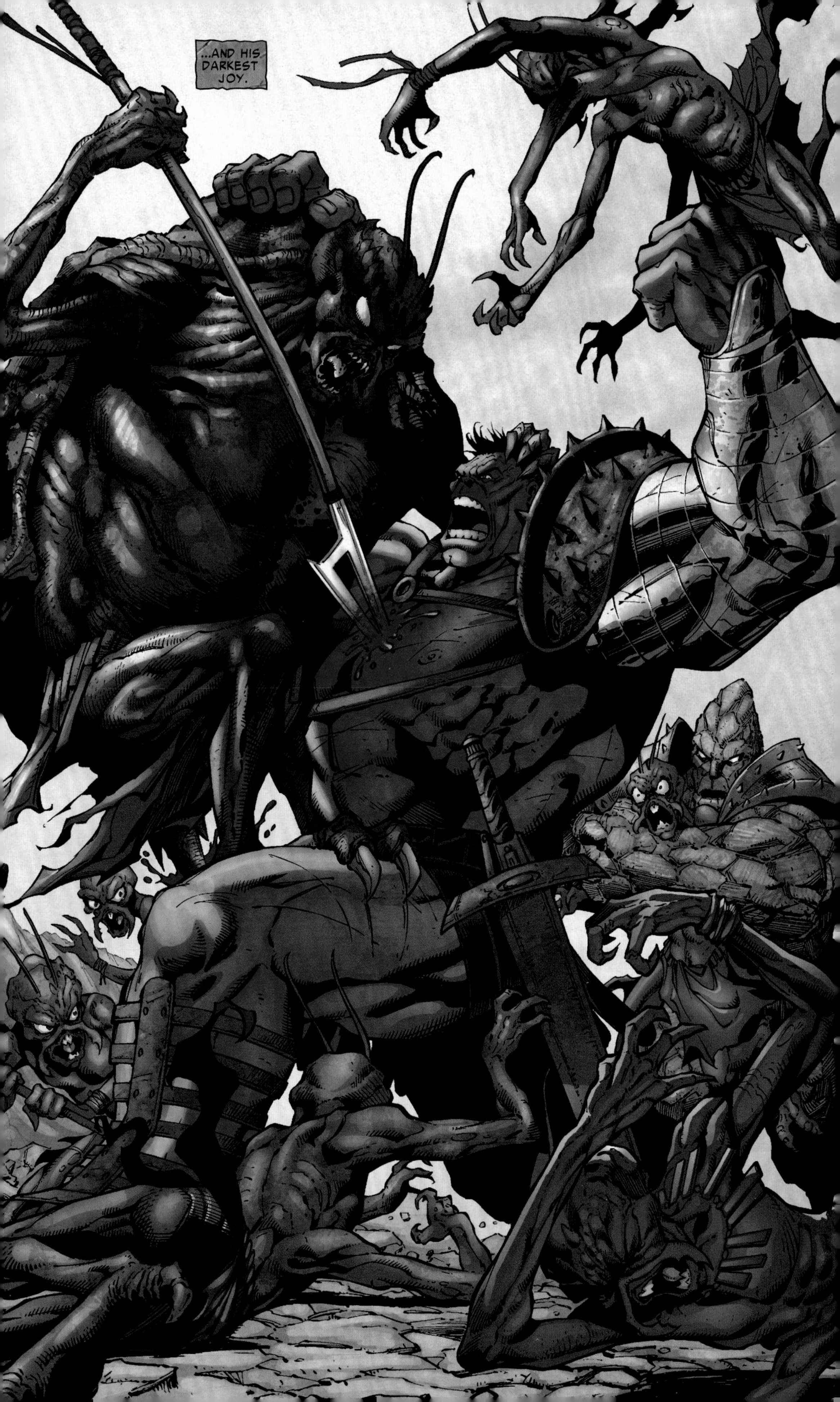
...AND HIS DARKEST JOY.

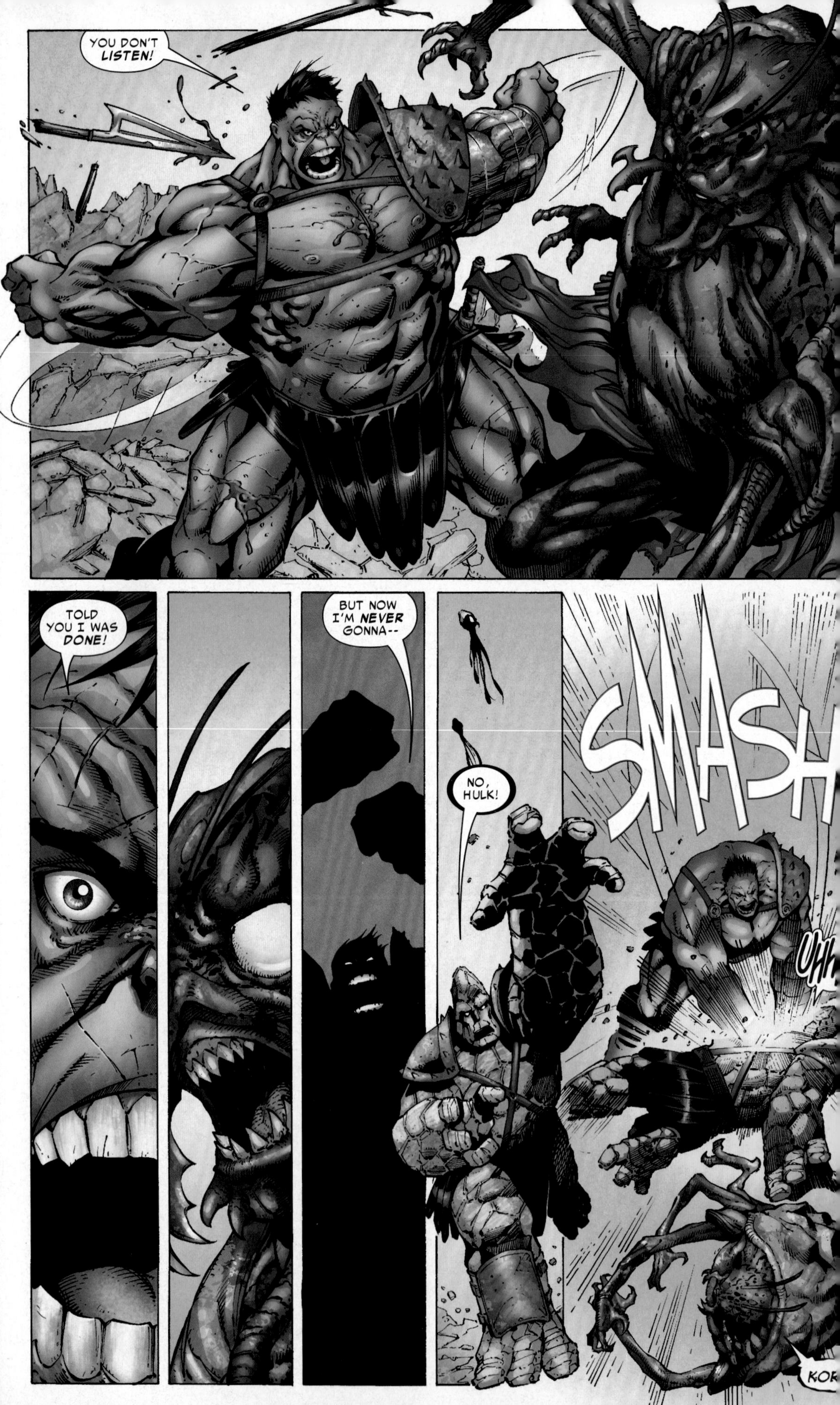
YOU DON'T LISTEN!
TOLD YOU I WAS DONE!
BUT NOW I'M NEVER GONNA--
NO, HULK!
SMASH

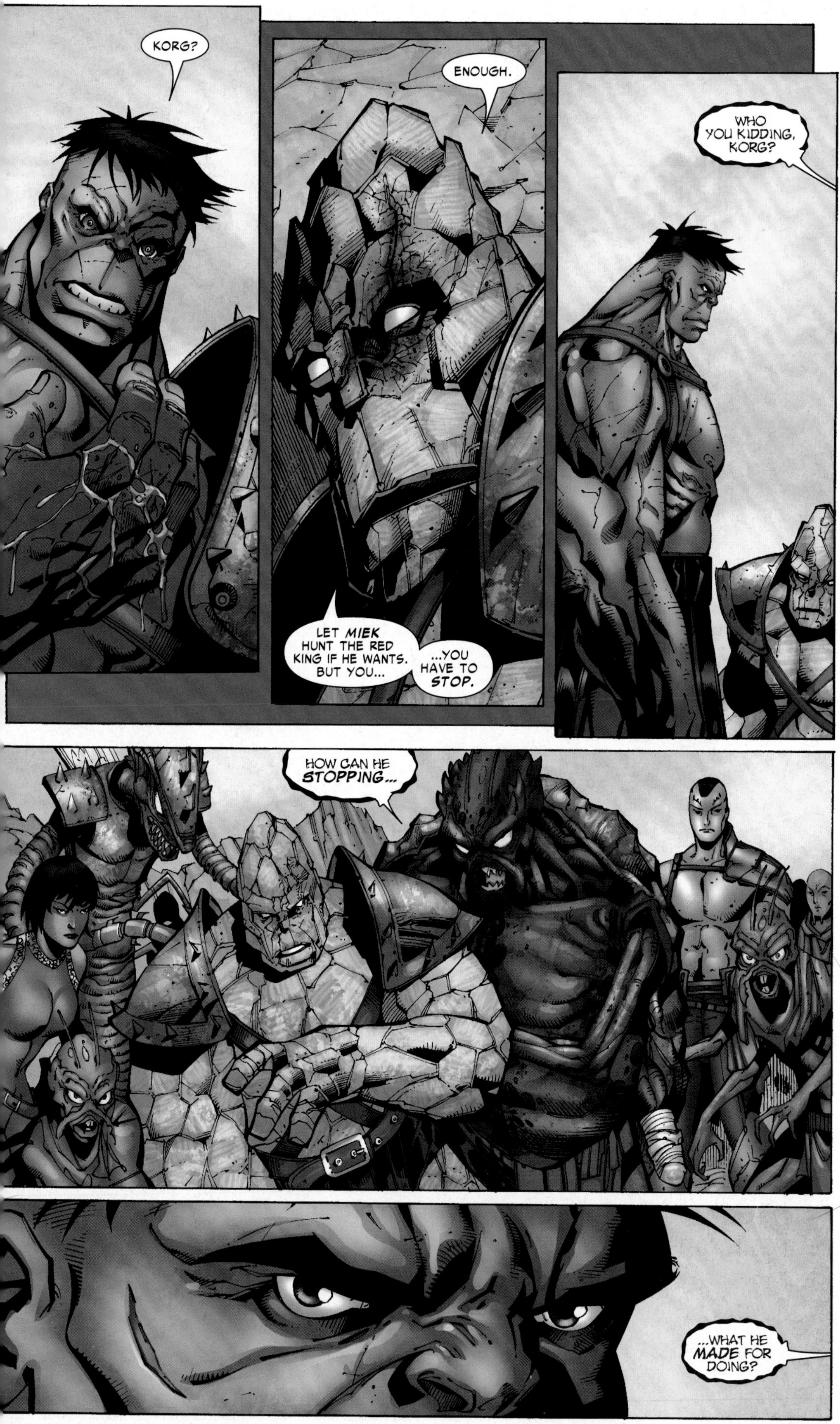
KORG?
ENOUGH.
LET MIEK HUNT THE RED KING IF HE WANTS. BUT YOU...
...YOU HAVE TO STOP.
WHO YOU KIDDING, KORG?
HOW CAN HE STOPPING...
...WHAT HE MADE FOR DOING?

EVER SINCE THE SPIKE WARS, THE STEPPES HAVE BEEN BARREN.

BUT A FEW DROPS OF THE GREEN SCAR'S BLOOD, AND THE ELEHA'AL VINES AWAKEN.

WHERE THEY GROW, OTHER PLANTS WILL FOLLOW.

THE REFUGEES... HE GIVES THEM *HOPE.* HE... GIVES *ME* HOPE.

MIEK IS WRONG. HULK SHOULD COME WITH US, INTO THE STEPPES WITH THE REFUGEES.

TO DO WHAT? PLANT CROPS? RAISE A FAMILY?

NO.

"THE GREEN SCAR GOES TO WAR."

WITH SIGNS UPON SIGNS POINTING THE WAY, HOW CAN WE HELP BUT BELIEVE? THESE ARE THE DAYS OF THE *SAKAARSON,* WHO WILL SAVE US, OR THE *WORLDBREAKER,* WHO WILL DESTROY US.

BUT THE PROPHET TELLS US TO LOOK *WITHIN* FOR THE SAKAARSON. IN OUR OWN HEARTS. WITH OUR OWN HANDS. BY OUR OWN BLOOD.

NO DESTI NO DOO FORETOLD. MAKE OU OWN CHOIC

TO SAVE OURSELVES. OR DESTROY OURSELVES.

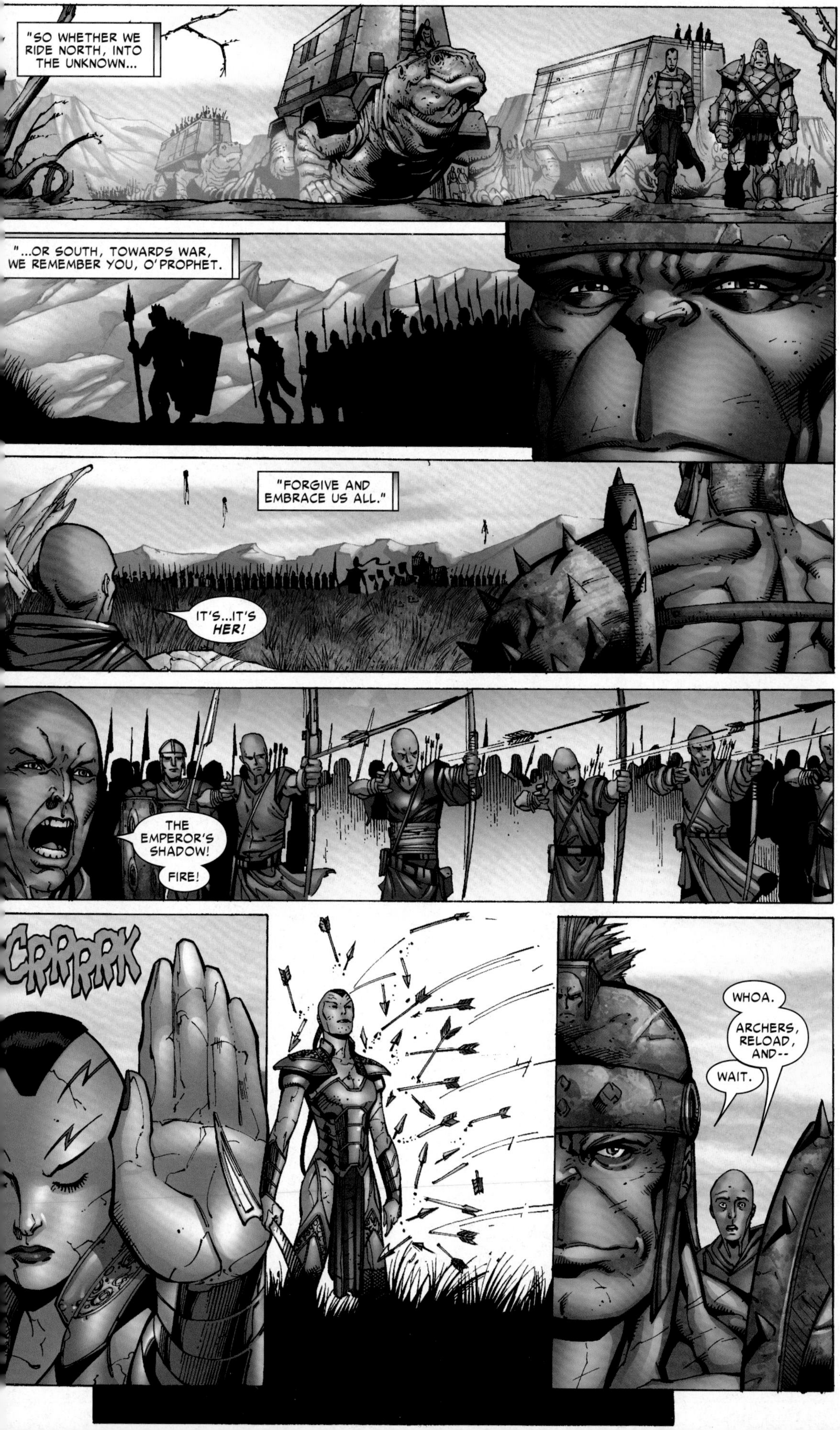

"SO WHETHER WE RIDE NORTH, INTO THE UNKNOWN...
"...OR SOUTH, TOWARDS WAR, WE REMEMBER YOU, O'PROPHET.
"FORGIVE AND EMBRACE US ALL."
IT'S...IT'S HER!
THE EMPEROR'S SHADOW!
FIRE!
CRRRRK
WHOA.
ARCHERS, RELOAD, AND--
WAIT.

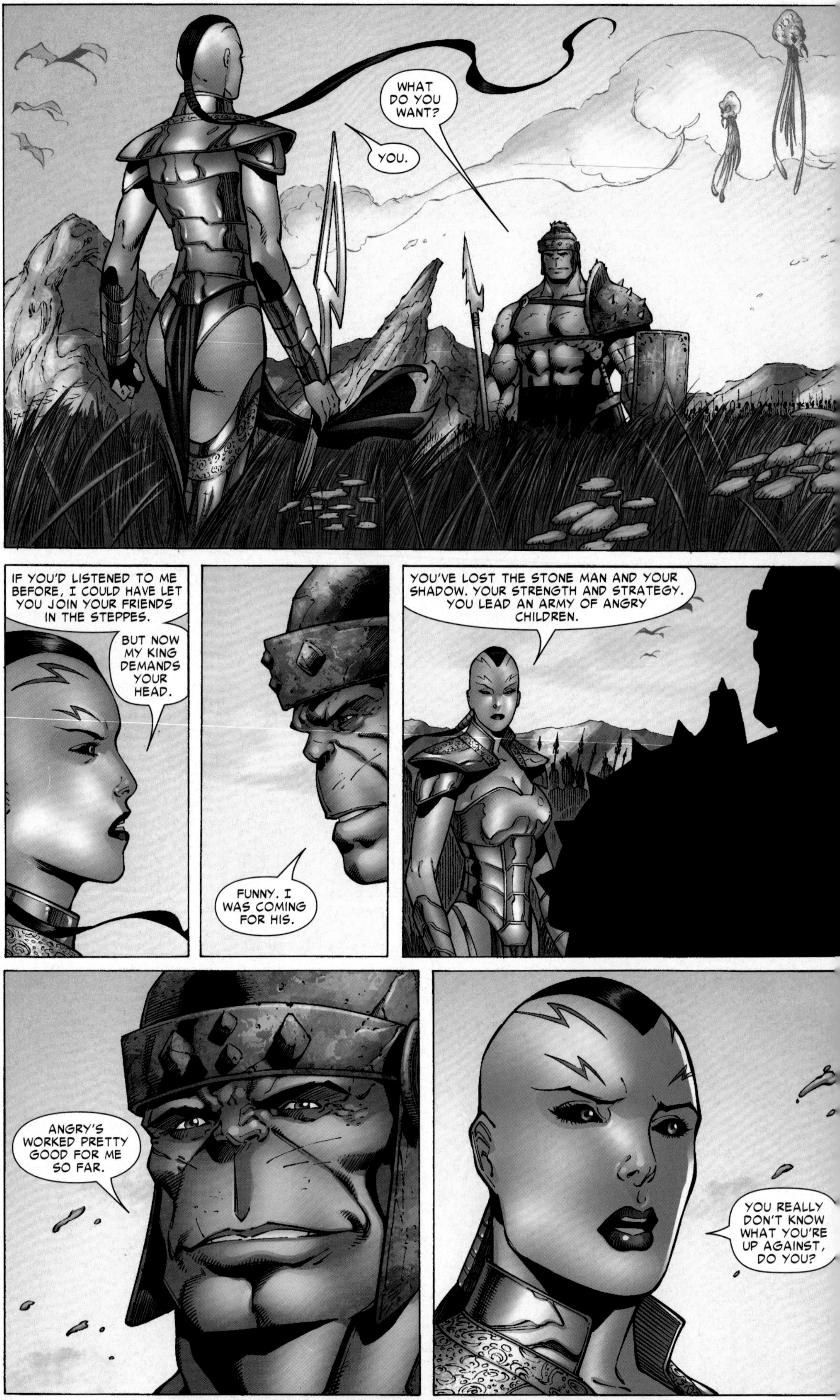
WHAT DO YOU WANT?
YOU.
IF YOU'D LISTENED TO ME BEFORE, I COULD HAVE LET YOU JOIN YOUR FRIENDS IN THE STEPPES.
BUT NOW MY KING DEMANDS YOUR HEAD.
FUNNY. I WAS COMING FOR HIS.
YOU'VE LOST THE STONE MAN AND YOUR SHADOW. YOUR STRENGTH AND STRATEGY. YOU LEAD AN ARMY OF ANGRY CHILDREN.
ANGRY'S WORKED PRETTY GOOD FOR ME SO FAR.
YOU REALLY DON'T KNOW WHAT YOU'RE UP AGAINST, DO YOU?

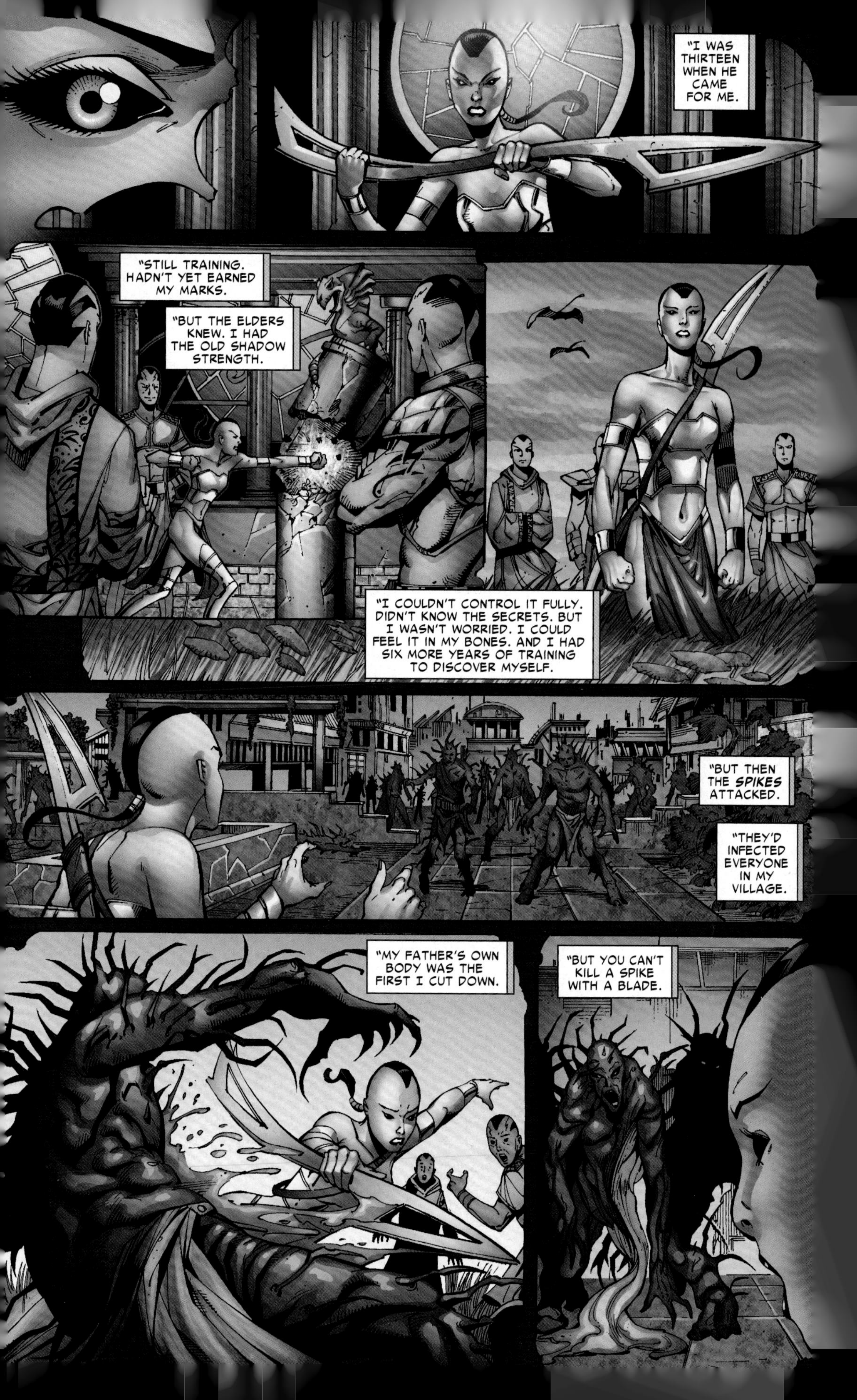
"I WAS THIRTEEN WHEN HE CAME FOR ME.
"STILL TRAINING. HADN'T YET EARNED MY MARKS.
"BUT THE ELDERS KNEW. I HAD THE OLD SHADOW STRENGTH.
"I COULDN'T CONTROL IT FULLY. DIDN'T KNOW THE SECRETS. BUT I WASN'T WORRIED. I COULD FEEL IT IN MY BONES. AND I HAD SIX MORE YEARS OF TRAINING TO DISCOVER MYSELF.
"BUT THEN THE SPIKES ATTACKED.
"THEY'D INFECTED EVERYONE IN MY VILLAGE.
"MY FATHER'S OWN BODY WAS THE FIRST I CUT DOWN.
"BUT YOU CAN'T KILL A SPIKE WITH A BLADE.

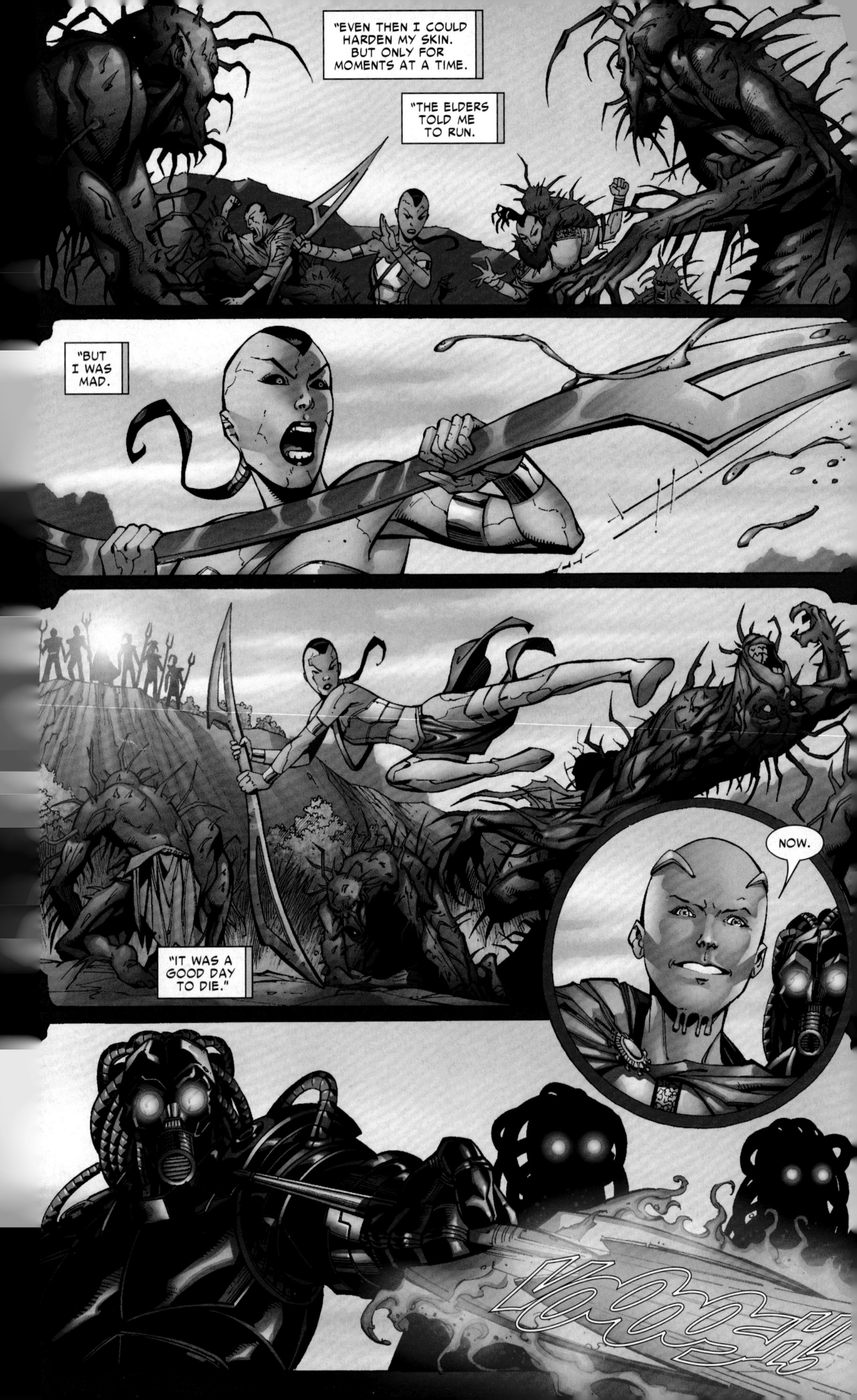
"EVEN THEN I COULD HARDEN MY SKIN. BUT ONLY FOR MOMENTS AT A TIME.
"THE ELDERS TOLD ME TO RUN.
"BUT I WAS MAD.
"IT WAS A GOOD DAY TO DIE."
NOW.

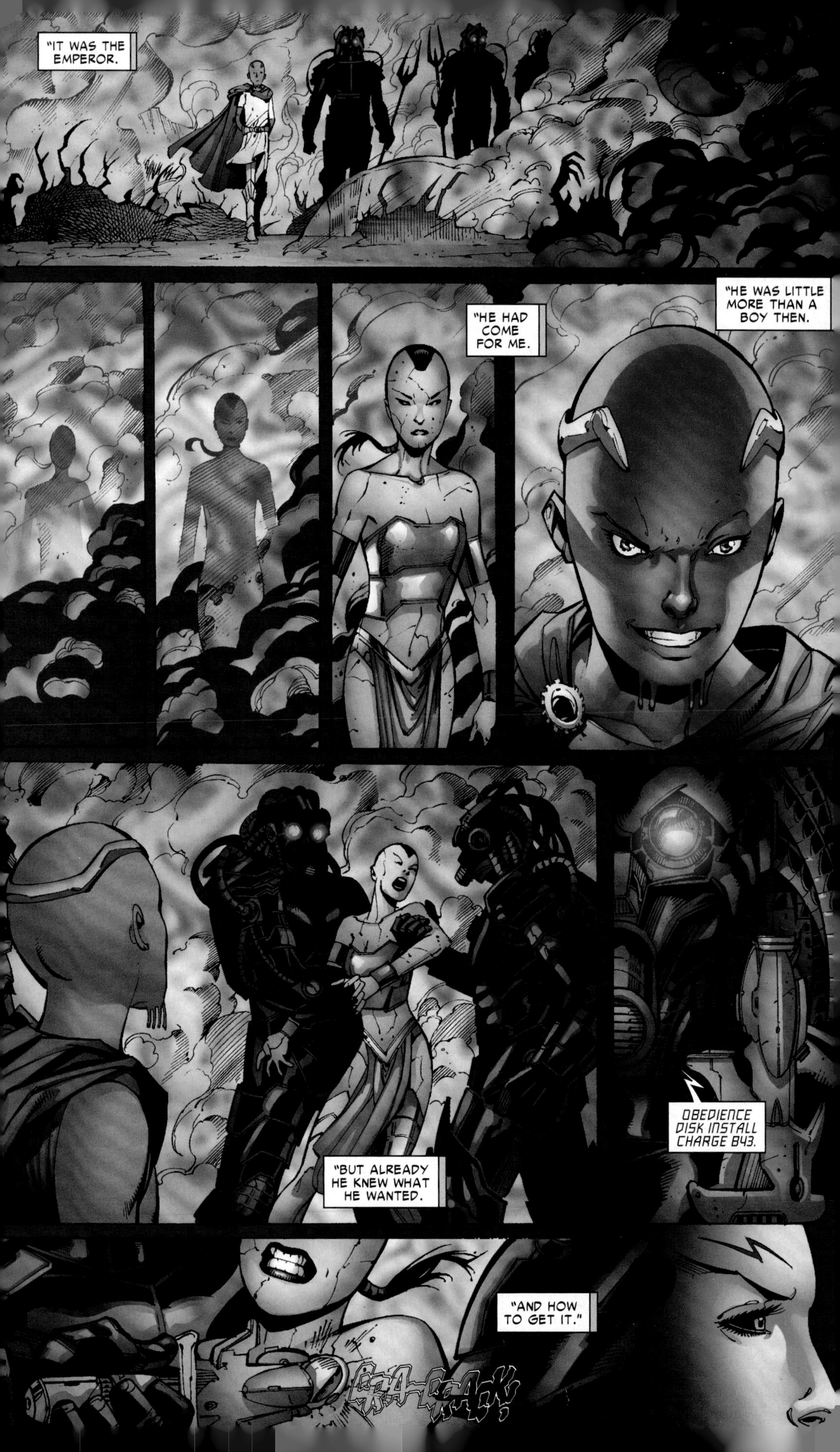
"IT WAS THE EMPEROR.
"HE HAD COME FOR ME.
"HE WAS LITTLE MORE THAN A BOY THEN.
"BUT ALREADY HE KNEW WHAT HE WANTED.
OBEDIENCE DISK INSTALL CHARGE B43.
"AND HOW TO GET IT."
CRA-CRACK!

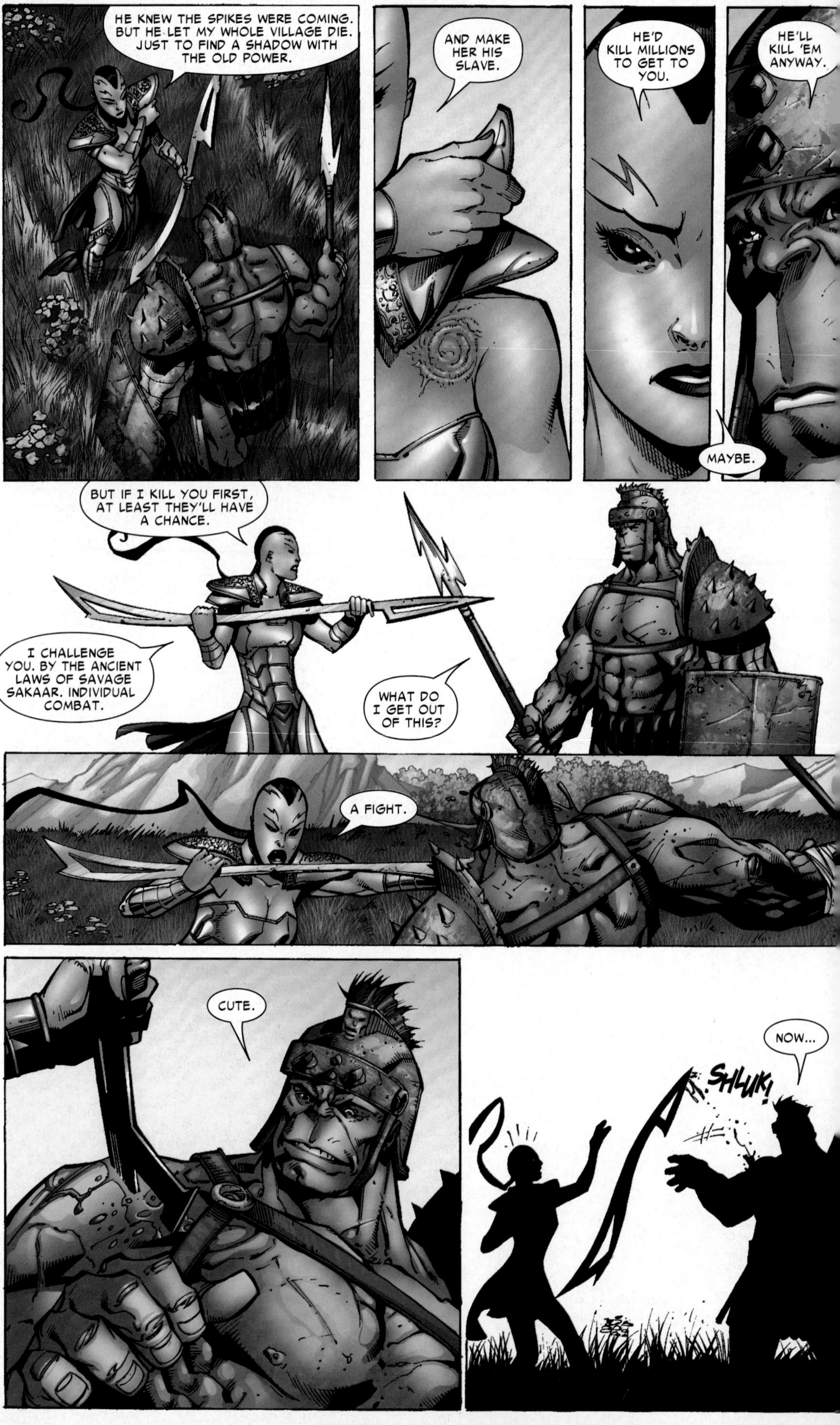
HE KNEW THE SPIKES WERE COMING. BUT HE LET MY WHOLE VILLAGE DIE. JUST TO FIND A SHADOW WITH THE OLD POWER.
AND MAKE HER HIS SLAVE.
HE'D KILL MILLIONS TO GET TO YOU.
HE'LL KILL 'EM ANYWAY.
MAYBE.
BUT IF I KILL YOU FIRST, AT LEAST THEY'LL HAVE A CHANCE.
I CHALLENGE YOU. BY THE ANCIENT LAWS OF SAVAGE SAKAAR. INDIVIDUAL COMBAT.
WHAT DO I GET OUT OF THIS?
A FIGHT.
CUTE.
NOW...
SHLUK!

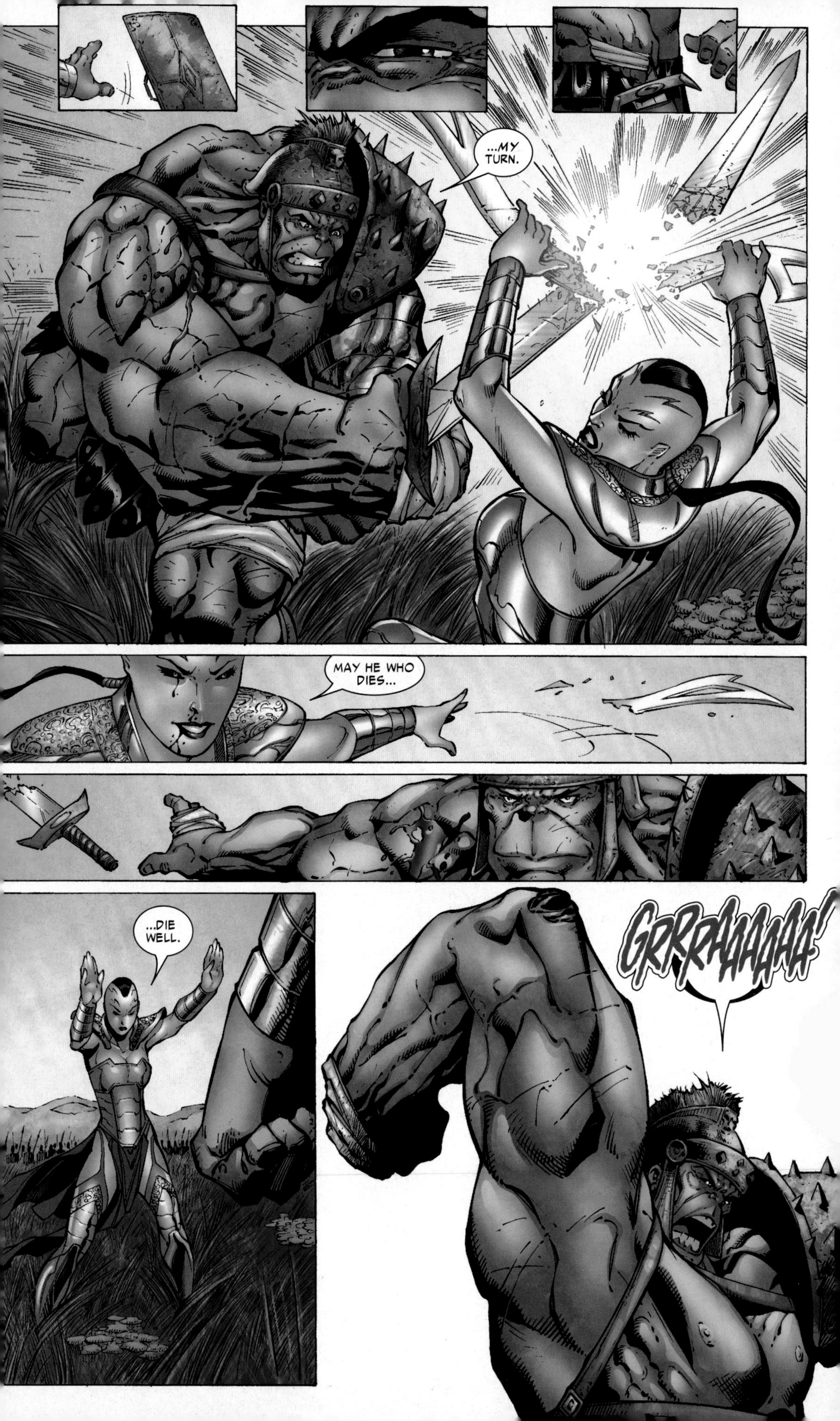
...MY TURN.
MAY HE WHO DIES...
...DIE WELL.
GRRRAAAAAA!

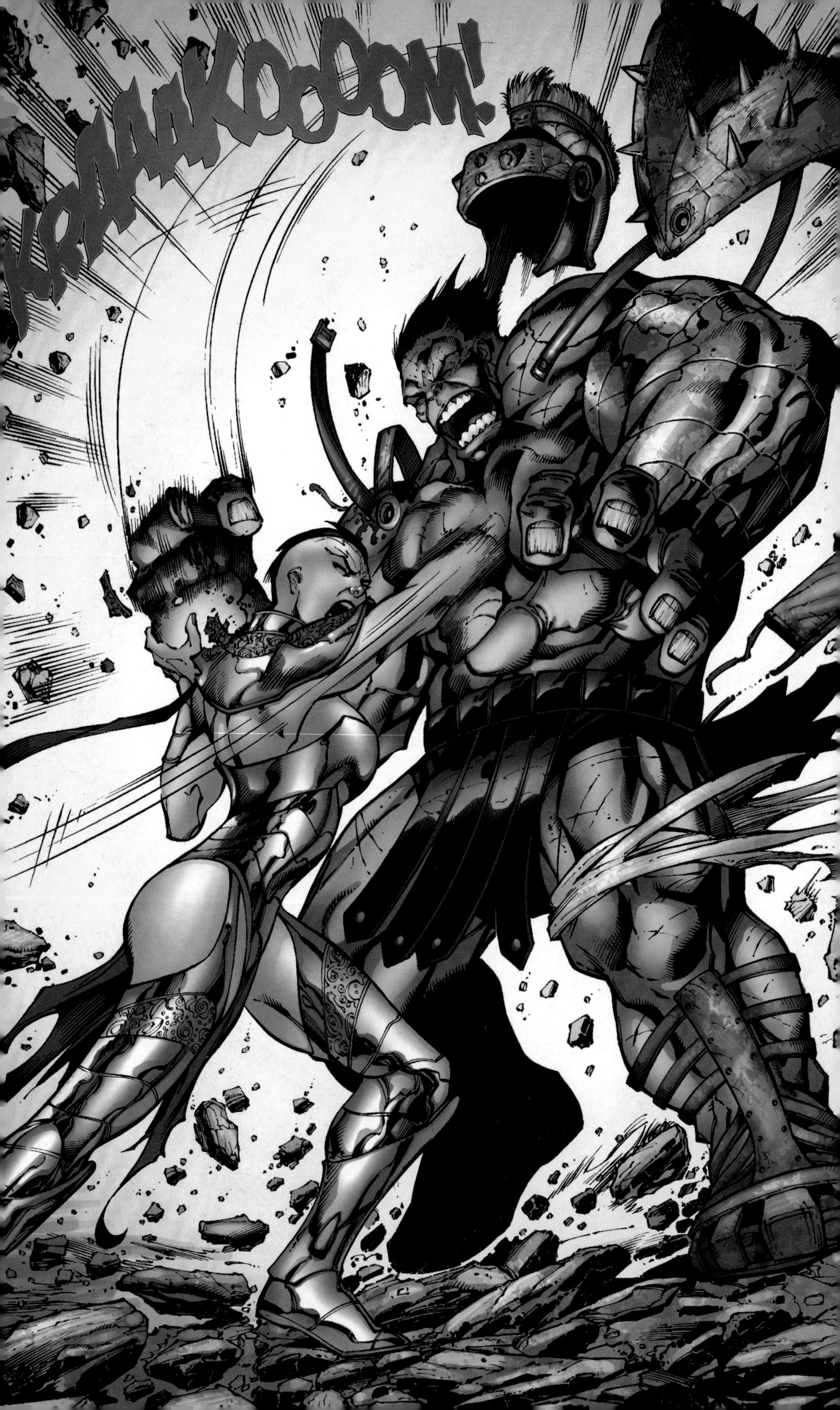
KRAAAKOOOOM!

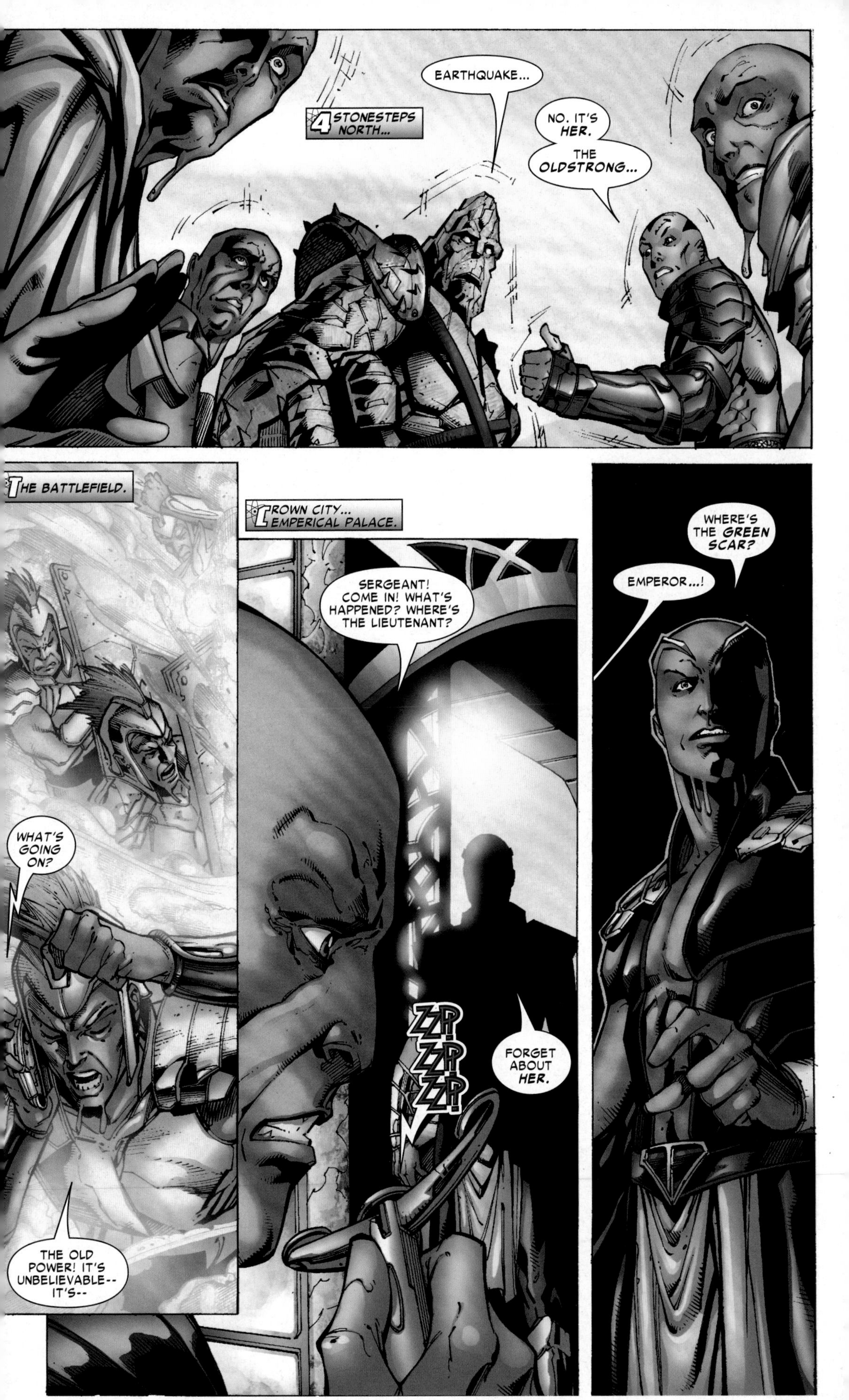
STONESTEPS NORTH...
EARTHQUAKE...
NO. IT'S HER. THE OLDSTRONG...
THE BATTLEFIELD.
WHAT'S GOING ON?
THE OLD POWER! IT'S UNBELIEVABLE-- IT'S--
CROWN CITY... EMPERICAL PALACE.
SERGEANT! COME IN! WHAT'S HAPPENED? WHERE'S THE LIEUTENANT?
ZZR! ZZR! ZZZR!
FORGET ABOUT HER.
EMPEROR...!
WHERE'S THE GREEN SCAR?

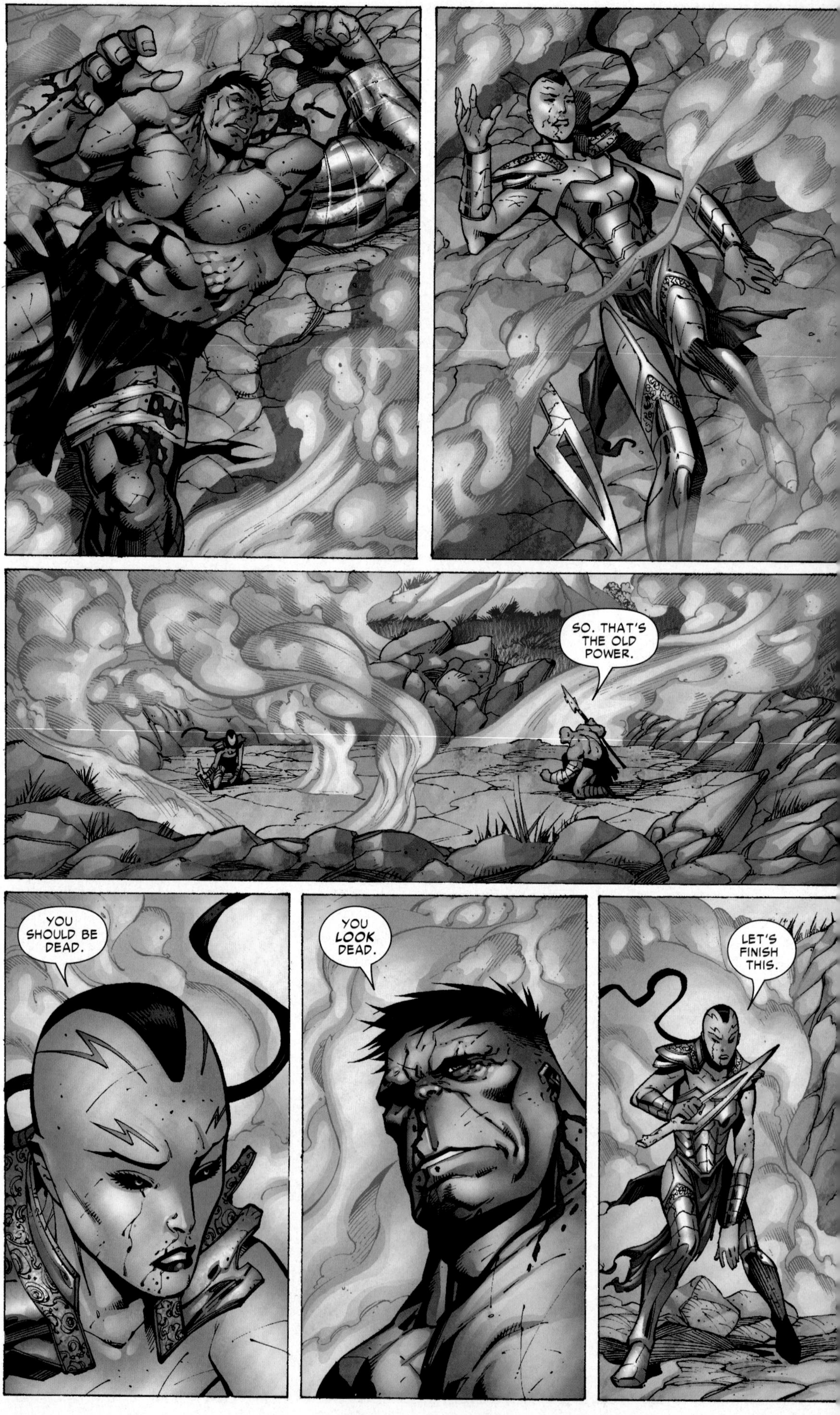
SO. THAT'S THE OLD POWER.
YOU SHOULD BE DEAD.
YOU LOOK DEAD.
LET'S FINISH THIS.

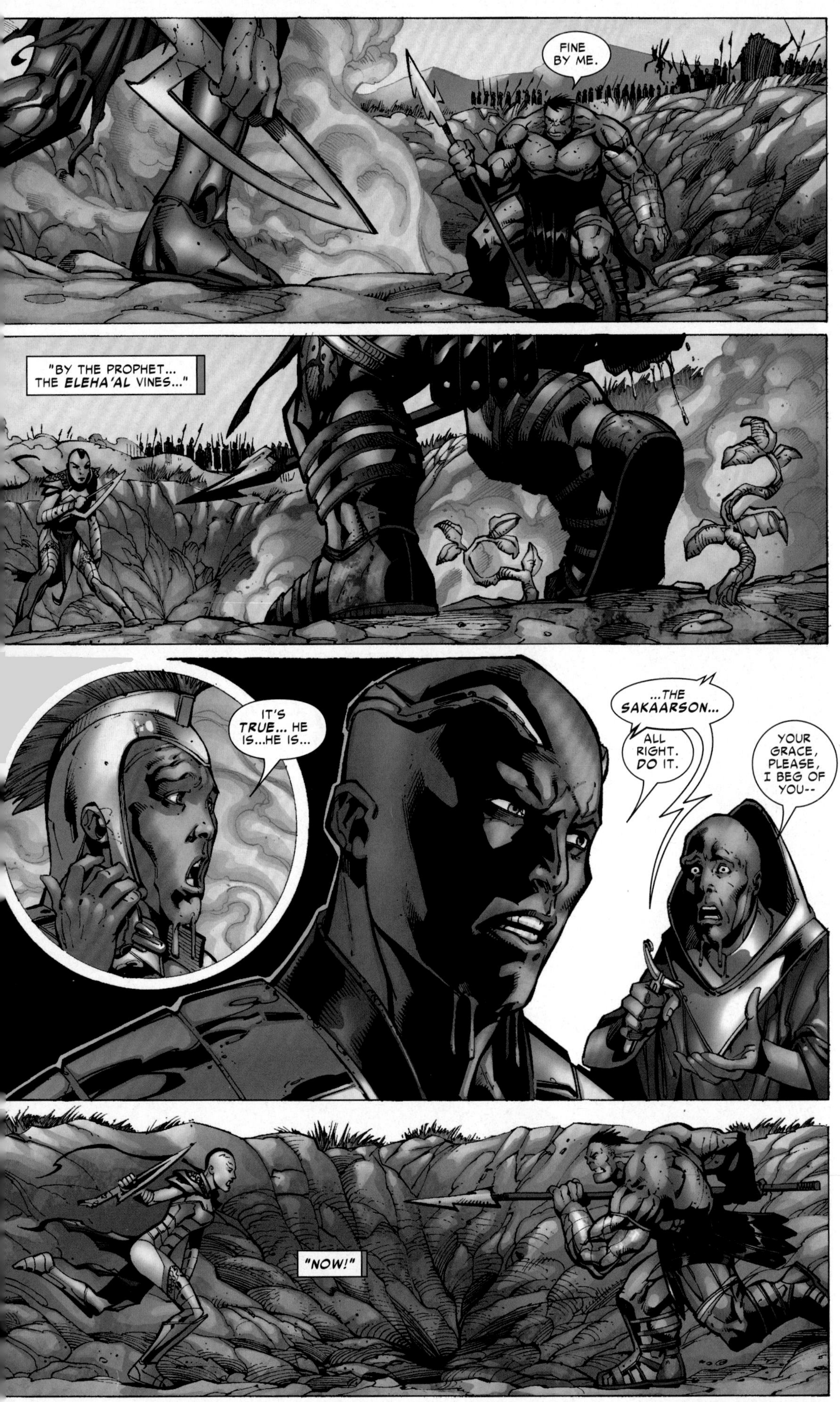
FINE BY ME.
"BY THE PROPHET... THE ELEHA'AL VINES..."
IT'S TRUE... HE IS...HE IS...
...THE SAKAARSON...
ALL RIGHT. DO IT.
YOUR GRACE, PLEASE, I BEG OF YOU--
"NOW!"

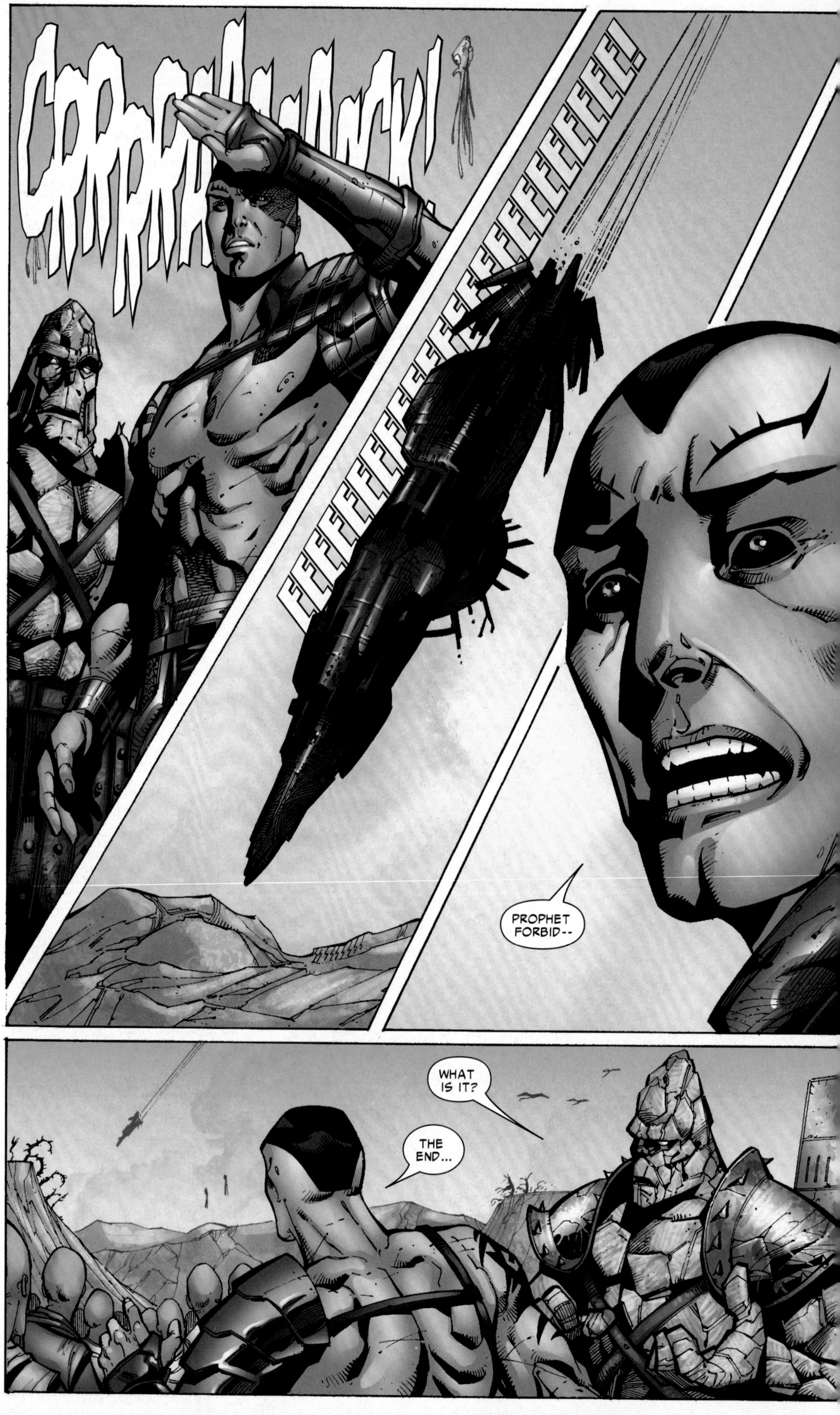
CRRRAAAACK!
EEEEEEEEEEEEEEEEEEEEEEEEEEEEE!
PROPHET FORBID--
WHAT IS IT?
THE END...

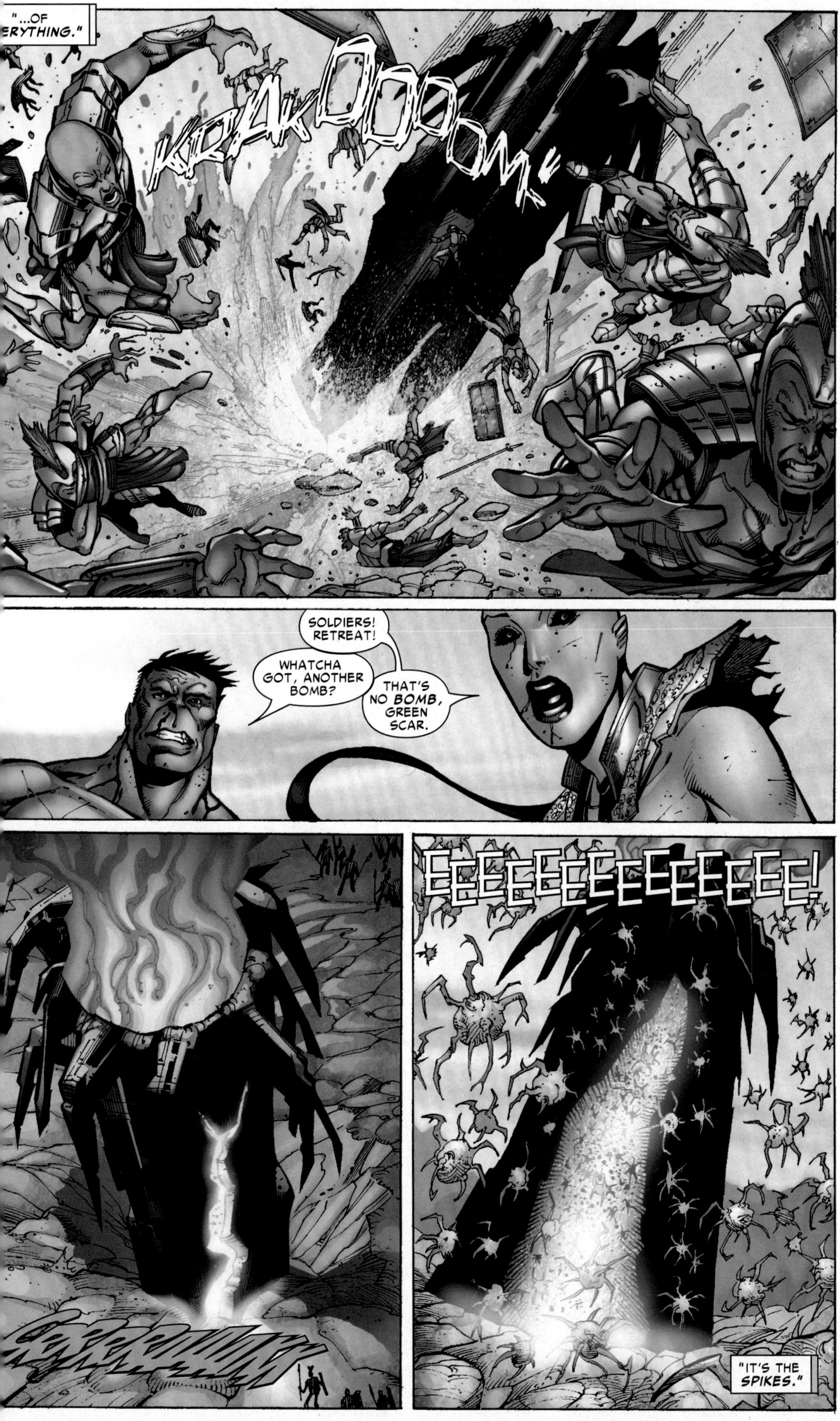

"...OF
ERYTHING."
KRAKDOOOOM!
SOLDIERS! RETREAT!
WHATCHA GOT, ANOTHER BOMB?
THAT'S NO BOMB, GREEN SCAR.
EEEEEEEEEEEEEEEE!
"IT'S THE SPIKES."

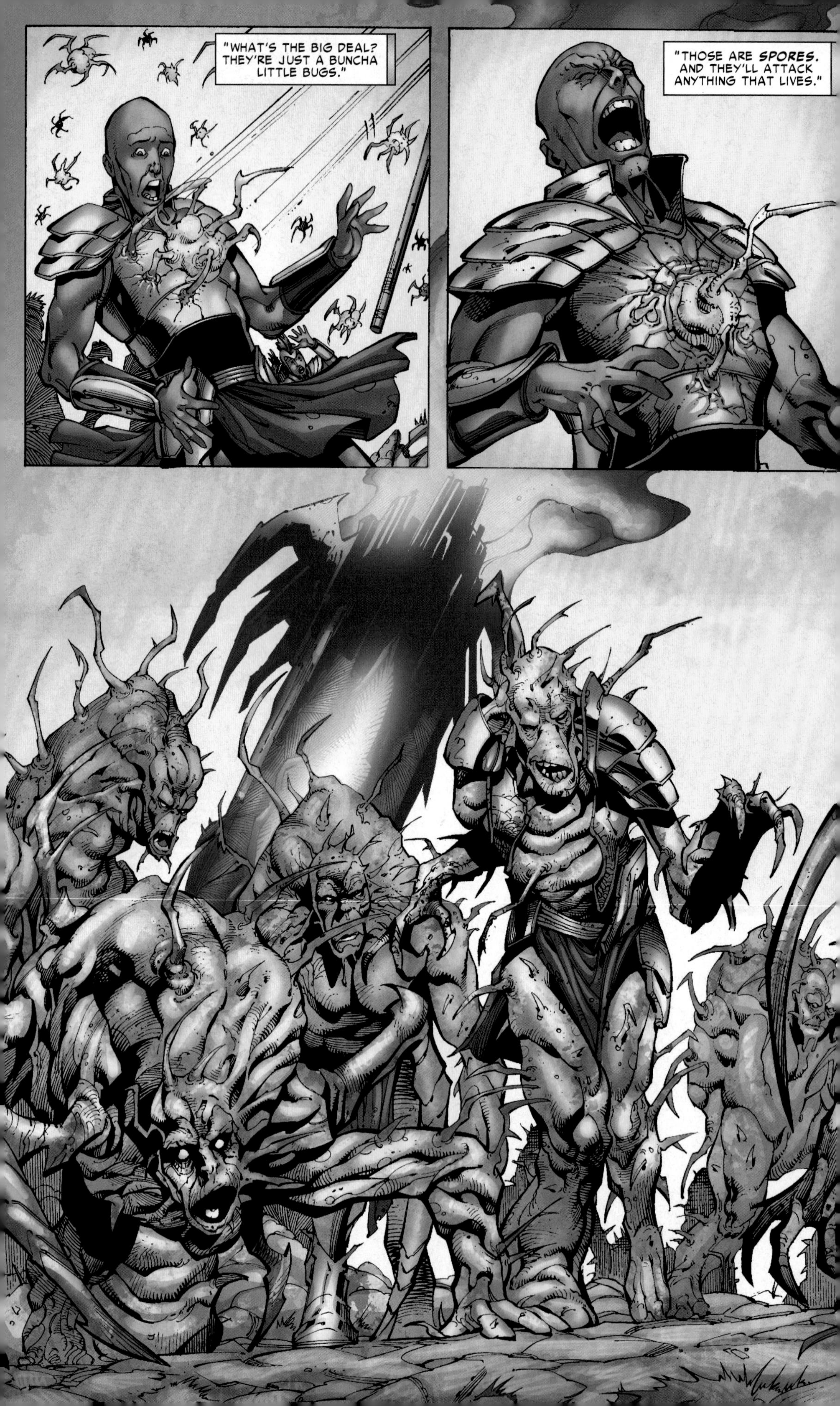
"WHAT'S THE BIG DEAL? THEY'RE JUST A BUNCHA LITTLE BUGS."
"THOSE ARE SPORES. AND THEY'LL ATTACK ANYTHING THAT LIVES."

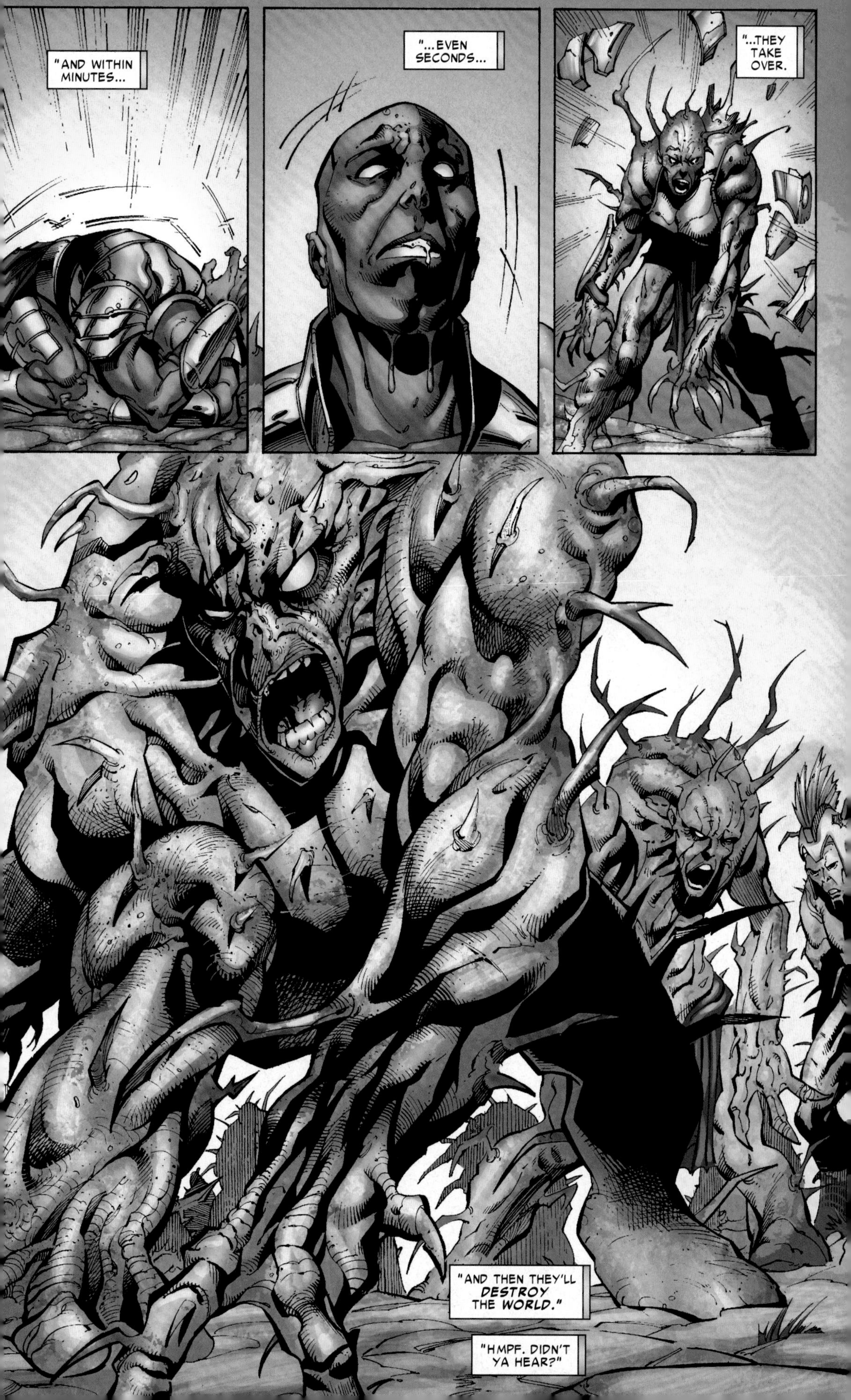
"AND WITHIN MINUTES...
"...EVEN SECONDS...
"...THEY TAKE OVER.
"AND THEN THEY'LL DESTROY THE WORLD."
"HMPF. DIDN'T YA HEAR?"

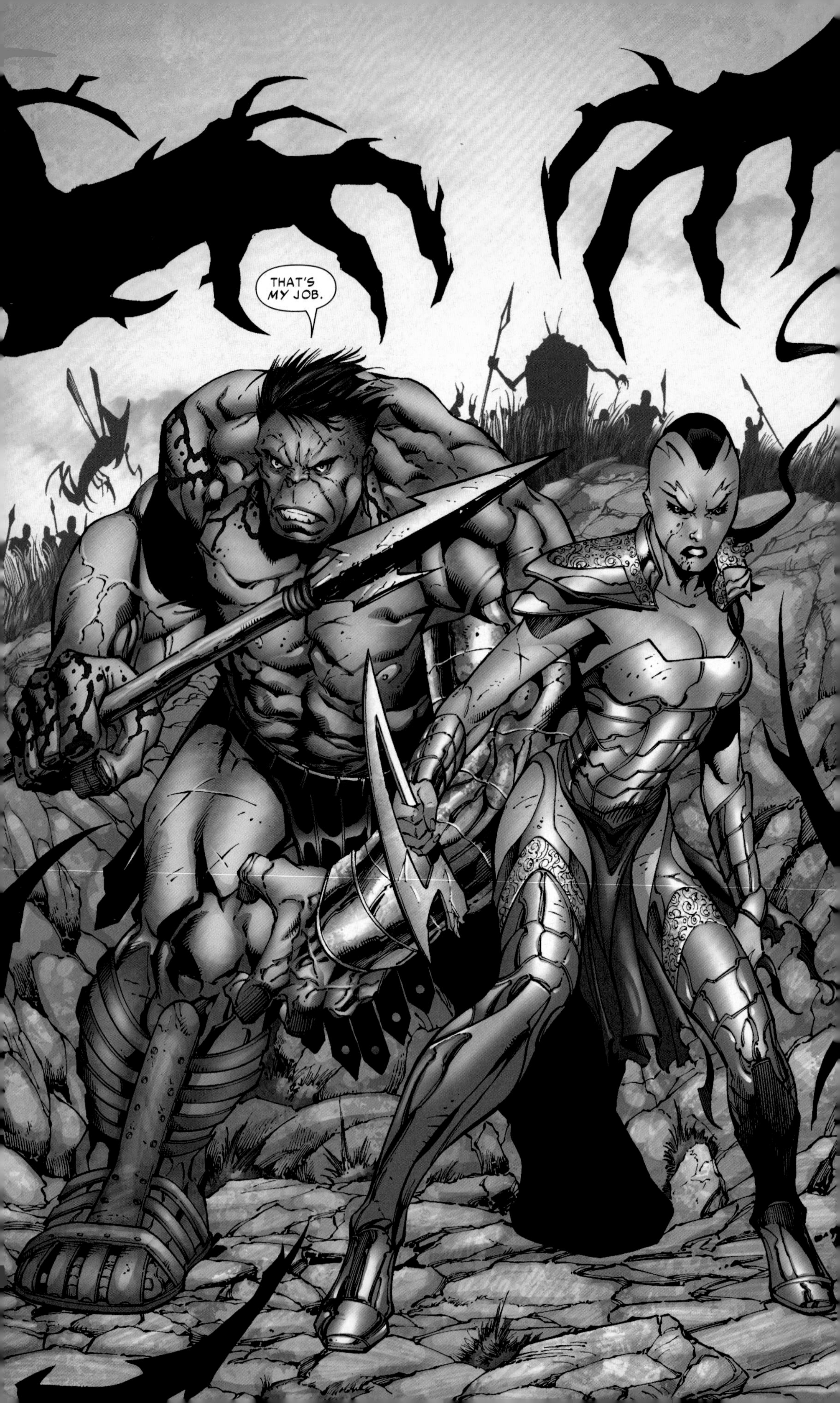
THAT'S MY JOB.

#99

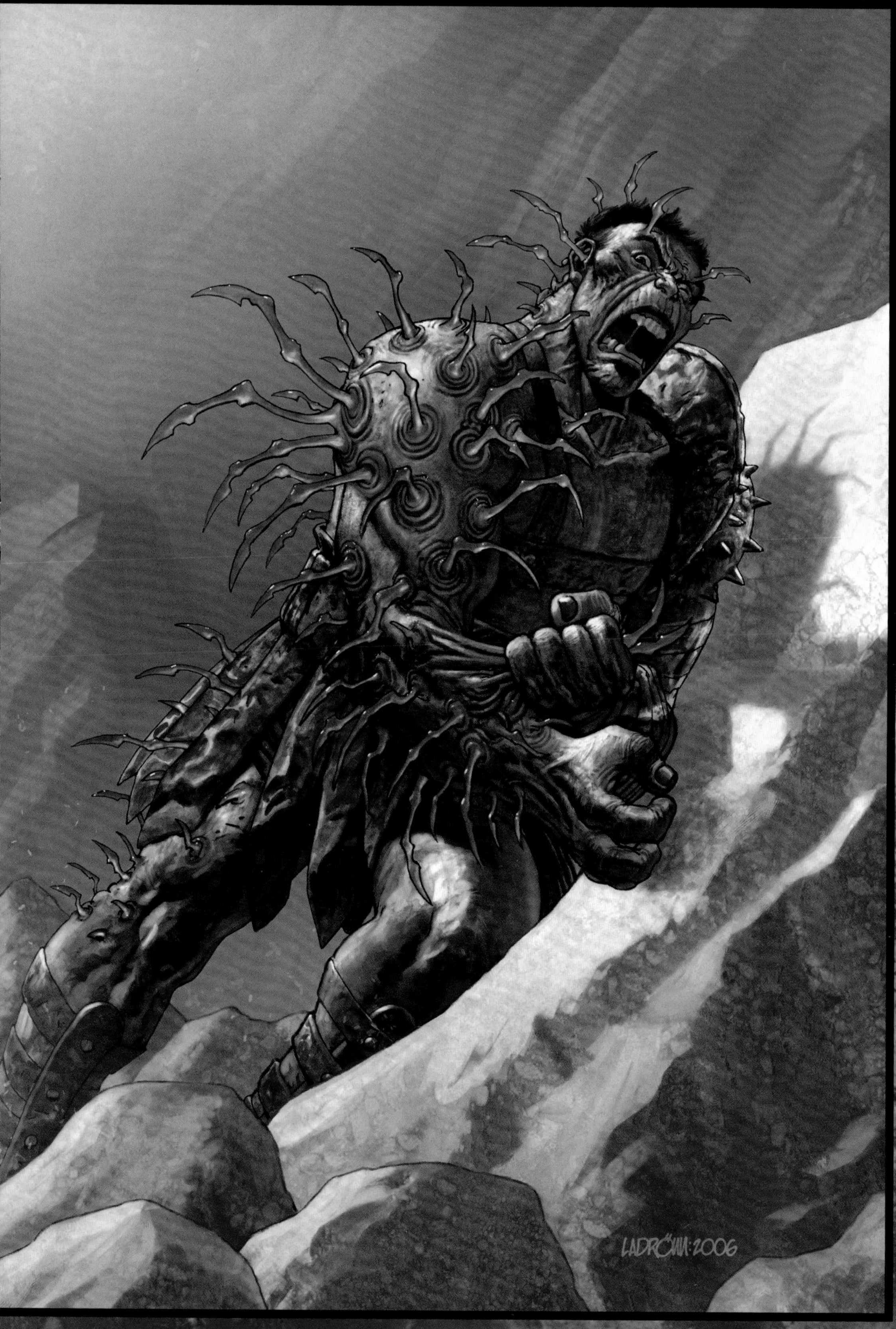
LADRÖNN·2006

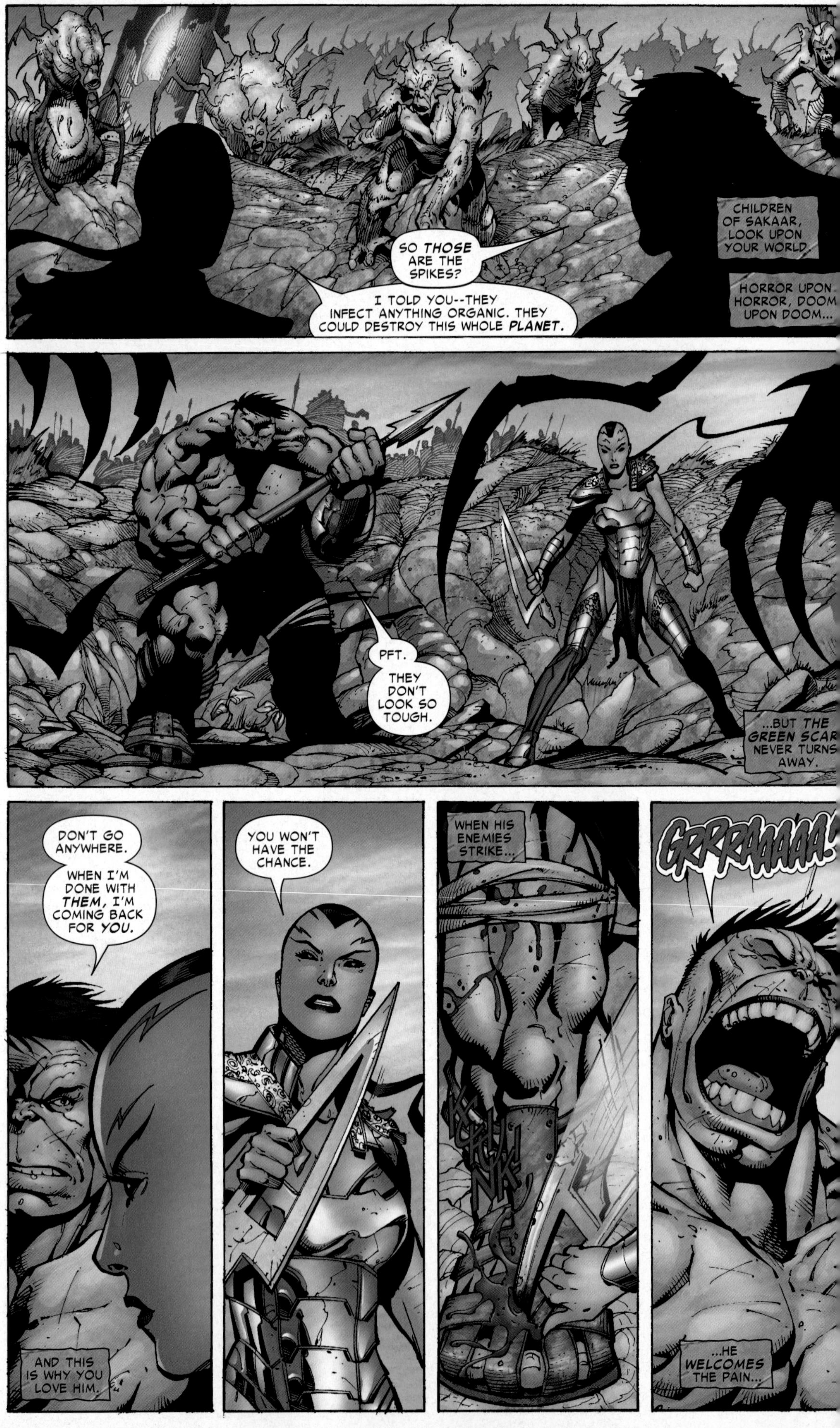
CHILDREN OF SAKAAR, LOOK UPON YOUR WORLD.
HORROR UPON HORROR, DOOM UPON DOOM...
SO THOSE ARE THE SPIKES?
I TOLD YOU--THEY INFECT ANYTHING ORGANIC. THEY COULD DESTROY THIS WHOLE PLANET.
PFT.
THEY DON'T LOOK SO TOUGH.
...BUT THE GREEN SCAR NEVER TURNS AWAY.
DON'T GO ANYWHERE.
WHEN I'M DONE WITH THEM, I'M COMING BACK FOR YOU.
AND THIS IS WHY YOU LOVE HIM.
YOU WON'T HAVE THE CHANCE.
WHEN HIS ENEMIES STRIKE...
GRRRAAAAA!
...HE WELCOMES THE PAIN...

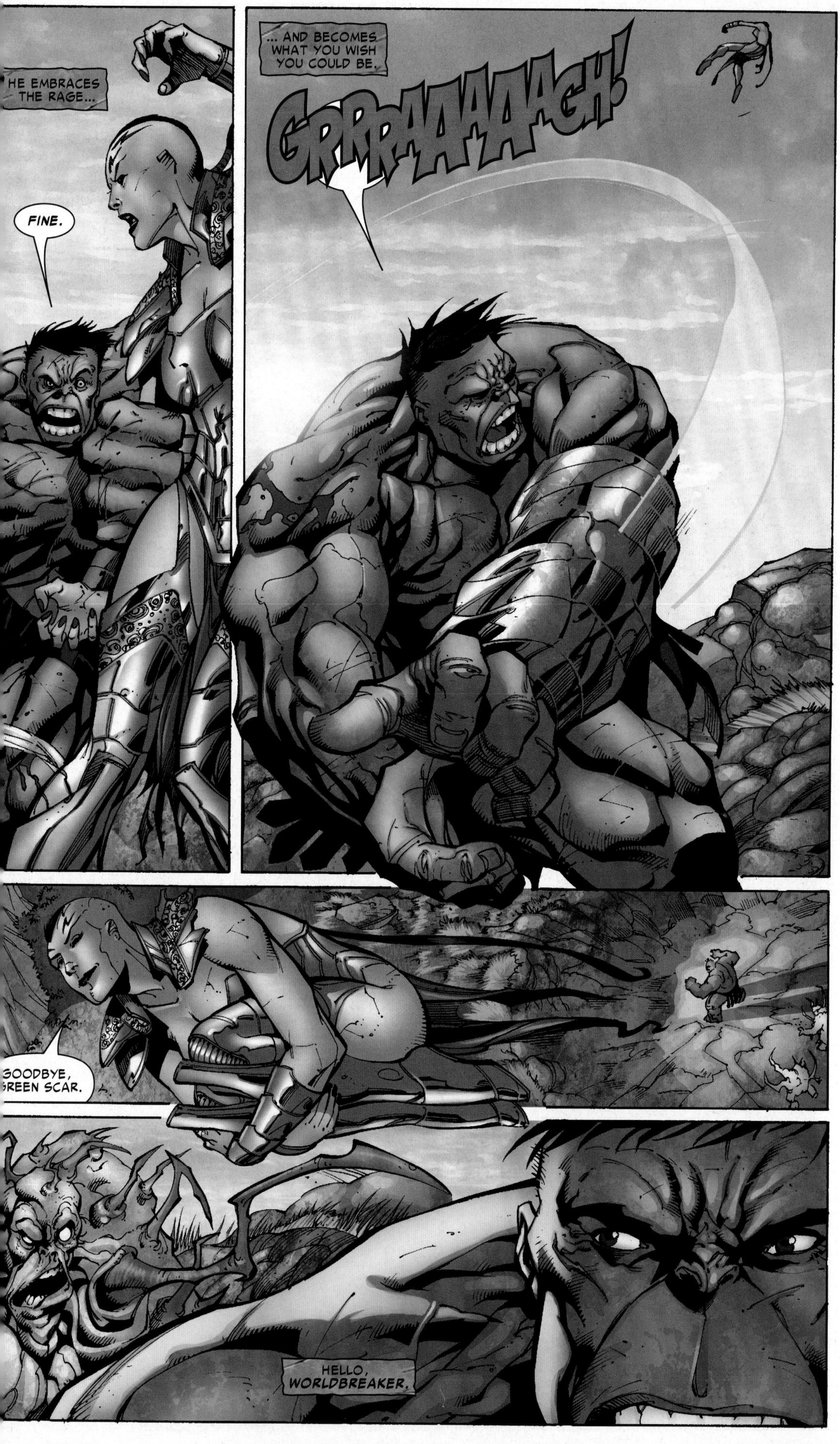
HE EMBRACES THE RAGE...
FINE.
... AND BECOMES WHAT YOU WISH YOU COULD BE.
GRRRAAAAAGH!
GOODBYE, GREEN SCAR.
HELLO, WORLDBREAKER.

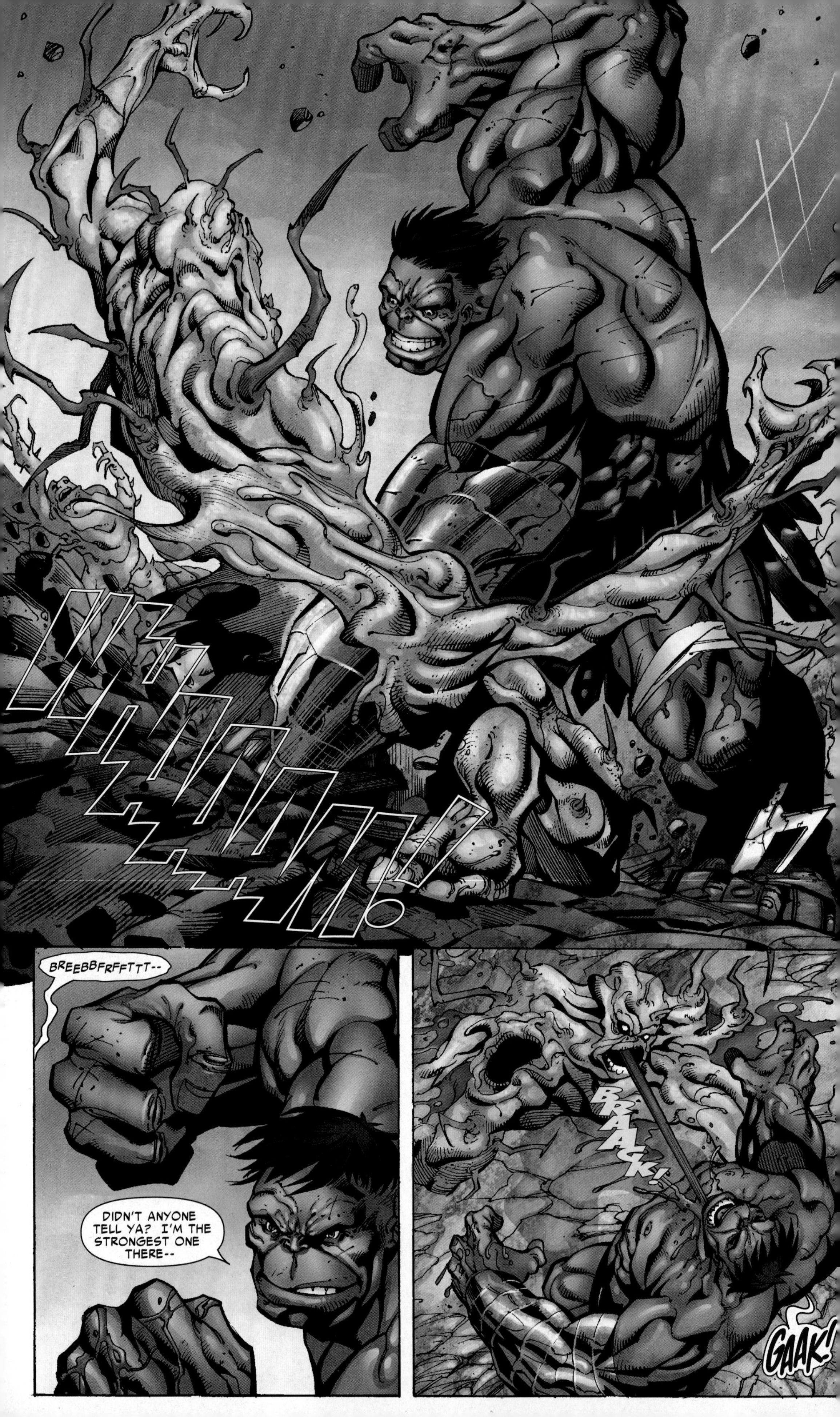
BREEBBFRFFTTT--
DIDN'T ANYONE TELL YA? I'M THE STRONGEST ONE THERE--
BRAACK!
GAAK!

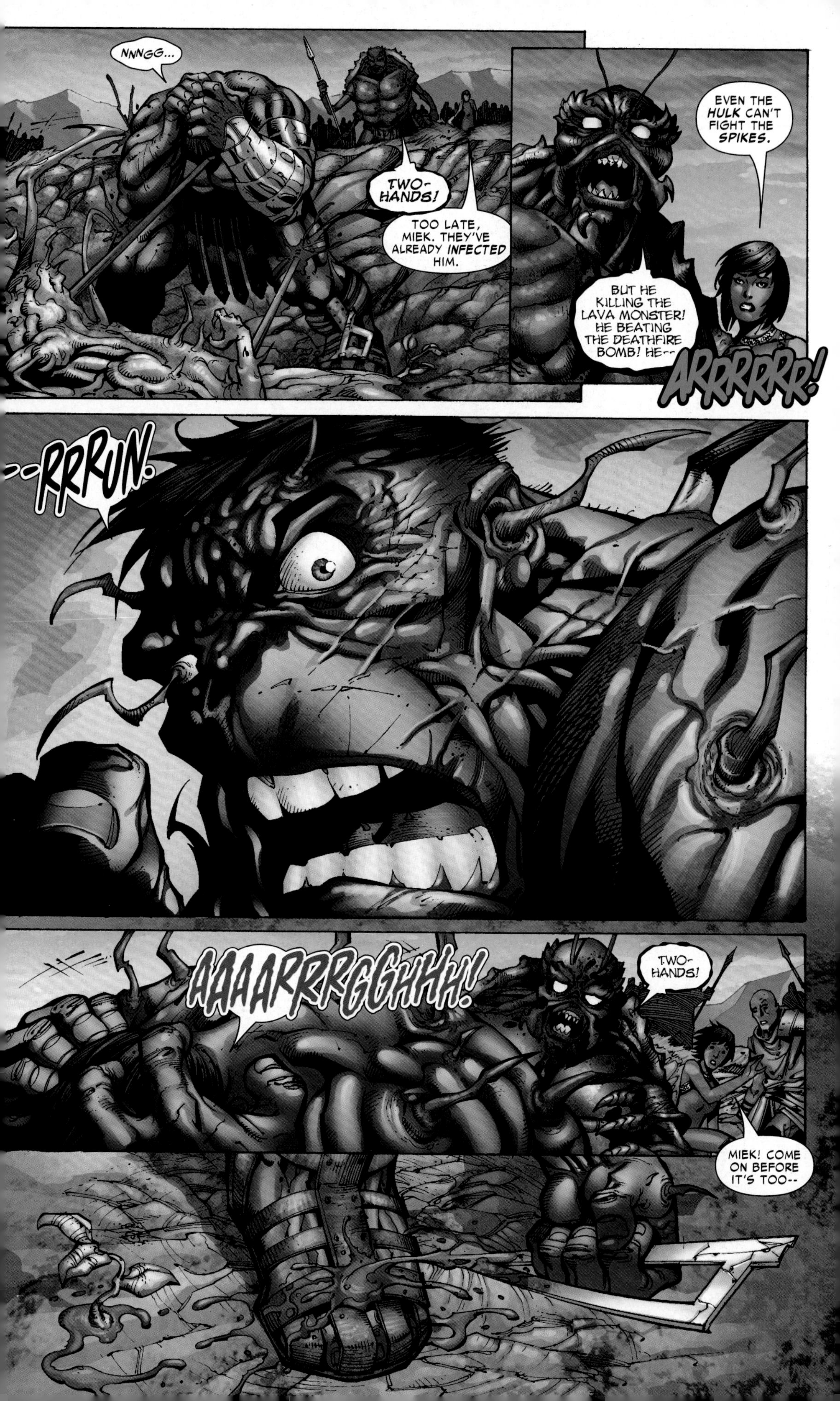
NNNGG...
TWO-HANDS!
TOO LATE, MIEK. THEY'VE ALREADY INFECTED HIM.
EVEN THE HULK CAN'T FIGHT THE SPIKES.
BUT HE KILLING THE LAVA MONSTER! HE BEATING THE DEATHFIRE BOMB! HE--
ARRRRRR!
--RRRUN.
AAAARRRGGHHH!
TWO-HANDS!
MIEK! COME ON BEFORE IT'S TOO--

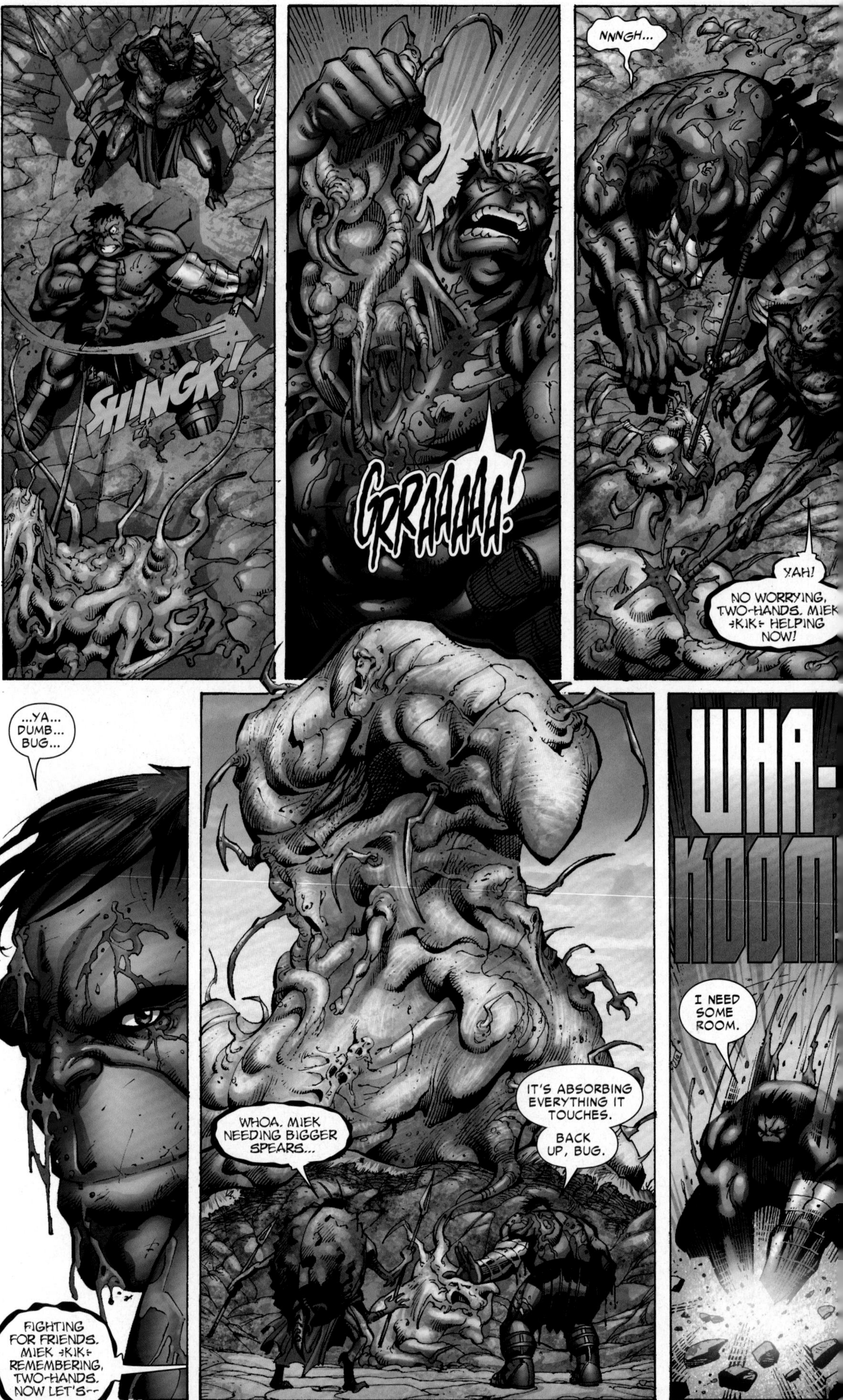
SHINGK!
GRAAAAA!
NNNGH...
YAH!
NO WORRYING, TWO-HANDS. MIEK ✢KIK✢ HELPING NOW!
...YA... DUMB... BUG...
FIGHTING FOR FRIENDS. MIEK ✢KIK✢ REMEMBERING, TWO-HANDS. NOW LET'S--
WHOA. MIEK NEEDING BIGGER SPEARS...
IT'S ABSORBING EVERYTHING IT TOUCHES.
BACK UP, BUG.
WHA-KOOM
I NEED SOME ROOM.

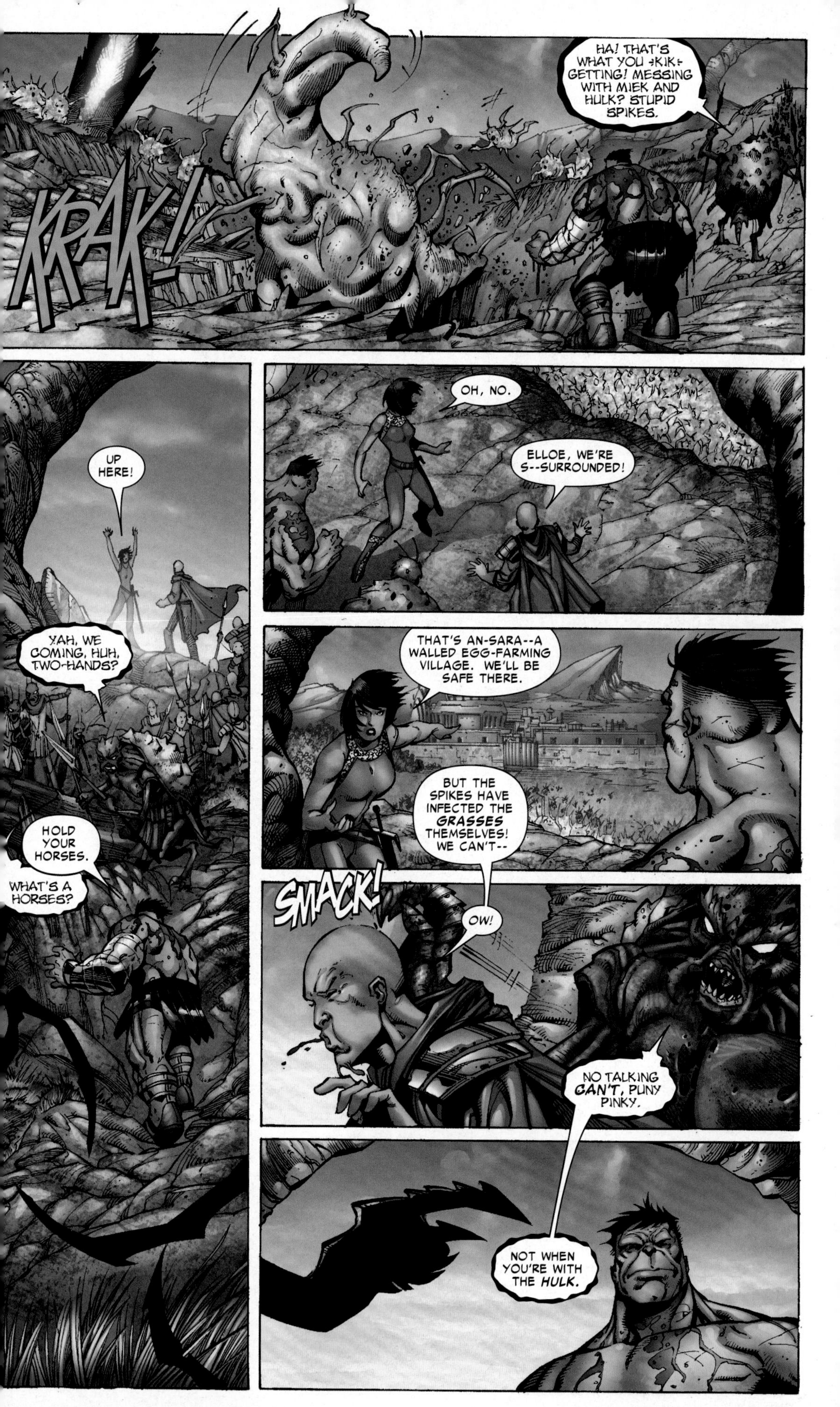
KRAK!
HA! THAT'S WHAT YOU ⁜KIK⁜ GETTING! MESSING WITH MIEK AND HULK? STUPID SPIKES.
UP HERE!
OH, NO.
ELLOE, WE'RE S--SURROUNDED!
YAH, WE COMING, HUH, TWO-HANDS?
HOLD YOUR HORSES.
WHAT'S A HORSES?
THAT'S AN-SARA--A WALLED EGG-FARMING VILLAGE. WE'LL BE SAFE THERE.
BUT THE SPIKES HAVE INFECTED THE GRASSES THEMSELVES! WE CAN'T--
SMACK!
OW!
NO TALKING CAN'T, PUNY PINKY.
NOT WHEN YOU'RE WITH THE HULK.

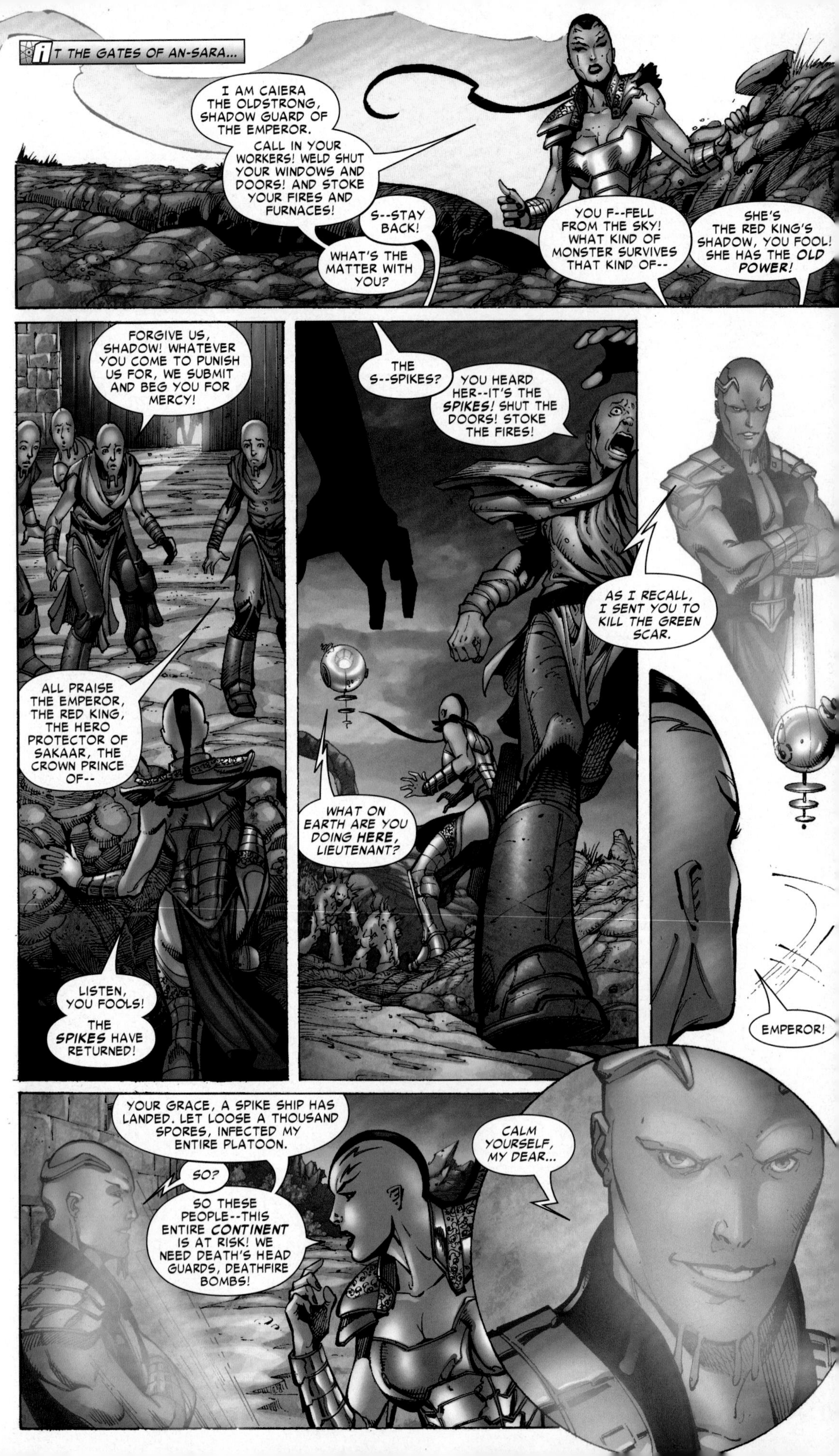
AT THE GATES OF AN-SARA...
I AM CAIERA THE OLDSTRONG, SHADOW GUARD OF THE EMPEROR.
CALL IN YOUR WORKERS! WELD SHUT YOUR WINDOWS AND DOORS! AND STOKE YOUR FIRES AND FURNACES!
S--STAY BACK!
WHAT'S THE MATTER WITH YOU?
YOU F--FELL FROM THE SKY! WHAT KIND OF MONSTER SURVIVES THAT KIND OF--
SHE'S THE RED KING'S SHADOW, YOU FOOL! SHE HAS THE OLD POWER!
FORGIVE US, SHADOW! WHATEVER YOU COME TO PUNISH US FOR, WE SUBMIT AND BEG YOU FOR MERCY!
ALL PRAISE THE EMPEROR, THE RED KING, THE HERO PROTECTOR OF SAKAAR, THE CROWN PRINCE OF--
LISTEN, YOU FOOLS!
THE SPIKES HAVE RETURNED!
THE S--SPIKES?
YOU HEARD HER--IT'S THE SPIKES! SHUT THE DOORS! STOKE THE FIRES!
WHAT ON EARTH ARE YOU DOING HERE, LIEUTENANT?
AS I RECALL, I SENT YOU TO KILL THE GREEN SCAR.
EMPEROR!
YOUR GRACE, A SPIKE SHIP HAS LANDED. LET LOOSE A THOUSAND SPORES, INFECTED MY ENTIRE PLATOON.
SO?
SO THESE PEOPLE--THIS ENTIRE CONTINENT IS AT RISK! WE NEED DEATH'S HEAD GUARDS, DEATHFIRE BOMBS!
CALM YOURSELF, MY DEAR...

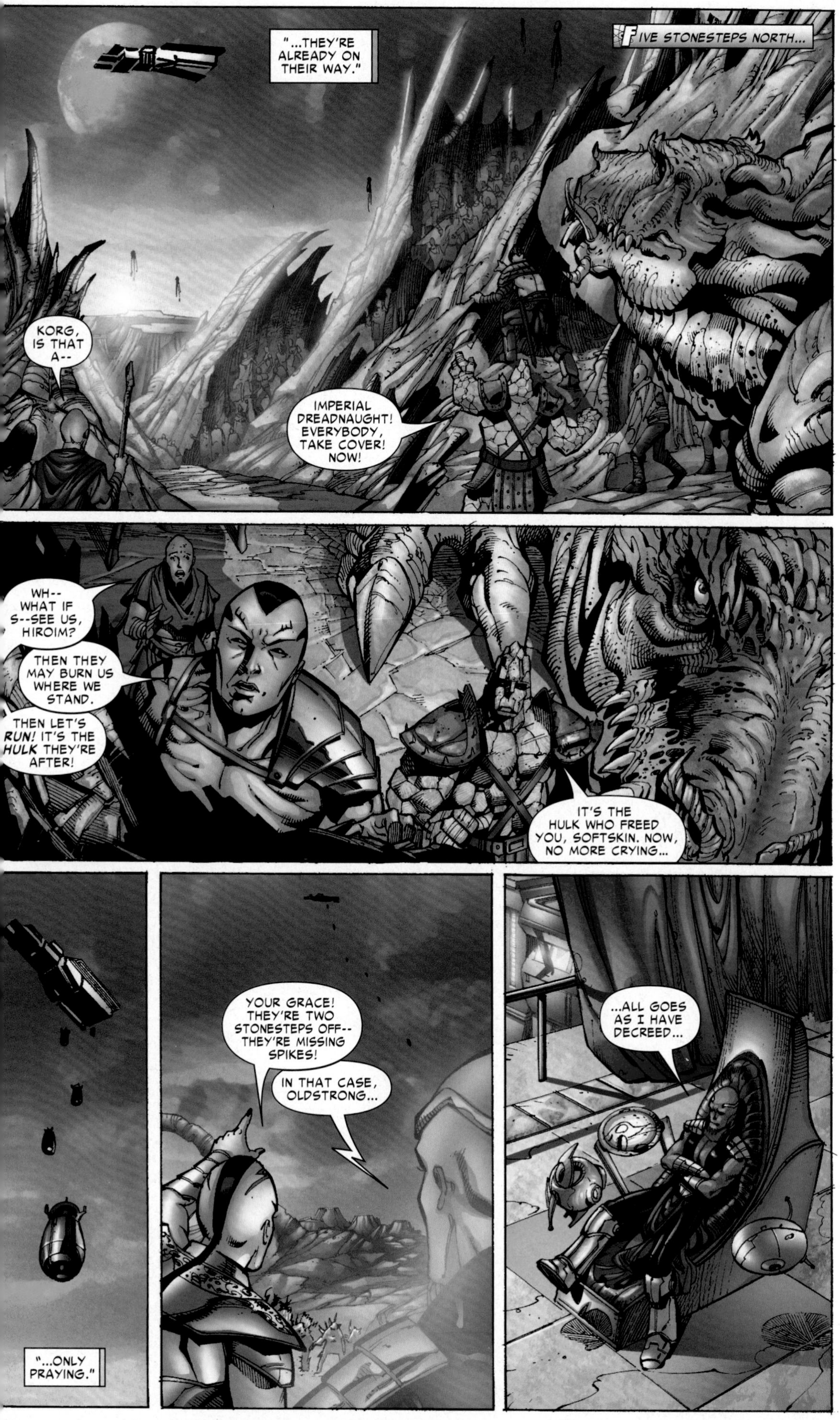
FIVE STONESTEPS NORTH...
"...THEY'RE ALREADY ON THEIR WAY."
KORG, IS THAT A--
IMPERIAL DREADNAUGHT! EVERYBODY, TAKE COVER! NOW!
WH-- WHAT IF S--SEE US, HIROIM?
THEN THEY MAY BURN US WHERE WE STAND.
THEN LET'S RUN! IT'S THE HULK THEY'RE AFTER!
IT'S THE HULK WHO FREED YOU, SOFTSKIN. NOW, NO MORE CRYING...
"...ONLY PRAYING."
YOUR GRACE! THEY'RE TWO STONESTEPS OFF-- THEY'RE MISSING SPIKES!
IN THAT CASE, OLDSTRONG...
...ALL GOES AS I HAVE DECREED...

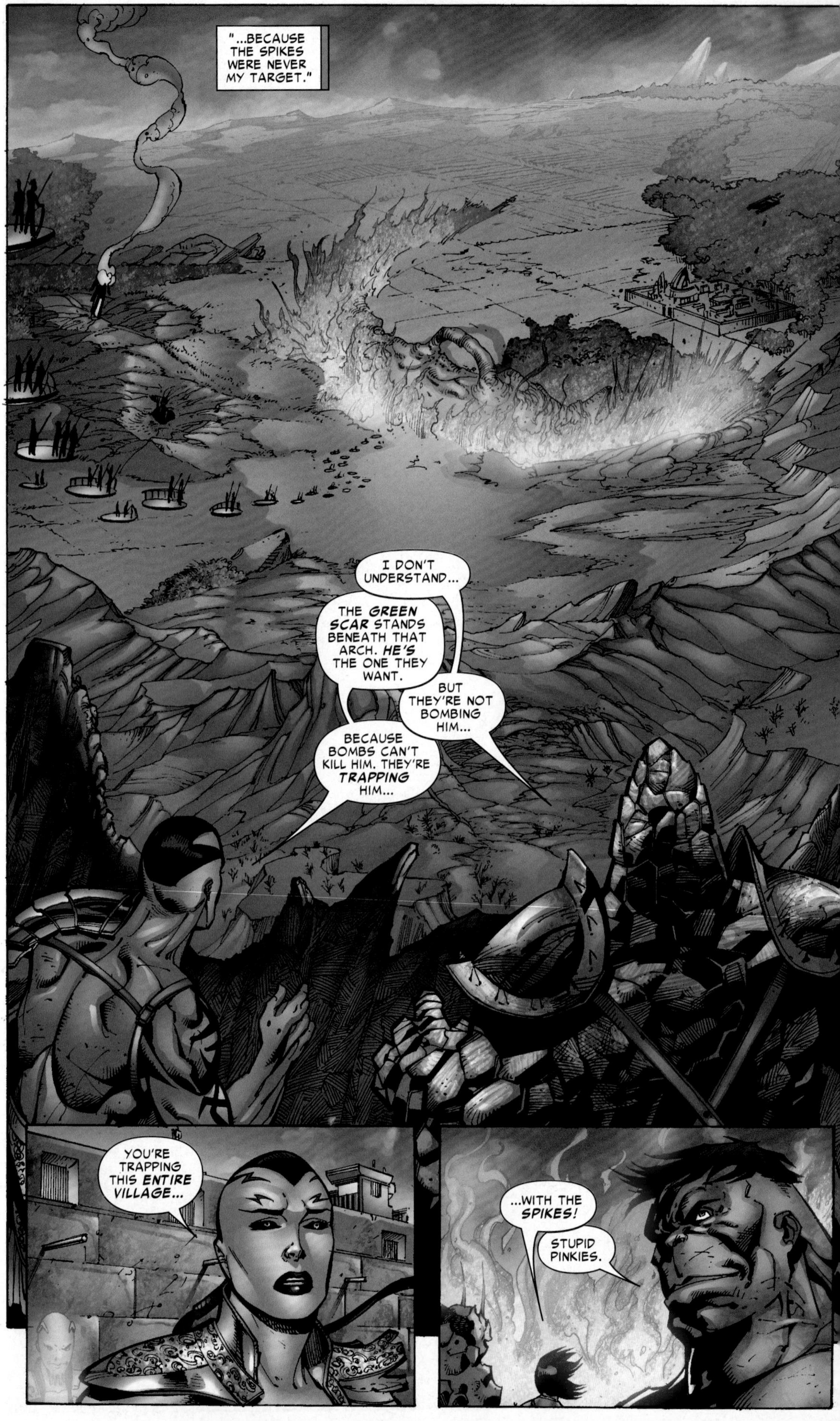
"...BECAUSE THE SPIKES WERE NEVER MY TARGET."
I DON'T UNDERSTAND...
THE GREEN SCAR STANDS BENEATH THAT ARCH. HE'S THE ONE THEY WANT.
BUT THEY'RE NOT BOMBING HIM...
BECAUSE BOMBS CAN'T KILL HIM. THEY'RE TRAPPING HIM...
YOU'RE TRAPPING THIS ENTIRE VILLAGE...
...WITH THE SPIKES!
STUPID PINKIES.

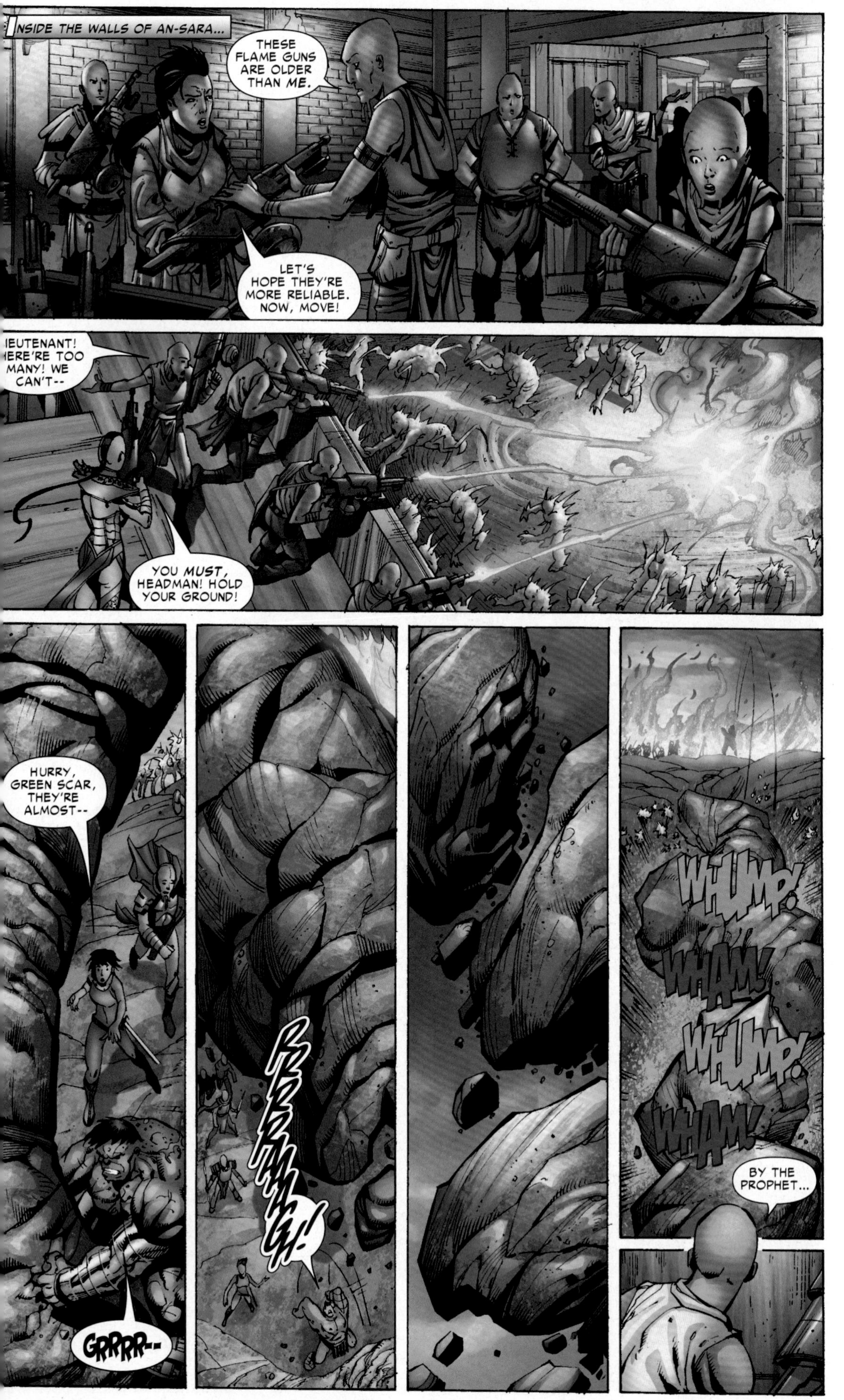

INSIDE THE WALLS OF AN-SARA...
THESE FLAME GUNS ARE OLDER THAN ME.
LET'S HOPE THEY'RE MORE RELIABLE. NOW, MOVE!
IEUTENANT! HERE'RE TOO MANY! WE CAN'T--
YOU MUST, HEADMAN! HOLD YOUR GROUND!
HURRY, GREEN SCAR, THEY'RE ALMOST--
GRRRR--
WHUMP!
WHAM!
WHUMP!
WHAM!
BY THE PROPHET...

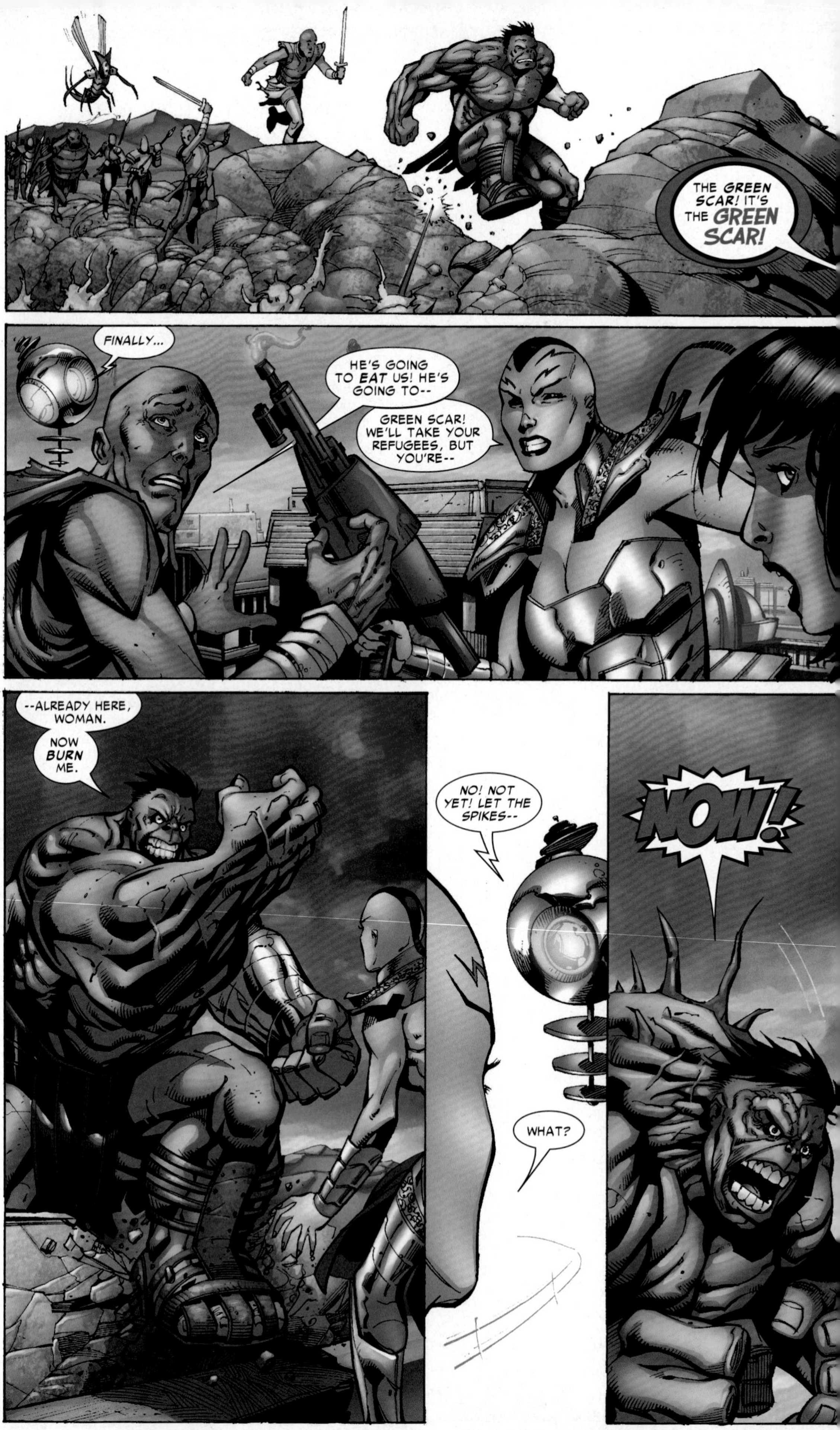
THE GREEN SCAR! IT'S THE GREEN SCAR!
FINALLY...
HE'S GOING TO EAT US! HE'S GOING TO--
GREEN SCAR! WE'LL TAKE YOUR REFUGEES, BUT YOU'RE--
--ALREADY HERE, WOMAN.
NOW BURN ME.
NO! NOT YET! LET THE SPIKES--
WHAT?
NOW!

QUEE! QUEE! QUEE!

VOOOOOSH!

THANKS. THOSE WERE STARTING TO ITCH.

BACK UP, YA STUPID PINKIES!

Y-- YES, SIR, M-- MR. SCAR!

NOW, WHILE HE'S PLAYING HERO-- YOU STILL HAVE A CHANCE--

GIVE ME THAT.

UTENANT! HAT ARE YOU--

LIEUTENANT!

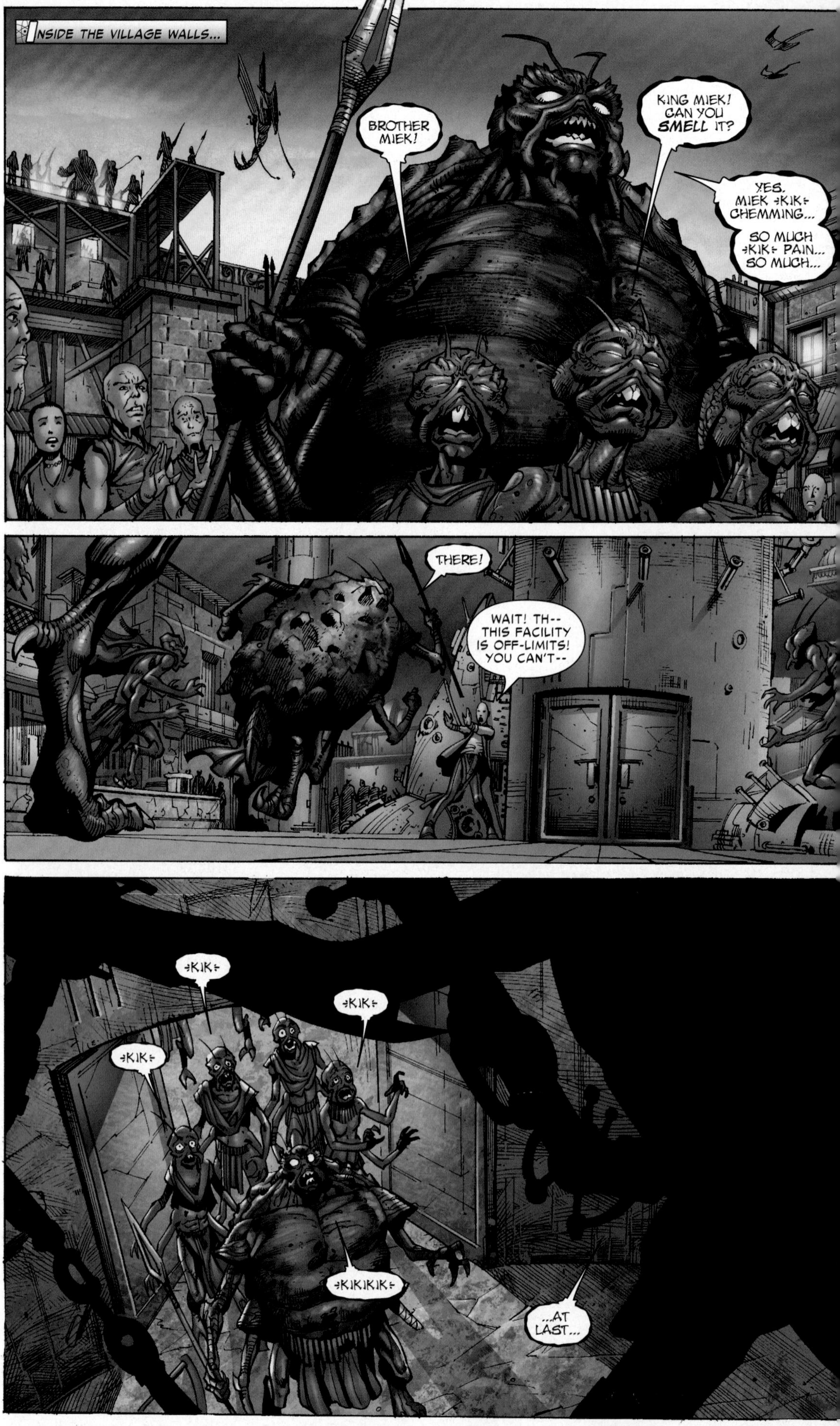
INSIDE THE VILLAGE WALLS...
BROTHER MIEK!
KING MIEK! CAN YOU SMELL IT?
YES. MIEK -KIK- CHEMMING...
SO MUCH -KIK- PAIN... SO MUCH...
THERE!
WAIT! TH-- THIS FACILITY IS OFF-LIMITS! YOU CAN'T--
-KIK-
-KIK-
-KIK-
-KIKIKIK-
...AT LAST...

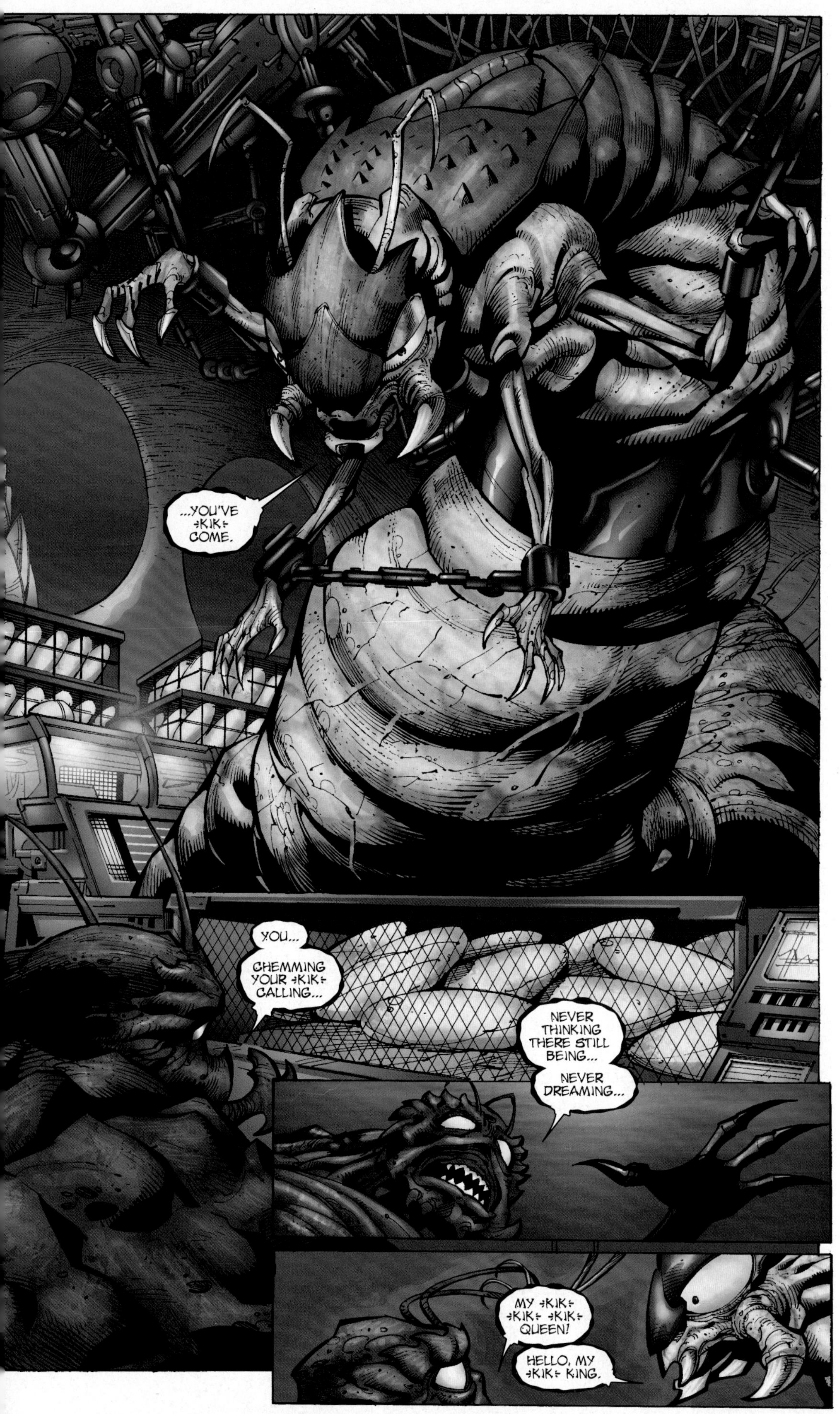
...YOU'VE ‹KIK› COME.
YOU...
CHEMMING YOUR ‹KIK› CALLING...
NEVER THINKING THERE STILL BEING...
NEVER DREAMING...
MY ‹KIK› ‹KIK› ‹KIK› QUEEN!
HELLO, MY ‹KIK› KING.

DIRTY, PUNY PINKIES!

MIEK ⸘KIK⸘ KILLING ALL OF YOU! ALL OF YOU!

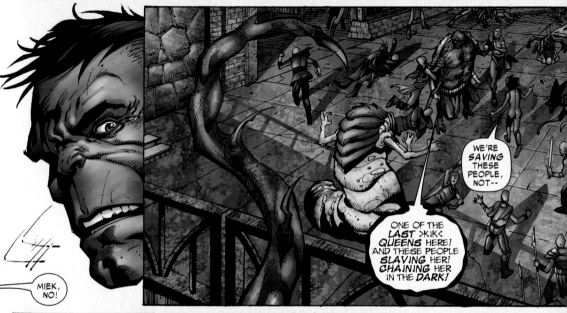

MIEK, NO!

WE'RE SAVING THESE PEOPLE, NOT--

ONE OF THE LAST ⸘KIK⸘ QUEENS HERE! AND THESE PEOPLE SLAVING HER! CHAINING HER IN THE DARK!

MAKING HER LAY. ⸘KIK⸘ ⸘KIK⸘ ⸘KIK⸘

EATING HER EGGS!

NOW MIEK EATING YOU!

AAAAHH!

KIKKEEEEEEE!

SHORK!

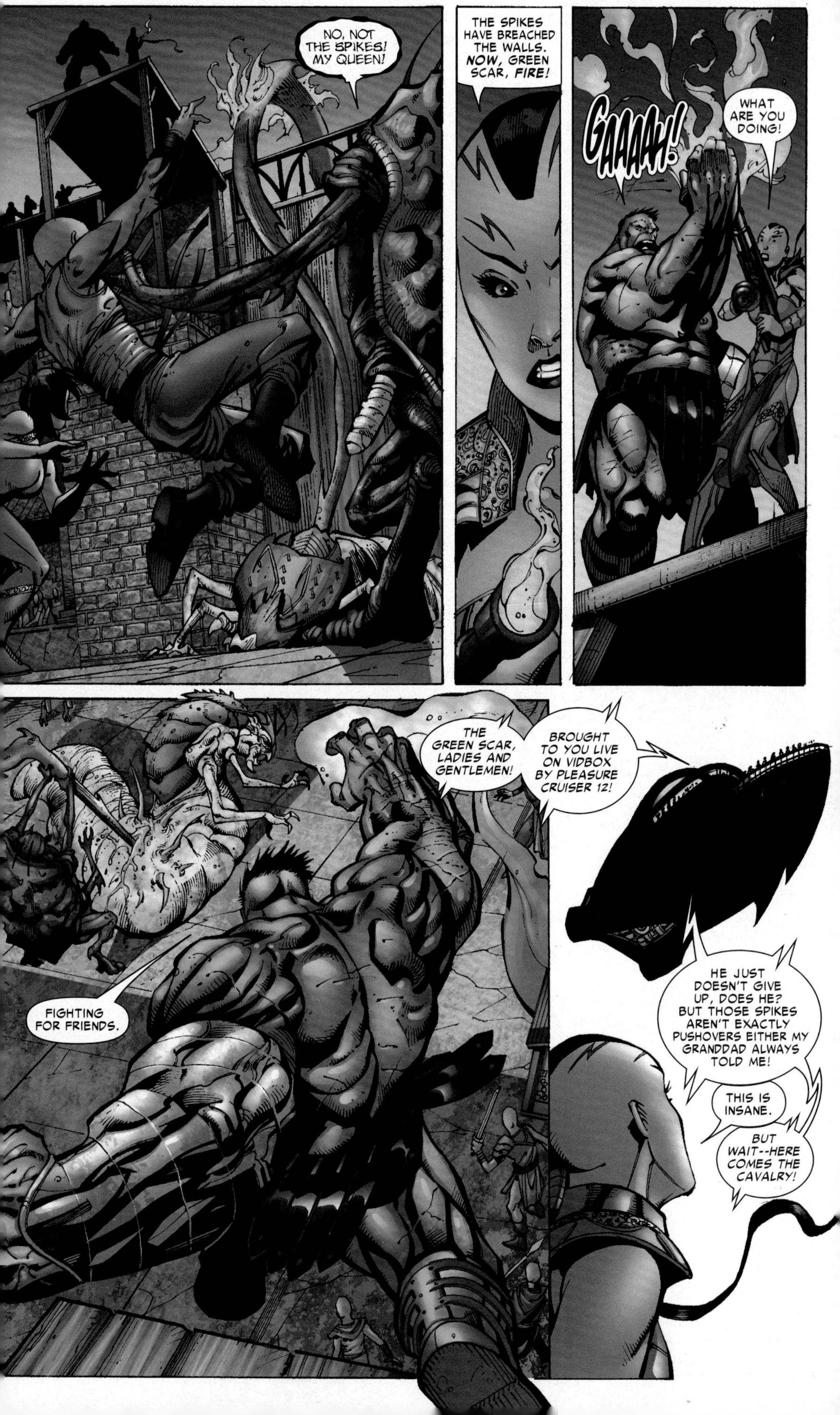
NO, NOT THE SPIKES! MY QUEEN!
THE SPIKES HAVE BREACHED THE WALLS. NOW, GREEN SCAR, FIRE!
GAAAAH!
WHAT ARE YOU DOING!
THE GREEN SCAR, LADIES AND GENTLEMEN!
BROUGHT TO YOU LIVE ON VIDBOX BY PLEASURE CRUISER 12!
FIGHTING FOR FRIENDS.
HE JUST DOESN'T GIVE UP, DOES HE? BUT THOSE SPIKES AREN'T EXACTLY PUSHOVERS EITHER MY GRANDDAD ALWAYS TOLD ME!
THIS IS INSANE.
BUT WAIT--HERE COMES THE CAVALRY!

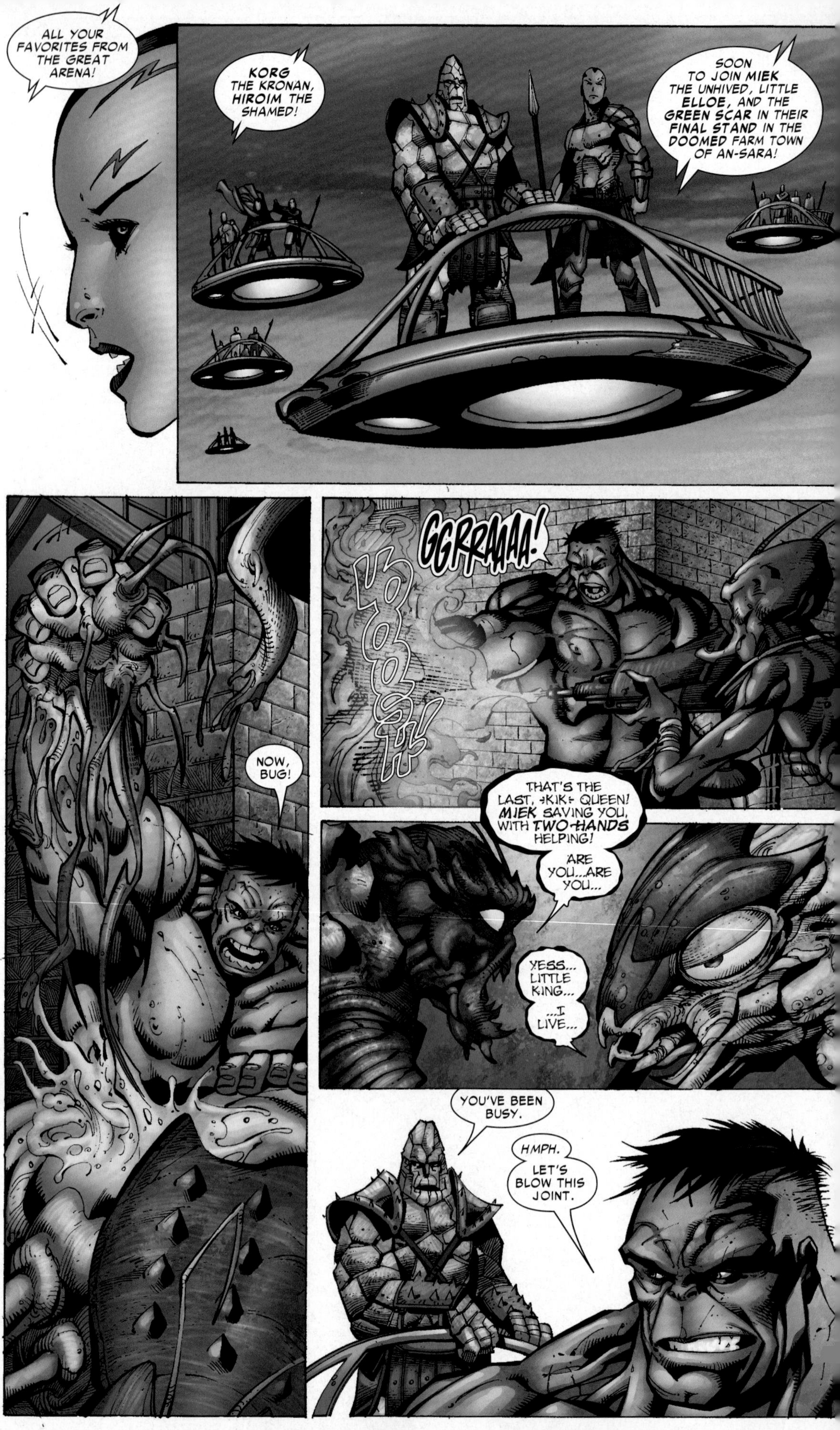
ALL YOUR FAVORITES FROM THE GREAT ARENA!
KORG THE KRONAN, HIROIM THE SHAMED!
SOON TO JOIN MIEK THE UNHIVED, LITTLE ELLOE, AND THE GREEN SCAR IN THEIR FINAL STAND IN THE DOOMED FARM TOWN OF AN-SARA!
NOW, BUG!
GGRRAAAA!
THAT'S THE LAST, ‡KIK‡ QUEEN! MIEK SAVING YOU, WITH TWO-HANDS HELPING!
ARE YOU...ARE YOU...
YESS... LITTLE KING...
...I LIVE...
YOU'VE BEEN BUSY.
HMPH.
LET'S BLOW THIS JOINT.

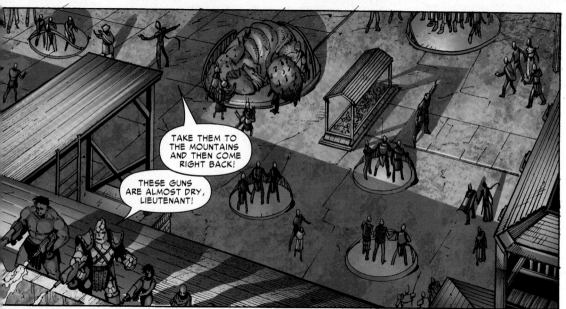

TAKE THEM TO THE MOUNTAINS AND THEN COME RIGHT BACK!

THESE GUNS ARE ALMOST DRY, LIEUTENANT!

ALMOST THERE! JUST ANOTHER HUNDRED TO EVACUATE!

WORKING WITH THE ENEMY, NOW, LIEUTENANT?

I HAVE NOT FORGOTTEN MY OATH TO YOU, YOUR GRACE.

ONCE YOUR SUBJECTS ARE SAFE, I'LL KILL THE GREEN SCAR.

ARE YOU REALLY SO STUPID?

WE'VE SEEN YOU TRY--YOU CAN'T KILL THE HULK.

THAT'S WHY I RELEASED THE SPIKES.

WHAT, YOU--

--AND NOW YOU AND YOUR PRECIOUS CIVILIANS ARE JUST GETTING IN THE WAY.

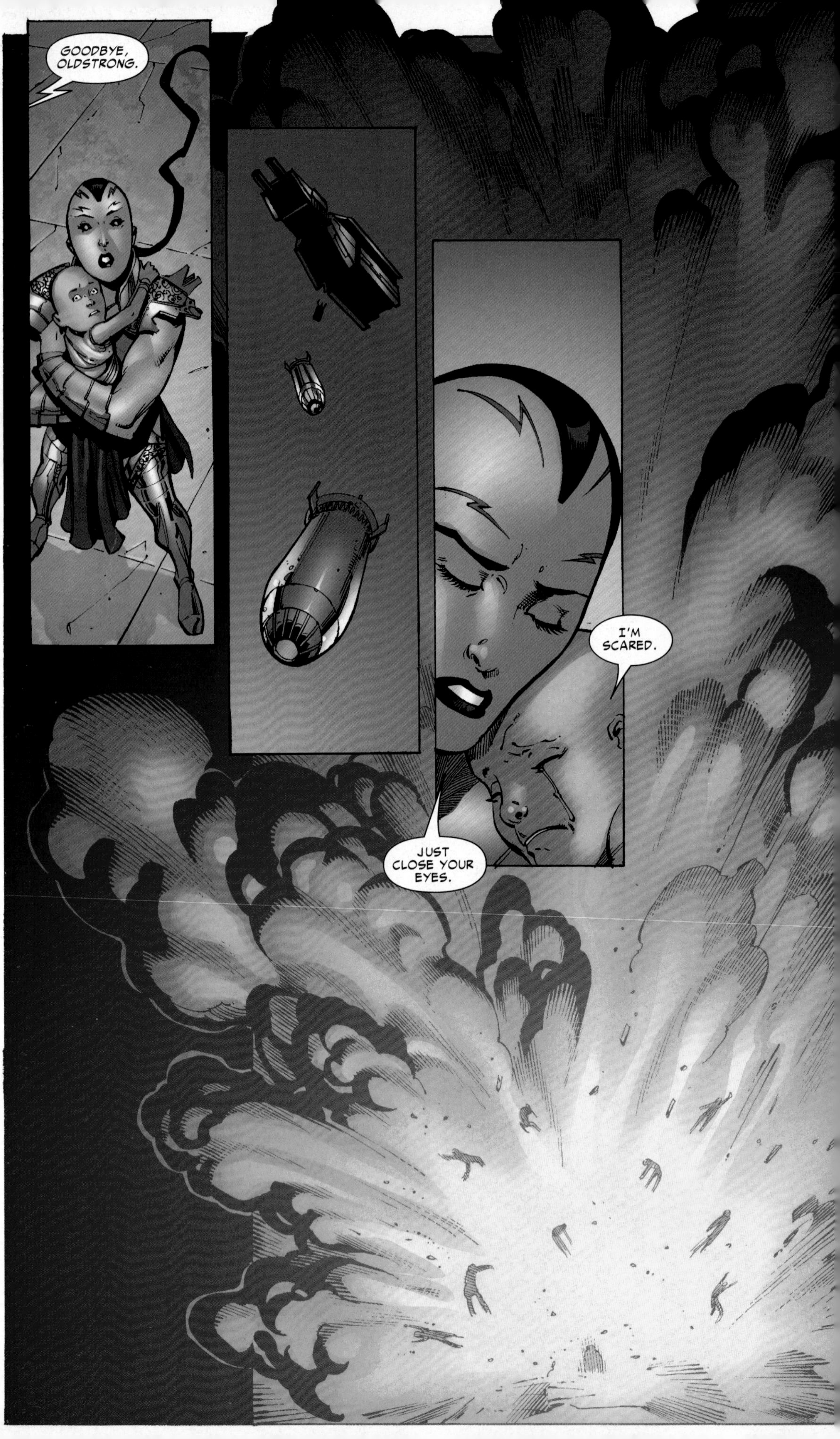
GOODBYE, OLDSTRONG.
I'M SCARED.
JUST CLOSE YOUR EYES.

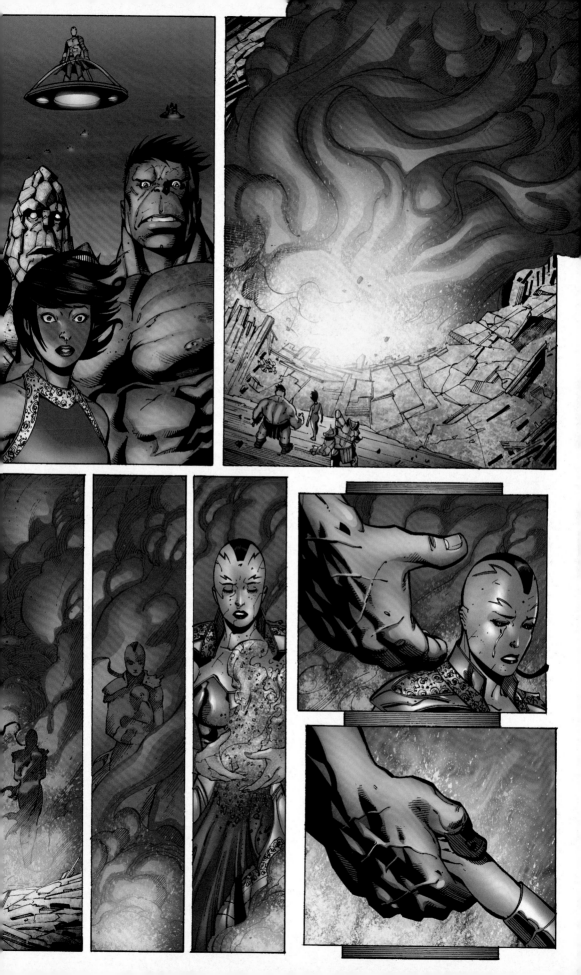

I AM CAIERA THE OLDSTRONG, ONCE THE EMPEROR'S SHADOW.

NOW I'LL FIGHT BY YOUR SIDE. UNTIL WE ALL ARE DEAD...

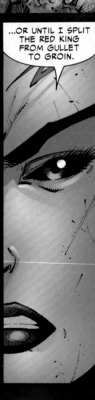

...OR UNTIL I SPLIT THE RED KING FROM GULLET TO GROIN.

WORKS FOR ME.

YOU WHO WOULD BE WARBOUND. SPEAK YOUR TRUE NAME AND BE BOUND TO US FOREVER.

COME HERE, YOU STUPID PINKIES!

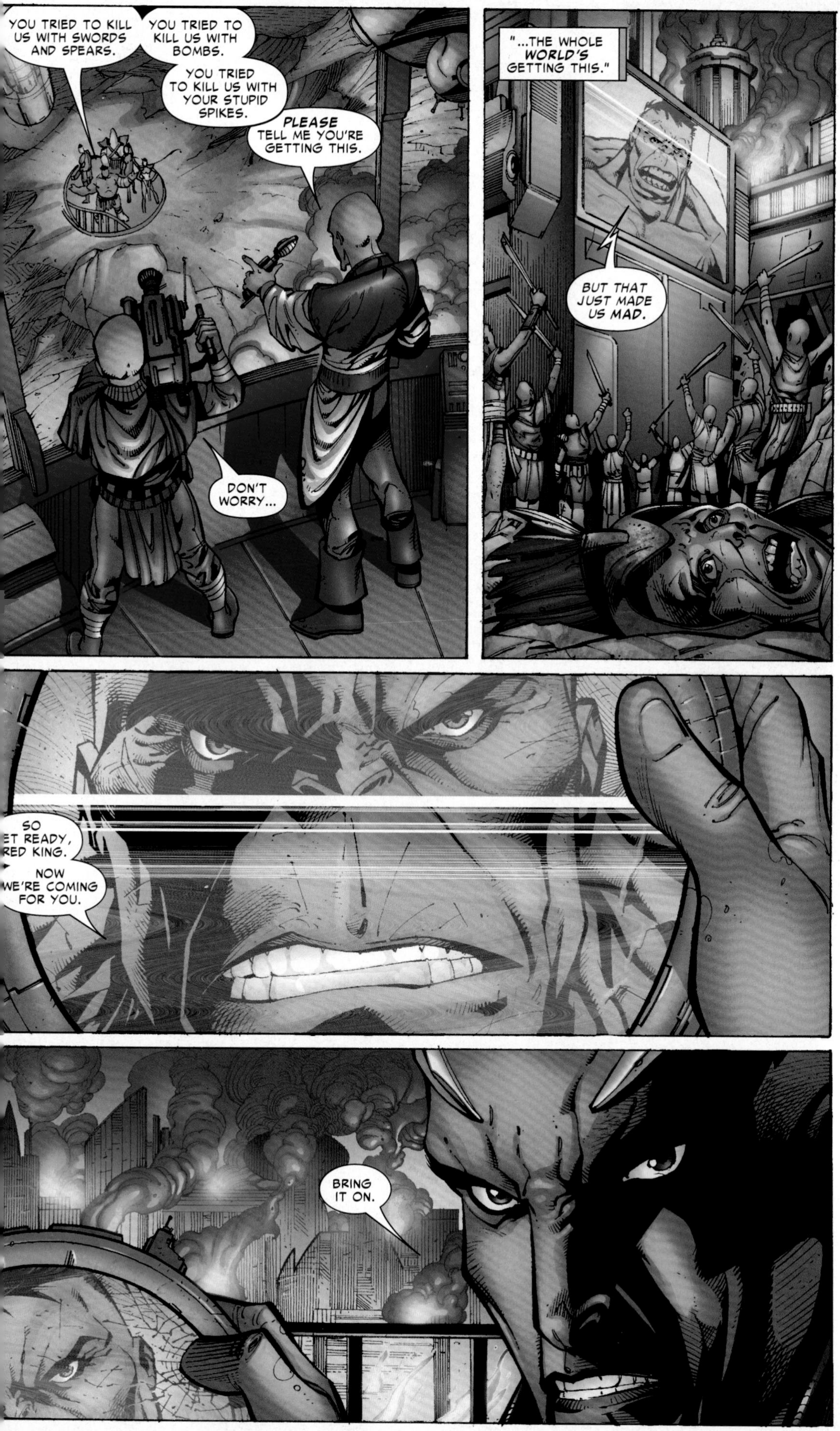
YOU TRIED TO KILL US WITH SWORDS AND SPEARS.
YOU TRIED TO KILL US WITH BOMBS.
YOU TRIED TO KILL US WITH YOUR STUPID SPIKES.
PLEASE TELL ME YOU'RE GETTING THIS.
DON'T WORRY...
"...THE WHOLE WORLD'S GETTING THIS."
BUT THAT JUST MADE US MAD.
SO ET READY, RED KING.
NOW WE'RE COMING FOR YOU.
BRING IT ON.

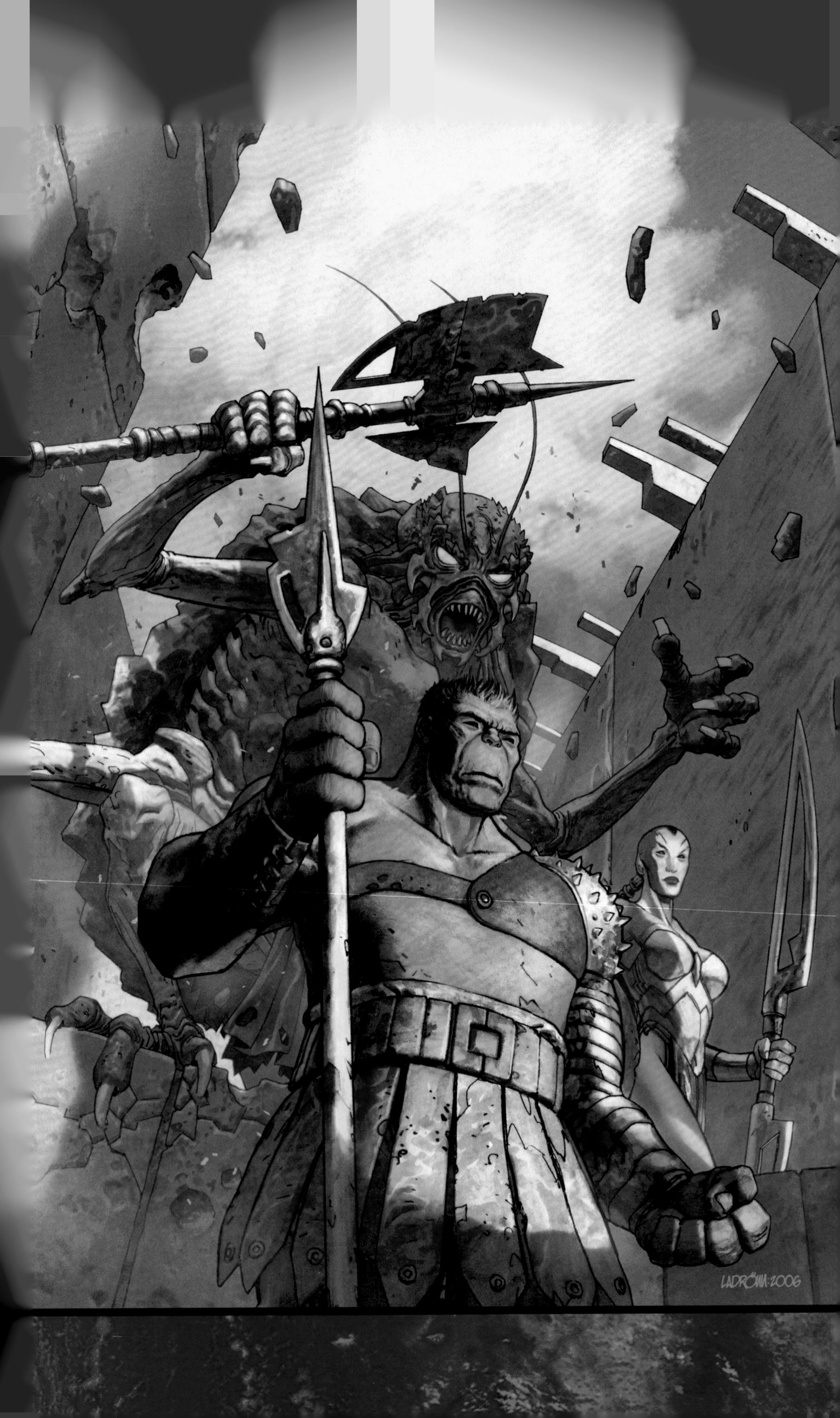
LADRÖNN 2006

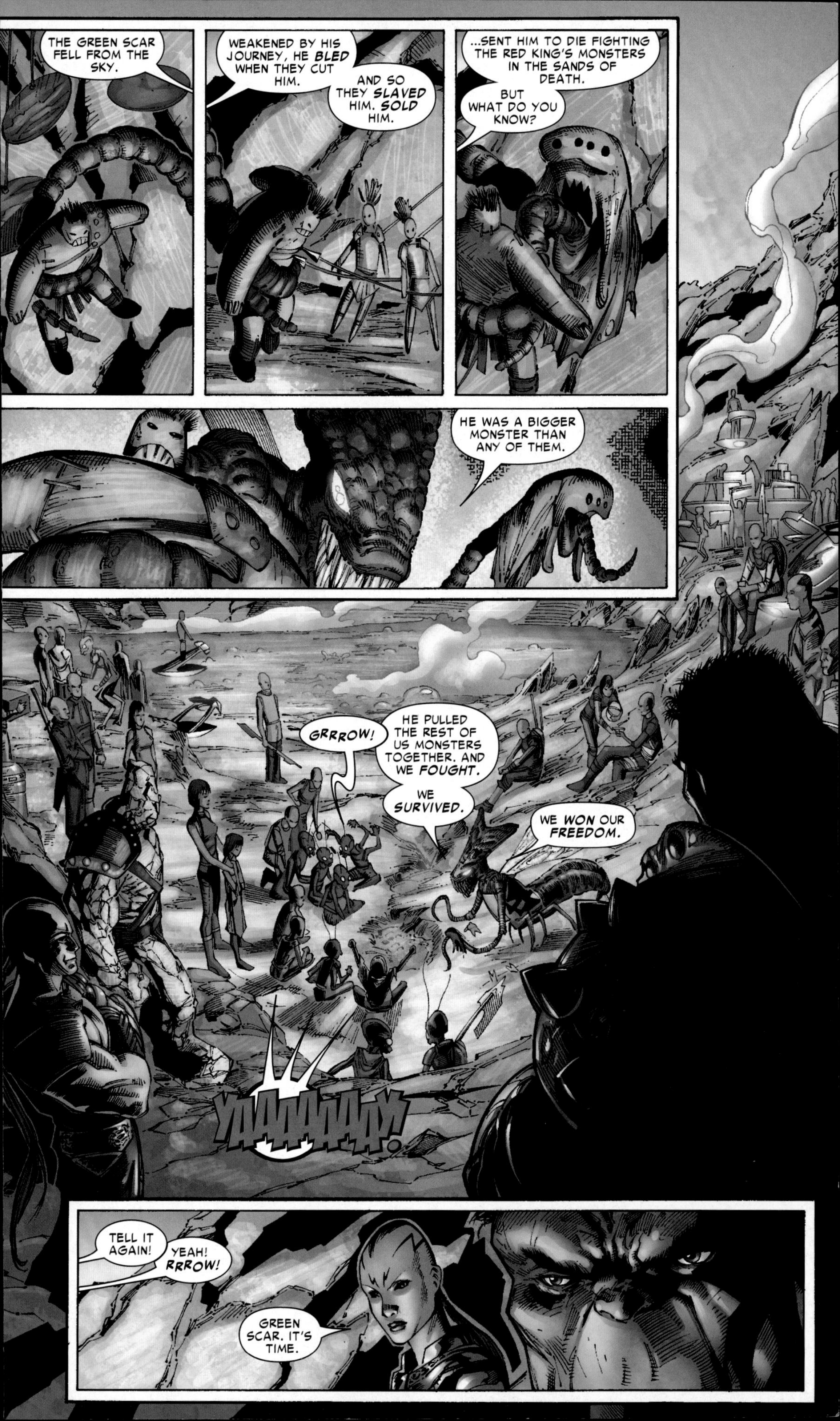
THE GREEN SCAR FELL FROM THE SKY.
WEAKENED BY HIS JOURNEY, HE BLED WHEN THEY CUT HIM.
AND SO THEY SLAVED HIM. SOLD HIM.
...SENT HIM TO DIE FIGHTING THE RED KING'S MONSTERS IN THE SANDS OF DEATH.
BUT WHAT DO YOU KNOW?
HE WAS A BIGGER MONSTER THAN ANY OF THEM.
GRRROW!
HE PULLED THE REST OF US MONSTERS TOGETHER. AND WE FOUGHT.
WE SURVIVED.
WE WON OUR FREEDOM.
YAAAAAAAAY!
TELL IT AGAIN!
YEAH! RRROW!
GREEN SCAR. IT'S TIME.

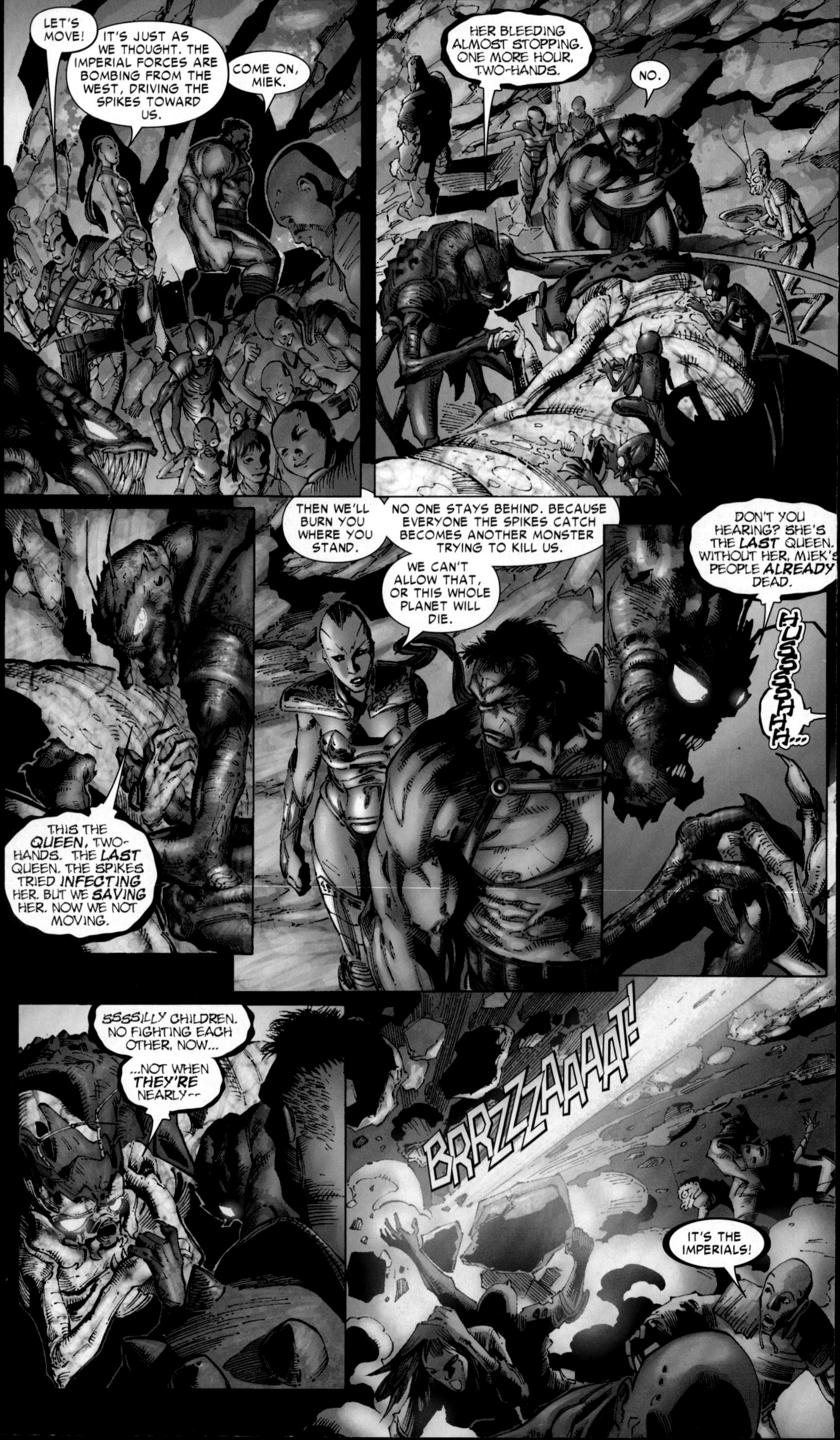
LET'S MOVE!
IT'S JUST AS WE THOUGHT. THE IMPERIAL FORCES ARE BOMBING FROM THE WEST, DRIVING THE SPIKES TOWARD US.
COME ON, MIEK.
HER BLEEDING ALMOST STOPPING. ONE MORE HOUR, TWO-HANDS.
NO.
THIS THE QUEEN, TWO-HANDS. THE LAST QUEEN. THE SPIKES TRIED INFECTING HER. BUT WE SAVING HER. NOW WE NOT MOVING.
THEN WE'LL BURN YOU WHERE YOU STAND.
NO ONE STAYS BEHIND. BECAUSE EVERYONE THE SPIKES CATCH BECOMES ANOTHER MONSTER TRYING TO KILL US.
WE CAN'T ALLOW THAT, OR THIS WHOLE PLANET WILL DIE.
DON'T YOU HEARING? SHE'S THE LAST QUEEN. WITHOUT HER, MIEK'S PEOPLE ALREADY DEAD.
HUSSSSHHH...
SSSSILLY CHILDREN. NO FIGHTING EACH OTHER, NOW...
...NOT WHEN THEY'RE NEARLY--
BRRZZZAAAAT!
IT'S THE IMPERIALS!

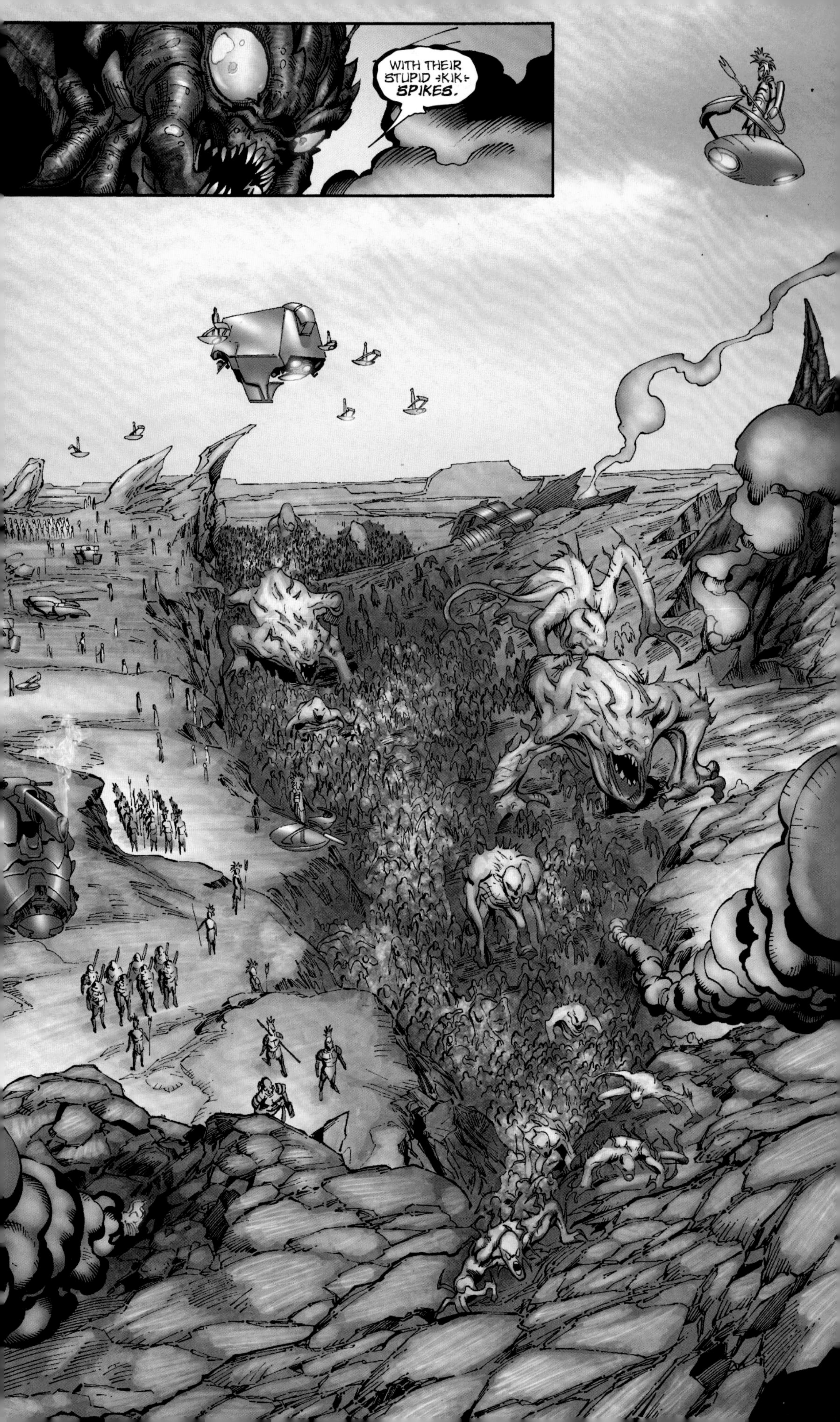
WITH THEIR STUPID ÷KIK÷ SPIKES.

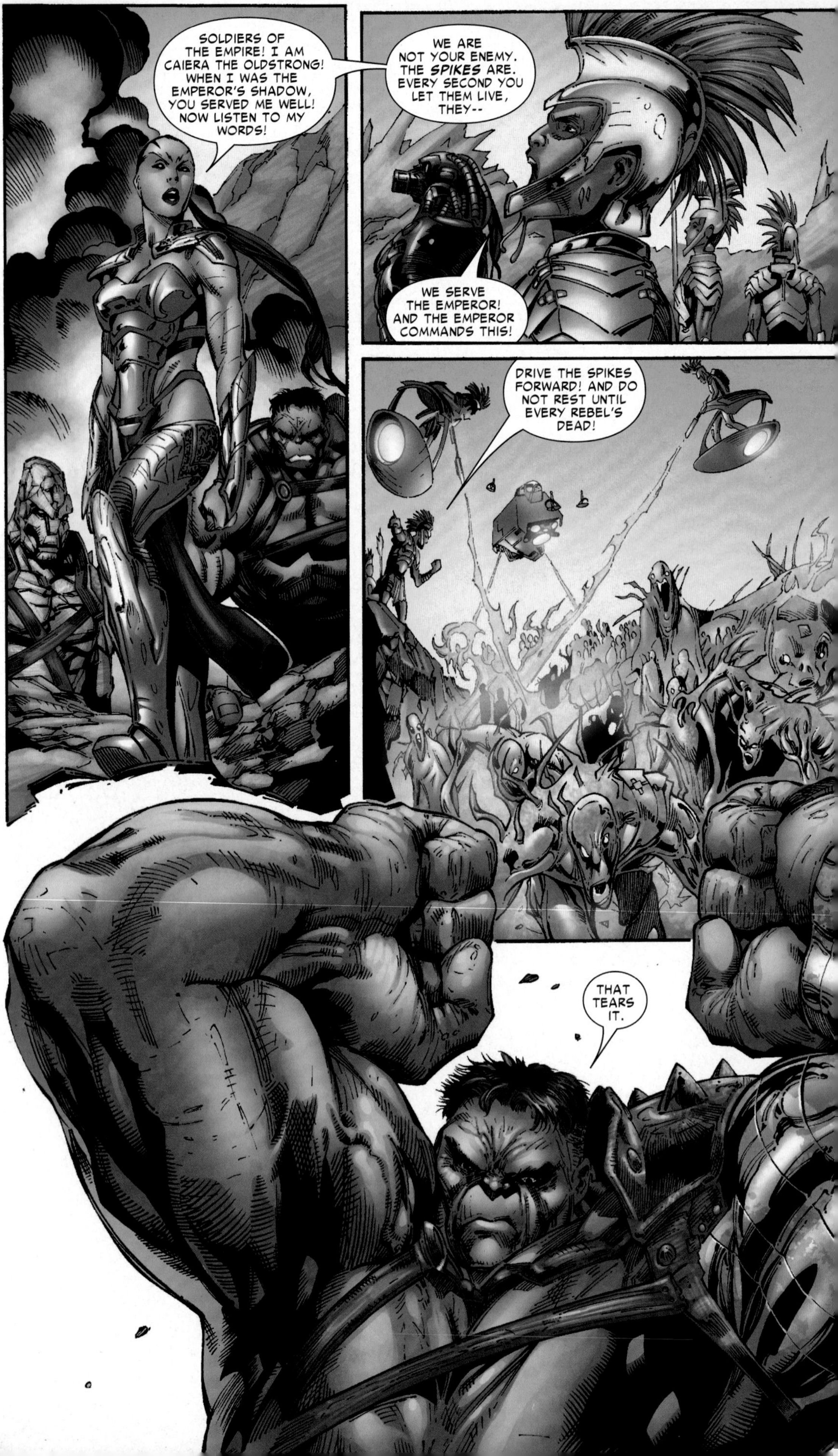
SOLDIERS OF THE EMPIRE! I AM CAIERA THE OLDSTRONG! WHEN I WAS THE EMPEROR'S SHADOW, YOU SERVED ME WELL! NOW LISTEN TO MY WORDS!
WE ARE NOT YOUR ENEMY. THE *SPIKES* ARE. EVERY SECOND YOU LET THEM LIVE, THEY--
WE SERVE THE EMPEROR! AND THE EMPEROR COMMANDS THIS!
DRIVE THE SPIKES FORWARD! AND DO NOT REST UNTIL EVERY REBEL'S DEAD!
THAT TEARS IT.

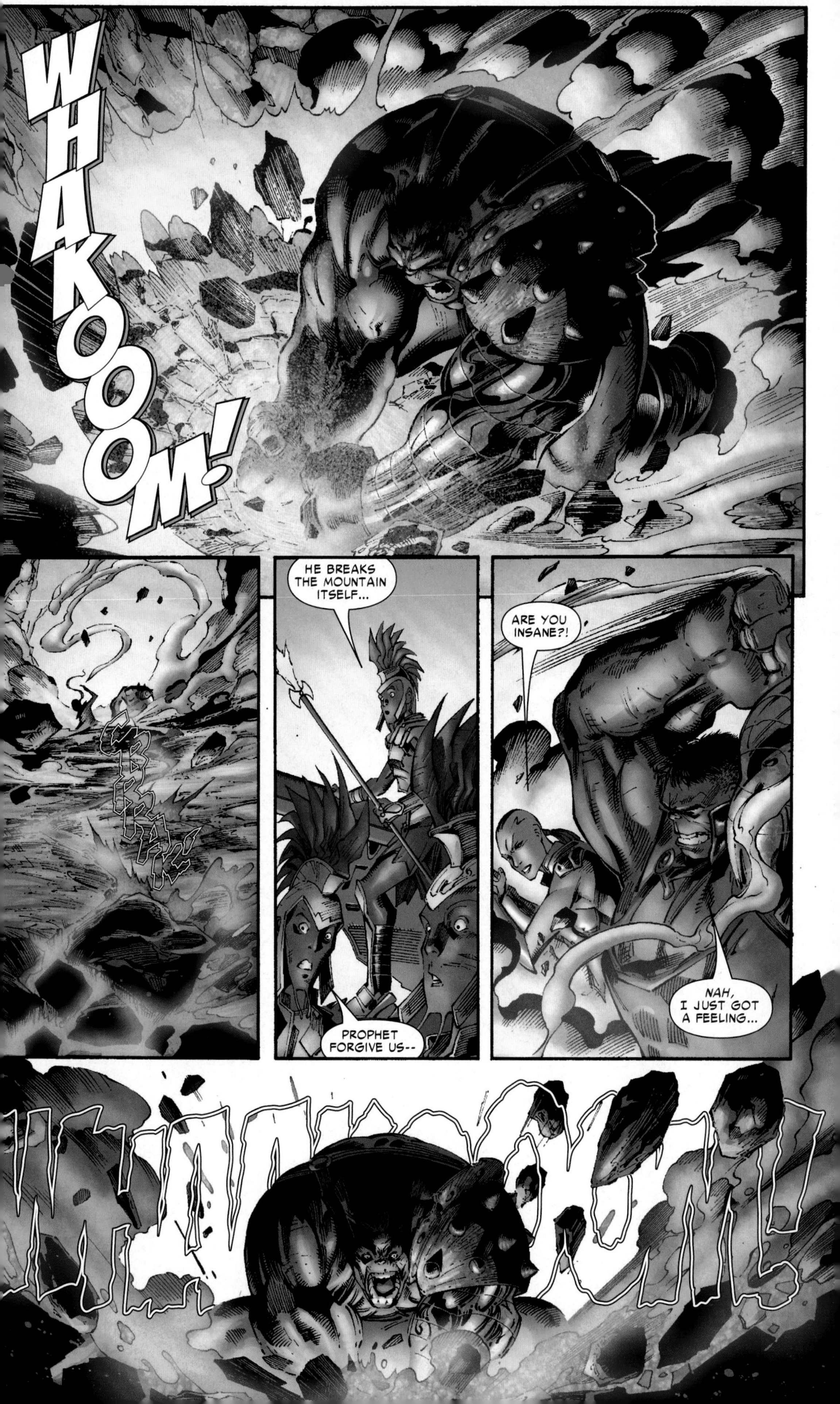
WHAKOOOOM!
HE BREAKS THE MOUNTAIN ITSELF...
PROPHET FORGIVE US--
ARE YOU INSANE?!
NAH, I JUST GOT A FEELING...

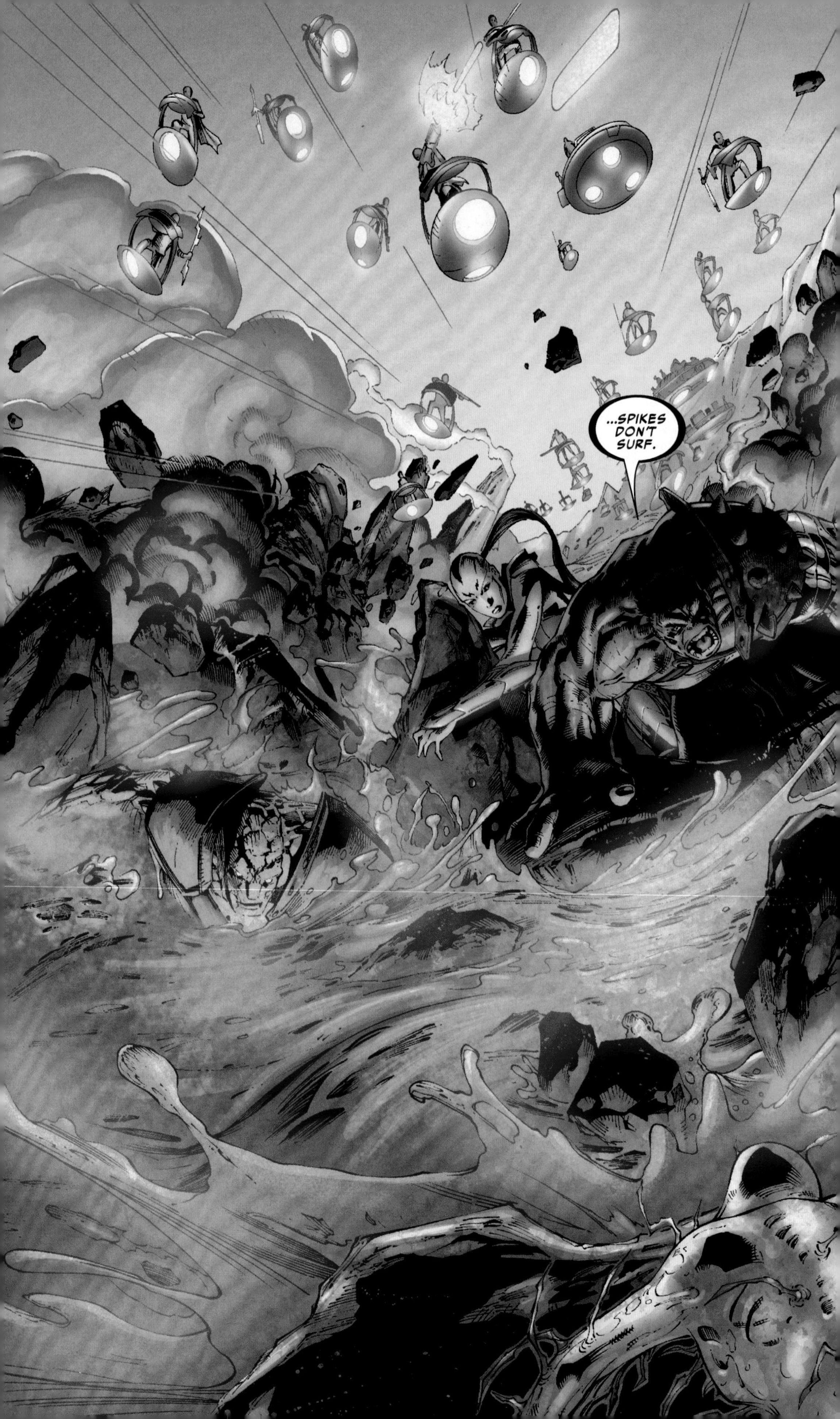
...SPIKES DON'T SURF.

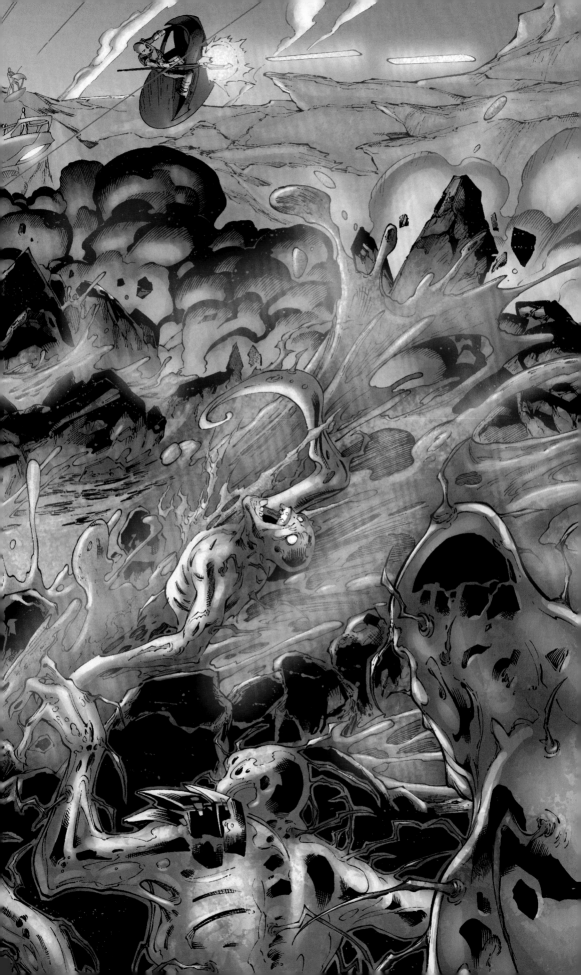

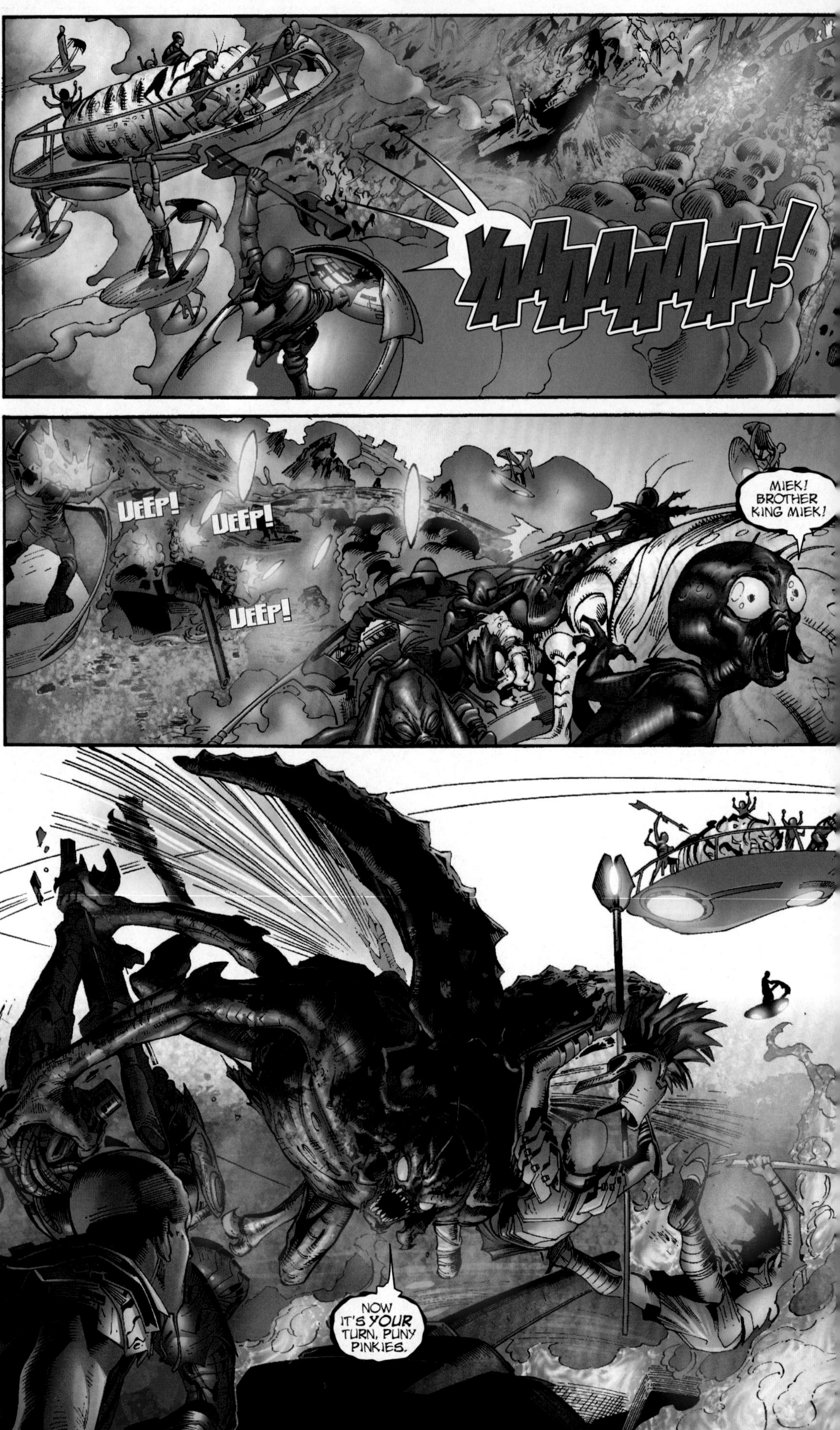
YAAAAAAAH!
VEEP!
VEEP!
VEEP!
MIEK! BROTHER KING MIEK!
NOW IT'S YOUR TURN, PUNY PINKIES.

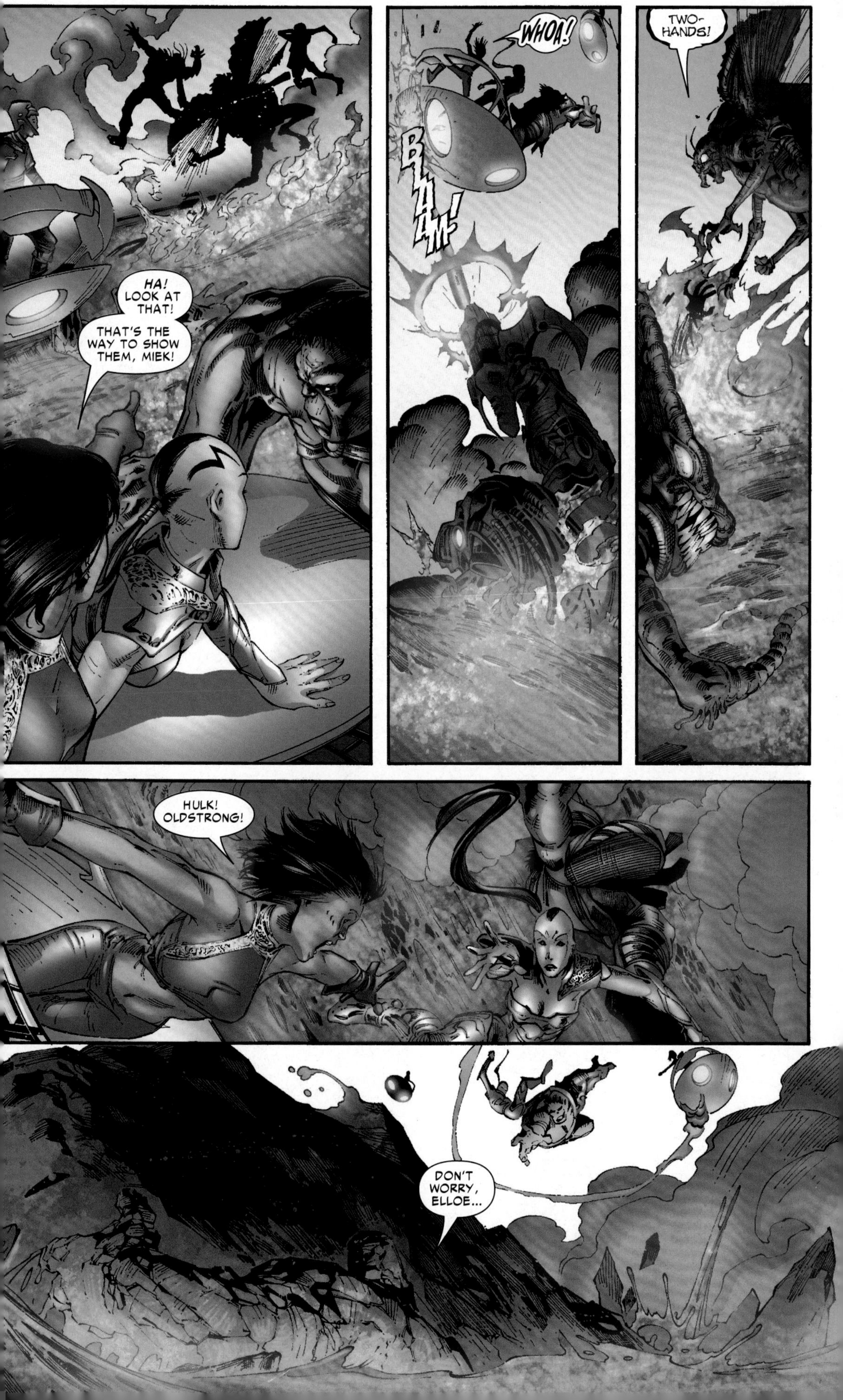
HA! LOOK AT THAT!
THAT'S THE WAY TO SHOW THEM, MIEK!
WHOA!
BLAAM!
TWO-HANDS!
HULK! OLDSTRONG!
DON'T WORRY, ELLOE...

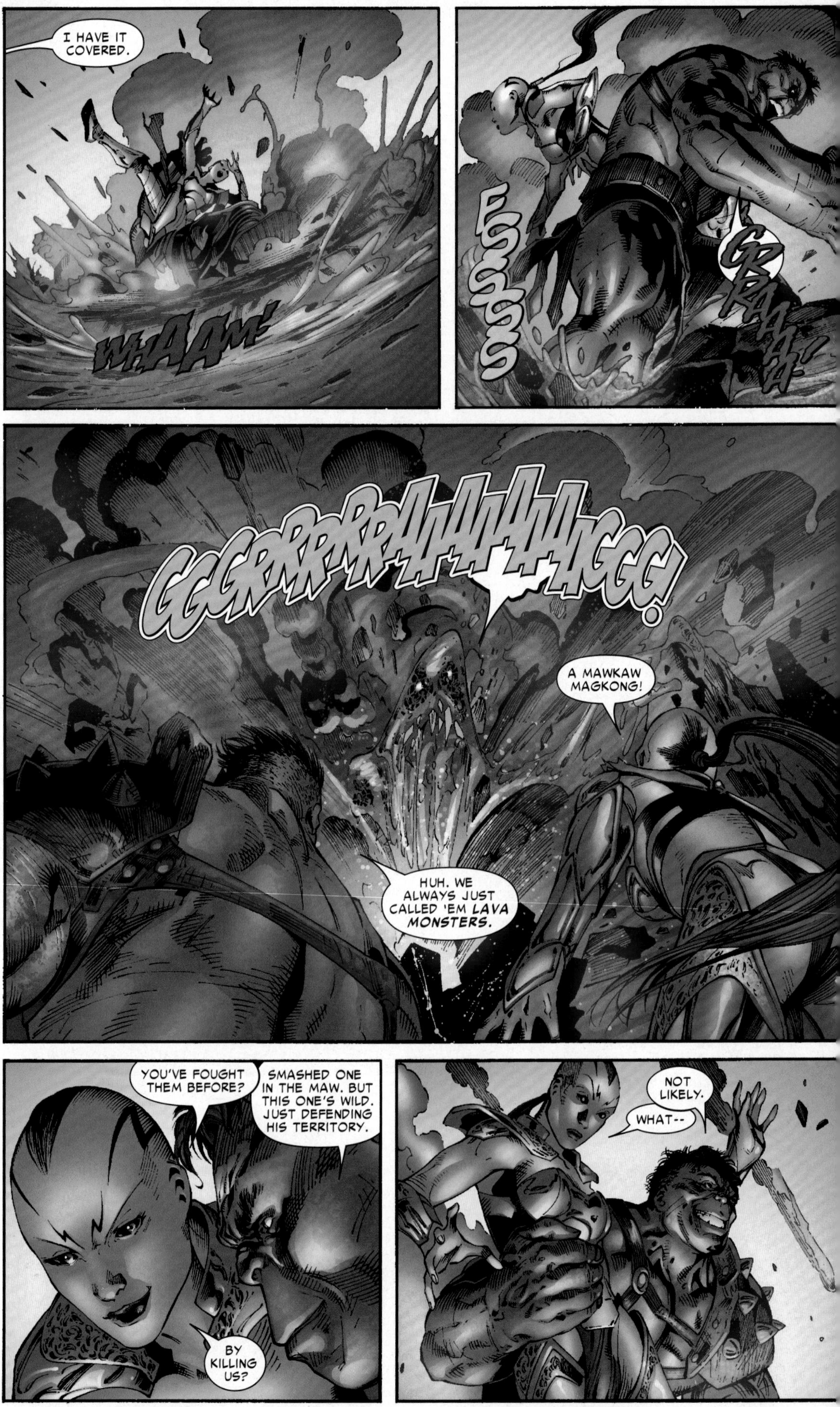
I HAVE IT COVERED.
WHAAM!
ESSSSSS
GRRAAAA!
GGGRRRRRAAAAAAAGGG!
A MAWKAW MAGKONG!
HUH. WE ALWAYS JUST CALLED 'EM LAVA MONSTERS.
YOU'VE FOUGHT THEM BEFORE?
SMASHED ONE IN THE MAW. BUT THIS ONE'S WILD. JUST DEFENDING HIS TERRITORY.
BY KILLING US?
NOT LIKELY.
WHAT--

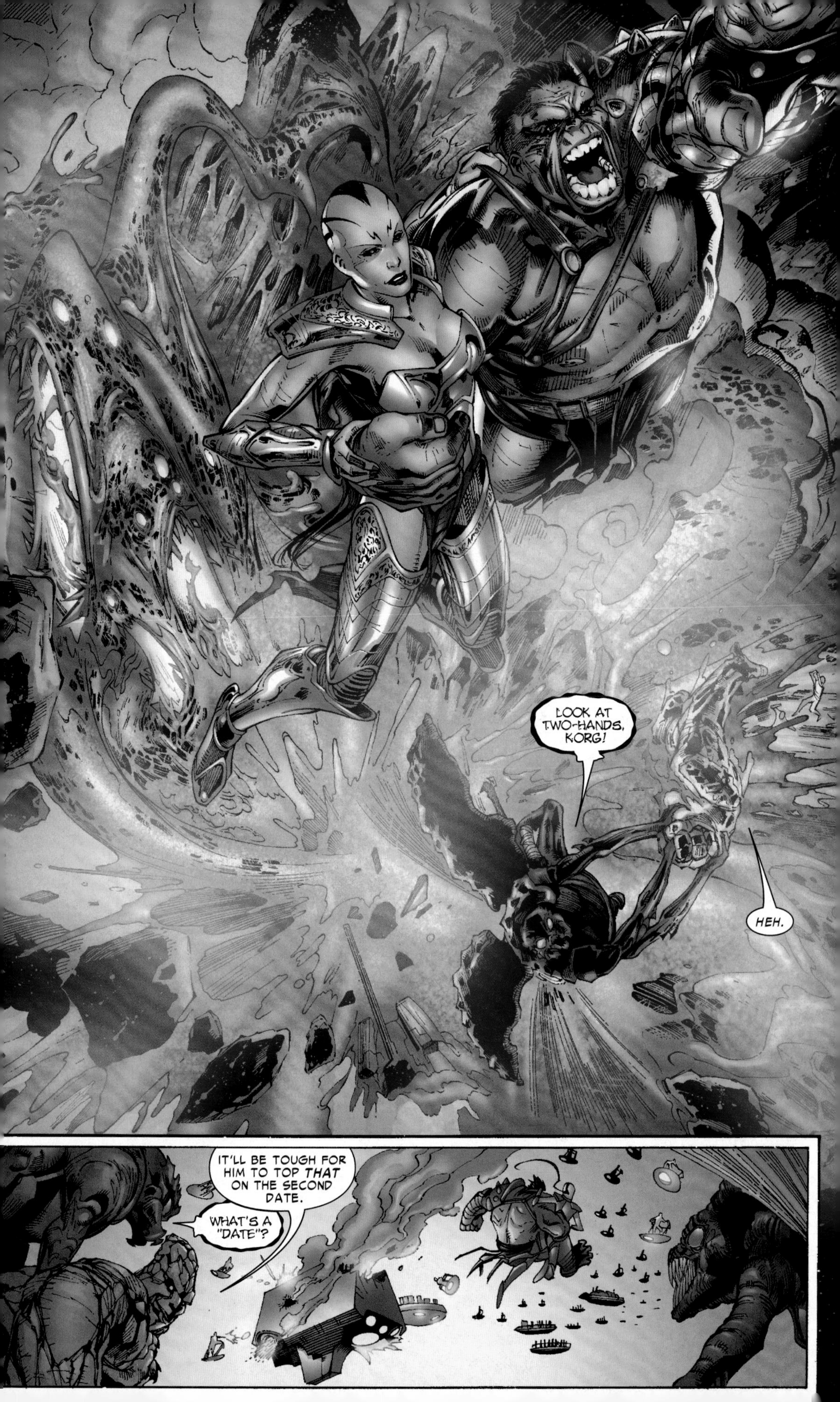
LOOK AT TWO-HANDS, KORG!
HEH.
IT'LL BE TOUGH FOR HIM TO TOP THAT ON THE SECOND DATE.
WHAT'S A "DATE"?

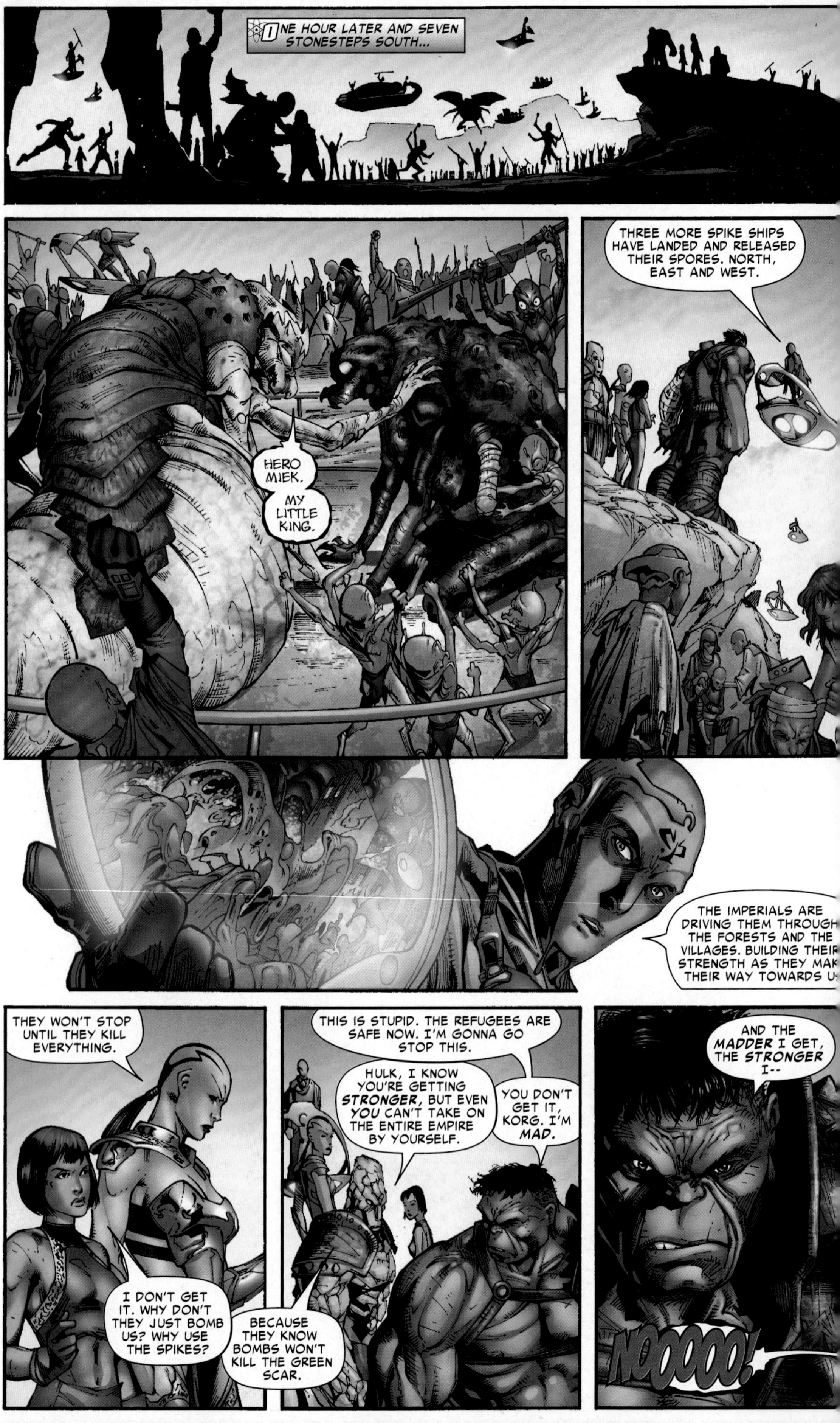
ONE HOUR LATER AND SEVEN STONESTEPS SOUTH...
HERO MIEK.
MY LITTLE KING.
THREE MORE SPIKE SHIPS HAVE LANDED AND RELEASED THEIR SPORES. NORTH, EAST AND WEST.
THE IMPERIALS ARE DRIVING THEM THROUGH THE FORESTS AND THE VILLAGES. BUILDING THEIR STRENGTH AS THEY MAKE THEIR WAY TOWARDS US.
THEY WON'T STOP UNTIL THEY KILL EVERYTHING.
I DON'T GET IT. WHY DON'T THEY JUST BOMB US? WHY USE THE SPIKES?
BECAUSE THEY KNOW BOMBS WON'T KILL THE GREEN SCAR.
THIS IS STUPID. THE REFUGEES ARE SAFE NOW. I'M GONNA GO STOP THIS.
HULK, I KNOW YOU'RE GETTING STRONGER, BUT EVEN YOU CAN'T TAKE ON THE ENTIRE EMPIRE BY YOURSELF.
YOU DON'T GET IT, KORG. I'M MAD.
AND THE MADDER I GET, THE STRONGER I--
NOOOOO!

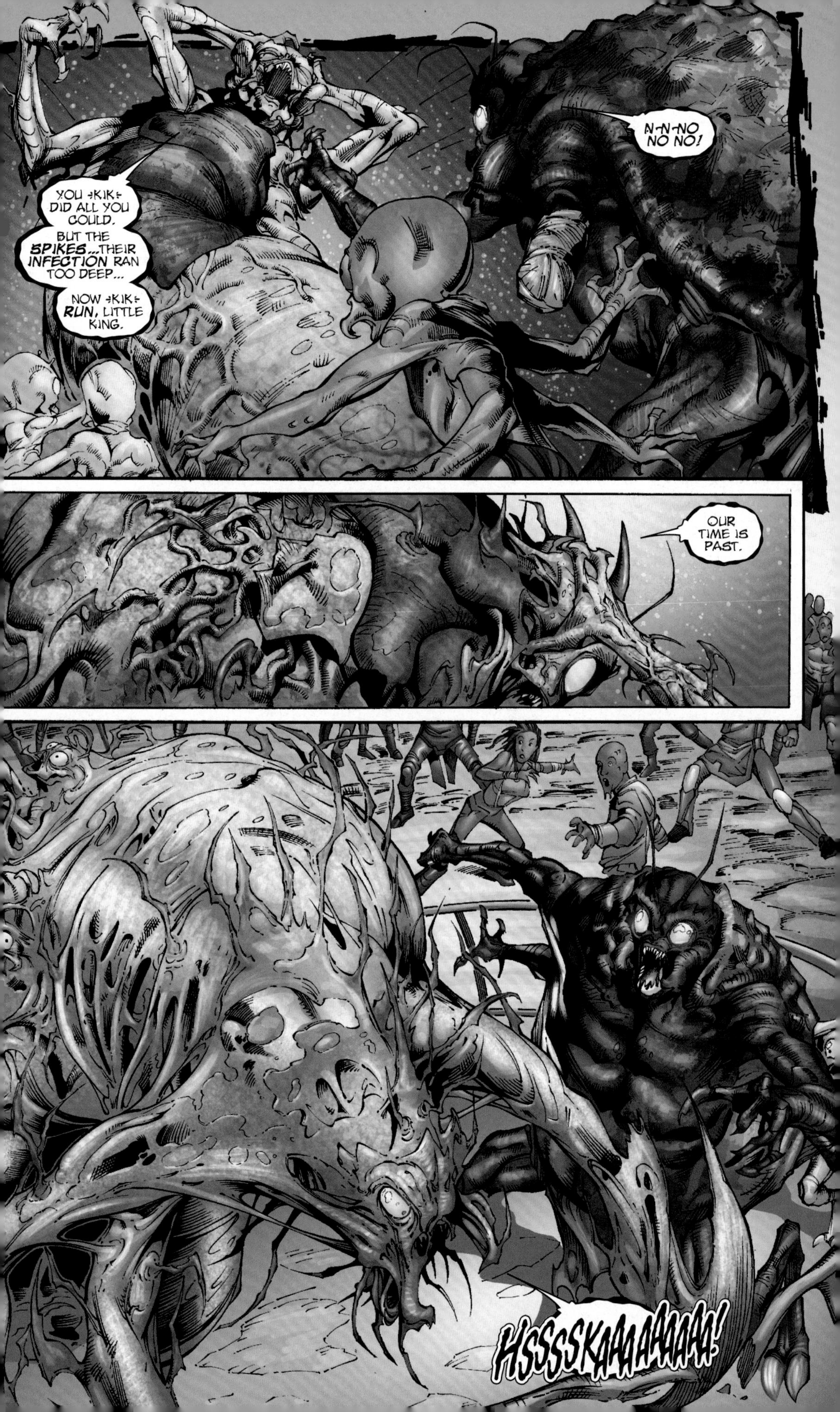
YOU ≠KIK≠ DID ALL YOU COULD.
BUT THE SPIKES... THEIR INFECTION RAN TOO DEEP...
NOW ≠KIK≠ RUN, LITTLE KING.
N-N-NO NO NO!
OUR TIME IS PAST.
HSSSSKAAAAAAAA!

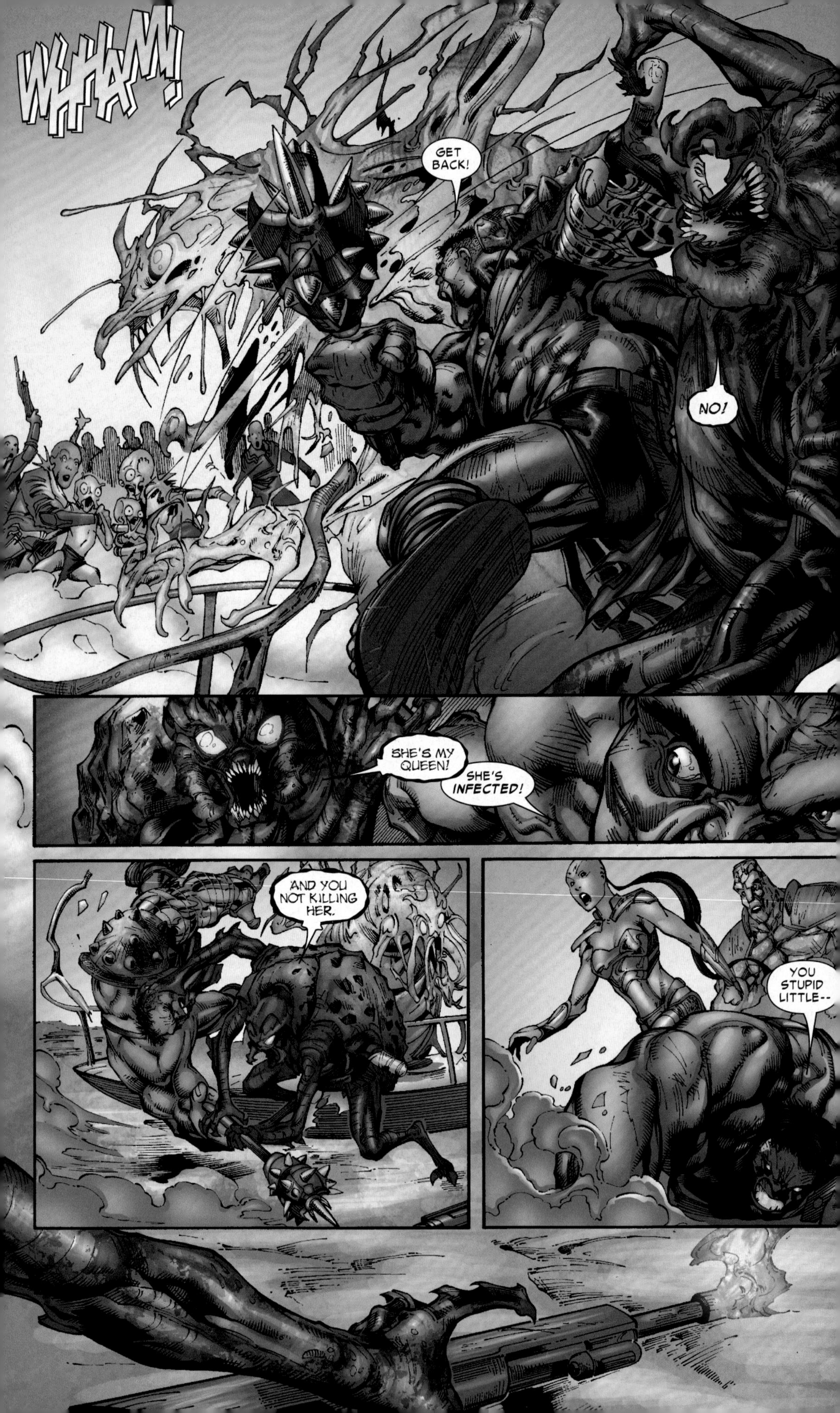
WHAM!
GET BACK!
NO!
SHE'S MY QUEEN!
SHE'S INFECTED!
AND YOU NOT KILLING HER.
YOU STUPID LITTLE--

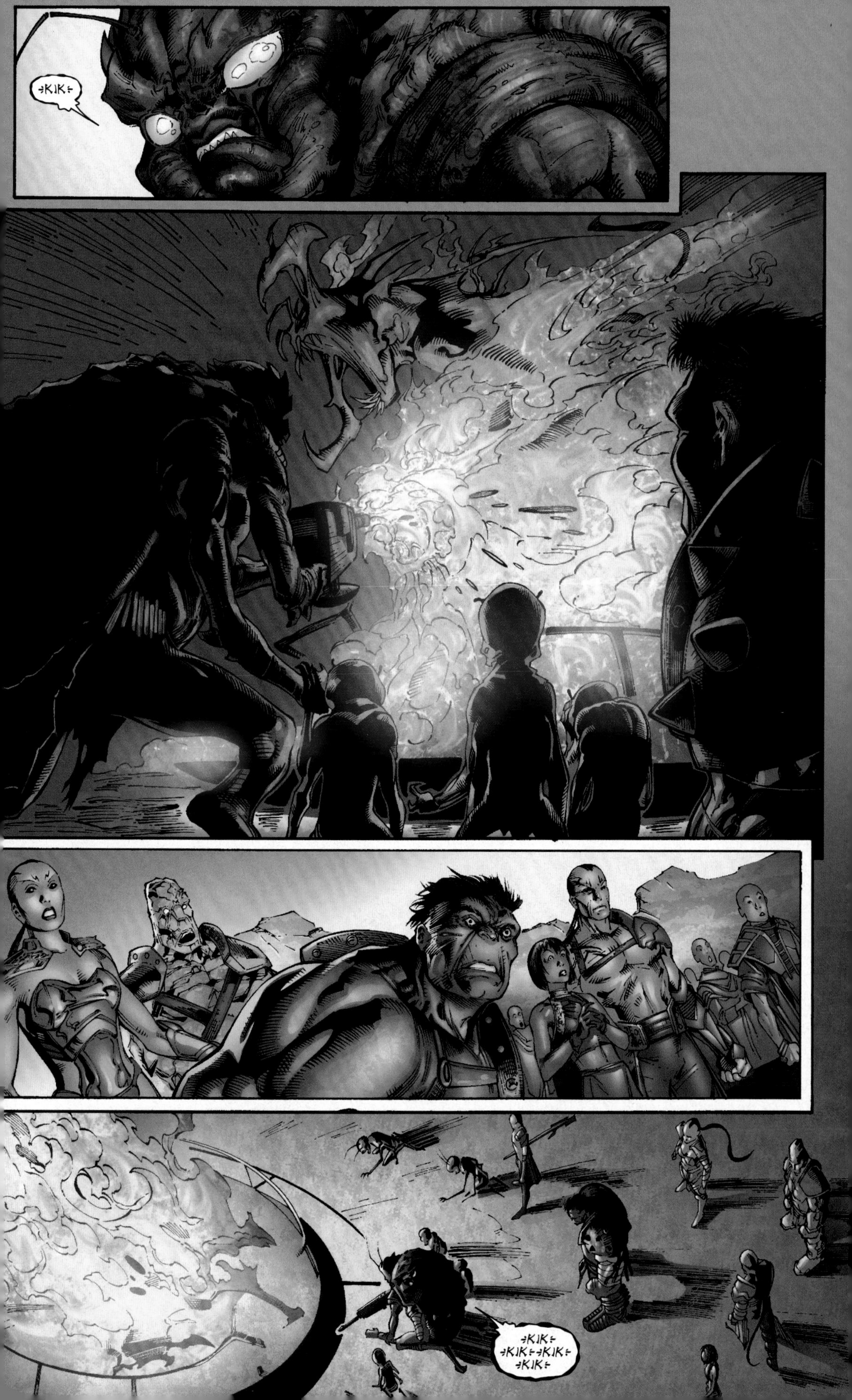

KIK
KIK KIK KIK KIK

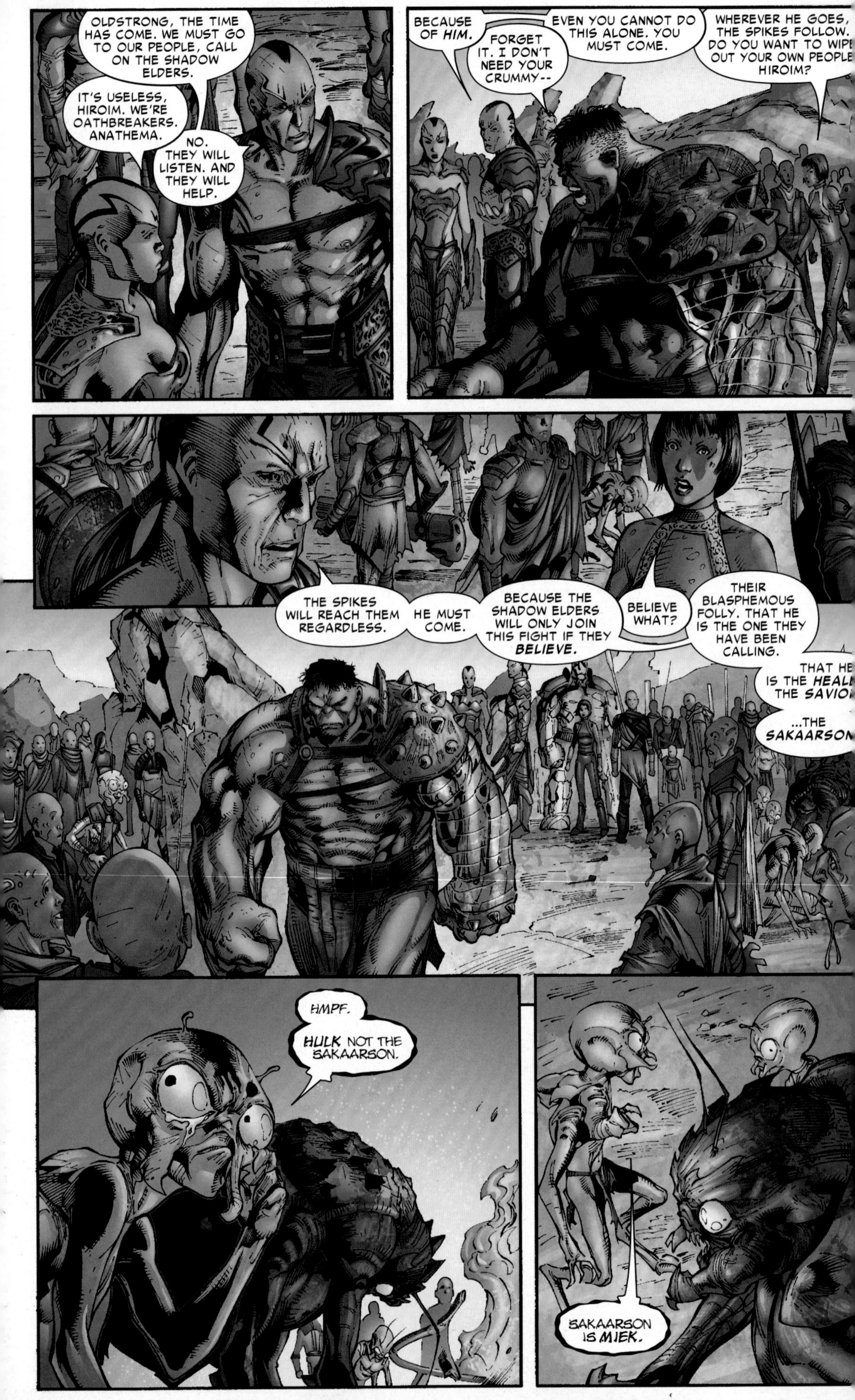

OLDSTRONG, THE TIME HAS COME. WE MUST GO TO OUR PEOPLE, CALL ON THE SHADOW ELDERS.
IT'S USELESS, HIROIM. WE'RE OATHBREAKERS. ANATHEMA.
NO. THEY WILL LISTEN. AND THEY WILL HELP.
BECAUSE OF HIM.
FORGET IT. I DON'T NEED YOUR CRUMMY--
EVEN YOU CANNOT DO THIS ALONE. YOU MUST COME.
WHEREVER HE GOES, THE SPIKES FOLLOW. DO YOU WANT TO WIPE OUT YOUR OWN PEOPLE HIROIM?
THE SPIKES WILL REACH THEM REGARDLESS.
HE MUST COME.
BECAUSE THE SHADOW ELDERS WILL ONLY JOIN THIS FIGHT IF THEY BELIEVE.
BELIEVE WHAT?
THEIR BLASPHEMOUS FOLLY. THAT HE IS THE ONE THEY HAVE BEEN CALLING.
THAT HE IS THE HEAL THE SAVIO
...THE SAKAARSON
HMPF.
HULK NOT THE SAKAARSON.
SAKAARSON IS MIEK.

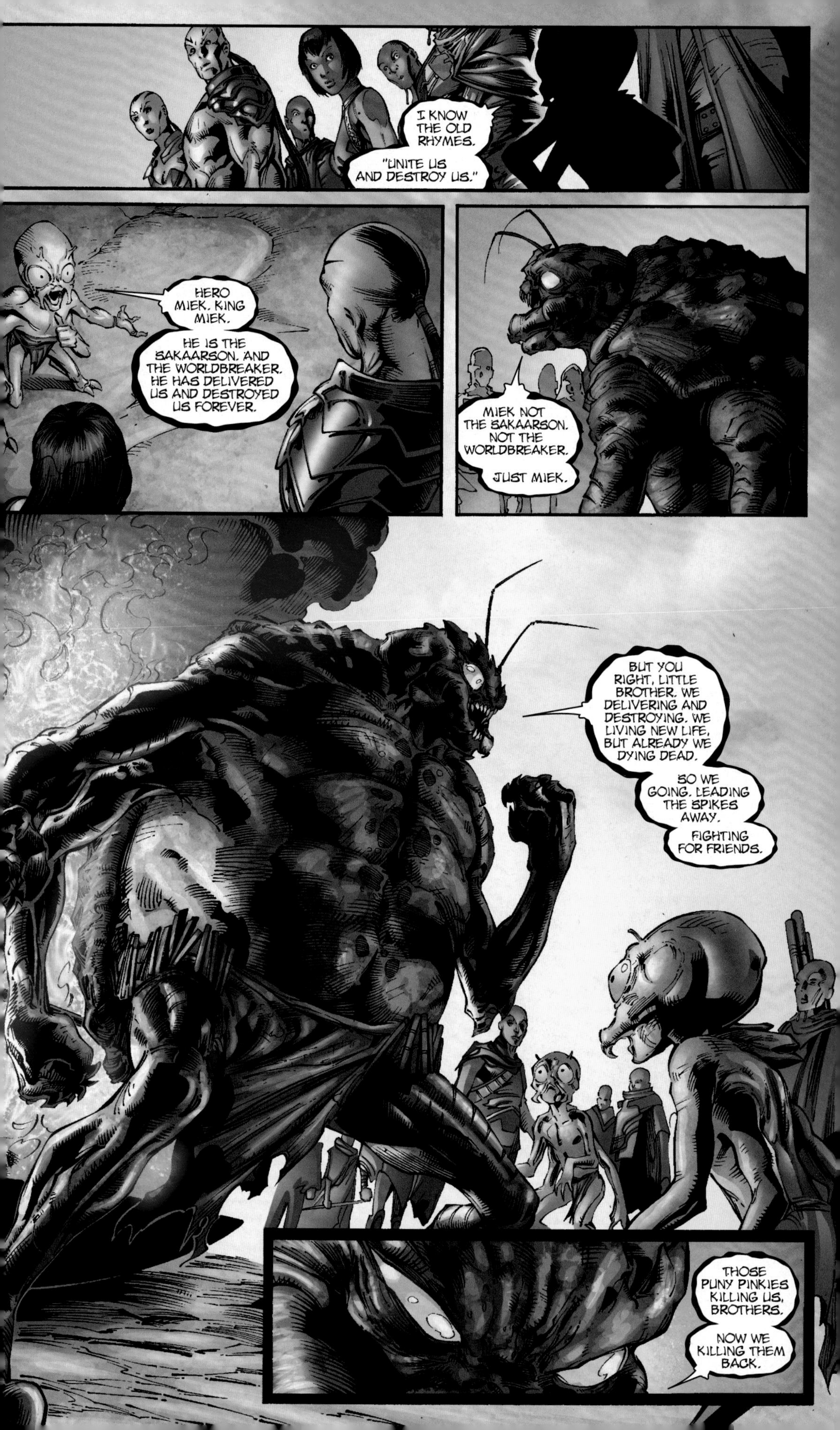
I KNOW THE OLD RHYMES.
"UNITE US AND DESTROY US."
HERO MIEK. KING MIEK.
HE IS THE SAKAARSON. AND THE WORLDBREAKER. HE HAS DELIVERED US AND DESTROYED US FOREVER.
MIEK NOT THE SAKAARSON. NOT THE WORLDBREAKER.
JUST MIEK.
BUT YOU RIGHT, LITTLE BROTHER. WE DELIVERING AND DESTROYING. WE LIVING NEW LIFE, BUT ALREADY WE DYING DEAD.
SO WE GOING. LEADING THE SPIKES AWAY.
FIGHTING FOR FRIENDS.
THOSE PUNY PINKIES KILLING US, BROTHERS.
NOW WE KILLING THEM BACK.

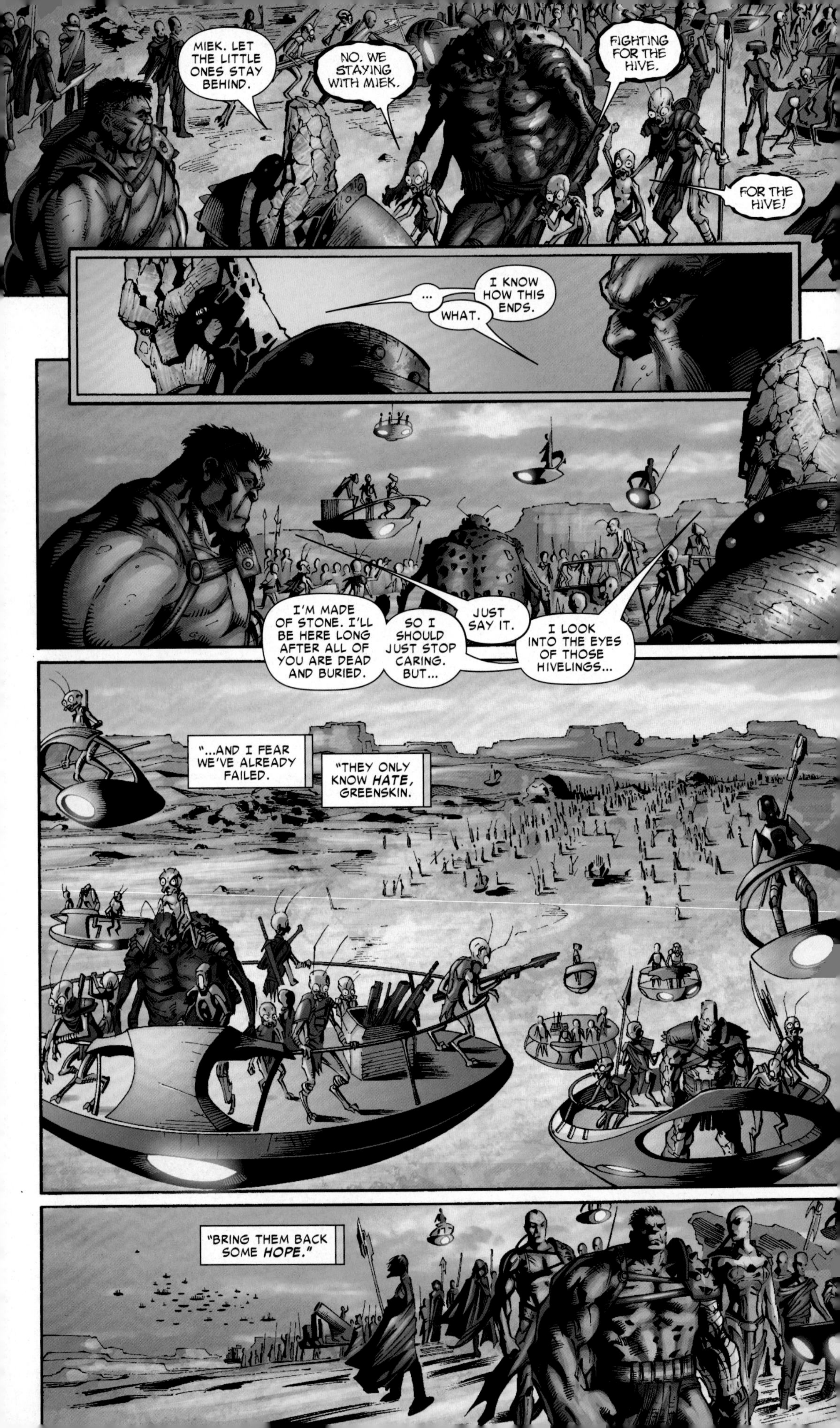
MIEK. LET THE LITTLE ONES STAY BEHIND.
NO. WE STAYING WITH MIEK.
FIGHTING FOR THE HIVE.
FOR THE HIVE!
...
I KNOW HOW THIS ENDS.
WHAT.
JUST SAY IT.
I'M MADE OF STONE. I'LL BE HERE LONG AFTER ALL OF YOU ARE DEAD AND BURIED.
SO I SHOULD JUST STOP CARING. BUT...
I LOOK INTO THE EYES OF THOSE HIVELINGS...
"...AND I FEAR WE'VE ALREADY FAILED.
"THEY ONLY KNOW *HATE*, GREENSKIN.
"BRING THEM BACK SOME *HOPE*."

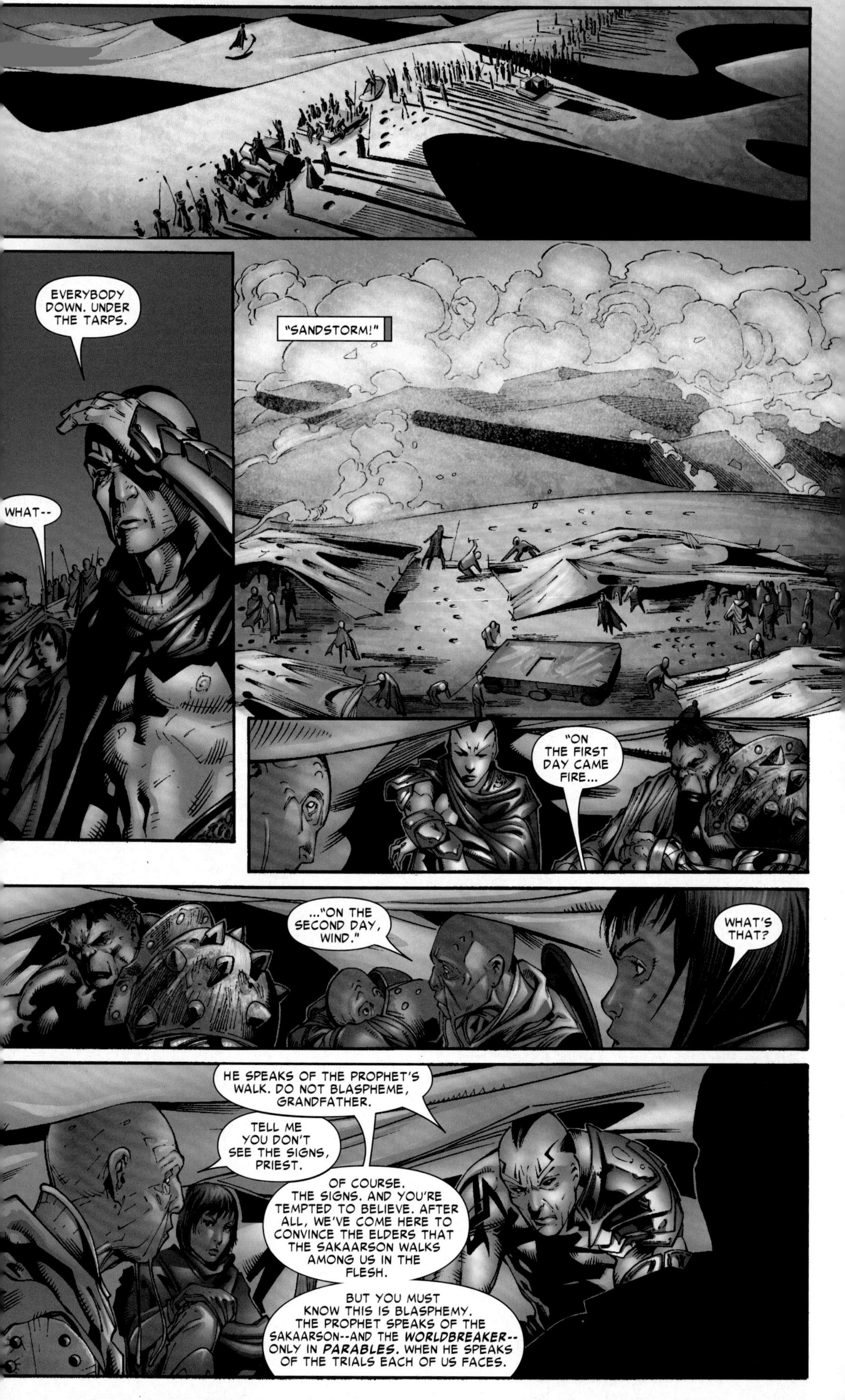

EVERYBODY DOWN. UNDER THE TARPS.
"SANDSTORM!"
WHAT--
"ON THE FIRST DAY CAME FIRE...
..."ON THE SECOND DAY, WIND."
WHAT'S THAT?
HE SPEAKS OF THE PROPHET'S WALK. DO NOT BLASPHEME, GRANDFATHER.
TELL ME YOU DON'T SEE THE SIGNS, PRIEST.
OF COURSE. THE SIGNS. AND YOU'RE TEMPTED TO BELIEVE. AFTER ALL, WE'VE COME HERE TO CONVINCE THE ELDERS THAT THE SAKAARSON WALKS AMONG US IN THE FLESH.
BUT YOU MUST KNOW THIS IS BLASPHEMY. THE PROPHET SPEAKS OF THE SAKAARSON--AND THE WORLDBREAKER--ONLY IN PARABLES. WHEN HE SPEAKS OF THE TRIALS EACH OF US FACES.

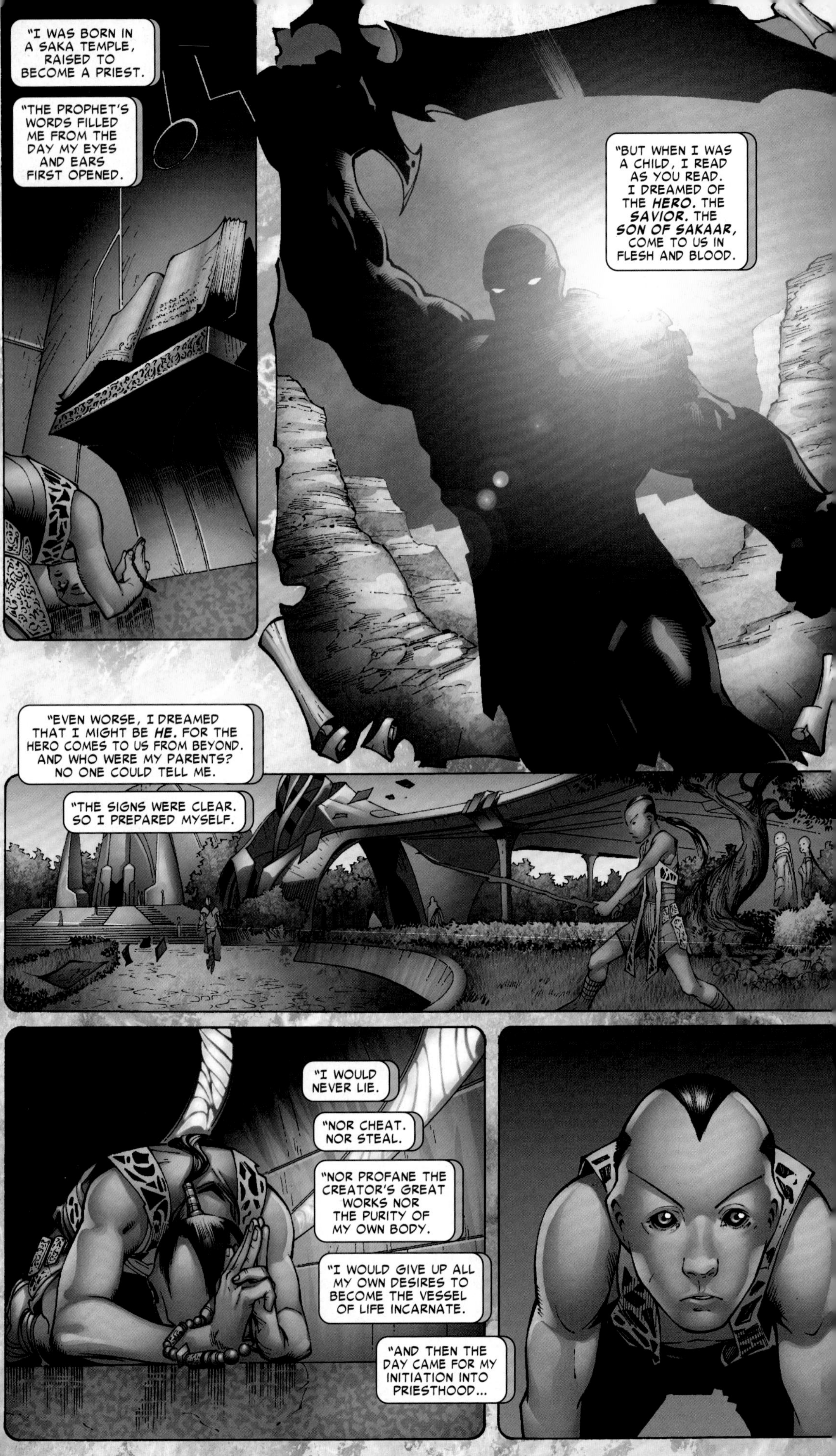
"I WAS BORN IN A SAKA TEMPLE, RAISED TO BECOME A PRIEST.
"THE PROPHET'S WORDS FILLED ME FROM THE DAY MY EYES AND EARS FIRST OPENED.
"BUT WHEN I WAS A CHILD, I READ AS YOU READ. I DREAMED OF THE HERO. THE SAVIOR. THE SON OF SAKAAR, COME TO US IN FLESH AND BLOOD.
"EVEN WORSE, I DREAMED THAT I MIGHT BE HE. FOR THE HERO COMES TO US FROM BEYOND. AND WHO WERE MY PARENTS? NO ONE COULD TELL ME.
"THE SIGNS WERE CLEAR. SO I PREPARED MYSELF.
"I WOULD NEVER LIE.
"NOR CHEAT. NOR STEAL.
"NOR PROFANE THE CREATOR'S GREAT WORKS NOR THE PURITY OF MY OWN BODY.
"I WOULD GIVE UP ALL MY OWN DESIRES TO BECOME THE VESSEL OF LIFE INCARNATE.
"AND THEN THE DAY CAME FOR MY INITIATION INTO PRIESTHOOD...

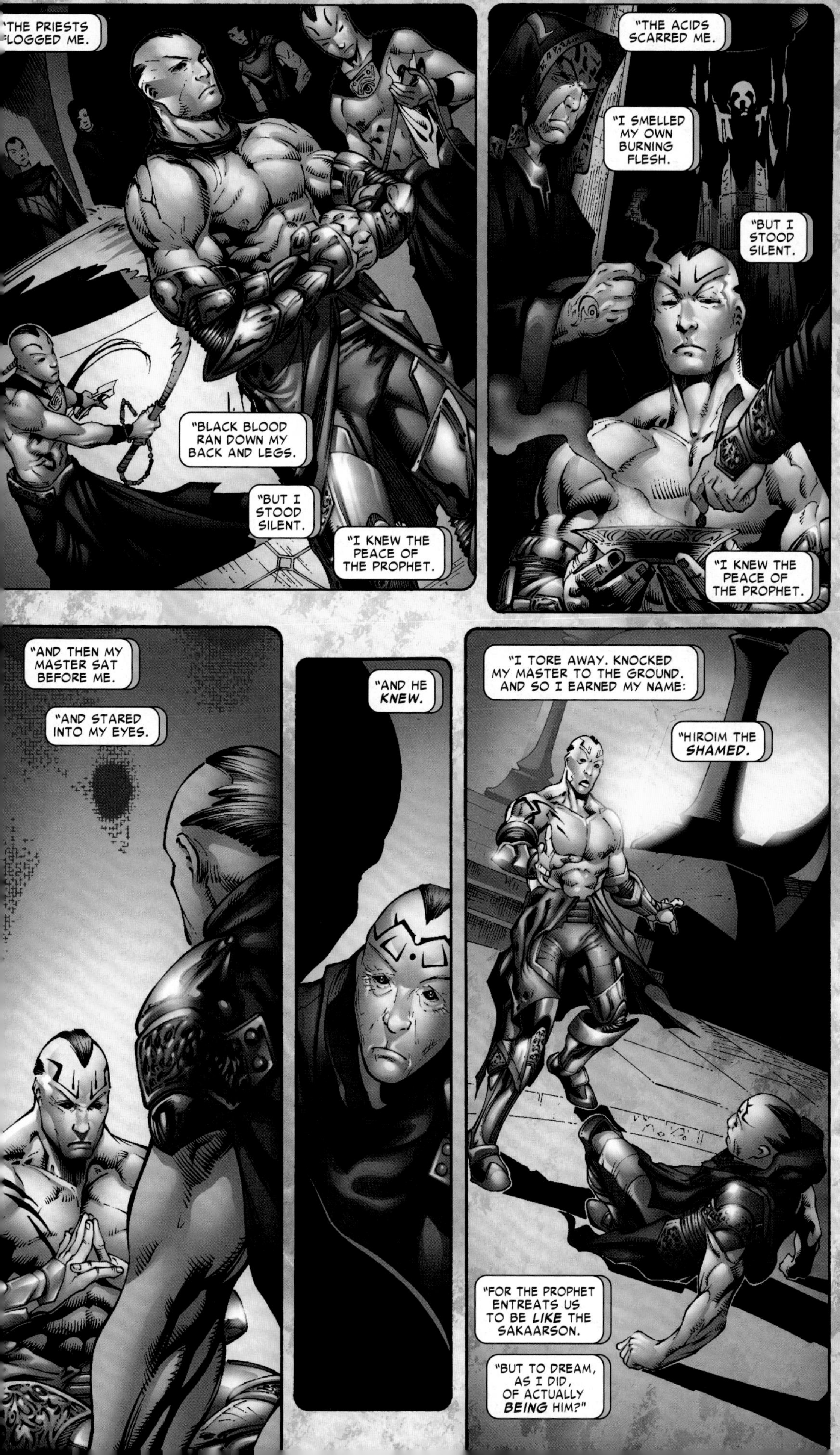
"THE PRIESTS FLOGGED ME.
"BLACK BLOOD RAN DOWN MY BACK AND LEGS.
"BUT I STOOD SILENT.
"I KNEW THE PEACE OF THE PROPHET.
"THE ACIDS SCARRED ME.
"I SMELLED MY OWN BURNING FLESH.
"BUT I STOOD SILENT.
"I KNEW THE PEACE OF THE PROPHET.
"AND THEN MY MASTER SAT BEFORE ME.
"AND STARED INTO MY EYES.
"AND HE *KNEW.*
"I TORE AWAY. KNOCKED MY MASTER TO THE GROUND. AND SO I EARNED MY NAME:
"HIROIM THE *SHAMED.*
"FOR THE PROPHET ENTREATS US TO BE *LIKE* THE SAKAARSON.
"BUT TO DREAM, AS I DID, OF ACTUALLY *BEING* HIM?"

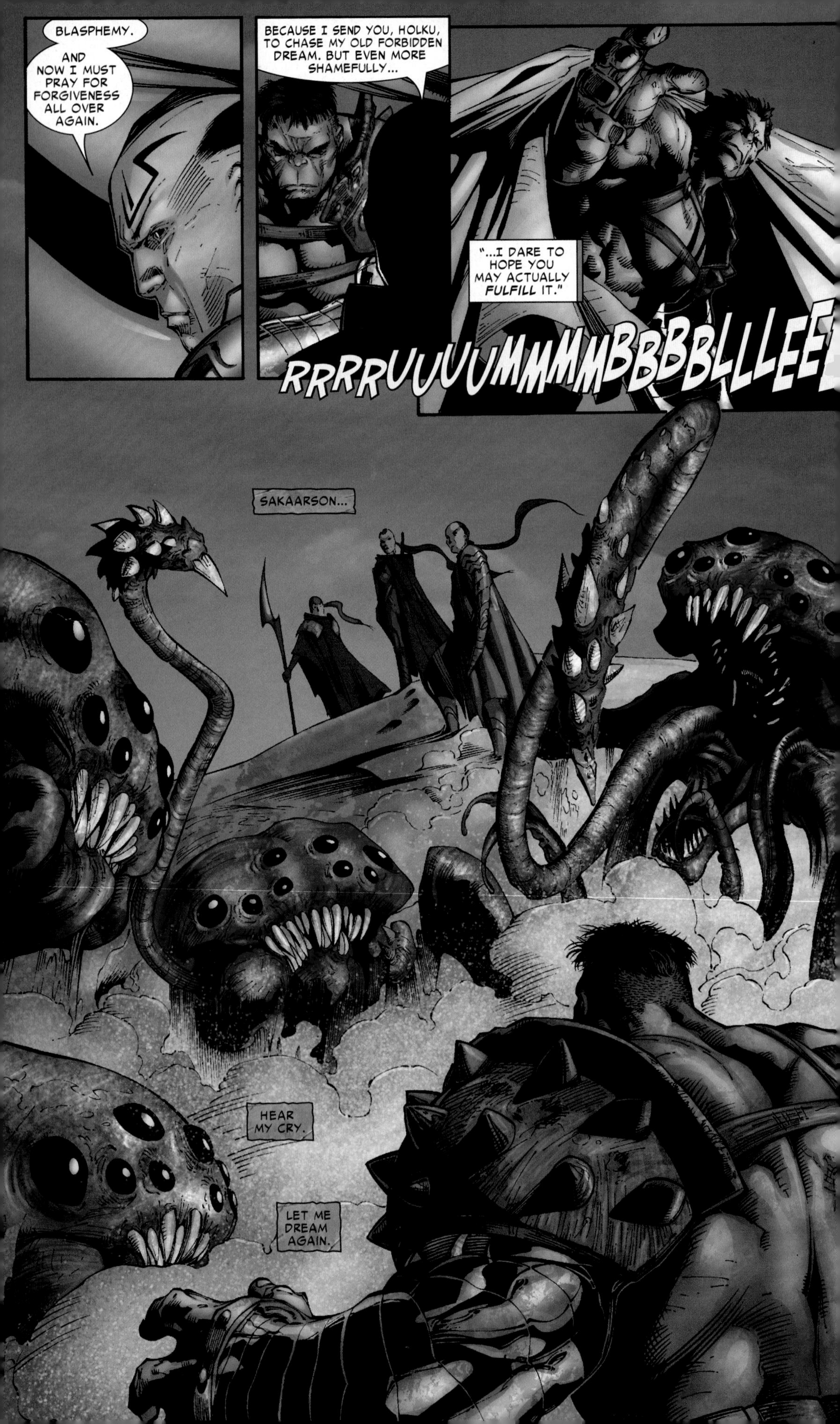
BLASPHEMY.
AND NOW I MUST PRAY FOR FORGIVENESS ALL OVER AGAIN.
BECAUSE I SEND YOU, HOLKU, TO CHASE MY OLD FORBIDDEN DREAM. BUT EVEN MORE SHAMEFULLY...
"...I DARE TO HOPE YOU MAY ACTUALLY *FULFILL* IT."
RRRRUUUUMMMMBBBBLLLEE
SAKAARSON...
HEAR MY CRY.
LET ME DREAM AGAIN.

#101

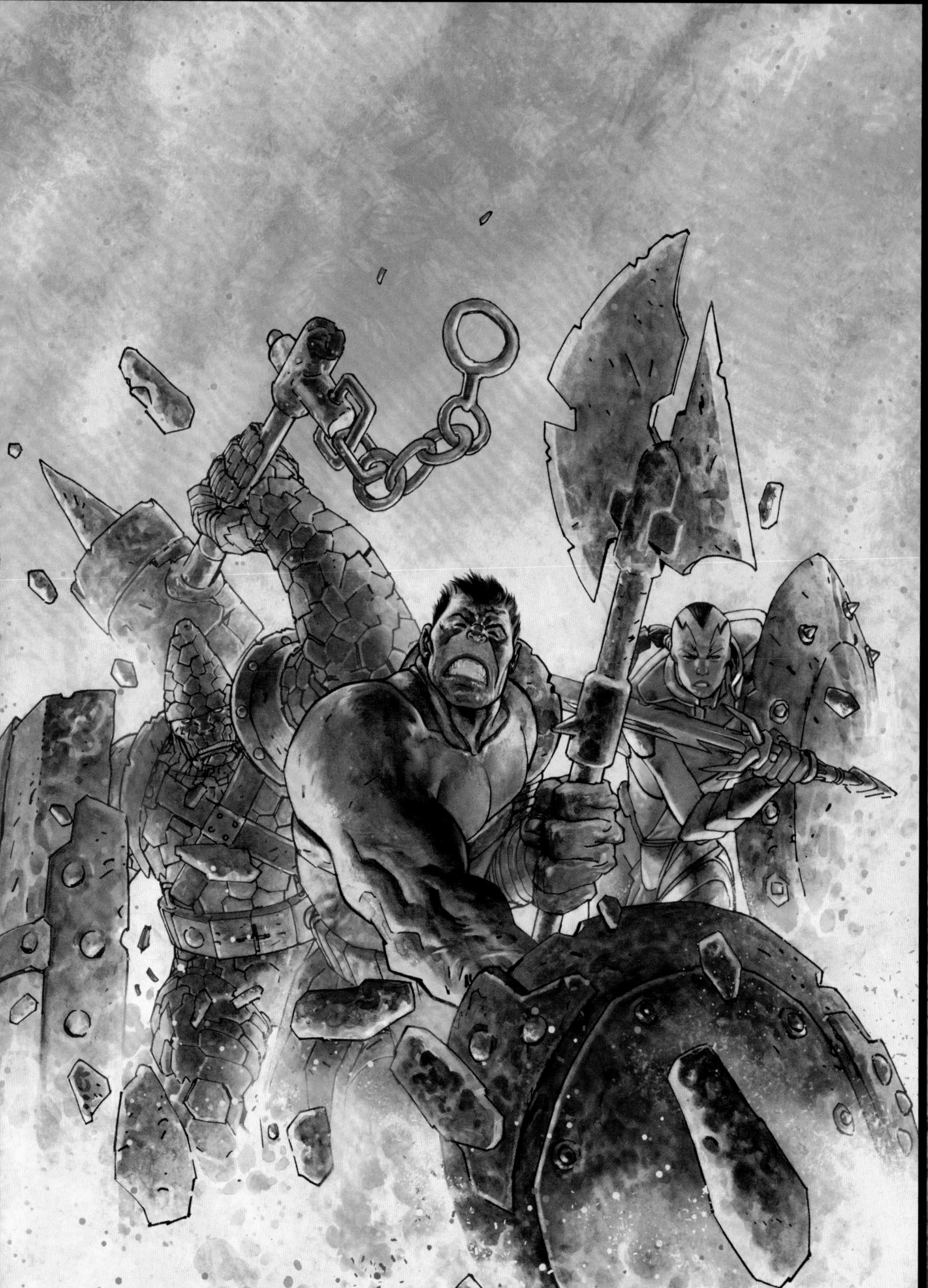
LADRÖNN:2006

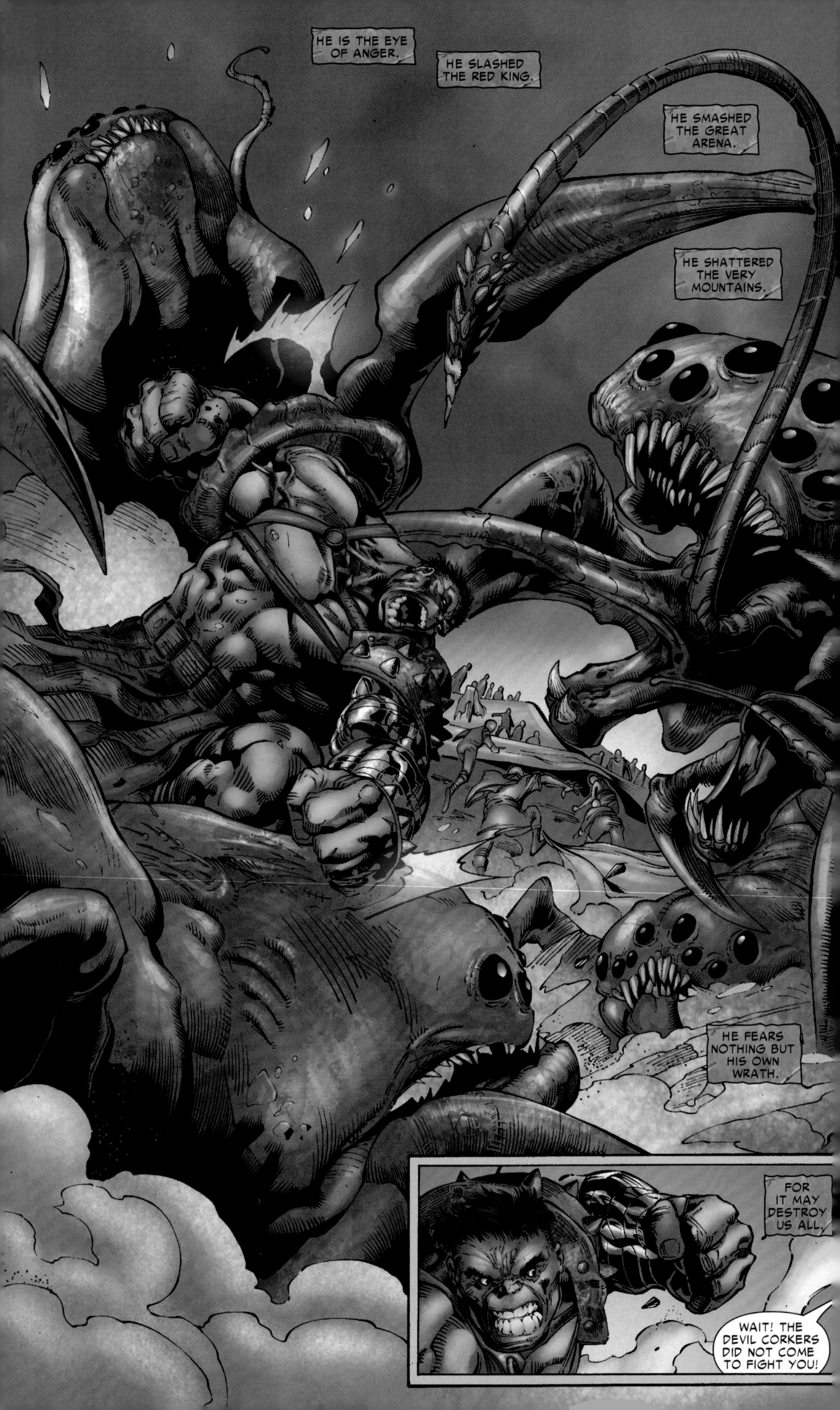
HE IS THE EYE OF ANGER.
HE SLASHED THE RED KING.
HE SMASHED THE GREAT ARENA.
HE SHATTERED THE VERY MOUNTAINS.
HE FEARS NOTHING BUT HIS OWN WRATH.
FOR IT MAY DESTROY US ALL.
WAIT! THE DEVIL CORKERS DID NOT COME TO FIGHT YOU!

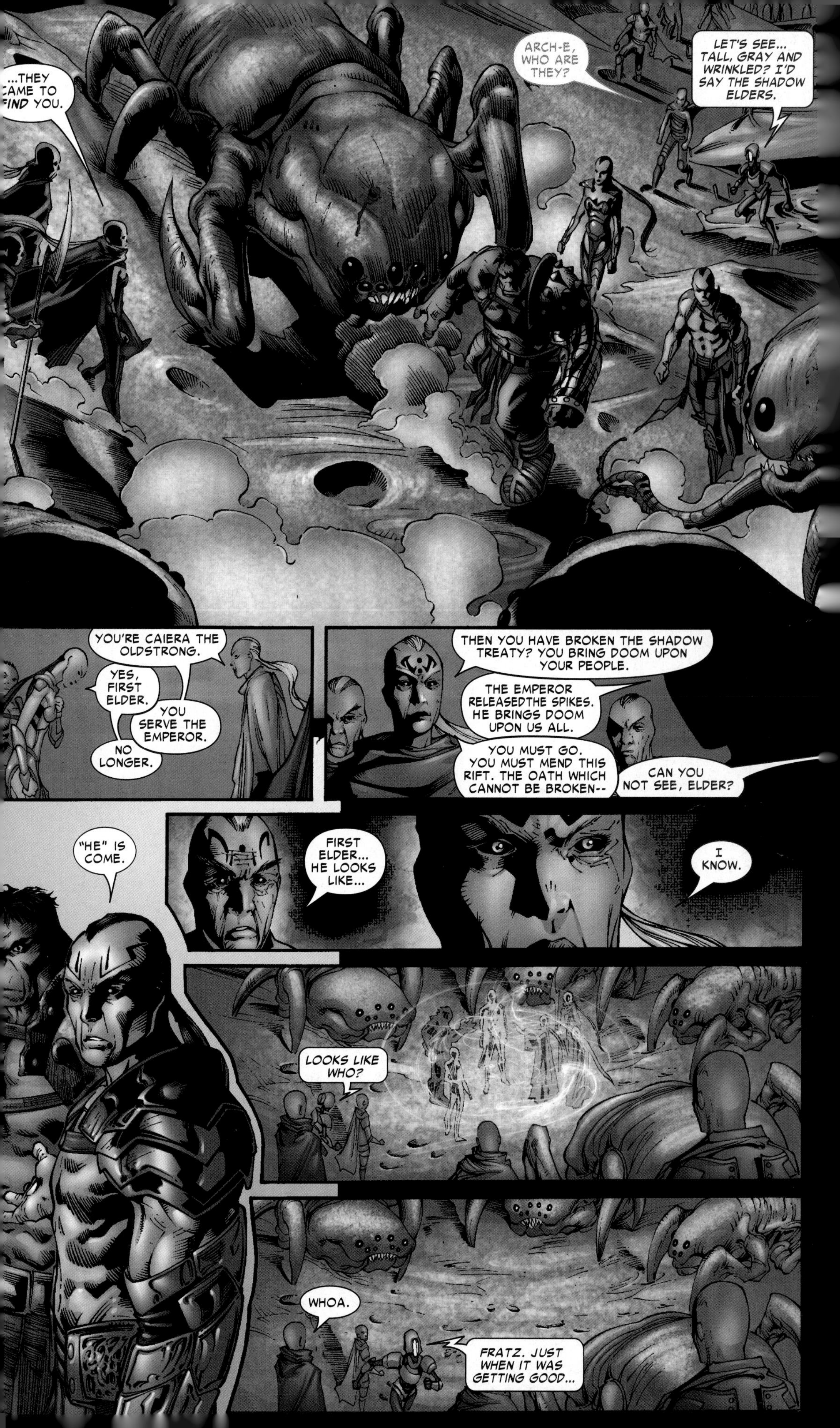
...THEY CAME TO FIND YOU.
ARCH-E, WHO ARE THEY?
LET'S SEE... TALL, GRAY AND WRINKLED? I'D SAY THE SHADOW ELDERS.
YOU'RE CAIERA THE OLDSTRONG.
YES, FIRST ELDER.
YOU SERVE THE EMPEROR.
NO LONGER.
THEN YOU HAVE BROKEN THE SHADOW TREATY? YOU BRING DOOM UPON YOUR PEOPLE.
THE EMPEROR RELEASEDTHE SPIKES. HE BRINGS DOOM UPON US ALL.
YOU MUST GO. YOU MUST MEND THIS RIFT. THE OATH WHICH CANNOT BE BROKEN--
CAN YOU NOT SEE, ELDER?
"HE" IS COME.
FIRST ELDER... HE LOOKS LIKE...
I KNOW.
LOOKS LIKE WHO?
WHOA.
FRATZ. JUST WHEN IT WAS GETTING GOOD...

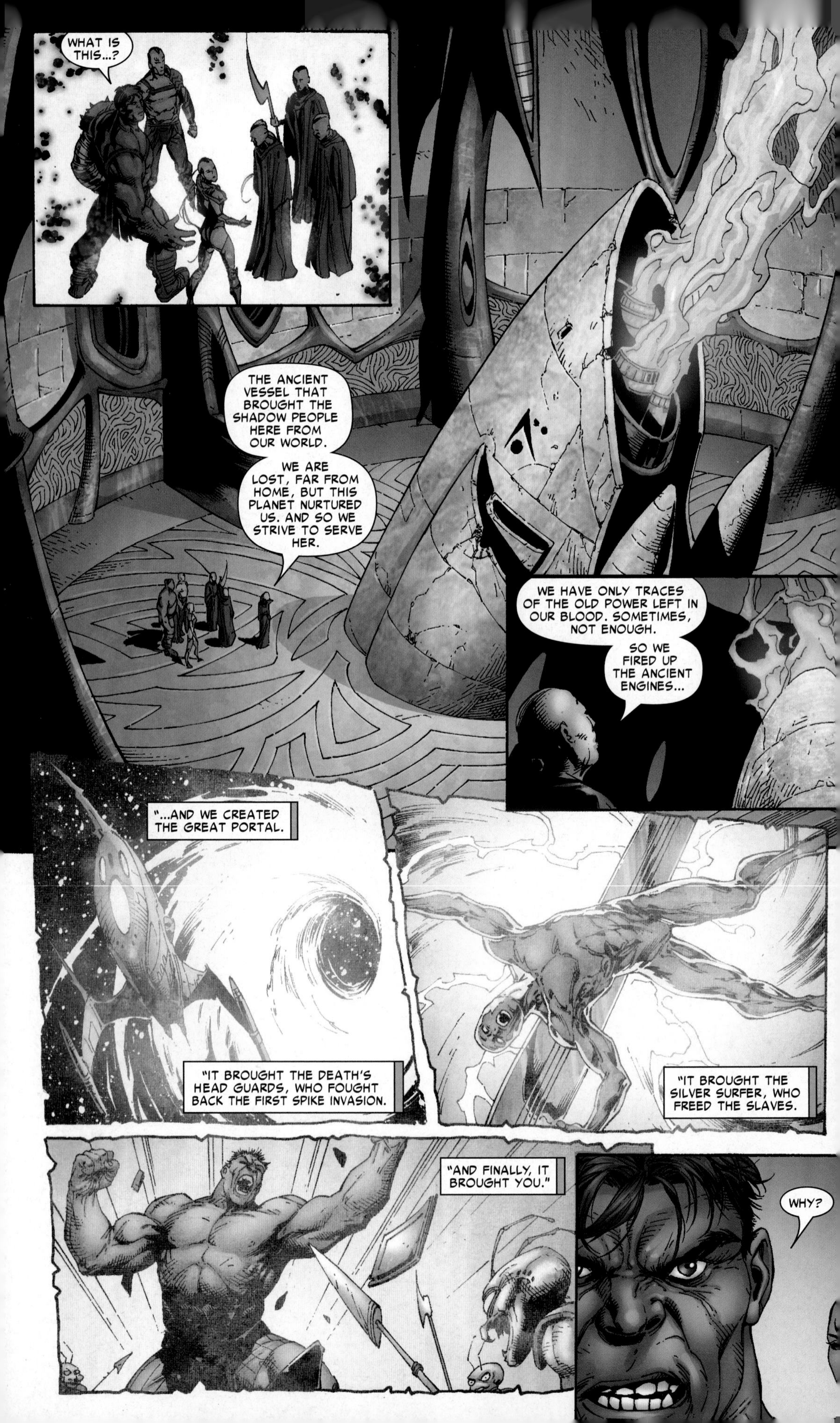
WHAT IS THIS...?
THE ANCIENT VESSEL THAT BROUGHT THE SHADOW PEOPLE HERE FROM OUR WORLD.
WE ARE LOST, FAR FROM HOME, BUT THIS PLANET NURTURED US. AND SO WE STRIVE TO SERVE HER.
WE HAVE ONLY TRACES OF THE OLD POWER LEFT IN OUR BLOOD. SOMETIMES, NOT ENOUGH.
SO WE FIRED UP THE ANCIENT ENGINES...
"...AND WE CREATED THE GREAT PORTAL.
"IT BROUGHT THE DEATH'S HEAD GUARDS, WHO FOUGHT BACK THE FIRST SPIKE INVASION.
"IT BROUGHT THE SILVER SURFER, WHO FREED THE SLAVES.
"AND FINALLY, IT BROUGHT YOU."
WHY?

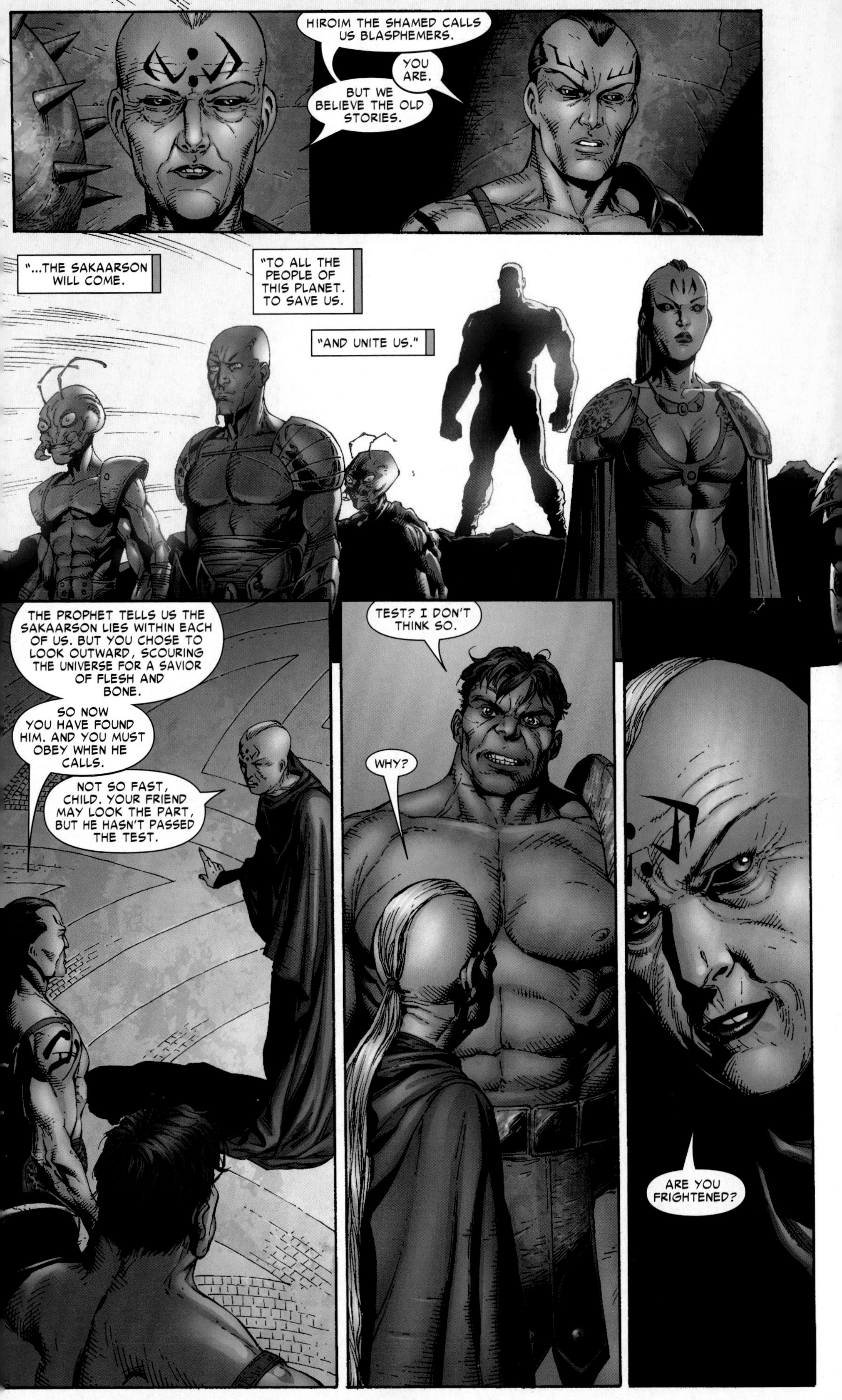
HIROIM THE SHAMED CALLS US BLASPHEMERS.
YOU ARE.
BUT WE BELIEVE THE OLD STORIES.
"...THE SAKAARSON WILL COME.
"TO ALL THE PEOPLE OF THIS PLANET. TO SAVE US.
"AND UNITE US."
THE PROPHET TELLS US THE SAKAARSON LIES WITHIN EACH OF US. BUT YOU CHOSE TO LOOK OUTWARD, SCOURING THE UNIVERSE FOR A SAVIOR OF FLESH AND BONE.
SO NOW YOU HAVE FOUND HIM. AND YOU MUST OBEY WHEN HE CALLS.
NOT SO FAST, CHILD. YOUR FRIEND MAY LOOK THE PART, BUT HE HASN'T PASSED THE TEST.
TEST? I DON'T THINK SO.
WHY?
ARE YOU FRIGHTENED?

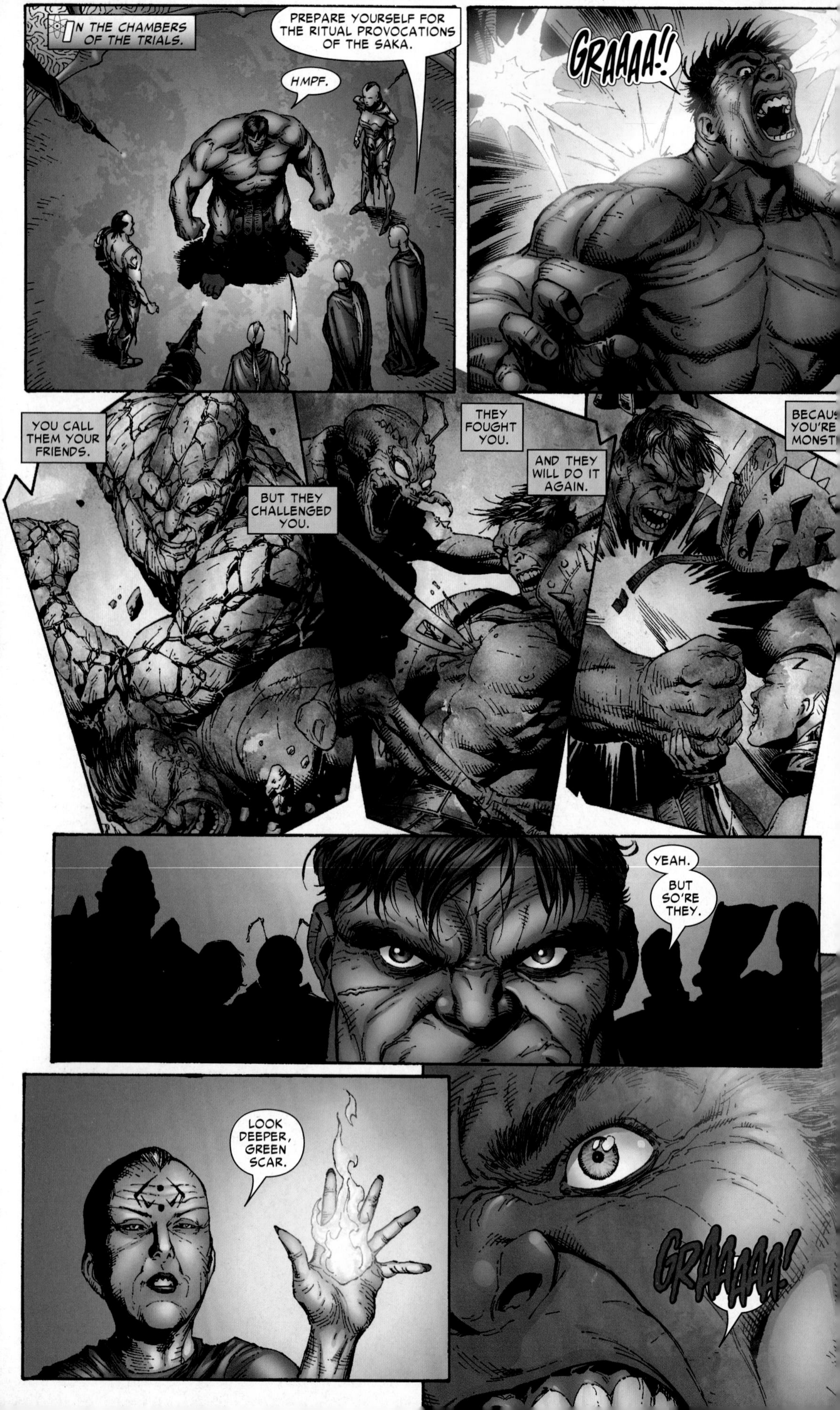
IN THE CHAMBERS OF THE TRIALS.
PREPARE YOURSELF FOR THE RITUAL PROVOCATIONS OF THE SAKA.
HMPF.
GRAAAA!!
YOU CALL THEM YOUR FRIENDS.
BUT THEY CHALLENGED YOU.
THEY FOUGHT YOU.
AND THEY WILL DO IT AGAIN.
YEAH.
BUT SO'RE THEY.
LOOK DEEPER, GREEN SCAR.
GRAAAAA!

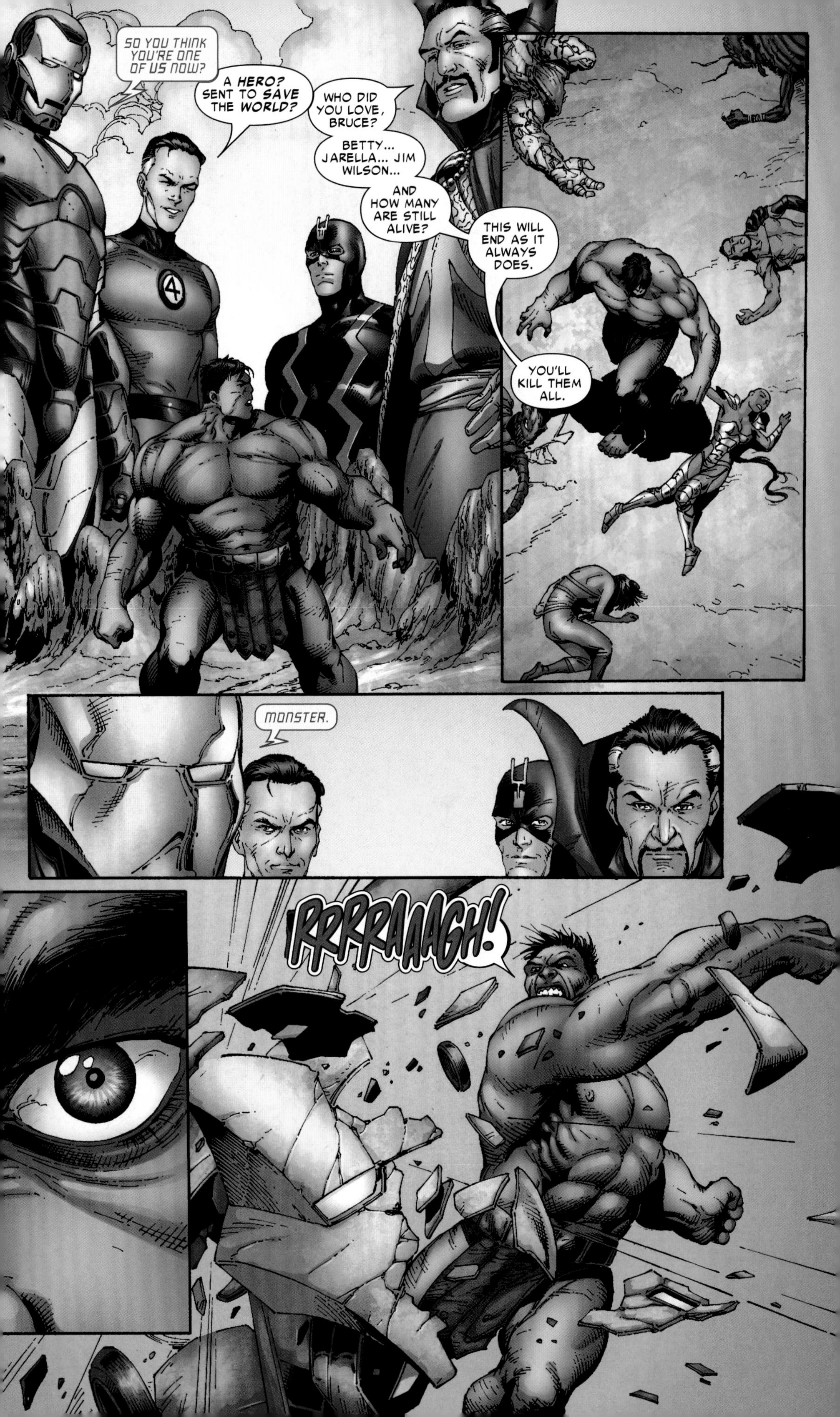
SO YOU THINK YOU'RE ONE OF US NOW?
A HERO? SENT TO SAVE THE WORLD?
WHO DID YOU LOVE, BRUCE?
BETTY... JARELLA... JIM WILSON...
AND HOW MANY ARE STILL ALIVE?
THIS WILL END AS IT ALWAYS DOES.
YOU'LL KILL THEM ALL.
MONSTER.
RRRRAAAGH!

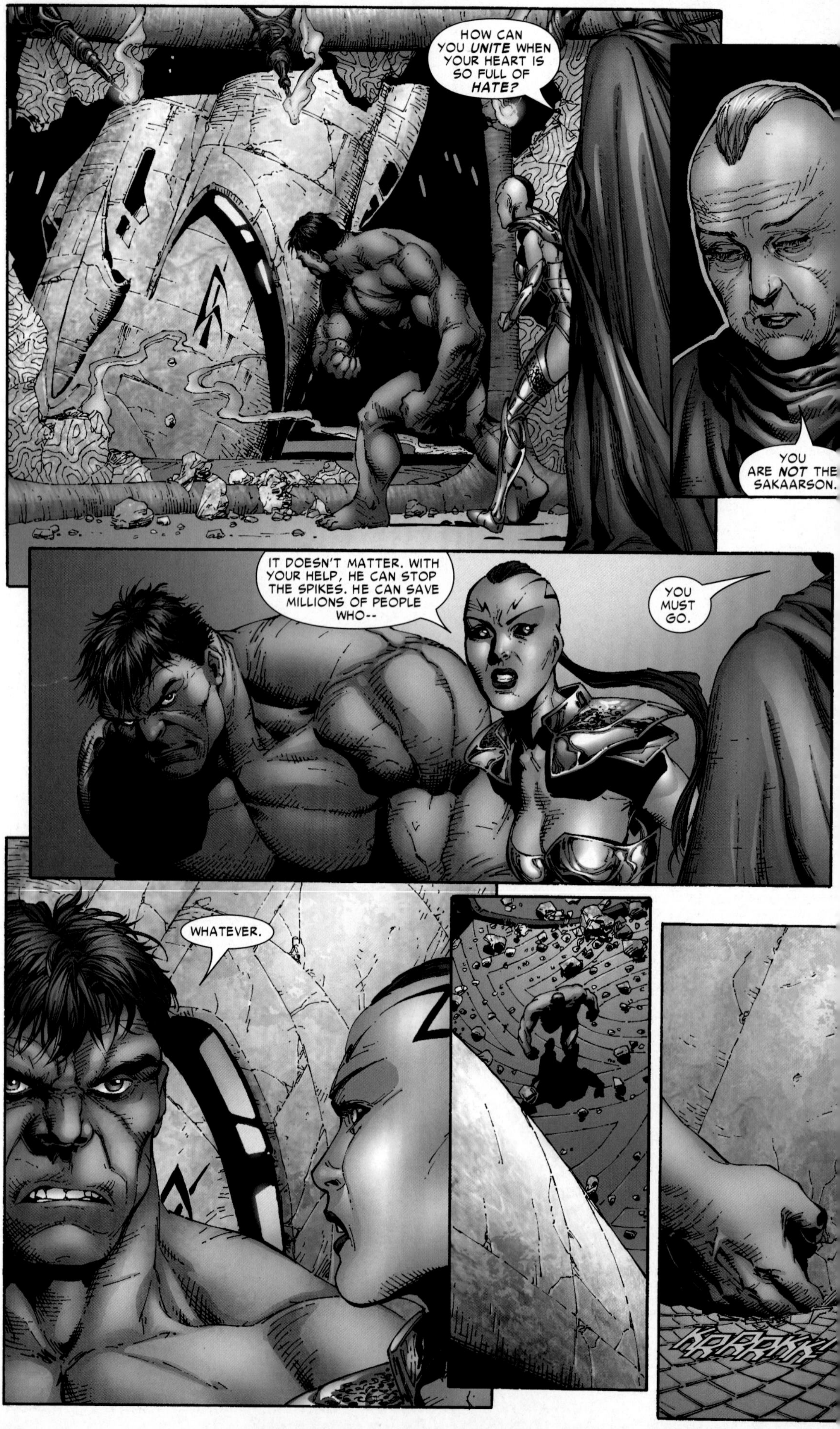
HOW CAN YOU UNITE WHEN YOUR HEART IS SO FULL OF HATE?
YOU ARE NOT THE SAKAARSON.
IT DOESN'T MATTER. WITH YOUR HELP, HE CAN STOP THE SPIKES. HE CAN SAVE MILLIONS OF PEOPLE WHO--
YOU MUST GO.
WHATEVER.
KRRKKK!

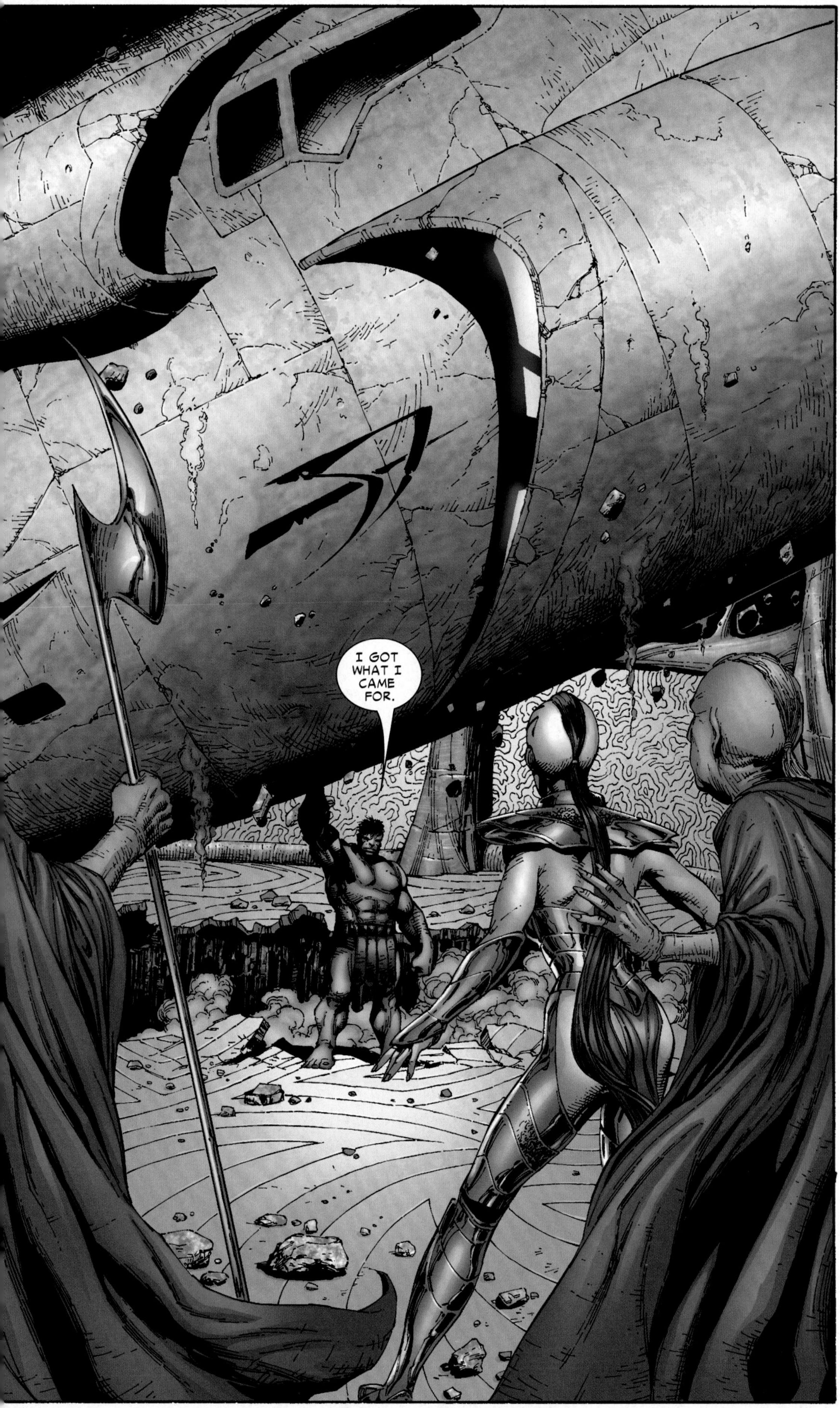
I GOT WHAT I CAME FOR.

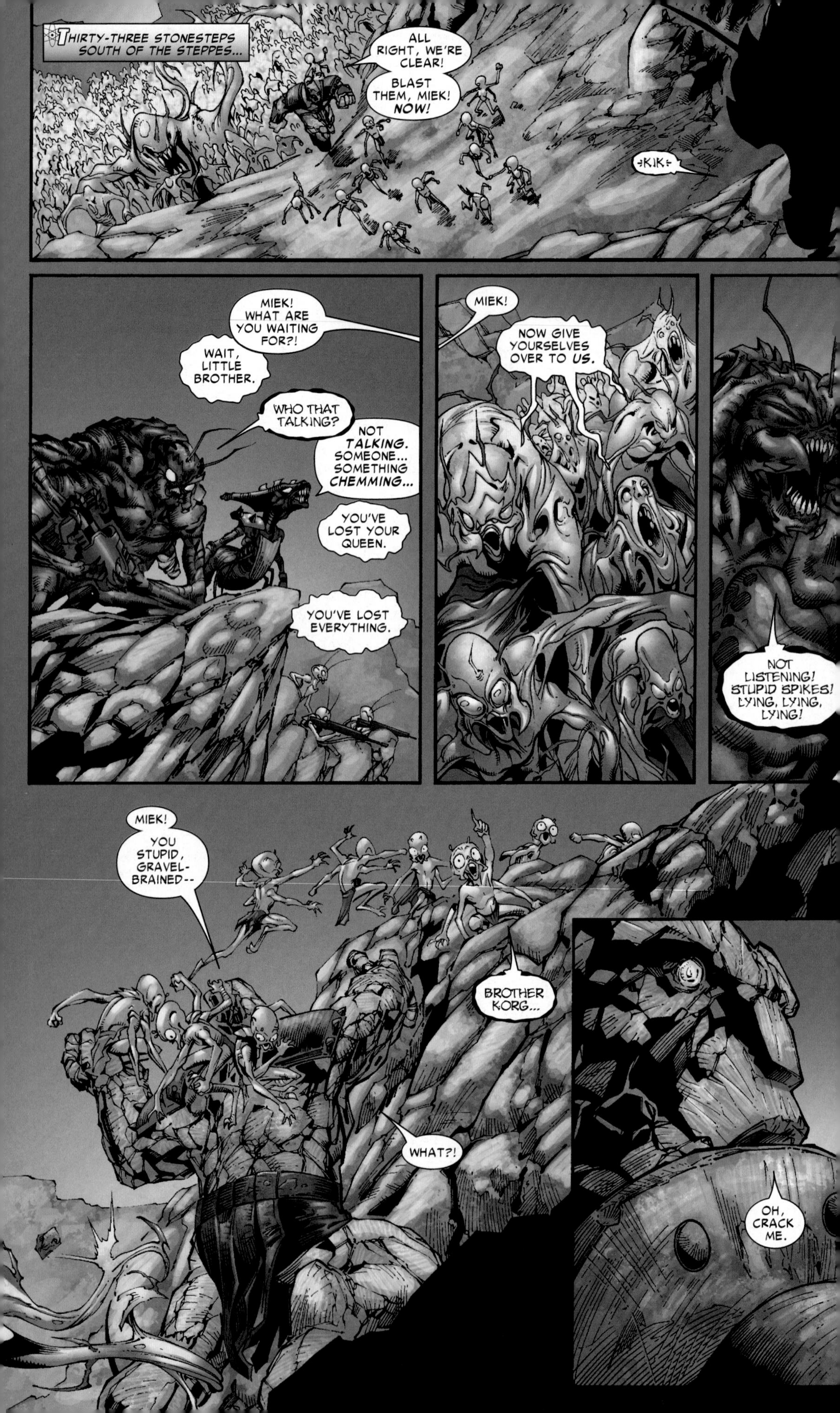
THIRTY-THREE STONESTEPS SOUTH OF THE STEPPES...
ALL RIGHT, WE'RE CLEAR!
BLAST THEM, MIEK! NOW!
⁝KIK⁝
MIEK! WHAT ARE YOU WAITING FOR?!
WAIT, LITTLE BROTHER.
WHO THAT TALKING?
NOT TALKING. SOMEONE... SOMETHING CHEMMING...
YOU'VE LOST YOUR QUEEN.
YOU'VE LOST EVERYTHING.
MIEK!
NOW GIVE YOURSELVES OVER TO US.
NOT LISTENING! STUPID SPIKES! LYING, LYING, LYING!
MIEK!
YOU STUPID, GRAVEL-BRAINED--
BROTHER KORG...
WHAT?!
OH, CRACK ME.

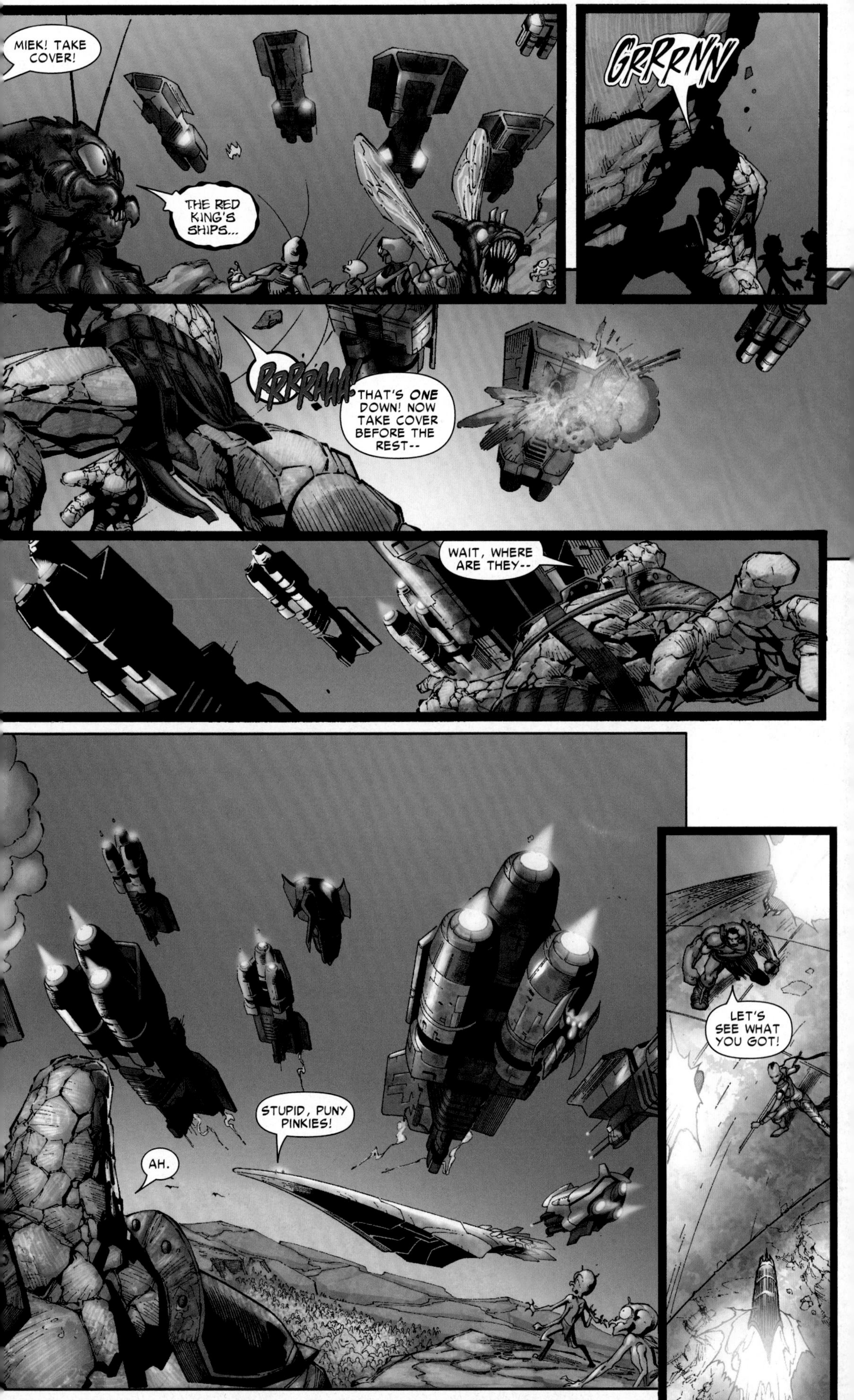
MIEK! TAKE COVER!
THE RED KING'S SHIPS...
GRRRNN
RRRRAAA!
THAT'S *ONE* DOWN! NOW TAKE COVER BEFORE THE REST--
WAIT, WHERE ARE THEY--
STUPID, PUNY PINKIES!
AH.
LET'S SEE WHAT YOU GOT!

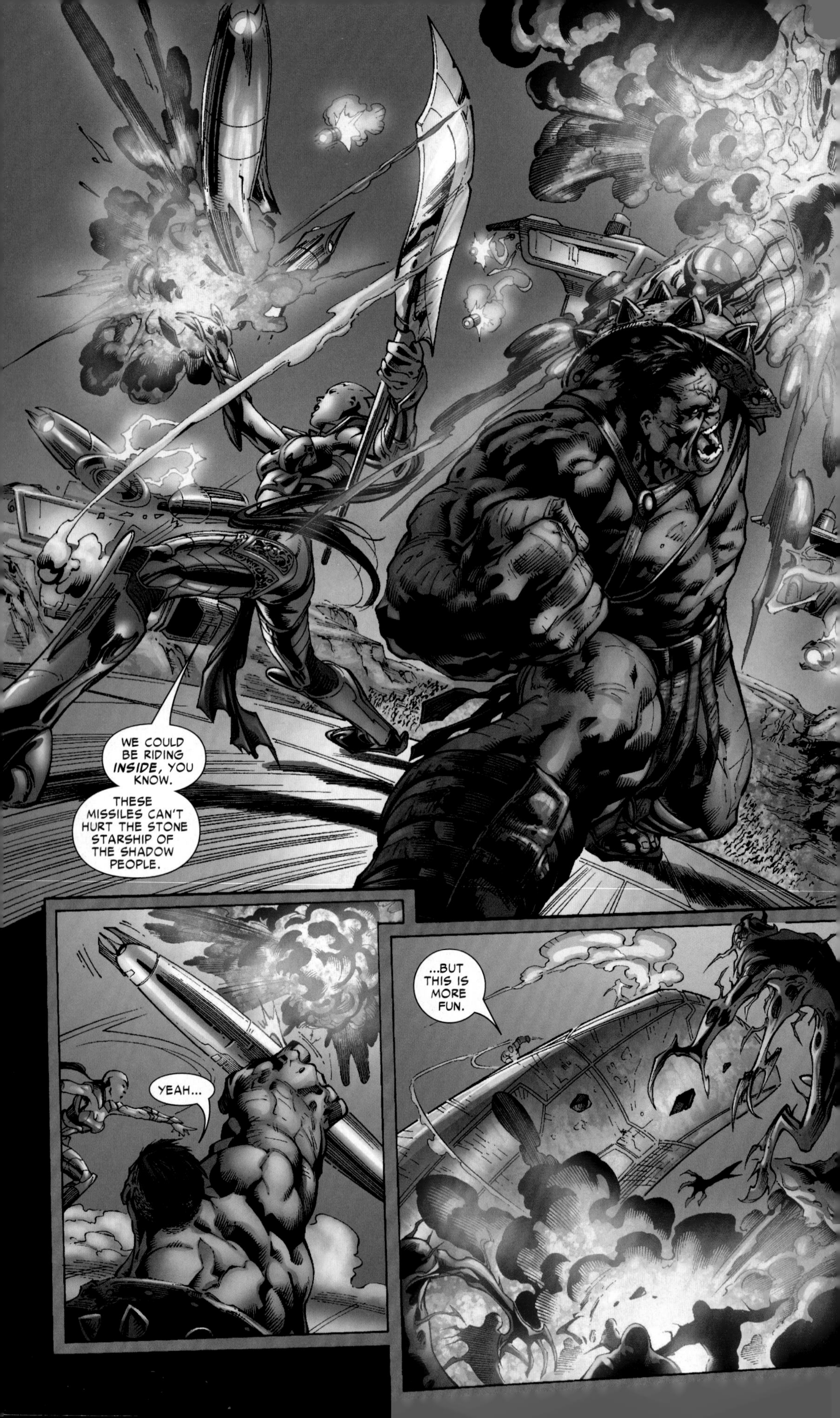
WE COULD BE RIDING *INSIDE*, YOU KNOW.
THESE MISSILES CAN'T HURT THE STONE STARSHIP OF THE SHADOW PEOPLE.
YEAH...
...BUT THIS IS MORE FUN.

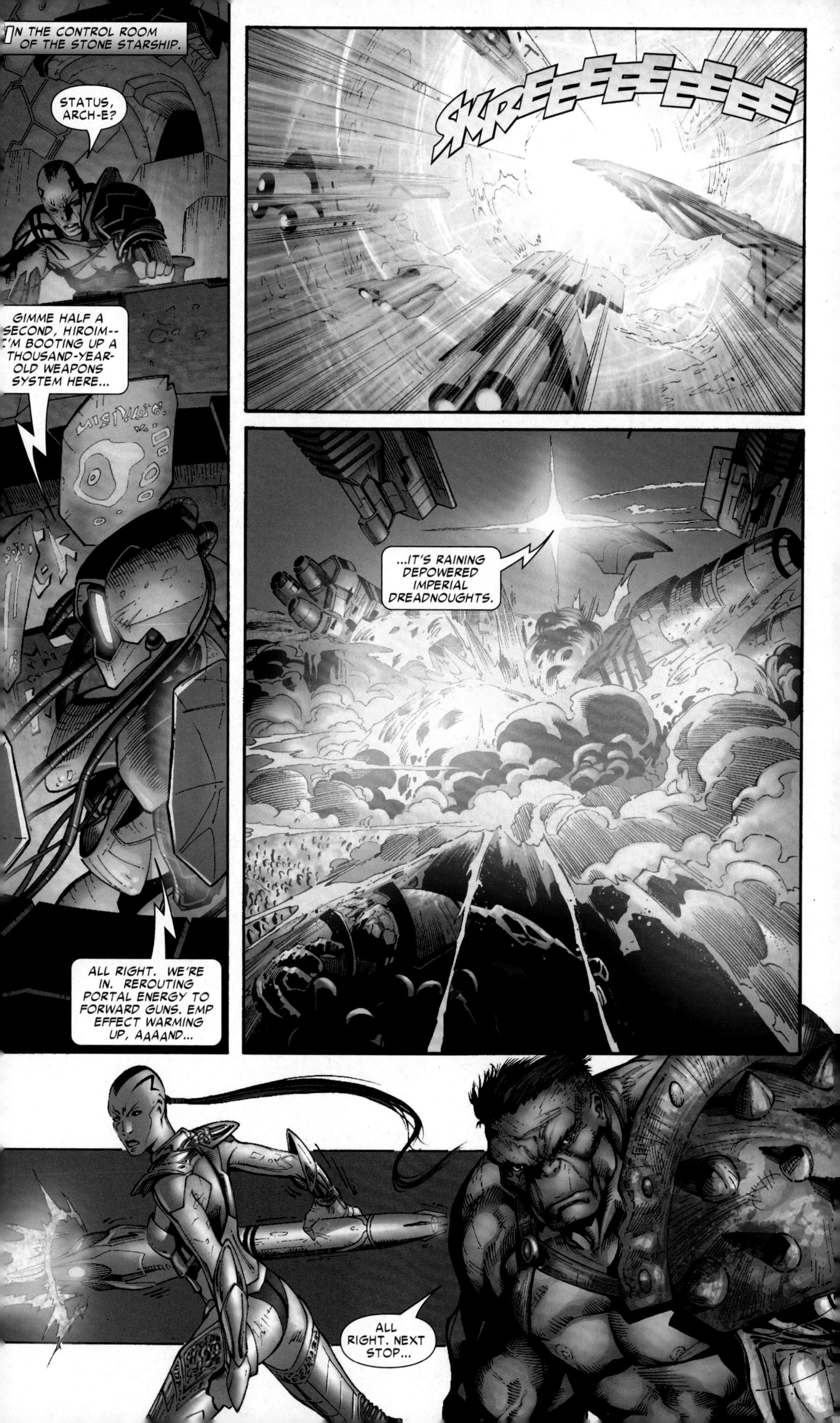
IN THE CONTROL ROOM OF THE STONE STARSHIP.
STATUS, ARCH-E?
GIMME HALF A SECOND, HIROIM-- I'M BOOTING UP A THOUSAND-YEAR-OLD WEAPONS SYSTEM HERE...
ALL RIGHT. WE'RE IN. REROUTING PORTAL ENERGY TO FORWARD GUNS. EMP EFFECT WARMING UP, AAAAND...
SKREEEEEEEEEE
...IT'S RAINING DEPOWERED IMPERIAL DREADNOUGHTS.
ALL RIGHT. NEXT STOP...

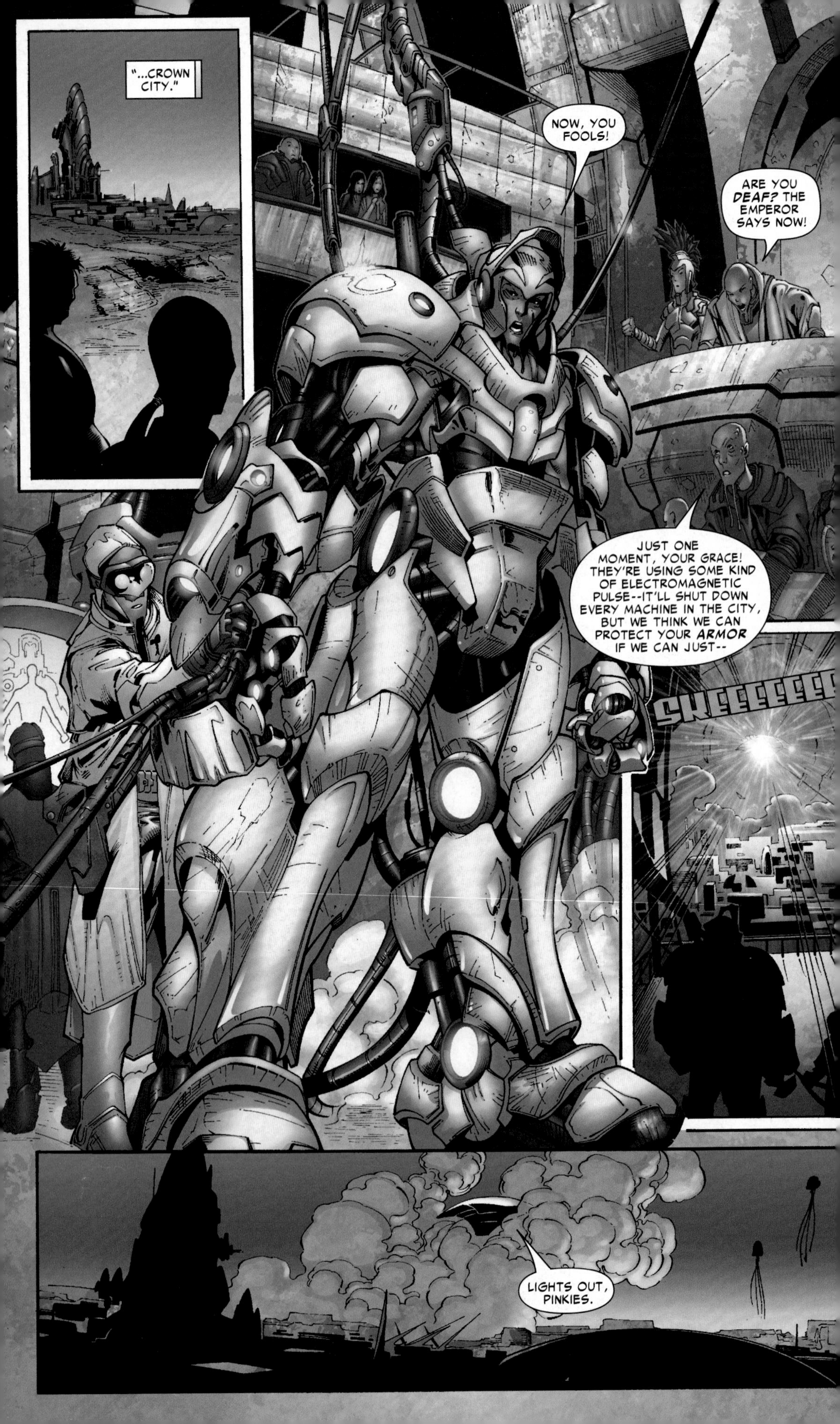
"...CROWN CITY."
NOW, YOU FOOLS!
ARE YOU DEAF? THE EMPEROR SAYS NOW!
JUST ONE MOMENT, YOUR GRACE! THEY'RE USING SOME KIND OF ELECTROMAGNETIC PULSE--IT'LL SHUT DOWN EVERY MACHINE IN THE CITY, BUT WE THINK WE CAN PROTECT YOUR ARMOR IF WE CAN JUST--
SKEEEEEE
LIGHTS OUT, PINKIES.

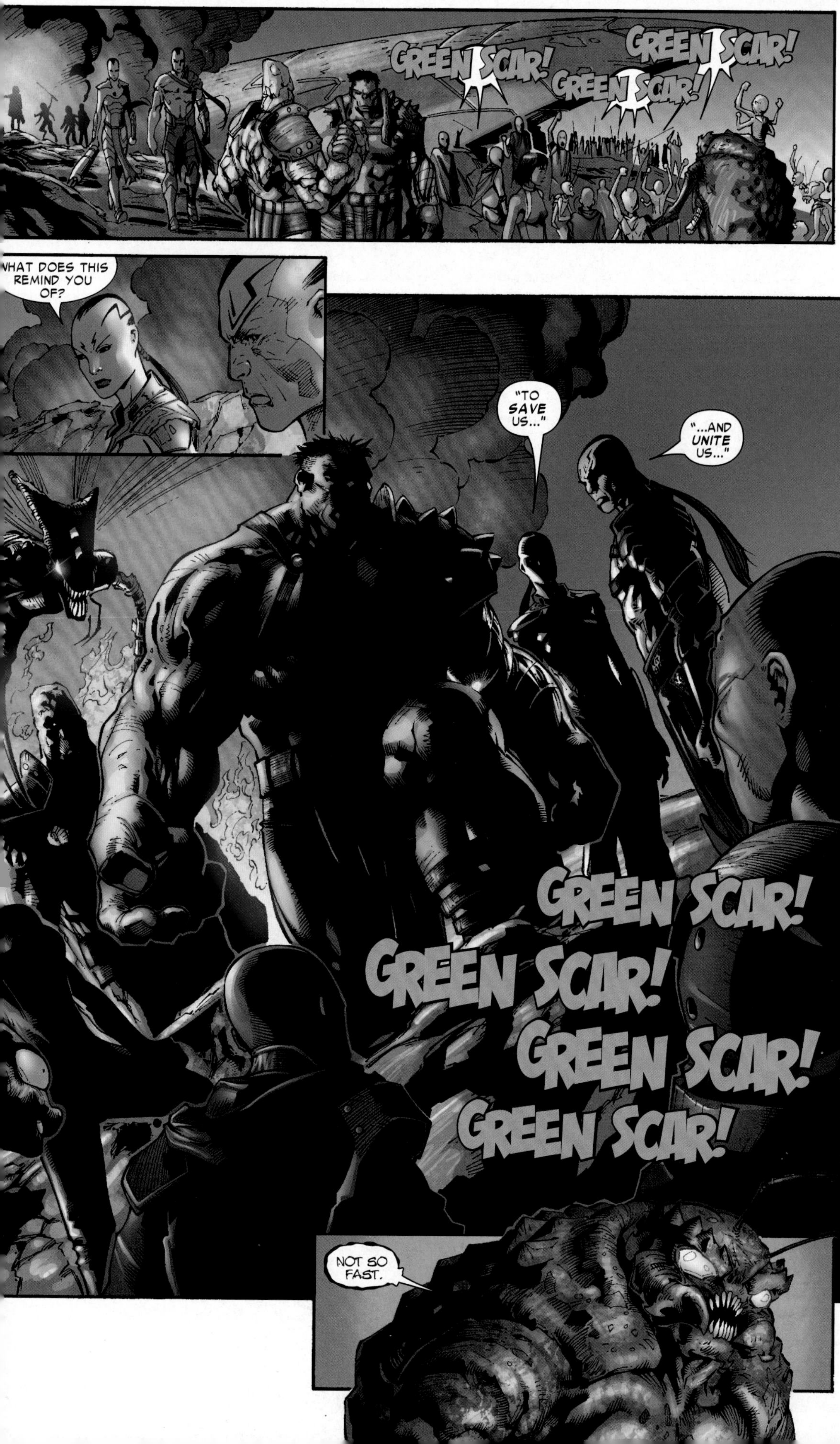
GREEN SCAR!
GREEN SCAR!
GREEN SCAR!
WHAT DOES THIS REMIND YOU OF?
"TO SAVE US..."
"...AND UNITE US..."
GREEN SCAR!
GREEN SCAR!
GREEN SCAR!
GREEN SCAR!
NOT SO FAST.

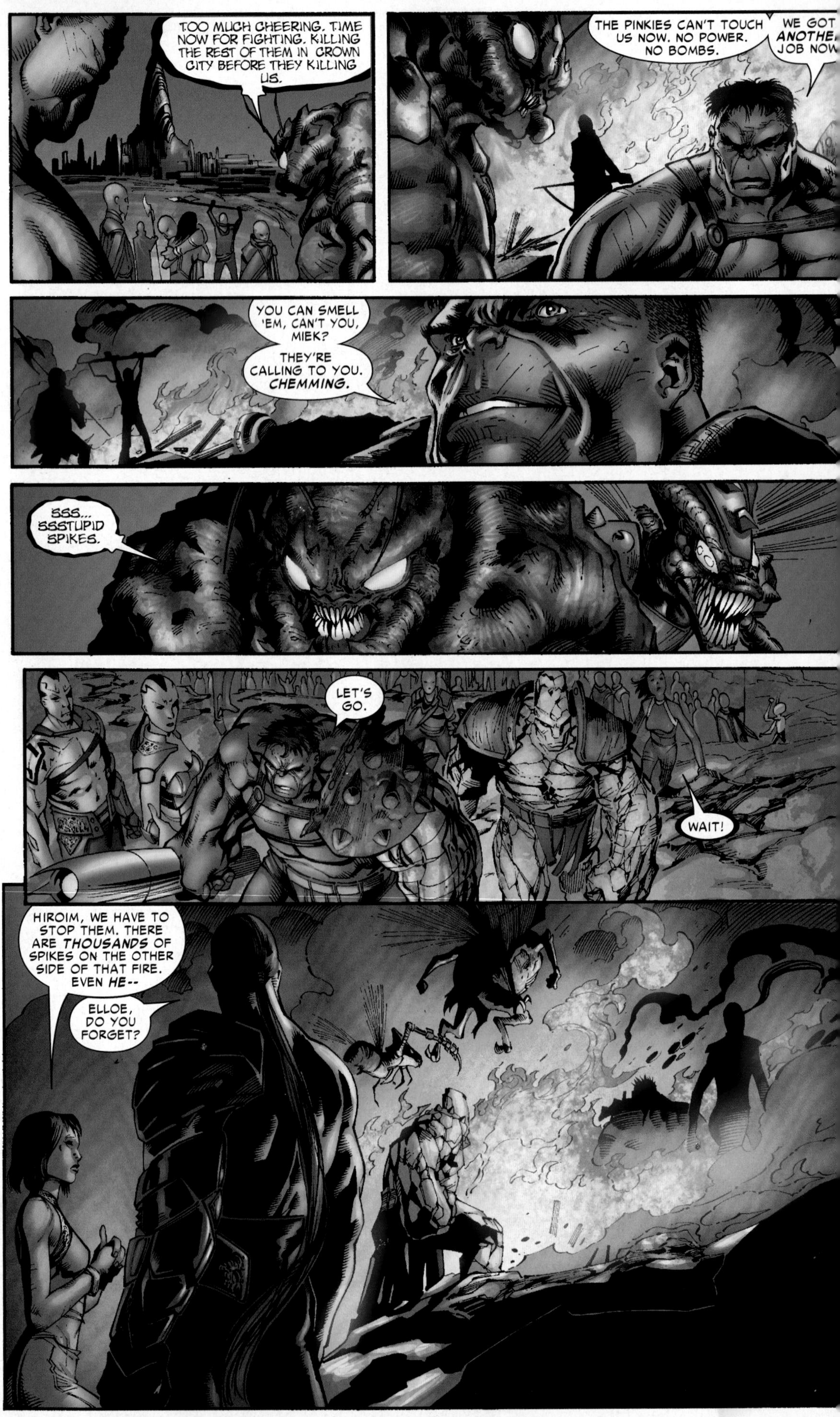
TOO MUCH CHEERING. TIME NOW FOR FIGHTING. KILLING THE REST OF THEM IN CROWN CITY BEFORE THEY KILLING US.
THE PINKIES CAN'T TOUCH US NOW. NO POWER. NO BOMBS.
YOU CAN SMELL 'EM, CAN'T YOU, MIEK?
THEY'RE CALLING TO YOU. CHEMMING.
SSS... SSSTUPID SPIKES.
LET'S GO.
WAIT!
HIROIM, WE HAVE TO STOP THEM. THERE ARE THOUSANDS OF SPIKES ON THE OTHER SIDE OF THAT FIRE. EVEN HE--
ELLOE, DO YOU FORGET?

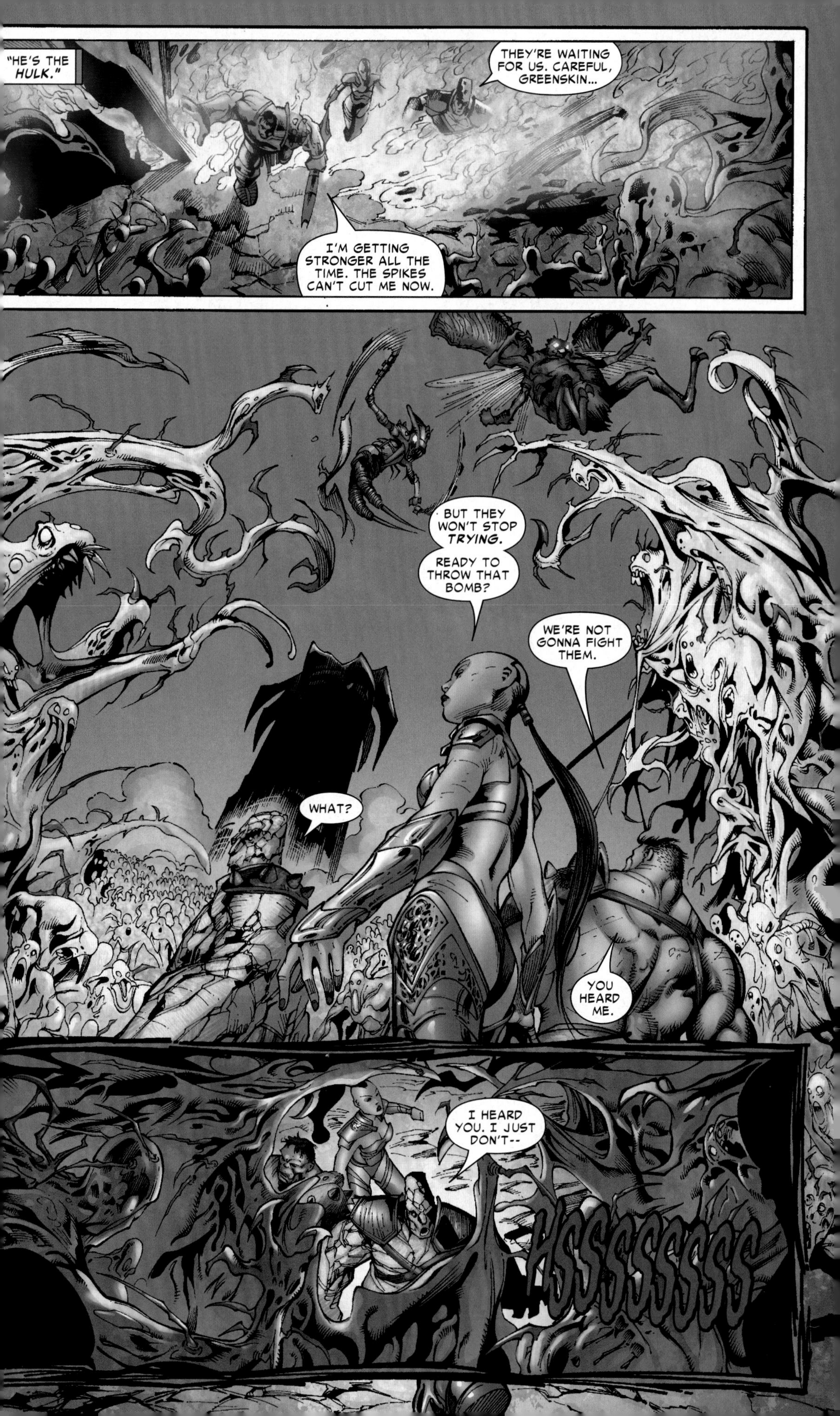
"HE'S THE *HULK*."
THEY'RE WAITING FOR US. CAREFUL, GREENSKIN...
I'M GETTING STRONGER ALL THE TIME. THE SPIKES CAN'T CUT ME NOW.
BUT THEY WON'T STOP *TRYING*.
READY TO THROW THAT BOMB?
WE'RE NOT GONNA FIGHT THEM.
WHAT?
YOU HEARD ME.
I HEARD YOU. I JUST DON'T--
HSSSSSSSS

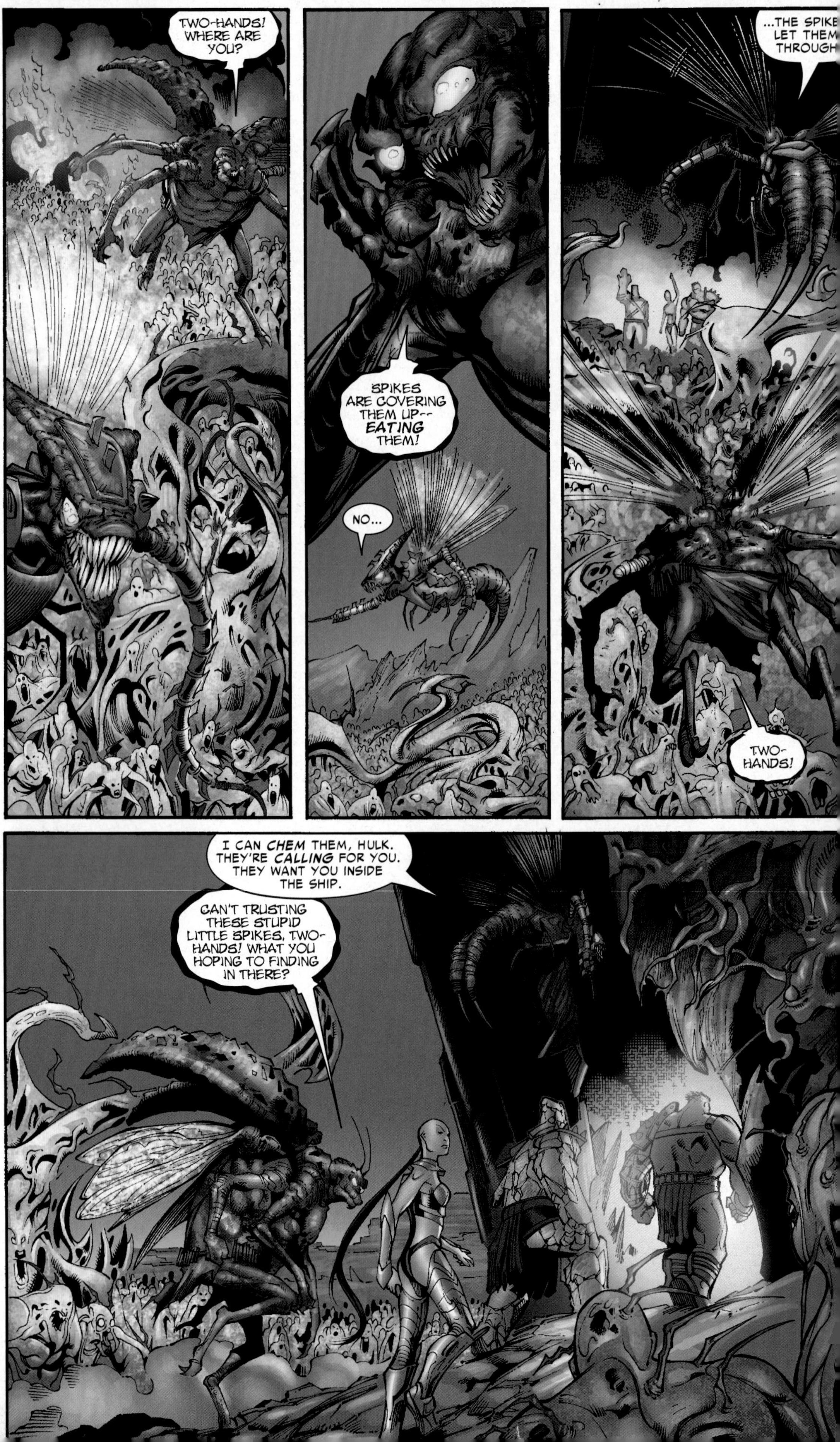

TWO-HANDS! WHERE ARE YOU?
SPIKES ARE COVERING THEM UP-- EATING THEM!
NO...
...THE SPIKE LET THEM THROUGH
TWO-HANDS!
I CAN CHEM THEM, HULK. THEY'RE CALLING FOR YOU. THEY WANT YOU INSIDE THE SHIP.
CAN'T TRUSTING THESE STUPID LITTLE SPIKES, TWO-HANDS! WHAT YOU HOPING TO FINDING IN THERE?

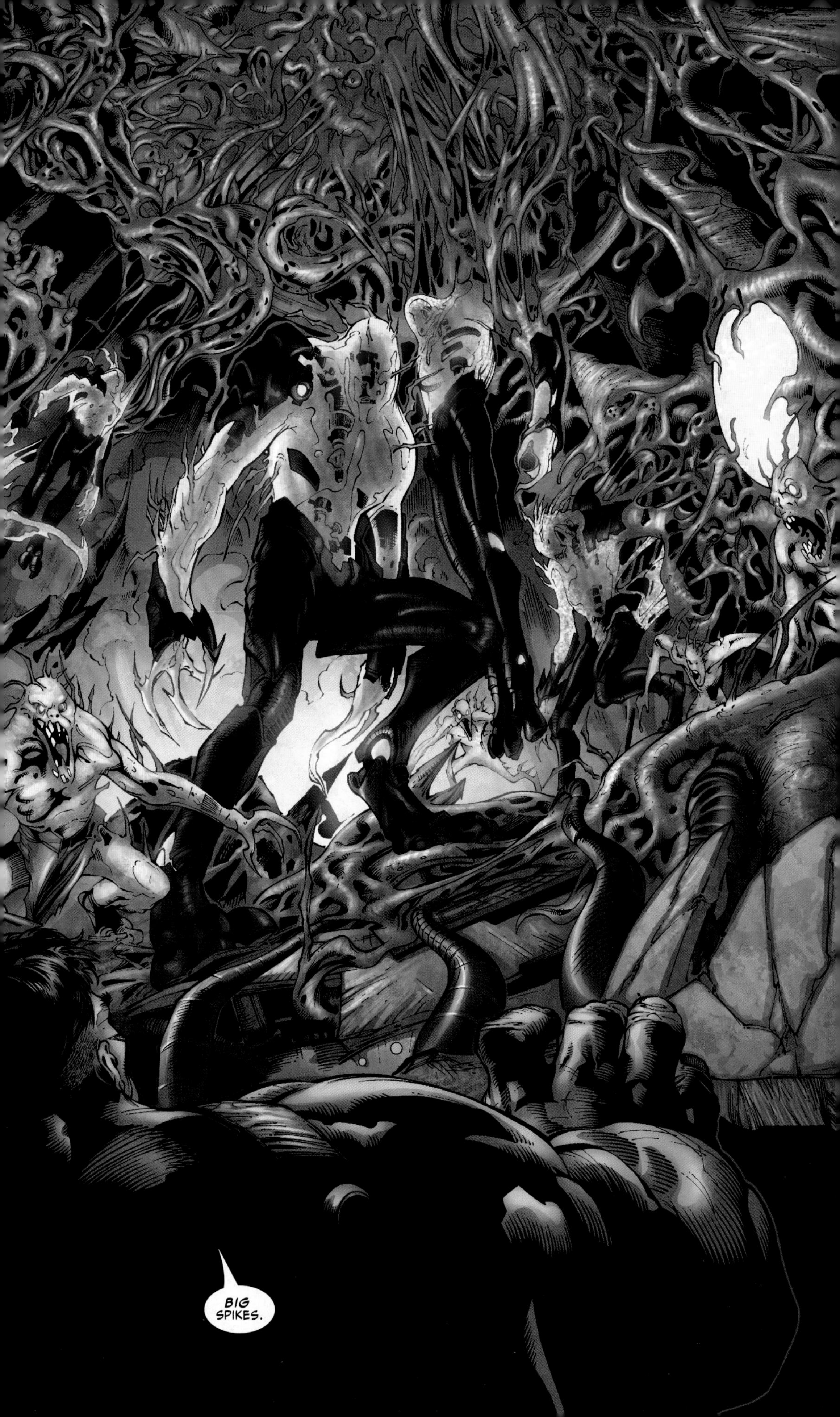
BIG SPIKES.

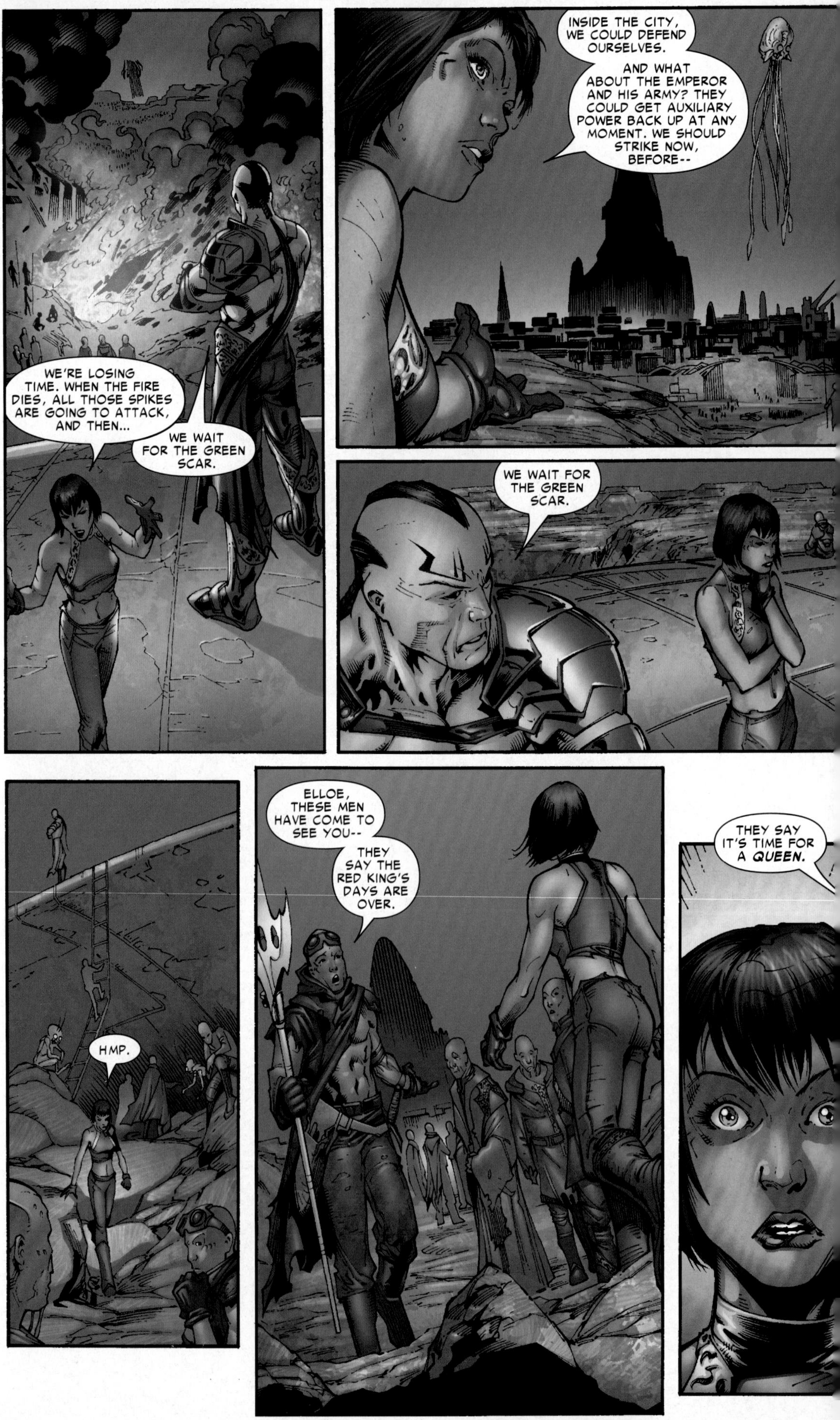
WE'RE LOSING TIME. WHEN THE FIRE DIES, ALL THOSE SPIKES ARE GOING TO ATTACK, AND THEN...
WE WAIT FOR THE GREEN SCAR.
INSIDE THE CITY, WE COULD DEFEND OURSELVES.
AND WHAT ABOUT THE EMPEROR AND HIS ARMY? THEY COULD GET AUXILIARY POWER BACK UP AT ANY MOMENT. WE SHOULD STRIKE NOW, BEFORE--
WE WAIT FOR THE GREEN SCAR.
HMP.
ELLOE, THESE MEN HAVE COME TO SEE YOU--
THEY SAY THE RED KING'S DAYS ARE OVER.
THEY SAY IT'S TIME FOR A QUEEN.

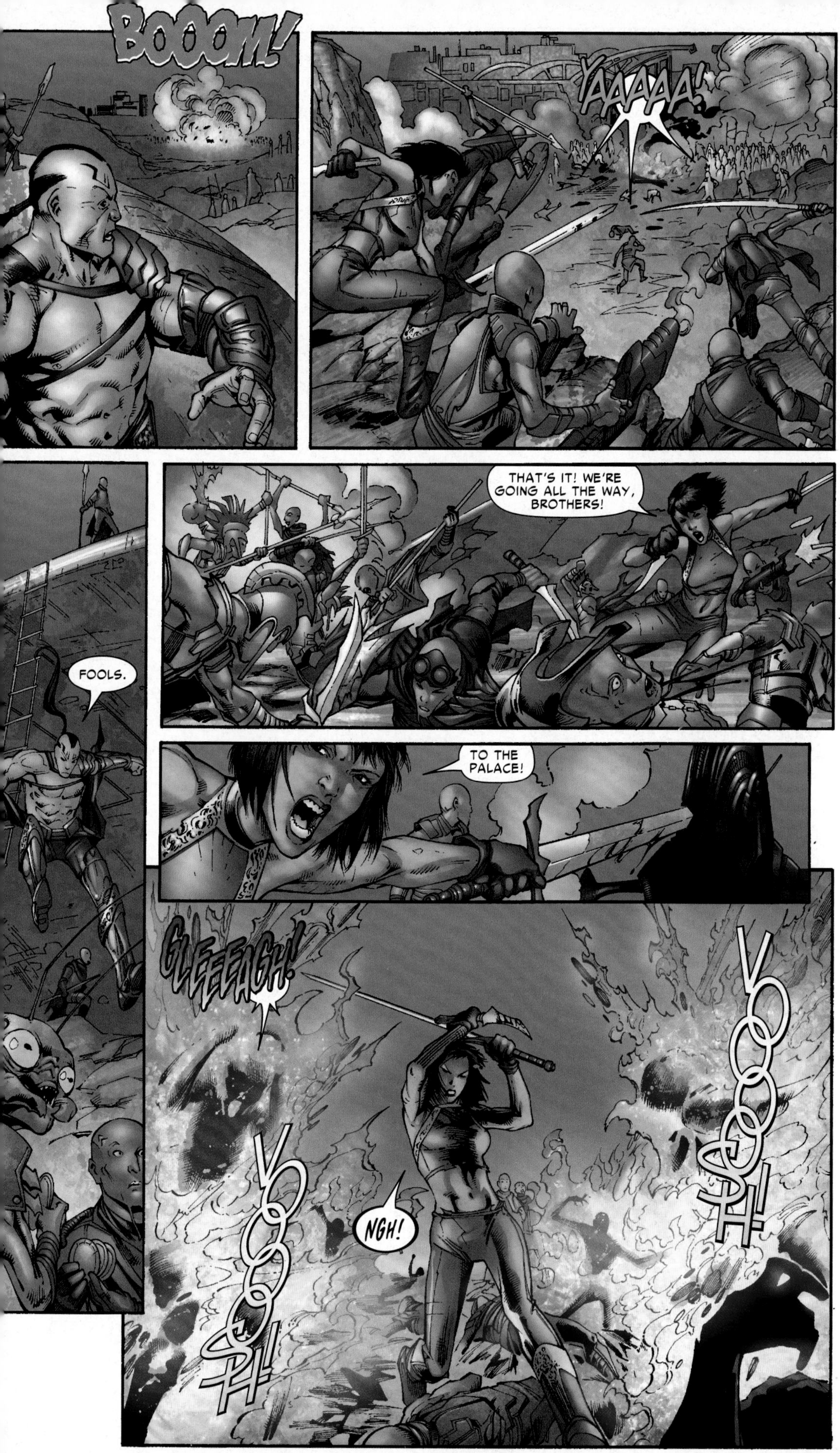
BOOOM!
YAAAAA!
FOOLS.
THAT'S IT! WE'RE GOING ALL THE WAY, BROTHERS!
TO THE PALACE!
GLEEEAGH!
VOOOOOSH!
NGH!
VOOOOOSH!

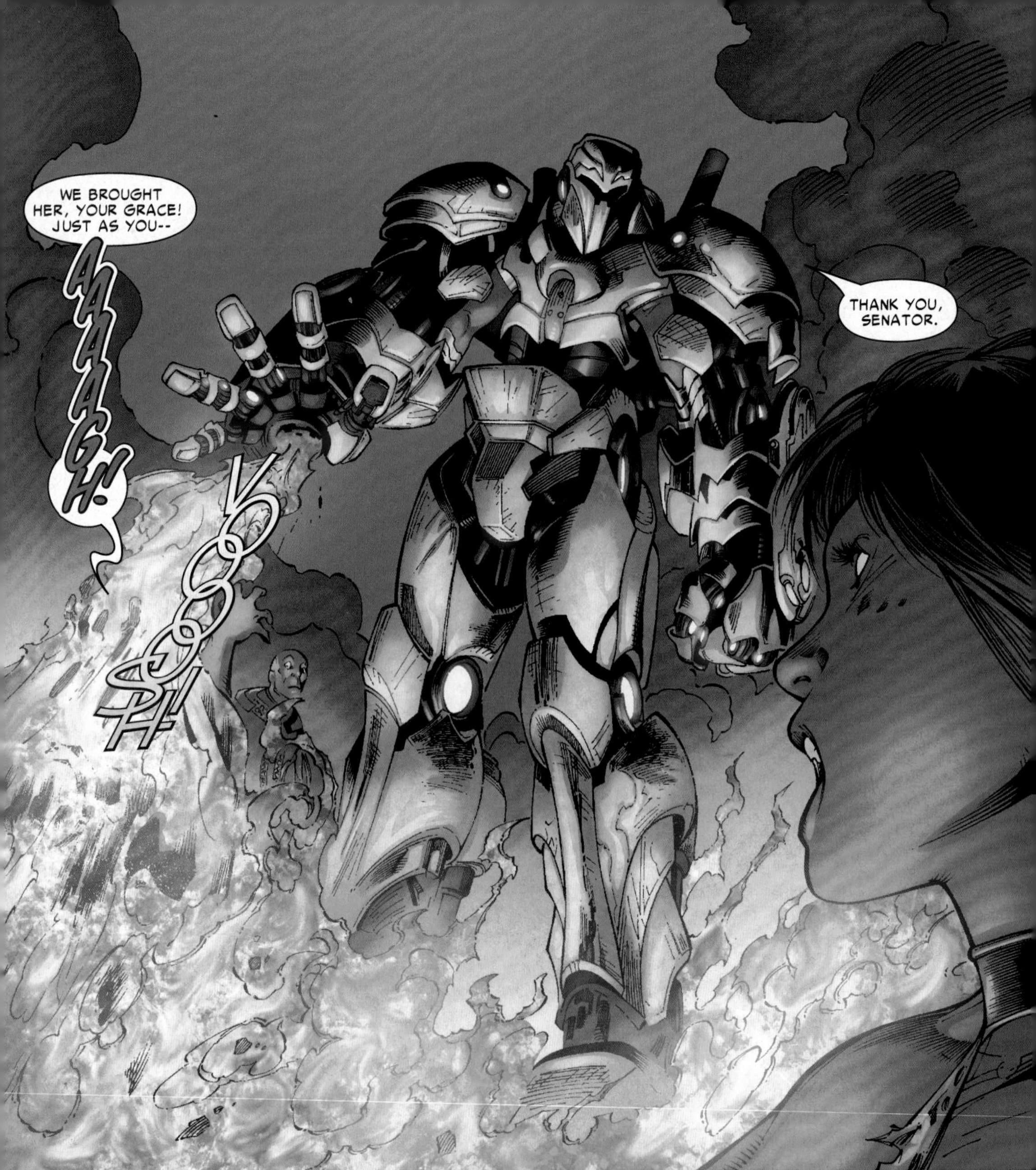
WE BROUGHT HER, YOUR GRACE! JUST AS YOU--
AAAAAGH!
VOOOOSH!
THANK YOU, SENATOR.

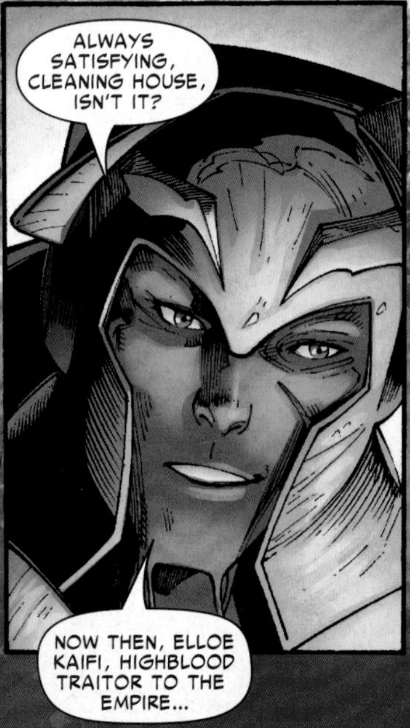
ALWAYS SATISFYING, CLEANING HOUSE, ISN'T IT?
NOW THEN, ELLOE KAIFI, HIGHBLOOD TRAITOR TO THE EMPIRE...

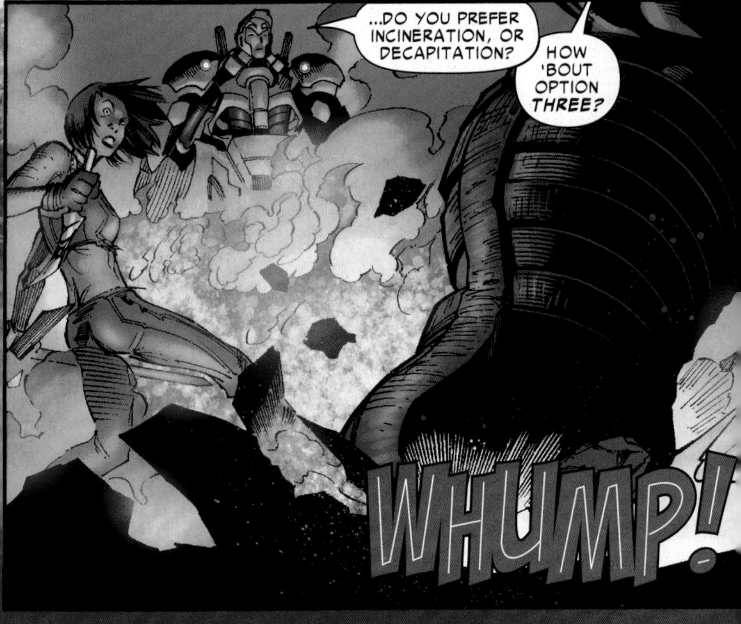
...DO YOU PREFER INCINERATION, OR DECAPITATION?
HOW 'BOUT OPTION THREE?
WHUMP!

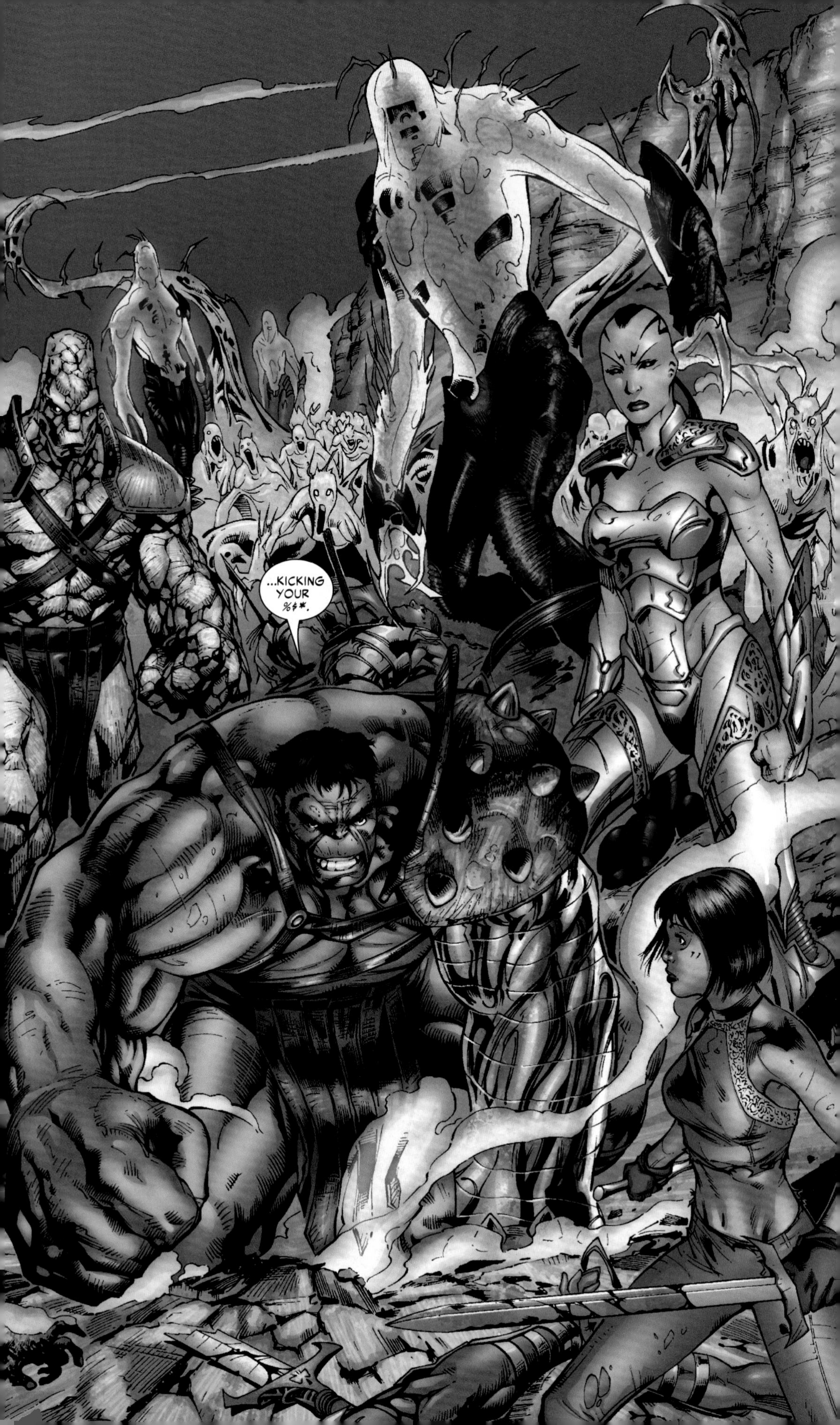
...KICKING YOUR %$*.

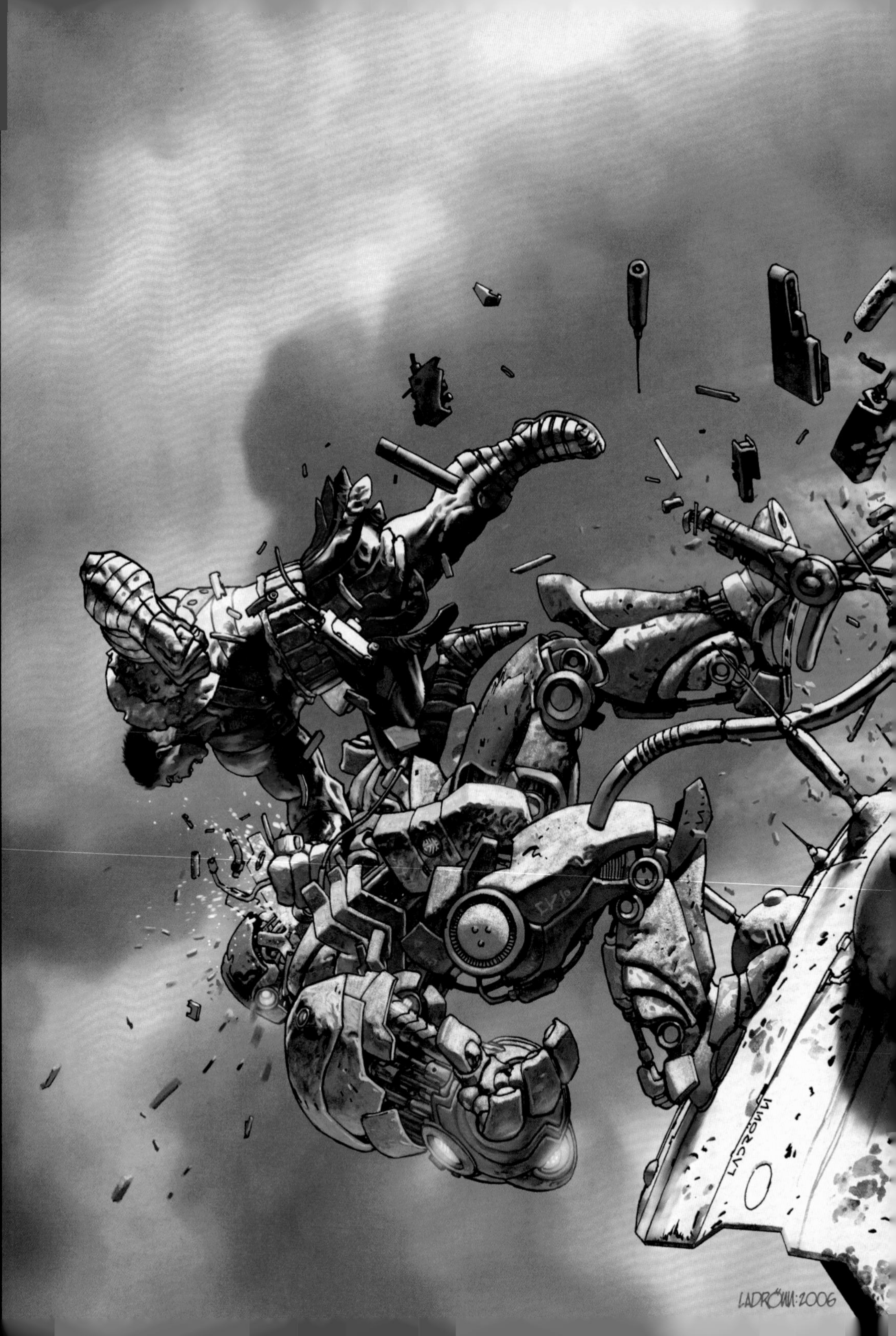
LADRÖNN:2006

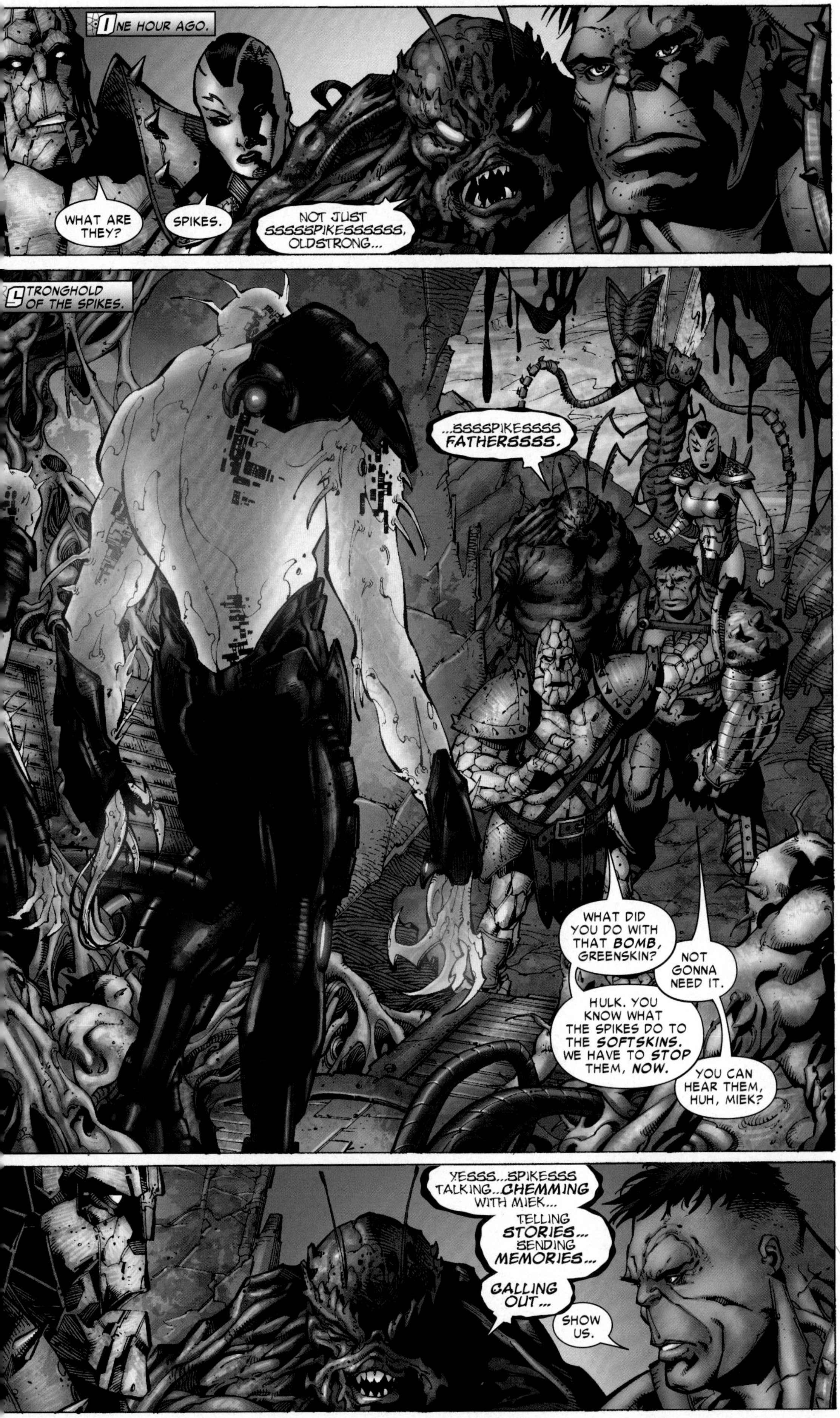
ONE HOUR AGO.
WHAT ARE THEY?
SPIKES.
NOT JUST SSSSSPIKESSSSSS, OLDSTRONG...
STRONGHOLD OF THE SPIKES.
...SSSSPIKESSSS FATHERSSSS.
WHAT DID YOU DO WITH THAT BOMB, GREENSKIN?
NOT GONNA NEED IT.
HULK. YOU KNOW WHAT THE SPIKES DO TO THE SOFTSKINS. WE HAVE TO STOP THEM, NOW.
YOU CAN HEAR THEM, HUH, MIEK?
YESSS...SPIKESSS TALKING...CHEMMING WITH MIEK...
TELLING STORIES... SENDING MEMORIES...
CALLING OUT...
SHOW US.

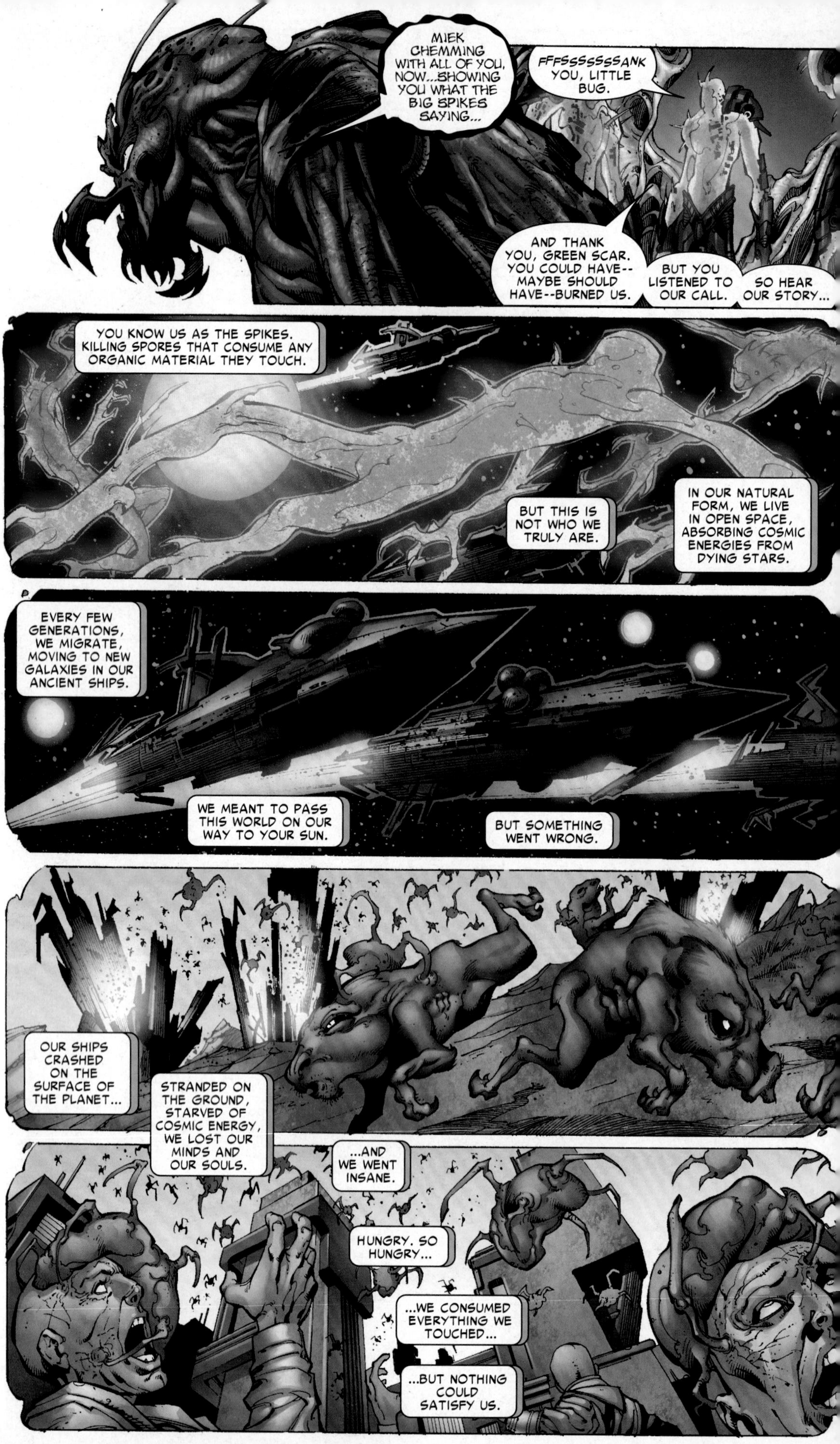
MIEK CHEMMING WITH ALL OF YOU, NOW...SHOWING YOU WHAT THE BIG SPIKES SAYING...
FFFSSSSSSSANK YOU, LITTLE BUG.
AND THANK YOU, GREEN SCAR. YOU COULD HAVE-- MAYBE SHOULD HAVE--BURNED US.
BUT YOU LISTENED TO OUR CALL.
SO HEAR OUR STORY...
YOU KNOW US AS THE SPIKES. KILLING SPORES THAT CONSUME ANY ORGANIC MATERIAL THEY TOUCH.
BUT THIS IS NOT WHO WE TRULY ARE.
IN OUR NATURAL FORM, WE LIVE IN OPEN SPACE, ABSORBING COSMIC ENERGIES FROM DYING STARS.
EVERY FEW GENERATIONS, WE MIGRATE, MOVING TO NEW GALAXIES IN OUR ANCIENT SHIPS.
WE MEANT TO PASS THIS WORLD ON OUR WAY TO YOUR SUN.
BUT SOMETHING WENT WRONG.
OUR SHIPS CRASHED ON THE SURFACE OF THE PLANET...
STRANDED ON THE GROUND, STARVED OF COSMIC ENERGY, WE LOST OUR MINDS AND OUR SOULS.
...AND WE WENT INSANE.
HUNGRY. SO HUNGRY...
...WE CONSUMED EVERYTHING WE TOUCHED...
...BUT NOTHING COULD SATISFY US.

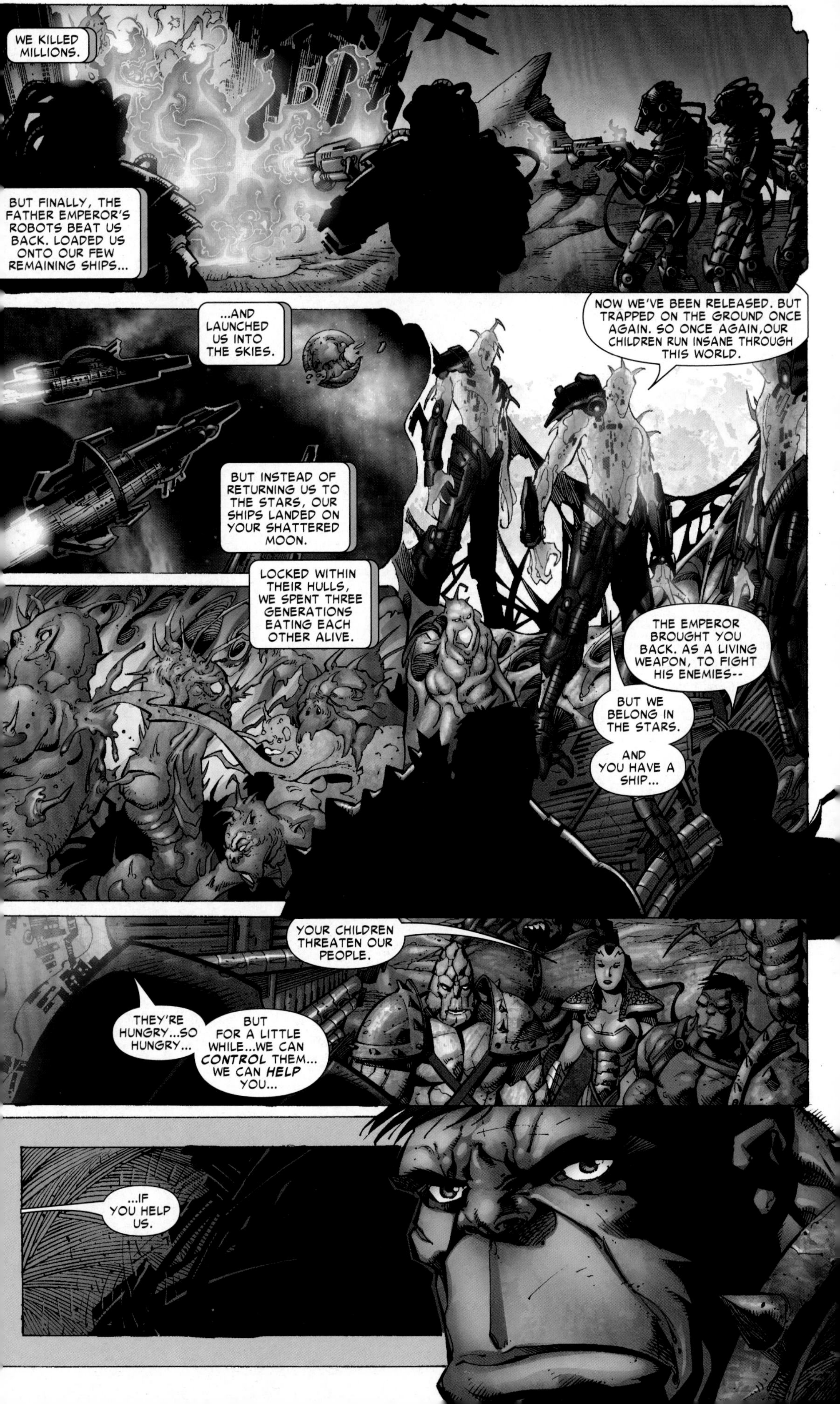
WE KILLED MILLIONS.
BUT FINALLY, THE FATHER EMPEROR'S ROBOTS BEAT US BACK. LOADED US ONTO OUR FEW REMAINING SHIPS...
...AND LAUNCHED US INTO THE SKIES.
BUT INSTEAD OF RETURNING US TO THE STARS, OUR SHIPS LANDED ON YOUR SHATTERED MOON.
NOW WE'VE BEEN RELEASED. BUT TRAPPED ON THE GROUND ONCE AGAIN. SO ONCE AGAIN,OUR CHILDREN RUN INSANE THROUGH THIS WORLD.
LOCKED WITHIN THEIR HULLS, WE SPENT THREE GENERATIONS EATING EACH OTHER ALIVE.
THE EMPEROR BROUGHT YOU BACK. AS A LIVING WEAPON, TO FIGHT HIS ENEMIES--
BUT WE BELONG IN THE STARS.
AND YOU HAVE A SHIP...
YOUR CHILDREN THREATEN OUR PEOPLE.
THEY'RE HUNGRY...SO HUNGRY...
BUT FOR A LITTLE WHILE...WE CAN *CONTROL* THEM... WE CAN *HELP* YOU...
...IF YOU HELP US.

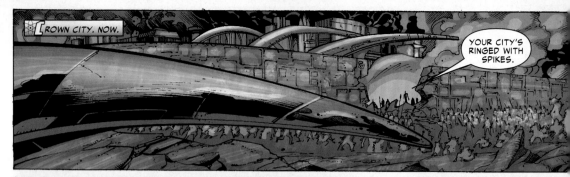

YOUR CITY'S RINGED WITH SPIKES.

AND THEY'RE FIGHTING FOR US NOW.

GIVE UP, RED KING.

PROTECT HIS GRACE! THE GREEN SCAR MUST NOT--

GGAKK!

OUT OF MY WAY, SLAVES.

THE GREEN SCAR IS MINE.

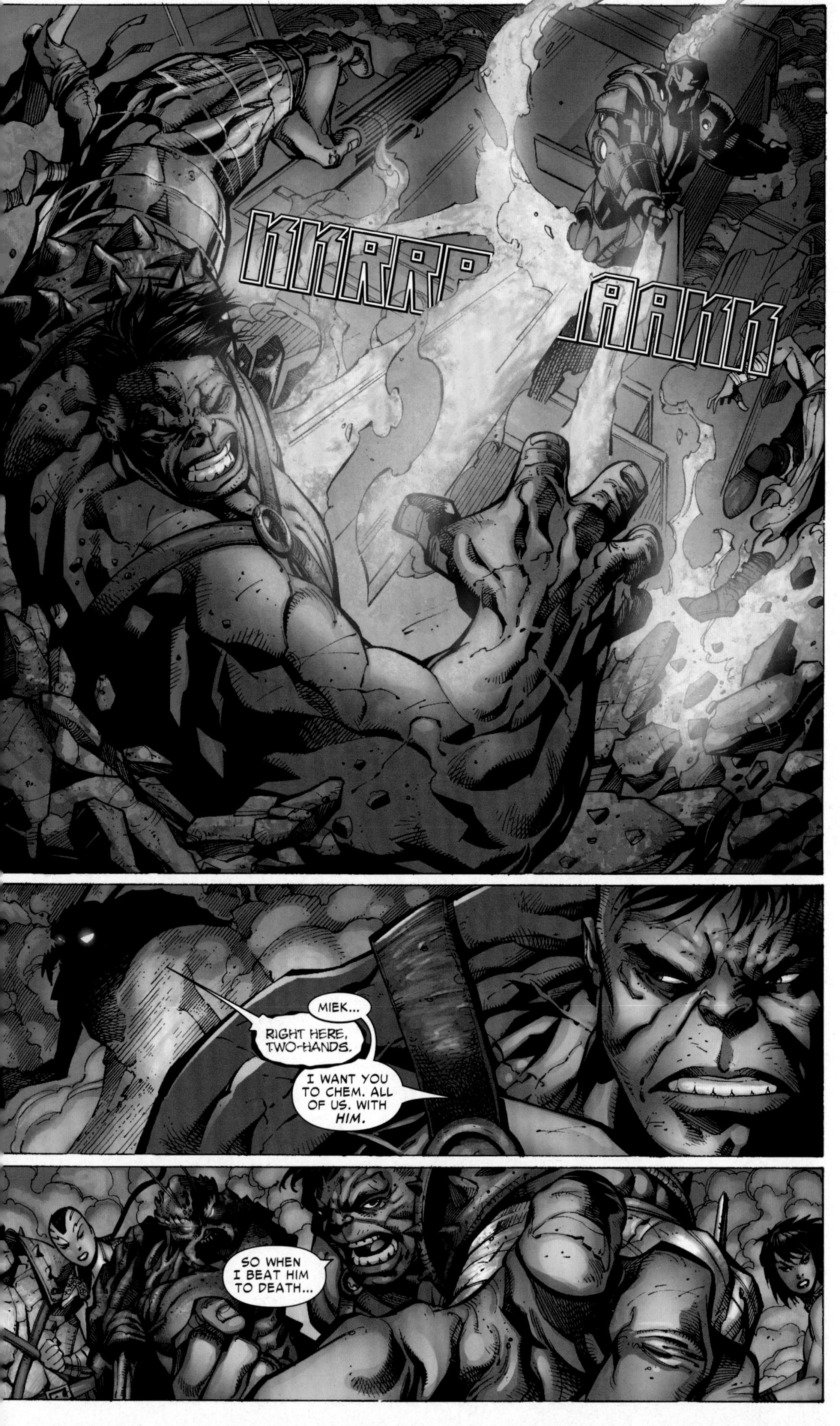
KKRRP
AAKK
MIEK...
RIGHT HERE, TWO-HANDS.
I WANT YOU TO CHEM. ALL OF US. WITH *HIM*.
SO WHEN I BEAT HIM TO DEATH...

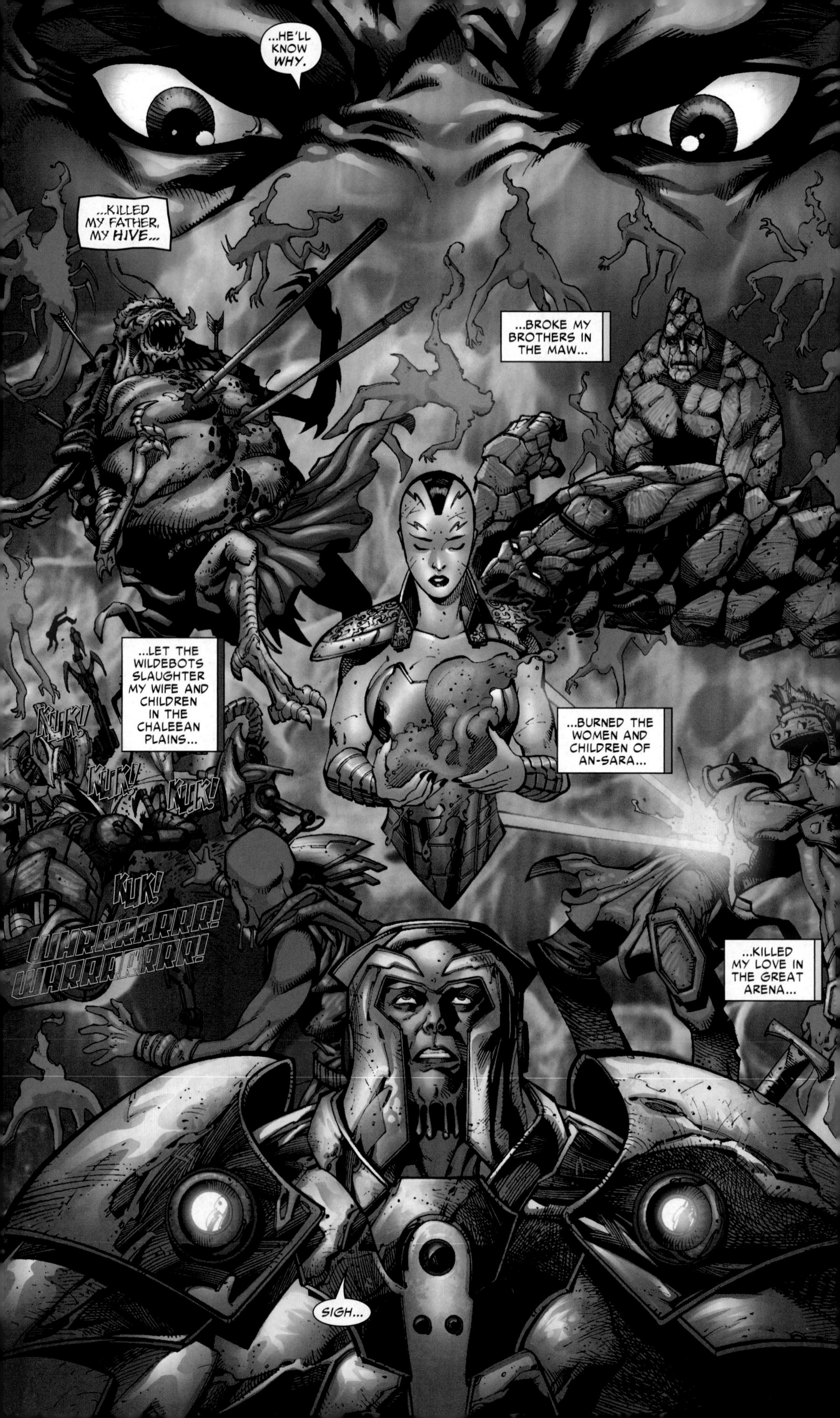
...HE'LL KNOW WHY.
...KILLED MY FATHER, MY HIVE...
...BROKE MY BROTHERS IN THE MAW...
...LET THE WILDEBOTS SLAUGHTER MY WIFE AND CHILDREN IN THE CHALEEAN PLAINS...
...BURNED THE WOMEN AND CHILDREN OF AN-SARA...
KLIK!
KLIK!
KLIK!
KLIK!
WHRRRRRRR!
WHRRRRRRR!
...KILLED MY LOVE IN THE GREAT ARENA...
SIGH...

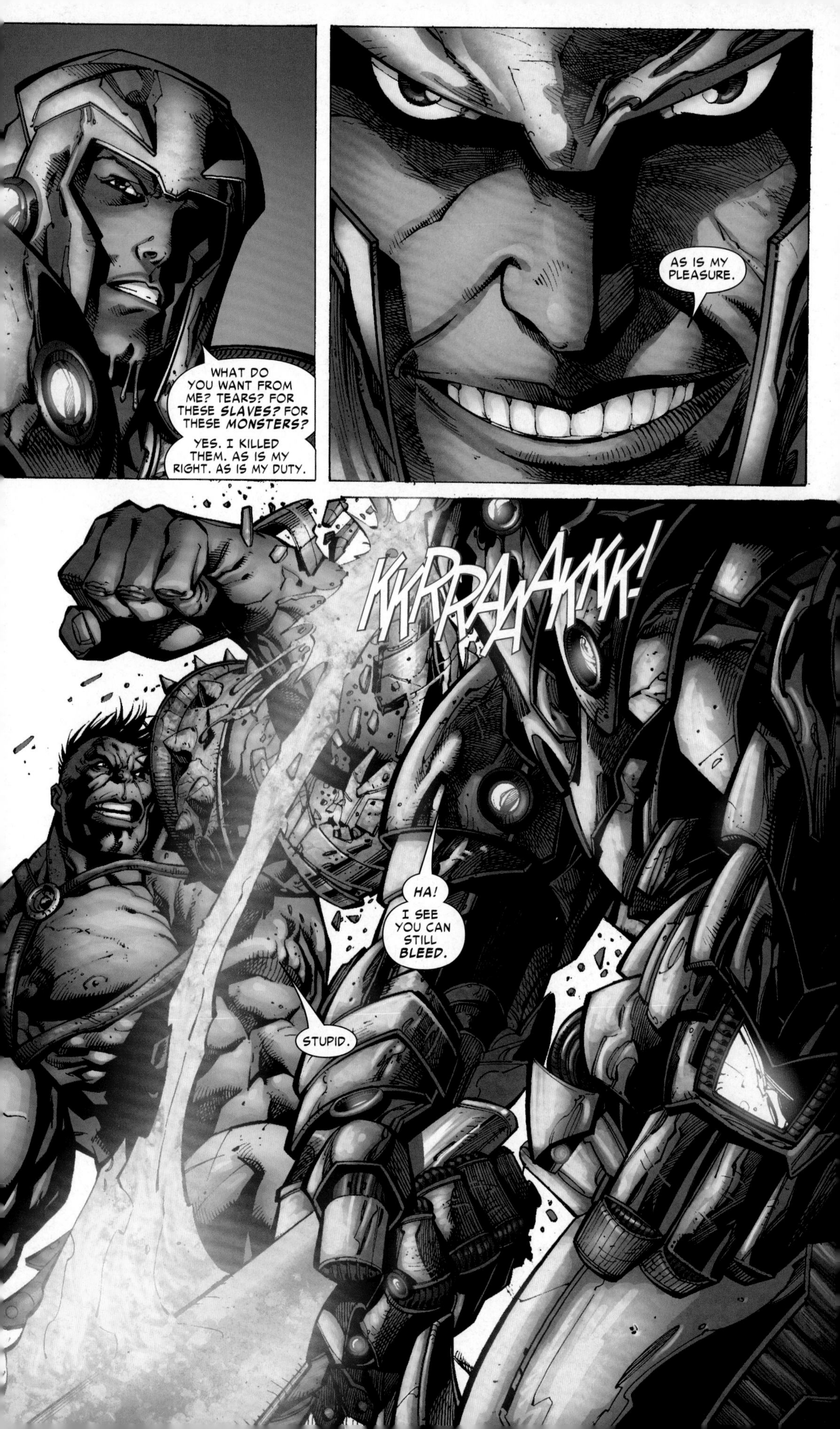
WHAT DO YOU WANT FROM ME? TEARS? FOR THESE *SLAVES?* FOR THESE *MONSTERS?*
YES. I KILLED THEM. AS IS MY RIGHT. AS IS MY DUTY.
AS IS MY PLEASURE.
KKRRAAAKKK!
HA! I SEE YOU CAN STILL *BLEED*.
STUPID.

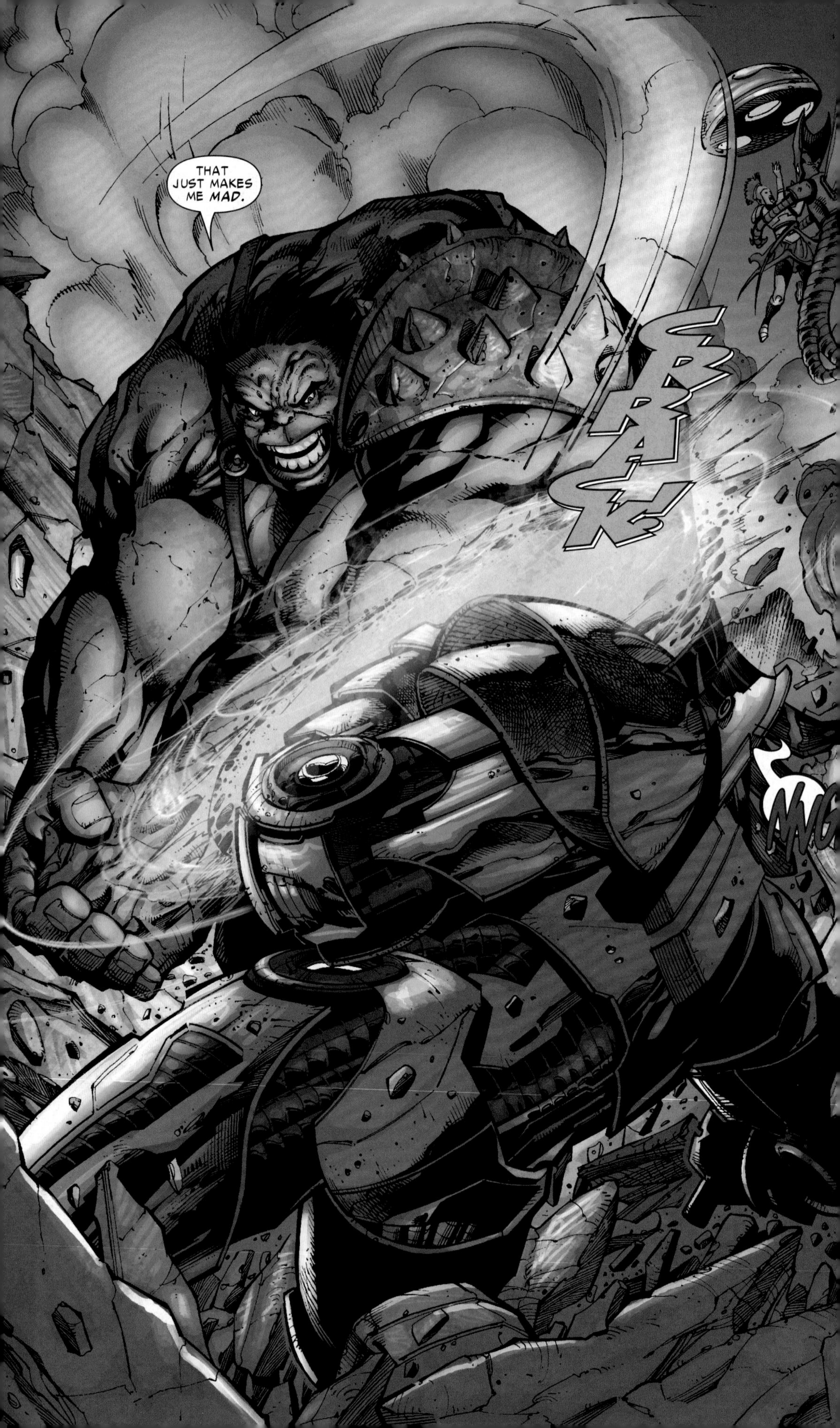
THAT JUST MAKES ME MAD.
CRACK!

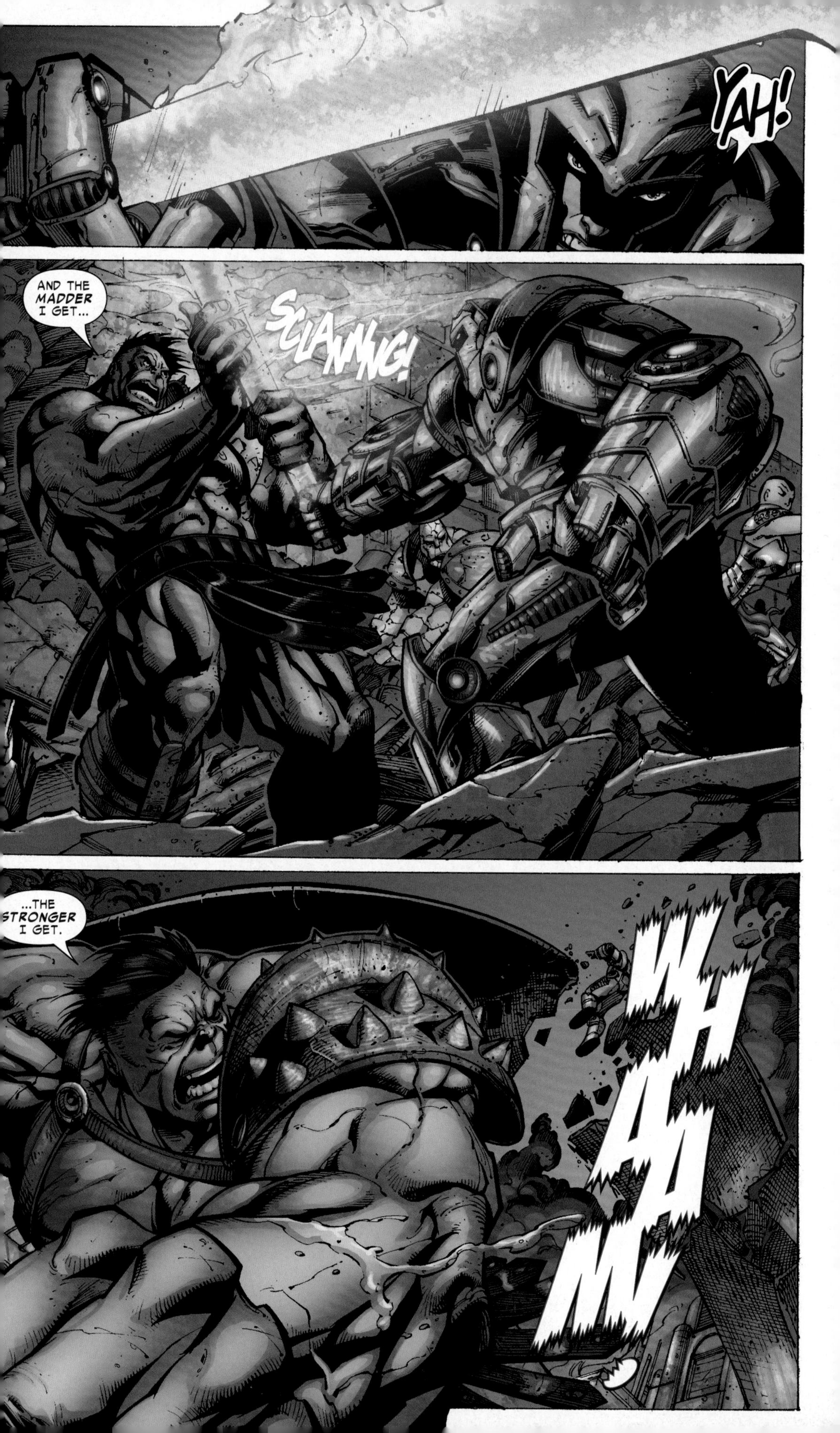
YAH!
AND THE MADDER I GET...
SCLANNNG!
...THE STRONGER I GET.
WHAM

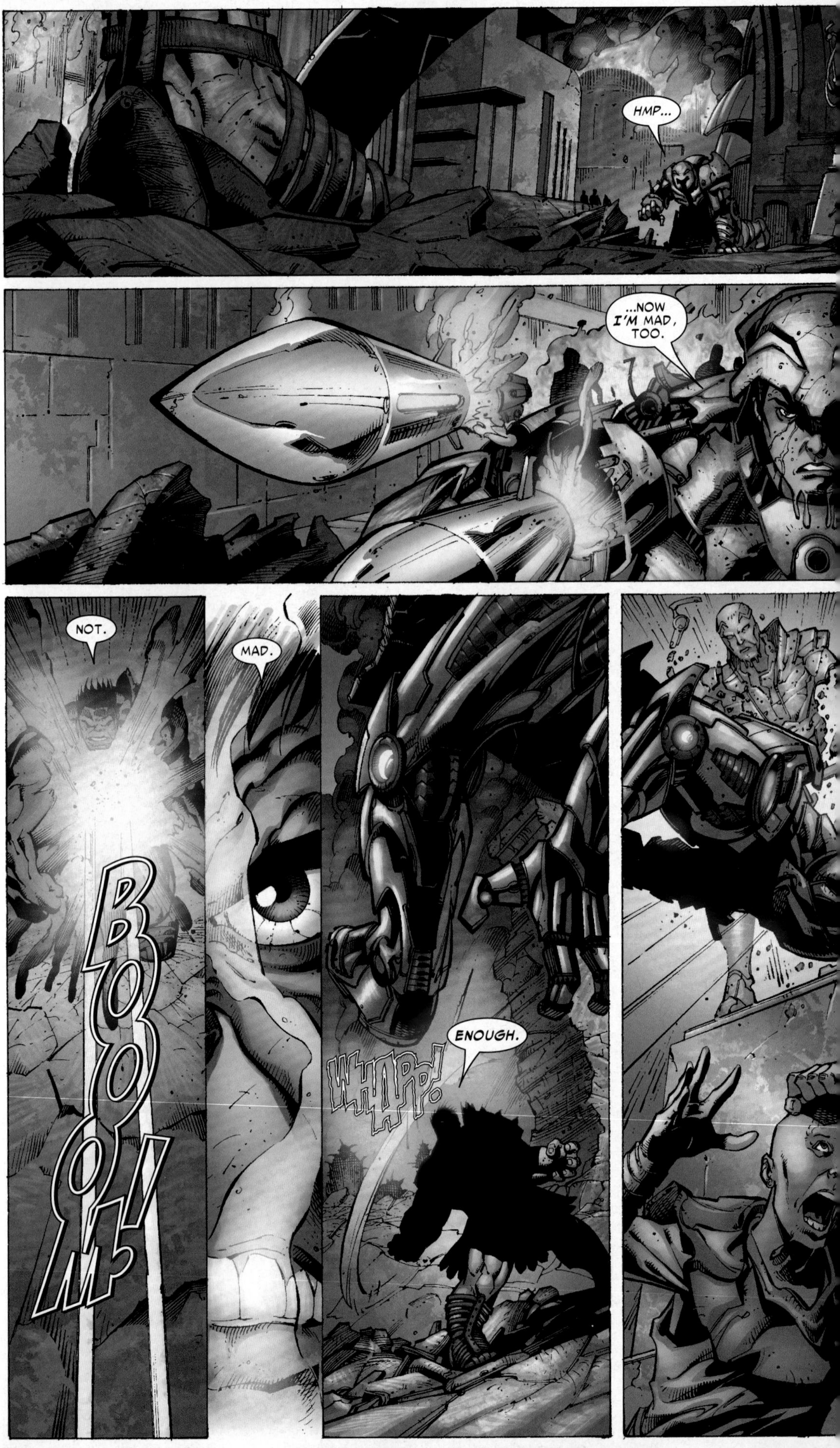
HMP...
...NOW I'M MAD, TOO.
NOT.
BOOOOM!
MAD.
WHAPP!
ENOUGH.

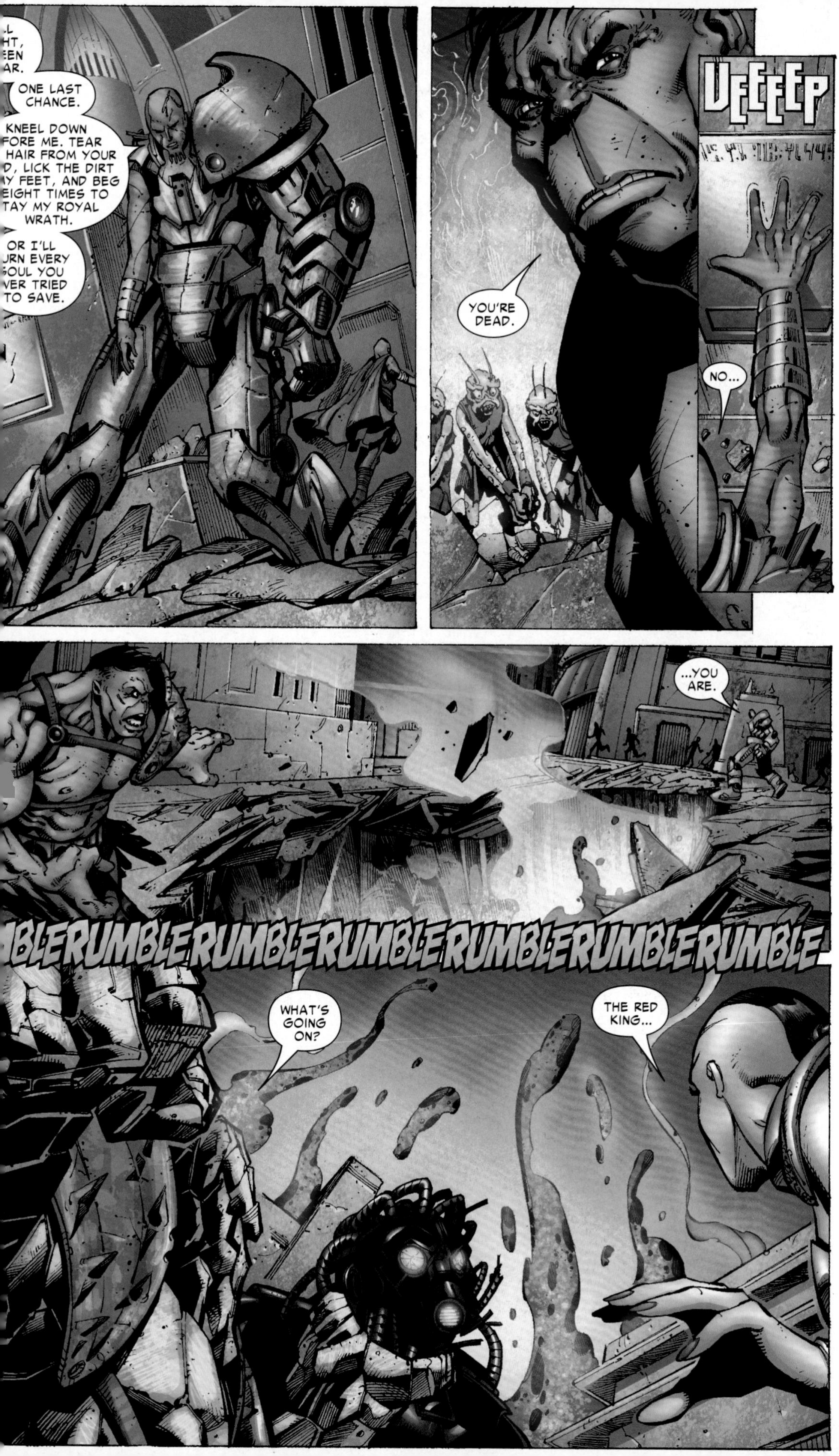

ONE LAST CHANCE.
KNEEL DOWN FORE ME. TEAR HAIR FROM YOUR D, LICK THE DIRT Y FEET, AND BEG EIGHT TIMES TO TAY MY ROYAL WRATH.
OR I'LL URN EVERY SOUL YOU VER TRIED TO SAVE.
YOU'RE DEAD.
VEEEEP
NO...
...YOU ARE.
BLERUMBLERUMBLERUMBLERUMBLERUMBLE
WHAT'S GOING ON?
THE RED KING...

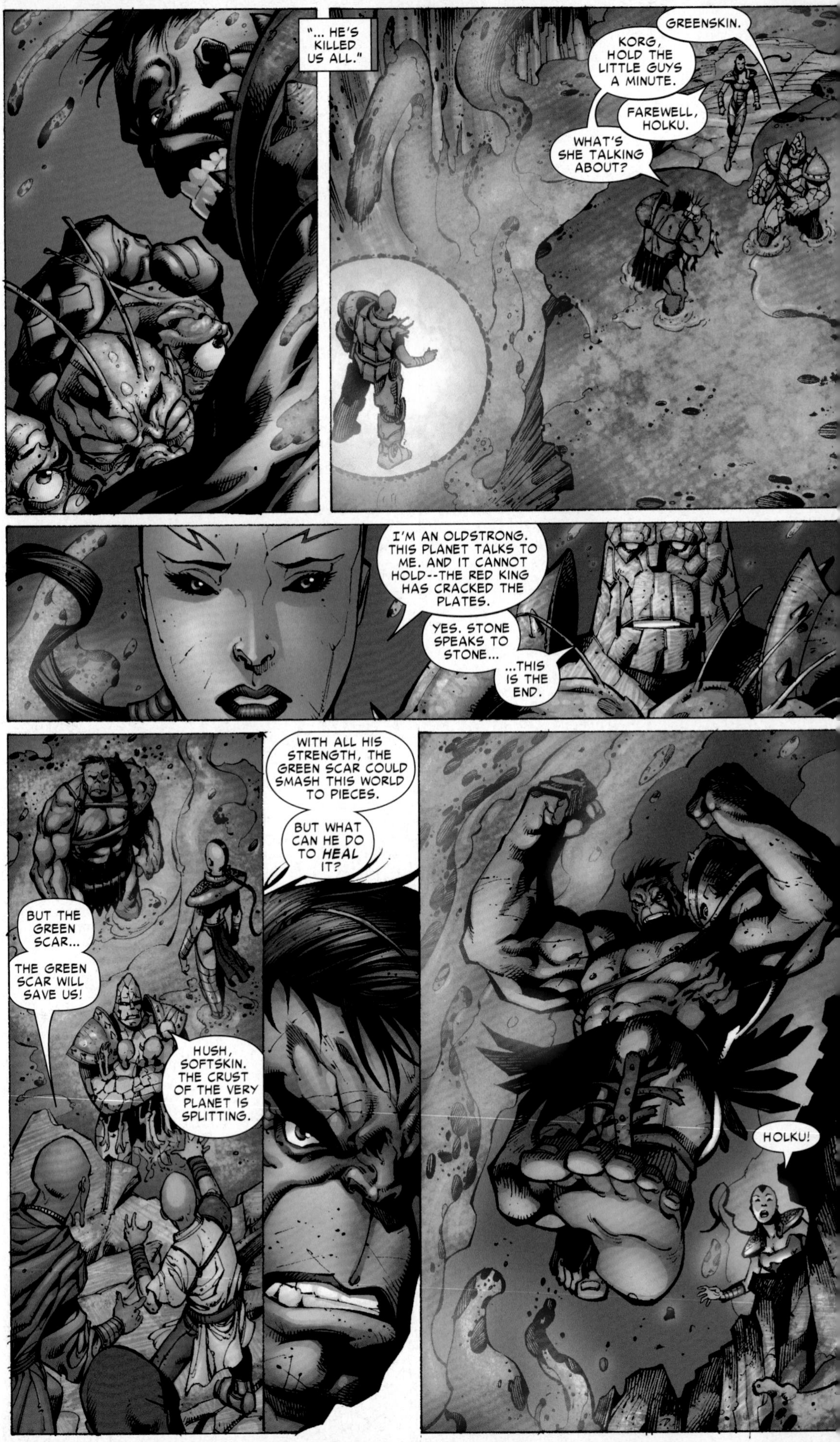
"... HE'S KILLED US ALL."
GREENSKIN.
KORG, HOLD THE LITTLE GUYS A MINUTE.
FAREWELL, HOLKU.
WHAT'S SHE TALKING ABOUT?
I'M AN OLDSTRONG. THIS PLANET TALKS TO ME. AND IT CANNOT HOLD--THE RED KING HAS CRACKED THE PLATES.
YES. STONE SPEAKS TO STONE...
...THIS IS THE END.
BUT THE GREEN SCAR...
THE GREEN SCAR WILL SAVE US!
HUSH, SOFTSKIN. THE CRUST OF THE VERY PLANET IS SPLITTING.
WITH ALL HIS STRENGTH, THE GREEN SCAR COULD SMASH THIS WORLD TO PIECES.
BUT WHAT CAN HE DO TO *HEAL* IT?
HOLKU!

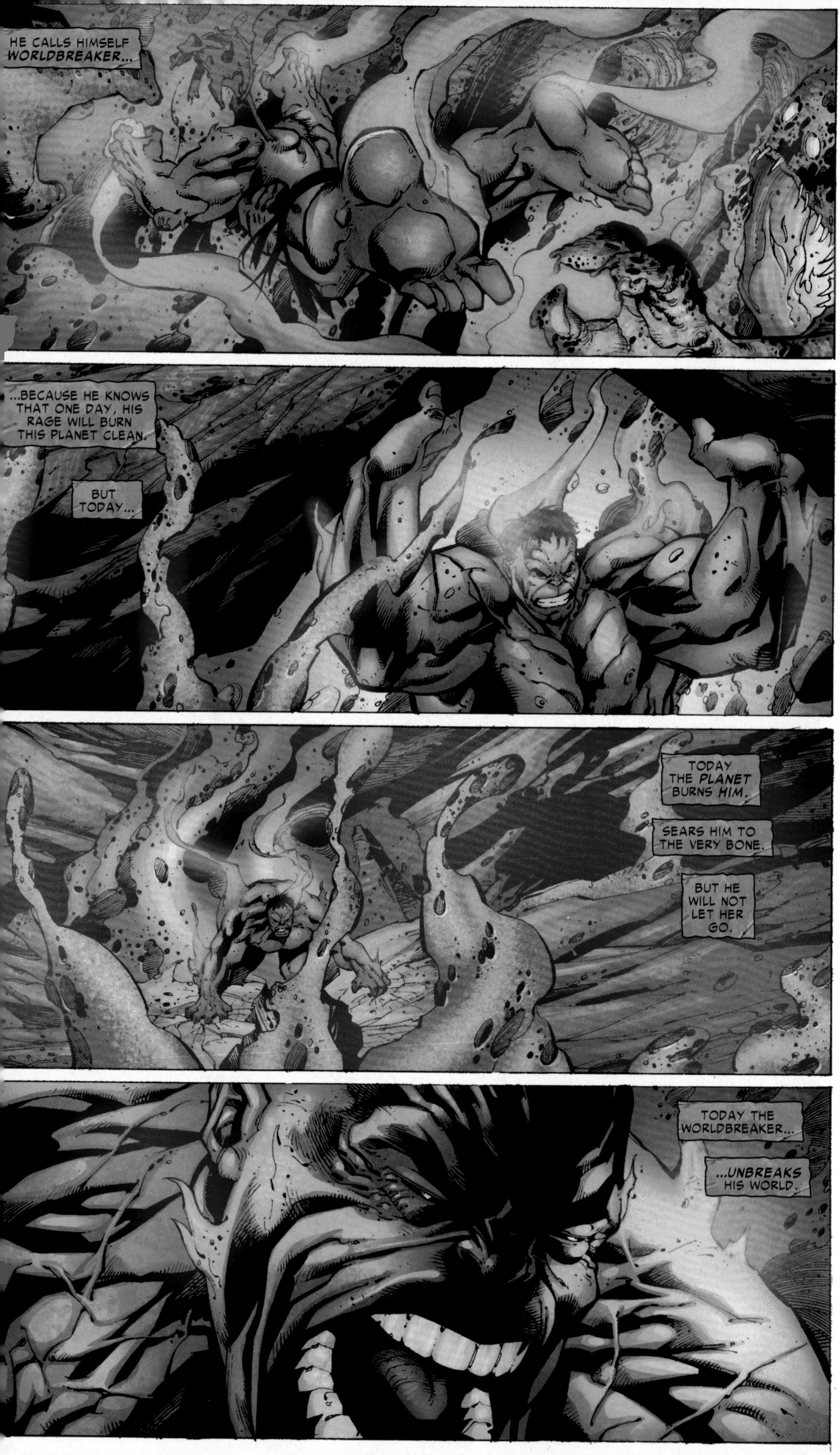
HE CALLS HIMSELF *WORLDBREAKER*...
...BECAUSE HE KNOWS THAT ONE DAY, HIS RAGE WILL BURN THIS PLANET CLEAN.
BUT TODAY...
TODAY THE *PLANET* BURNS *HIM*.
SEARS HIM TO THE VERY BONE.
BUT HE WILL NOT LET HER GO.
TODAY THE WORLDBREAKER...
...*UNBREAKS* HIS WORLD.

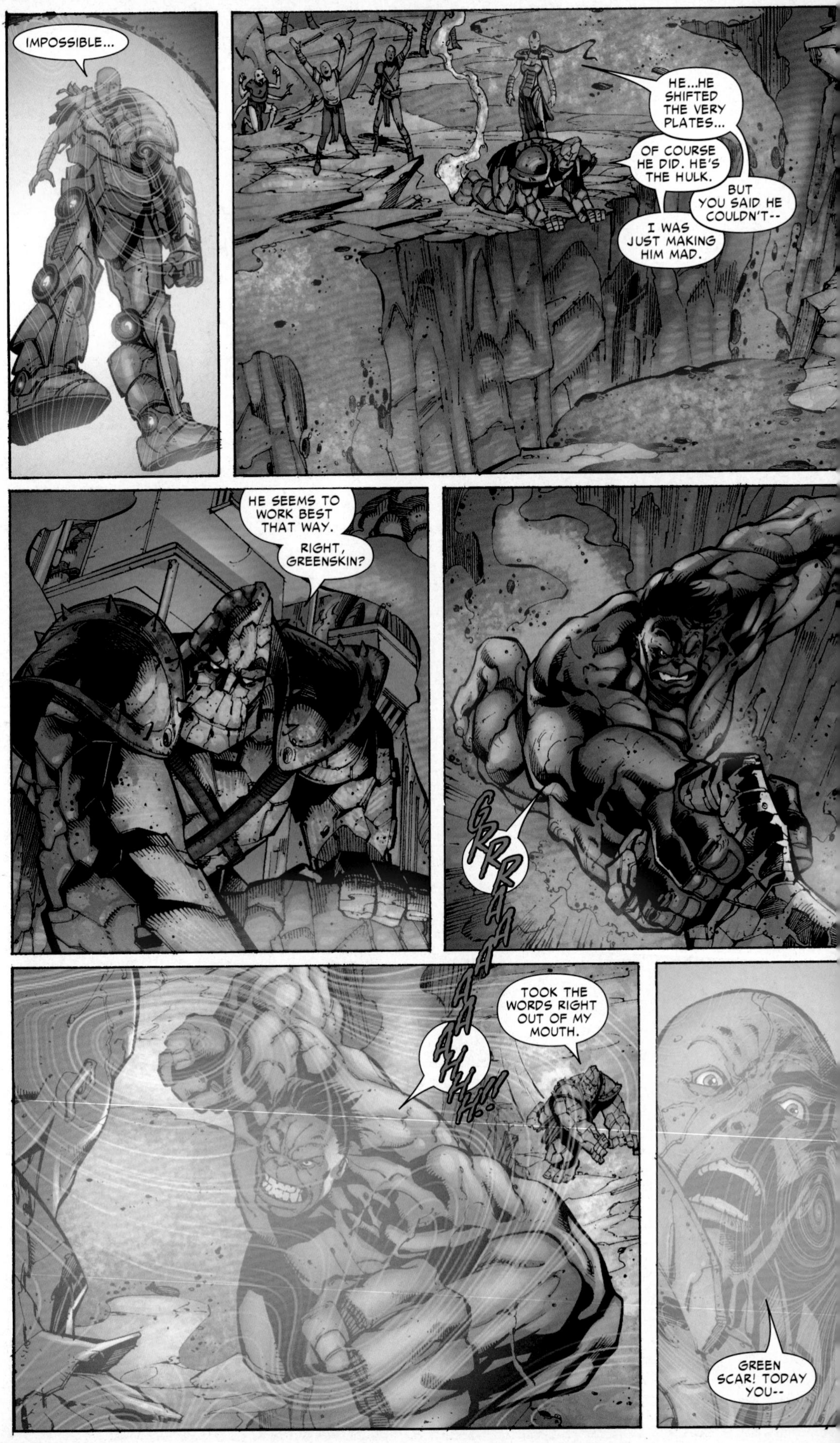

IMPOSSIBLE...
HE...HE SHIFTED THE VERY PLATES...
OF COURSE HE DID. HE'S THE HULK.
BUT YOU SAID HE COULDN'T--
I WAS JUST MAKING HIM MAD.
HE SEEMS TO WORK BEST THAT WAY.
RIGHT, GREENSKIN?
GRRRAAAAAAAHHH!
TOOK THE WORDS RIGHT OUT OF MY MOUTH.
GREEN SCAR! TODAY YOU--

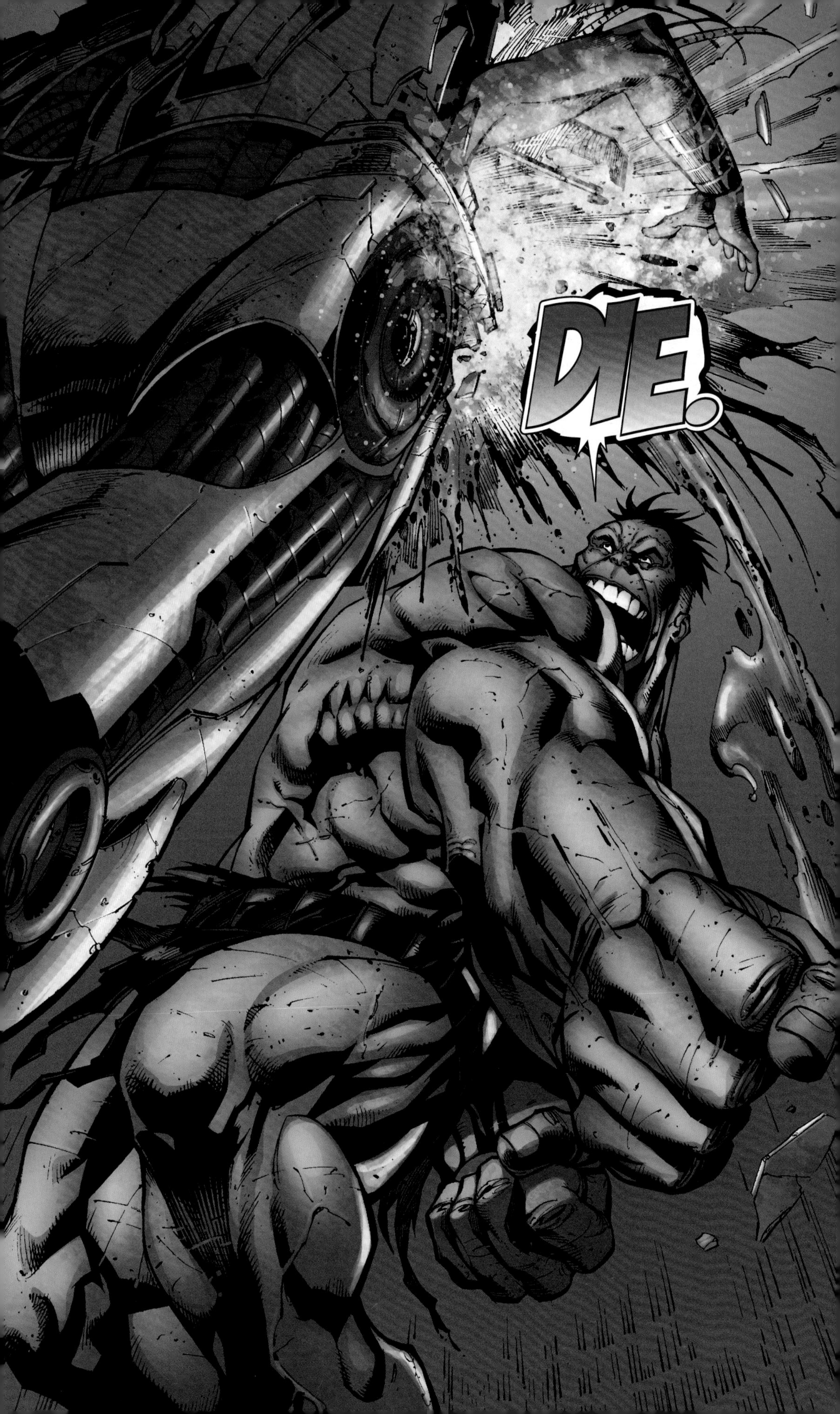
DIE.

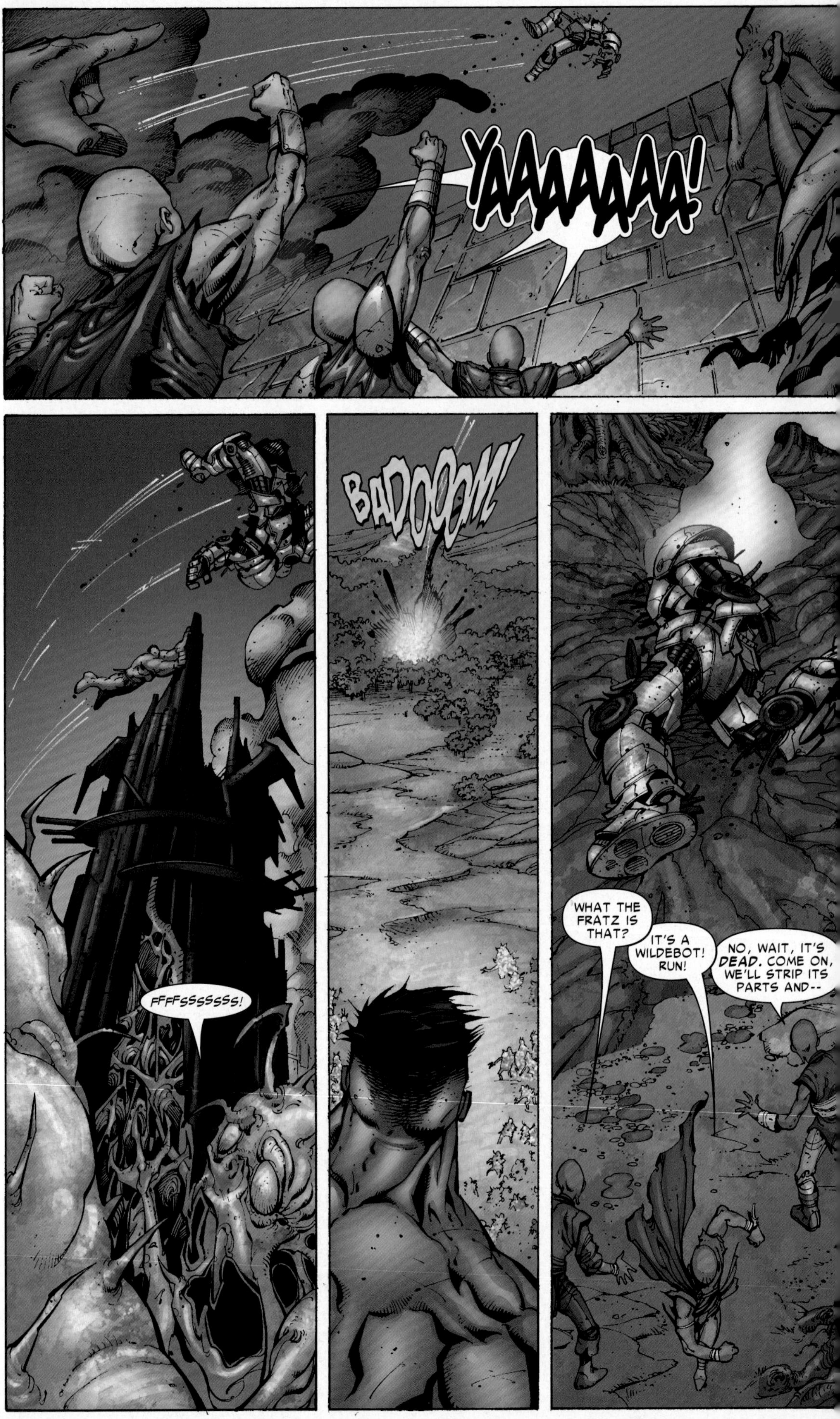
YAAAAAAA!
FFFFSSSSSSS!
BADOOOM!
WHAT THE FRATZ IS THAT?
IT'S A WILDEBOT! RUN!
NO, WAIT, IT'S *DEAD.* COME ON, WE'LL STRIP ITS PARTS AND--

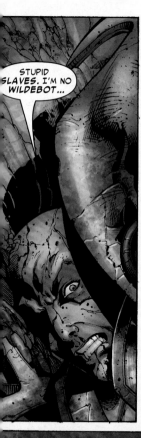

STUPID SLAVES. I'M NO WILDEBOT...

...I AM THE HERO PROTECTOR. THE CROWN PRINCE, THE RED KING, THE EMPEROR OF SAKAAR!

I AM GOD IN FLESH AND BLOOD!

KUK! KUK! KUK! KUK! KUK! KUK!

AND YOU CANNOT--

KUK! KUK! KUK!

SCHAAK

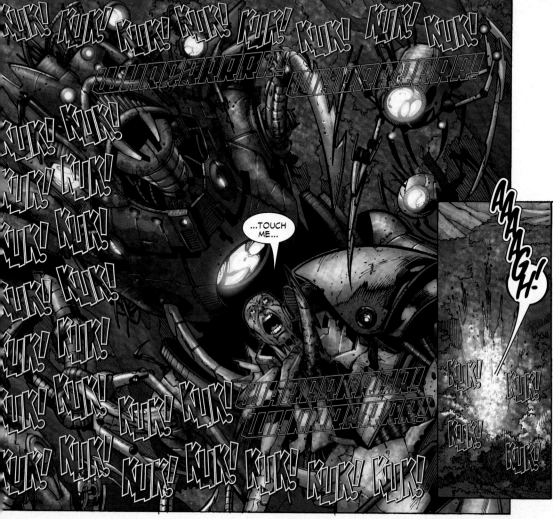

KUK! KUK! KUK! KUK! KUK! KUK! KUK! KUK!

UHRRRRRRR! UHRRARRRR!

KUK! KUK! KUK! KUK!

KUK! KUK!

...TOUCH ME...

KUK! KUK! KUK! KUK!

UHRRRRRRR! UHRRRRRRR!

KUK! KUK! KUK! KUK! KUK!

AAAAGH!

KUK! KUK!

KUK! KUK!

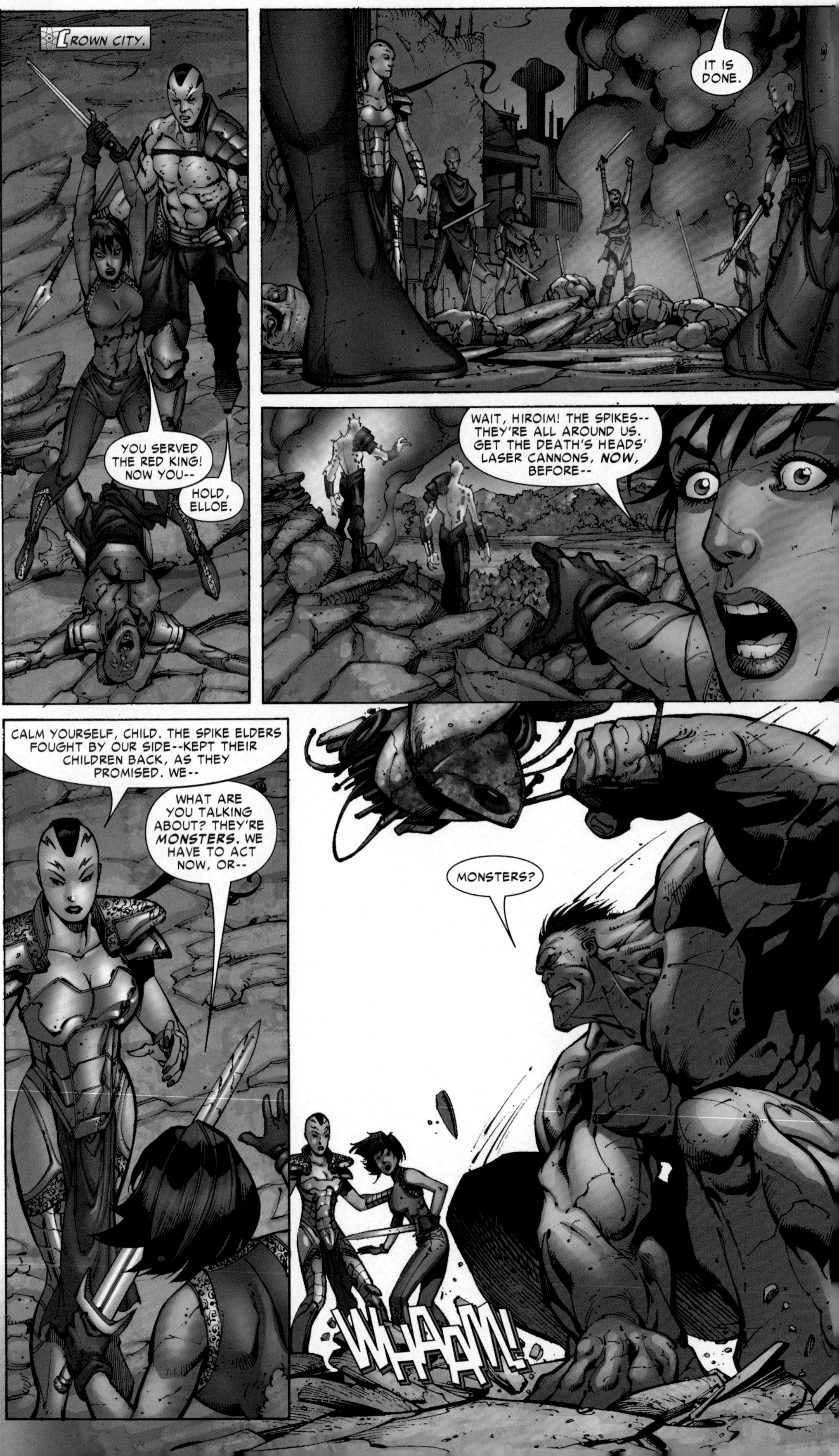
CROWN CITY.
YOU SERVED THE RED KING! NOW YOU--
HOLD, ELLOE.
IT IS DONE.
WAIT, HIROIM! THE SPIKES-- THEY'RE ALL AROUND US. GET THE DEATH'S HEADS' LASER CANNONS, NOW, BEFORE--
CALM YOURSELF, CHILD. THE SPIKE ELDERS FOUGHT BY OUR SIDE--KEPT THEIR CHILDREN BACK, AS THEY PROMISED. WE--
WHAT ARE YOU TALKING ABOUT? THEY'RE MONSTERS. WE HAVE TO ACT NOW, OR--
MONSTERS?
WHAAM!

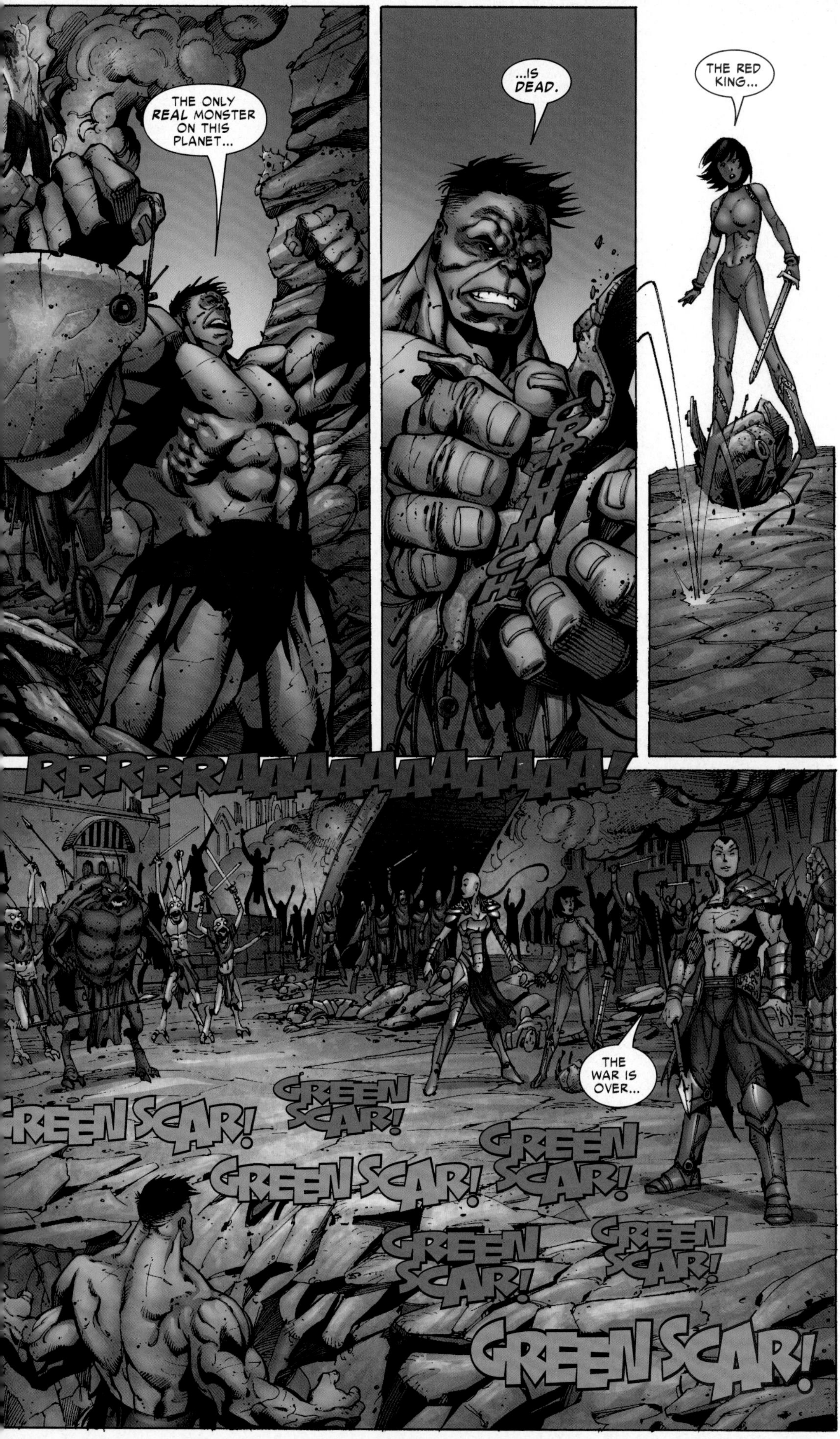
THE ONLY REAL MONSTER ON THIS PLANET...
...IS DEAD.
CRRUNCH!
THE RED KING...
RRRRRAAAAAAAAAAAA!
THE WAR IS OVER...
GREEN SCAR!
GREEN SCAR!
GREEN SCAR!
GREEN SCAR!
GREEN SCAR!
GREEN SCAR!
GREEN SCAR!

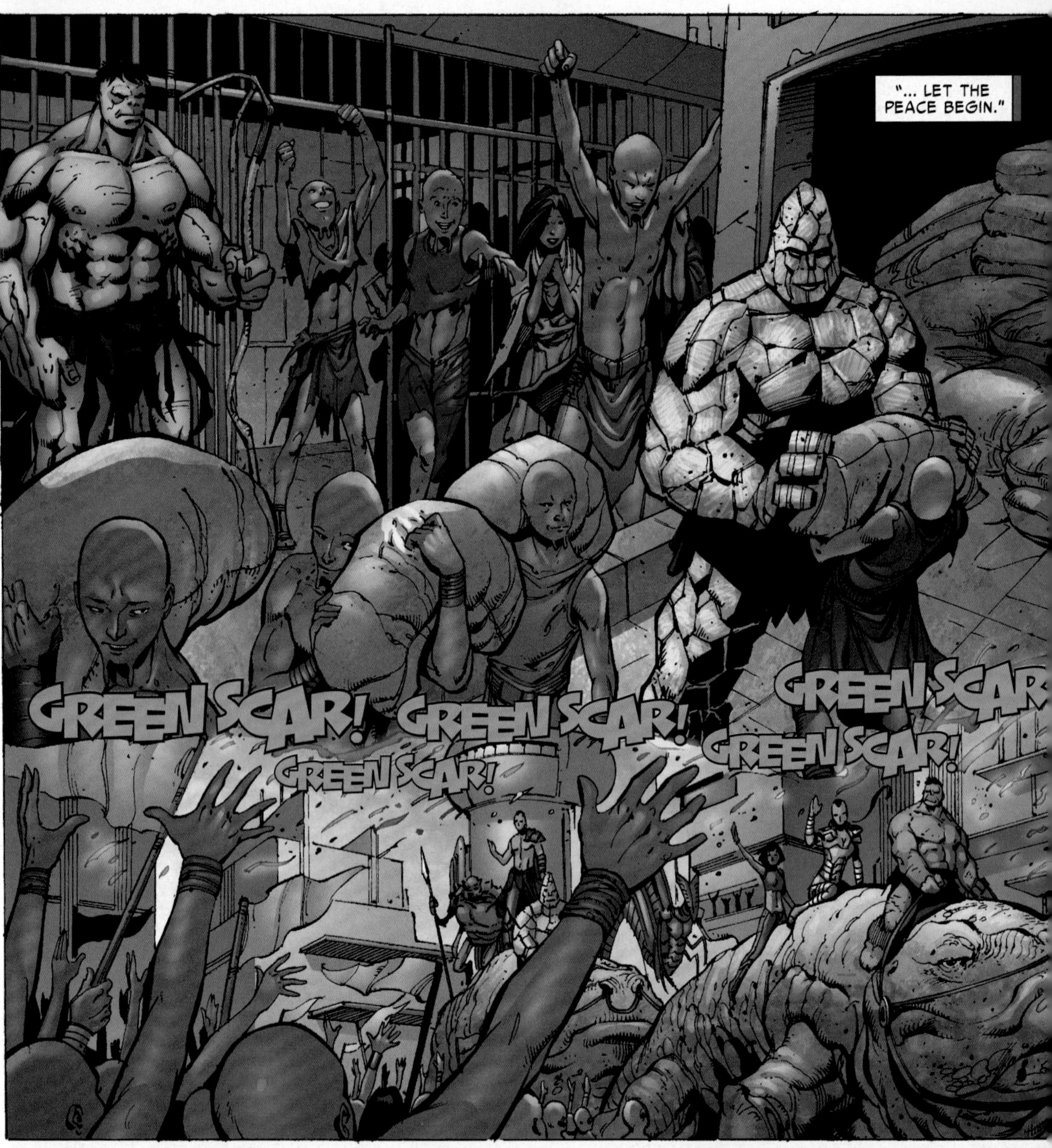
"... LET THE PEACE BEGIN."
GREEN SCAR! GREEN SCAR!
GREEN SCAR!
GREEN SCAR!
GREEN SCAR!

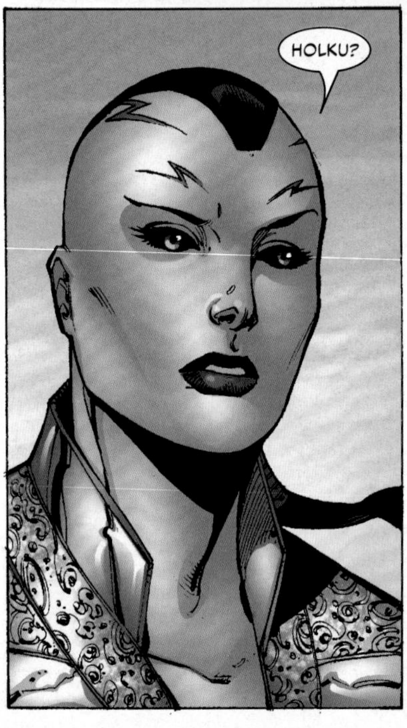
HOLKU?

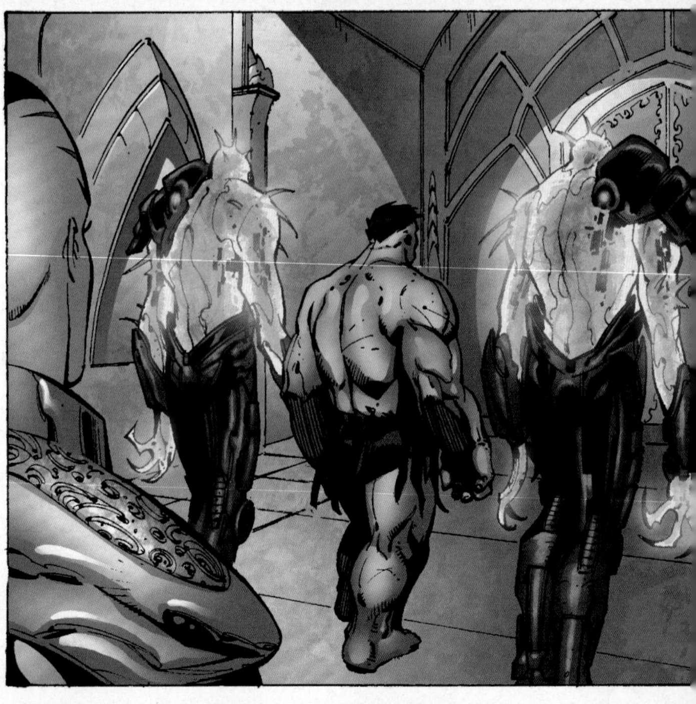

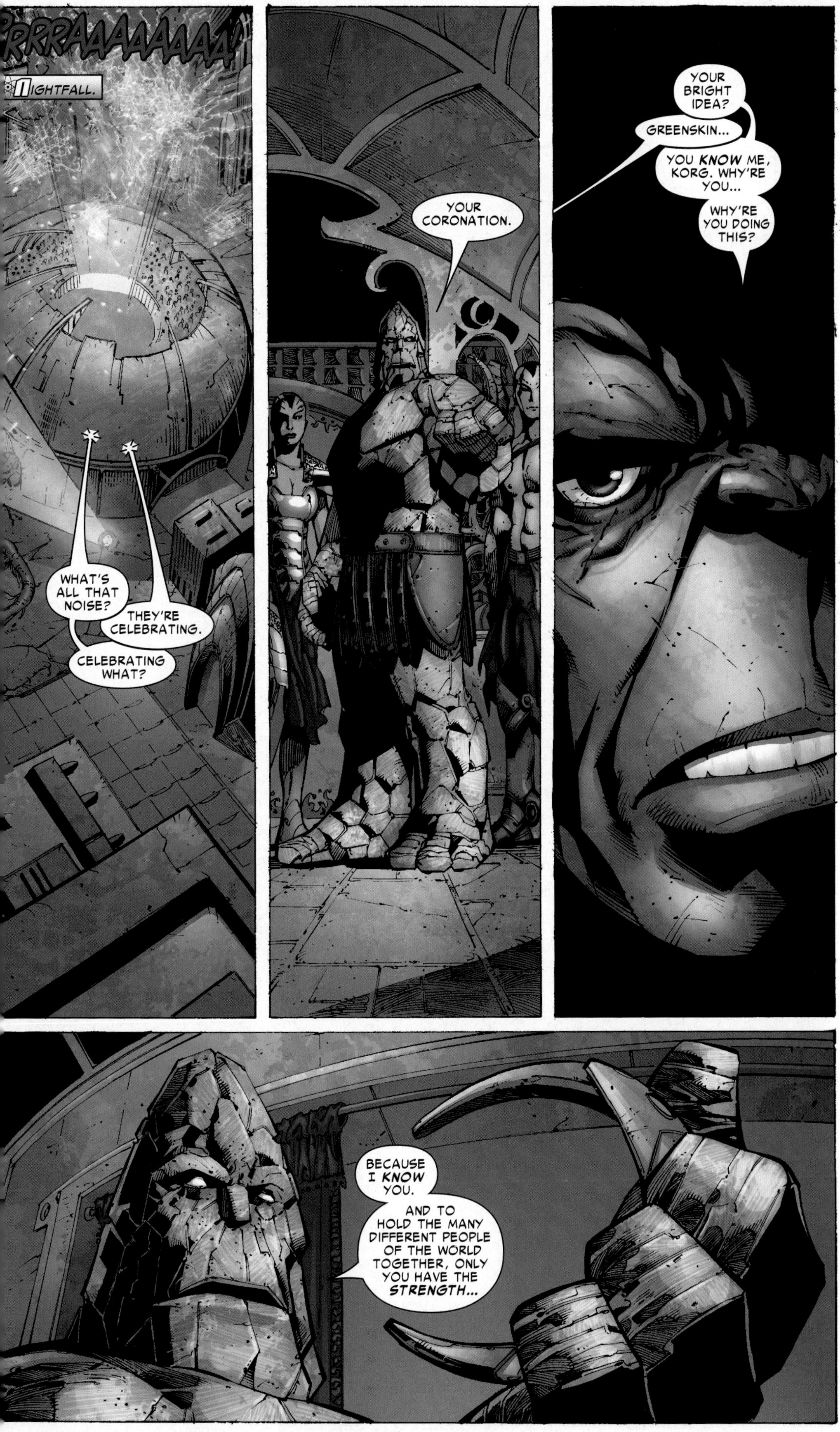
RRRAAAAAAAA!
NIGHTFALL.
WHAT'S ALL THAT NOISE?
THEY'RE CELEBRATING.
CELEBRATING WHAT?
YOUR CORONATION.
YOUR BRIGHT IDEA?
GREENSKIN...
YOU KNOW ME, KORG. WHY'RE YOU...
WHY'RE YOU DOING THIS?
BECAUSE I KNOW YOU.
AND TO HOLD THE MANY DIFFERENT PEOPLE OF THE WORLD TOGETHER, ONLY YOU HAVE THE STRENGTH...

...AND ONLY YOU HAVE THE WILL.

FORGIVE US, GREEN SCAR.

SO... HUNGRY...

FOR U

HOLKU...

WHILE THE SPIKE ELDERS FEED ON HIM, THE SPIKE CHILDREN OUTSIDE ARE QUIET.

BUT HE CAN'T...HE CAN'T BEAR EVERY BURDEN OF THIS WORLD...

SAYS WHO?

GRRRAAGH...

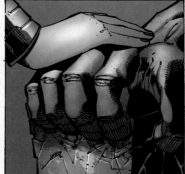

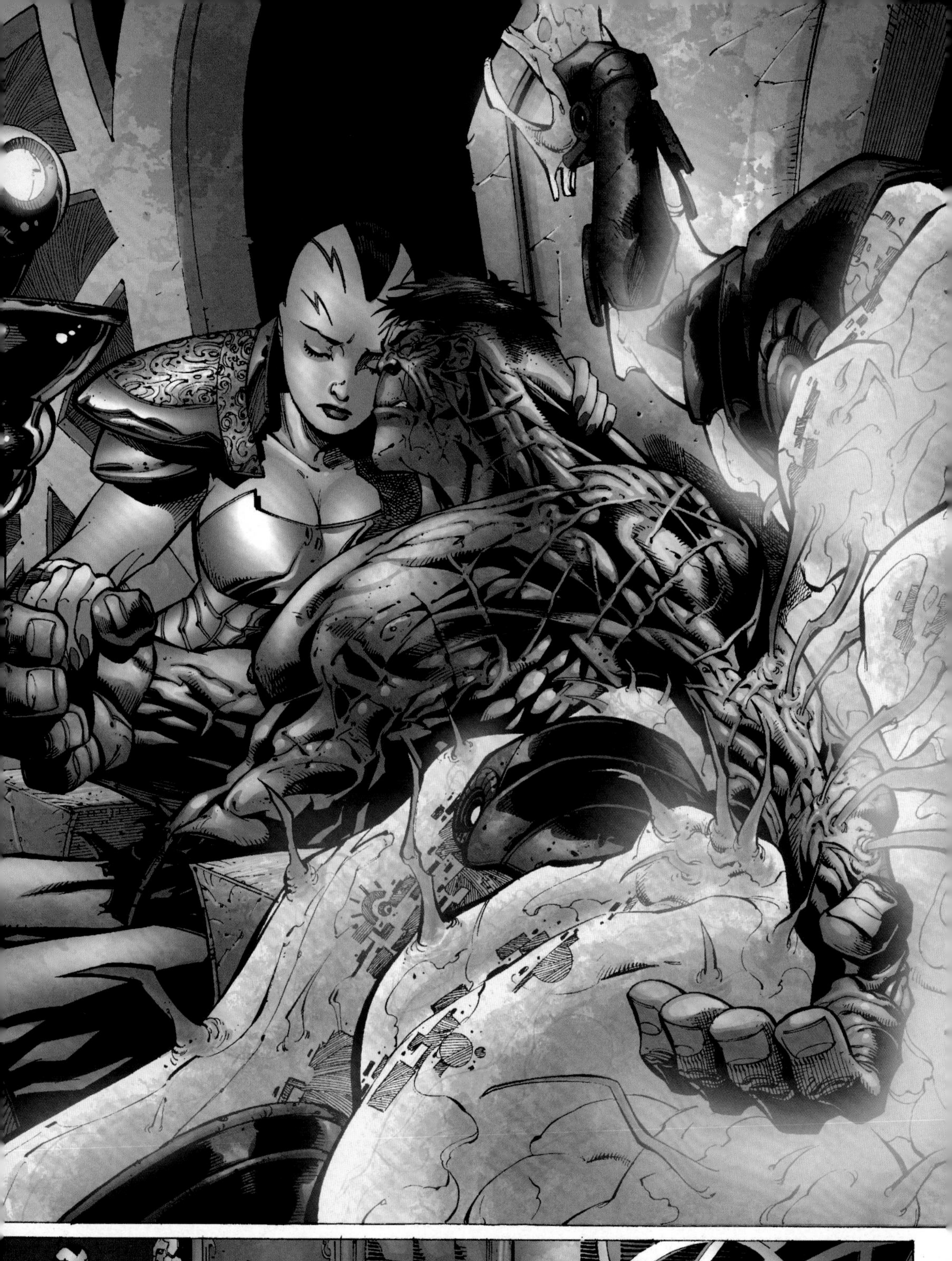

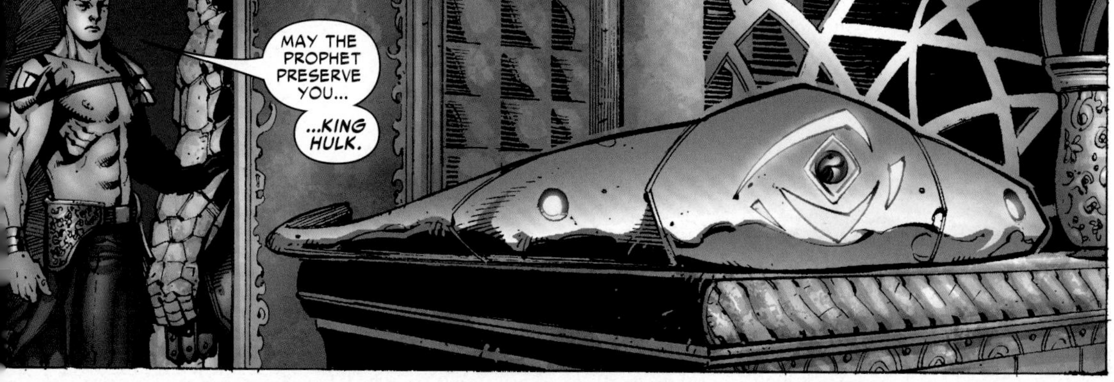
MAY THE PROPHET PRESERVE YOU...
...KING HULK.

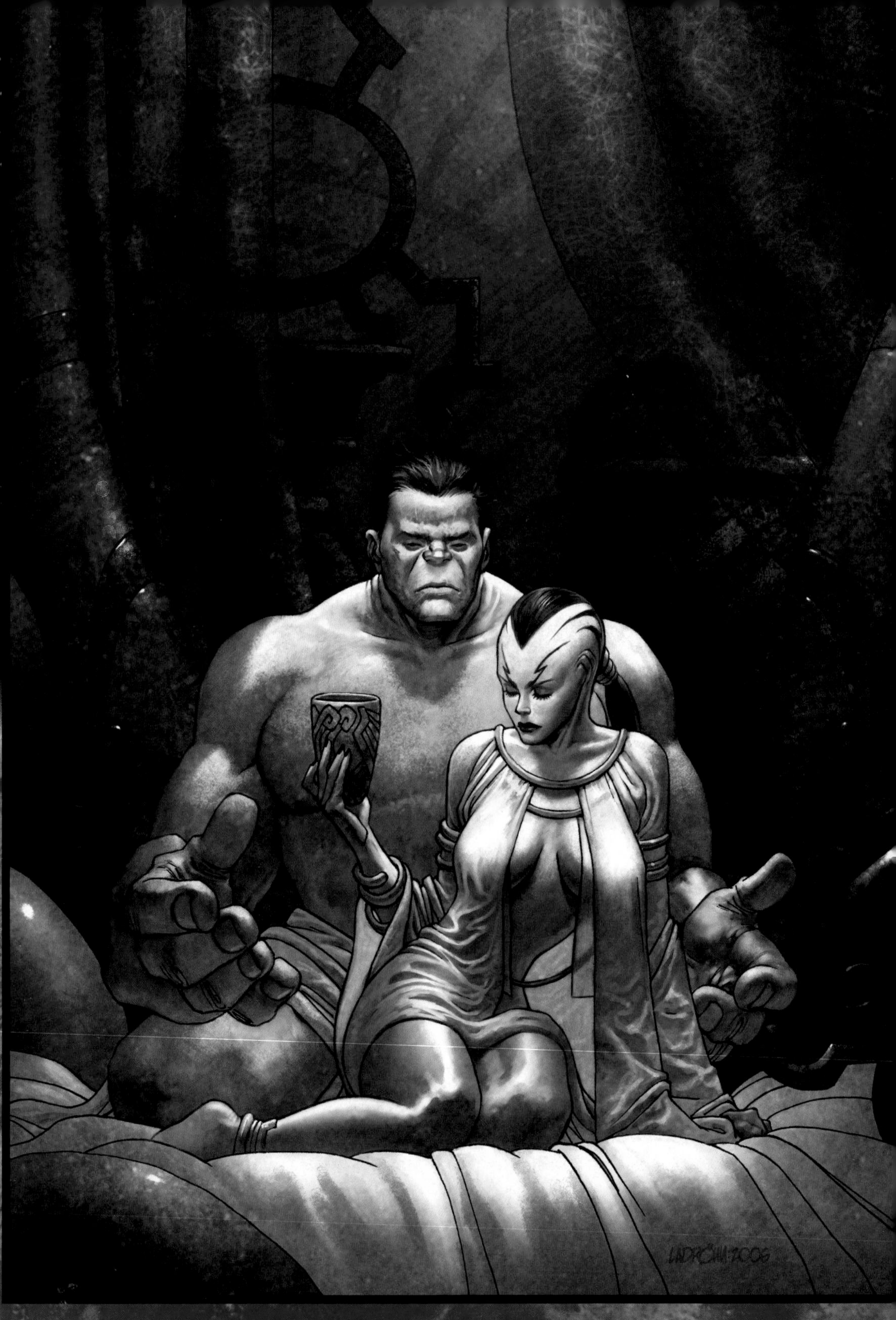

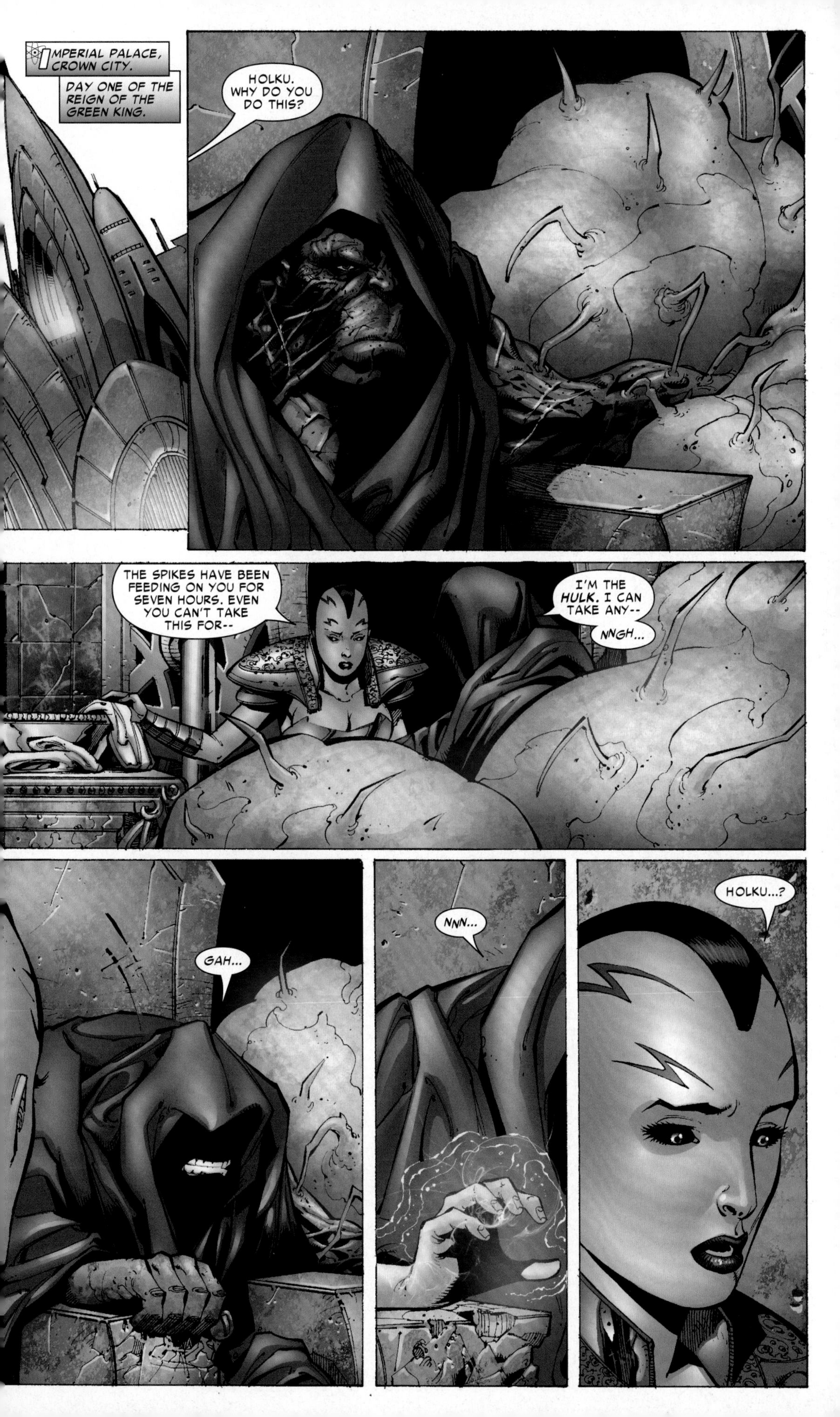
IMPERIAL PALACE, CROWN CITY.
DAY ONE OF THE REIGN OF THE GREEN KING.
HOLKU. WHY DO YOU DO THIS?
THE SPIKES HAVE BEEN FEEDING ON YOU FOR SEVEN HOURS. EVEN YOU CAN'T TAKE THIS FOR--
I'M THE HULK. I CAN TAKE ANY--
NNGH...
GAH...
NNN...
HOLKU...?

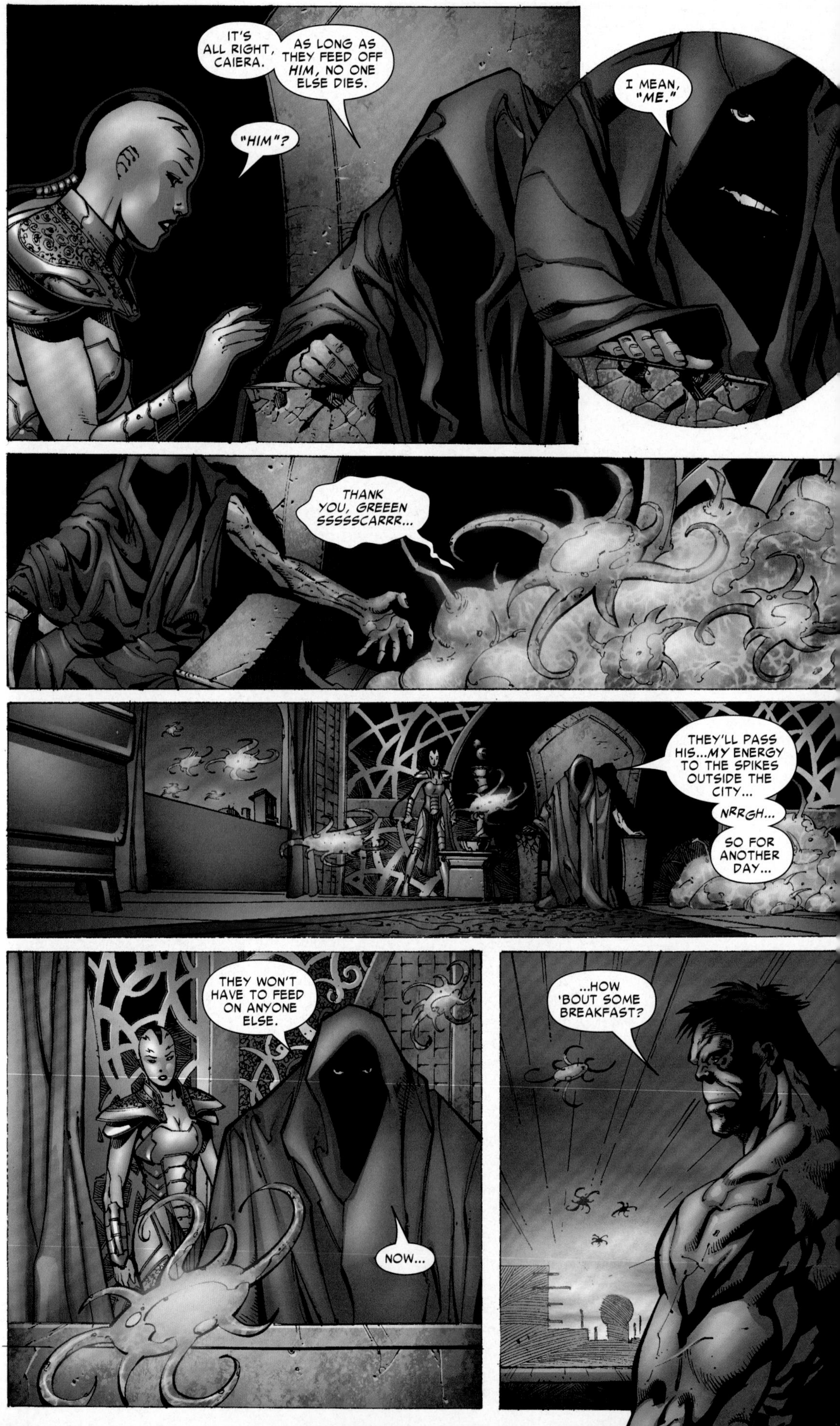
IT'S ALL RIGHT, CAIERA.
AS LONG AS THEY FEED OFF *HIM*, NO ONE ELSE DIES.
"HIM"?
I MEAN, "*ME*."
THANK YOU, GREEEN SSSSSCARRR...
THEY'LL PASS HIS...*MY* ENERGY TO THE SPIKES OUTSIDE THE CITY...
NRRGH...
SO FOR ANOTHER DAY...
THEY WON'T HAVE TO FEED ON ANYONE ELSE.
NOW...
...HOW 'BOUT SOME BREAKFAST?

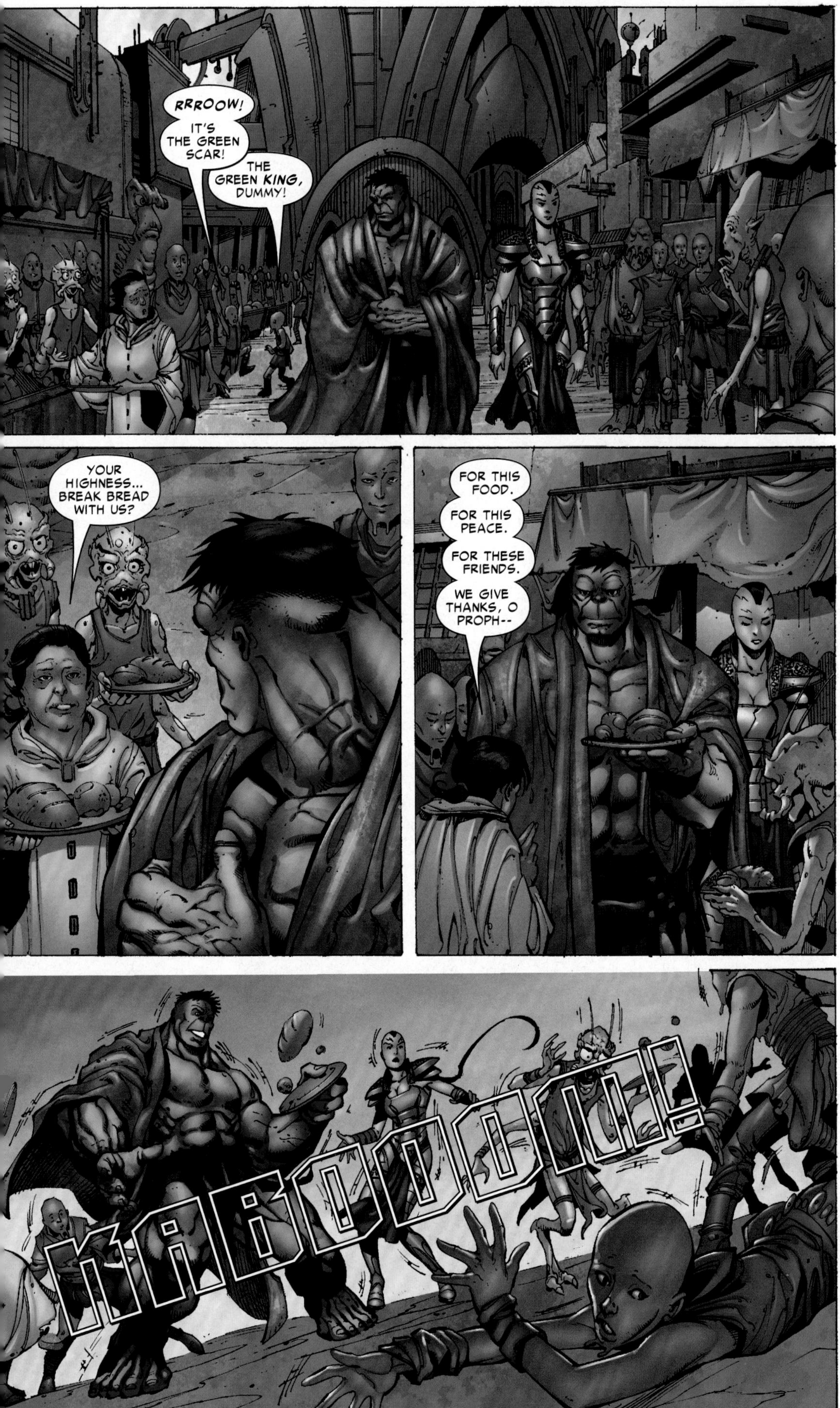
RRROOW!
IT'S THE GREEN SCAR!
THE GREEN KING, DUMMY!
YOUR HIGHNESS... BREAK BREAD WITH US?
FOR THIS FOOD.
FOR THIS PEACE.
FOR THESE FRIENDS.
WE GIVE THANKS, O PROPH--
KRAOOOM!

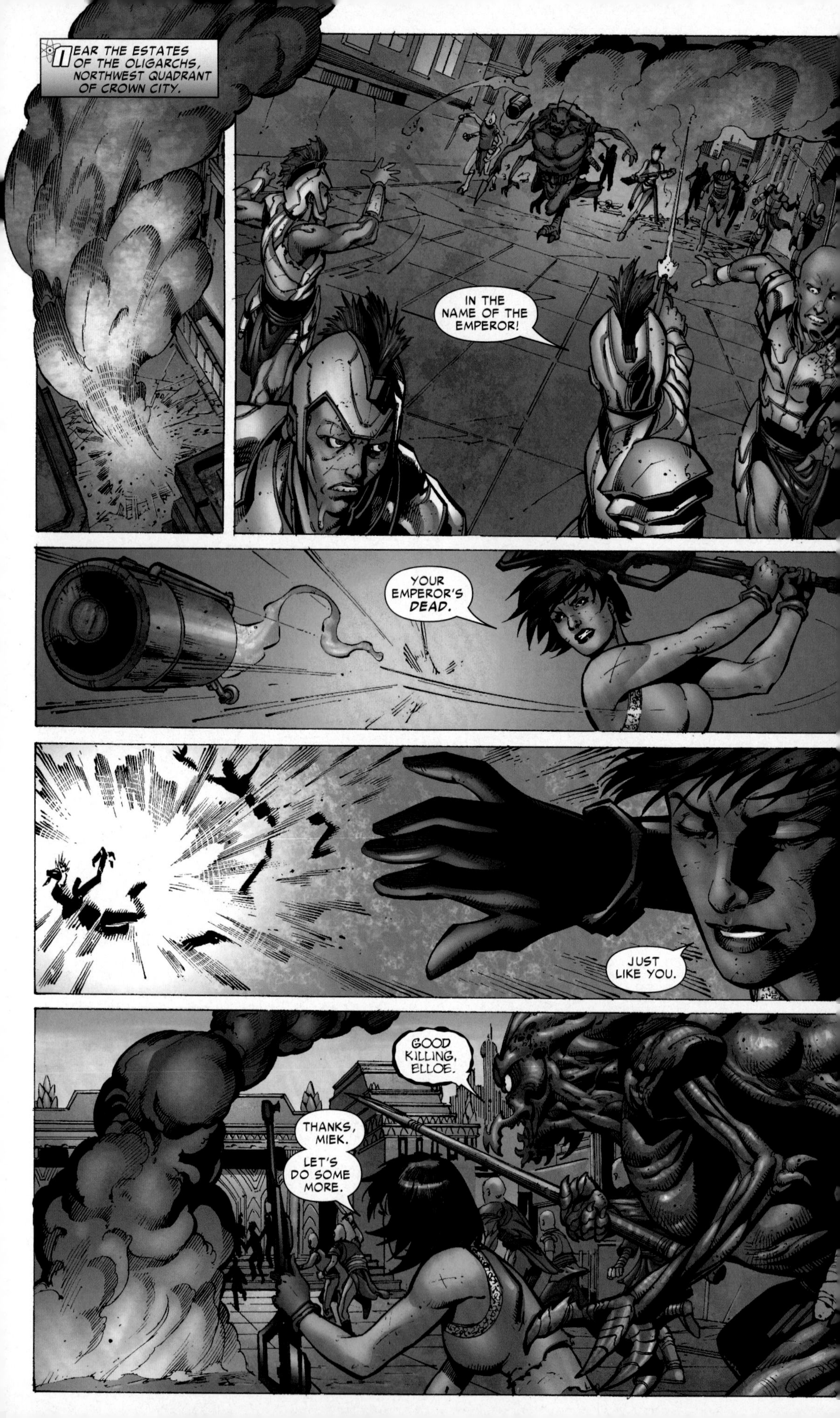
NEAR THE ESTATES OF THE OLIGARCHS, NORTHWEST QUADRANT OF CROWN CITY.
IN THE NAME OF THE EMPEROR!
YOUR EMPEROR'S DEAD.
JUST LIKE YOU.
GOOD KILLING, ELLOE.
THANKS, MIEK.
LET'S DO SOME MORE.

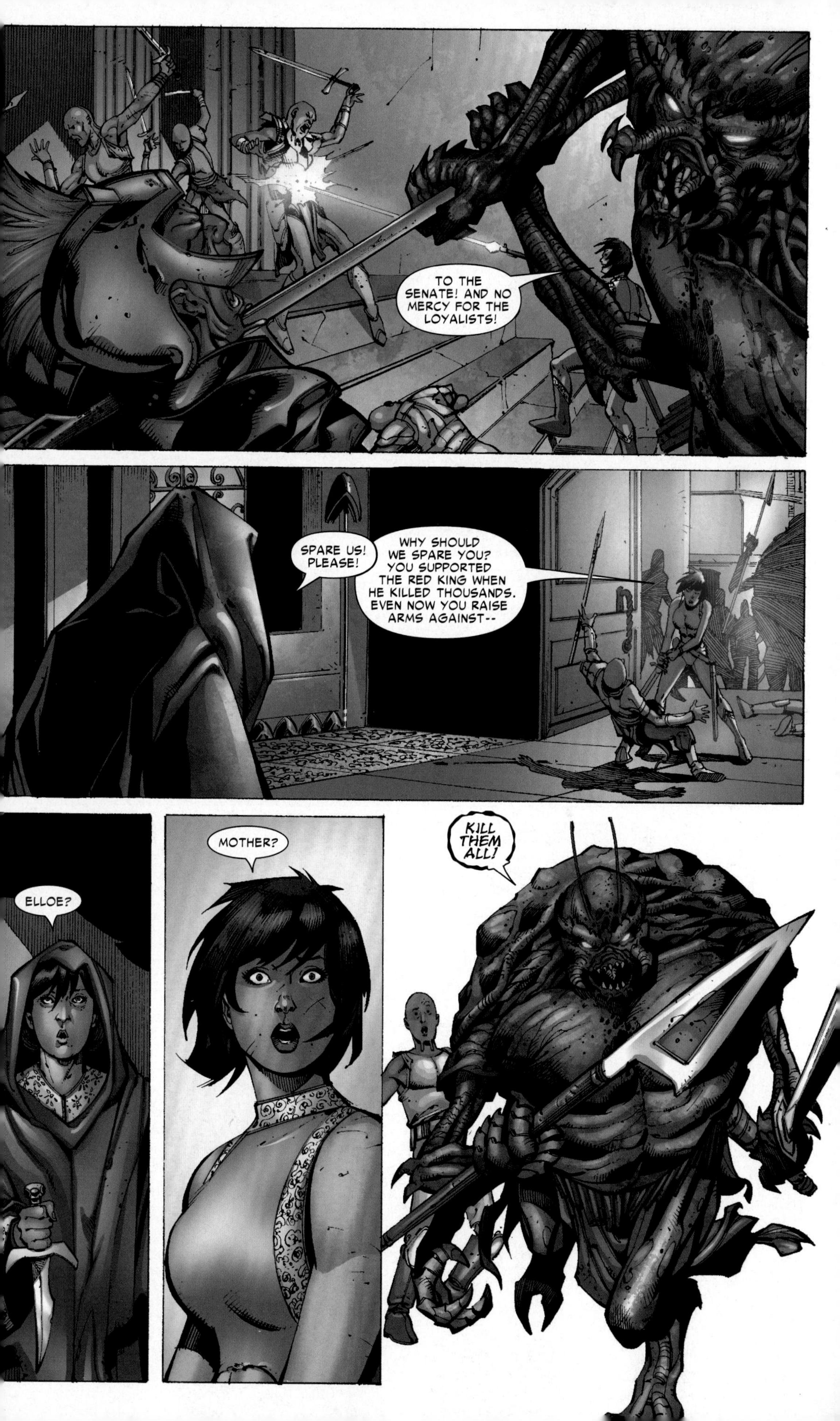
TO THE SENATE! AND NO MERCY FOR THE LOYALISTS!
SPARE US! PLEASE!
WHY SHOULD WE SPARE YOU? YOU SUPPORTED THE RED KING WHEN HE KILLED THOUSANDS. EVEN NOW YOU RAISE ARMS AGAINST--
ELLOE?
MOTHER?
KILL THEM ALL!

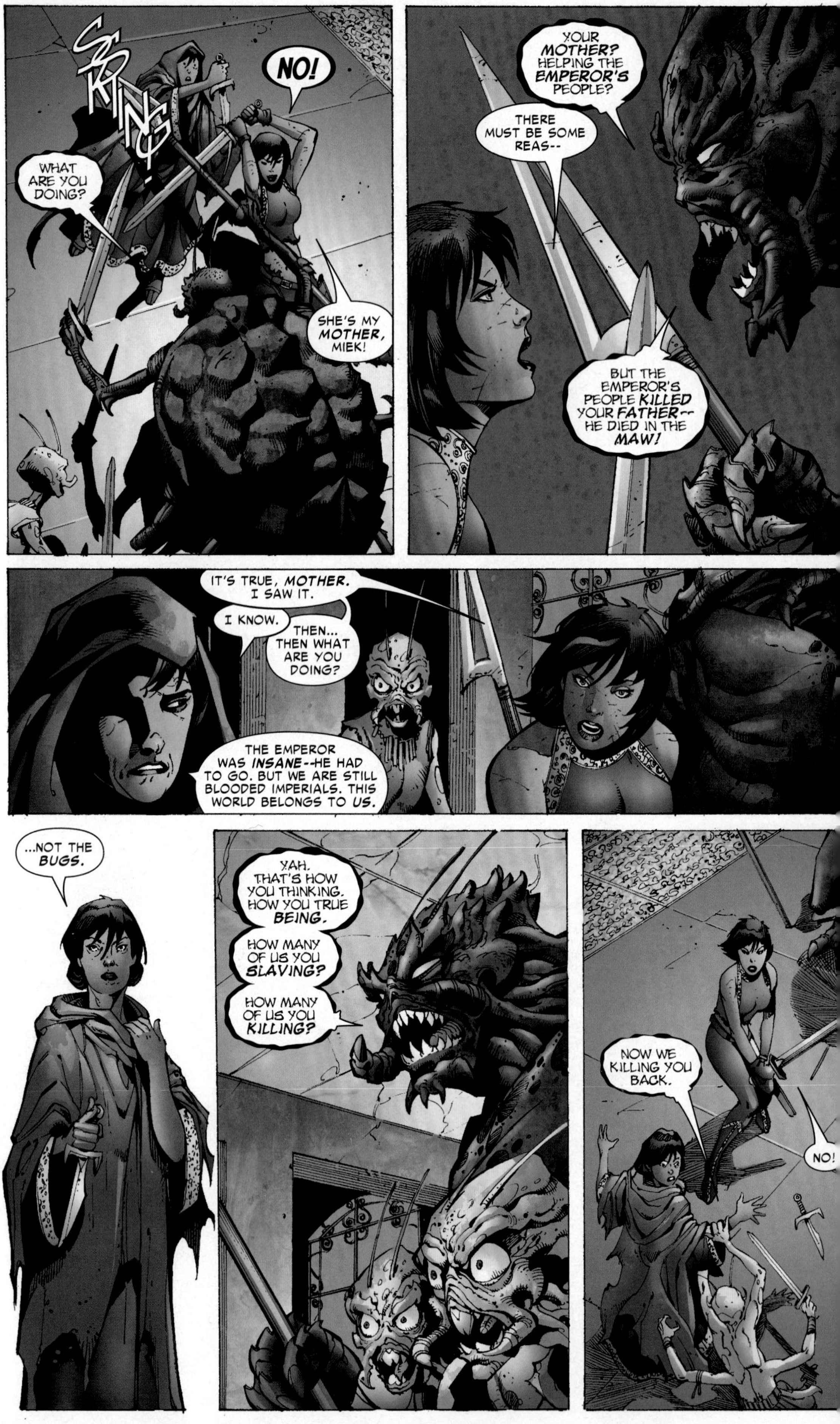
SCHRING!
NO!
WHAT ARE YOU DOING?
SHE'S MY MOTHER, MIEK!
YOUR MOTHER? HELPING THE EMPEROR'S PEOPLE?
THERE MUST BE SOME REAS--
BUT THE EMPEROR'S PEOPLE KILLED YOUR FATHER--HE DIED IN THE MAW!
IT'S TRUE, MOTHER. I SAW IT.
I KNOW.
THEN... THEN WHAT ARE YOU DOING?
THE EMPEROR WAS INSANE--HE HAD TO GO. BUT WE ARE STILL BLOODED IMPERIALS. THIS WORLD BELONGS TO US.
...NOT THE BUGS.
YAH. THAT'S HOW YOU THINKING. HOW YOU TRUE BEING.
HOW MANY OF US YOU SLAVING?
HOW MANY OF US YOU KILLING?
NOW WE KILLING YOU BACK.
NO!

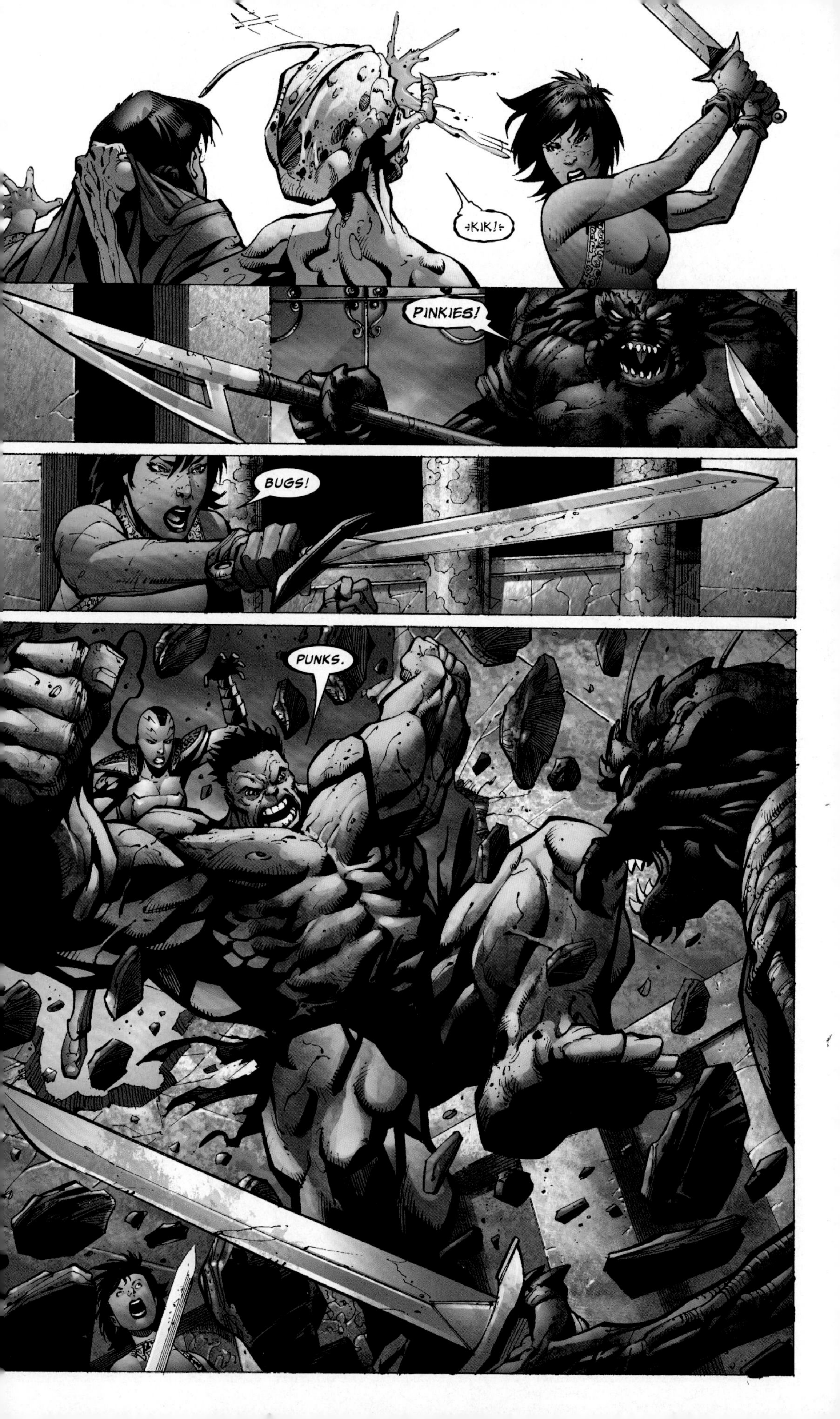
KIK!
PINKIES!
BUGS!
PUNKS.

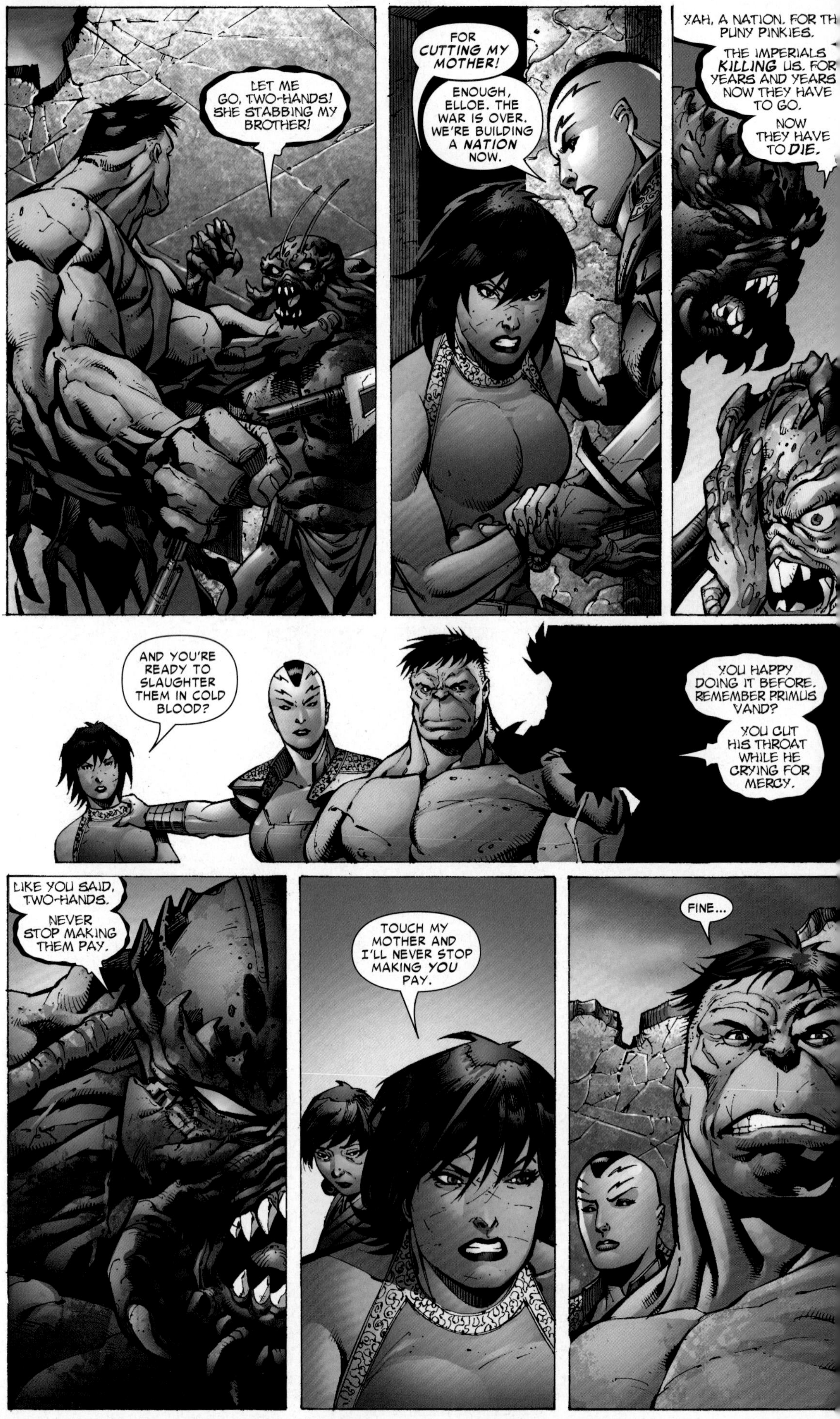
LET ME GO, TWO-HANDS! SHE STABBING MY BROTHER!
FOR CUTTING MY MOTHER!
ENOUGH, ELLOE. THE WAR IS OVER. WE'RE BUILDING A NATION NOW.
YAH, A NATION. FOR TH PUNY PINKIES.
THE IMPERIALS KILLING US. FOR YEARS AND YEARS NOW THEY HAVE TO GO.
NOW THEY HAVE TO DIE.
AND YOU'RE READY TO SLAUGHTER THEM IN COLD BLOOD?
YOU HAPPY DOING IT BEFORE. REMEMBER PRIMUS VAND?
YOU CUT HIS THROAT WHILE HE CRYING FOR MERCY.
LIKE YOU SAID, TWO-HANDS.
NEVER STOP MAKING THEM PAY.
TOUCH MY MOTHER AND I'LL NEVER STOP MAKING YOU PAY.
FINE...

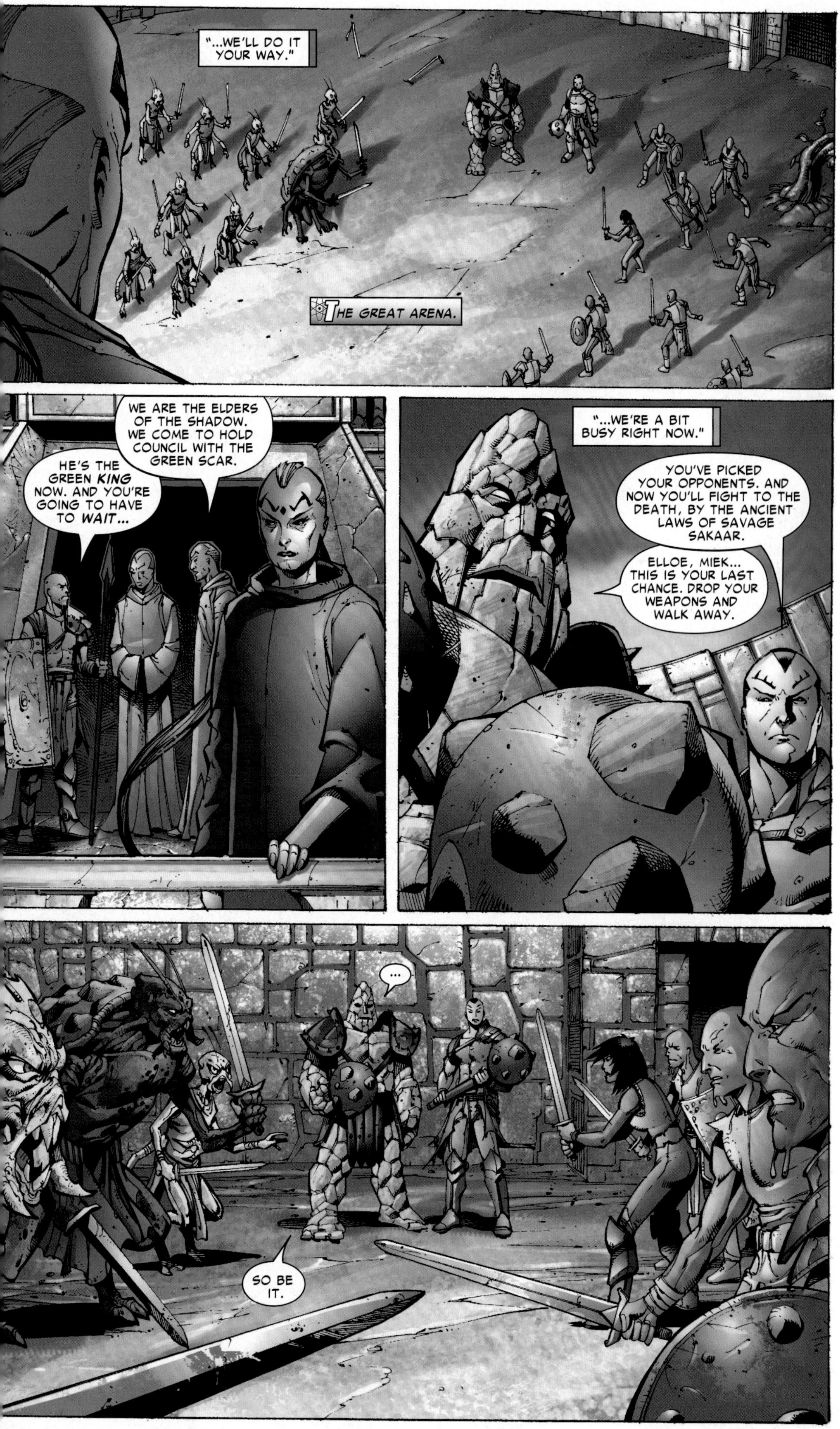
"...WE'LL DO IT YOUR WAY."
THE GREAT ARENA.
WE ARE THE ELDERS OF THE SHADOW. WE COME TO HOLD COUNCIL WITH THE GREEN SCAR.
HE'S THE GREEN KING NOW. AND YOU'RE GOING TO HAVE TO WAIT...
"...WE'RE A BIT BUSY RIGHT NOW."
YOU'VE PICKED YOUR OPPONENTS. AND NOW YOU'LL FIGHT TO THE DEATH, BY THE ANCIENT LAWS OF SAVAGE SAKAAR.
ELLOE, MIEK... THIS IS YOUR LAST CHANCE. DROP YOUR WEAPONS AND WALK AWAY.
...
SO BE IT.

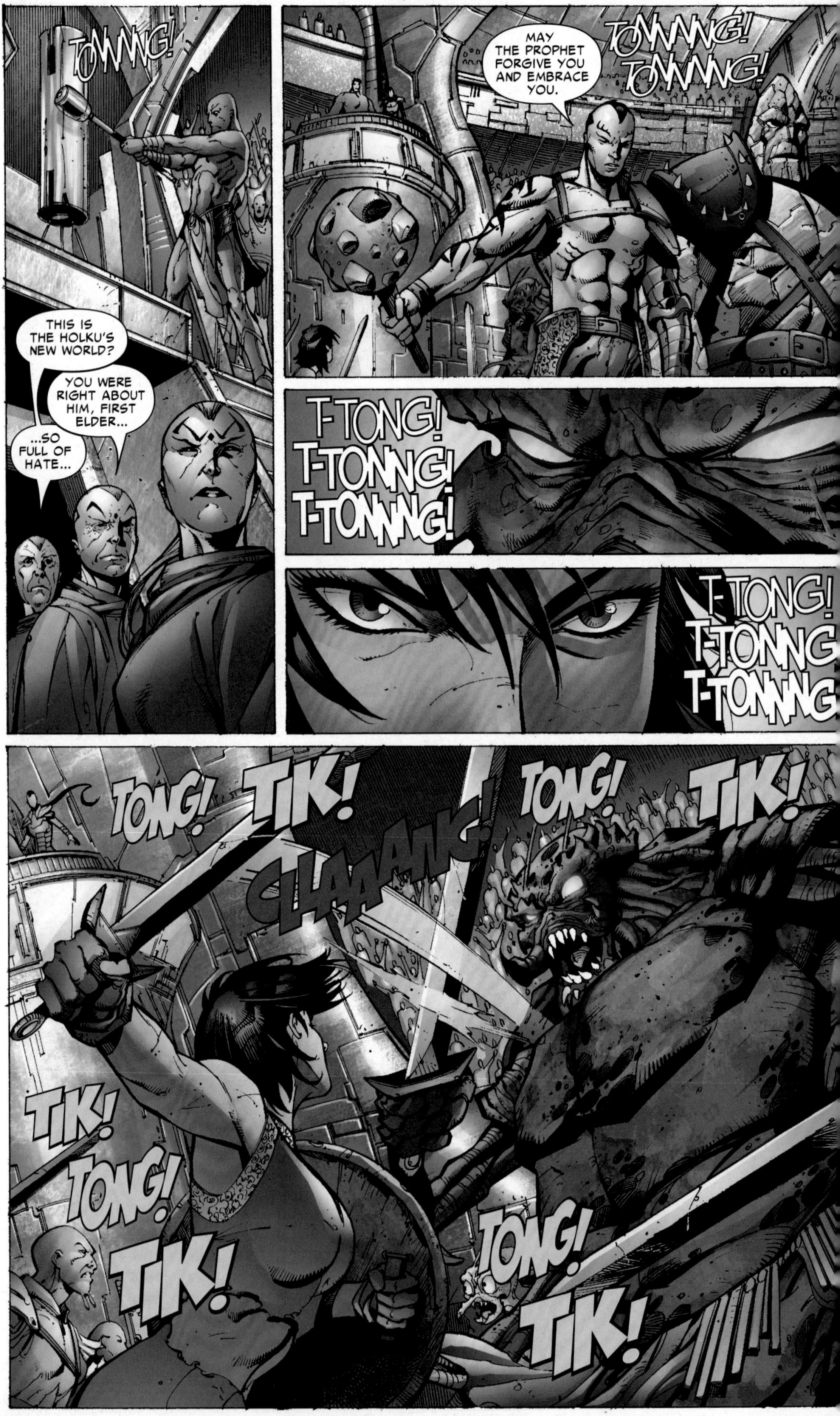
TONNNG!
MAY THE PROPHET FORGIVE YOU AND EMBRACE YOU.
TONNNG! TONNNG!
THIS IS THE HOLKU'S NEW WORLD?
YOU WERE RIGHT ABOUT HIM, FIRST ELDER...
...SO FULL OF HATE...
T-TONG! T-TONNG! T-TONNNG!
T-TONG! T-TONNG T-TONNNG
TONG! TIK!
CLAAANG!
TONG! TIK!
TIK! TONG! TIK!
TONG! TIK!

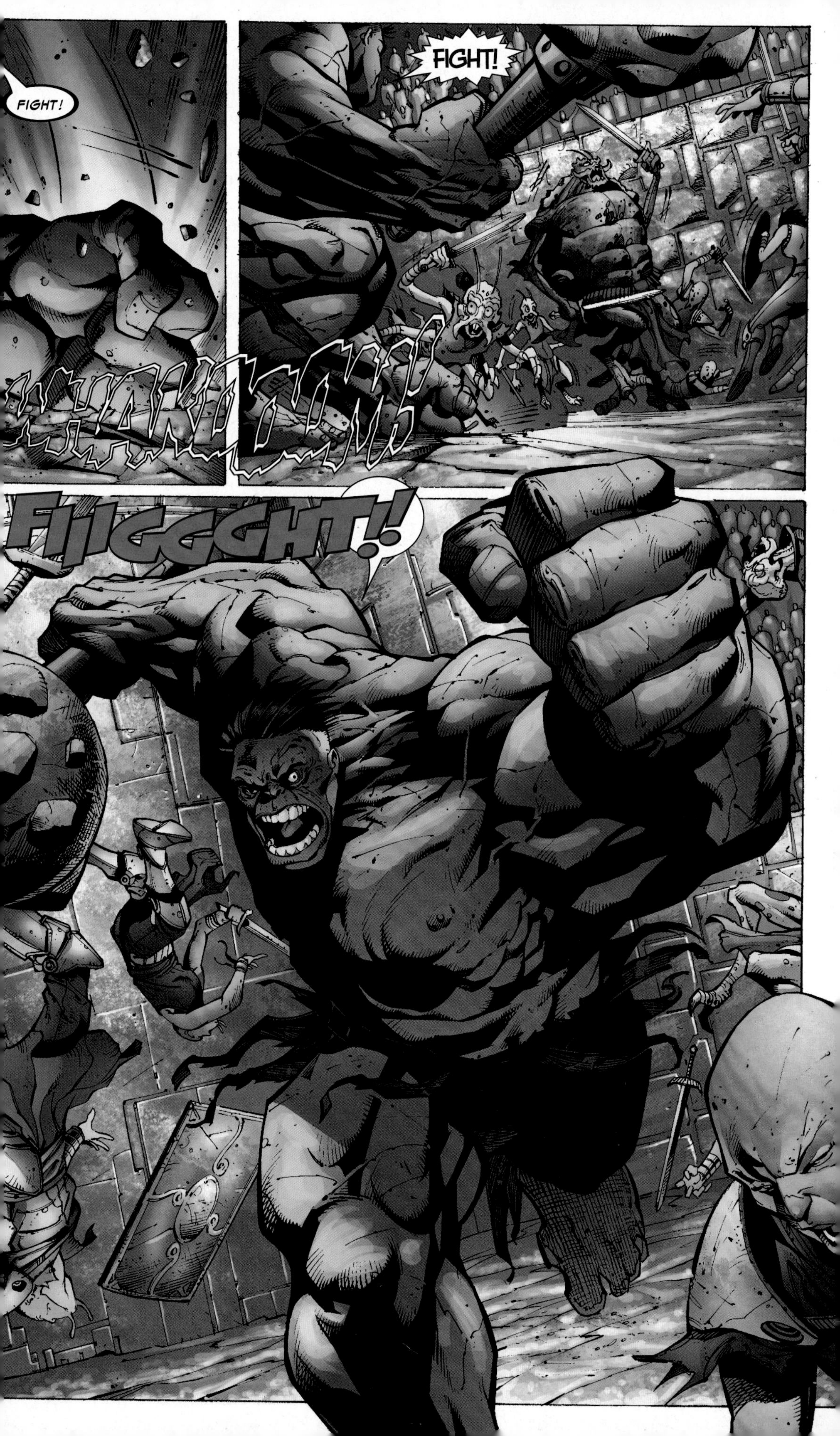

FIGHT!
FIGHT!
FIIIGGGHT!!

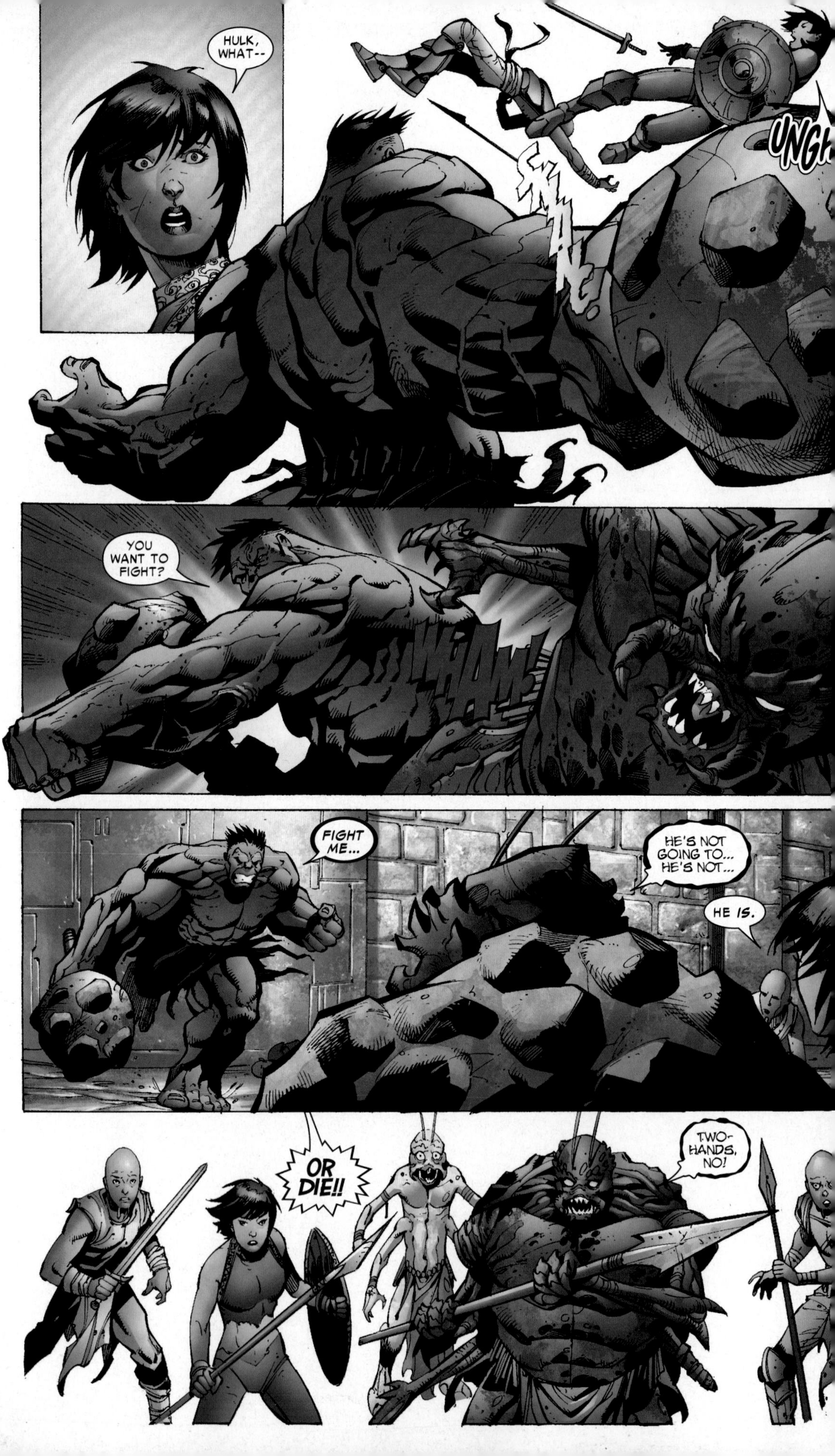
HULK, WHAT--
UNGH
SHANG!
YOU WANT TO FIGHT?
WHAM!
FIGHT ME...
HE'S NOT GOING TO... HE'S NOT...
HE IS.
OR DIE!!
TWO-HANDS, NO!

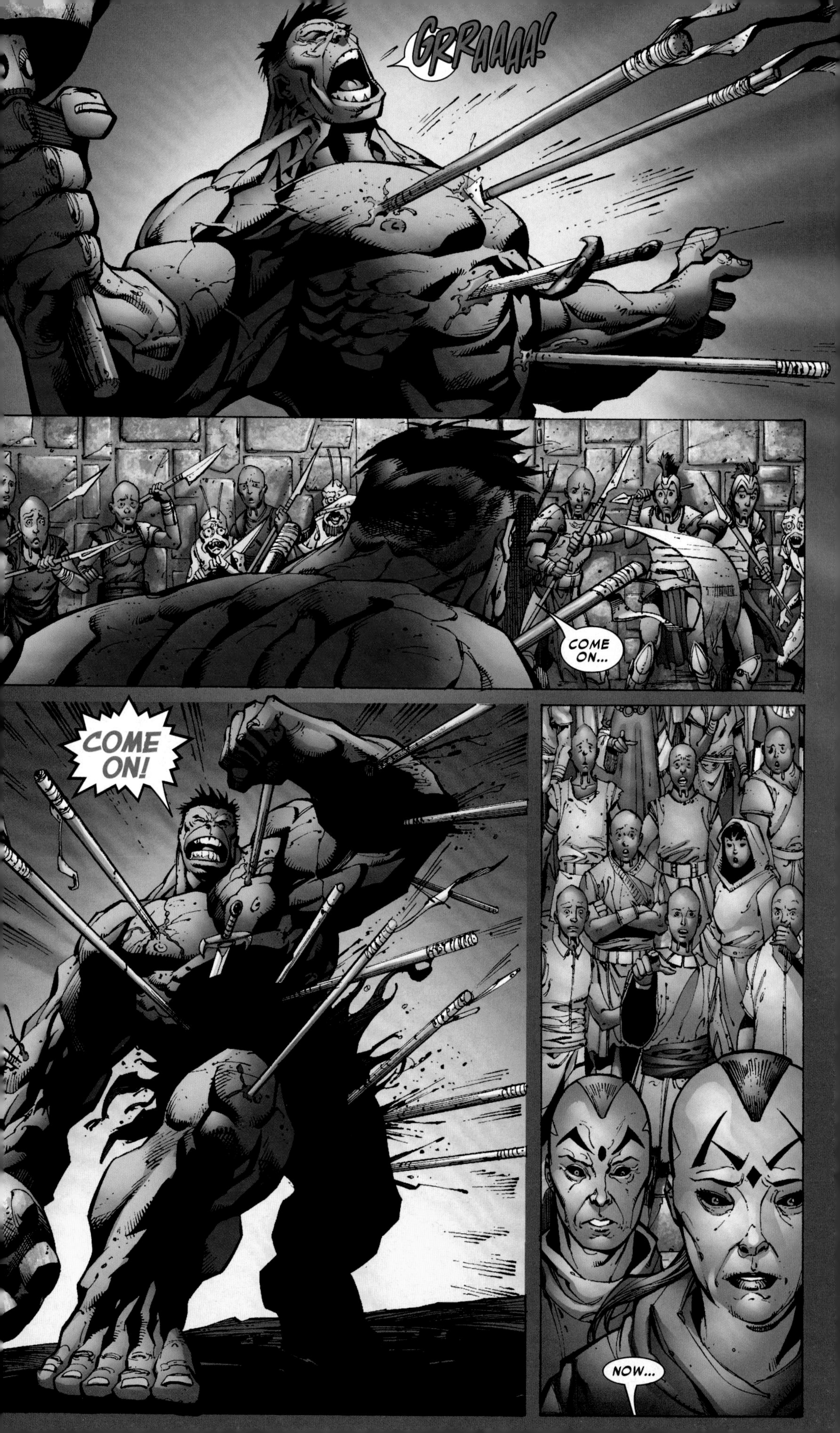

GRRAAAA!
COME ON...
COME ON!
NOW...

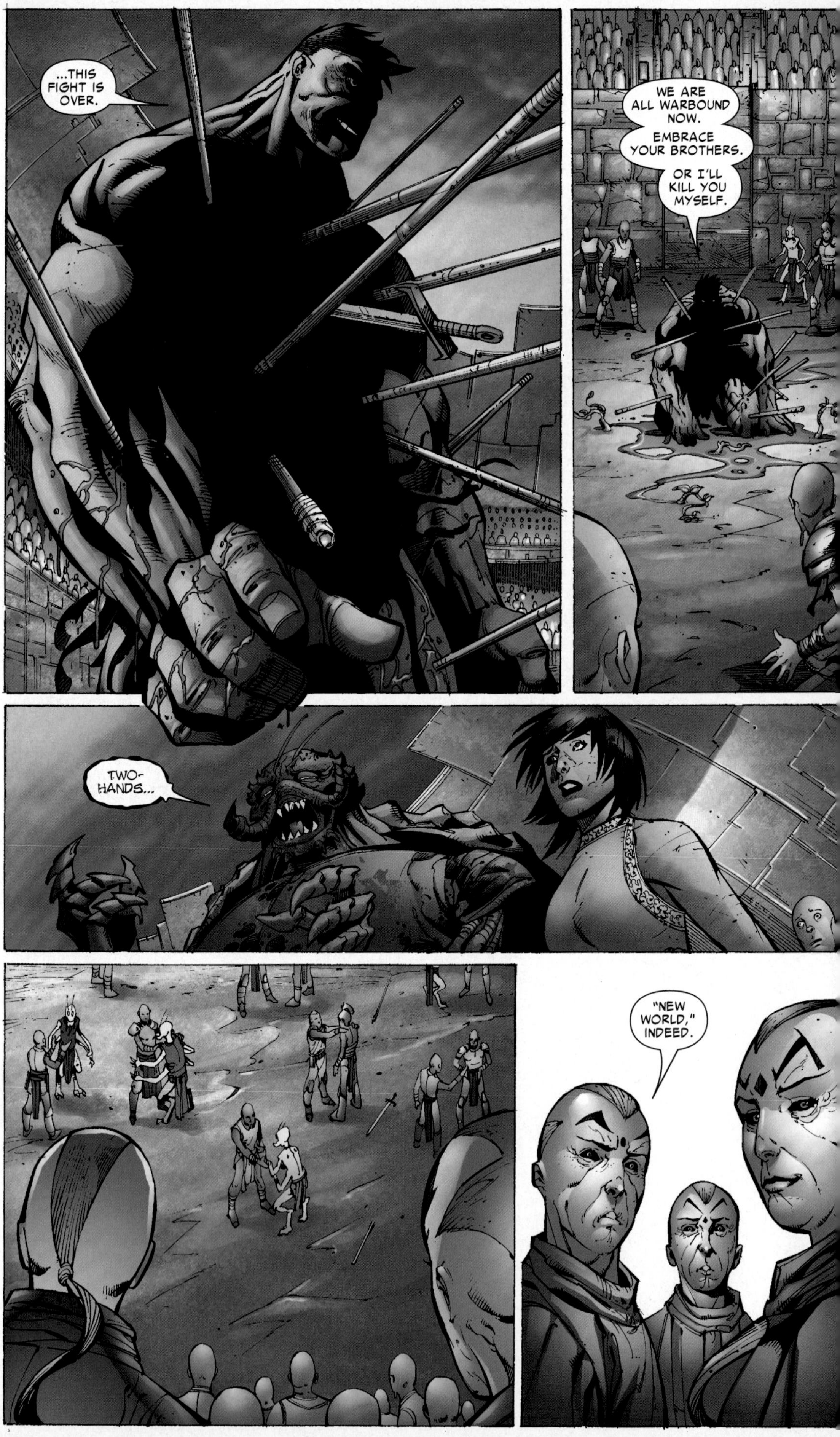
...THIS FIGHT IS OVER.
WE ARE ALL WARBOUND NOW.
EMBRACE YOUR BROTHERS.
OR I'LL KILL YOU MYSELF.
TWO-HANDS...
"NEW WORLD," INDEED.

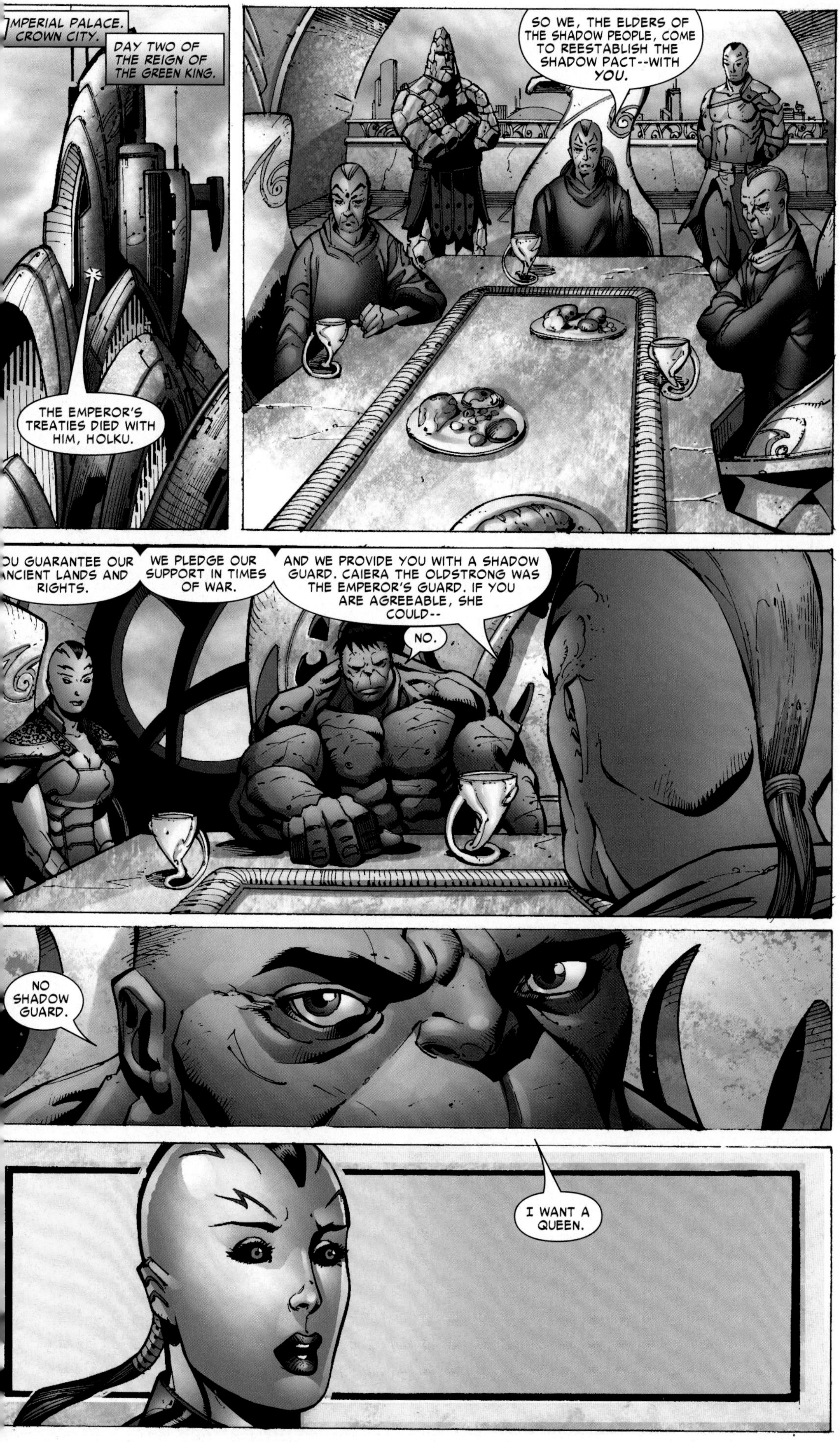
MPERIAL PALACE. CROWN CITY.
DAY TWO OF THE REIGN OF THE GREEN KING.
THE EMPEROR'S TREATIES DIED WITH HIM, HOLKU.
SO WE, THE ELDERS OF THE SHADOW PEOPLE, COME TO REESTABLISH THE SHADOW PACT--WITH YOU.
OU GUARANTEE OUR NCIENT LANDS AND RIGHTS.
WE PLEDGE OUR SUPPORT IN TIMES OF WAR.
AND WE PROVIDE YOU WITH A SHADOW GUARD. CAIERA THE OLDSTRONG WAS THE EMPEROR'S GUARD. IF YOU ARE AGREEABLE, SHE COULD--
NO.
NO SHADOW GUARD.
I WANT A QUEEN.

HOLKU...

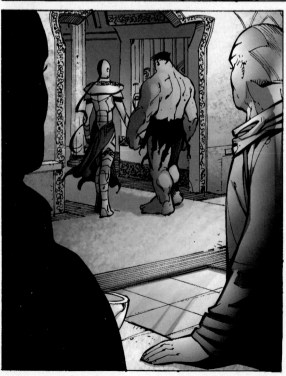

I...BELIEVE WE HAVE OURSELVES A TREATY.

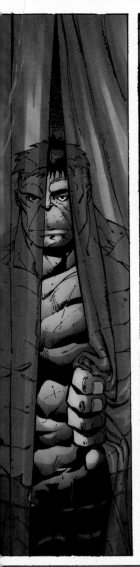

I AM SHADOW. FOR THIS MARRIAGE TO BE TRUE, WE MUST COMPLETE THE SHADOW CEREMONY.

WILL YOU KNEEL WITH ME AS I KNEEL WITH YOU?

...

I WILL.

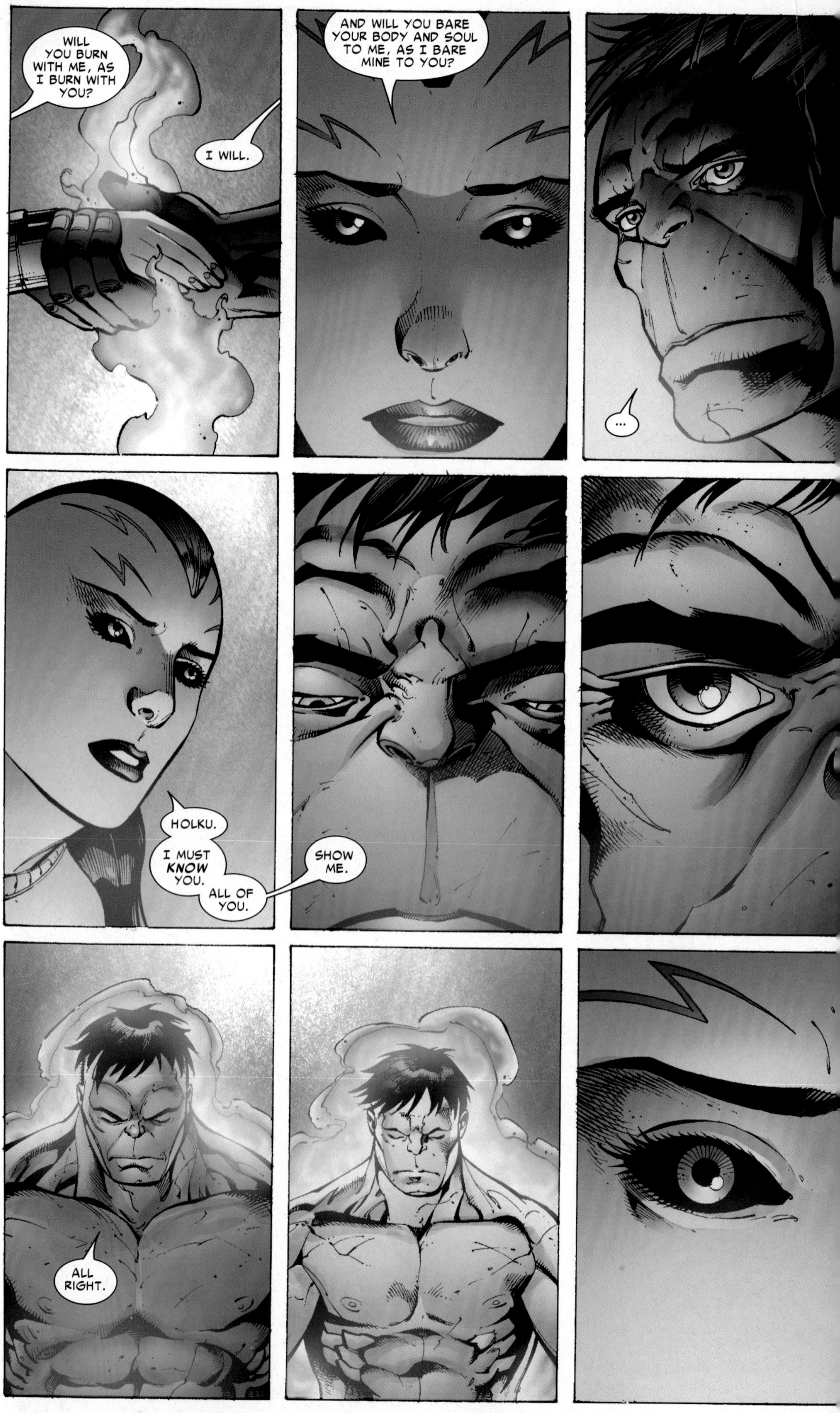
WILL YOU BURN WITH ME, AS I BURN WITH YOU?
I WILL.
AND WILL YOU BARE YOUR BODY AND SOUL TO ME, AS I BARE MINE TO YOU?
...
HOLKU.
I MUST KNOW YOU.
ALL OF YOU.
SHOW ME.
ALL RIGHT.

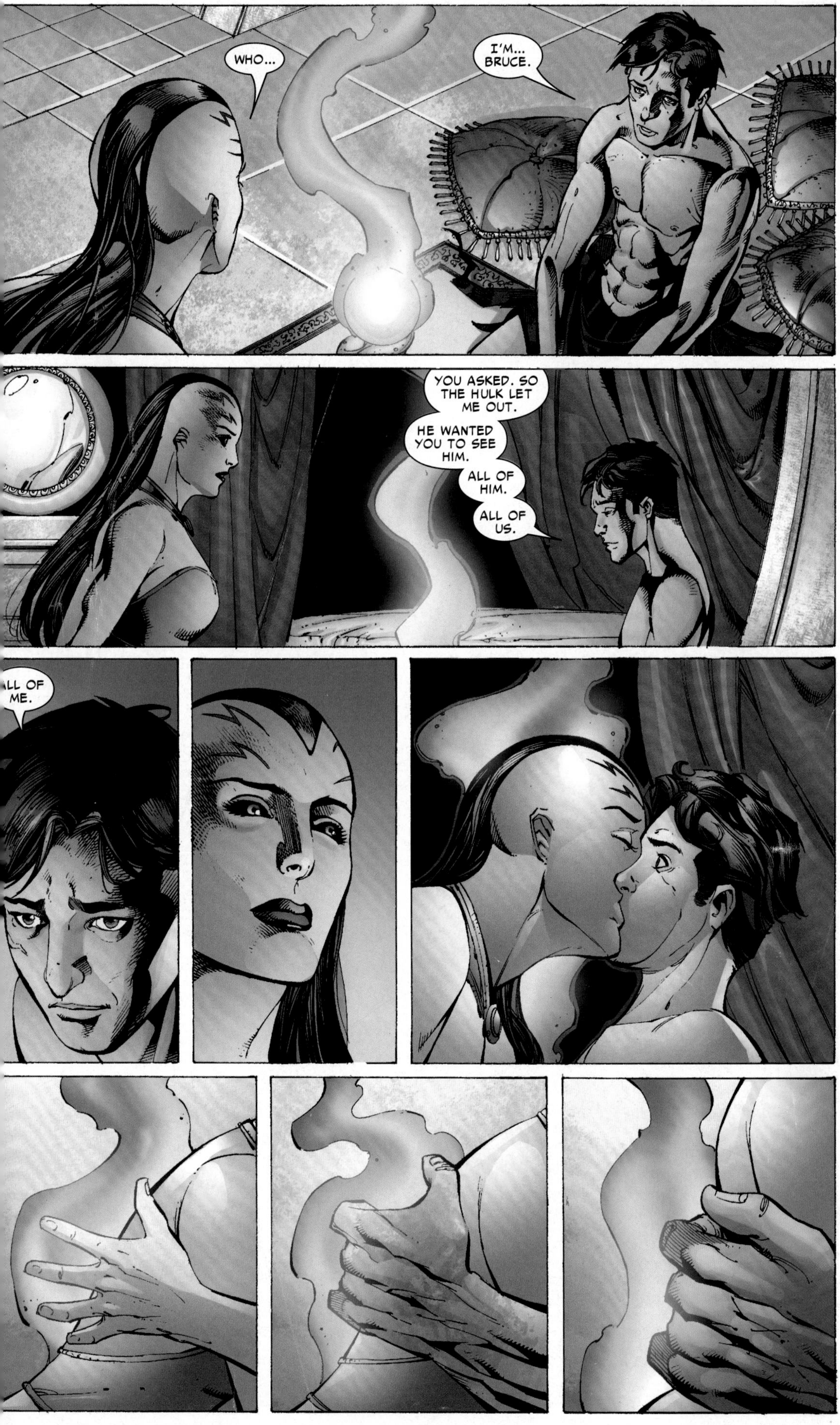
WHO...
I'M... BRUCE.
YOU ASKED. SO THE HULK LET ME OUT.
HE WANTED YOU TO SEE HIM.
ALL OF HIM.
ALL OF US.
ALL OF ME.

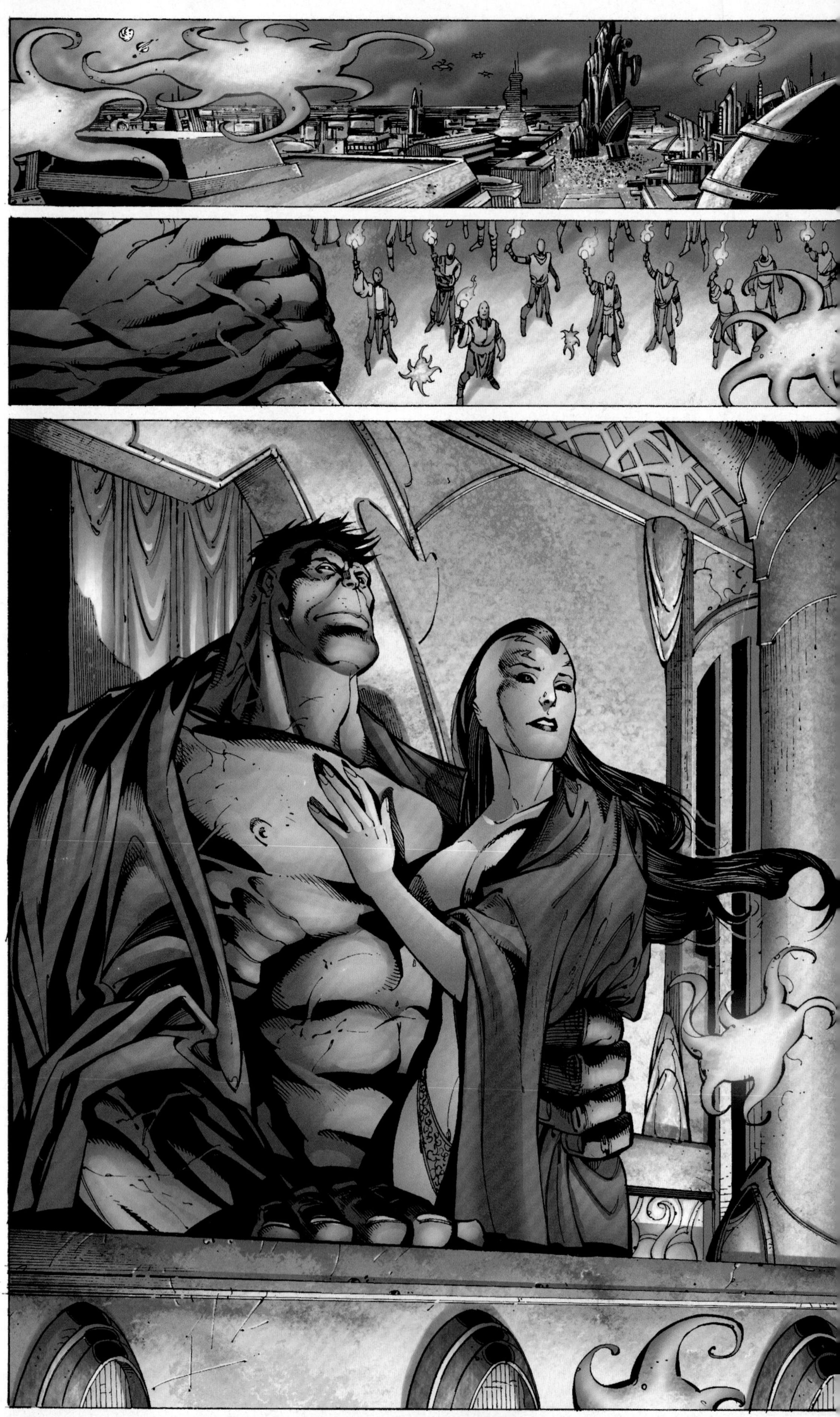

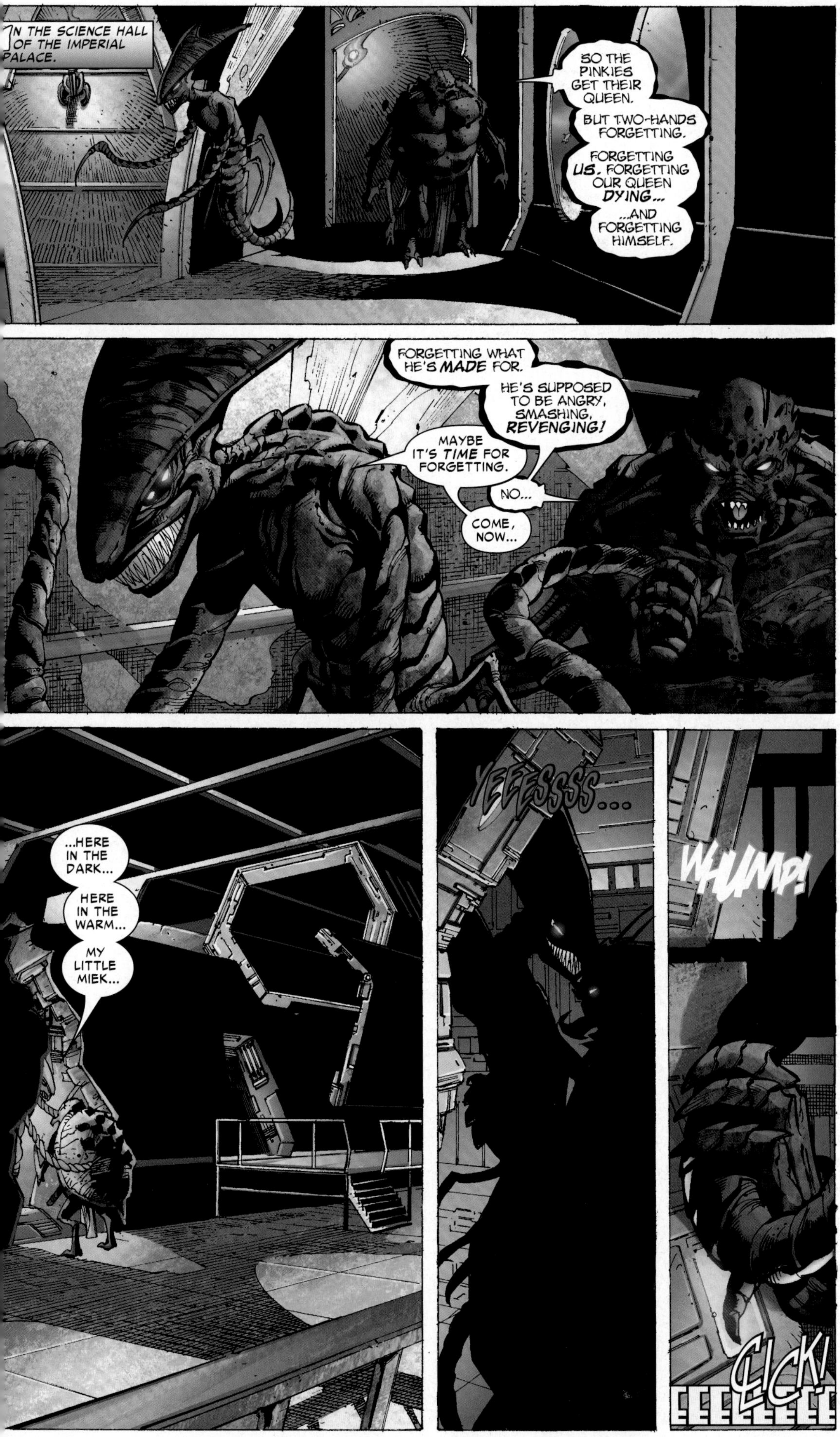
IN THE SCIENCE HALL OF THE IMPERIAL PALACE.
SO THE PINKIES GET THEIR QUEEN.
BUT TWO-HANDS FORGETTING.
FORGETTING US. FORGETTING OUR QUEEN DYING...
...AND FORGETTING HIMSELF.
FORGETTING WHAT HE'S MADE FOR.
HE'S SUPPOSED TO BE ANGRY, SMASHING, REVENGING!
MAYBE IT'S TIME FOR FORGETTING.
NO...
COME, NOW...
...HERE IN THE DARK...
HERE IN THE WARM...
MY LITTLE MIEK...
YEEESSSS...
WHUMP!
CLICK!

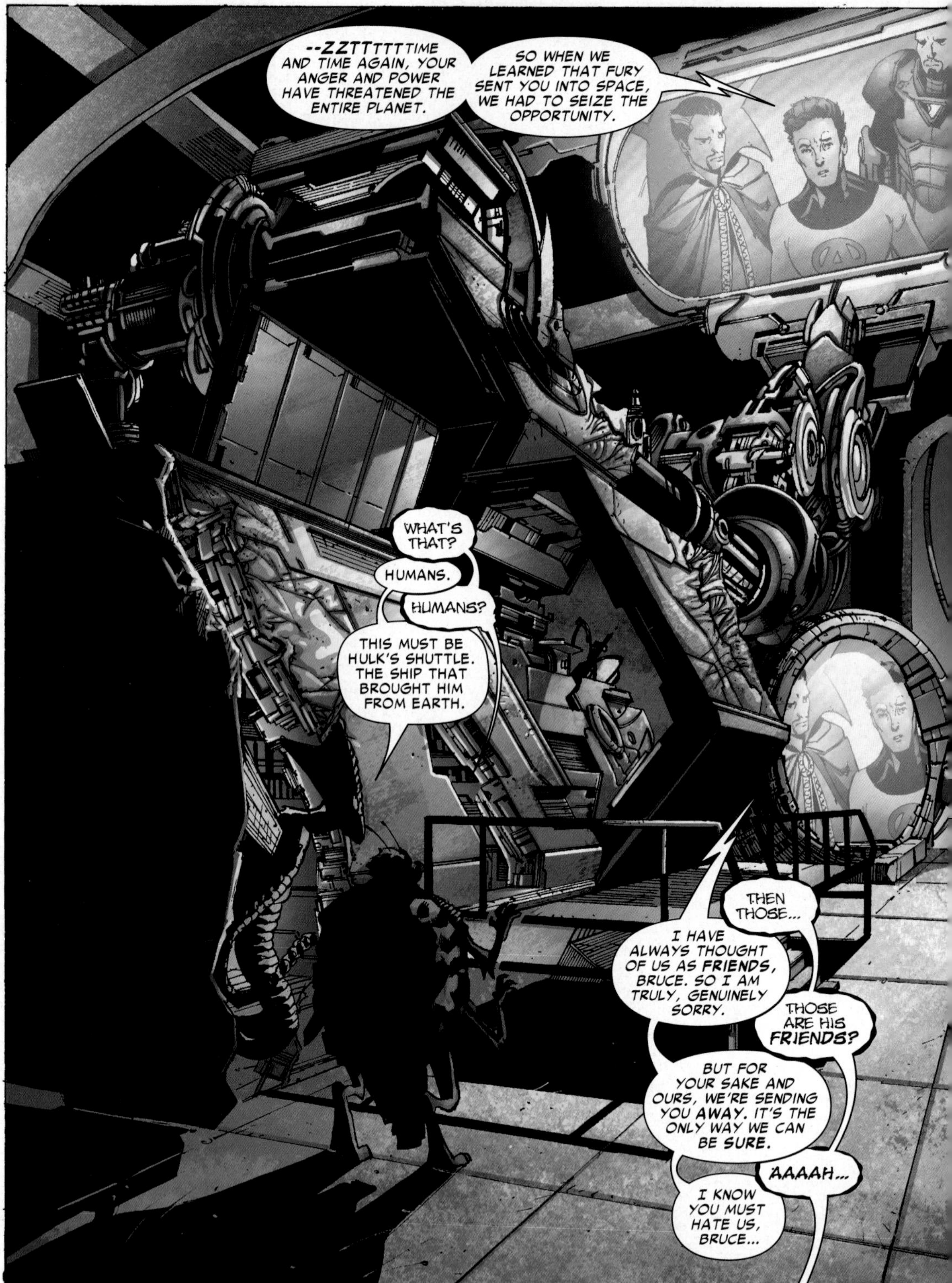
--ZZTTTTTTIME AND TIME AGAIN, YOUR ANGER AND POWER HAVE THREATENED THE ENTIRE PLANET.
SO WHEN WE LEARNED THAT FURY SENT YOU INTO SPACE, WE HAD TO SEIZE THE OPPORTUNITY.
WHAT'S THAT?
HUMANS.
HUMANS?
THIS MUST BE HULK'S SHUTTLE. THE SHIP THAT BROUGHT HIM FROM EARTH.
THEN THOSE...
I HAVE ALWAYS THOUGHT OF US AS FRIENDS, BRUCE. SO I AM TRULY, GENUINELY SORRY.
THOSE ARE HIS FRIENDS?
BUT FOR YOUR SAKE AND OURS, WE'RE SENDING YOU AWAY. IT'S THE ONLY WAY WE CAN BE SURE.
AAAAH...
I KNOW YOU MUST HATE US, BRUCE...

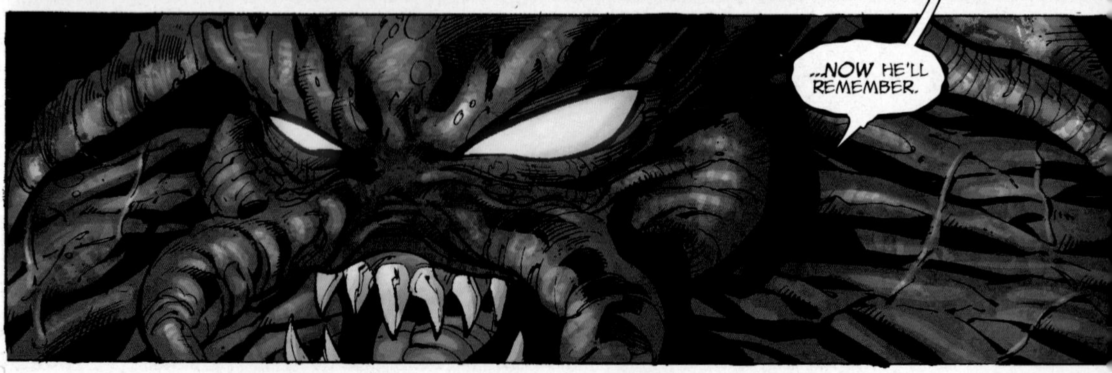
...NOW HE'LL REMEMBER.

#104

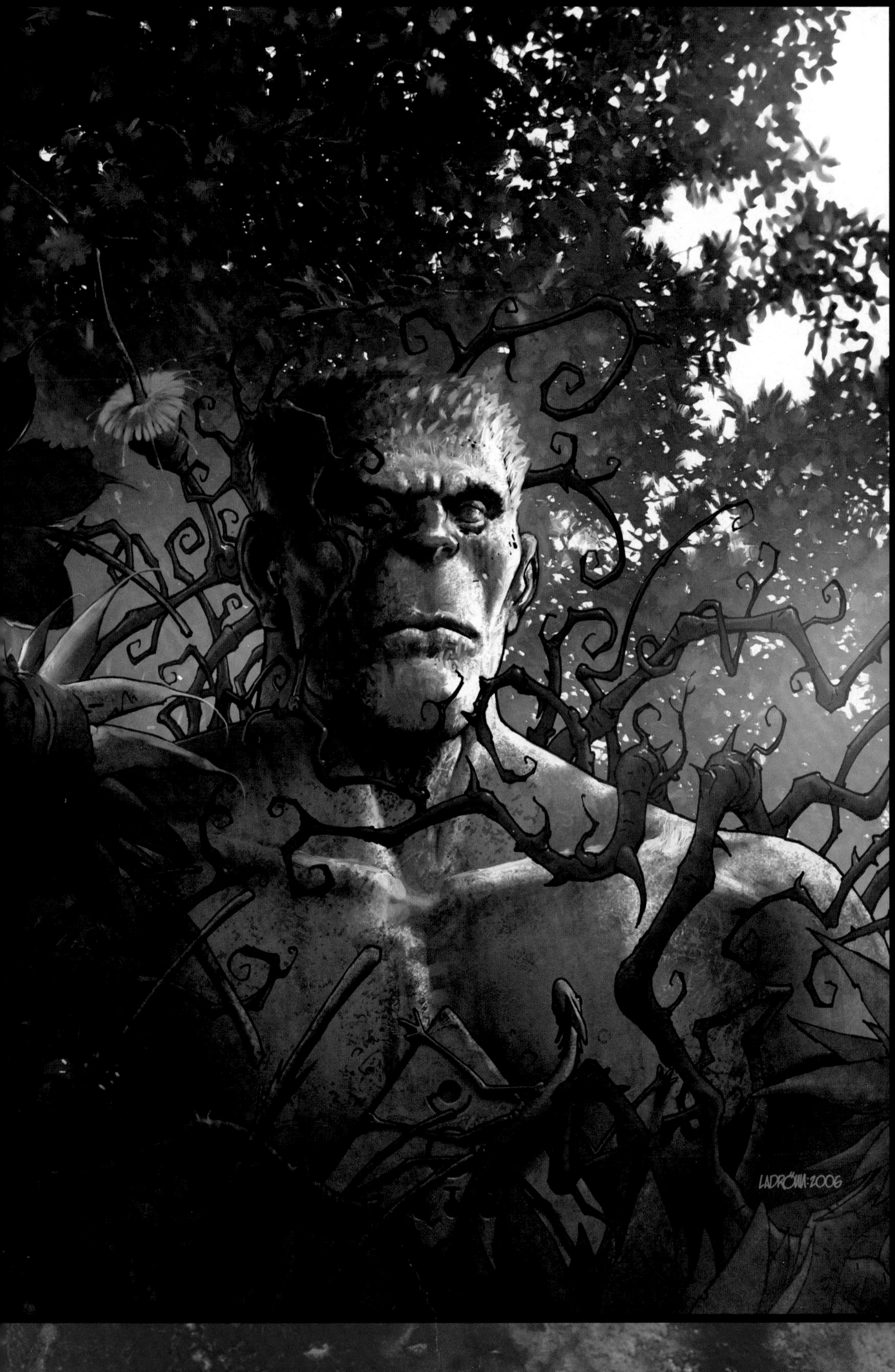
LADRÖNN 2006

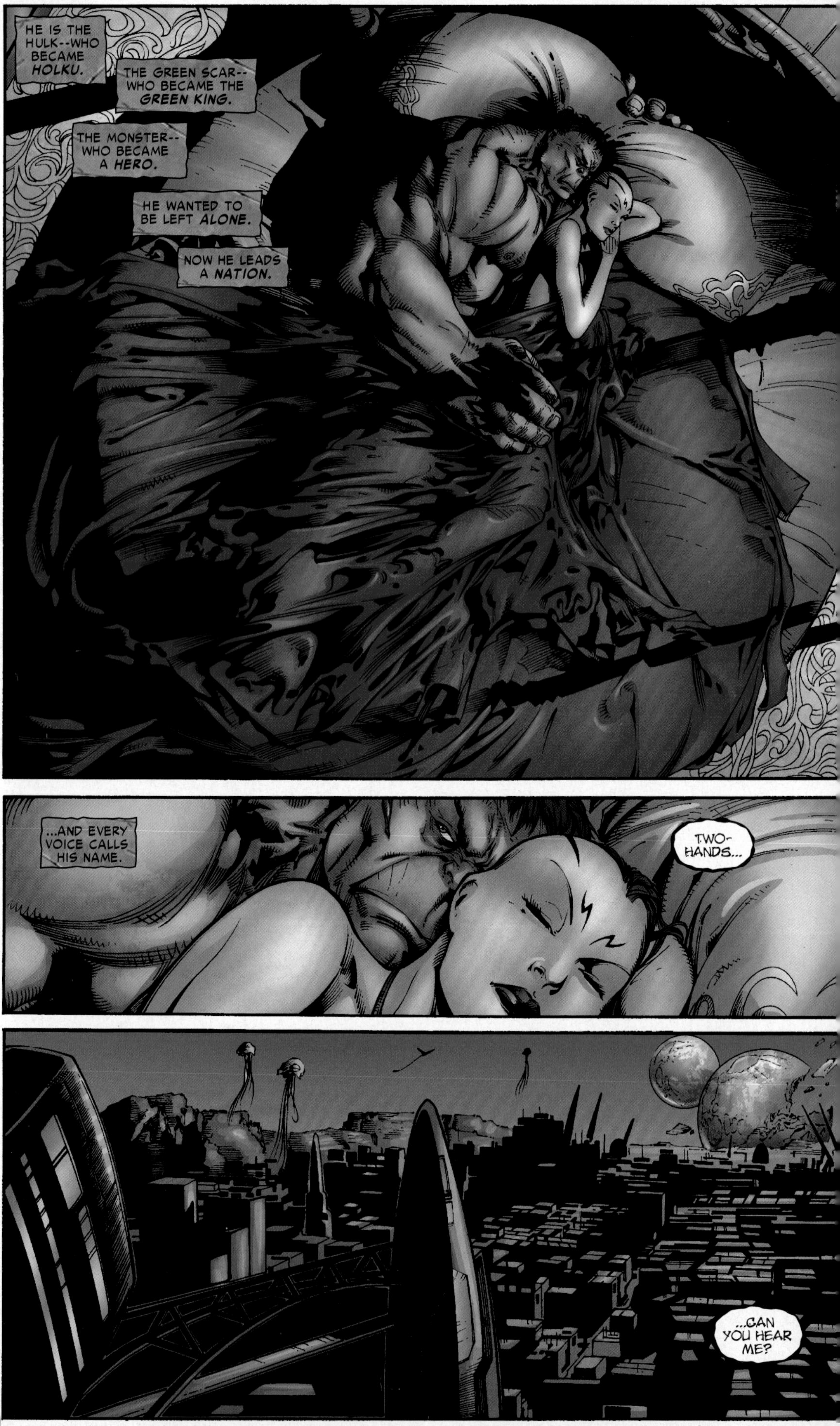
HE IS THE HULK--WHO BECAME HOLKU.
THE GREEN SCAR--WHO BECAME THE GREEN KING.
THE MONSTER--WHO BECAME A HERO.
HE WANTED TO BE LEFT ALONE.
NOW HE LEADS A NATION.
...AND EVERY VOICE CALLS HIS NAME.
TWO-HANDS...
...CAN YOU HEAR ME?

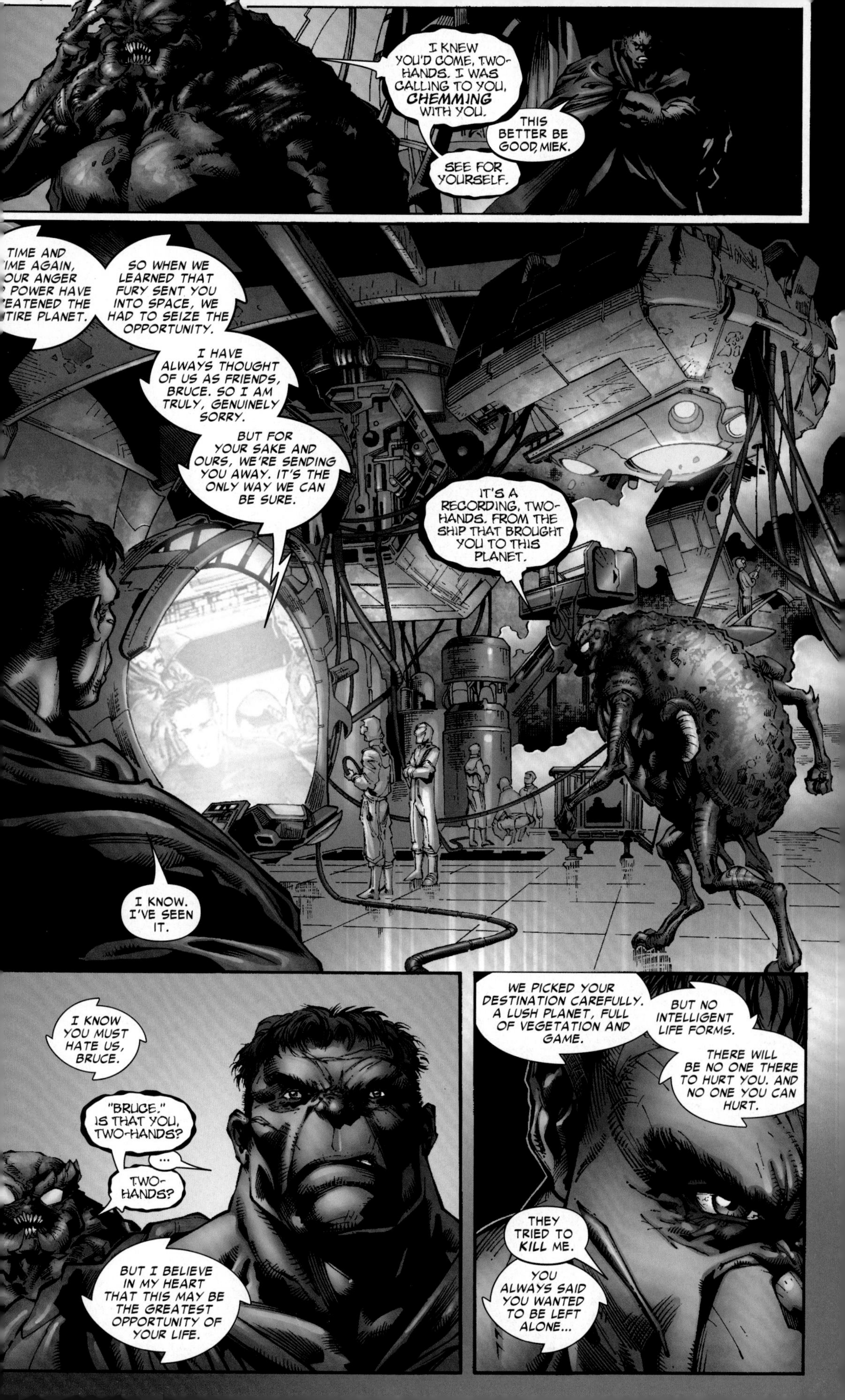

I KNEW YOU'D COME, TWO-HANDS. I WAS CALLING TO YOU, CHEMMING WITH YOU.
THIS BETTER BE GOOD, MIEK.
SEE FOR YOURSELF.
TIME AND TIME AGAIN, OUR ANGER POWER HAVE EATENED THE TIRE PLANET.
SO WHEN WE LEARNED THAT FURY SENT YOU INTO SPACE, WE HAD TO SEIZE THE OPPORTUNITY.
I HAVE ALWAYS THOUGHT OF US AS FRIENDS, BRUCE. SO I AM TRULY, GENUINELY SORRY.
BUT FOR YOUR SAKE AND OURS, WE'RE SENDING YOU AWAY. IT'S THE ONLY WAY WE CAN BE SURE.
IT'S A RECORDING, TWO-HANDS. FROM THE SHIP THAT BROUGHT YOU TO THIS PLANET.
I KNOW. I'VE SEEN IT.
I KNOW YOU MUST HATE US, BRUCE.
"BRUCE." IS THAT YOU, TWO-HANDS?
...
TWO-HANDS?
BUT I BELIEVE IN MY HEART THAT THIS MAY BE THE GREATEST OPPORTUNITY OF YOUR LIFE.
WE PICKED YOUR DESTINATION CAREFULLY. A LUSH PLANET, FULL OF VEGETATION AND GAME.
BUT NO INTELLIGENT LIFE FORMS.
THERE WILL BE NO ONE THERE TO HURT YOU. AND NO ONE YOU CAN HURT.
THEY TRIED TO KILL ME.
YOU ALWAYS SAID YOU WANTED TO BE LEFT ALONE...

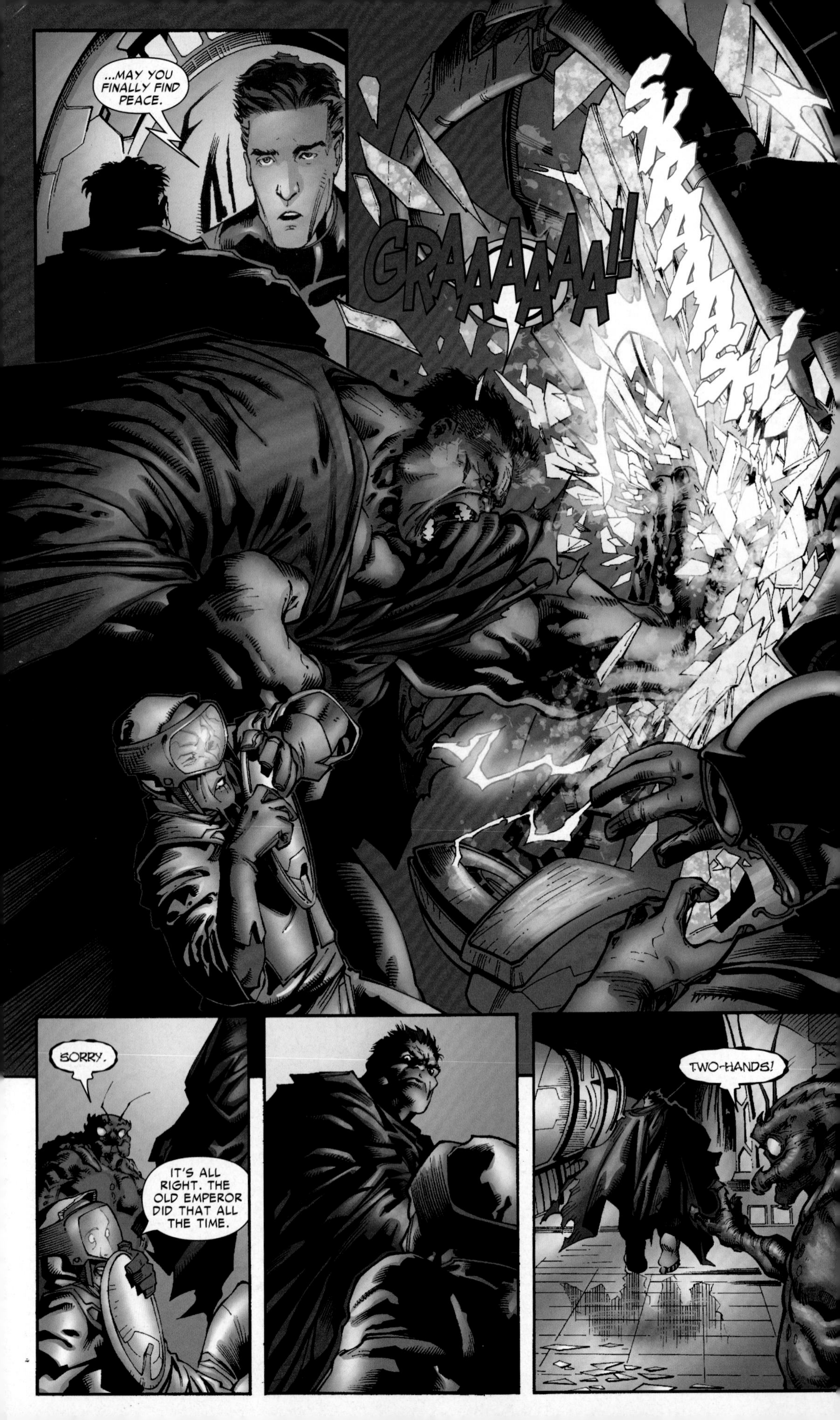
...MAY YOU FINALLY FIND PEACE.
GRAAAAAA!!
SKRAAASH!
SORRY.
IT'S ALL RIGHT. THE OLD EMPEROR DID THAT ALL THE TIME.
TWO-HANDS!

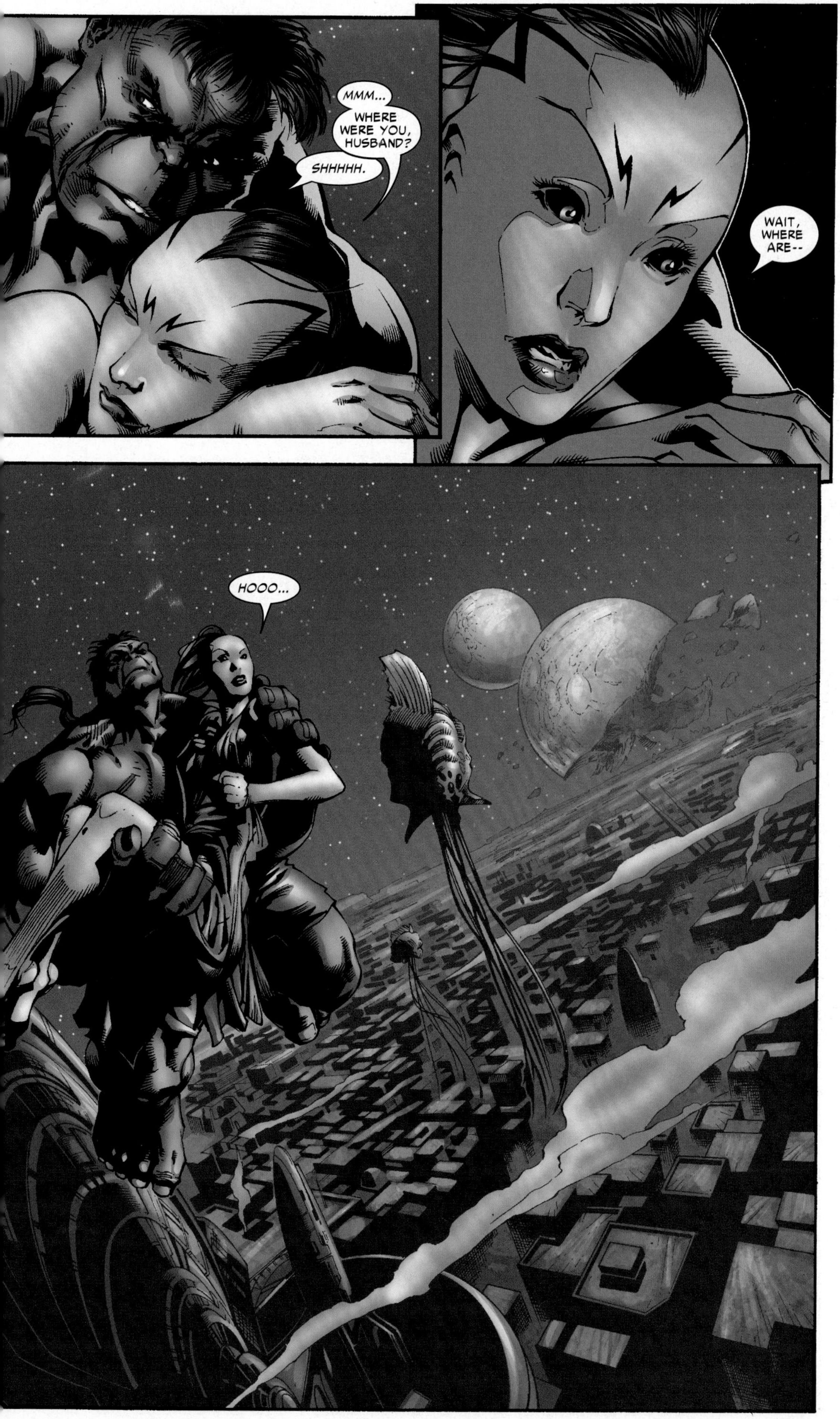
MMM...
WHERE WERE YOU, HUSBAND?
SHHHHH.
WAIT, WHERE ARE--
HOOO...

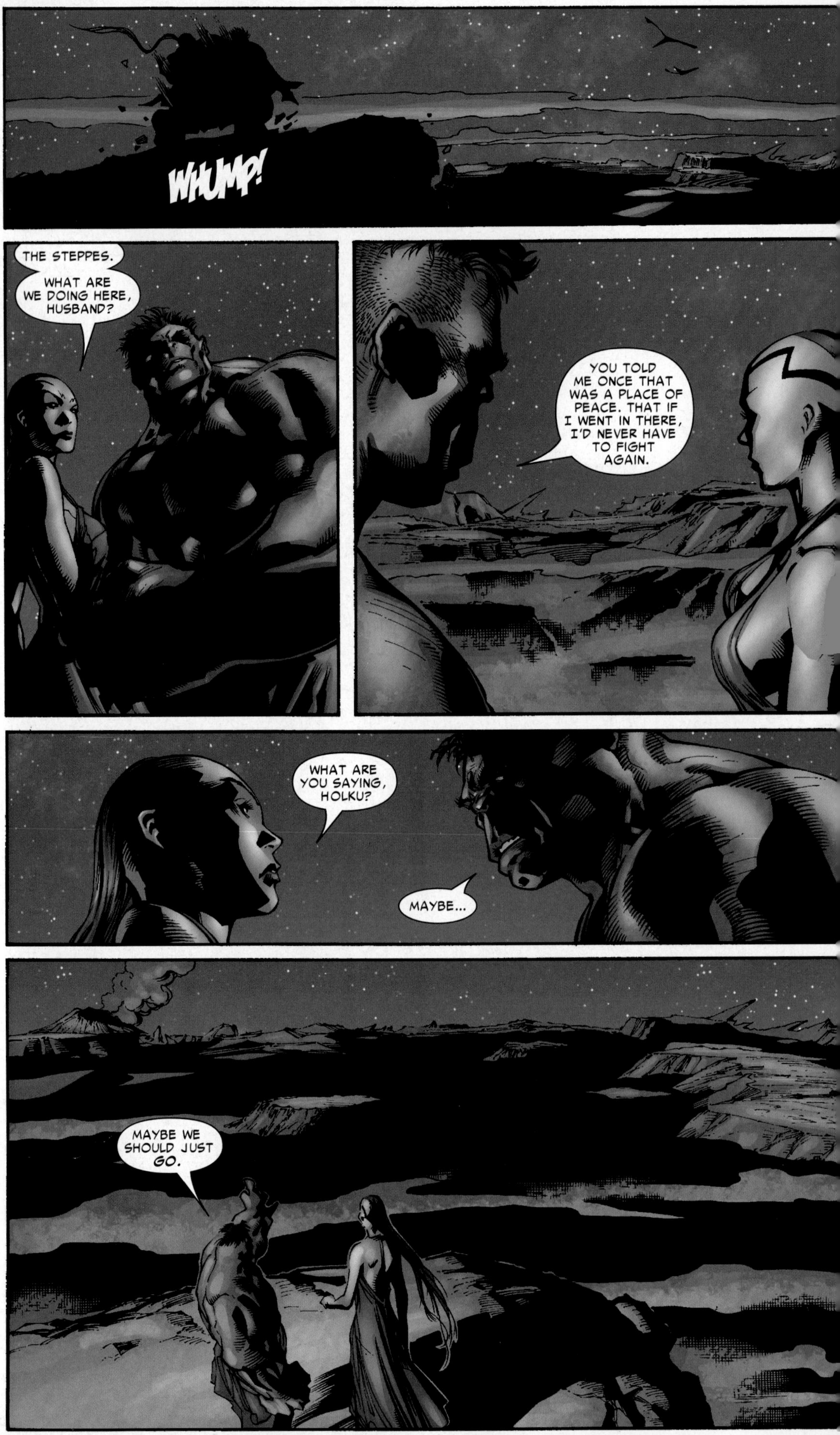
WHUMP!
THE STEPPES.
WHAT ARE WE DOING HERE, HUSBAND?
YOU TOLD ME ONCE THAT WAS A PLACE OF PEACE. THAT IF I WENT IN THERE, I'D NEVER HAVE TO FIGHT AGAIN.
WHAT ARE YOU SAYING, HOLKU?
MAYBE...
MAYBE WE SHOULD JUST GO.

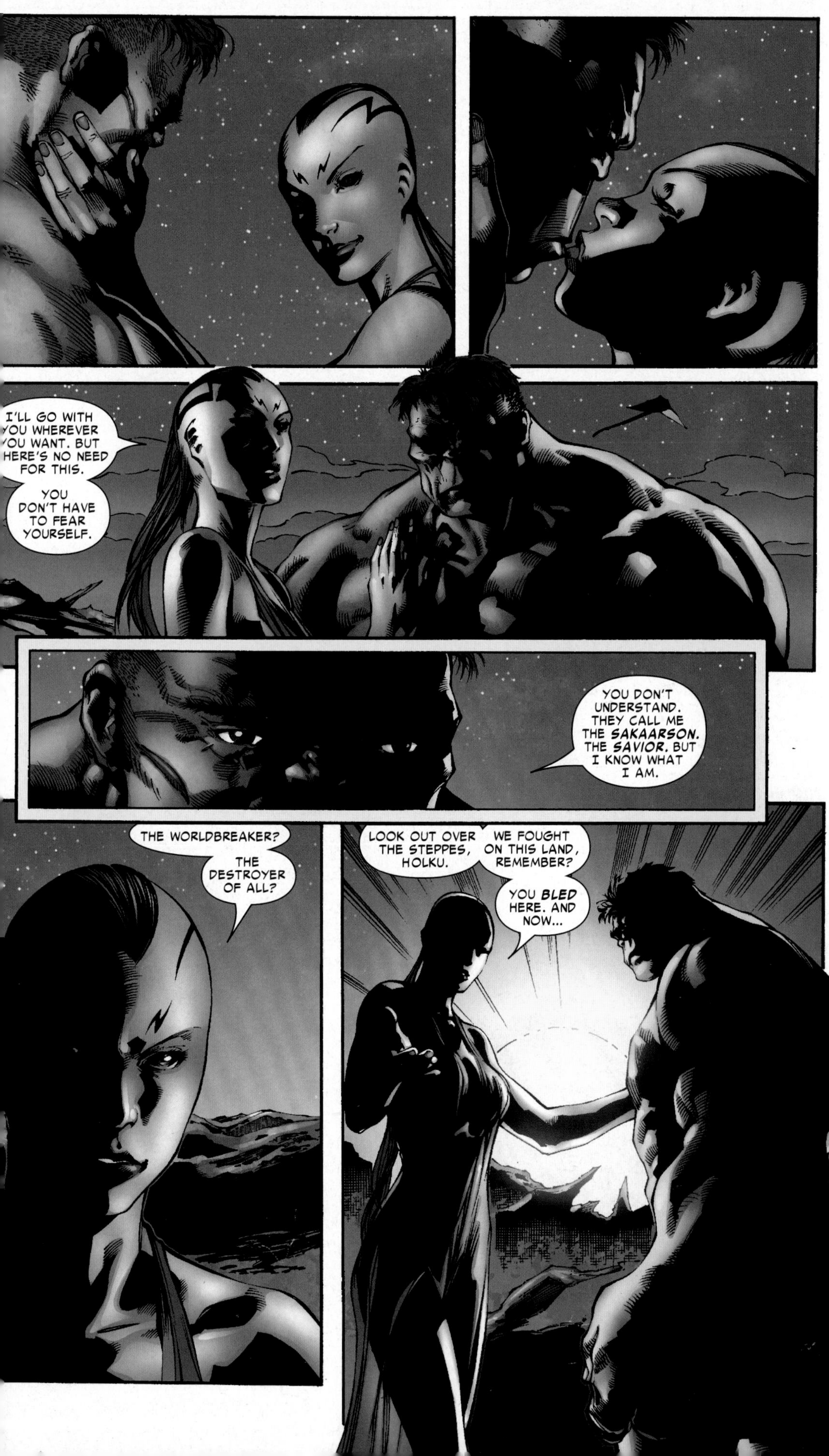
I'LL GO WITH YOU WHEREVER YOU WANT. BUT THERE'S NO NEED FOR THIS.
YOU DON'T HAVE TO FEAR YOURSELF.
YOU DON'T UNDERSTAND. THEY CALL ME THE SAKAARSON. THE SAVIOR. BUT I KNOW WHAT I AM.
THE WORLDBREAKER?
THE DESTROYER OF ALL?
LOOK OUT OVER THE STEPPES, HOLKU.
WE FOUGHT ON THIS LAND, REMEMBER?
YOU BLED HERE. AND NOW...

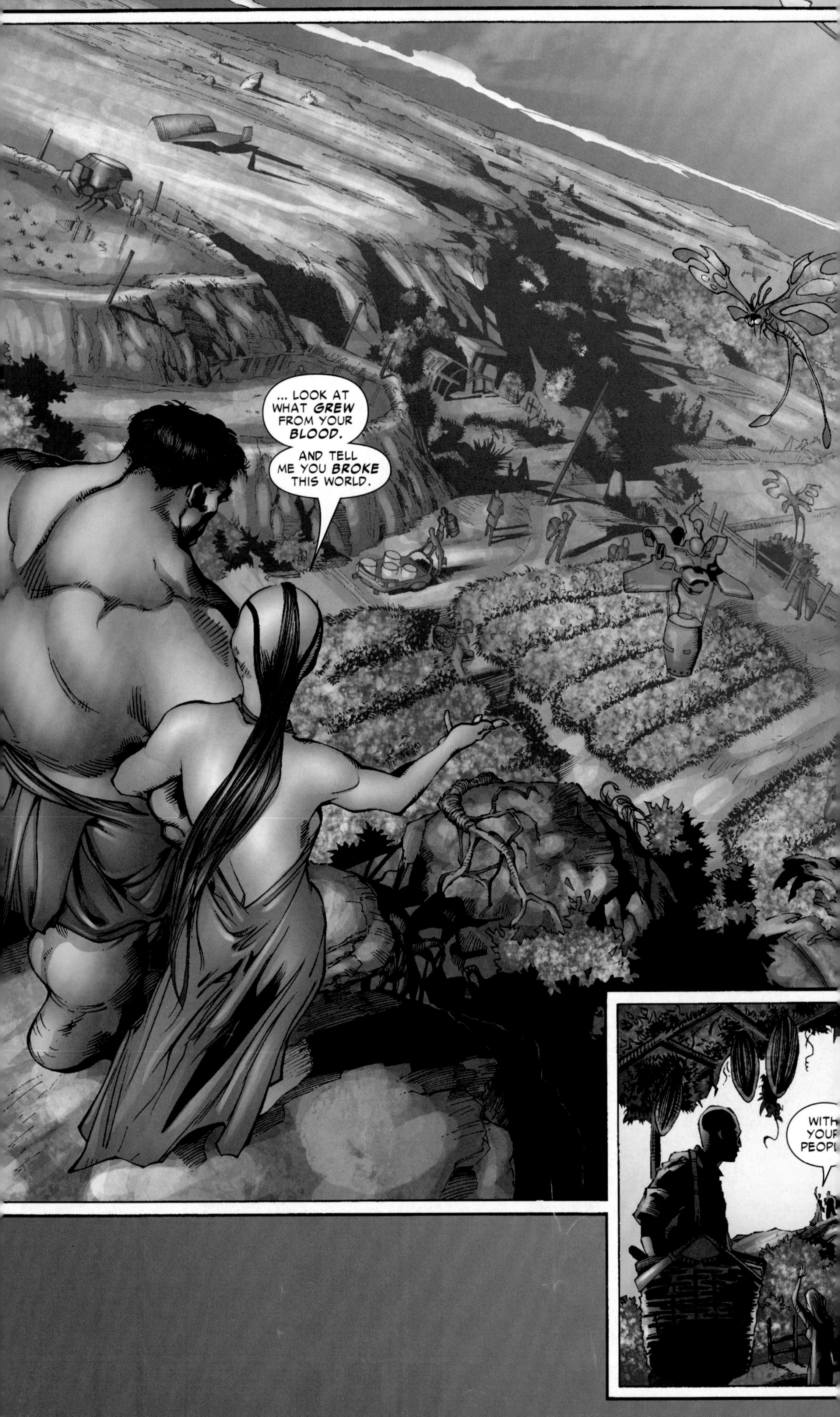
... LOOK AT WHAT GREW FROM YOUR BLOOD.
AND TELL ME YOU BROKE THIS WORLD.

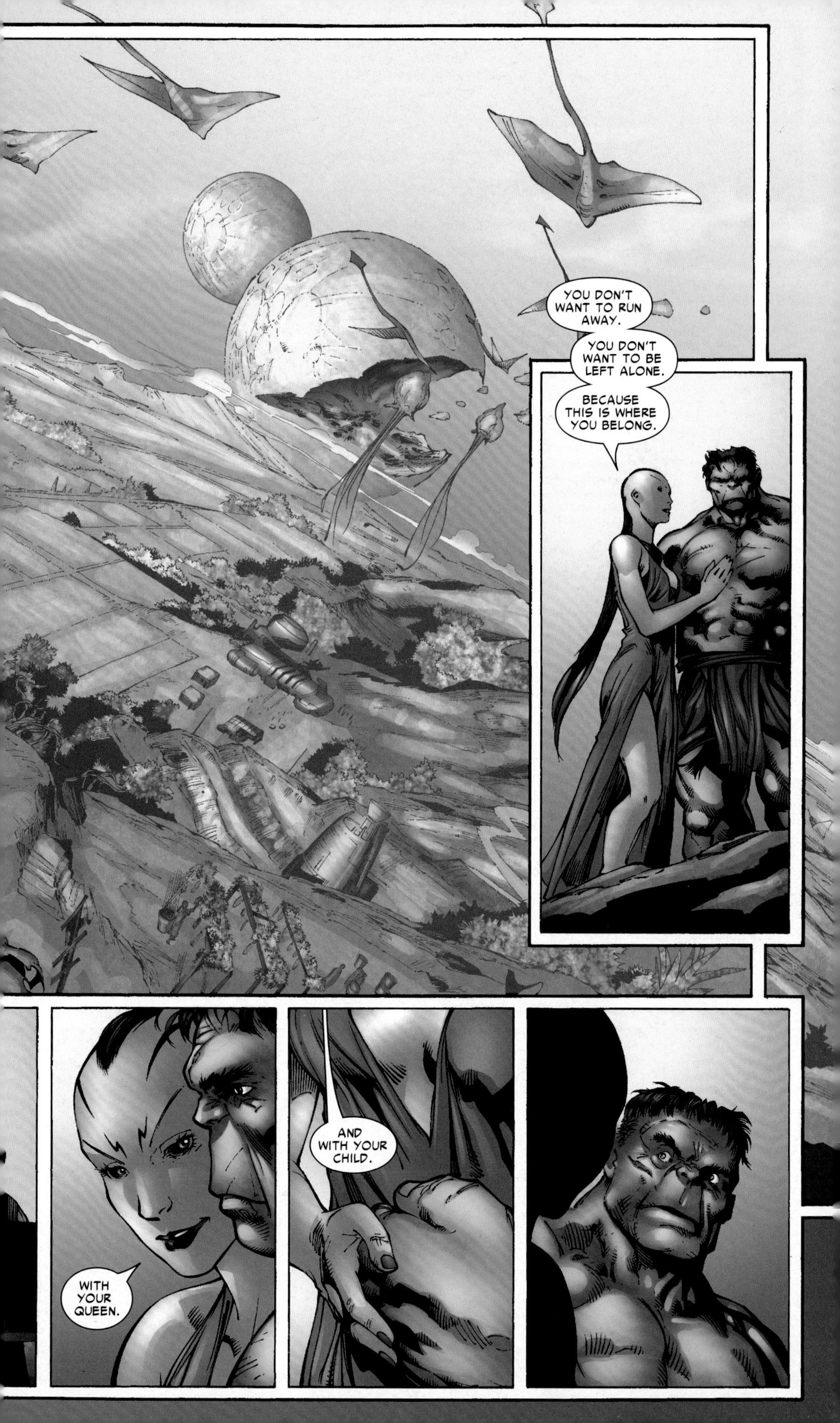
YOU DON'T WANT TO RUN AWAY.
YOU DON'T WANT TO BE LEFT ALONE.
BECAUSE THIS IS WHERE YOU BELONG.
WITH YOUR QUEEN.
AND WITH YOUR CHILD.

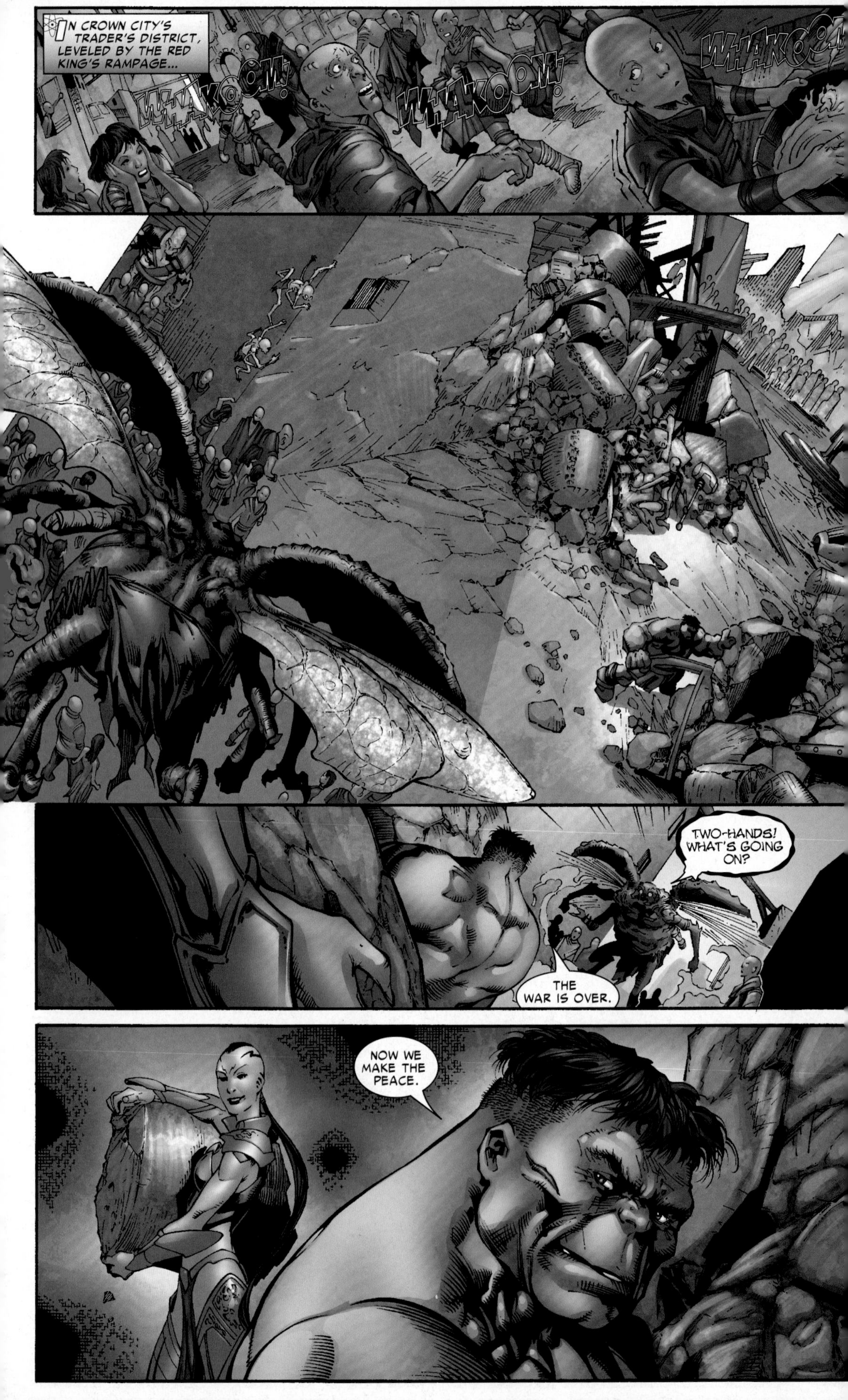
IN CROWN CITY'S TRADER'S DISTRICT, LEVELED BY THE RED KING'S RAMPAGE...
WHAKOOM!
WHAKOOM!
WHAKOOM!
T.WO-HANDS! WHAT'S GOING ON?
THE WAR IS OVER.
NOW WE MAKE THE PEACE.

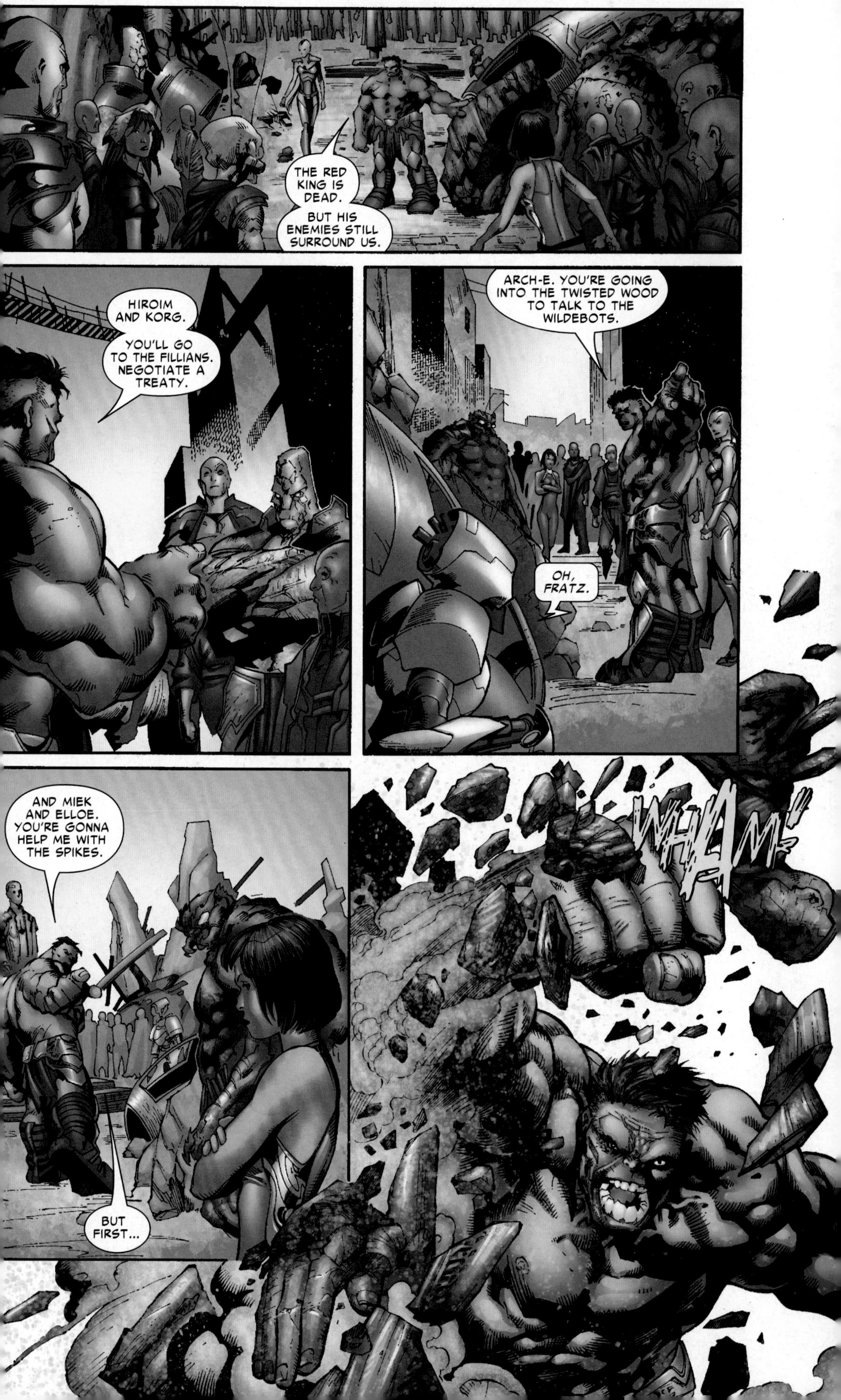
THE RED KING IS DEAD.
BUT HIS ENEMIES STILL SURROUND US.
HIROIM AND KORG.
YOU'LL GO TO THE FILLIANS. NEGOTIATE A TREATY.
ARCH-E. YOU'RE GOING INTO THE TWISTED WOOD TO TALK TO THE WILDEBOTS.
OH, FRATZ.
AND MIEK AND ELLOE. YOU'RE GONNA HELP ME WITH THE SPIKES.
BUT FIRST...
WHAM!

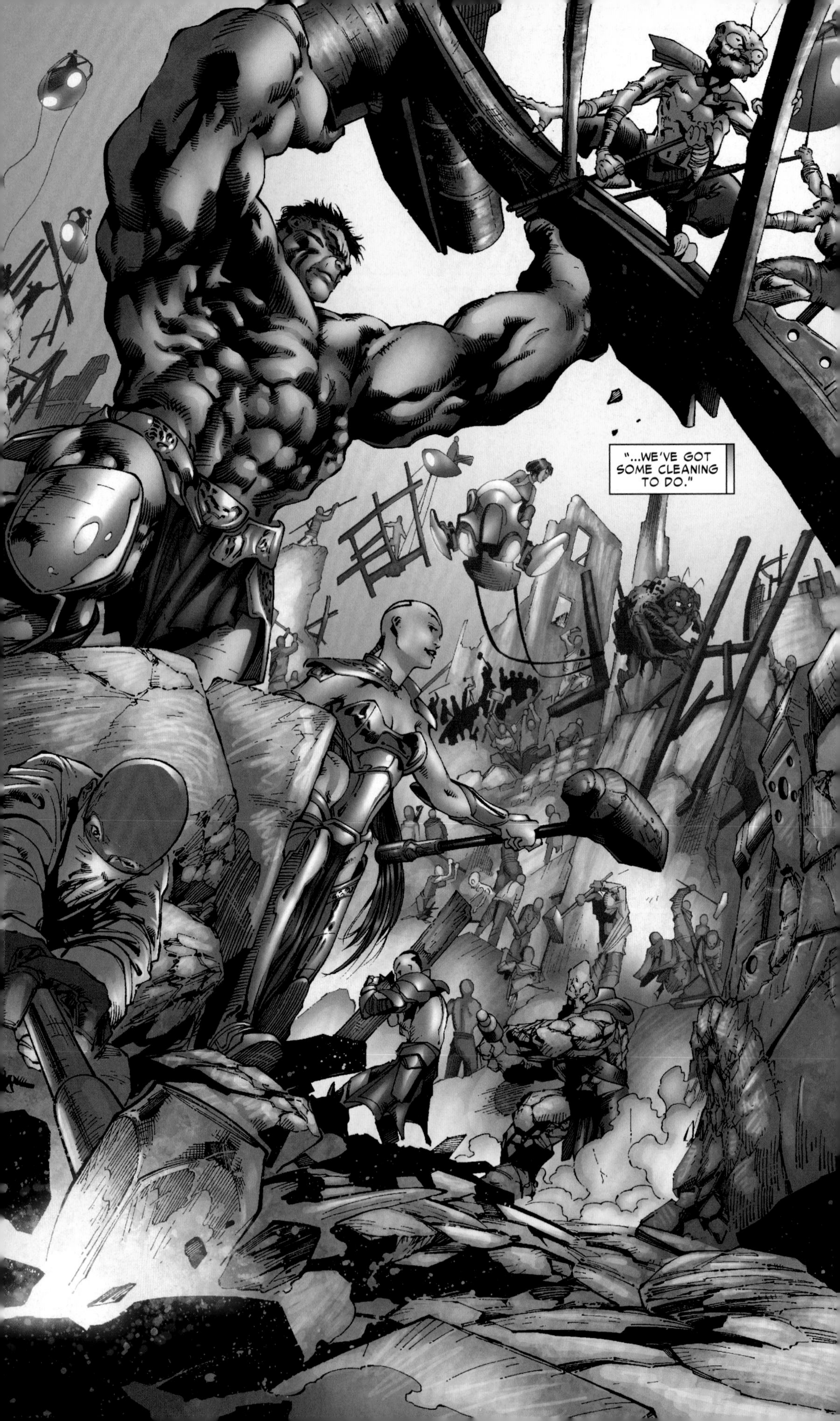
"...WE'VE GOT SOME CLEANING TO DO."

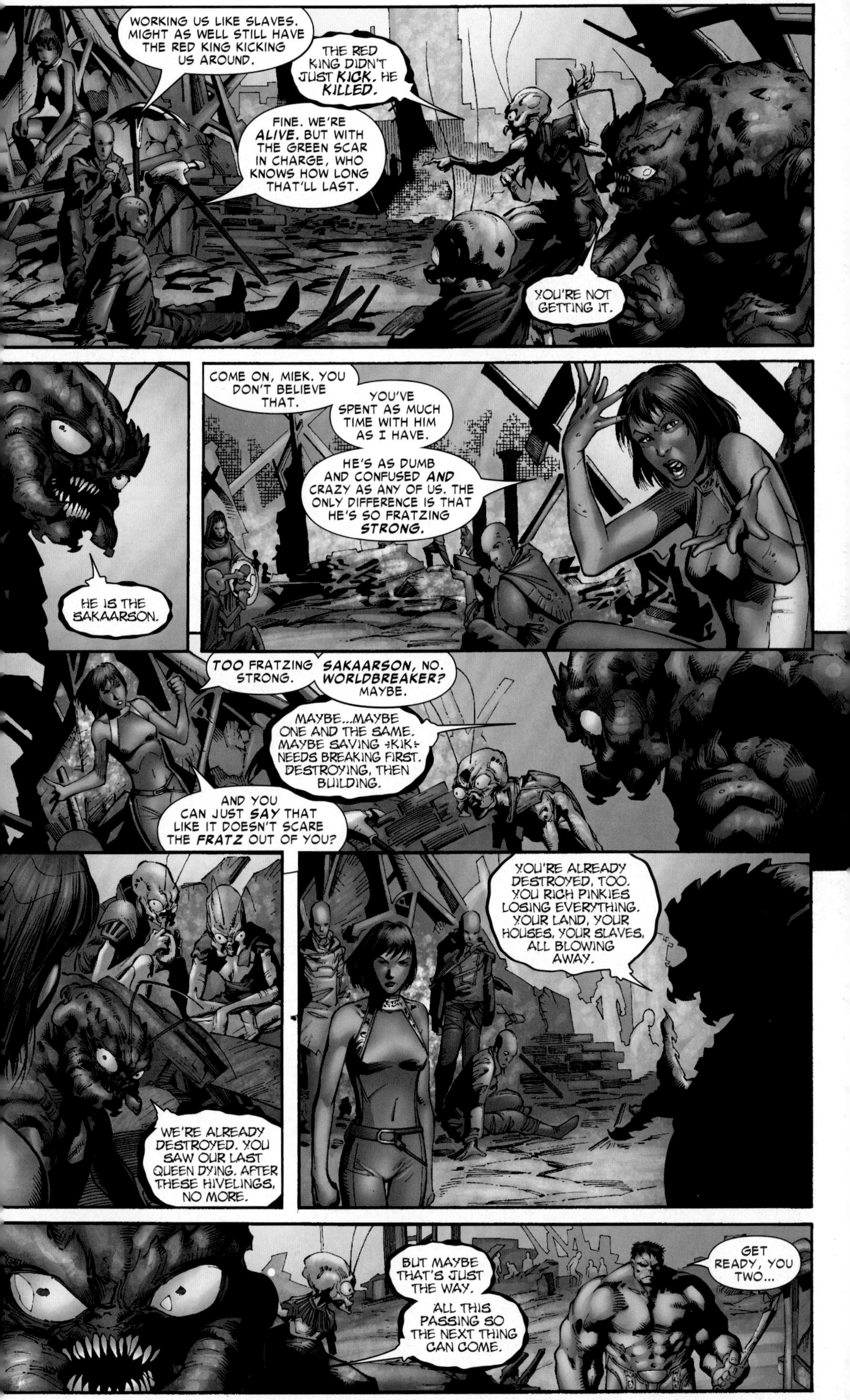
WORKING US LIKE SLAVES. MIGHT AS WELL STILL HAVE THE RED KING KICKING US AROUND.
THE RED KING DIDN'T JUST KICK. HE KILLED.
FINE. WE'RE ALIVE. BUT WITH THE GREEN SCAR IN CHARGE, WHO KNOWS HOW LONG THAT'LL LAST.
YOU'RE NOT GETTING IT.
HE IS THE SAKAARSON.
COME ON, MIEK. YOU DON'T BELIEVE THAT.
YOU'VE SPENT AS MUCH TIME WITH HIM AS I HAVE.
HE'S AS DUMB AND CONFUSED AND CRAZY AS ANY OF US. THE ONLY DIFFERENCE IS THAT HE'S SO FRATZING STRONG.
TOO FRATZING STRONG.
SAKAARSON, NO. WORLDBREAKER? MAYBE.
MAYBE...MAYBE ONE AND THE SAME. MAYBE SAVING ÷KIK÷ NEEDS BREAKING FIRST. DESTROYING, THEN BUILDING.
AND YOU CAN JUST SAY THAT LIKE IT DOESN'T SCARE THE FRATZ OUT OF YOU?
WE'RE ALREADY DESTROYED. YOU SAW OUR LAST QUEEN DYING. AFTER THESE HIVELINGS, NO MORE.
YOU'RE ALREADY DESTROYED, TOO. YOU RICH PINKIES LOSING EVERYTHING. YOUR LAND, YOUR HOUSES, YOUR SLAVES, ALL BLOWING AWAY.
BUT MAYBE THAT'S JUST THE WAY.
ALL THIS PASSING SO THE NEXT THING CAN COME.
GET READY, YOU TWO...

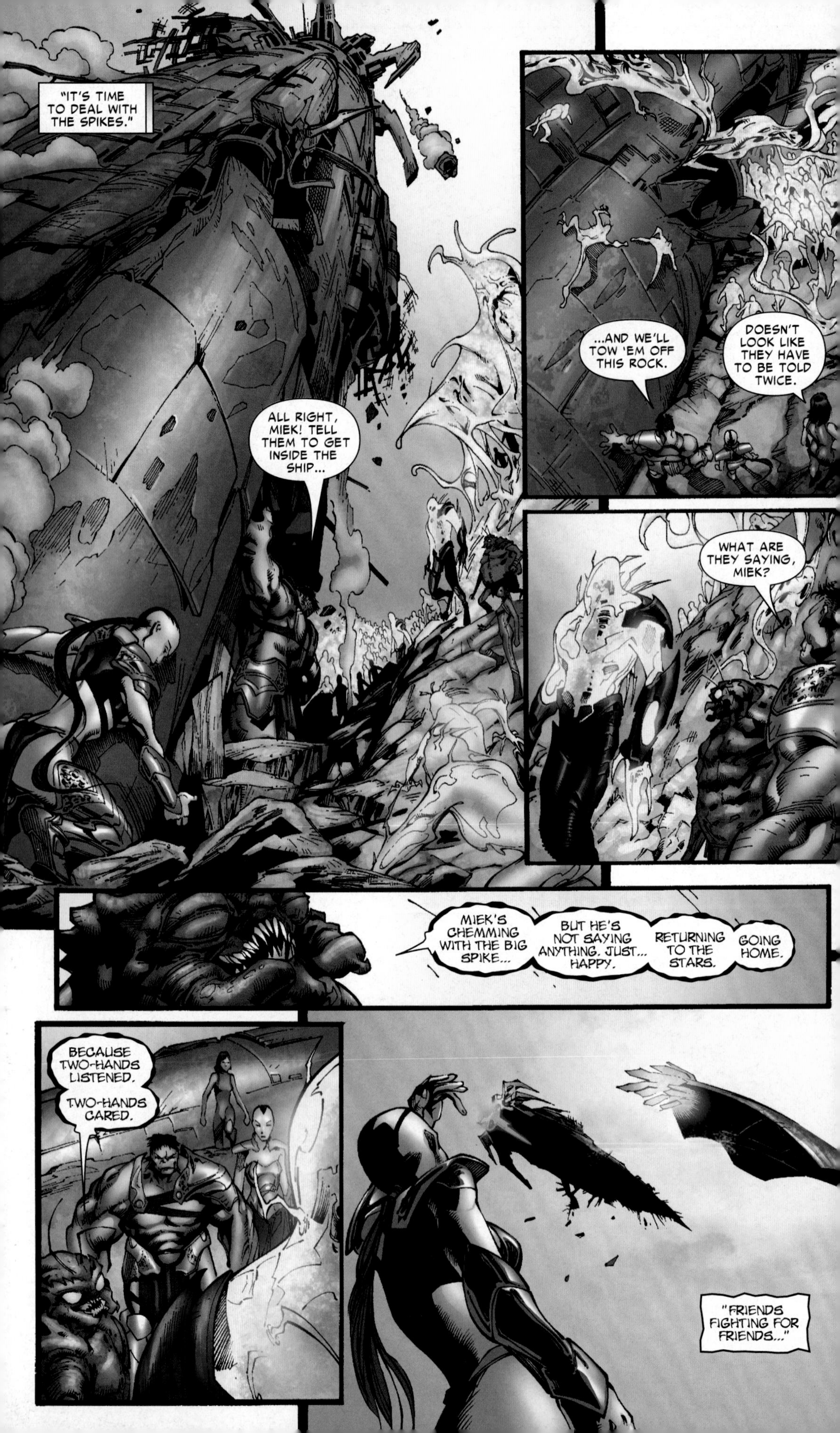
"IT'S TIME TO DEAL WITH THE SPIKES."
ALL RIGHT, MIEK! TELL THEM TO GET INSIDE THE SHIP...
...AND WE'LL TOW 'EM OFF THIS ROCK.
DOESN'T LOOK LIKE THEY HAVE TO BE TOLD TWICE.
WHAT ARE THEY SAYING, MIEK?
MIEK'S CHEMMING WITH THE BIG SPIKE...
BUT HE'S NOT SAYING ANYTHING. JUST... HAPPY.
RETURNING TO THE STARS.
GOING HOME.
BECAUSE TWO-HANDS LISTENED.
TWO-HANDS CARED.
"FRIENDS FIGHTING FOR FRIENDS..."

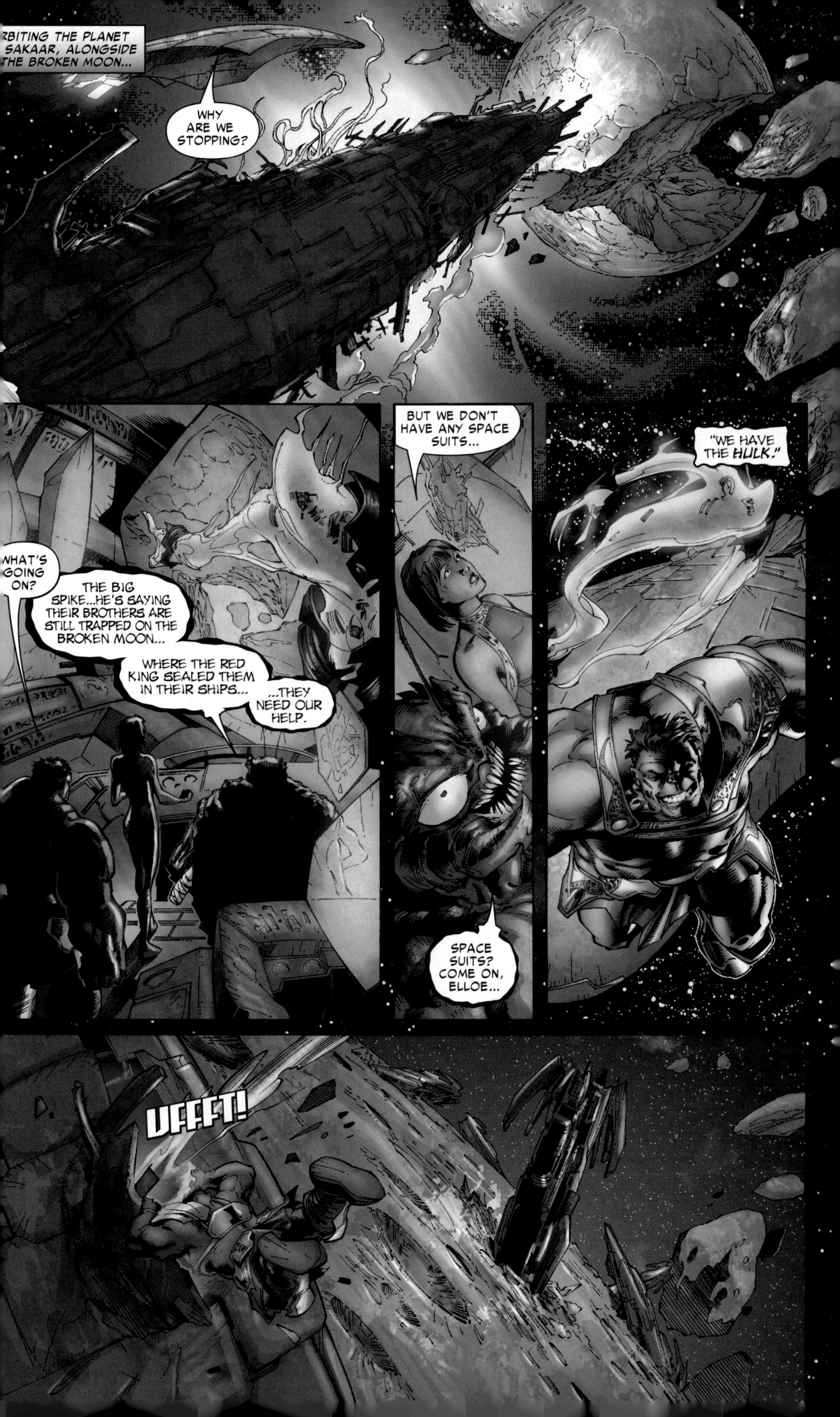
RBITING THE PLANET SAKAAR, ALONGSIDE THE BROKEN MOON...
WHY ARE WE STOPPING?
WHAT'S GOING ON?
THE BIG SPIKE...HE'S SAYING THEIR BROTHERS ARE STILL TRAPPED ON THE BROKEN MOON...
WHERE THE RED KING SEALED THEM IN THEIR SHIPS...
...THEY NEED OUR HELP.
BUT WE DON'T HAVE ANY SPACE SUITS...
SPACE SUITS? COME ON, ELLOE...
"WE HAVE THE HULK."
UFFFT!

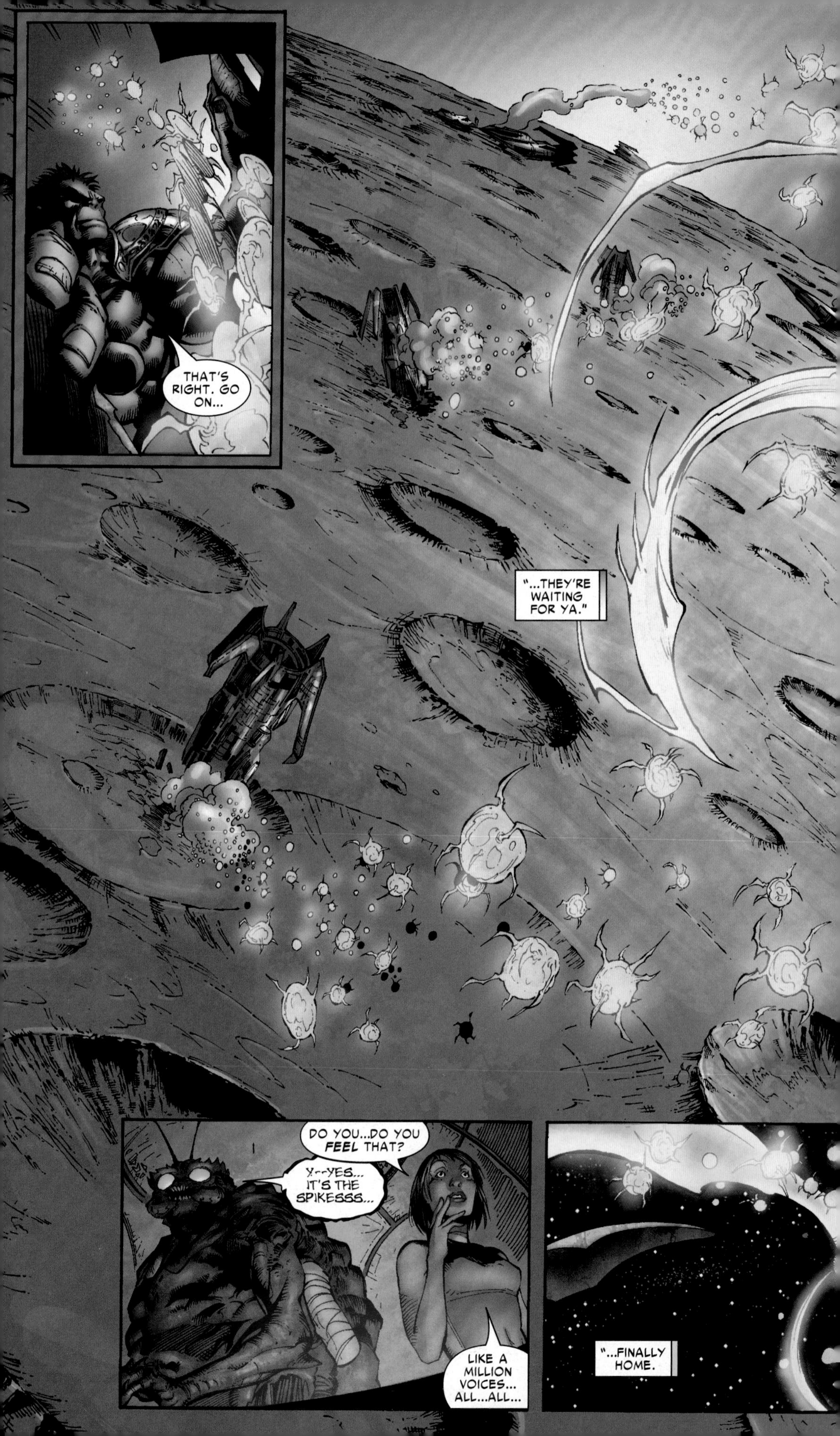
THAT'S RIGHT. GO ON...
"...THEY'RE WAITING FOR YA."
DO YOU...DO YOU FEEL THAT?
Y--YES... IT'S THE SPIKESSS...
LIKE A MILLION VOICES... ALL...ALL...
"...FINALLY HOME.

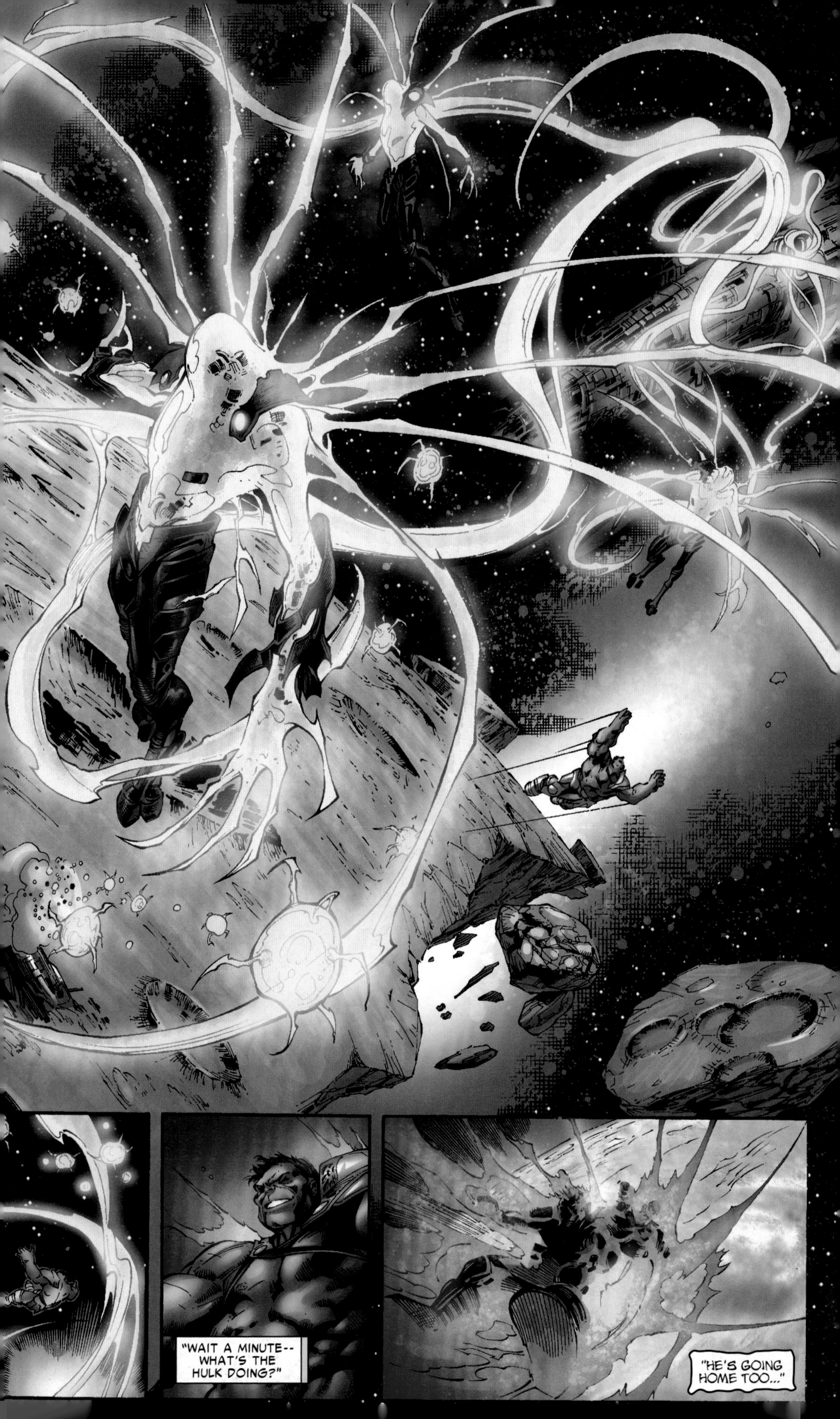
"WAIT A MINUTE--
WHAT'S THE
HULK DOING?"
"HE'S GOING
HOME TOO..."

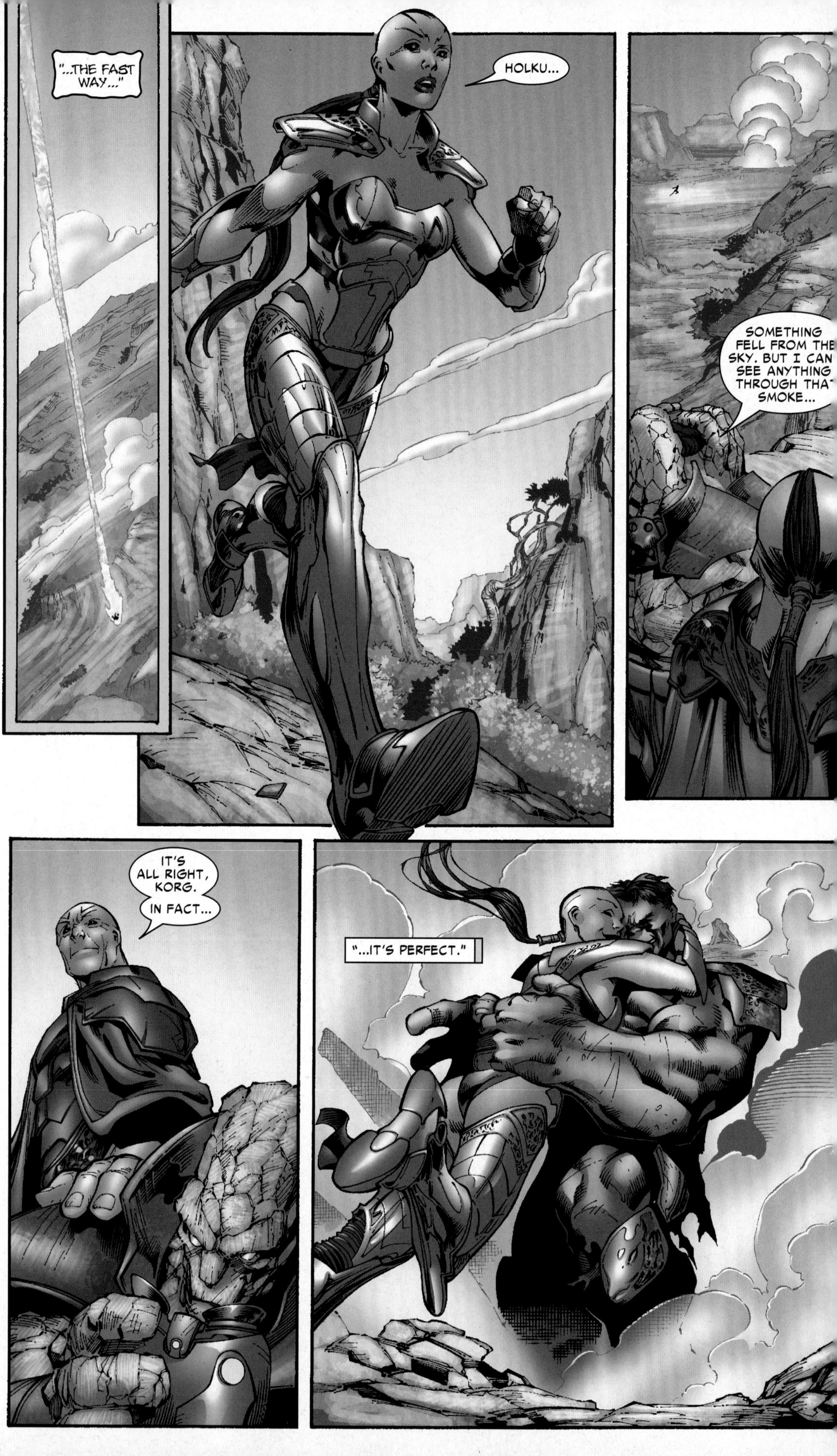

"...THE FAST WAY..."
HOLKU...
SOMETHING FELL FROM THE SKY. BUT I CAN SEE ANYTHING THROUGH THAT SMOKE...
IT'S ALL RIGHT, KORG.
IN FACT...
"...IT'S PERFECT."

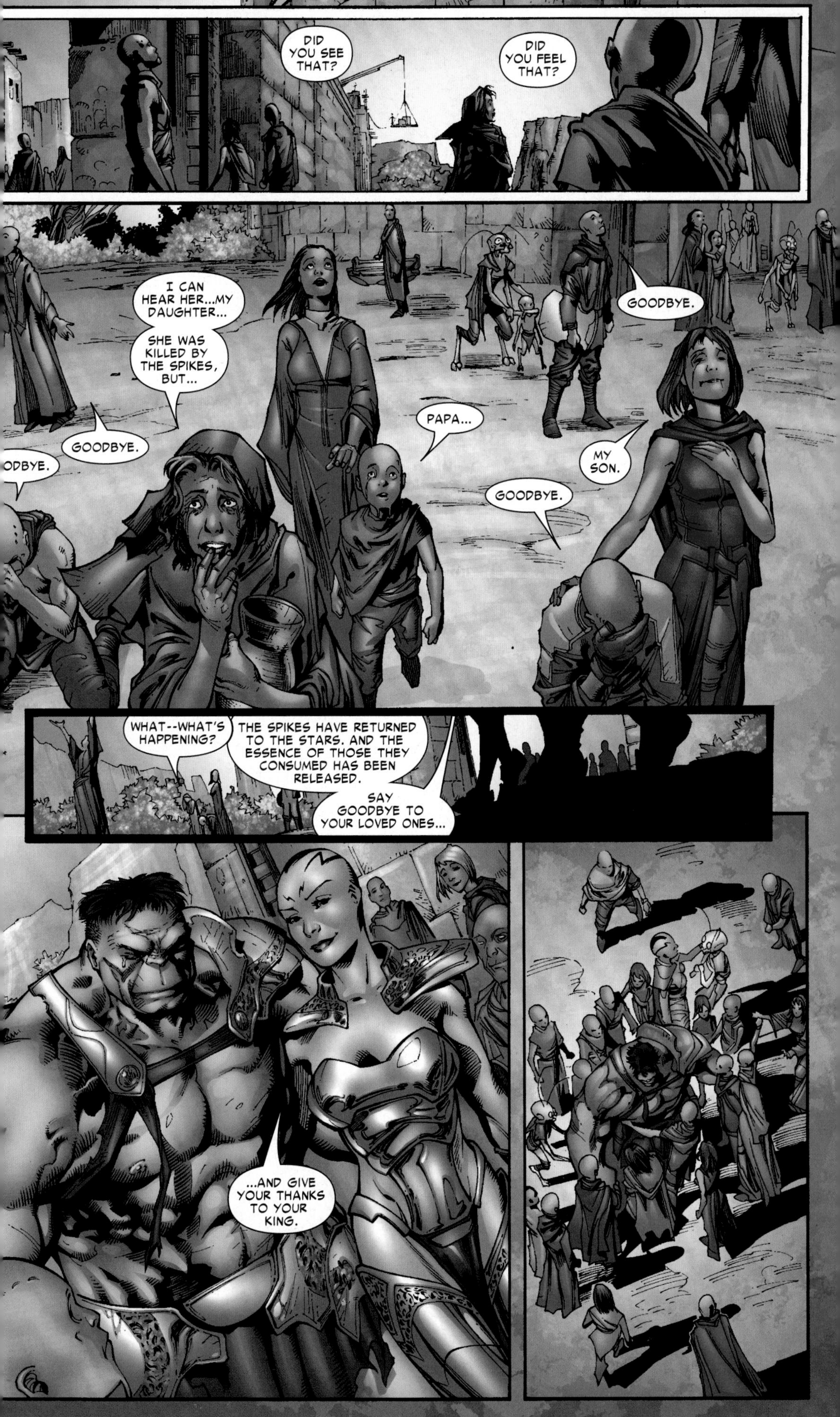

DID YOU SEE THAT?
DID YOU FEEL THAT?
I CAN HEAR HER...MY DAUGHTER...
SHE WAS KILLED BY THE SPIKES, BUT...
GOODBYE.
PAPA...
GOODBYE.
MY SON.
GOODBYE.
ODBYE.
WHAT--WHAT'S HAPPENING?
THE SPIKES HAVE RETURNED TO THE STARS. AND THE ESSENCE OF THOSE THEY CONSUMED HAS BEEN RELEASED.
SAY GOODBYE TO YOUR LOVED ONES...
...AND GIVE YOUR THANKS TO YOUR KING.

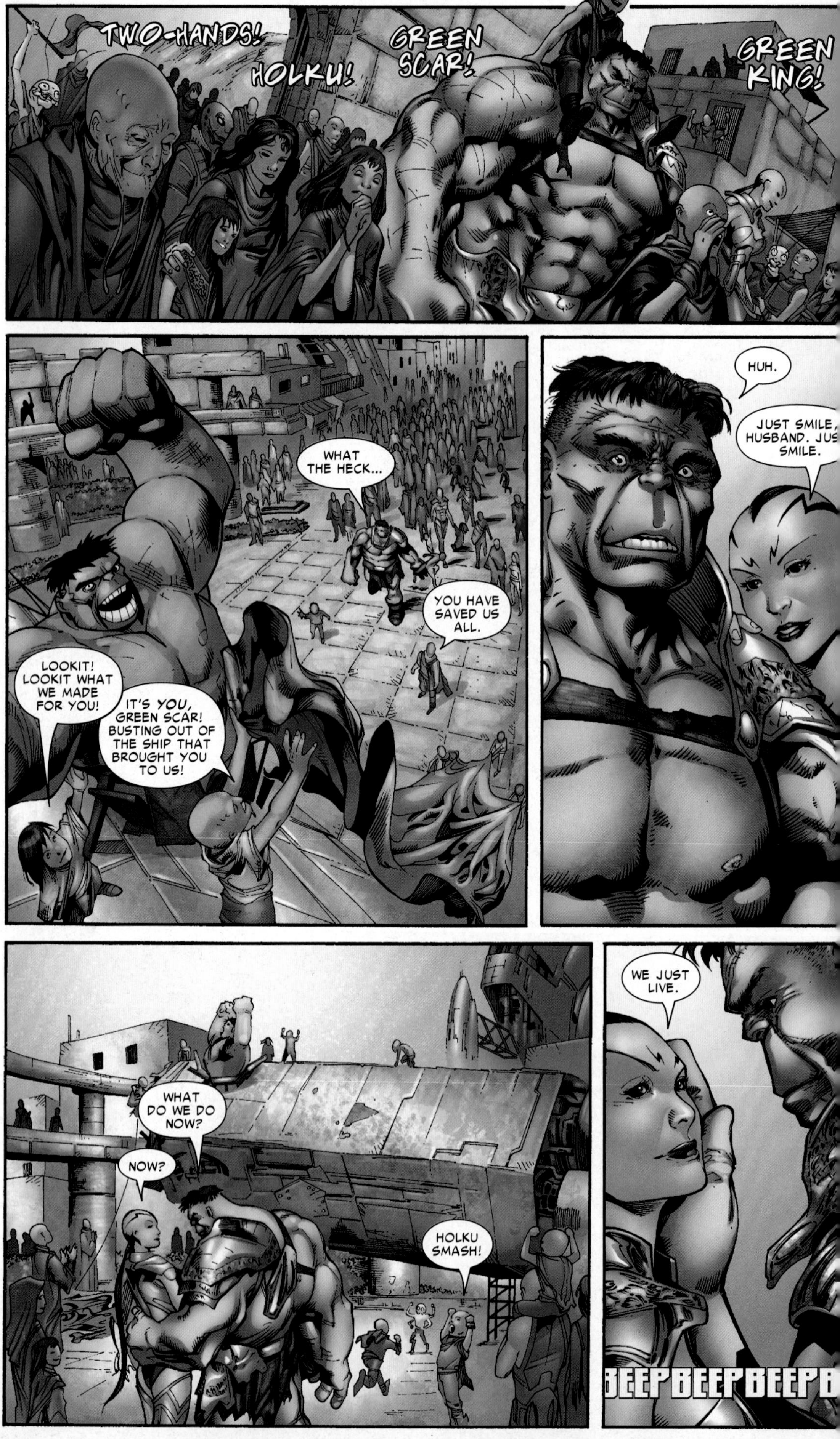
TWO-HANDS!
HOLKU!
GREEN SCAR!
GREEN KING!
WHAT THE HECK...
YOU HAVE SAVED US ALL.
LOOKIT! LOOKIT WHAT WE MADE FOR YOU!
IT'S YOU, GREEN SCAR! BUSTING OUT OF THE SHIP THAT BROUGHT YOU TO US!
HUH.
JUST SMILE, HUSBAND. JUS SMILE.
WHAT DO WE DO NOW?
NOW?
HOLKU SMASH!
WE JUST LIVE.
BEEPBEEPBEEPB

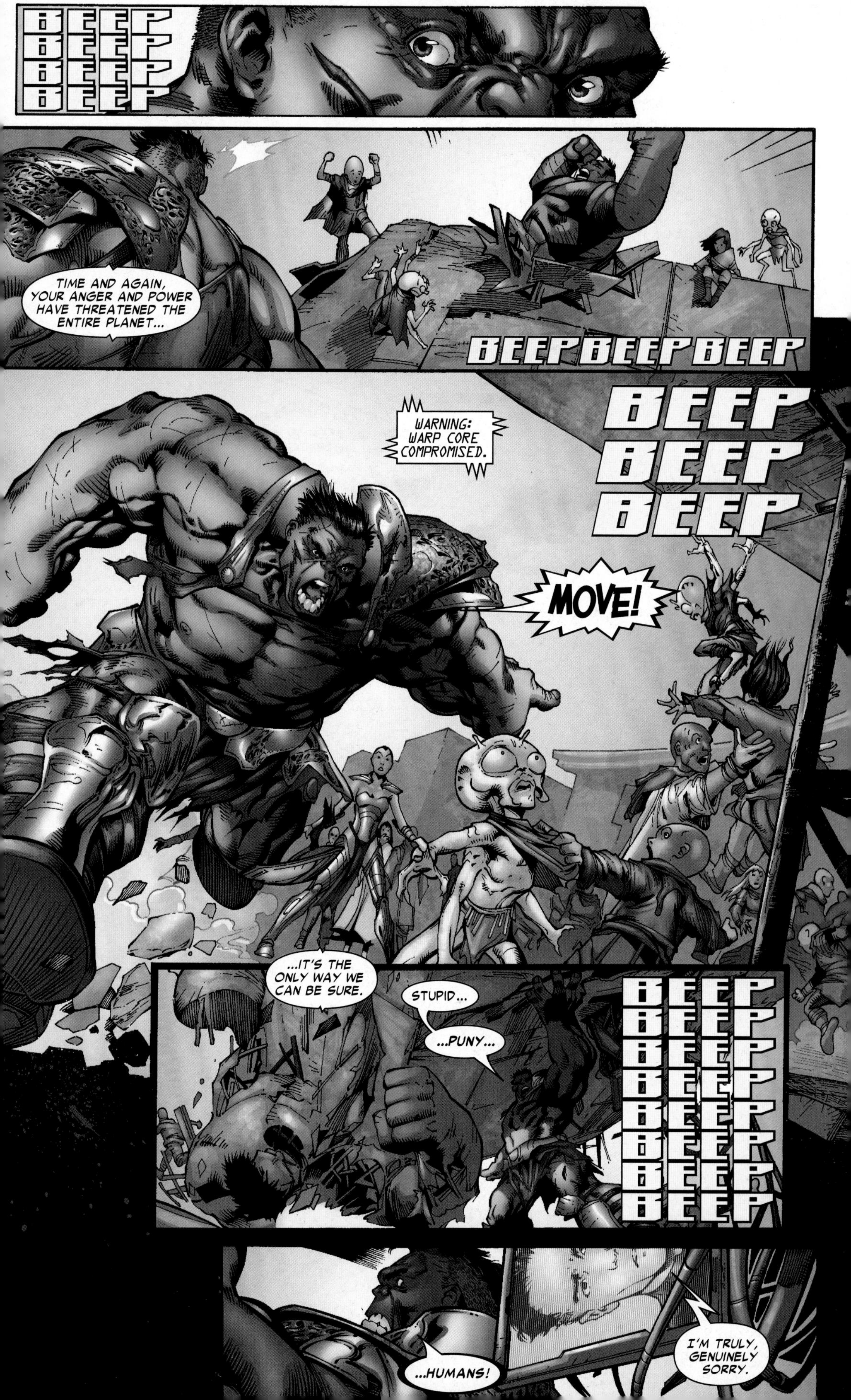
BEEP
BEEP
BEEP
BEEP
TIME AND AGAIN, YOUR ANGER AND POWER HAVE THREATENED THE ENTIRE PLANET...
BEEPBEEPBEEP
BEEP
BEEP
BEEP
WARNING: WARP CORE COMPROMISED.
MOVE!
...IT'S THE ONLY WAY WE CAN BE SURE.
STUPID...
...PUNY...
BEEP
BEEP
BEEP
BEEP
BEEP
BEEP
BEEP
BEEP
...HUMANS!
I'M TRULY, GENUINELY SORRY.

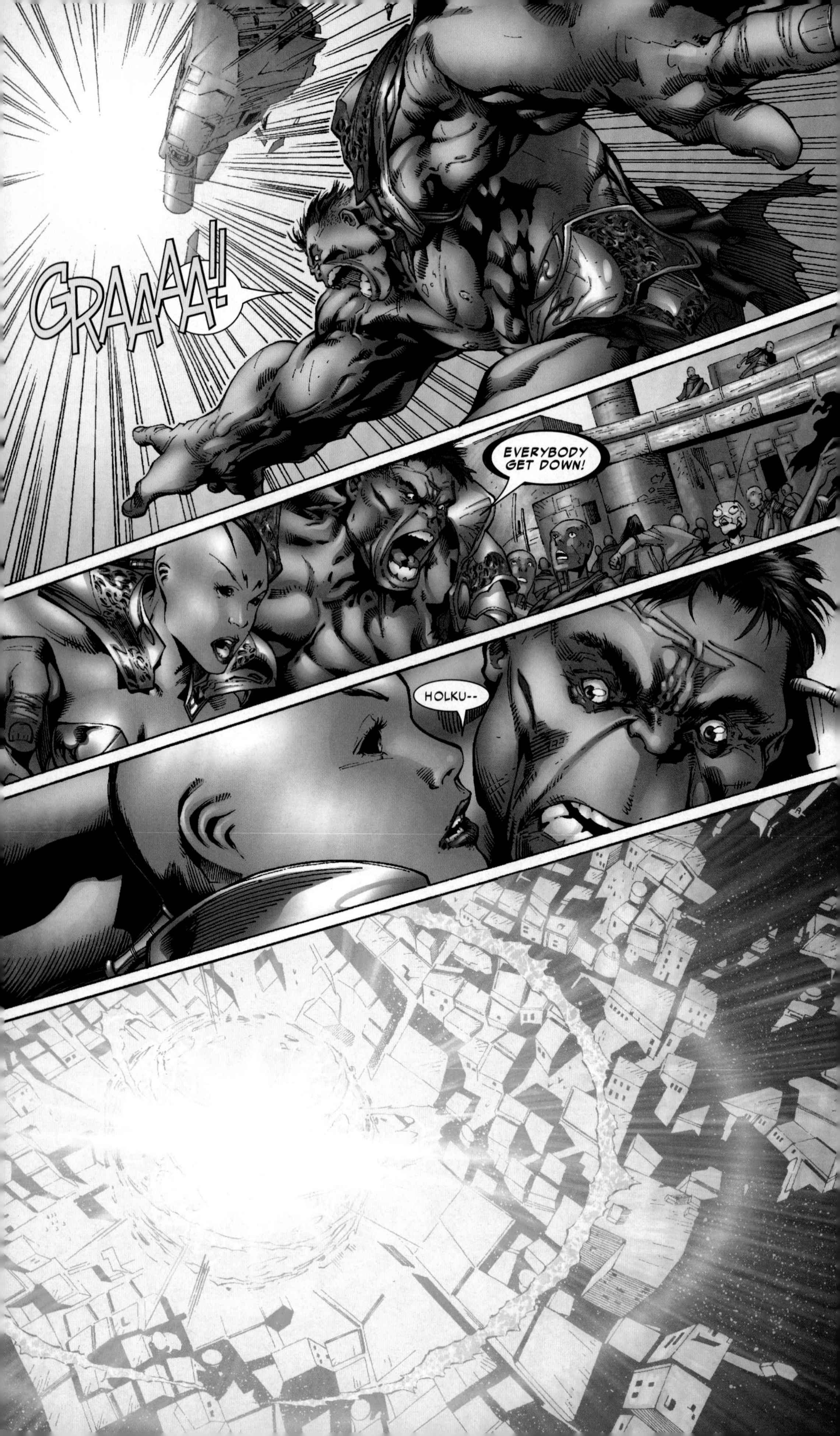
GRAAAA!!
EVERYBODY GET DOWN!
HOLKU--

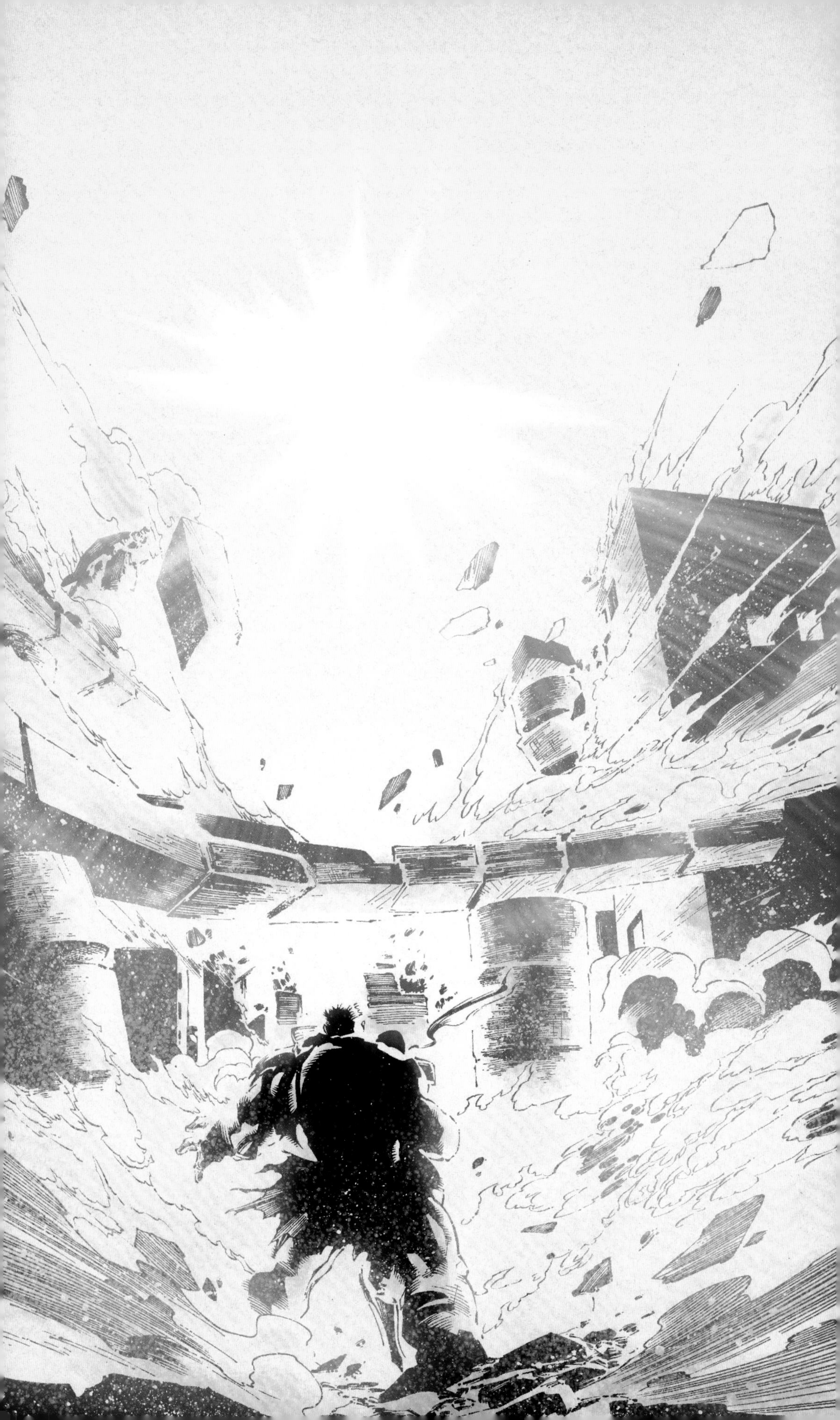

100 VARIANTS

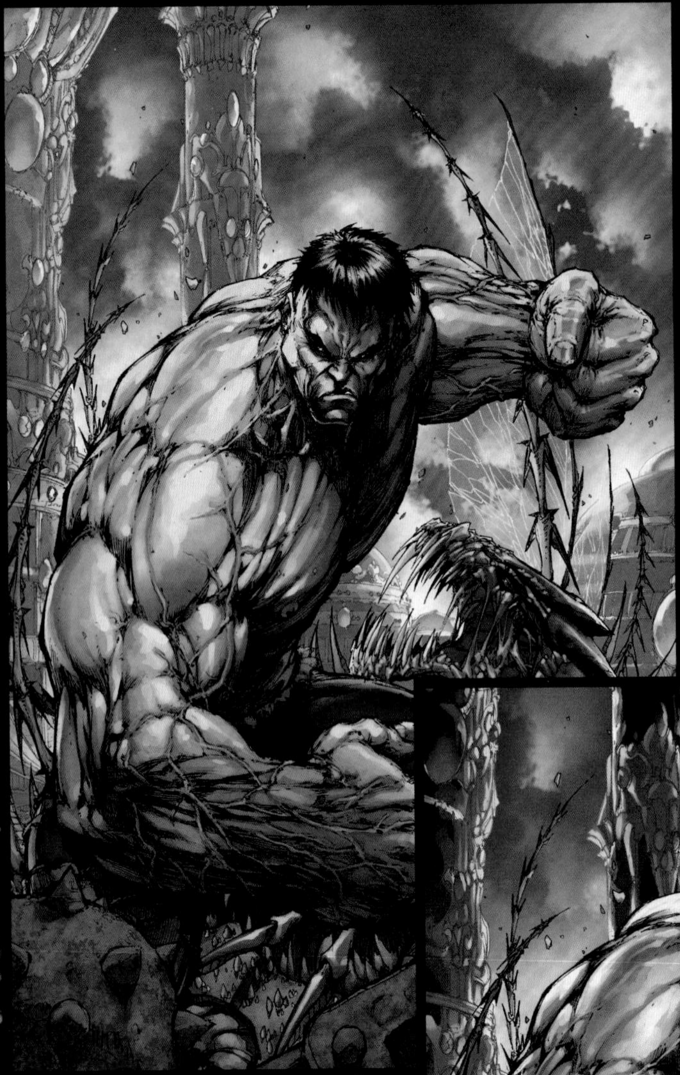

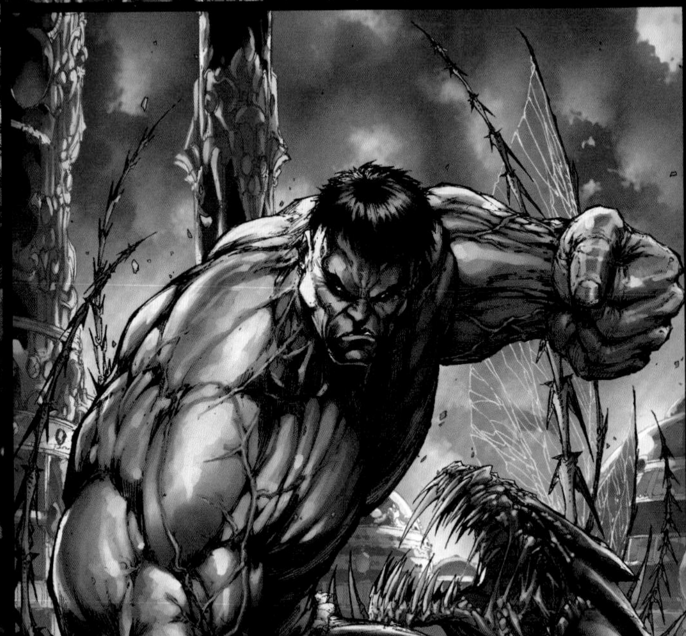
MICHAEL TURNER

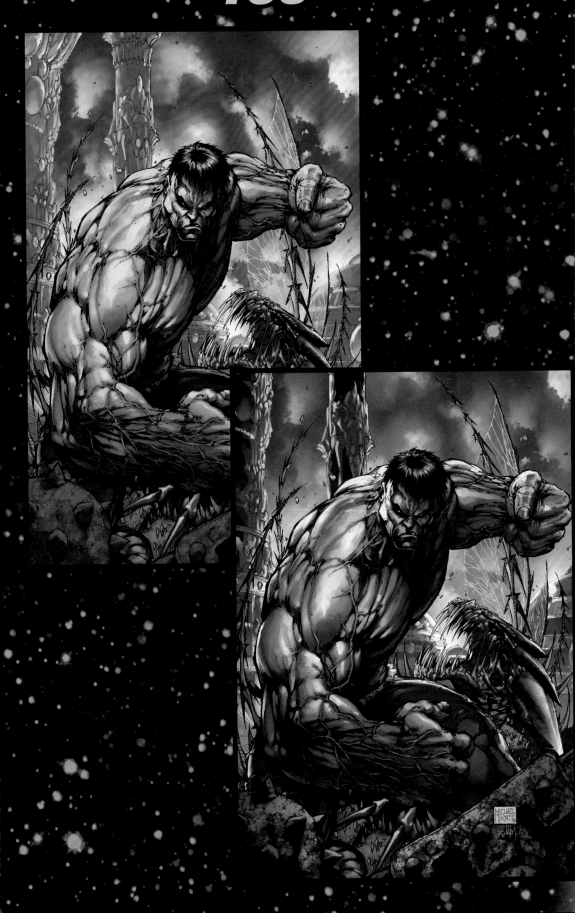

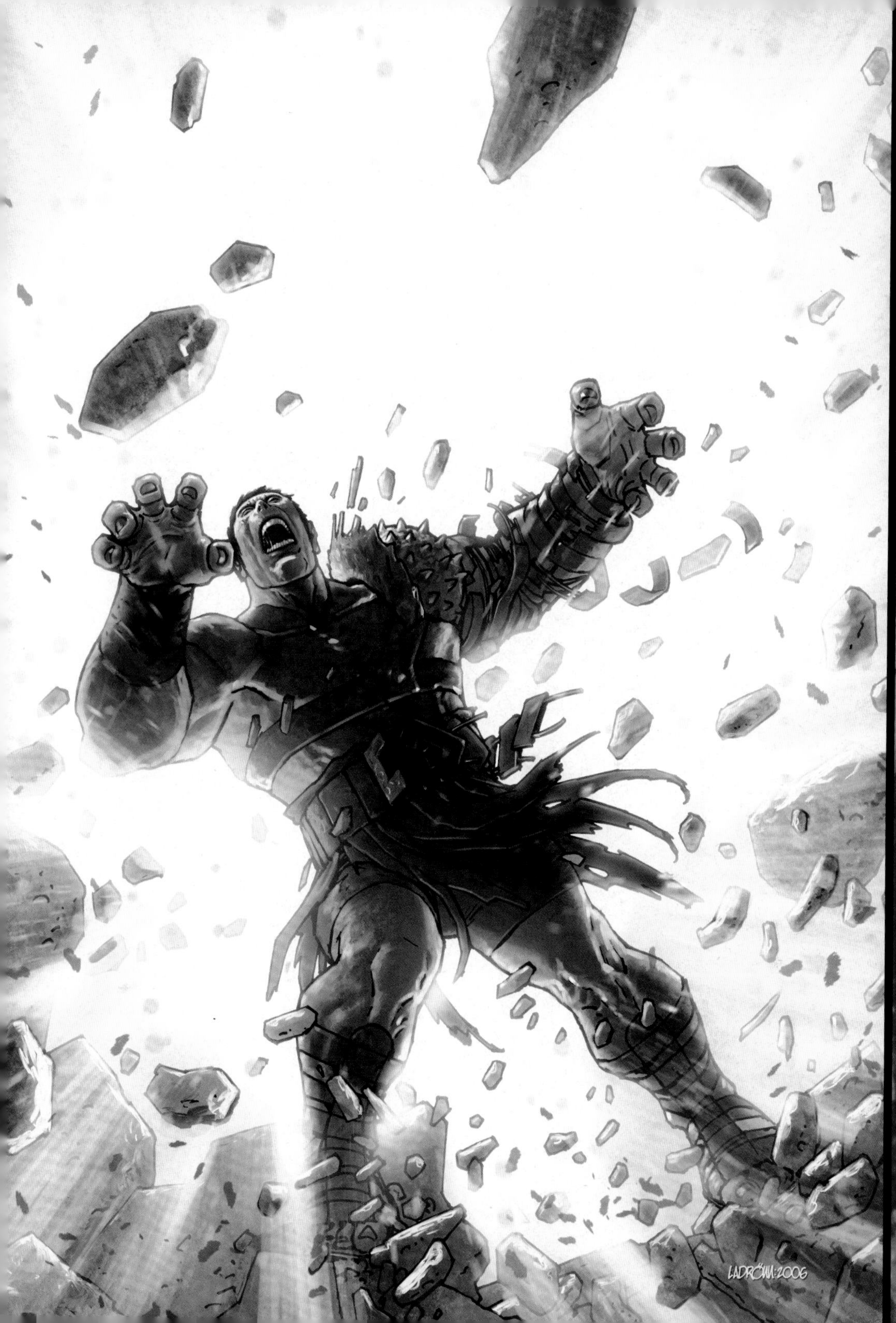
LADRÖNN:2006

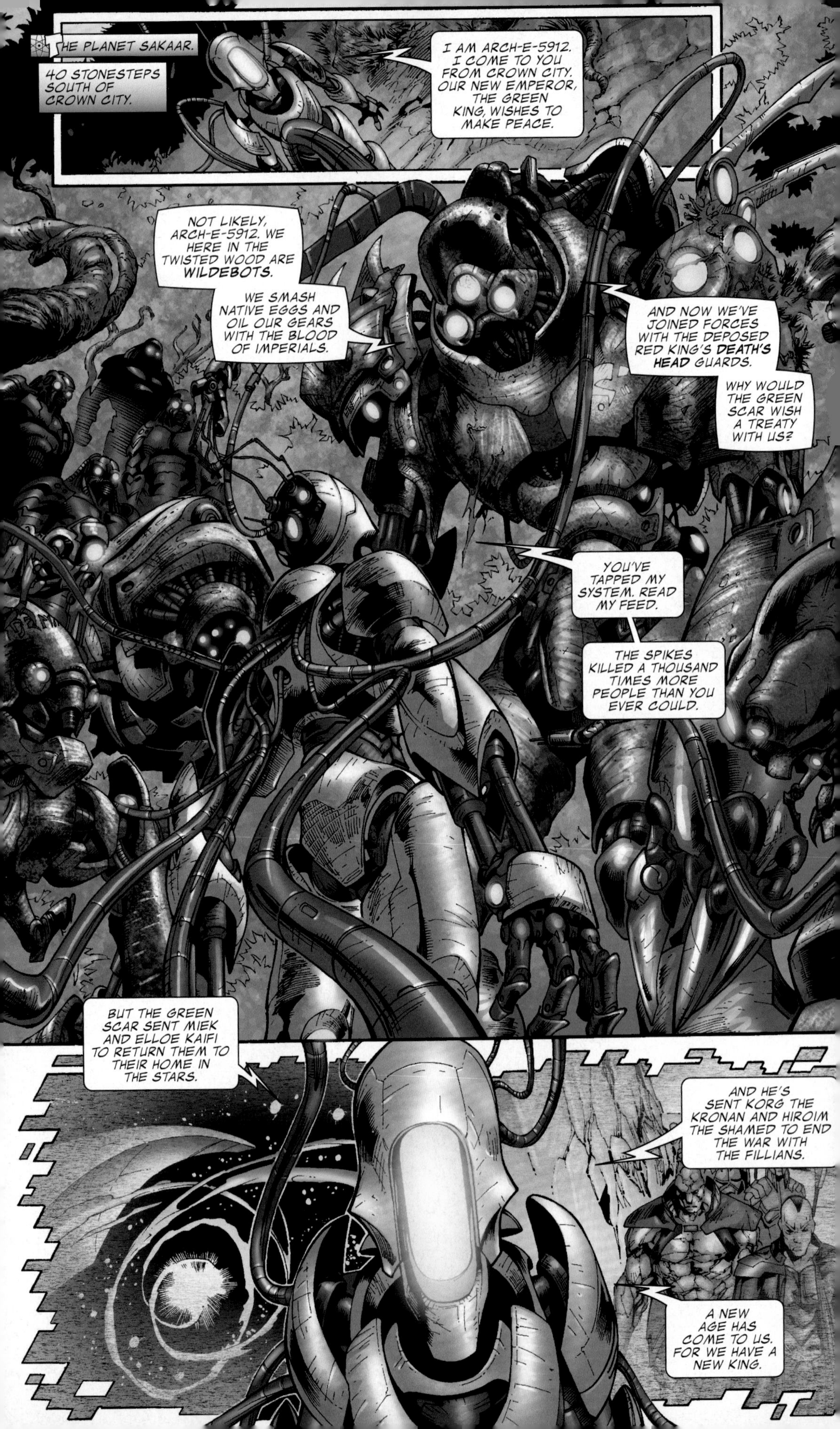
THE PLANET SAKAAR.
40 STONESTEPS SOUTH OF CROWN CITY.
I AM ARCH-E-5912. I COME TO YOU FROM CROWN CITY. OUR NEW EMPEROR, THE GREEN KING, WISHES TO MAKE PEACE.
NOT LIKELY, ARCH-E-5912. WE HERE IN THE TWISTED WOOD ARE WILDEBOTS.
WE SMASH NATIVE EGGS AND OIL OUR GEARS WITH THE BLOOD OF IMPERIALS.
AND NOW WE'VE JOINED FORCES WITH THE DEPOSED RED KING'S DEATH'S HEAD GUARDS.
WHY WOULD THE GREEN SCAR WISH A TREATY WITH US?
YOU'VE TAPPED MY SYSTEM. READ MY FEED.
THE SPIKES KILLED A THOUSAND TIMES MORE PEOPLE THAN YOU EVER COULD.
BUT THE GREEN SCAR SENT MIEK AND ELLOE KAIFI TO RETURN THEM TO THEIR HOME IN THE STARS.
AND HE'S SENT KORG THE KRONAN AND HIROIM THE SHAMED TO END THE WAR WITH THE FILLIANS.
A NEW AGE HAS COME TO US. FOR WE HAVE A NEW KING.

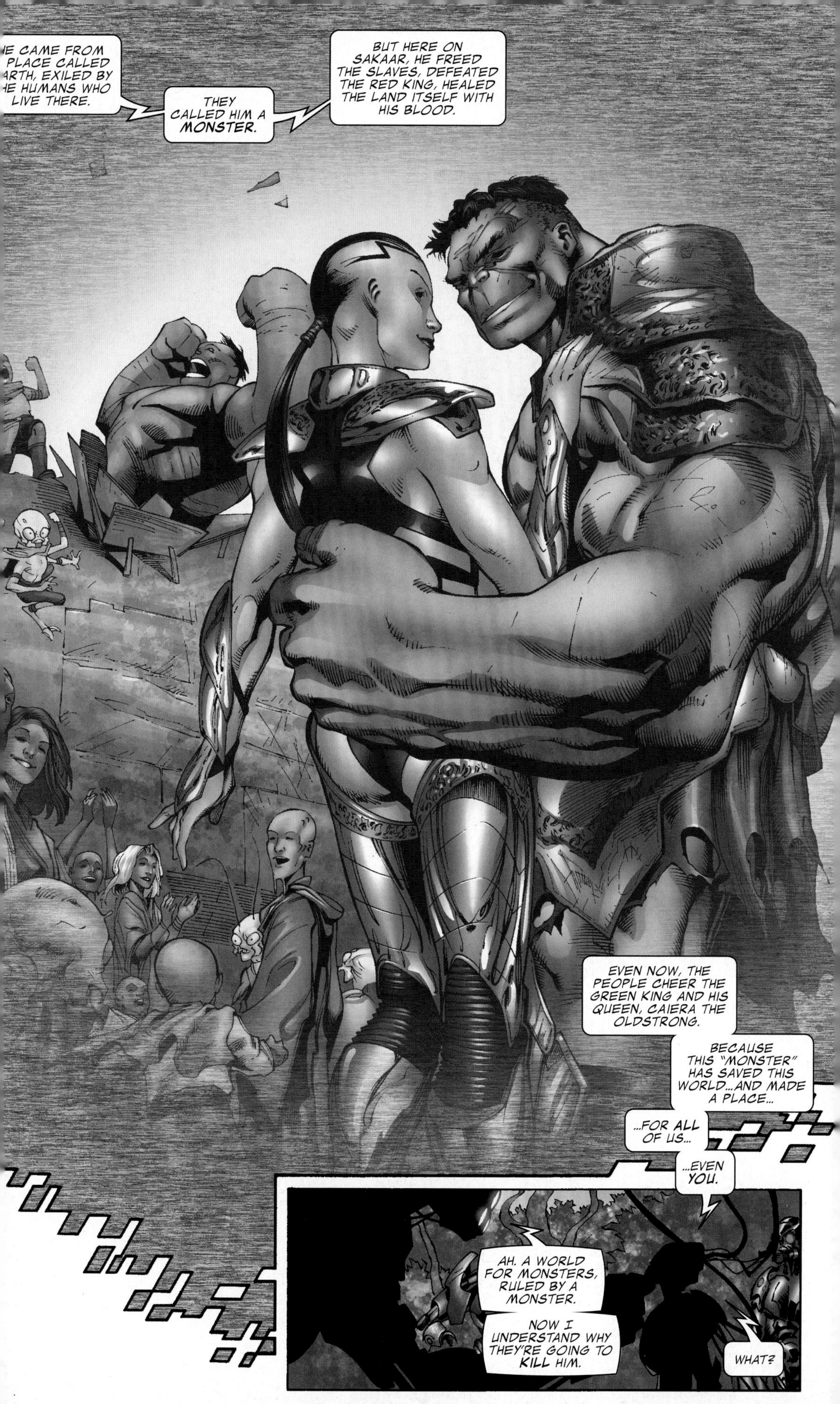
E CAME FROM PLACE CALLED ARTH, EXILED BY HE HUMANS WHO LIVE THERE.
THEY CALLED HIM A MONSTER.
BUT HERE ON SAKAAR, HE FREED THE SLAVES, DEFEATED THE RED KING, HEALED THE LAND ITSELF WITH HIS BLOOD.
EVEN NOW, THE PEOPLE CHEER THE GREEN KING AND HIS QUEEN, CAIERA THE OLDSTRONG.
BECAUSE THIS "MONSTER" HAS SAVED THIS WORLD...AND MADE A PLACE...
...FOR ALL OF US...
...EVEN YOU.
AH. A WORLD FOR MONSTERS, RULED BY A MONSTER.
NOW I UNDERSTAND WHY THEY'RE GOING TO KILL HIM.
WHAT?

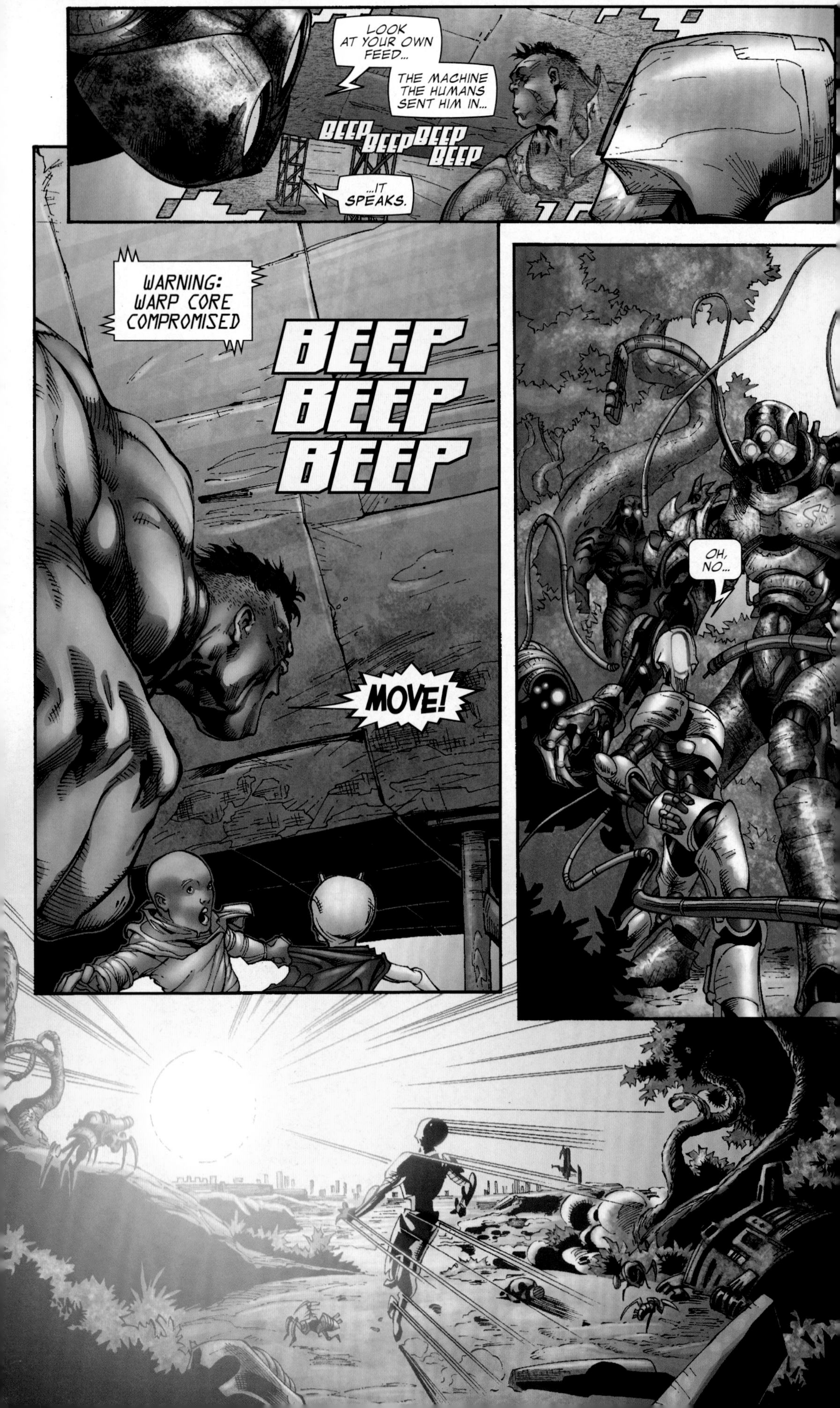
LOOK AT YOUR OWN FEED...
THE MACHINE THE HUMANS SENT HIM IN...
BEEP BEEP BEEP BEEP
...IT SPEAKS.
WARNING: WARP CORE COMPROMISED
BEEP BEEP BEEP
MOVE!
OH, NO...

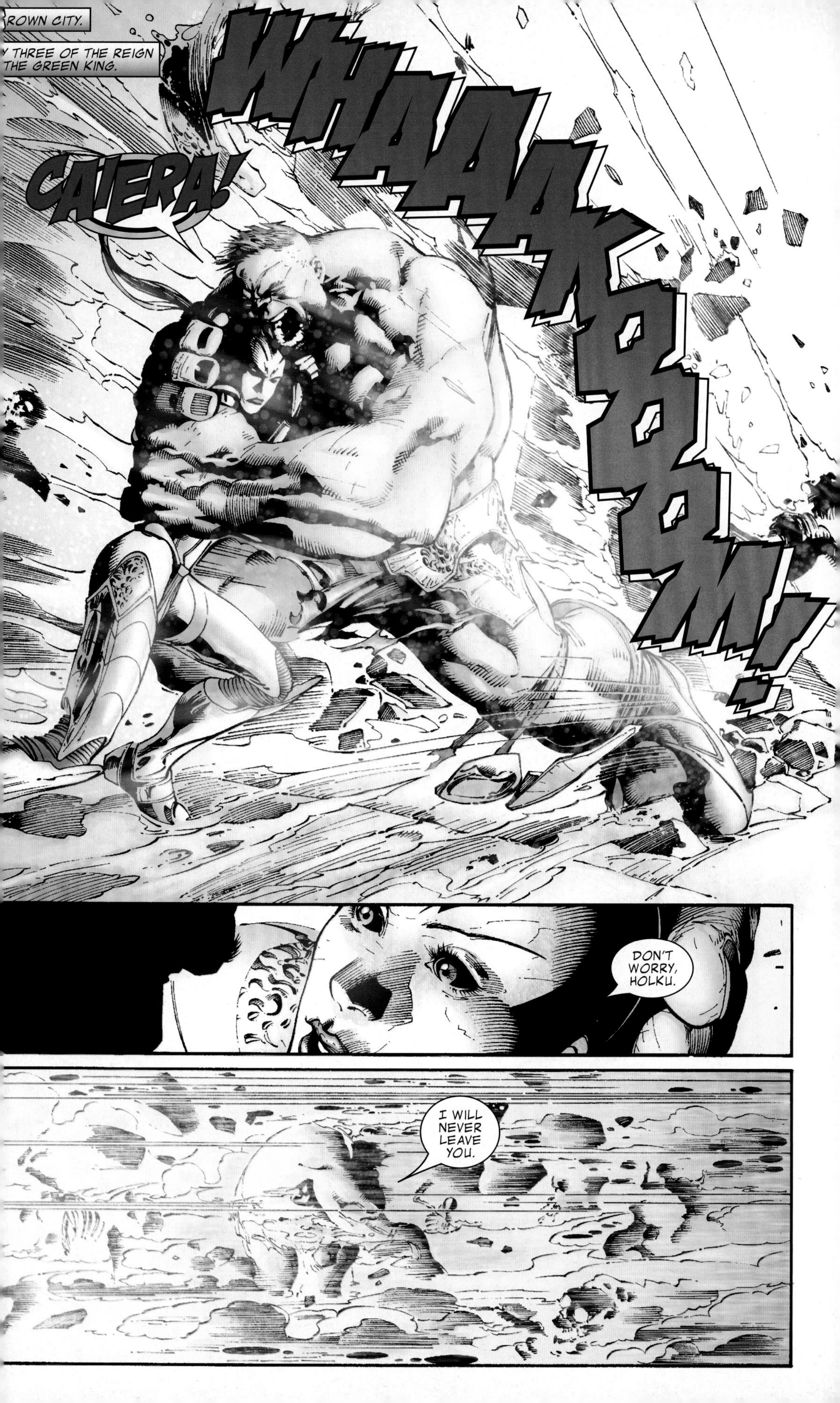

ROWN CITY.
Y THREE OF THE REIGN
THE GREEN KING.
WHAAAAKOOOM!
CAIERA!
DON'T WORRY, HOLKU.
I WILL NEVER LEAVE YOU.

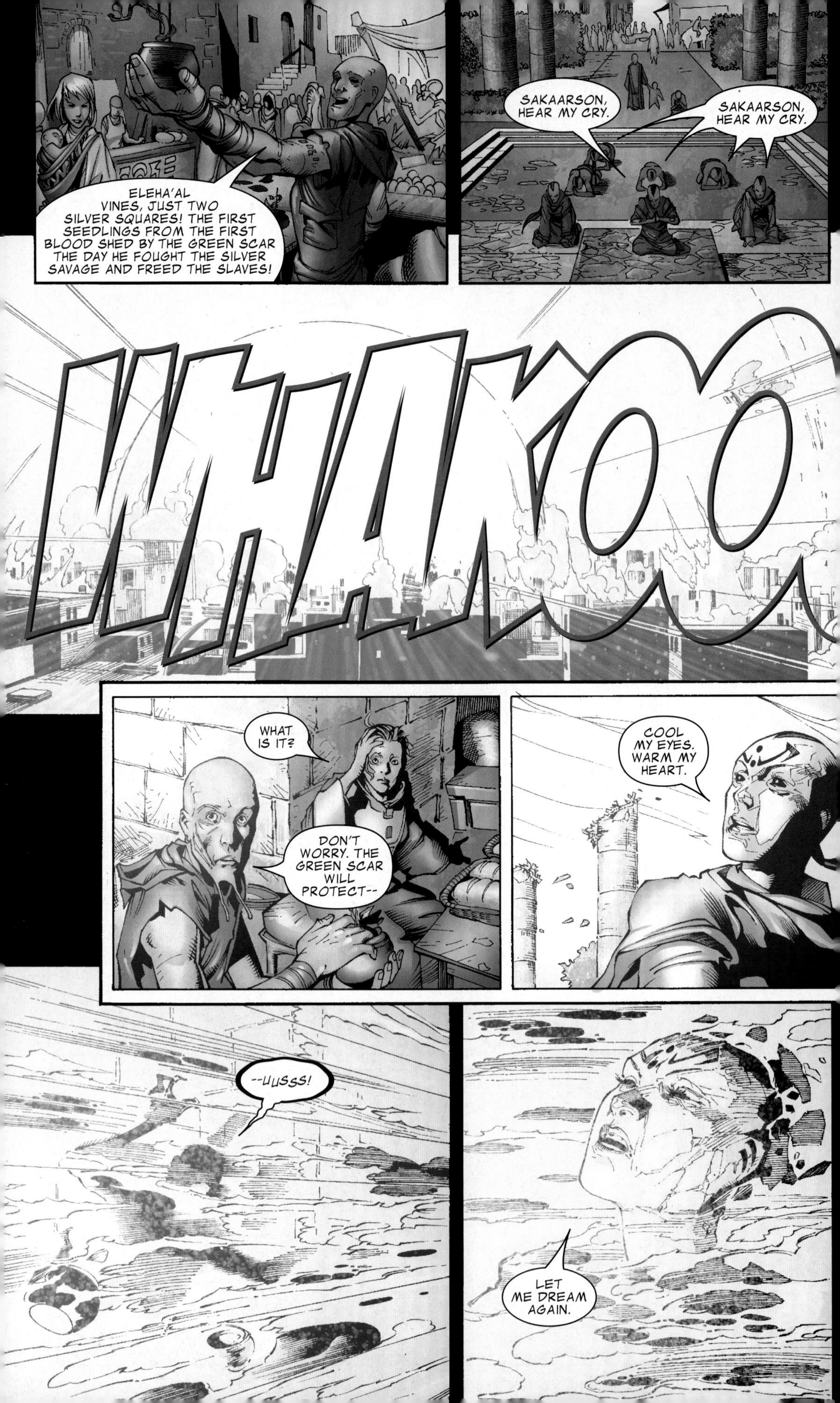

ELEHA'AL VINES, JUST TWO SILVER SQUARES! THE FIRST SEEDLINGS FROM THE FIRST BLOOD SHED BY THE GREEN SCAR THE DAY HE FOUGHT THE SILVER SAVAGE AND FREED THE SLAVES!
SAKAARSON, HEAR MY CRY.
SAKAARSON, HEAR MY CRY.
WHAKOOO
WHAT IS IT?
DON'T WORRY. THE GREEN SCAR WILL PROTECT--
COOL MY EYES. WARM MY HEART.
--UUSSS!
LET ME DREAM AGAIN.

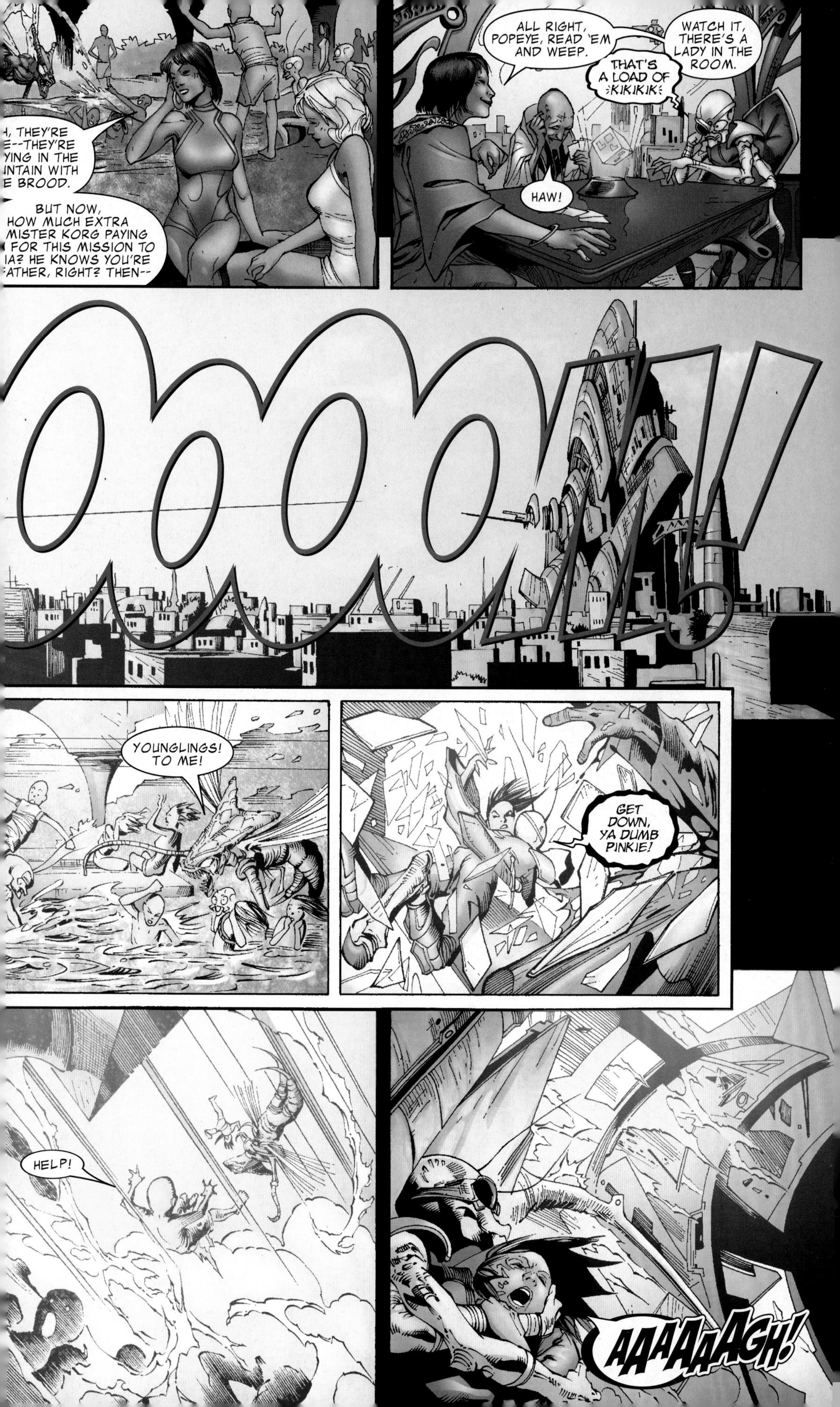

H, THEY'RE
E--THEY'RE
YING IN THE
NTAIN WITH
E BROOD.
BUT NOW,
HOW MUCH EXTRA
MISTER KORG PAYING
FOR THIS MISSION TO
IA? HE KNOWS YOU'RE
FATHER, RIGHT? THEN--
ALL RIGHT, POPEYE, READ 'EM AND WEEP.
WATCH IT, THERE'S A LADY IN THE ROOM.
THAT'S A LOAD OF KIKIKIK
HAW!
YOUNGLINGS! TO ME!
GET DOWN, YA DUMB PINKIE!
HELP!
AAAAAAGH!

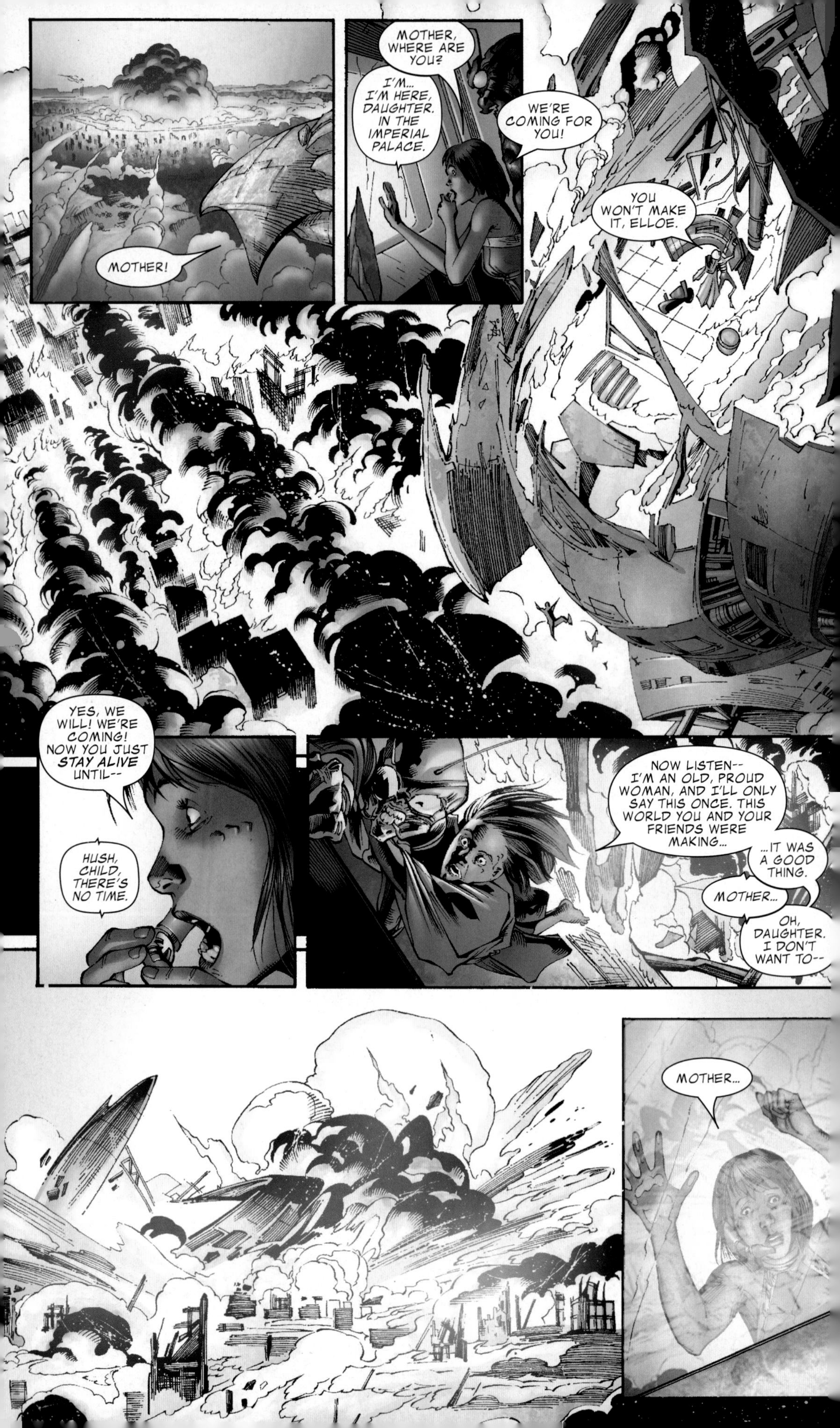
MOTHER!
MOTHER, WHERE ARE YOU?
I'M... I'M HERE, DAUGHTER. IN THE IMPERIAL PALACE.
WE'RE COMING FOR YOU!
YOU WON'T MAKE IT, ELLOE.
YES, WE WILL! WE'RE COMING! NOW YOU JUST STAY ALIVE UNTIL--
HUSH, CHILD, THERE'S NO TIME.
NOW LISTEN-- I'M AN OLD, PROUD WOMAN, AND I'LL ONLY SAY THIS ONCE. THIS WORLD YOU AND YOUR FRIENDS WERE MAKING...
...IT WAS A GOOD THING.
MOTHER...
OH, DAUGHTER. I DON'T WANT TO--
MOTHER...

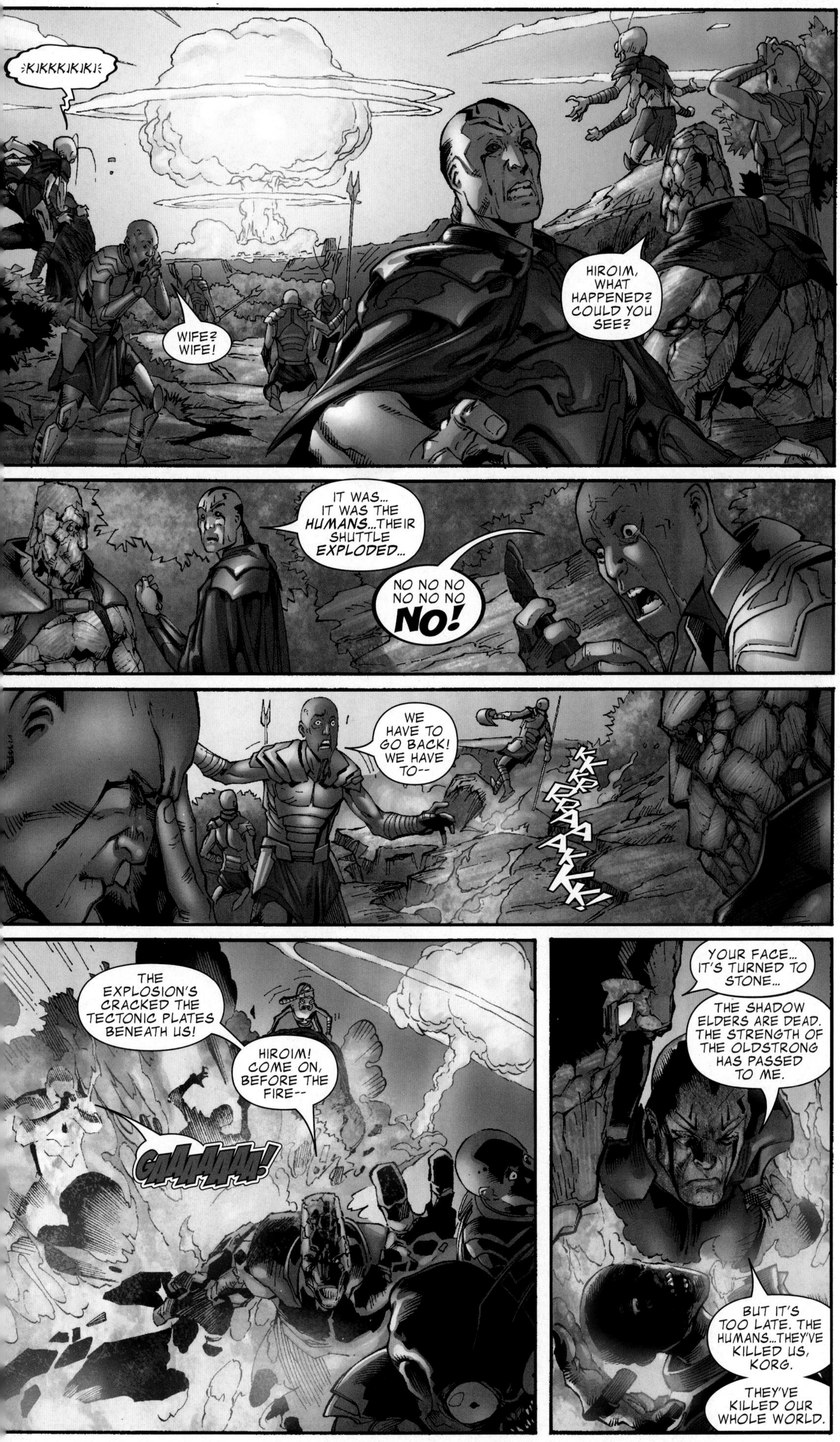
KIKKKIKIKI
WIFE? WIFE!
HIROIM, WHAT HAPPENED? COULD YOU SEE?
IT WAS... IT WAS THE HUMANS...THEIR SHUTTLE EXPLODED...
NO NO NO NO NO NO NO!
WE HAVE TO GO BACK! WE HAVE TO--
KKRRRAAAKKK!
THE EXPLOSION'S CRACKED THE TECTONIC PLATES BENEATH US!
HIROIM! COME ON, BEFORE THE FIRE--
GAAAAAA!
YOUR FACE... IT'S TURNED TO STONE...
THE SHADOW ELDERS ARE DEAD. THE STRENGTH OF THE OLDSTRONG HAS PASSED TO ME.
BUT IT'S TOO LATE. THE HUMANS...THEY'VE KILLED US, KORG.
THEY'VE KILLED OUR WHOLE WORLD.

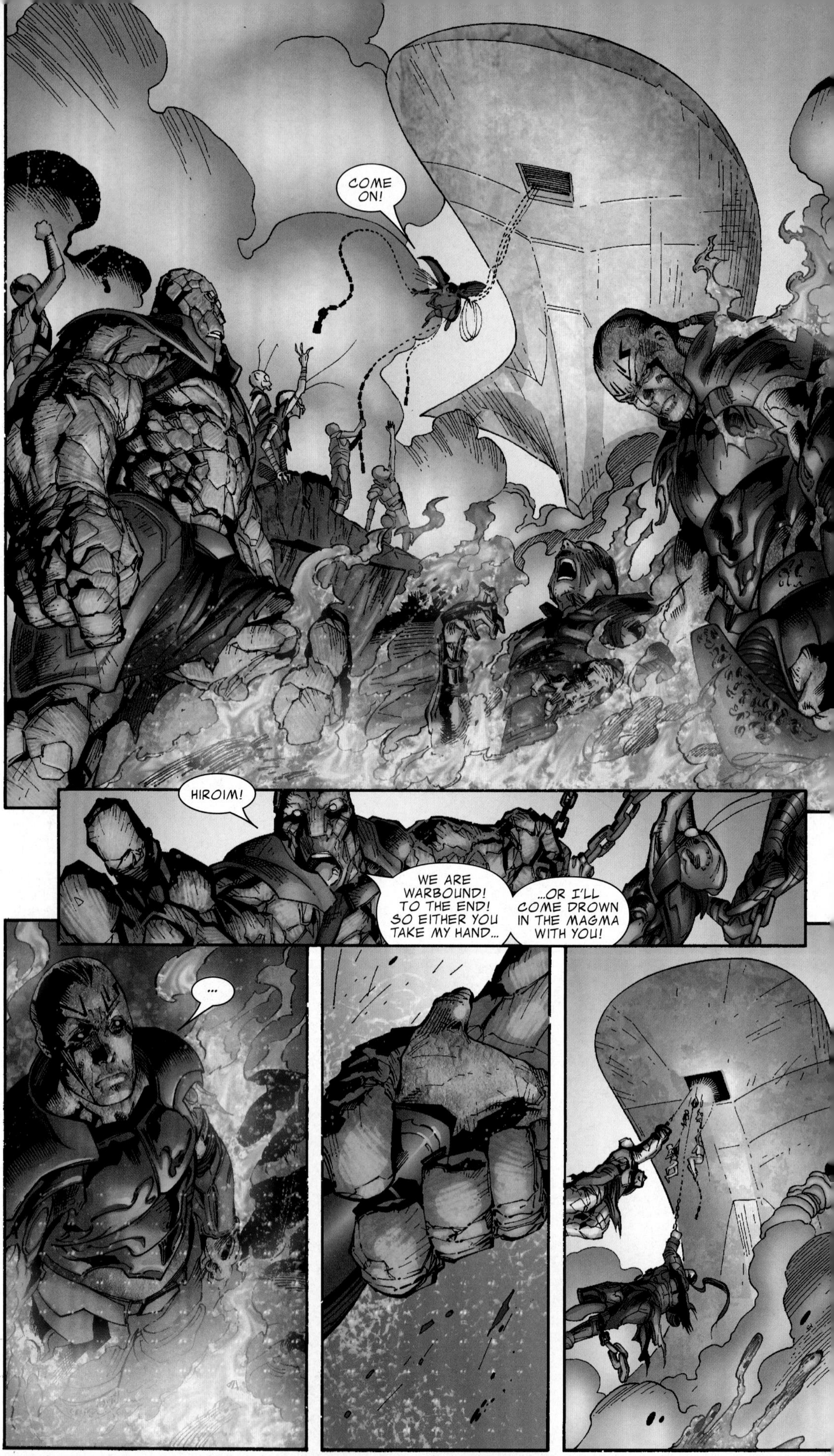
COME ON!
HIROIM!
WE ARE WARBOUND! TO THE END! SO EITHER YOU TAKE MY HAND...
...OR I'LL COME DROWN IN THE MAGMA WITH YOU!
...

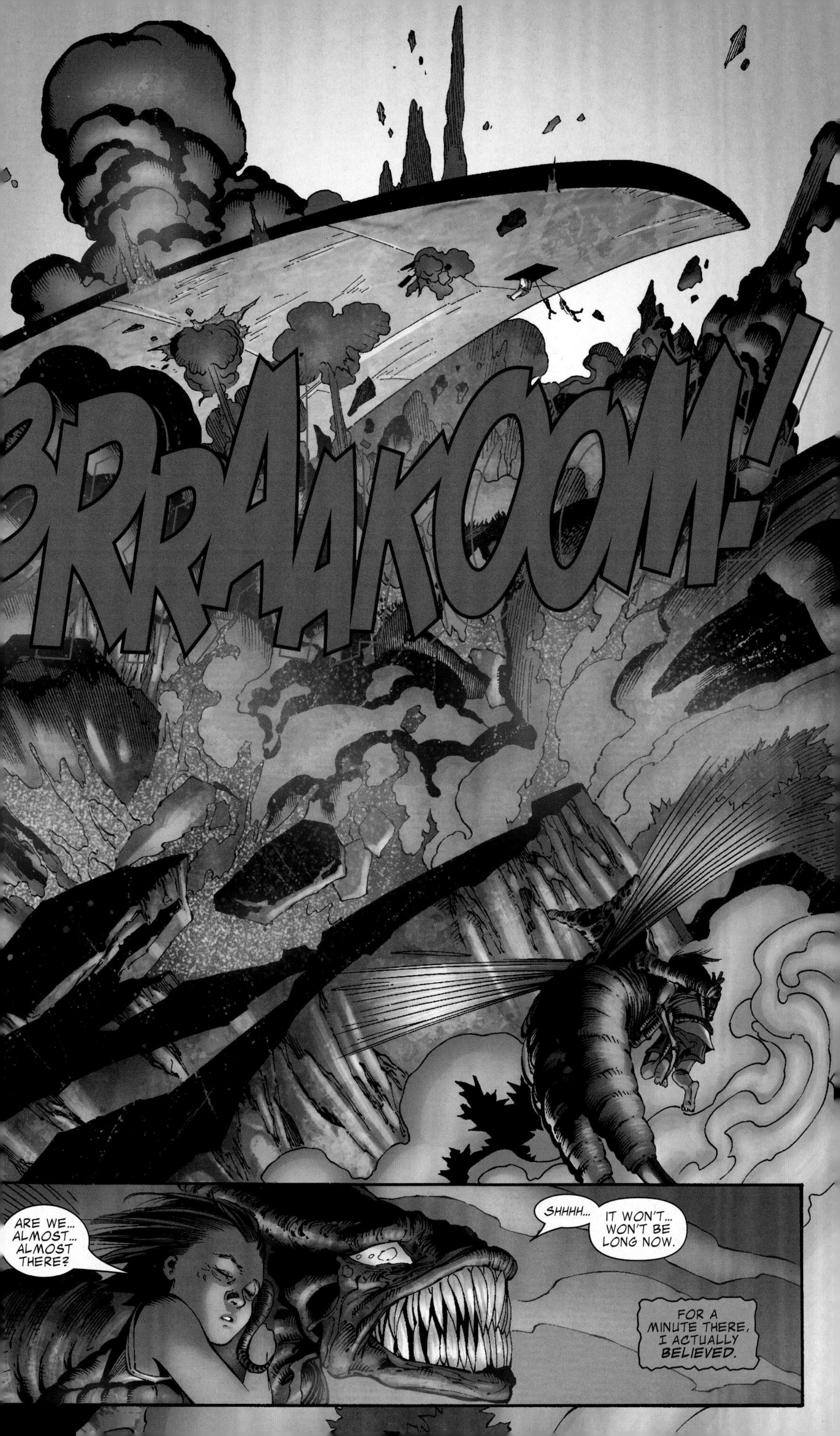

BRRAAKOOM!
ARE WE... ALMOST... ALMOST THERE?
SHHHH...
IT WON'T... WON'T BE LONG NOW.
FOR A MINUTE THERE, I ACTUALLY BELIEVED.

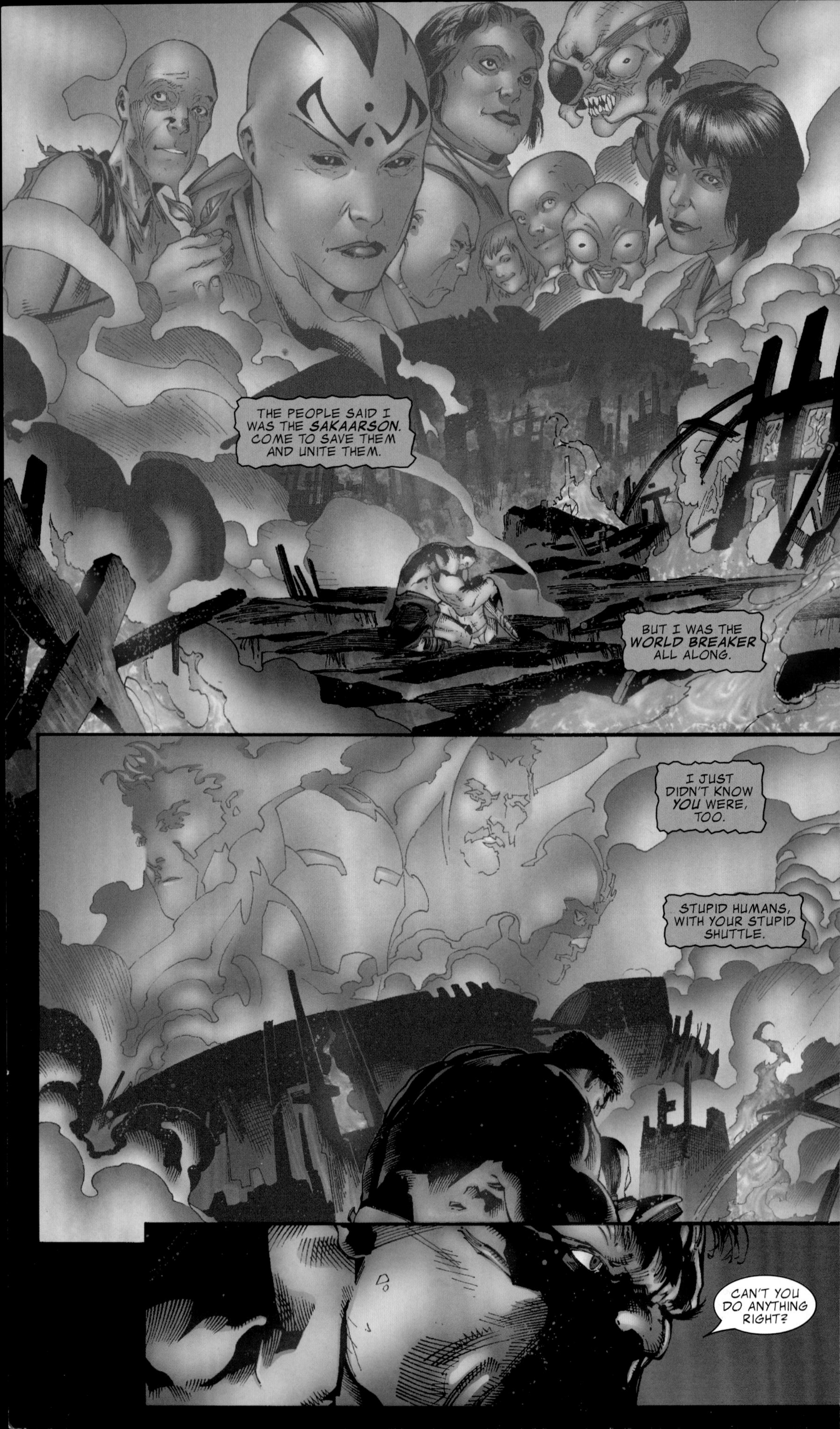
THE PEOPLE SAID I WAS THE SAKAARSON. COME TO SAVE THEM AND UNITE THEM.
BUT I WAS THE WORLD BREAKER ALL ALONG.
I JUST DIDN'T KNOW YOU WERE, TOO.
STUPID HUMANS, WITH YOUR STUPID SHUTTLE.
CAN'T YOU DO ANYTHING RIGHT?

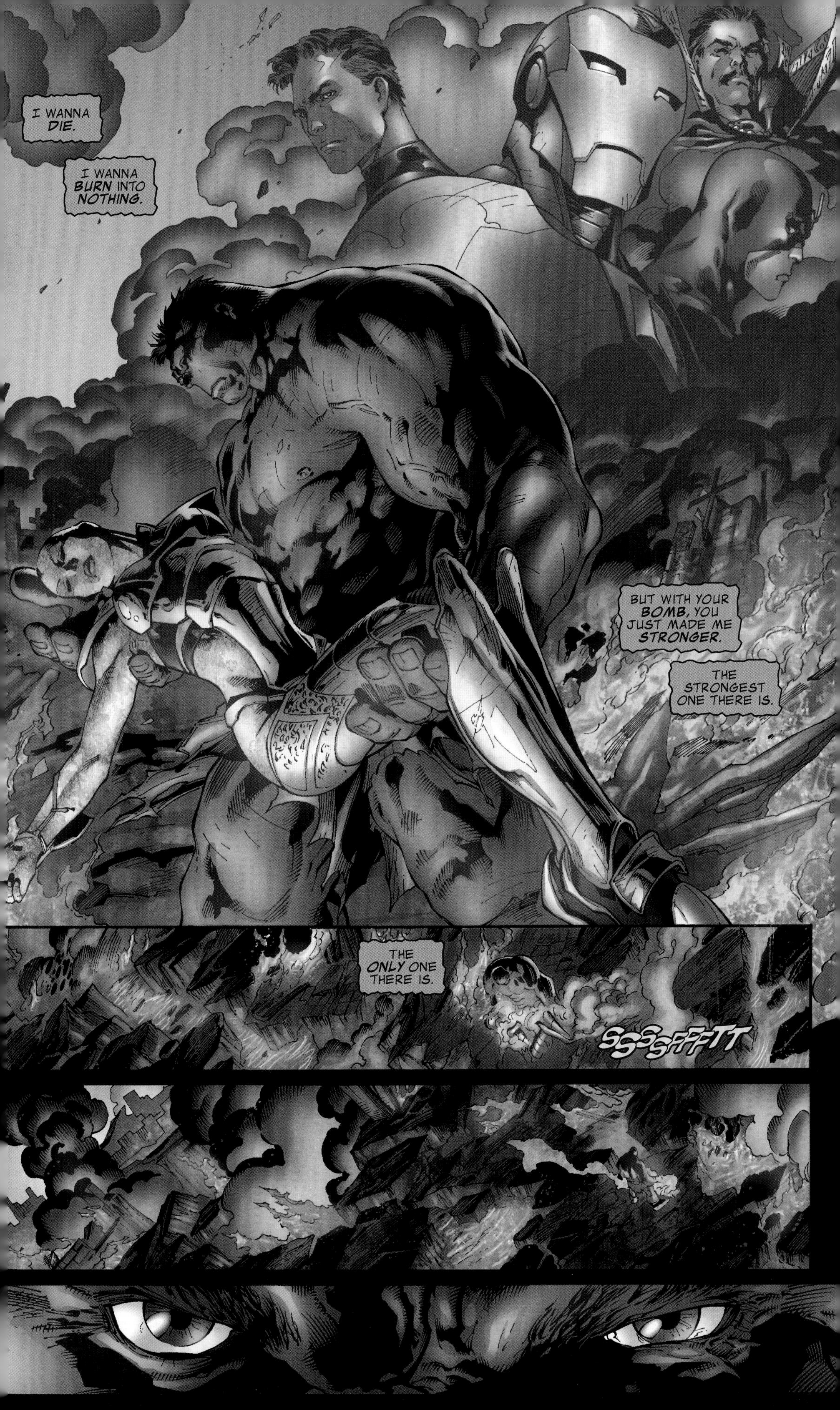
I WANNA DIE.
I WANNA BURN INTO NOTHING.
BUT WITH YOUR BOMB, YOU JUST MADE ME STRONGER.
THE STRONGEST ONE THERE IS.
THE ONLY ONE THERE IS.
SSSSFFFFTT

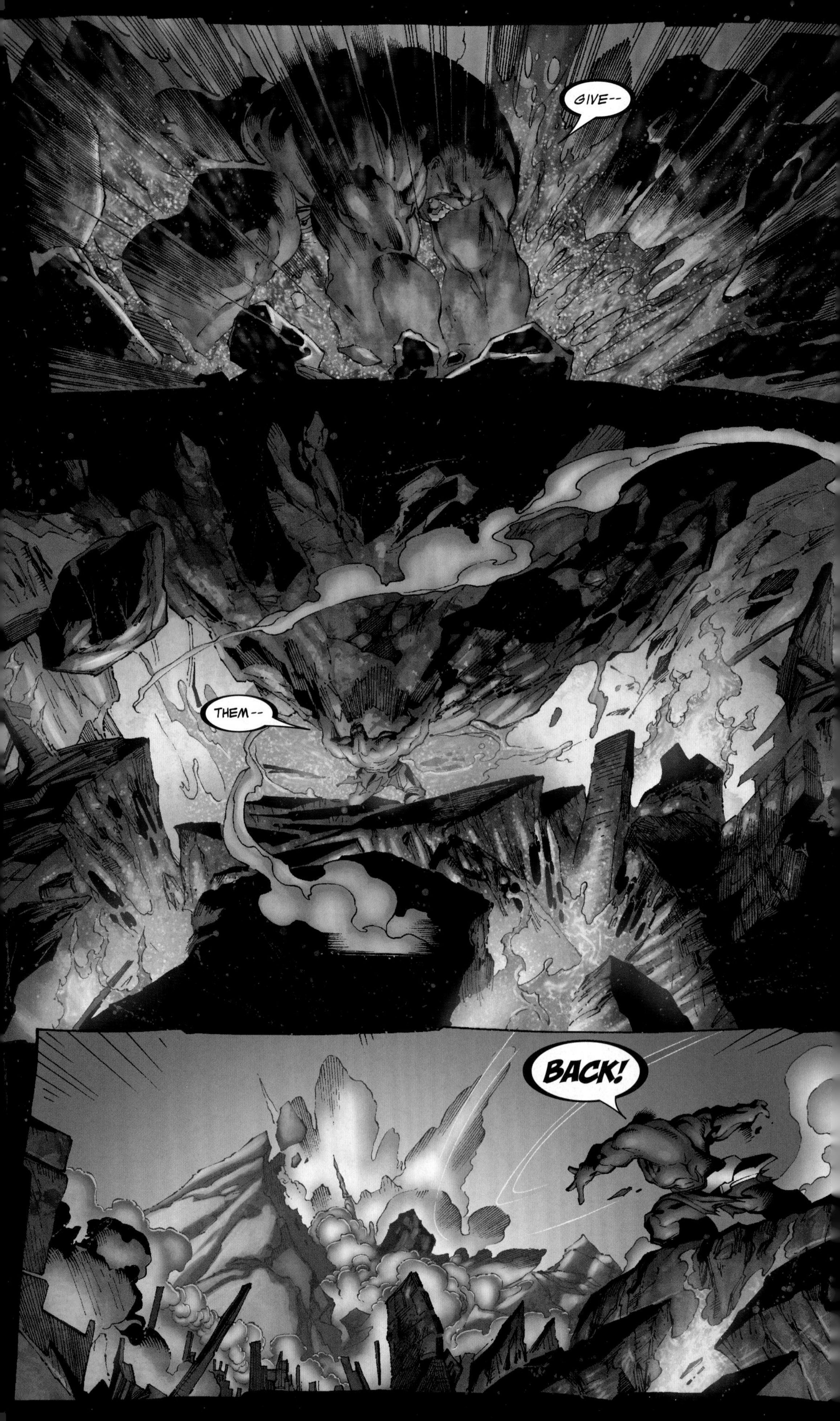
GIVE--
THEM--
BACK!

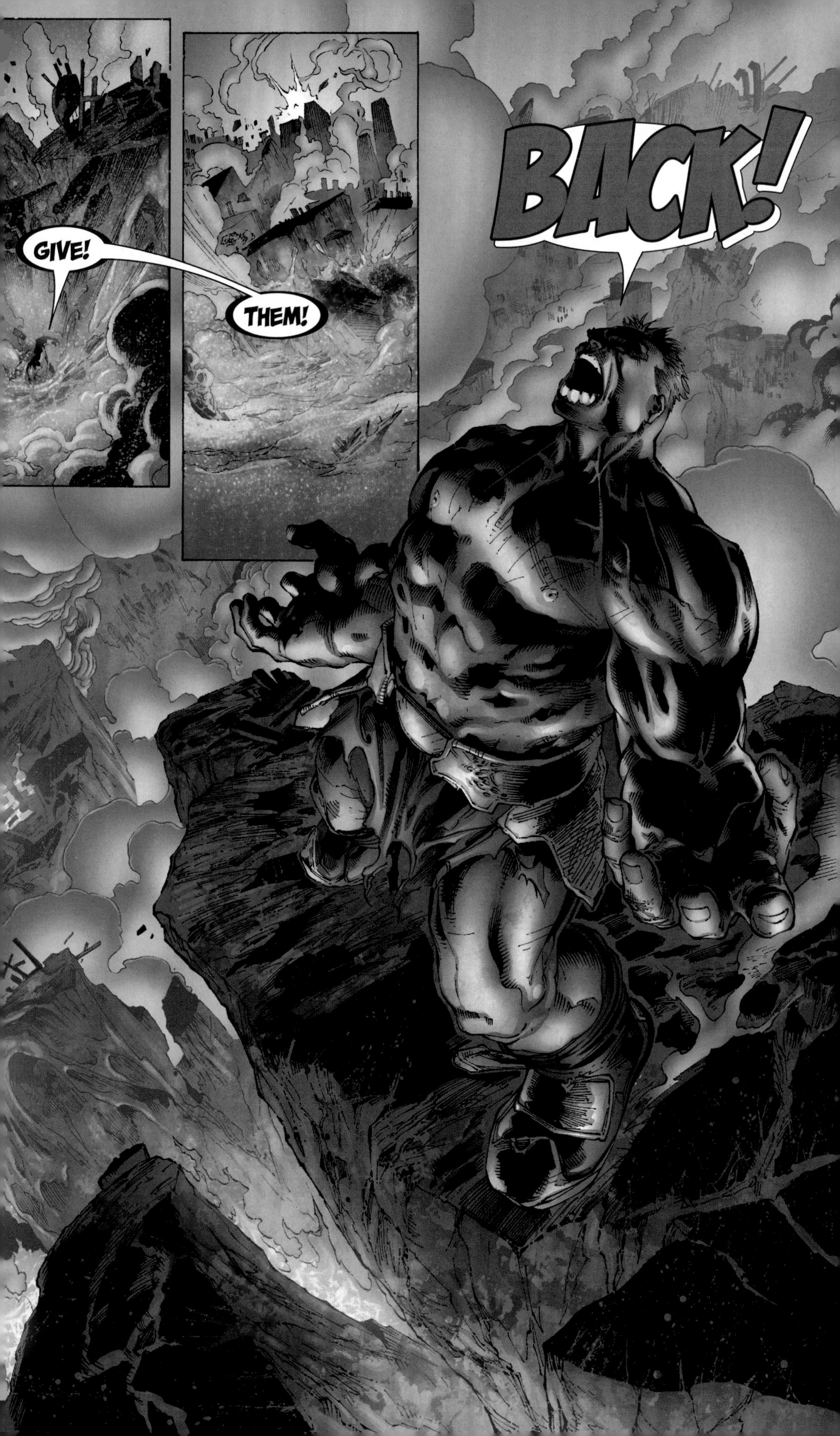
GIVE!
THEM!
BACK!

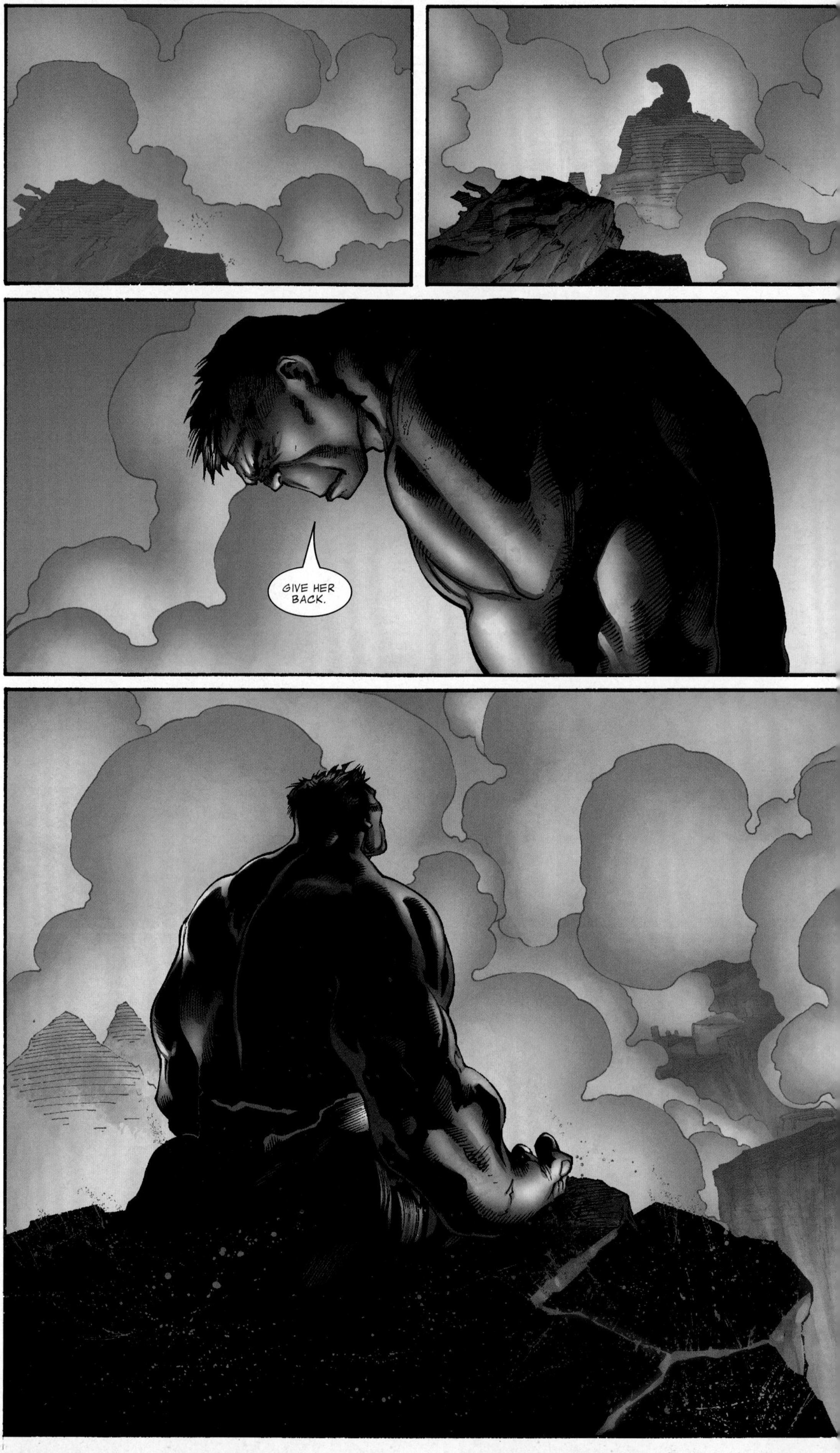
GIVE HER BACK.

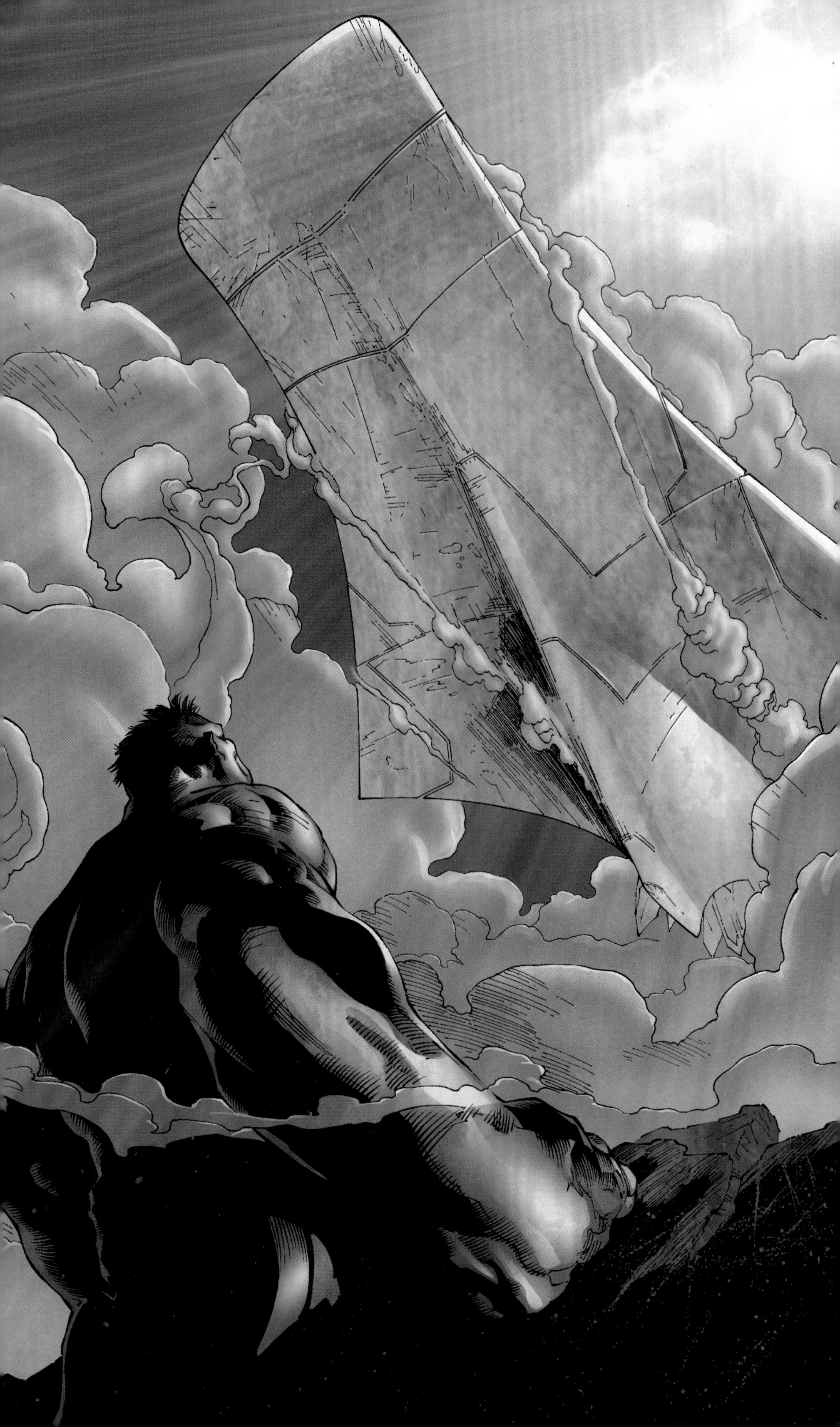

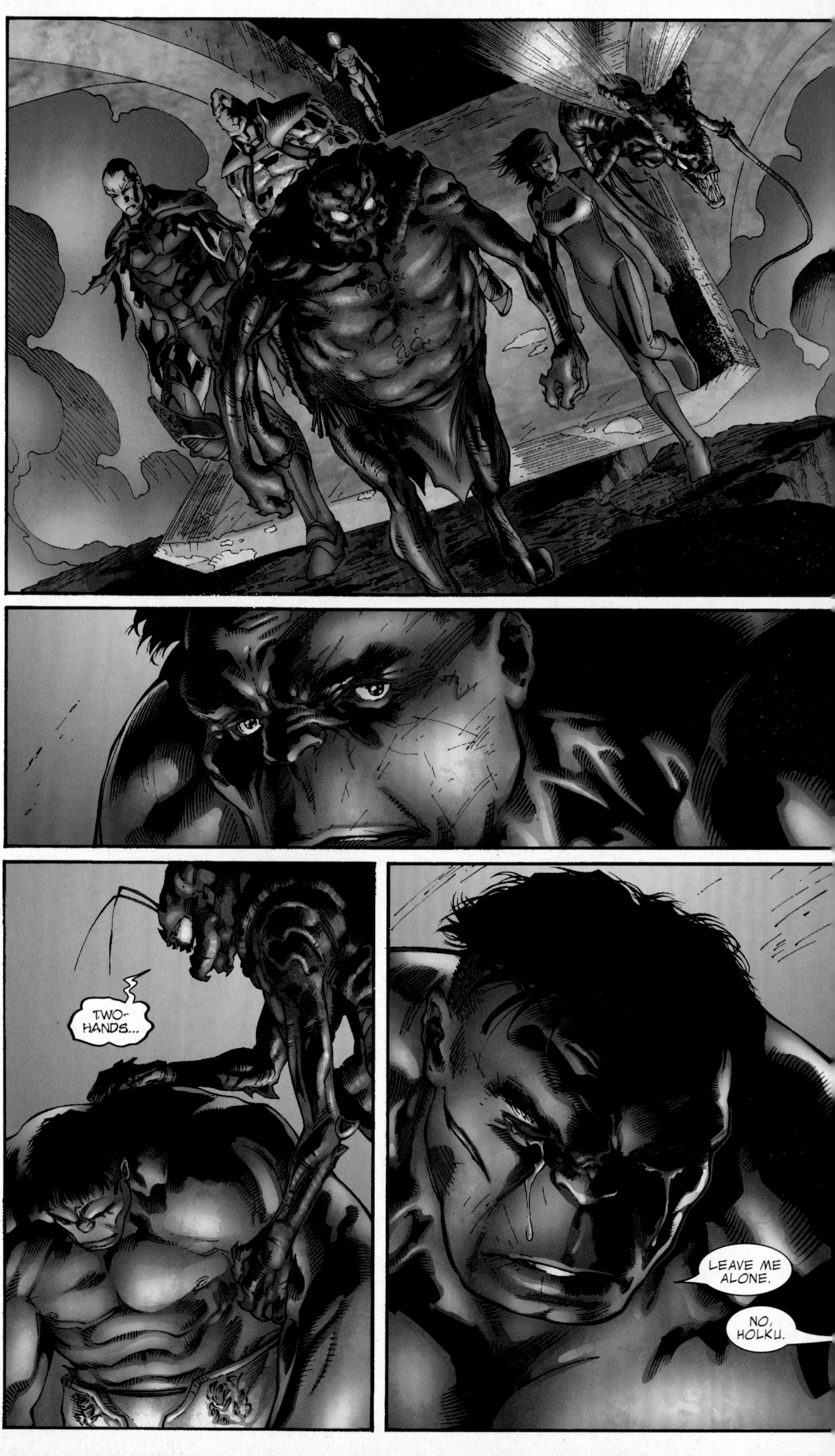
TWO-HANDS...
LEAVE ME ALONE.
NO, HOLKU.

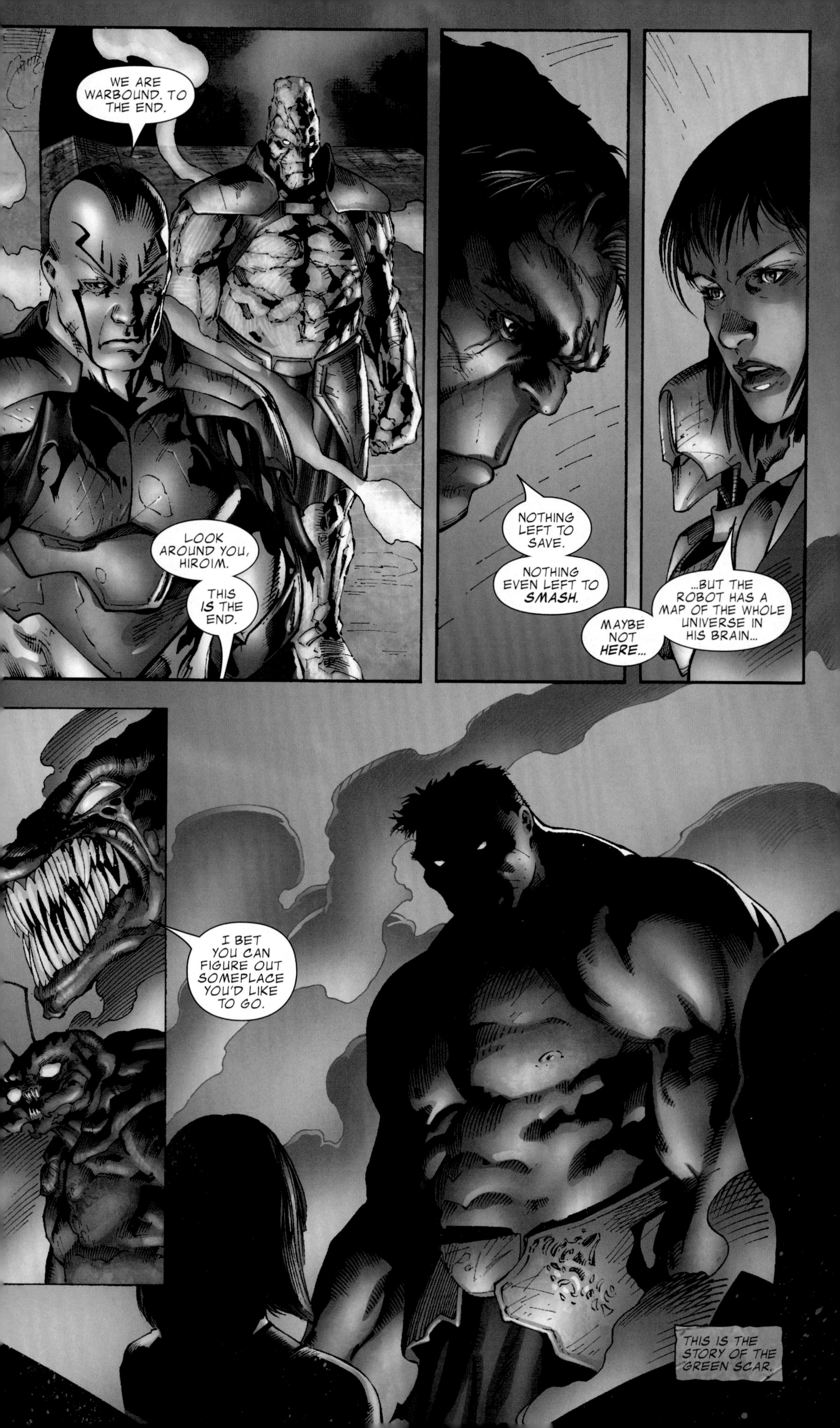
WE ARE WARBOUND. TO THE END.
LOOK AROUND YOU, HIROIM.
THIS IS THE END.
NOTHING LEFT TO SAVE.
NOTHING EVEN LEFT TO SMASH.
MAYBE NOT HERE...
...BUT THE ROBOT HAS A MAP OF THE WHOLE UNIVERSE IN HIS BRAIN...
I BET YOU CAN FIGURE OUT SOMEPLACE YOU'D LIKE TO GO.
THIS IS THE STORY OF THE GREEN SCAR.

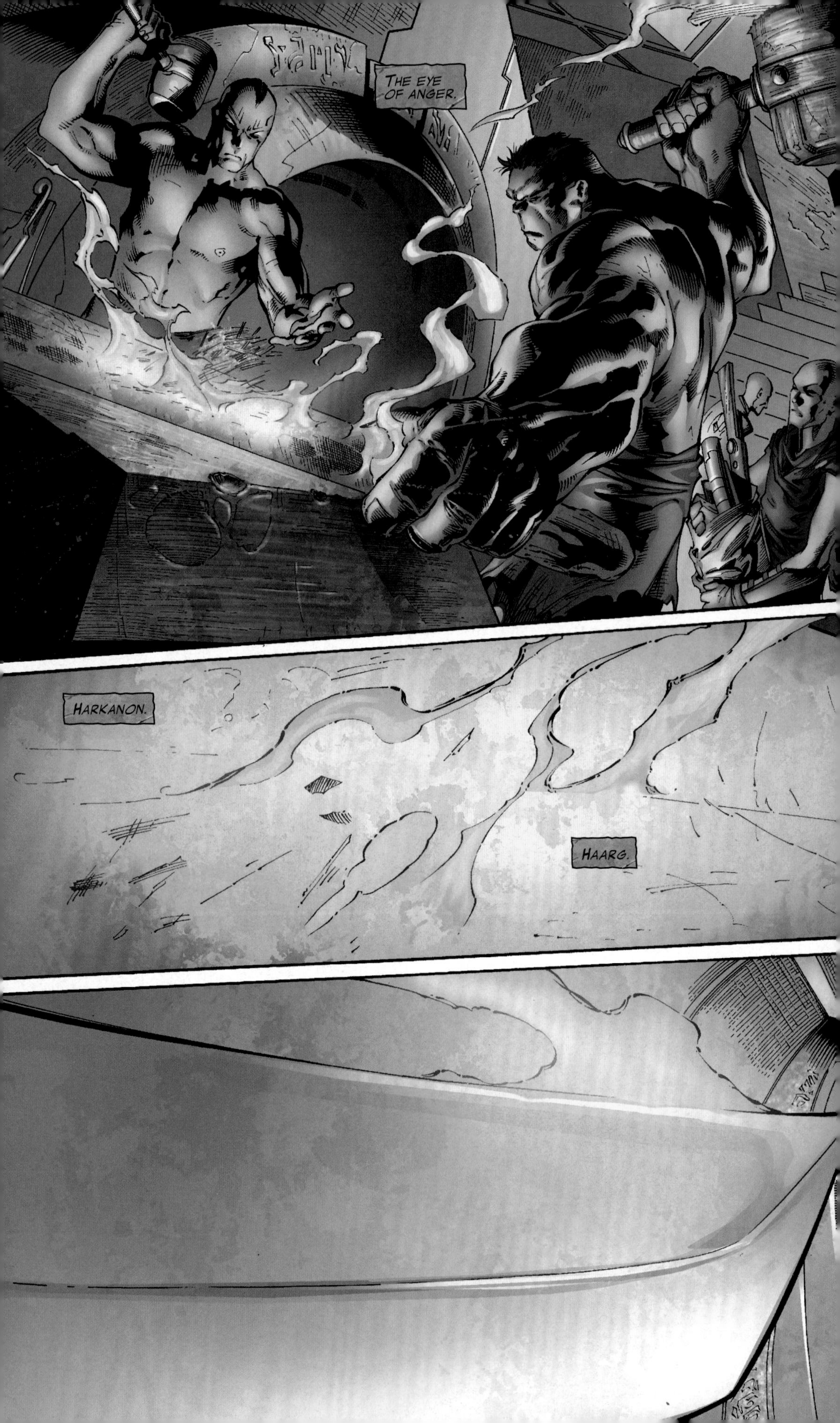
THE EYE OF ANGER.
HARKANON.
HAARG.

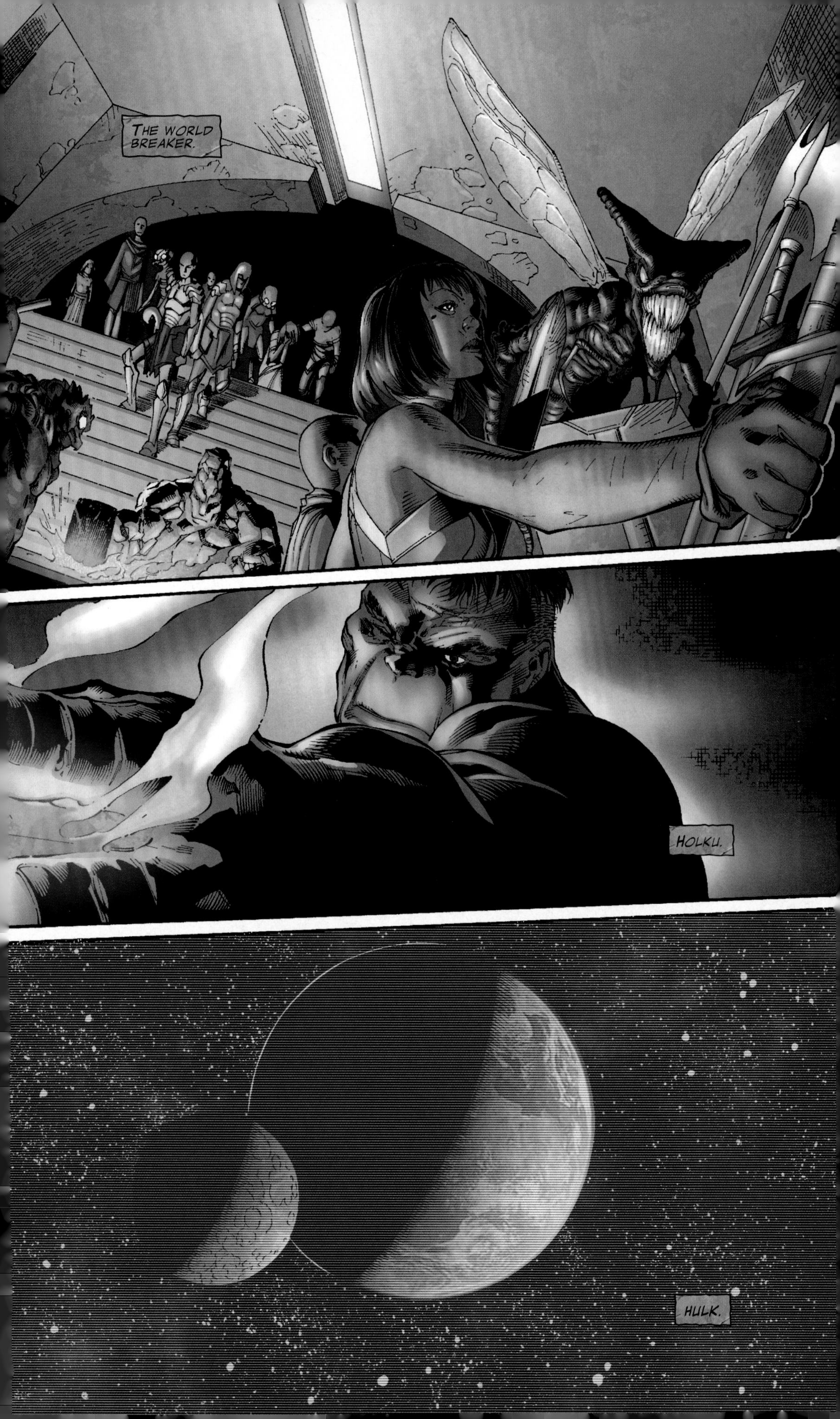
THE WORLD BREAKER.
HOLKU.
HULK.

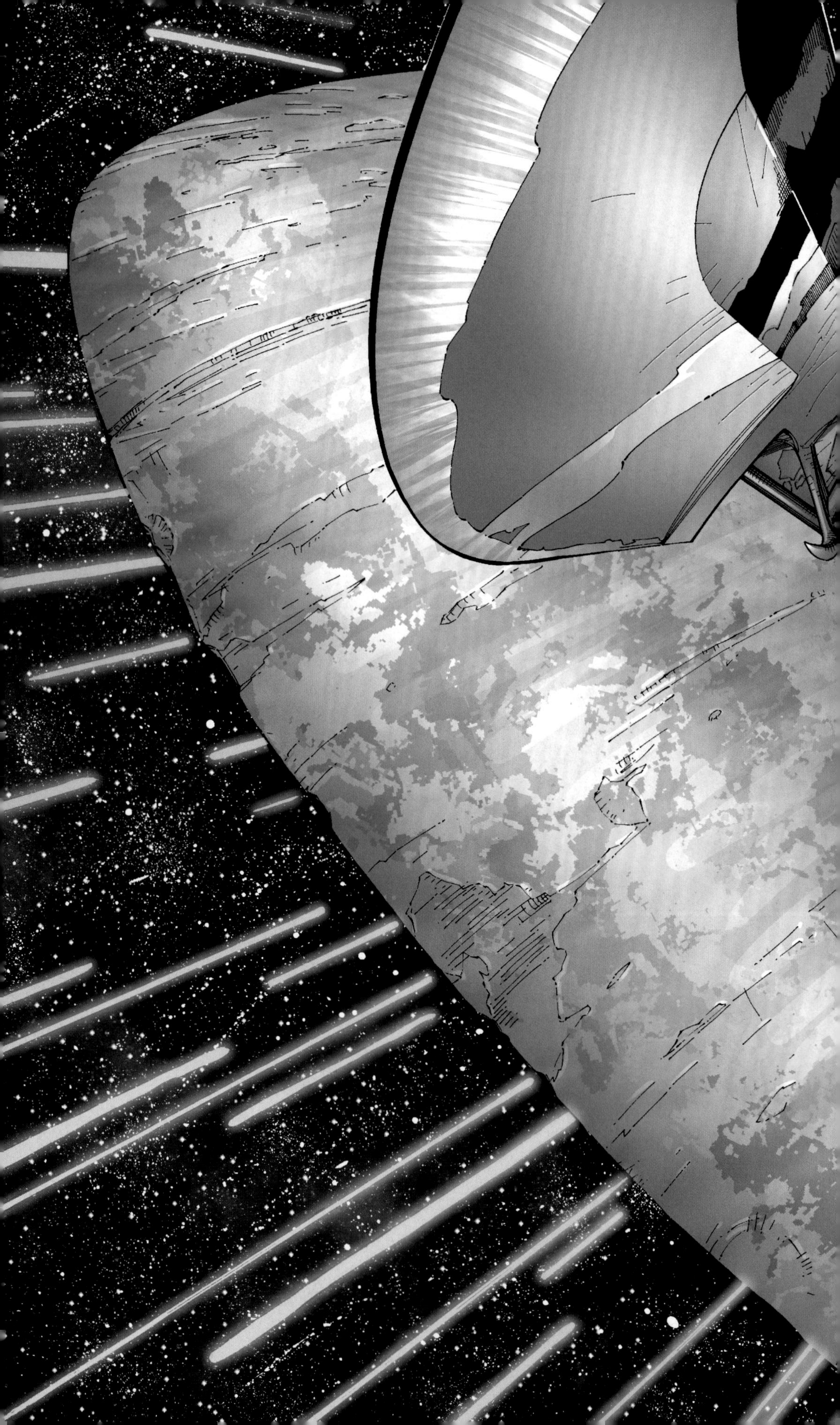

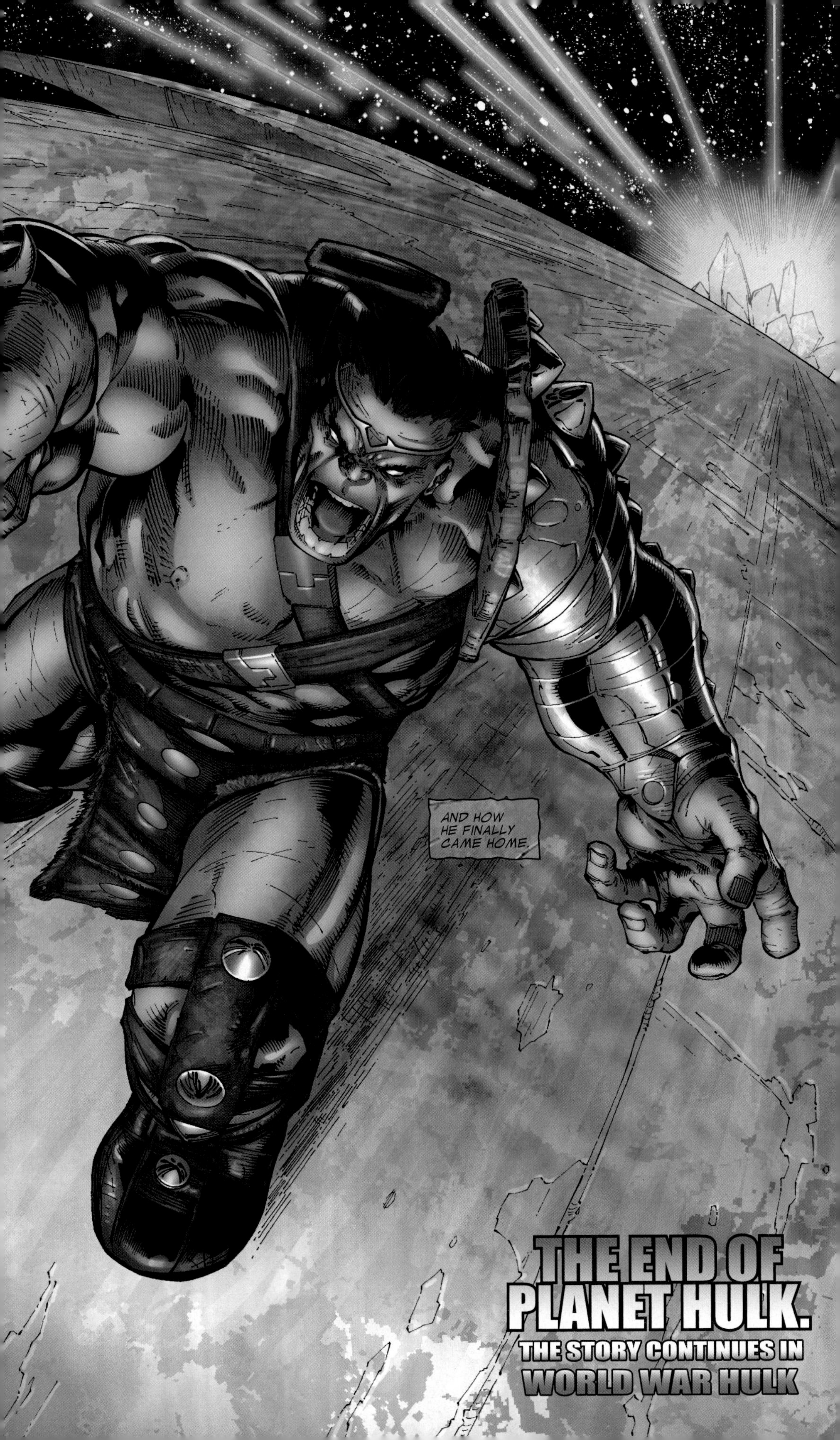
AND HOW HE FINALLY CAME HOME.
THE END OF PLANET HULK.
THE STORY CONTINUES IN WORLD WAR HULK

AMAZING FANTASY # 15

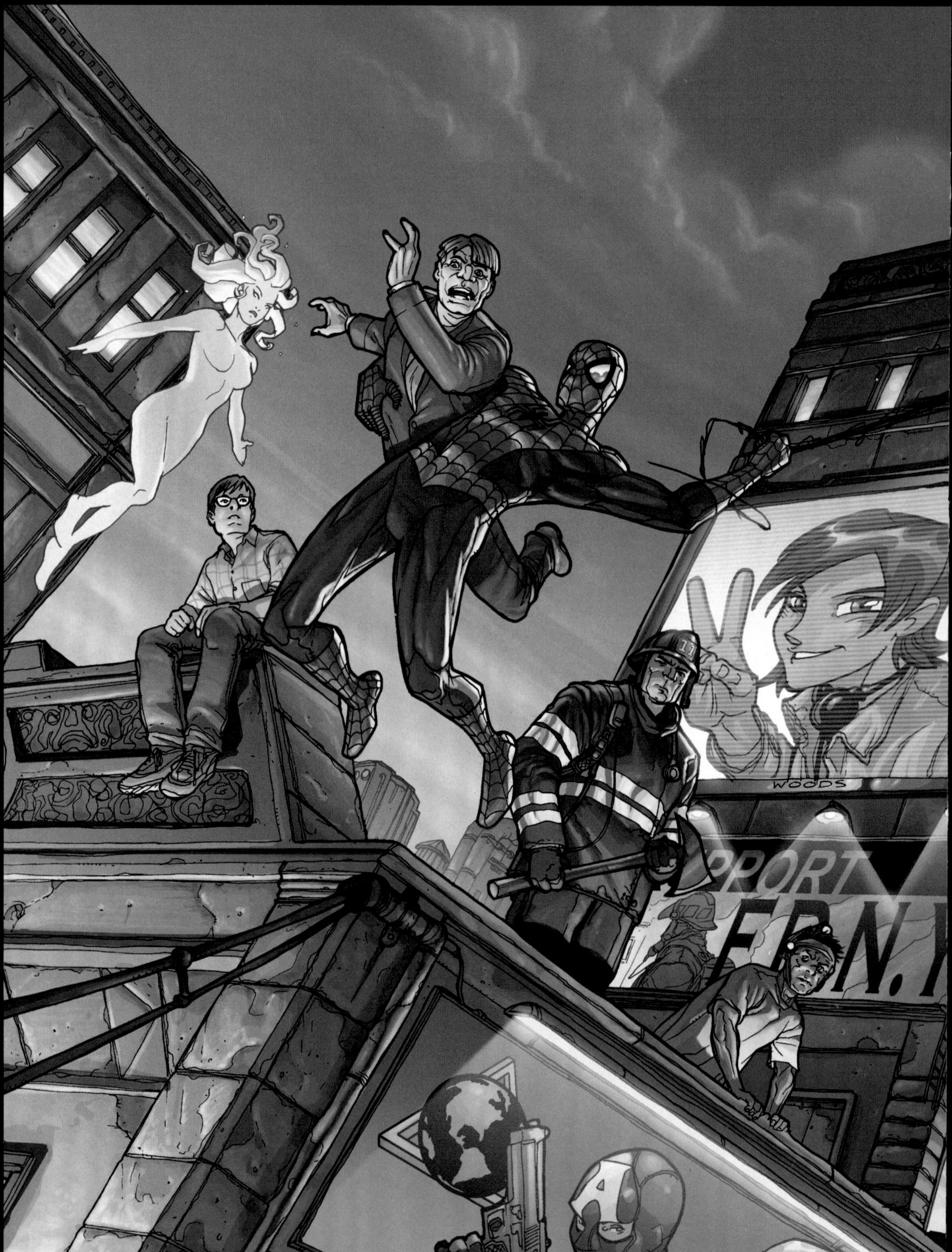
WOODS

JUST TELL US WHERE YOU ARE, AMADEUS. WE CAN BE ANYWHERE IN THE COUNTRY WITHIN AN HOUR.

MASTERMIND EXCELLO

WHY DON'T YOU MEET ME AT MY HOUSE? NO, WAIT, THAT'S NOT GONNA WORK... BECAUSE YOU *BLEW IT UP.*

WE DIDN'T DO THAT, AMADEUS. THAT WAS THE ENEMY.

THE "ENEMY"? HOW STUPID DO YOU THINK I AM?

NOT VERY. YOU WERE SMART ENOUGH TO GET ON OUR RADAR. SMART ENOUGH TO SLIP THROUGH OUR PERIMETER. SMART ENOUGH TO CALL ME ON A LINE WHICH THREE ROOMFULS OF OUR TOP PEOPLE CAN'T SEEM TO TRACE.

TO BE PRECISE, WE THINK YOU'RE THE SEVENTH SMARTEST PERSON ON THE PLANET.

WHICH IS WHY WE WANT YOU TO WORK FOR *US.* AND WHY THE *ENEMY* WANTS YOU DEAD.

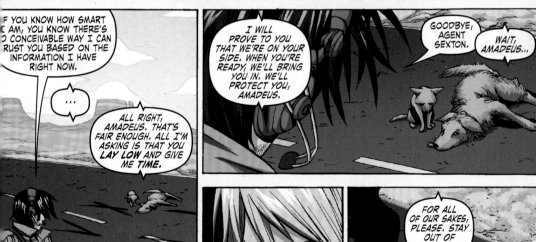

IF YOU KNOW HOW SMART I AM, YOU KNOW THERE'S NO CONCEIVABLE WAY I CAN TRUST YOU BASED ON THE INFORMATION I HAVE RIGHT NOW.

...

ALL RIGHT, AMADEUS. THAT'S FAIR ENOUGH. ALL I'M ASKING IS THAT YOU *LAY LOW* AND GIVE ME *TIME.*

I WILL PROVE TO YOU THAT WE'RE ON YOUR SIDE. WHEN YOU'RE READY, WE'LL BRING YOU IN. WE'LL PROTECT YOU, AMADEUS.

GOODBYE, AGENT SEXTON.

WAIT, AMADEUS...

IF THEY CATCH YOU, THEY'LL USE YOU TO DESTROY THE WORLD AS WE KNOW IT.

FOR ALL OF OUR SAKES, PLEASE. STAY OUT OF TROUBLE.

STAY OUT OF TROUBLE.

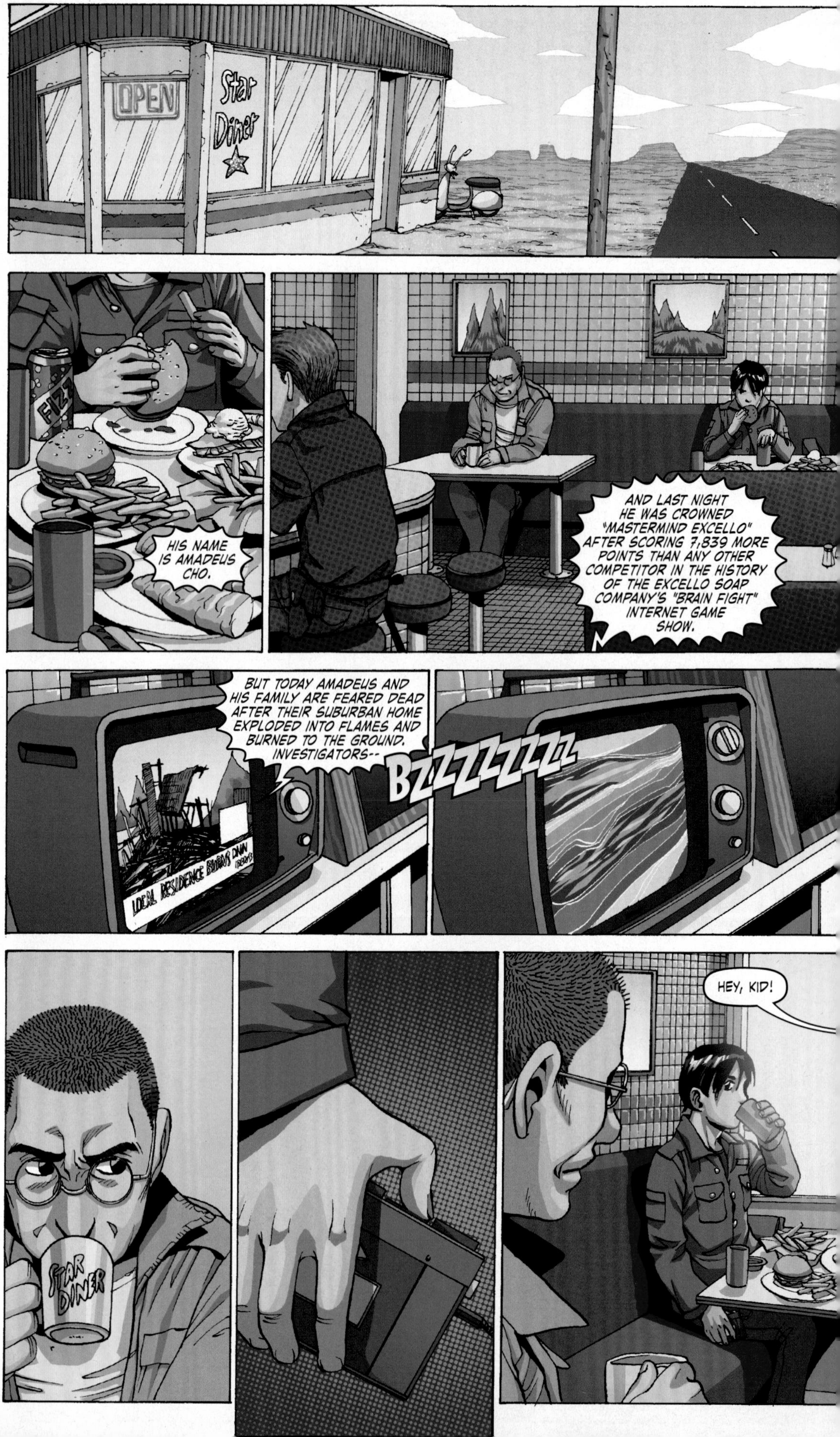
OPEN
Star Diner
FIZZ
HIS NAME IS AMADEUS CHO.
AND LAST NIGHT HE WAS CROWNED "MASTERMIND EXCELLO" AFTER SCORING 7,839 MORE POINTS THAN ANY OTHER COMPETITOR IN THE HISTORY OF THE EXCELLO SOAP COMPANY'S "BRAIN FIGHT" INTERNET GAME SHOW.
BUT TODAY AMADEUS AND HIS FAMILY ARE FEARED DEAD AFTER THEIR SUBURBAN HOME EXPLODED INTO FLAMES AND BURNED TO THE GROUND. INVESTIGATORS--
LOCAL RESIDENCE BURNS DOWN
BZZZZZZZZz
STAR DINER
HEY, KID!

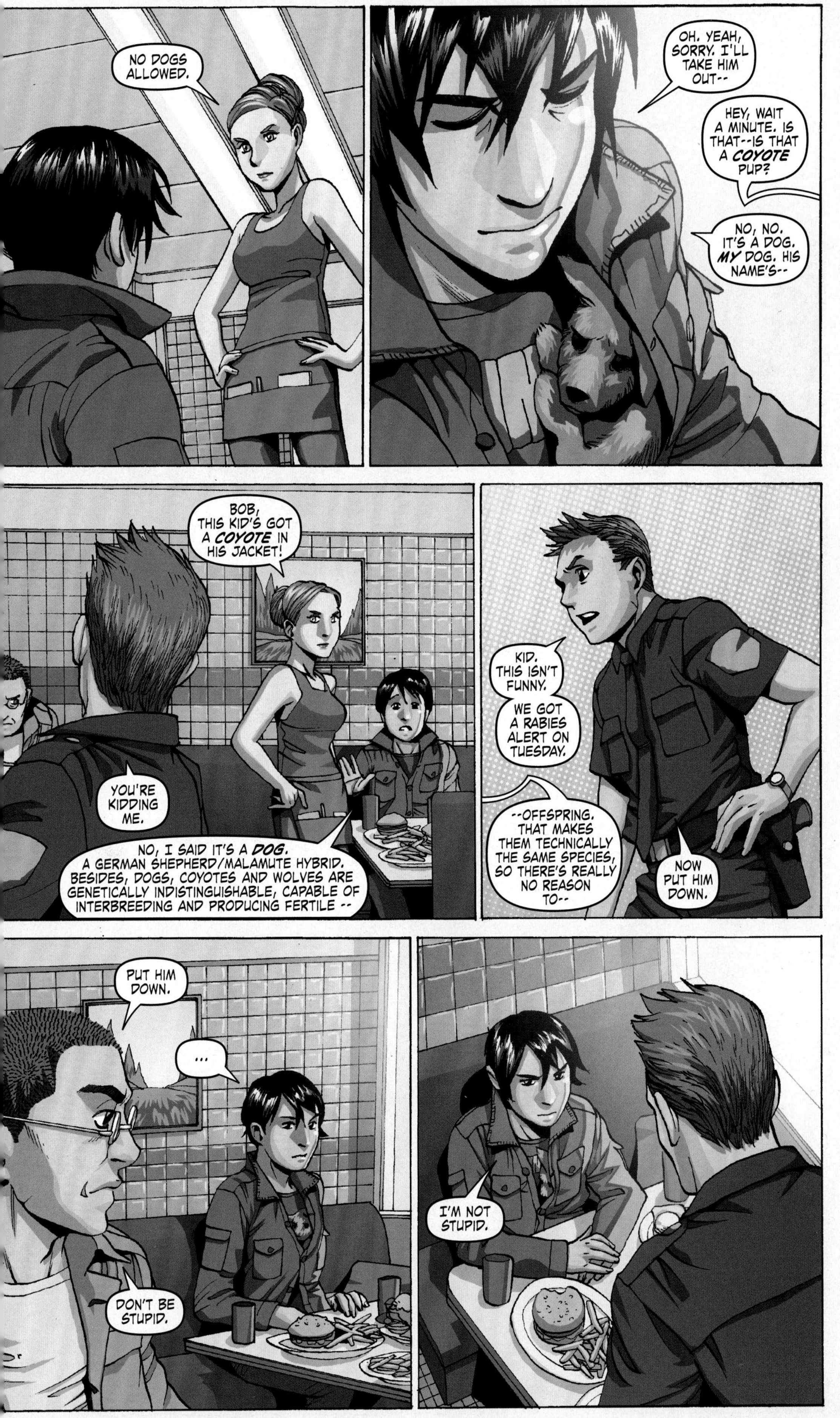
NO DOGS ALLOWED.
OH. YEAH, SORRY. I'LL TAKE HIM OUT--
HEY, WAIT A MINUTE. IS THAT--IS THAT A COYOTE PUP?
NO, NO. IT'S A DOG. MY DOG. HIS NAME'S--
BOB, THIS KID'S GOT A COYOTE IN HIS JACKET!
YOU'RE KIDDING ME.
NO, I SAID IT'S A DOG. A GERMAN SHEPHERD/MALAMUTE HYBRID. BESIDES, DOGS, COYOTES AND WOLVES ARE GENETICALLY INDISTINGUISHABLE, CAPABLE OF INTERBREEDING AND PRODUCING FERTILE --
KID. THIS ISN'T FUNNY.
WE GOT A RABIES ALERT ON TUESDAY.
--OFFSPRING. THAT MAKES THEM TECHNICALLY THE SAME SPECIES, SO THERE'S REALLY NO REASON TO--
NOW PUT HIM DOWN.
PUT HIM DOWN.
...
DON'T BE STUPID.
I'M NOT STUPID.

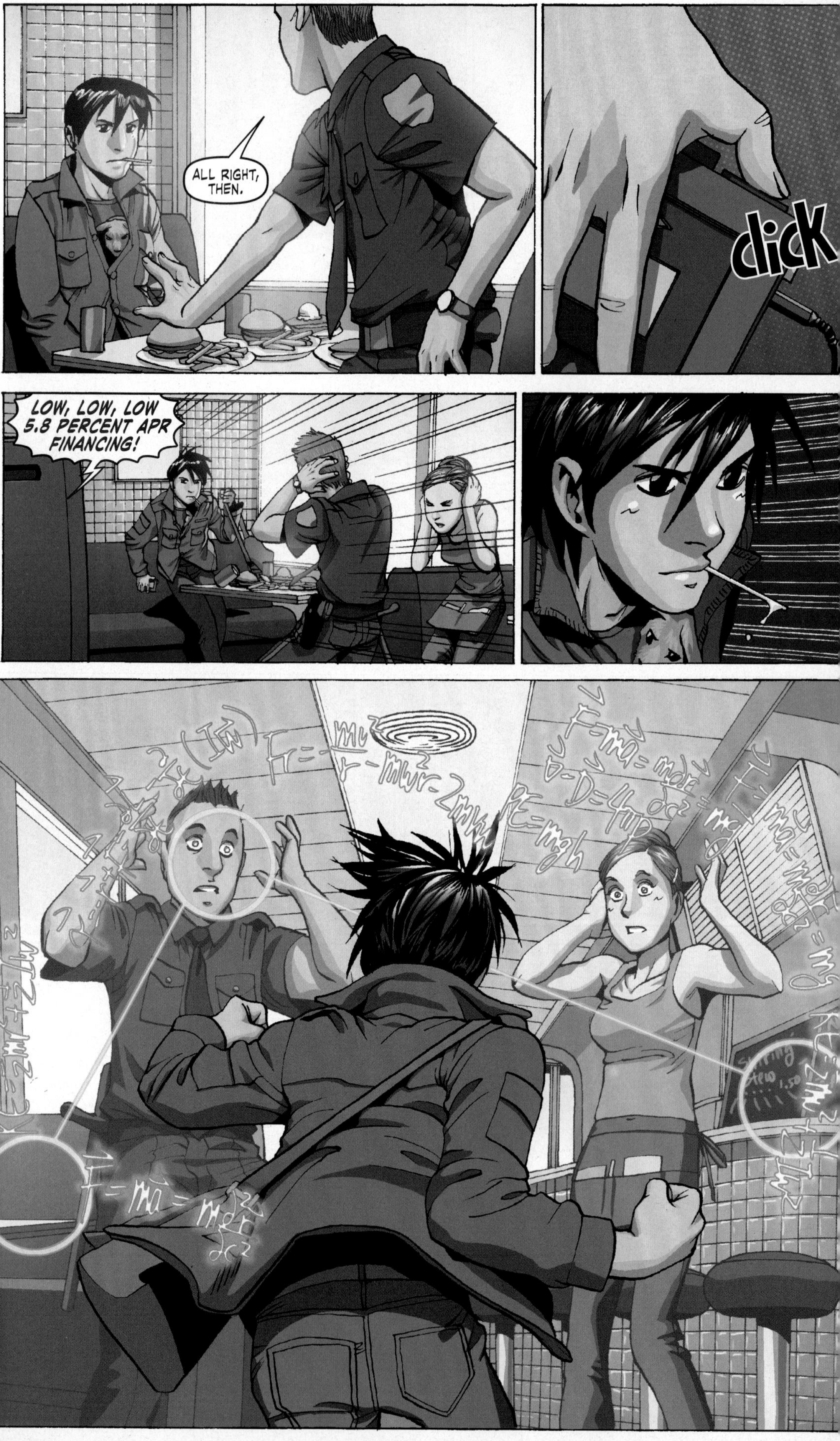
ALL RIGHT, THEN.
click
LOW, LOW, LOW 5.8 PERCENT APR FINANCING!

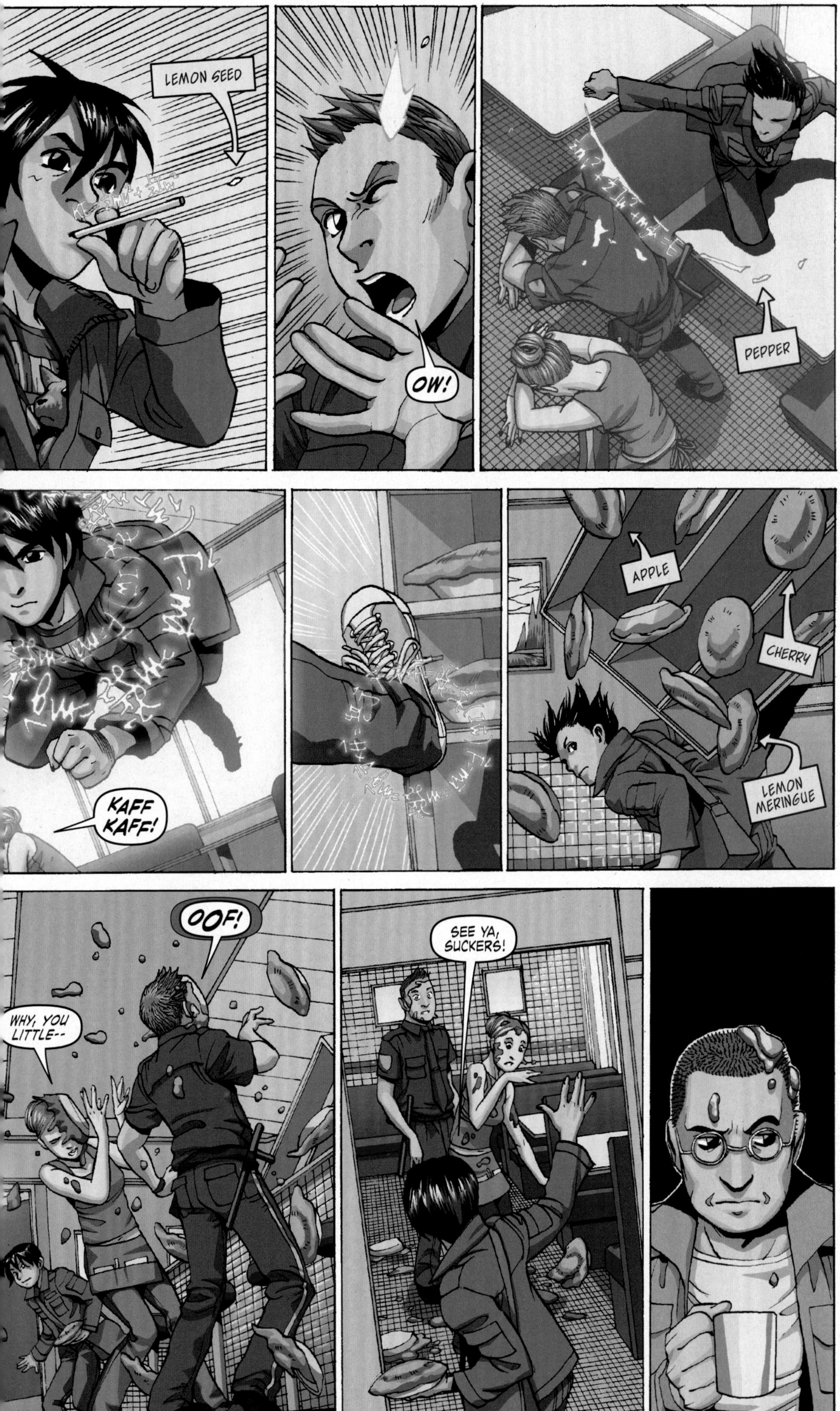

LEMON SEED
OW!
PEPPER
KAFF KAFF!
APPLE
CHERRY
LEMON MERINGUE
OOF!
WHY, YOU LITTLE--
SEE YA, SUCKERS!

STAR DINER

YEAH, EXACTLY, A SKINNY ASIAN KID...

... JUST LIKE ON THE TEE VEE.

THAT'S THE LOCAL POLICE BAND. SHOULD BE CLOSE--

GOT HIM.

UH OH...

LASER SIGHT.

REARVIEW MIRROR

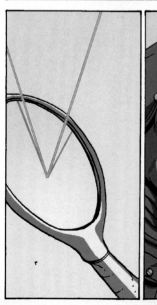

WHA--

PANICCIA 135mm M72 PORTABLE WARHEAD

GAH!

AW, MAN...

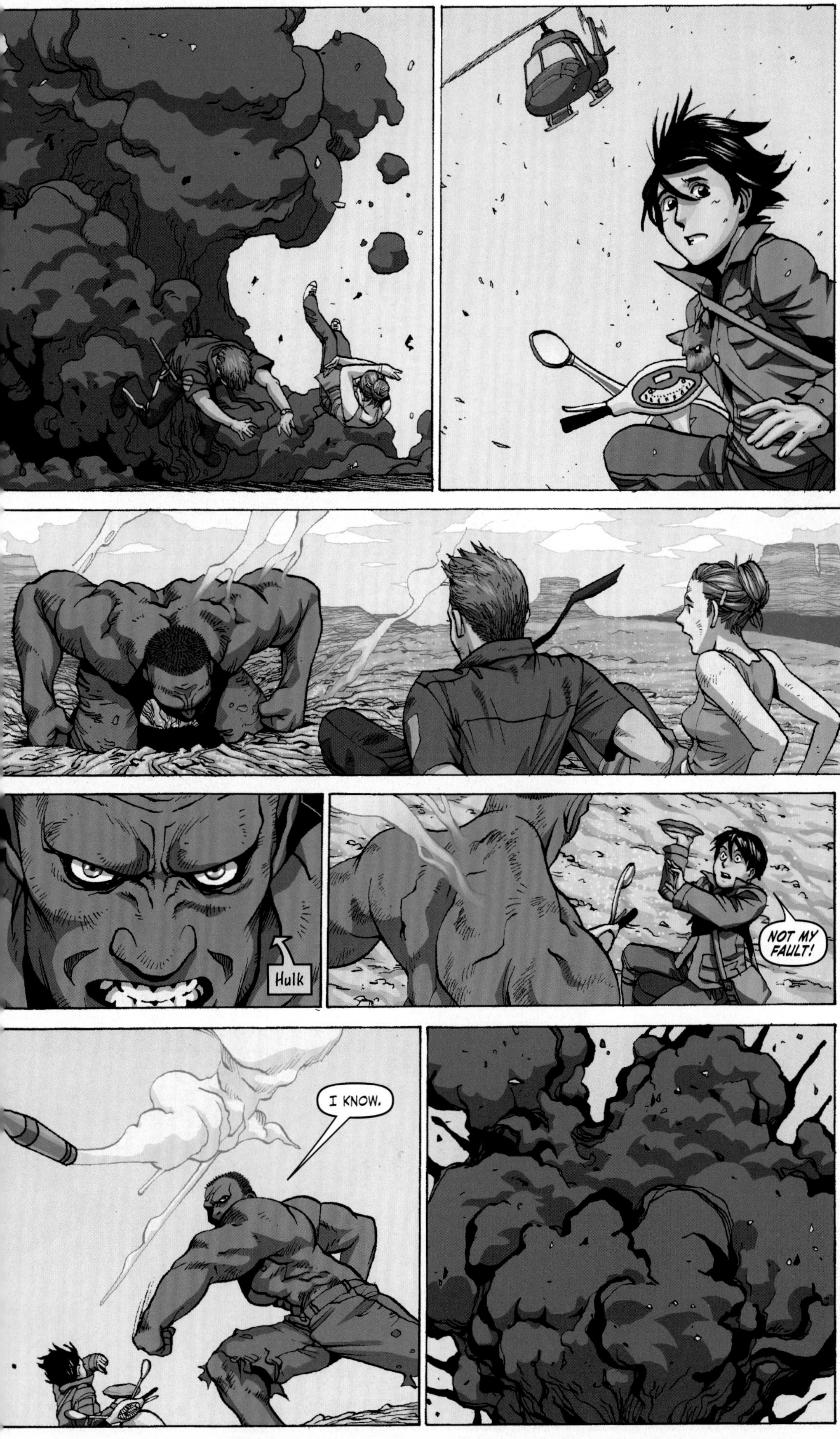
Hulk
NOT MY FAULT!
I KNOW.

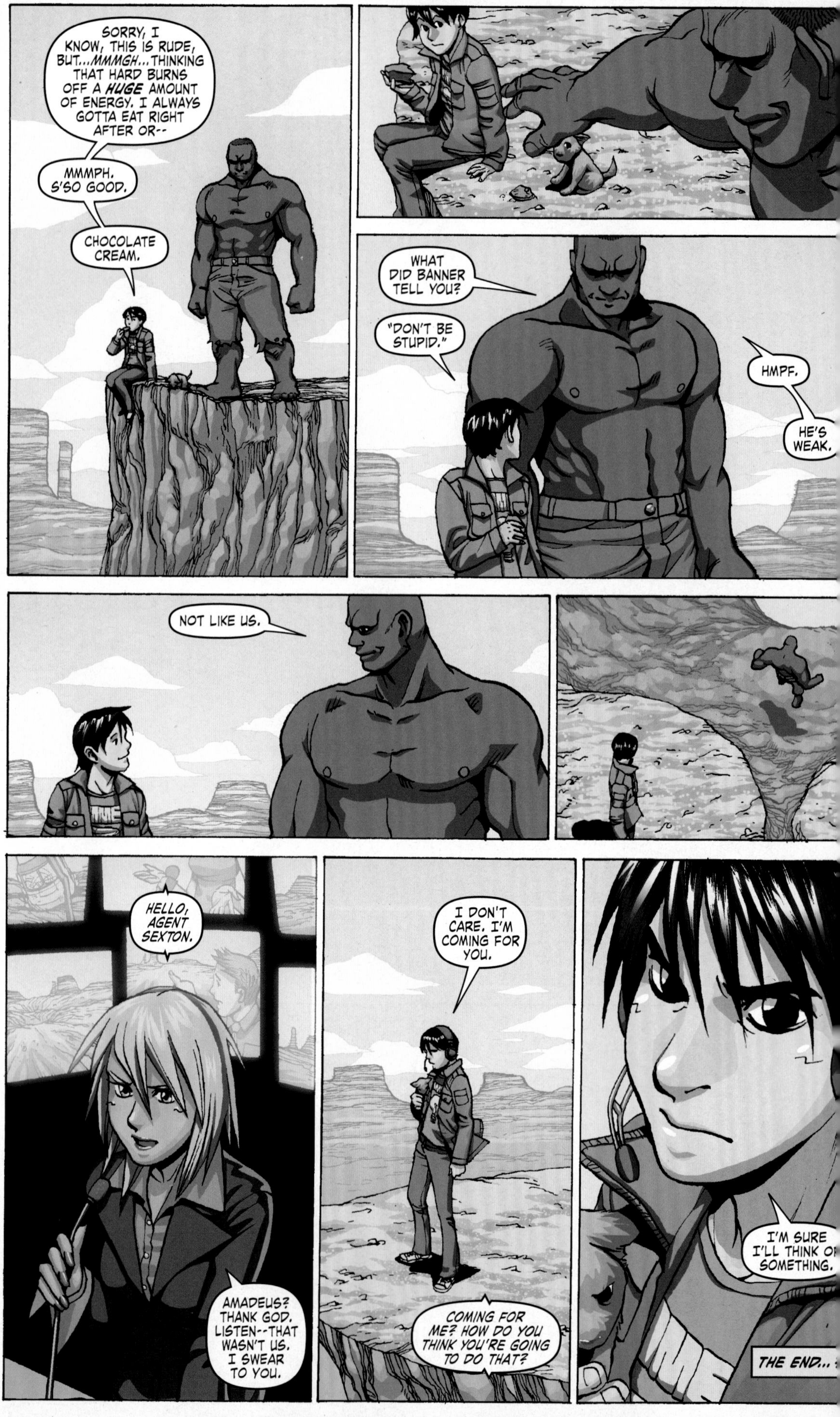
SORRY, I KNOW, THIS IS RUDE, BUT...MMMGH...THINKING THAT HARD BURNS OFF A HUGE AMOUNT OF ENERGY. I ALWAYS GOTTA EAT RIGHT AFTER OR--
MMMPH. S'SO GOOD.
CHOCOLATE CREAM.
WHAT DID BANNER TELL YOU?
"DON'T BE STUPID."
HMPF.
HE'S WEAK.
NOT LIKE US.
HELLO, AGENT SEXTON.
AMADEUS? THANK GOD. LISTEN--THAT WASN'T US. I SWEAR TO YOU.
I DON'T CARE. I'M COMING FOR YOU.
COMING FOR ME? HOW DO YOU THINK YOU'RE GOING TO DO THAT?
I'M SURE I'LL THINK OF SOMETHING.
THE END...

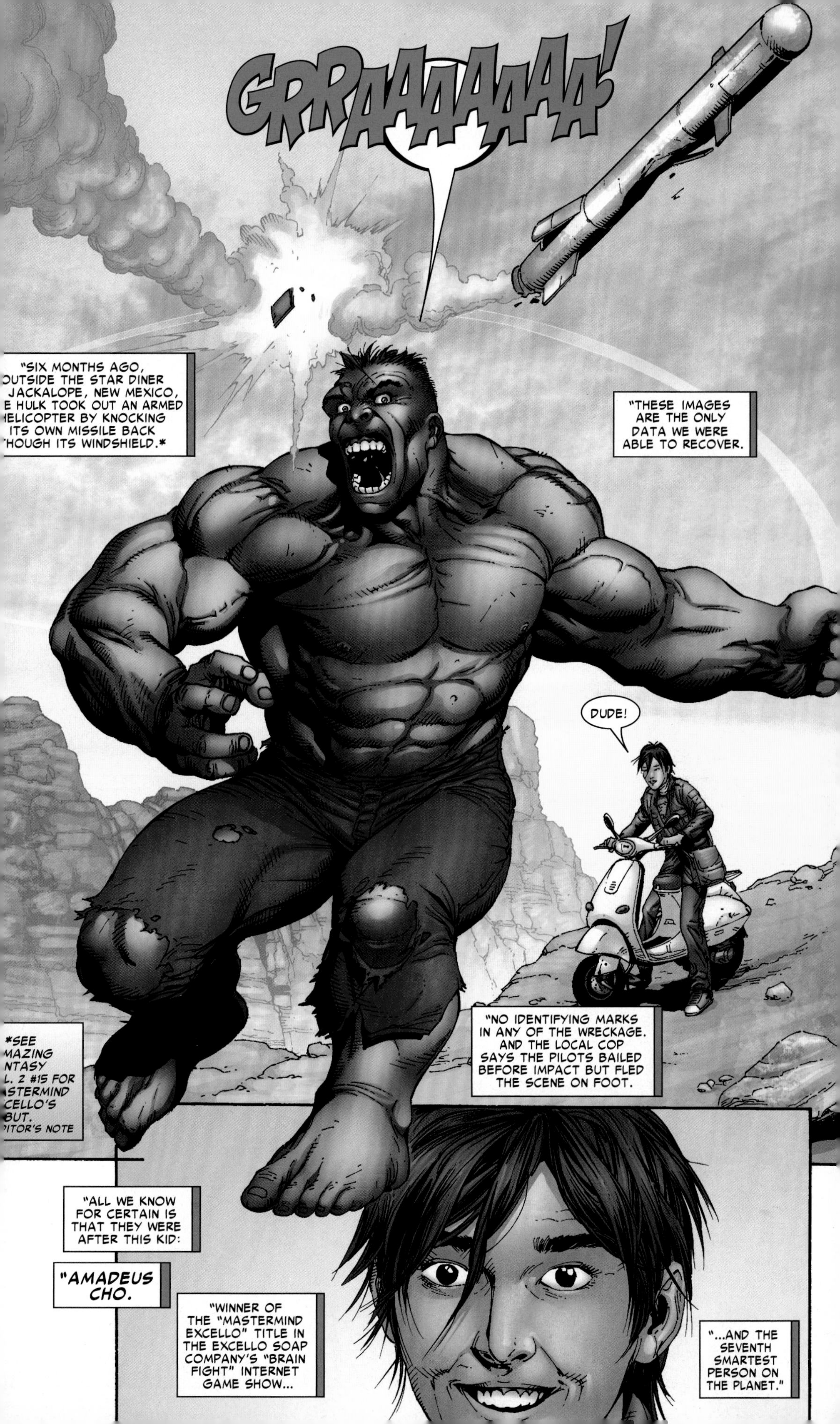
GRRAAAAAAA!
"SIX MONTHS AGO, OUTSIDE THE STAR DINER JACKALOPE, NEW MEXICO, E HULK TOOK OUT AN ARMED HELICOPTER BY KNOCKING ITS OWN MISSILE BACK THOUGH ITS WINDSHIELD.*
"THESE IMAGES ARE THE ONLY DATA WE WERE ABLE TO RECOVER.
DUDE!
"NO IDENTIFYING MARKS IN ANY OF THE WRECKAGE. AND THE LOCAL COP SAYS THE PILOTS BAILED BEFORE IMPACT BUT FLED THE SCENE ON FOOT.
*SEE MAZING NTASY L. 2 #15 FOR STERMIND CELLO'S BUT. DITOR'S NOTE
"ALL WE KNOW FOR CERTAIN IS THAT THEY WERE AFTER THIS KID:
"AMADEUS CHO.
"WINNER OF THE "MASTERMIND EXCELLO" TITLE IN THE EXCELLO SOAP COMPANY'S "BRAIN FIGHT" INTERNET GAME SHOW...
"...AND THE SEVENTH SMARTEST PERSON ON THE PLANET."

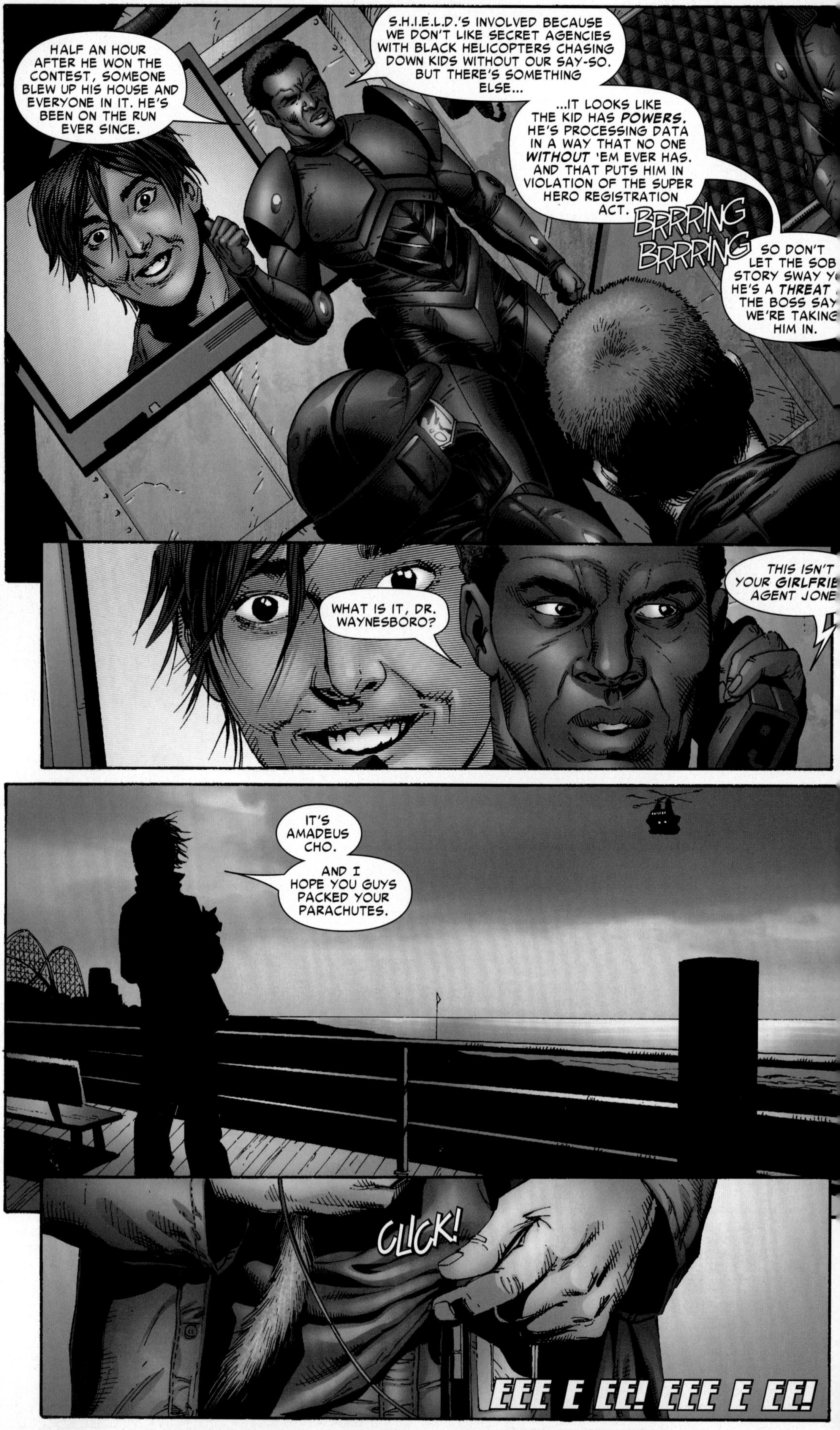
HALF AN HOUR AFTER HE WON THE CONTEST, SOMEONE BLEW UP HIS HOUSE AND EVERYONE IN IT. HE'S BEEN ON THE RUN EVER SINCE.
S.H.I.E.L.D.'S INVOLVED BECAUSE WE DON'T LIKE SECRET AGENCIES WITH BLACK HELICOPTERS CHASING DOWN KIDS WITHOUT OUR SAY-SO. BUT THERE'S SOMETHING ELSE...
...IT LOOKS LIKE THE KID HAS POWERS. HE'S PROCESSING DATA IN A WAY THAT NO ONE WITHOUT 'EM EVER HAS. AND THAT PUTS HIM IN VIOLATION OF THE SUPER HERO REGISTRATION ACT.
BRRRING BRRRING
SO DON'T LET THE SOB STORY SWAY Y HE'S A THREAT THE BOSS SAY WE'RE TAKING HIM IN.
WHAT IS IT, DR. WAYNESBORO?
THIS ISN'T YOUR GIRLFRIE AGENT JONE
IT'S AMADEUS CHO.
AND I HOPE YOU GUYS PACKED YOUR PARACHUTES.
CLICK!
EEE E EE! EEE E EE!

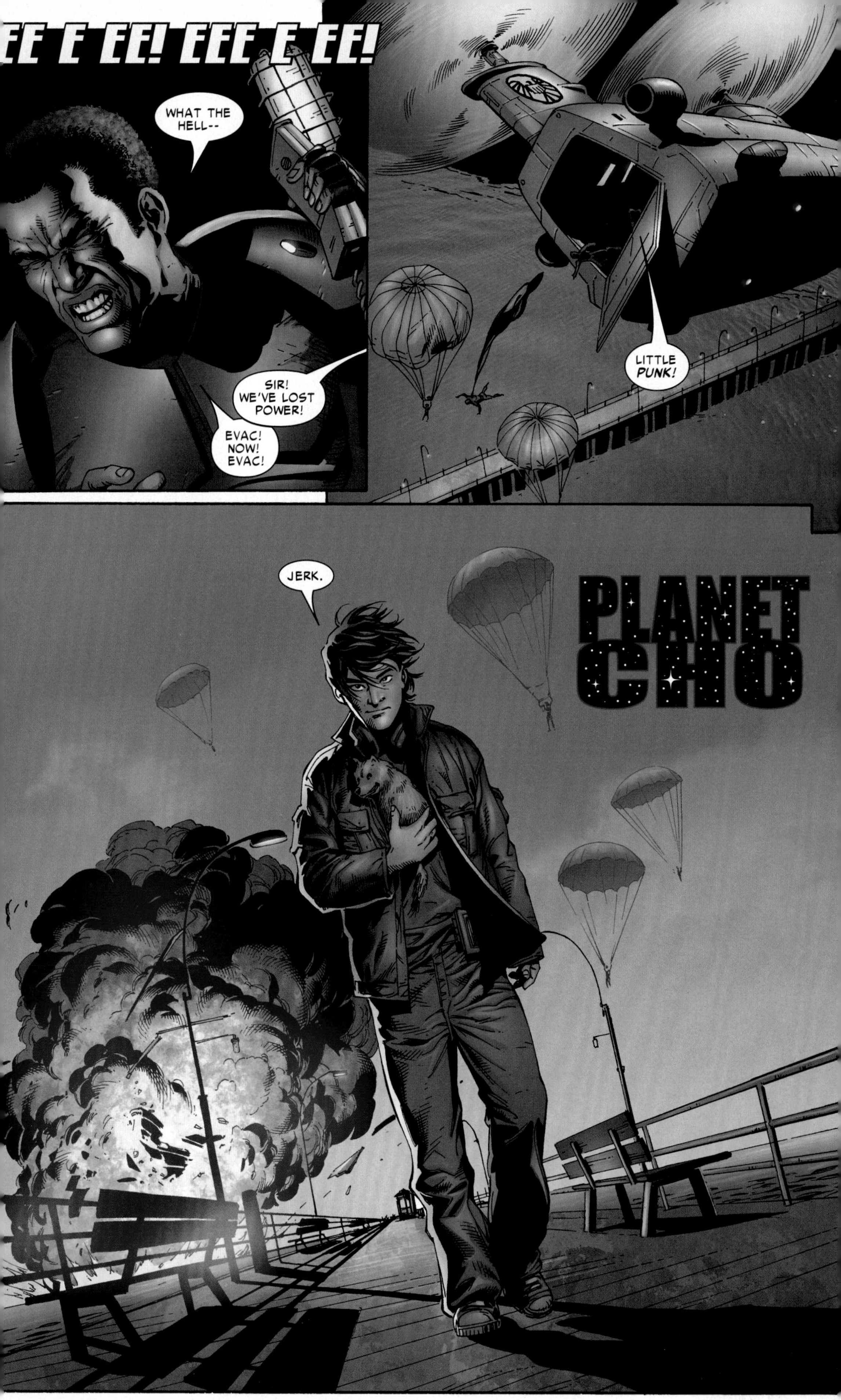

EE E EE! EEE E EE!
WHAT THE HELL--
SIR! WE'VE LOST POWER!
EVAC! NOW! EVAC!
LITTLE PUNK!
JERK.
PLANET CHO

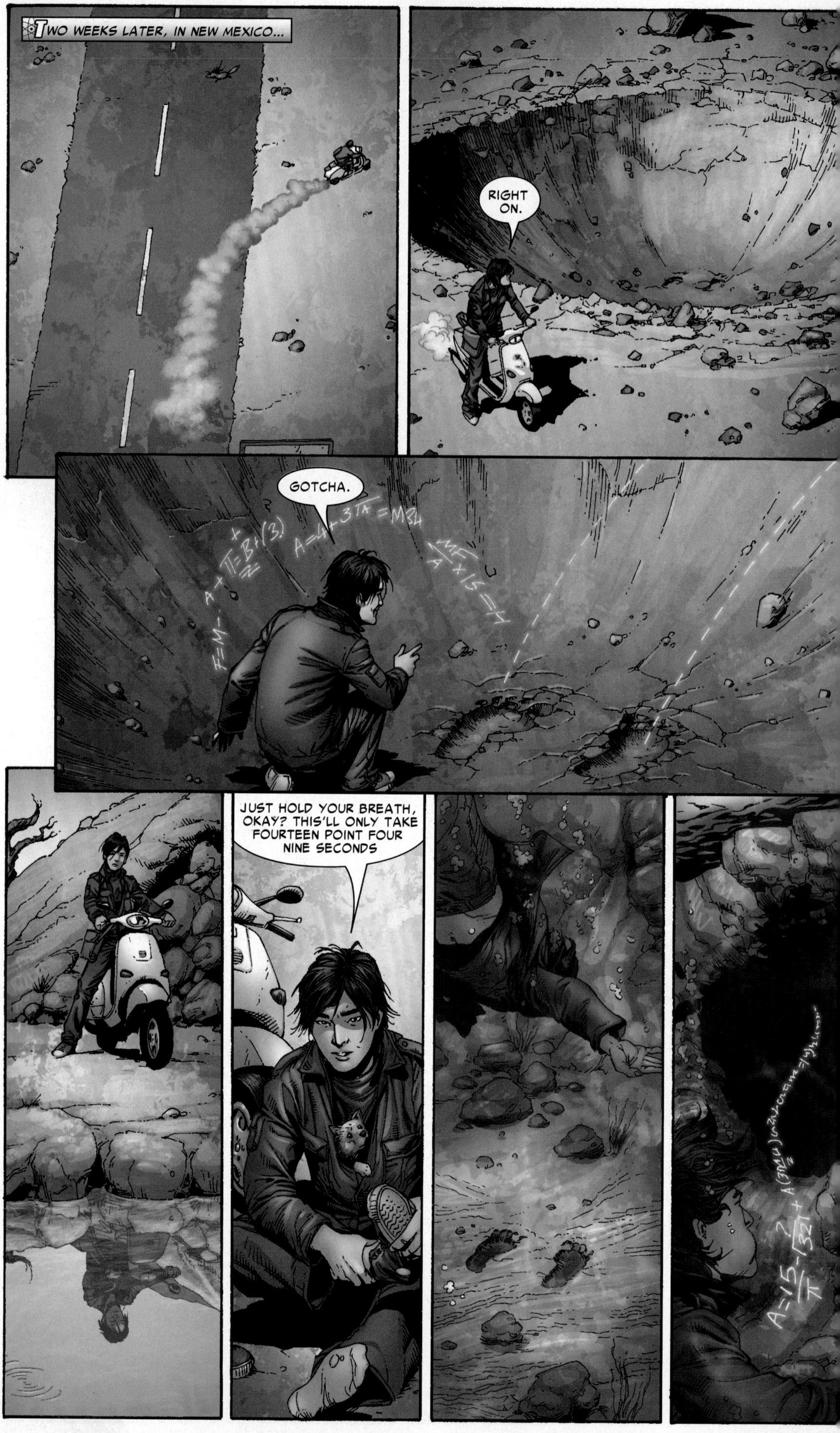
TWO WEEKS LATER, IN NEW MEXICO...
RIGHT ON.
GOTCHA.
JUST HOLD YOUR BREATH, OKAY? THIS'LL ONLY TAKE FOURTEEN POINT FOUR NINE SECONDS

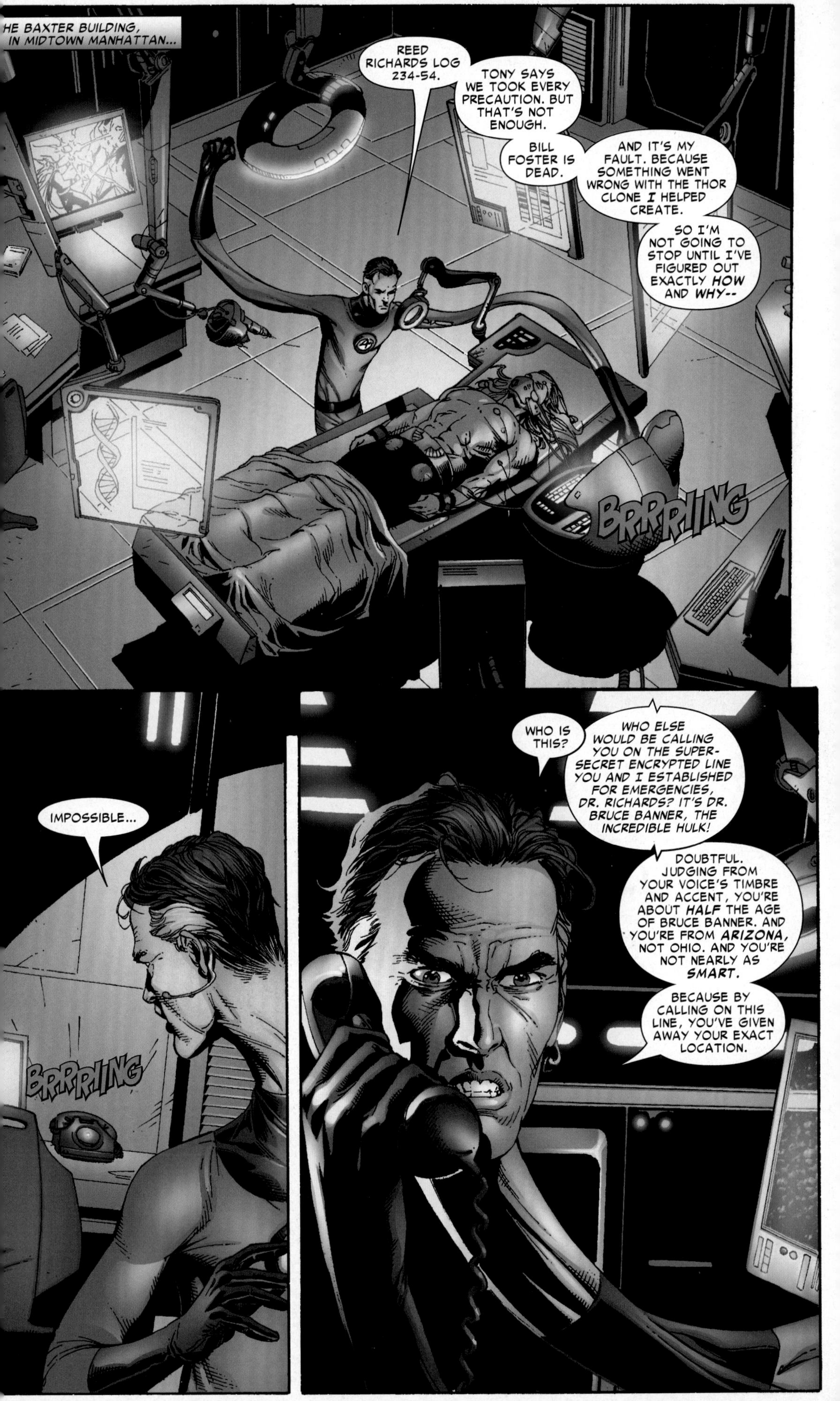
HE BAXTER BUILDING, IN MIDTOWN MANHATTAN...
REED RICHARDS LOG 234-54.
TONY SAYS WE TOOK EVERY PRECAUTION. BUT THAT'S NOT ENOUGH.
BILL FOSTER IS DEAD.
AND IT'S MY FAULT. BECAUSE SOMETHING WENT WRONG WITH THE THOR CLONE I HELPED CREATE.
SO I'M NOT GOING TO STOP UNTIL I'VE FIGURED OUT EXACTLY HOW AND WHY--
BRRRIIING
IMPOSSIBLE...
BRRRIIING
WHO IS THIS?
WHO ELSE WOULD BE CALLING YOU ON THE SUPER-SECRET ENCRYPTED LINE YOU AND I ESTABLISHED FOR EMERGENCIES, DR. RICHARDS? IT'S DR. BRUCE BANNER, THE INCREDIBLE HULK!
DOUBTFUL. JUDGING FROM YOUR VOICE'S TIMBRE AND ACCENT, YOU'RE ABOUT HALF THE AGE OF BRUCE BANNER. AND YOU'RE FROM ARIZONA, NOT OHIO. AND YOU'RE NOT NEARLY AS SMART.
BECAUSE BY CALLING ON THIS LINE, YOU'VE GIVEN AWAY YOUR EXACT LOCATION.

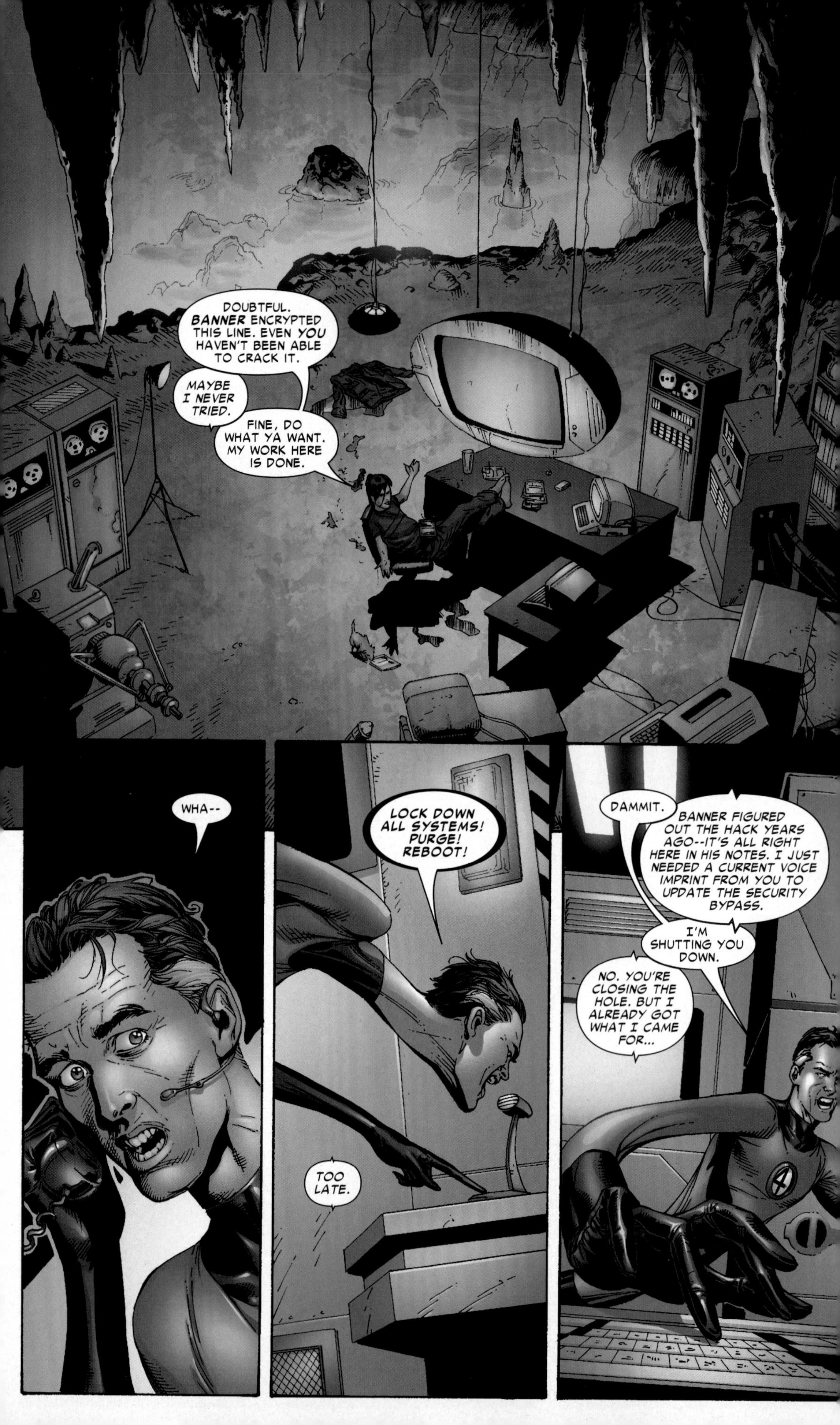
DOUBTFUL. BANNER ENCRYPTED THIS LINE. EVEN YOU HAVEN'T BEEN ABLE TO CRACK IT.
MAYBE I NEVER TRIED.
FINE, DO WHAT YA WANT. MY WORK HERE IS DONE.
WHA--
LOCK DOWN ALL SYSTEMS! PURGE! REBOOT!
TOO LATE.
DAMMIT.
BANNER FIGURED OUT THE HACK YEARS AGO--IT'S ALL RIGHT HERE IN HIS NOTES. I JUST NEEDED A CURRENT VOICE IMPRINT FROM YOU TO UPDATE THE SECURITY BYPASS.
I'M SHUTTING YOU DOWN.
NO. YOU'RE CLOSING THE HOLE. BUT I ALREADY GOT WHAT I CAME FOR...

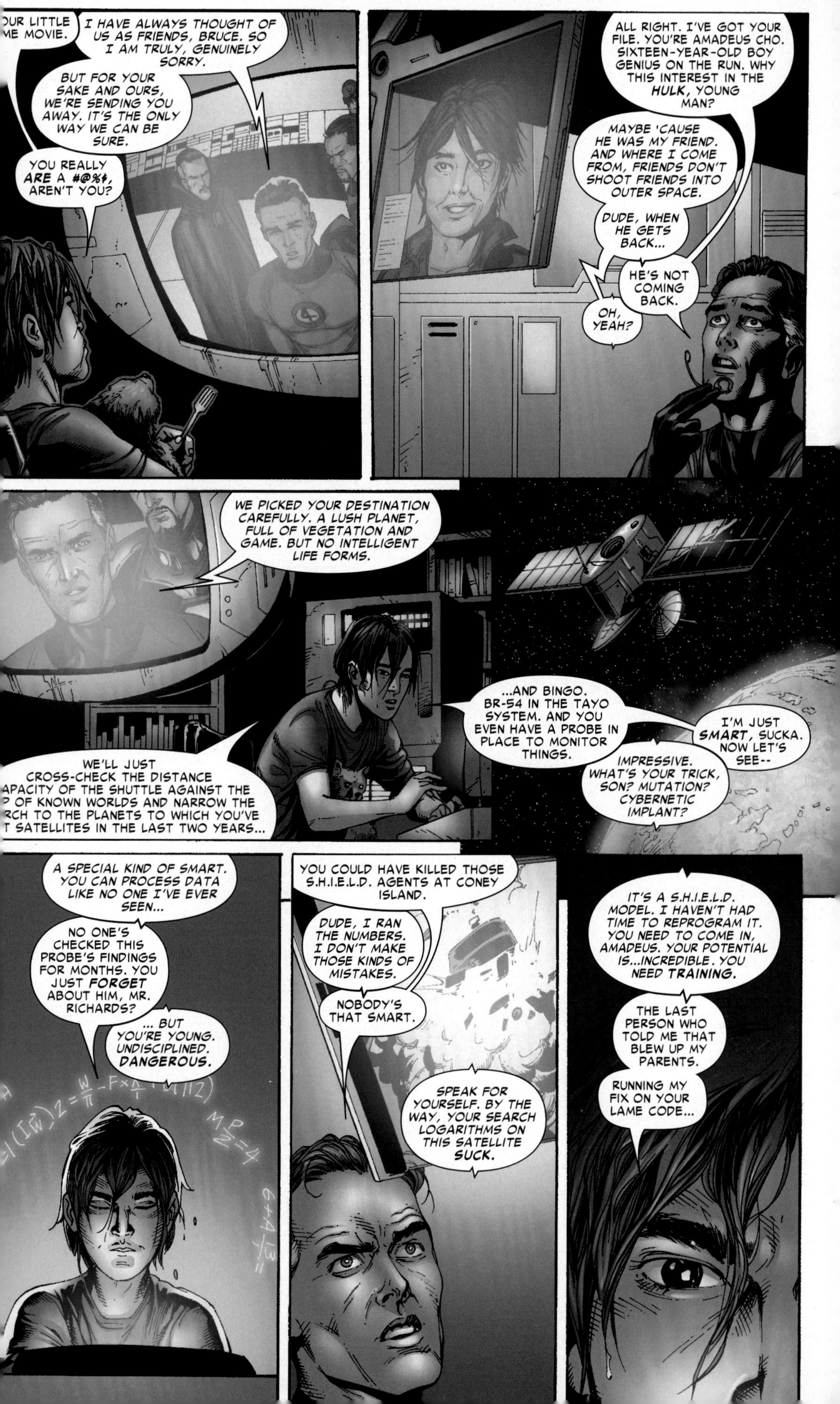

OUR LITTLE
ME MOVIE.
I HAVE ALWAYS THOUGHT OF US AS FRIENDS, BRUCE. SO I AM TRULY, GENUINELY SORRY.
BUT FOR YOUR SAKE AND OURS, WE'RE SENDING YOU AWAY. IT'S THE ONLY WAY WE CAN BE SURE.
YOU REALLY ARE A #@%¢, AREN'T YOU?
ALL RIGHT. I'VE GOT YOUR FILE. YOU'RE AMADEUS CHO. SIXTEEN-YEAR-OLD BOY GENIUS ON THE RUN. WHY THIS INTEREST IN THE HULK, YOUNG MAN?
MAYBE 'CAUSE HE WAS MY FRIEND. AND WHERE I COME FROM, FRIENDS DON'T SHOOT FRIENDS INTO OUTER SPACE.
DUDE, WHEN HE GETS BACK...
HE'S NOT COMING BACK.
OH, YEAH?
WE PICKED YOUR DESTINATION CAREFULLY. A LUSH PLANET, FULL OF VEGETATION AND GAME. BUT NO INTELLIGENT LIFE FORMS.
WE'LL JUST CROSS-CHECK THE DISTANCE
APACITY OF THE SHUTTLE AGAINST THE
P OF KNOWN WORLDS AND NARROW THE
RCH TO THE PLANETS TO WHICH YOU'VE
T SATELLITES IN THE LAST TWO YEARS...
...AND BINGO. BR-54 IN THE TAYO SYSTEM. AND YOU EVEN HAVE A PROBE IN PLACE TO MONITOR THINGS.
IMPRESSIVE. WHAT'S YOUR TRICK, SON? MUTATION? CYBERNETIC IMPLANT?
I'M JUST SMART, SUCKA. NOW LET'S SEE--
A SPECIAL KIND OF SMART. YOU CAN PROCESS DATA LIKE NO ONE I'VE EVER SEEN...
NO ONE'S CHECKED THIS PROBE'S FINDINGS FOR MONTHS. YOU JUST FORGET ABOUT HIM, MR. RICHARDS?
... BUT YOU'RE YOUNG. UNDISCIPLINED. DANGEROUS.
YOU COULD HAVE KILLED THOSE S.H.I.E.L.D. AGENTS AT CONEY ISLAND.
DUDE, I RAN THE NUMBERS. I DON'T MAKE THOSE KINDS OF MISTAKES.
NOBODY'S THAT SMART.
SPEAK FOR YOURSELF. BY THE WAY, YOUR SEARCH LOGARITHMS ON THIS SATELLITE SUCK.
IT'S A S.H.I.E.L.D. MODEL. I HAVEN'T HAD TIME TO REPROGRAM IT. YOU NEED TO COME IN, AMADEUS. YOUR POTENTIAL IS...INCREDIBLE. YOU NEED TRAINING.
THE LAST PERSON WHO TOLD ME THAT BLEW UP MY PARENTS.
RUNNING MY FIX ON YOUR LAME CODE...

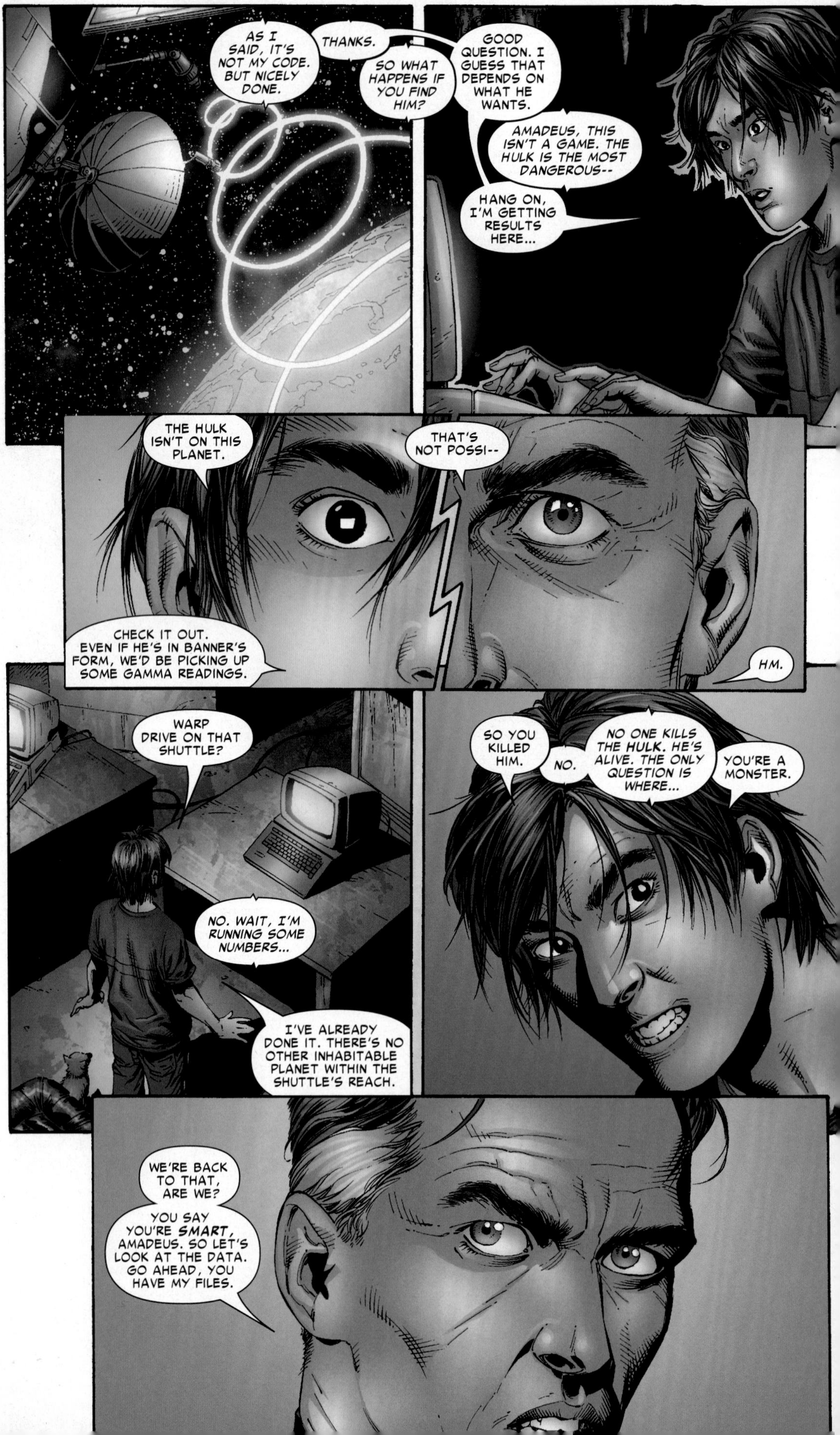
AS I SAID, IT'S NOT MY CODE. BUT NICELY DONE.
THANKS.
SO WHAT HAPPENS IF YOU FIND HIM?
GOOD QUESTION. I GUESS THAT DEPENDS ON WHAT HE WANTS.
AMADEUS, THIS ISN'T A GAME. THE HULK IS THE MOST DANGEROUS--
HANG ON, I'M GETTING RESULTS HERE...
THE HULK ISN'T ON THIS PLANET.
THAT'S NOT POSSI--
CHECK IT OUT. EVEN IF HE'S IN BANNER'S FORM, WE'D BE PICKING UP SOME GAMMA READINGS.
HM.
WARP DRIVE ON THAT SHUTTLE?
NO. WAIT, I'M RUNNING SOME NUMBERS...
I'VE ALREADY DONE IT. THERE'S NO OTHER INHABITABLE PLANET WITHIN THE SHUTTLE'S REACH.
SO YOU KILLED HIM.
NO.
NO ONE KILLS THE HULK. HE'S ALIVE. THE ONLY QUESTION IS WHERE...
YOU'RE A MONSTER.
WE'RE BACK TO THAT, ARE WE?
YOU SAY YOU'RE SMART, AMADEUS. SO LET'S LOOK AT THE DATA. GO AHEAD, YOU HAVE MY FILES.

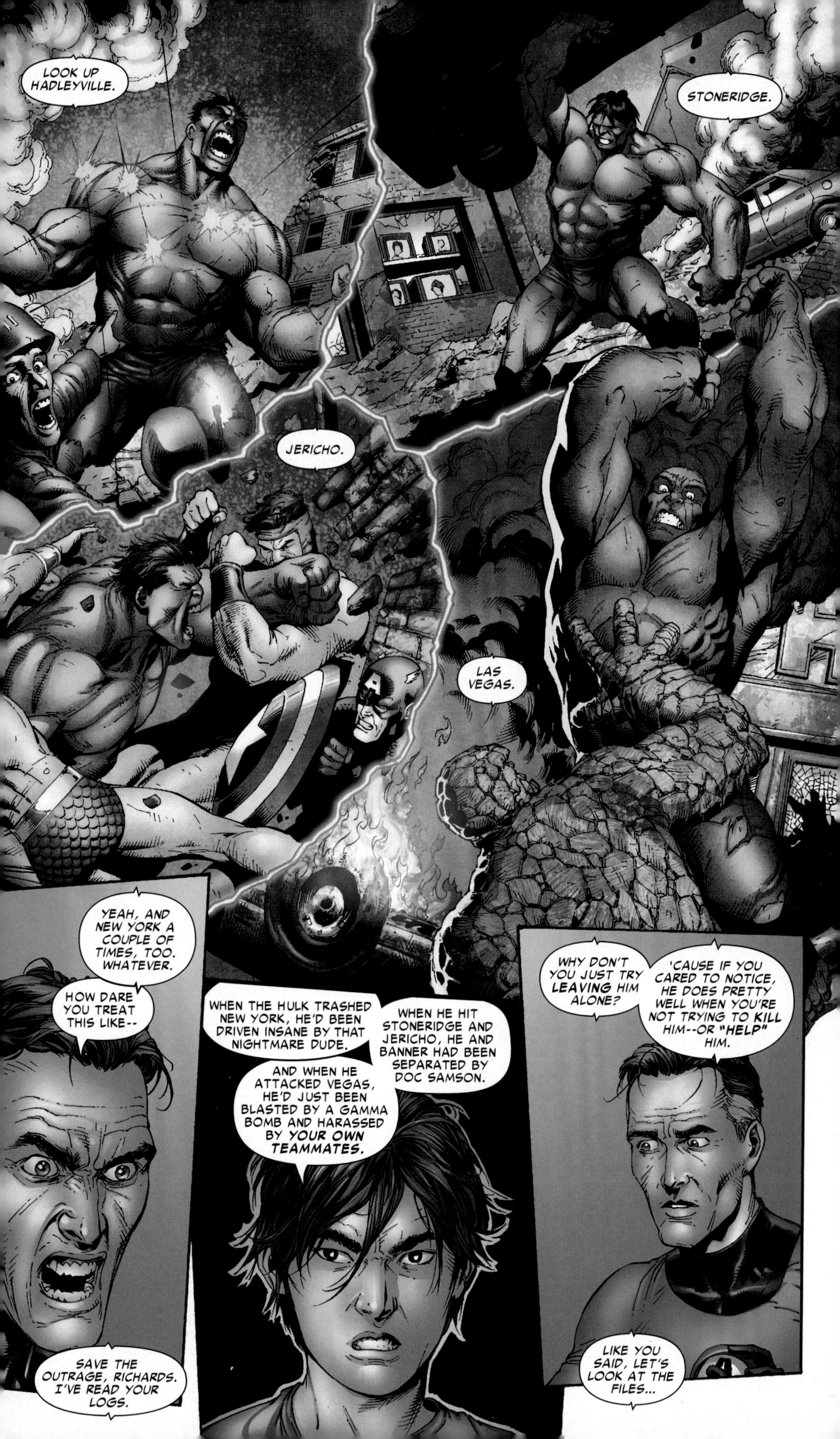
LOOK UP HADLEYVILLE.
STONERIDGE.
JERICHO.
LAS VEGAS.
YEAH, AND NEW YORK A COUPLE OF TIMES, TOO. WHATEVER.
HOW DARE YOU TREAT THIS LIKE--
WHEN THE HULK TRASHED NEW YORK, HE'D BEEN DRIVEN INSANE BY THAT NIGHTMARE DUDE.
WHEN HE HIT STONERIDGE AND JERICHO, HE AND BANNER HAD BEEN SEPARATED BY DOC SAMSON.
AND WHEN HE ATTACKED VEGAS, HE'D JUST BEEN BLASTED BY A GAMMA BOMB AND HARASSED BY *YOUR OWN TEAMMATES.*
WHY DON'T YOU JUST TRY **LEAVING** HIM ALONE?
'CAUSE IF YOU CARED TO NOTICE, HE DOES PRETTY WELL WHEN YOU'RE NOT TRYING TO **KILL** HIM--OR **"HELP"** HIM.
SAVE THE OUTRAGE, RICHARDS. I'VE READ YOUR LOGS.
LIKE YOU SAID, LET'S LOOK AT THE FILES...

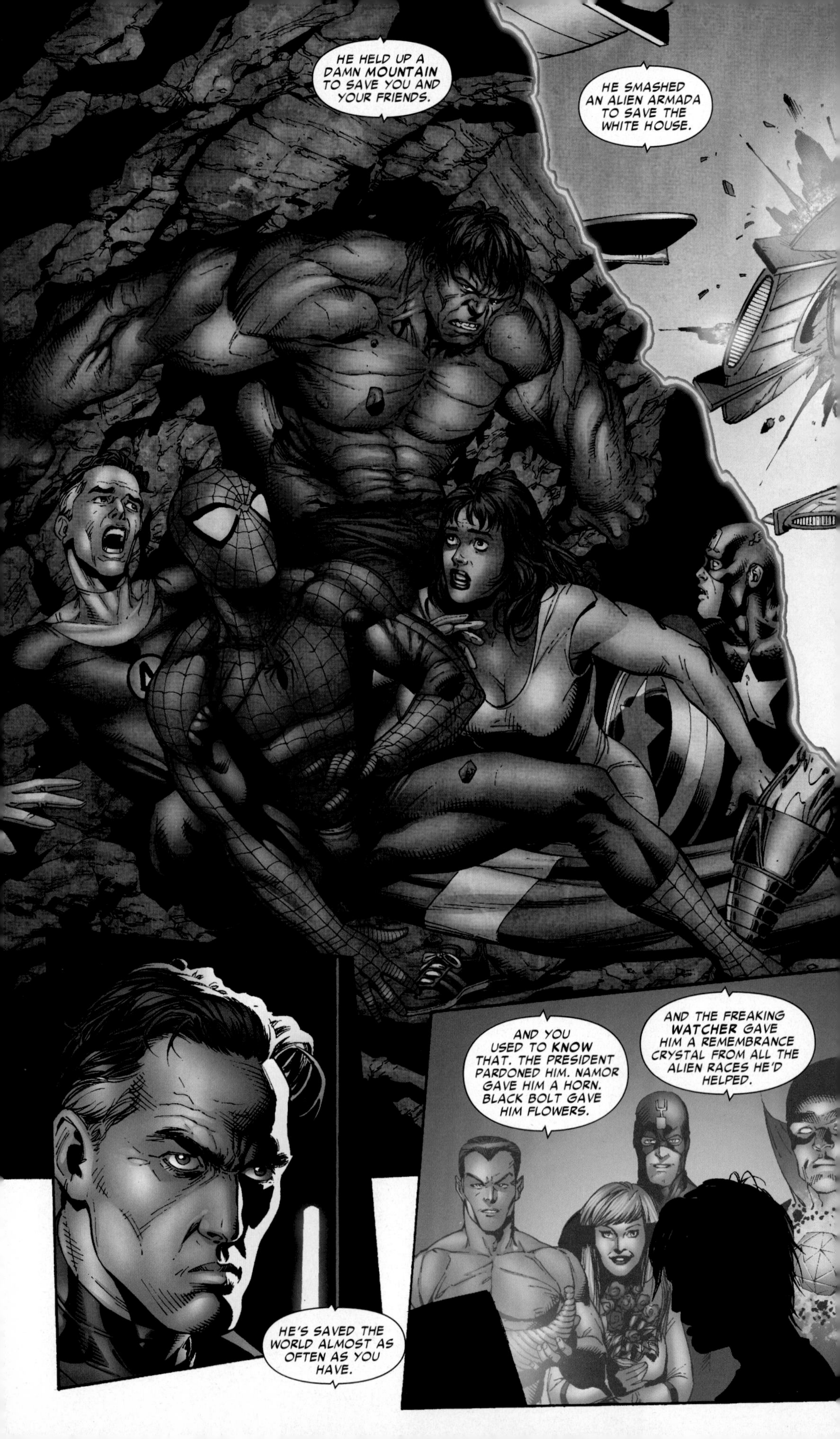
HE HELD UP A DAMN MOUNTAIN TO SAVE YOU AND YOUR FRIENDS.
HE SMASHED AN ALIEN ARMADA TO SAVE THE WHITE HOUSE.
HE'S SAVED THE WORLD ALMOST AS OFTEN AS YOU HAVE.
AND YOU USED TO KNOW THAT. THE PRESIDENT PARDONED HIM. NAMOR GAVE HIM A HORN. BLACK BOLT GAVE HIM FLOWERS.
AND THE FREAKING WATCHER GAVE HIM A REMEMBRANCE CRYSTAL FROM ALL THE ALIEN RACES HE'D HELPED.

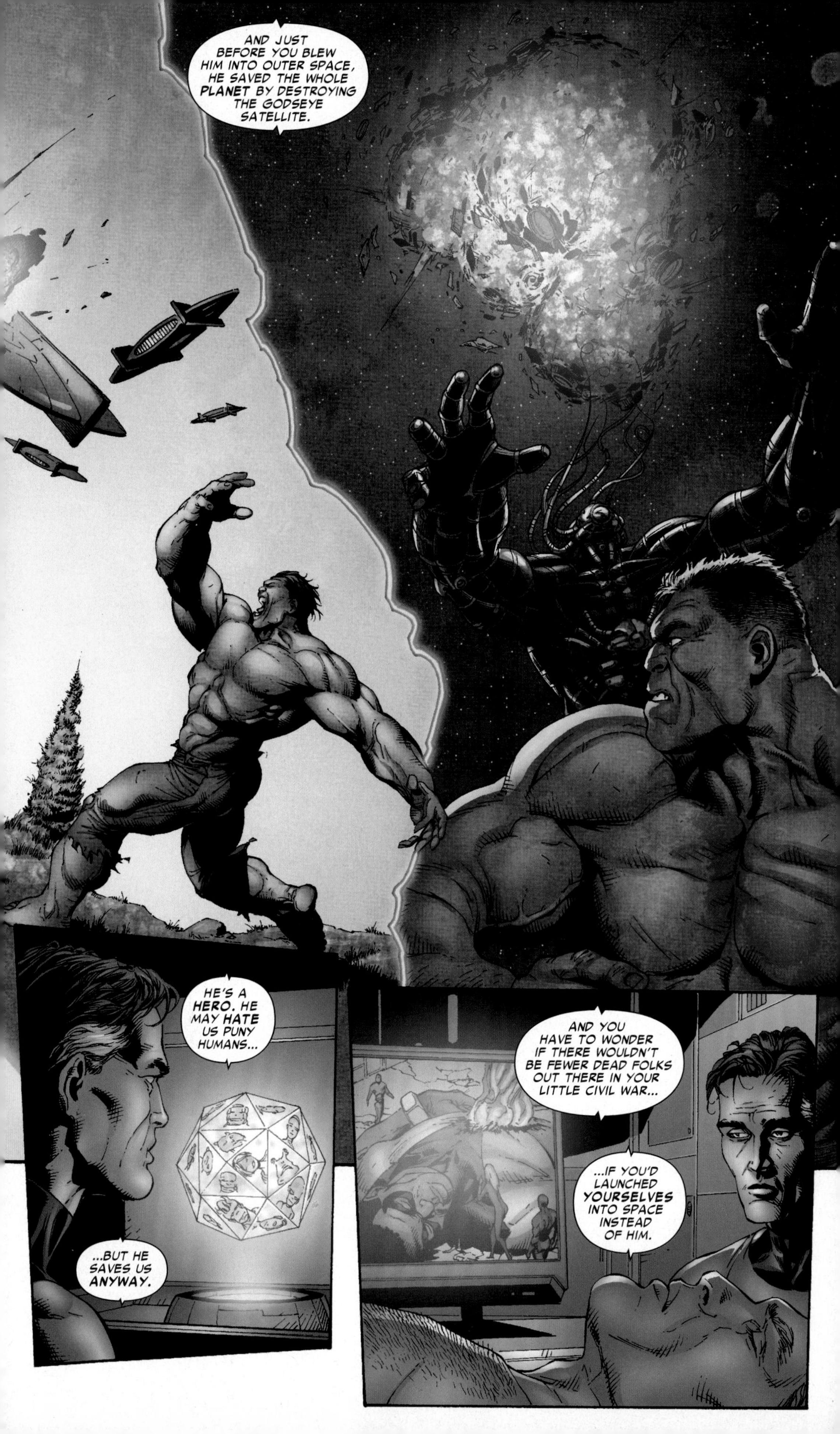
AND JUST BEFORE YOU BLEW HIM INTO OUTER SPACE, HE SAVED THE WHOLE PLANET BY DESTROYING THE GODSEYE SATELLITE.
HE'S A HERO. HE MAY HATE US PUNY HUMANS...
...BUT HE SAVES US ANYWAY.
AND YOU HAVE TO WONDER IF THERE WOULDN'T BE FEWER DEAD FOLKS OUT THERE IN YOUR LITTLE CIVIL WAR...
...IF YOU'D LAUNCHED YOURSELVES INTO SPACE INSTEAD OF HIM.

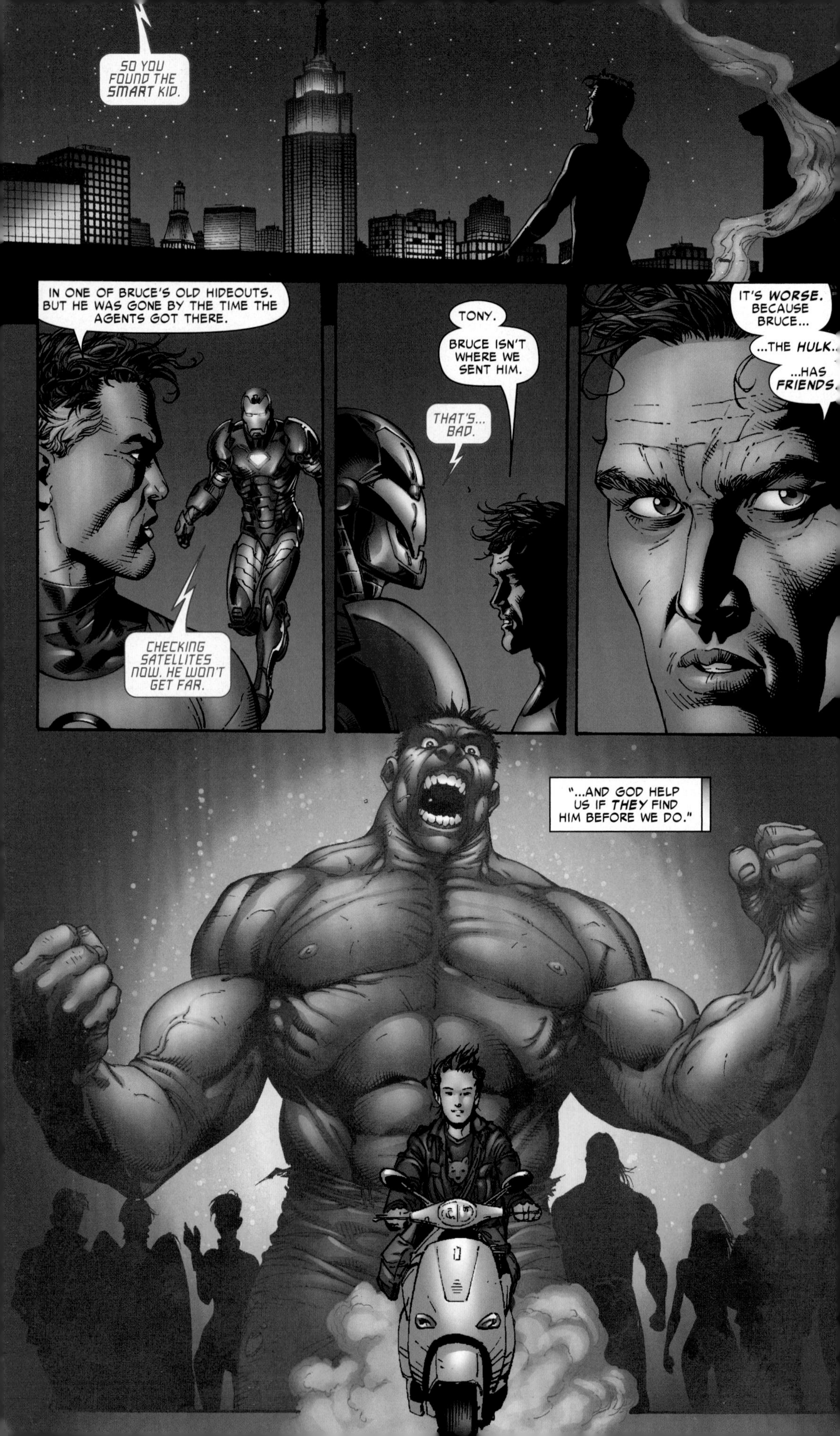
SO YOU FOUND THE SMART KID.
IN ONE OF BRUCE'S OLD HIDEOUTS. BUT HE WAS GONE BY THE TIME THE AGENTS GOT THERE.
CHECKING SATELLITES NOW. HE WON'T GET FAR.
TONY.
BRUCE ISN'T WHERE WE SENT HIM.
THAT'S... BAD.
IT'S WORSE. BECAUSE BRUCE...
...THE HULK...
...HAS FRIENDS.
"...AND GOD HELP US IF THEY FIND HIM BEFORE WE DO."

AFTERWORD

It's been almost two years since Marvel Editor-in-Chief Joe Quesada first told me about a little idea called "Planet Hulk." I can't remember Joe's exact phrasing, but I heard the words "Hulk," "battleaxe," and "alien planet." Then my head popped off.

From my first days as a Marvel writer, I'd been hungry to get my hands on the Hulk. I'm a sucker for all the great Marvel characters — misunderstood heroes whose powers create evocative metaphors and whose foibles lead to genuine, human storytelling. But the Hulk was something special. The metaphor driving the character is as pure and universal as it gets — who hasn't felt the transforming, terrifying power of anger?

And now my bosses weren't just giving me the Hulk — they were letting me take him to a savage alien planet for fourteen issues of epic adventure in which the Hulk would become slave, gladiator, rebel, and finally, conquering emperor? Whoa.

But what kicked "Planet Hulk" up from super-sweet-gig-I-can't-wait-to-start to unbelievably-awesome-project-that-will-become-my-creative-mission-in-life-for-the-next-year was that we weren't just telling a great sci-fi action story. We were building an emotional epic that confronted the question of whether a person who gives himself over to violent wrath, no matter how justified, is a hero — or a monster.

We love the Hulk because he does what we wish we could do — when faced with injustice or stupidity, he *smashes*. That's unacceptable behavior here on Earth. But "Planet Hulk" put our hero on a savage world where his rage and strength were virtues, where he just might find a place, a community, even a queen... But the terrible beauty of the story — that kernel of truth that great writers from Stan Lee to Bill Mantlo to Peter David have bequeathed us — is that rage, no matter how justified, always has a price.

By now, you know the price the Hulk pays at the end of "Planet Hulk." And if you're as hooked as we are, you can find the next epic chapter of our hero's life in the pages of "World War Hulk," wherein a certain group of so-called "heroes" on a puny planet called Earth learn the price of anger firsthand.

But first, a few words for the incredible team that's made "Planet Hulk" possible.

I bow down before Hulk editor extraordinaire Mark Paniccia, my constant co-conspirator, with whom I've hatched and nurtured all my crazy ideas. Every writer should be so lucky to have the kind of creative guidance and championing that Panic provides — I literally cannot imagine a better collaborator. And a tip of the hat to executive editor Tom Brevoort, who's read every script and provided key pointers along the way. And grateful genuflections to editor-in-chief Joe Quesada for all the inspiration, publisher Dan Buckley for all the support, and sales gurus David Gabriel and Jim McCann for their beautiful, dedicated shilling.

Pencilers Carlo Pagulayan and Aaron Lopresti — supported by primo inkers Jeffrey Huet, Danny Miki, and Sandu Florea — masterfully crammed an insane amount of detail, power, and emotion into every panel while designing a slew of new characters and environments that made planet Sakaar fresh and real. Thank you Carlo, for working through monsoons, and Aaron, for hitting me with layouts and pages every darn day without missing a beat.

Colorist Chris Sotomayor hatched the brilliant idea that the Hulk should be the only green thing on the planet — with the exception of the eyes of Hulk's future queen, Caiera the Oldstrong.

Assistant editor Nate Cosby and letterer Randy Gentile put up with multiple tweaks every month as we ensured that every word and every balloon placement were just right.

Cover artist Ladrönn created evocative, textured images that blew all our minds. And all of the guest artists knocked their segments out of the park — kudos to Gary Frank, Alex Nino, Mike Oeming, Mike Allred, and especially Marshall Rogers, may he rest in peace.

Anthony Flamini wrote page after page of the "Planet Hulk Gladiator Guidebook," giving Sakaar a depth and history thoroughly connected with the Marvel Universe.

The team behind the "Mastermind Excello" story helped me create eight little pages that represent one of my proudest moments in comics thus far. Penciler Takeshi Miyazawa, colorist Christina Strain, and letterer David Lanphear brought just the right touch to the story that launched Amadeus Cho, a new character with a big role to play in "World War Hulk" and beyond. Many thanks as well to the supercool Sandor Barna, who hooked us up with authentic physics formulae for the story, and to all the readers whose votes made Mastermind Excello the winner of Marvel's "Amazing Fantasy" #15 fan-favorite contest.

And of course, many thanks to everyone who's been buying, selling, reading, and writing about "Planet Hulk." Fans, retailers, reviewers, bloggers — your enthusiasm has inspired us — and helped ensure that the Marvel Universe hasn't seen the last of the themes, characters, and world of "Planet Hulk."

Finally, all hail the Eye of Anger. The King of Smash. Two-Hands, Holku, the Green Scar, the Green King —

The *Hulk*.

It's his planet — we're just visiting.

GREG PAK

April 2007

I grew up cartooning and love to doodle, but it's pretty rare that I send pencilers any of my drawings when I'm writing a comic book — I don't want to cramp their style by confusing them with my lame sketches. But every once in a while, words fail and I'll find myself doodling a li'l something. Below are a few of my favorite sketches from the "Planet Hulk" run.

g series
es and gladiators in a war agains

On an early draft of the "Planet Hulk" outline, I doodled this little guy, a prototype for what eventually became the insectivorid Natives.

5.

PAGE FIVE

PANEL ONE

Wide panel filling the first row. The Hulk plows through the aliens, tossing them into the air like bowling pins. We're look down at the scene ~~from~~ over the shoulders of a tall soldier standing on a rise. The man is the GOVERNOR.

GOVERNOR
Nara toru.

PANEL TWO

Second row, left. Reverse. Armed warriors stand on either side of the Governor, firing down on the Hulk.

SFX
Bam! Bam! Bam!

PANEL THREE

Second row, right. Reverse. Close on the Hulk as he turns, looking up. Darts are protruding from his back.

PANEL FOUR

Third row, left. Angle on the Governor.

GOVERNOR
Koiron! Shera ho fira kearrako know you can understand me.

PANEL FIVE

Third row, right. The Hulk's eyes widen.

GOVERNOR
(off panel)
Judging by the moronically stunned expression spreading over your ape-like features, I assume the Talkbots are in your brain by now. So.

PANEL SIX

Wide panel filling the fourth row. Angle on the Governor. He's holding a printed proclamation, reading from it with a bored air.

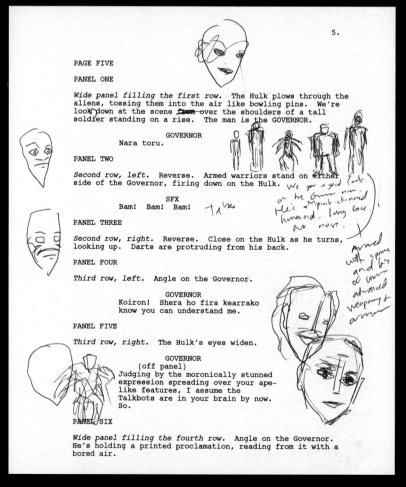

A page from an early draft of *Incredible Hulk #92*, the first chapter of "Planet Hulk." My favorite bit here is the lineup of silhouettes in the upper right — an early glance at the Hulk's team of Warbound allies and what kind of variety they might have.

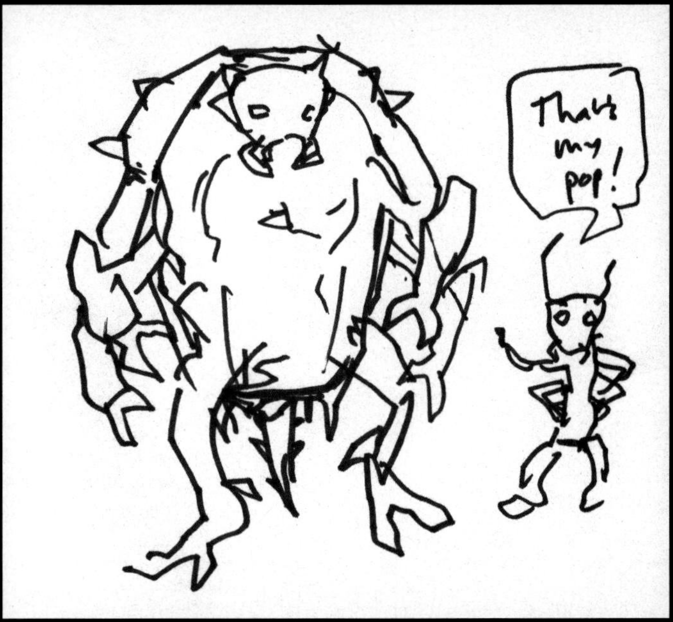
That's my pop!

I became obsessed with giant water bugs and the unfortunately named Cockchafer beetles while thinking about how Miek's father should look in the flashback scenes of *Incredible Hulk #96*.

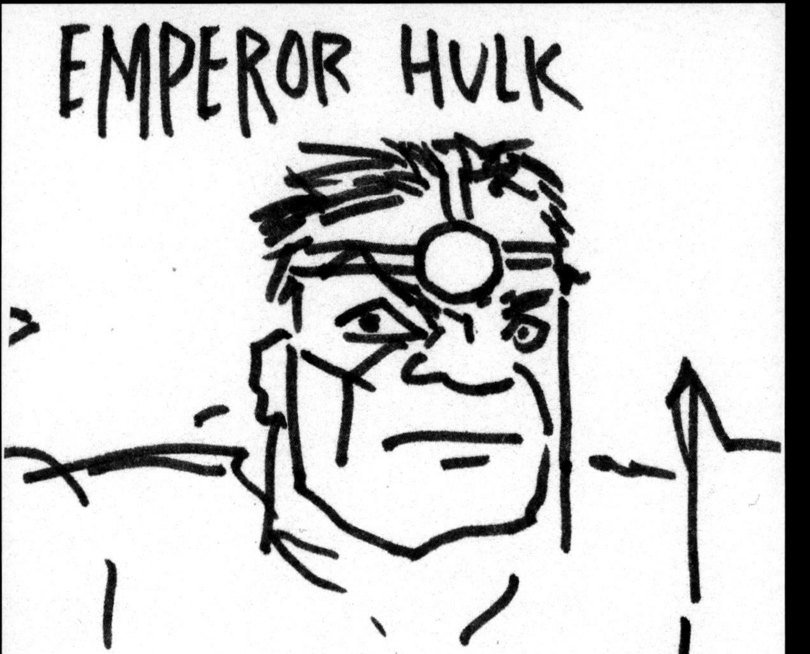
EMPEROR HULK

A quick sketch to figure out just how a diadem-style crown might work on the Green King.

PLANET HULK

GLADIATOR GUIDEBOOK

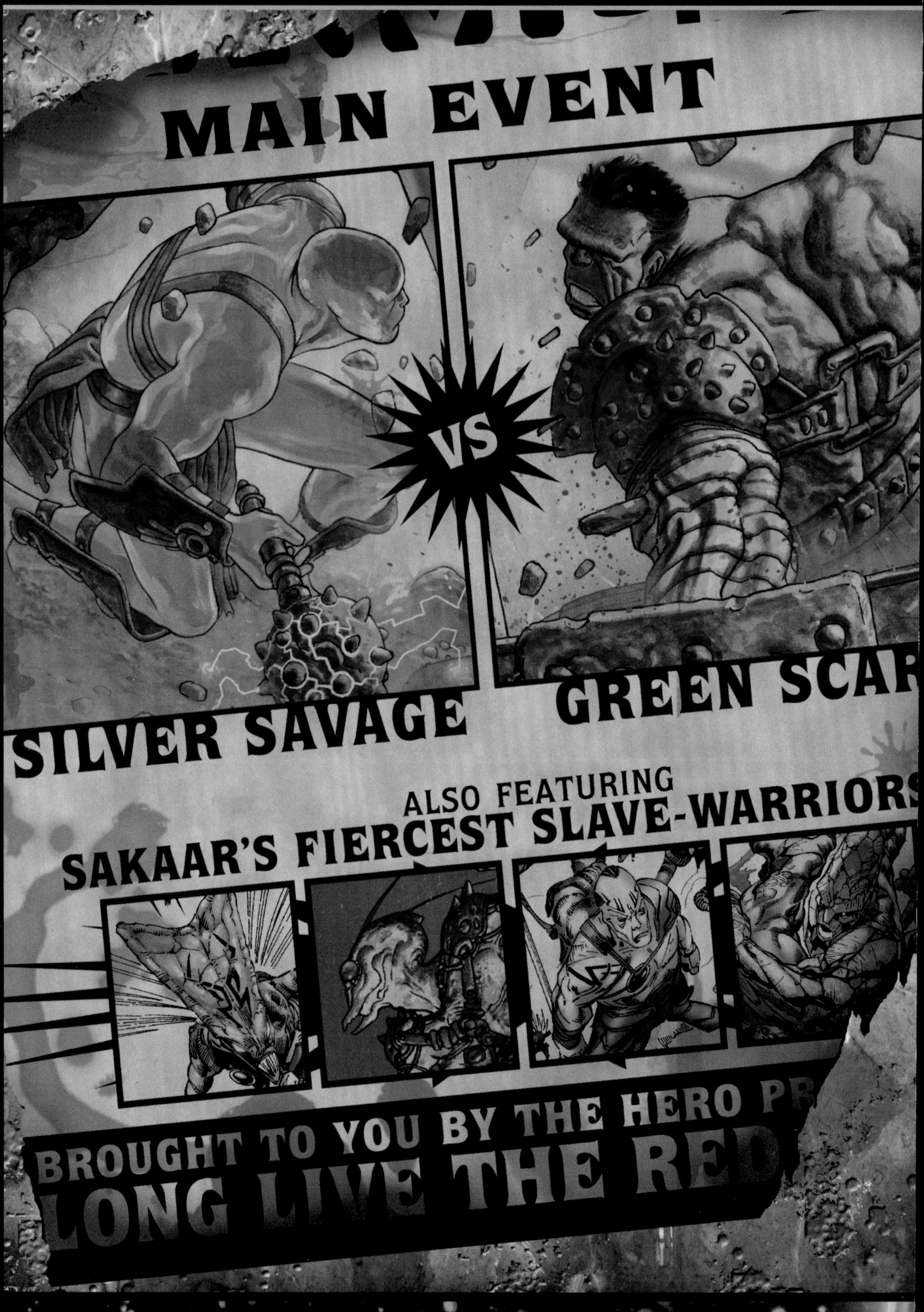
MAIN EVENT
VS
SILVER SAVAGE
GREEN SCAR
ALSO FEATURING
SAKAAR'S FIERCEST SLAVE-WARRIORS
BROUGHT TO YOU BY THE HERO PR
LONG LIVE THE RED

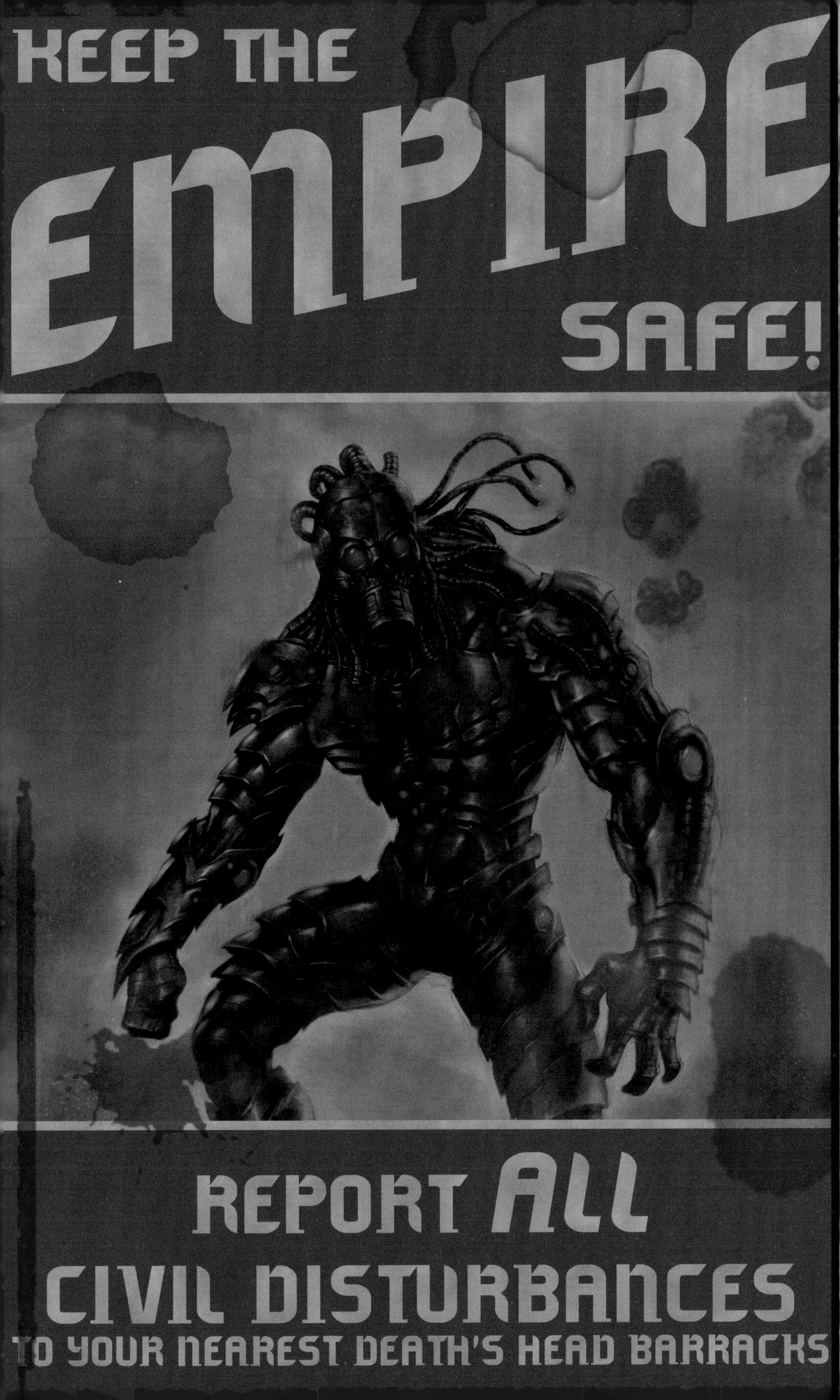
KEEP THE
EMPIRE
SAFE!
REPORT ALL
CIVIL DISTURBANCES
TO YOUR NEAREST DEATH'S HEAD BARRACKS

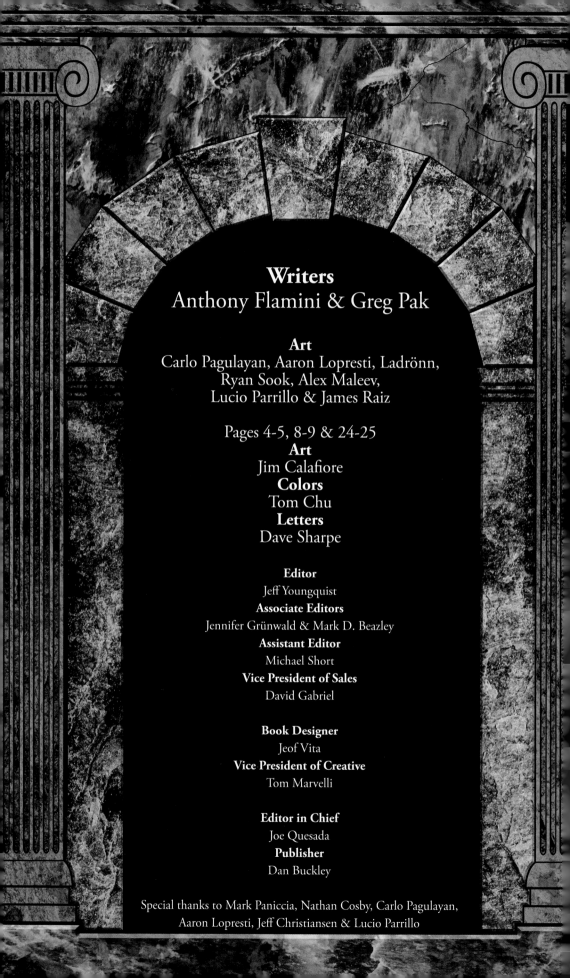

Writers
Anthony Flamini & Greg Pak

Art
Carlo Pagulayan, Aaron Lopresti, Ladrönn,
Ryan Sook, Alex Maleev,
Lucio Parrillo & James Raiz

Pages 4-5, 8-9 & 24-25
Art
Jim Calafiore
Colors
Tom Chu
Letters
Dave Sharpe

Editor
Jeff Youngquist
Associate Editors
Jennifer Grünwald & Mark D. Beazley
Assistant Editor
Michael Short
Vice President of Sales
David Gabriel

Book Designer
Jeof Vita
Vice President of Creative
Tom Marvelli

Editor in Chief
Joe Quesada
Publisher
Dan Buckley

Special thanks to Mark Paniccia, Nathan Cosby, Carlo Pagulayan,
Aaron Lopresti, Jeff Christiansen & Lucio Parrillo

WELCOME TO SAKAAR'S GREAT GAMES

reetings, Great Games aficionados!

or the past ten years, Guidebook Publications of Sakaar
as produced high-quality programs commemorating the
eroes of the annual Spring Games. But this year, 566 Post,
arks the centennial birthday of our beloved and departed
ther Emperor. So we thought it fitting to honor the
emory of the Father Emperor by producing a Guidebook
at would delve a bit deeper, not only providing in-depth
ofiles of the latest Spring Games sensations, but also
king a look back on our planet's history, culture, and
habitants.

ut the book you hold in your hands is vastly different
om the book we originally planned to publish. Perhaps
ue to the unplanned destruction of our editorial staff's
pedience disks at the conclusion of the Spring Games, we
ave chosen to speak the truth, as well as we know it, about
ur planet, our people, and, yes, our Emperor. Many of
e Empire's finest historians, scientists, and thinkers have
ined us in this effort — at the probable cost of all of our
es.

o enjoy, dear readers. Glory in the stories of our gladiatorial
ampions, marvel at our storied past, rage over the horrors
f the current regime, and join us as we march forward into
e terrifying unknown. And please keep an eye out for our
ext publication — "How to Keep Your Head When the
evolution Comes: The Underground Guide to the Green
car's Sakaar."

— The Staff
Guidebook Publications of Sakaar

UIDE TO THE SAKAARIAN CALENDAR SYSTEM

s a benefit to offlanders unfamiliar with the structure of
ur Sakaarian calendar, here is a brief explanation. At the
me of First Sakaarian Empire's founding, it became clear
at a uniform calendar system was needed to replace the
dividual calendar systems of the old Imperial kingdoms.
hus, the modern Sakaarian calendar was introduced and
omulgated. The calendar is a system of numbering years
om the year of the birth of the Father Emperor's oldest
nown ancestor, who was born approximately 566 years
go. All years subsequent to his birth are labeled "Post,"
hile all years precedent to his birth are labeled "Pre."
hus, the current year is "566 Post," 566 years after the
rth of the Father Emperor's oldest known ancestor.

SAKAAR:
THE TAYO STAR SYSTEM

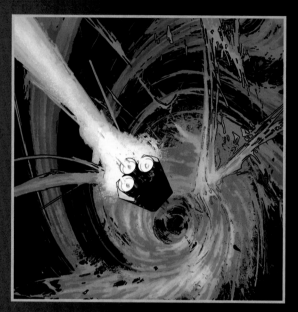

Jigokar is the planet whose orbit lies nearest Tayo. As Jigokar is a fiery world whose landscape is com exclusively of volcanoes and dark-colored lava rivers. surface temperatures ranging from 1,010° to 1,175°, Jig thought to be incapable of supporting any organic life. J is orbited by one satellite.

Since the rise of civilization on Sakaar, its inhabitants have remained largely ignorant of their star system, its planets, and its place in the larger universe. Although ancient legends suggest that the Shadow People arrived on Sakaar from off-planet, Imperial scientists have found no credible evidence to support this theory. Thus, although ancient Imperials developed crude telescopic devices to observe and name heavenly bodies within Sakaar's immediate vicinity, it was not until technology from other star-faring species arrived on Sakaar via the Great Portal that the Imperials learned any specific information about their star system.

Sakaar is the fourth planet from the star Tayo, a member of the grouping of eight major heavenly bodies that comprise the Tayo star system within the Fornax Galaxy. Tayo is the central member of the star system, a large star far outweighing all other members of the star system combined and holding all other members in orbit through its gravitational force. The remaining seven major members of the Tayo star system are planets, many of which are orbited by smaller satellite bodies of their own. All of the planets orbit Tayo in nearly the same plane, except for Glaciar, the outermost planet, whose elliptical orbit is slightly divergent.

The second closest planet to Tayo, Tuksnesis, is a barren world covered in constantly shifting "oceans" of quartz The smallest planet in the Tayo star system in both s area and mass, Tuksnesis has an arid climate with s temperatures ranging from 58° to 100°.

Gangalo is the third planet from Tayo, a humid world ov with exotic vegetation and fungal lifeforms. With an o? rich atmosphere and nearly 70% of the planet cove bodies of fresh water, Gangalo is thought to be a planet ca of supporting various forms of life. However, scans have unable to penetrate the planet's thick jungle canop determine whether there is any evidence of sentient l the planet. Gangalo is orbited by two satellites, both of share its climate and terrain.

Kaasu, the fifth planet in distance from Tayo, is a gas and the most massive planet in the star system. Com primarily of nitrogen, hydrogen, and methane, Kaas no solid surface and no topographical features. Althoug surface may appear solid from space, it is merely the eff layer upon layer of gaseous clouds surrounding a metallic Massive lightning storms, often visible from space, cons form in the planet's lower atmosphere. With the most pov

SAKAAR:
THE TAYO STAR SYSTEM

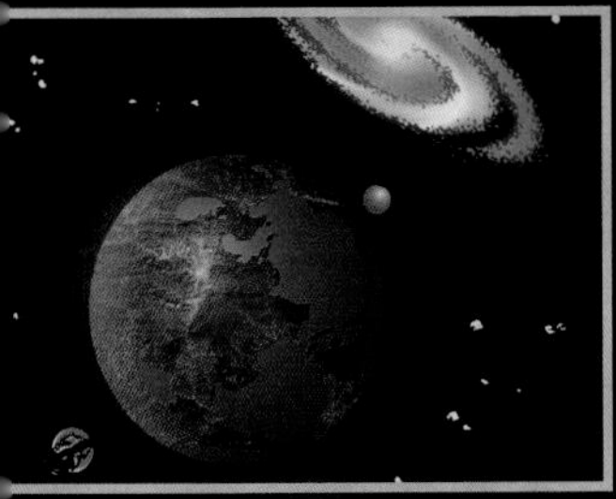
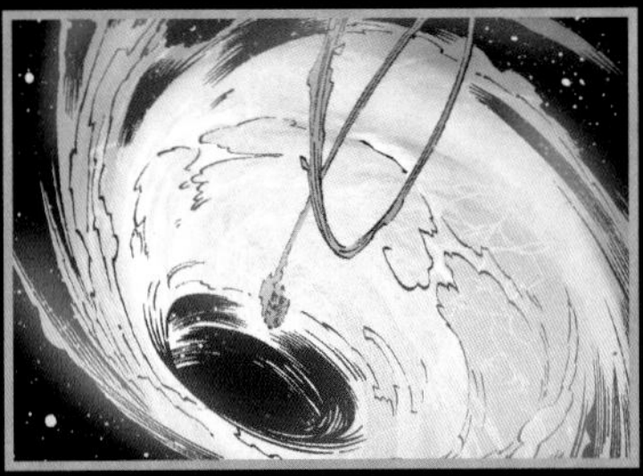
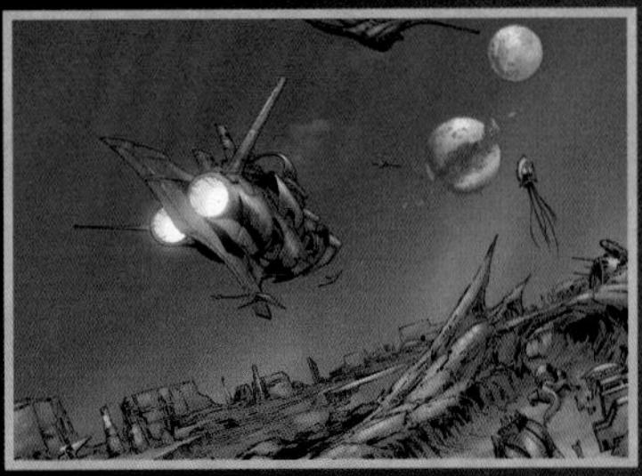

gnetic field of all the star system's planets, Kaasu is orbited three satellites.

the sixth planet in the Tayo star system, Suishus is devoid ny organic life. Its terrain is composed exclusively of metals precious stone deposits. Surface temperatures of the logically dormant planet range anywhere between -20° and Suishus has one satellite; however, the orbit of this satellite deviated over the centuries due to the magnetic pull of neighboring planet Kaasu. It is speculated that Kaasu's e powerful magnetic pull may one day draw the satellite pletely out of Suishus' orbit.

seventh and outermost planet in the Tayo star system Glaciar. With a unique elliptical orbit, Glaciar drifts the hest away from Tayo's life-giving light and, as such, has coldest climate of the Tayo planetoids, with temperatures ging between -250° and -200° (which can also be attributed he planet's atmospheric composition). The landscape of ciar is comprised entirely of enormous, crystallized glaciers ice shelves. Glaciar is orbited by two satellites.

ar is the only planet within the Tayo star system known e inhabited by sentient life. The planet and its moons are ently inhabited by four main sentient species, although question of which of these species is actually native to the et is a hotly debated topic among scientists. In addition, ous other off-world species have become stranded on the et's surface in recent years.

ar is considered a savage planet that is full of extremes. vever, it is the most geographically diverse planet in the star system. Outer regions once included great deserts incredible rock formations, tropical paradises at the foothills of steaming volcanoes, mountainous arctic wastelands, great archipelagos, lakes, and oceans. Sakaar exhibits vast expanses of untamed wilderness populated by a great variety of dangerous non-sentient creatures, both large and small. The planet is orbited by two satellites: Aakar and Sabyr ("the Broken Moon").

In the year 536 Post, during the height of the Spike War which plagued Sakaar for decades, a cosmic vortex opened in the planet's orbit. Upon the vortex's first appearance, it emitted a powerful blast of energy that shattered the moon Sabyr and caused massive earthquakes and tidal waves on Sakaar's surface. At first, the inhabitants of Sakaar, already beleaguered by the Spike War, viewed the arrival of the vortex as a sign of the end of their world. However, in time, the people of Sakaar learned that the vortex brought valuable detritus to their planet in the form of off-world technology and extraterrestrial species. Naming it the "Great Portal," the inhabitants soon came to view the vortex as a boon rather than a curse.

Imperial scientists have been unable to determine the cause of the Great Portal's arrival, but they theorize its first appearance was related to the Spikes, extraterrestrial invaders whose arrival on Sakaar triggered the Spike War in 504 Post. The Great Portal sporadically disappears and reappears, depositing technological detritus and exotic alien species from all corners of the universe onto the planet's surface upon reopening. However, the Great Portal has a negative side-effect on those who pass through it, as it drastically saps the physical strength of all organisms and disrupts all technological programming that it swallows. Although Imperial scientists have devoted much time to the study of the Great Portal, they have been unable to track its movement or fully explain its seemingly random coming and goings.

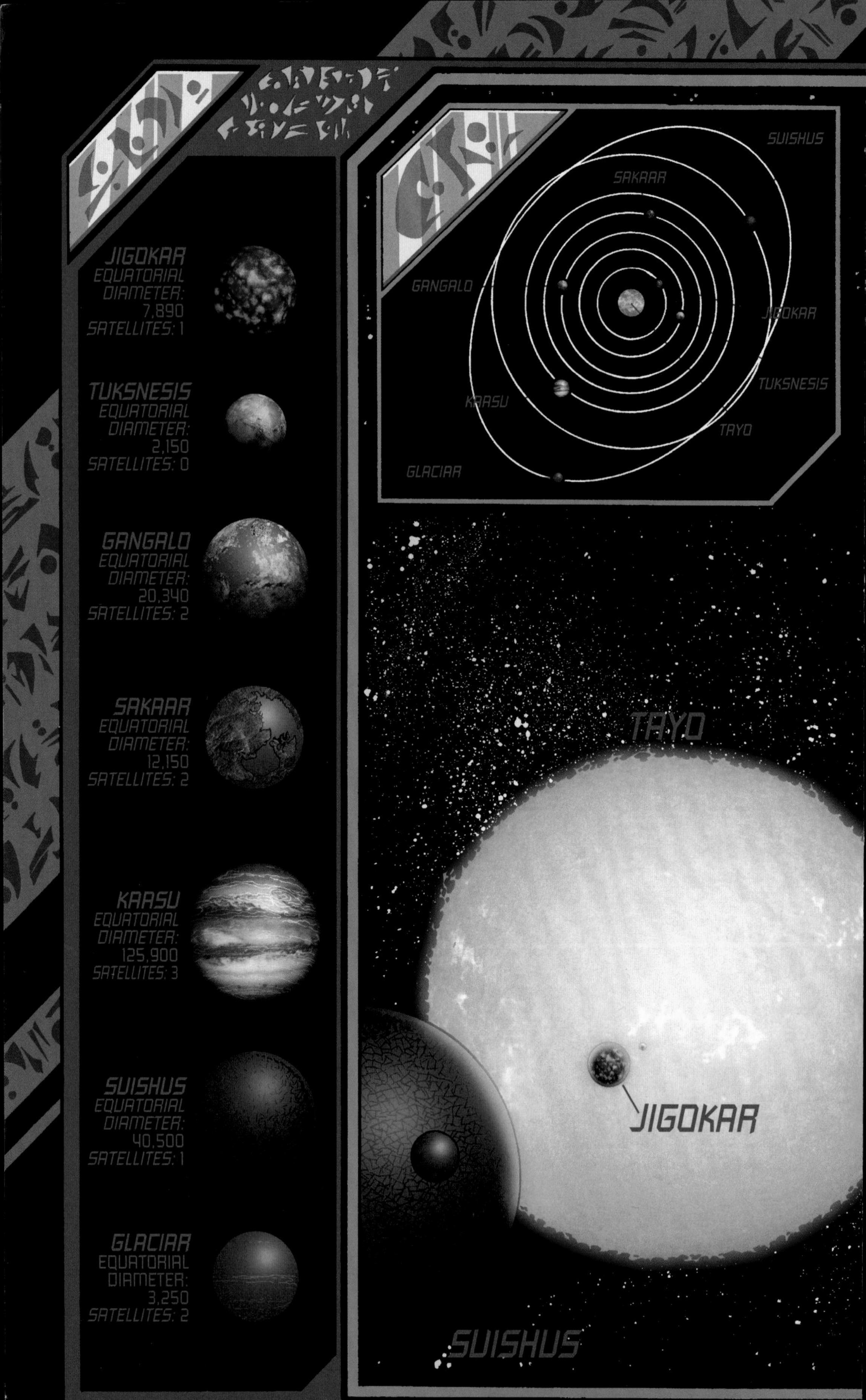

JIGOKAR
EQUATORIAL
DIAMETER:
7,890
SATELLITES: 1
TUKSNESIS
EQUATORIAL
DIAMETER:
2,150
SATELLITES: 0
GANGALO
EQUATORIAL
DIAMETER:
20,340
SATELLITES: 2
SAKAAR
EQUATORIAL
DIAMETER:
12,150
SATELLITES: 2
KAASU
EQUATORIAL
DIAMETER:
125,900
SATELLITES: 3
SUISHUS
EQUATORIAL
DIAMETER:
40,500
SATELLITES: 1
GLACIAR
EQUATORIAL
DIAMETER:
3,250
SATELLITES: 2
SUISHUS
SAKAAR
GANGALO
JIGOKAR
TUKSNESIS
KAASU
TAYO
GLACIAR
TAYO
JIGOKAR
SUISHUS

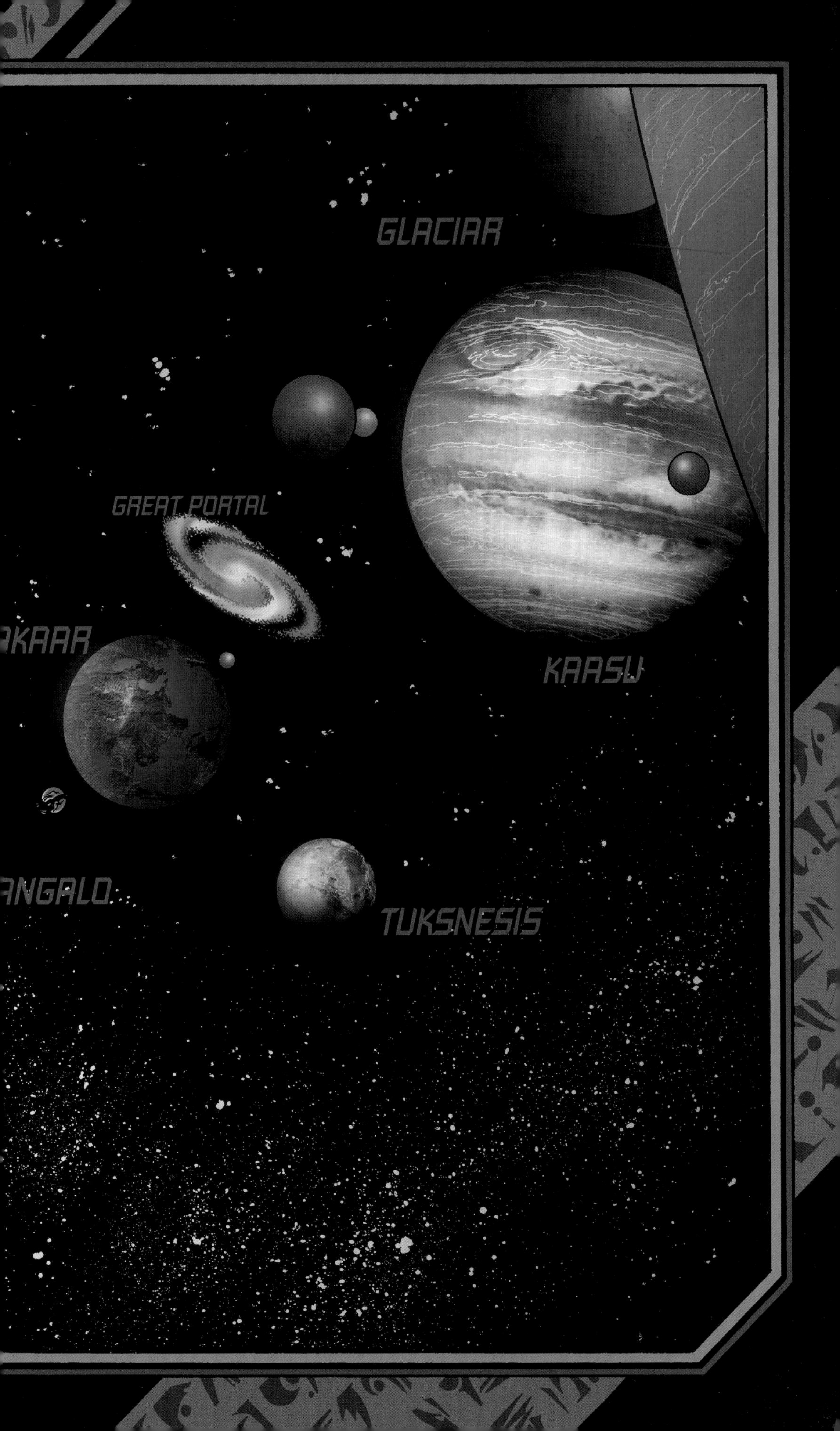
GLACIAR
GREAT PORTAL
KAAR
KAASU
ANGALO
TUKSNESIS

SAKAAR:
GEOGRAPHY

IMPERIA PROVINCE

The seat of the Imperial government, Imperia is home to Crown City, a bustling metropolis adorned with wide boulevards and monuments depicting the Emperor at every turn with the Imperial Palace at its center. But outside the affluent neighborhoods inhabited by the Imperial oligarchs, most of Crown City is a labyrinth of shacks and substandard dwellings. Outside the city walls exists a pristine countryside filled with sloping green hills and dotted with palatial estates where the richest Imperial oligarchs reside when they are not conducting business within the city. Directly to Crown City's east is the Imperial Canal, an artificial waterway constructed by slave labor so that the Empire could have easy access to the Fillian Sea.

WUKAR PROVINCE

Wukar is the smallest province within the Empire and the most loyal. Wukar is very weak compared to the other provinces and, as a result, depends on the Empire for protection and sustenance. Once the home of thriving timber and weapons-crafting industries, Wukar has fallen on hard times since the introduction of advanced technology into Imperial society. Wukar is characterized by thick, coniferous forests in its southernmost regions and an arid desert region adorned with magnificent rock formations along its northern border with the Maga Mountains.

OKINI PROVINCE

With the introduction of advanced technology into Imperial society via the Great Portal, Okini has established itself as the Empire's manufacturing center in the past 25 years. Most of the province has been deforested and the Torkaw River is now dotted with many hydroelectric power plants and primitive factory complexes dedicated to reverse-engineering all forms of alien technology that land on the planet, although a few small fishing and farming villages still exist along the Torkaw's fertile river banks. Okini is where many of the Empire's hi-tech vehicles are constructed and/or modified from intact off-worlder vessels.

THE WASTELANDS

Once home of the First Imperial Capital City, the area now known as the Wastelands was formerly known as Umegus, one of the most powerful Sakaarian city-states prior to the formation of the Empire. It was from Umegus that the Father Emperor waged his military campaign to unify Sakaar's rival Imperial kingdoms during the Wars of Empire. But shortly after the Empire was established, the Spike invaders attacked, eventually leading a ground assault that killed hundreds of thousands of Imperials and left the Empire's Capital City under Spike occupation. The Father Emperor survived the attack and temporarily relocated his base of operations to a volcanic crater deep in the Mawkaw Mountains. After acquiring a powerful alien war vessel from the Great Portal, the Father Emperor ordered that the vessel attack the Spike-controlled Capital City with Deathfire Bombs outfitted with biological warheads. Although the attack led to the Spike's ultimate defeat and ended the decades-long war, it also permanently destroyed the surrounding environment, transforming the once beautiful countryside into the Wastel we know today. All that remains o former capital city and its province desolate, 400-mile-wide circular radius surrounding the point where Deathfire Bombs struck.

LOWER VANDRO

Lower Vandro and its neighbor to north, Upper Vandro, began as unified Kingdom of Vandro. When s squares began to be used as currenc Sakaar, the silver mines discovered ir northwest corner of the Maga mour range quickly made the unified King of Vandro the most prosperous powerful kingdom on the pl Envious of Vandro's wealth, other states foolishly tried to conquer kingdom for generations, but Van superior military strength (fur by silver revenue) handily crushec challengers. But then General Angm Umegus (who would later become Father Emperor) concocted a plan weaken Vandro, planting Umegan s within Vandronese society to conv the citizens of Lower Vandro (sout the Vandro River) to take their ri and secede from Upper Vandro (n of the Vandro River). The plan wo and a civil war soon erupted w Upper Vandro attempted to preven Lower Vandro from seceding thro use of military force. The Vandro War came to an end years afte Father Emperor convinced the rule both Upper and Lower Vandro (t exhausted from years of war ag each other) to set aside their differe and join his new political entity their mutual benefit. Today, the s mining industry of Lower Vandro flourishes, with hundreds of prospe

ng towns and affluent cities in the of the province along the Maga ntains.

ER VANDRO

ke their neighbor to the south, er Vandro did not fare as well after eparation of the Vandro kingdoms. le Lower Vandro reaped the fall from the silver mines, Upper ro was forced to turn elsewhere rofit — so Imperials began farming leserts and sprawling plains that py most of the province. Upper lro was also the area where the most erful Native kingdoms once existed re the rise of Imperial society, so the ve population is more concentrated than in any other province and, as ult, competition between Natives Imperials for scarce resources has the bloodiest. Today, the plains of er Vandro are sparsely dotted with erial farming villages surrounded nan-made moats which are built in ttempt to protect the citizens from ebots, wild robots which inhabit the ted Wood and frequently venture the Chaleen Plains to attack villages terrorize hives. Many Native hive munities are still interspersed ng the Imperial farming villages, he Imperials view the Natives more nimals than as equals.

MA PROVINCE

a is known for its sprawling meadows nany hills. Since joining the Empire, na has become a training ground for Empire's armies and its resort towns once dotted the southern coast of illian Sea have since been converted military barracks since the start of Emperor's war against Fillia. Kuma

takes advantage of its proximity to the Mawkaw mountains and, while there are not any silver deposits located within the province, the Mawkaws do contain many other metals which are mined and then crafted into gladiator weapons and armor by Kumarian craftsmen. The weapons and armor are then sent directly to the Maw, which is only a short distance away in the Mawkaw Mountains

INDEPENDENT PROVINCE OF FILLIA

The northernmost known Imperial civilization is Fillia, the last of the Imperial kingdoms to resist being conquered by the Father Emperor until it was finally annexed in the year 500 Post after a costly four year war, marking the birth of the First Sakaarian Empire. Although the Fillians faithfully served the Empire during the Spike War, many local Fillian politicians began to question the Empire's authority in the years following the war. Relations between Fillia and the Empire have grown increasingly worse since then, with the Red King suspecting the Fillians of secretly plotting against him and harboring anti-Empire terrorists. Tensions came to a head when an Imperial Pleasure Cruiser was shot out of the sky near the Fillian city of I'tjam in 560 Post, killing all on board. Despite the fact that eyewitnesses claimed to have seen wildebots fire at the Pleasure Cruiser, the Red King was convinced it was the group of Fillian rebels who shot it down. The Red King used the tragedy as an excuse to go to war against his own province, and the Fillians immediately declared their intention to leave the Empire and establish themselves as an

independent city. In the past six years, the ground battle between the Empire and the Fillian rebels has reached a stalemate, but the Empire has recently gained an advantage.

THE GREAT DESERT

A harsh desert climate whose temperatures are too extreme for members of the Imperial race and even most Natives, the Great Desert is primarily inhabited by the nomadic Shadow People who view it as a Saka holy region. It is filled with great mountain ranges and hidden, oasis-like forests where Shadow People dwell in obscurity. One such mountain is known as "Prophet Rock," where, according to legend, the teachings forming the basis of the Saka religion were revealed millennia ago. Shadow People often make pilgrimages to Prophet Rock, which they view as the holiest of their holy sites.

NORTHERN STEPPES

The Northern Steppes is a very remote region largely removed from the Empire's conflicts and inhabited primarily by Shadow People, who have migrated here to remove themselves from encounters with the Empire. There are no permanent cities or towns in this area, only temporary encampments of the nomadic Shadow People and ancient Saka temples built into the tops of the unchartered mountain peaks of the far north.

THE TWISTED WOOD

A dense forest that begins near the Crown City and extends between the Maga and Mawkaw mountain ranges up into the Chaleen Plains, the Twisted Wood is feared by many travelers.

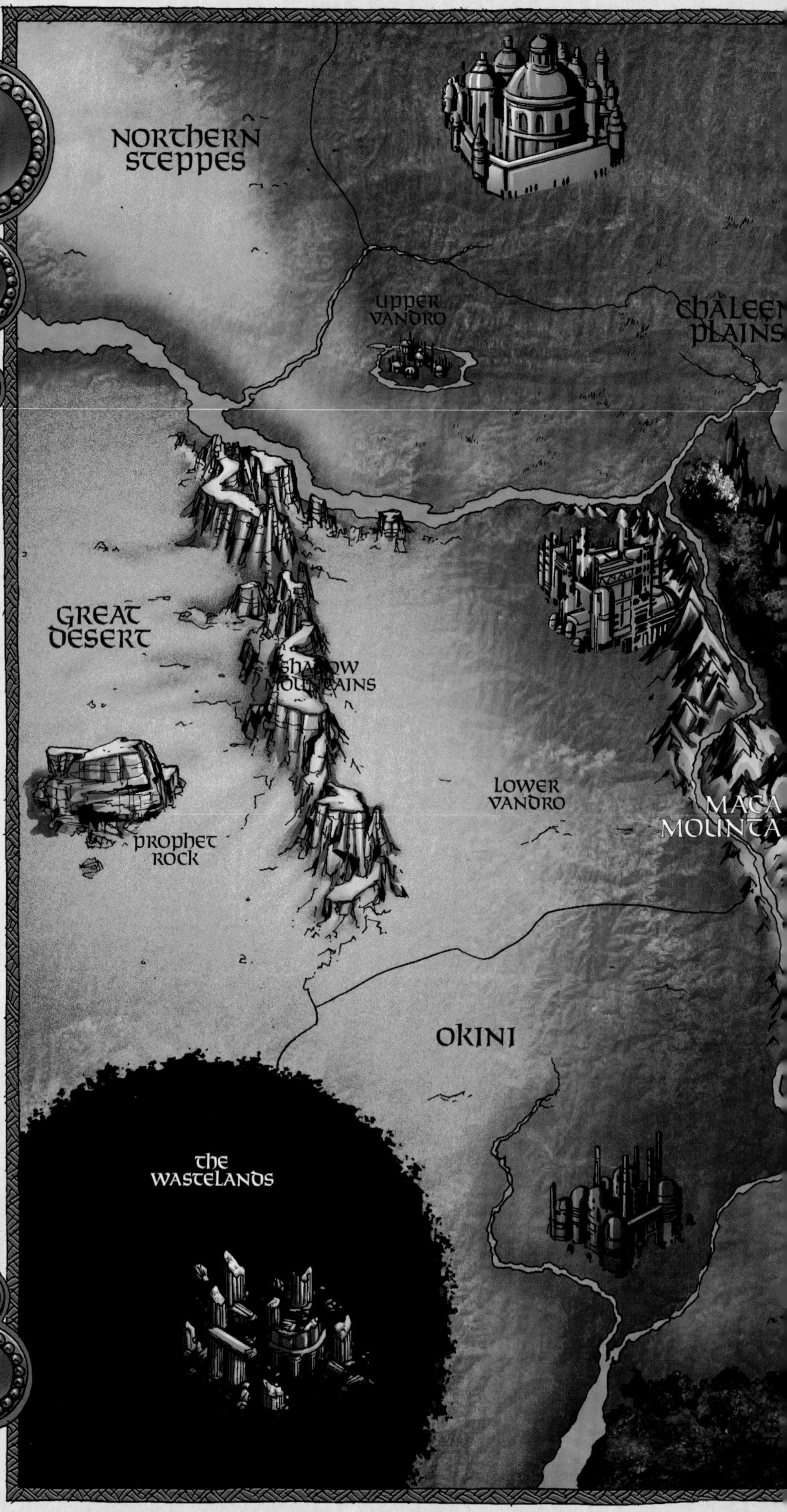
NORTHERN STEPPES
UPPER VANDRO
CHALEEN PLAINS
GREAT DESERT
SHADOW MOUNTAINS
PROPHET ROCK
LOWER VANDRO
MACA MOUNTA
OKINI
THE WASTELANDS

LIA

FILLIAN
SEA

M

AW

MAWKAW
MOUNTAINS

KUMA

WISTED
WOOD

IMPERIAL
CANAL

CROWN
CITY

UKAR

IMPERIA

SAKAAR

SAKAAR: SOCIETY

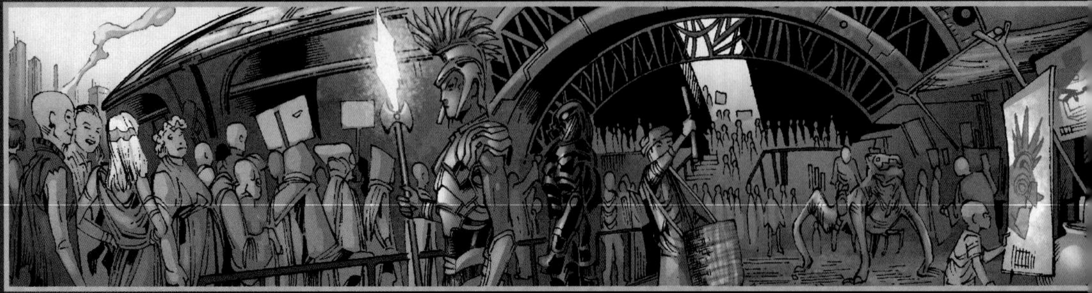

Today, there are four main sentient races that inhabit Sakaar and its moons. The Imperials, a race of pink-skinned humanoids, have become the dominant life form on the planet and control the Empire which subjugates all of the "lesser" races of Sakaar. The Natives, sentient, insectoid creatures who evolved from Sakaar's primitive insect lifeforms many millennia ago, once dominated the planet but have since dramatically declined under the harsh oppression of the Empire. The Shadow People, a race of grey-skinned, nomadic humanoid giants who flourish in the sparsely populated Great Desert, remain largely removed from affairs of the Empire, although they have entered into treaties with the Empire in the past. Finally, the Spikes are a race of gelatinous, shape-shifting xenophobes who arrived on Sakaar intending to feed on its organic materials, only to be defeated and banished to one of Sakaar's moons after a decades-long war against a coalition of the planet's other races.

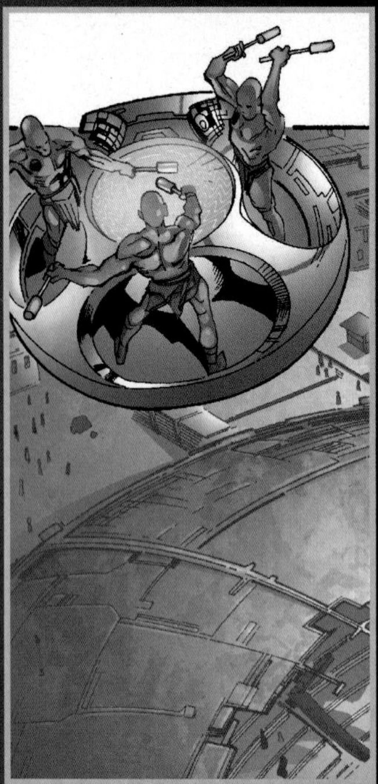

Of course, since the arrival of the Great Portal in 536 Post, which transports life forms and technology from all quadrants of the known universe, many other ser alien species have arrived on Sakaar in the last three dec While a majority of these offlanders have been sold into sl as laborers or forced to compete as gladiators for the amuse of the Empire's subjects, others have evaded enslavemen formed small alien communities in the shanty neighborh and ghettos of the Empire's major cities where they wc merchants and craftsmen.

A small percentage of the planet's population are citizens rest are conquered people or slaves. However, any gladiatc win his freedom and citizenship if he survives three roun the Great Games, a time-honored tradition in Imperial cu A modicum of civil rights and liberties are allotted to cit Slaves and conquered people are not afforded those r but because there is freedom in the immediate ambit c citizens and because the domestic slaves within the Em cities are relatively clean and docile, its citizens ratio that they live in a free and fair society. Meanwhile conquered people and slaves outside of the cities live ho lives of oppression, brutalization, rape, and murder. The majority of the Empire's citizens are from the upper cl the Imperial race, although a small percentage of beings other backgrounds and races have become citizens, prin through the citizenship provisions of the Great Games serve in the Imperial Senate and Imperial Guard. This non-Imperial participation in government also contribu the sense of a free and fair society.

Technologically speaking, Sakaar's civilizations were capa incredible feats of engineering by the year 536 Post, bu remained a pre-industrial society without internal combu engines or any other kinds of artificial energy sources. Bu

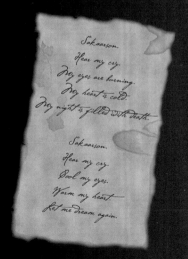

SAKAAR: SOCIETY

ːmergence of the Great Portal, the ːrials, and, to a lesser extent, the ves, embraced the highly advanced vorld technology that fell through Portal, making use of the futuristic s however they could. Today, nologically advanced weapons, cles, and devices can be found ughout the planet, refurbished and ified by the Empire's finest mechanics engineers. However, only a handful eings on the planet understand advanced workings of mechanical neering in any kind of fundamental ;, therefore significantly limiting amount of original manufacturing mplished. Many Sakaarians remain rstitious and suspicious of the new nology, and Sakaarians still fight swords and spears alongside their and blasters. Similarly, primitive ults are used side-by-side with nanized tanks and airborne Imperial dnoughts. There are a handful of solar panels providing some energy ne Imperial Crown City, but water hydroelectric power are provided ugh the Imperial Canal and a series nnecting aqueducts.

itionally, the Imperials, Natives, Shadow People have shared many non themes in their folklore and ous belief systems. The Prophet is chief religious figure in Saka, the ːnt religion of the Shadow People. rding to ancient Saka texts, in the 2150 Pre, the Prophet traveled to is today known as Prophet's Rock e he prayed and fasted for seven On the seventh day, what would me Saka's central precepts of peace, sin, and redemption were revealed to the Prophet, who then spent the rest of his life articulating and teaching these central precepts to others, forming the basis of the Saka religious movement.

There are also a set of additional stories in the form of fragmentary songs, poems, and prayers which are not necessarily part of Saka but which have permeated the planet's folk culture. These are the stories of the Sakaarson and the World Breaker. The World Breaker brings destruction while the Sakaarson brings redemption. Some theologians believe the figures are diametrically opposed, separate beings representing good and evil. Others believe the figures are actually the same person, pointing to the timeless notions that all beings have the capacity for good and evil, that every action leads to others, that life and death are part of the same continuum, and that the circle is the symbol for all.

Many Imperials are ardent believers in Saka as well, but the old religion has come to be considered gauche by the Imperial elite in recent years. In fact, Imperial clerics of Fillia have accused the Red King of going out of his way to eradicate practice of Saka. These critics claim that the Red King's hidden goal is to place himself as the recipient of all adulation by creating a secular society guided by a code of ethics in which service to the Empire is the greatest glory. Other more radical critics argue that the Emperor is actually planning to create a new religion that names him as the one and only god. Although most citizens reject these arguments as outlandish, many upper middle class Imperials have started shrines and temples dedicated to the Emperor himself, claiming that his bloodline is divine in hopes of gaining favor with the Red King. The Empire has tolerated these shrines without any official comment. Many Shadow People, Natives, and religious Imperials see this as terrible sacrilege.

Sakaarson.
Hear my cry.
My eyes are burning.
My heart is cold.
My night is filled with death.
Sakaarson.
Hear my cry.
Cool my eyes.
Warm my heart.
Let me dream again.

SAKAAR: WILDLIFE

AMEBID
(Balenus jelafus)

One of the most versatile animal species native to Sakaar, the amebids were once sea-dwelling creatures. But without any natural defense mechanisms, they were easy prey for the carnivorous aquatic beasts that inhabited Sakaar's oceans and seas. Over the millennia, the amebids adapted and developed the ability to inflate their bodies with the noxious waste gases they excreted, becoming balloon-like flyers who thrived in Sakaar's lower atmosphere.

The prolific amebids now inhabit nearly every known region of Sakaar, from the deserts to the urban jungles. Drifting slowly through the skies, the amebids change direction by subtly shifting the weight of the six prehensile tentacles that hang from their body. These tentacles are also used to collect airborne microscopic organisms, which the amebids filter through the rows of tiny, baleen-like, keratinized structures that adorn the opening to their oral cavity. Most recently, the Empire has begun using amebids in its war against the Fillians, strapping the unwitting animals with explosives and directing them toward Fillian encampments on suicide missions.

DRAMMOTH
(Kimodus burdonus)

Native to the Mawkaw and Maga mountain ranges, the gigantic drammoths are specially adapted for life in high elevations. The largest known lizard species native to Sakaar, the drammoths possess a lung capacity several times larger than that of other reptilian species and their scaly hide is thick enough to protect them from the most frigid temperatures of the elevations. In the wild, drammoths live in mixed herds of about 30-35 and feed on eggs, small mammals, and carrion. Female drammoths lay about six eggs per year, and the young are quickly assimilated into the herd upon hatching.

Although it is not known with certainty when the dramm were first domesticated by the Natives and Imperials, domesticated drammoths vastly outnumber their brethren. Natives use the docile drammoths as beasts of bu to plow their fields. The Imperials have taken advantage o drammoths' affinity for high elevations, breeding ther traction and using them as massive, lumbering slave trans Drammoths are most often used to transport gladiators t from the Maw.

GREAT DEVIL CORKER
(Cavaranthus mazorus)

Native to the plains of Upper Va the great devil corkers are both lo and feared as one of Sakaar's ferocious land predators. An elon arachnid species of ancient origin devil corkers have evolved very over the millennia. Of their four of segmented legs, the first pair are pincer-like and us both dig burrows and masticate food. Devil corkers s most of their time burrowed under the sandy soil o plains, biding their time until unsuspecting prey traverse ground above them. It is only then that the devil corkers forth from their subterranean dens and attack their vic With eight eyes, a spiked, projectile tongue, and four preh tentacles used to drag prey into its tooth-filled mouth devil corker has earned its place in the nightmares of chi throughout the Empire.

Ever since Native civilization first rose in the Chaleen P the Natives have lived in constant fear of devil corker att prompting Natives to never traverse the plains in groups c than eight. Today, the devil corkers terrorize both Native Imperials alike. Although the Empire once tasked the D Head Warguard with the mission of eradicating this loath species, the Empire has since refocused its attention o Emperor's War. Those devil corkers that the Empire ma to capture alive are taken to the Great Arena to ente onlookers at the Great Games.

SAKAAR: WILDLIFE

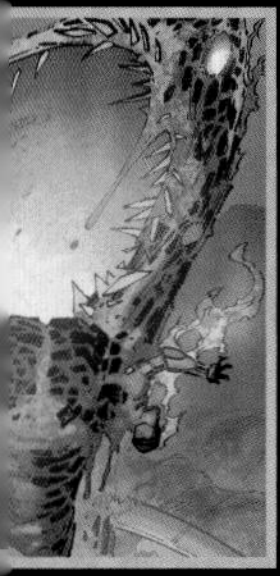

MAWKAW MAGKONG
(Plasmus eradicus)

The Mawkaw magkongs (commonly referred to as "lava monsters") were not discovered until very late in Sakaar's history. As its name implies, the Mawkaw magkong lives only within the hellish depths of the Mawkaw Mountains' remote volcano caverns. ›iscovered in the year 515 Post by soldiers of the newly ›ed Imperial Empire who were exploring the Mawkaw's ›noes in search of a new base of operations in their war ›st the Spikes, the territorial magkongs incinerated any ›r foolish enough to venture too close to the subterranean ›a rivers.

›ugh Imperial scientists have been unable to thoroughly › a living magkong specimen, it is believed the creatures ›normous, unicellular organisms lacking any sort of spine ›ntral nervous system and consisting solely of a large cell ›us surrounded by cytoplasm. It is their fireproof plasma ›brane that allows the magkongs to survive in their magma ›onment and gives them their burning appearance. ›ate that fact that the magkongs were discovered prior to ›ppearance of the Great Portal, some Sakaarian scientists ›naintain that the magkongs originated off-planet due to › dissimilarity with any other known species on Sakaar; ›ver, these scientists offer no explanation as to how the ›ongs would have arrived on Sakaar. Today, the Empire ›ly feeds disobedient gladiators and slaves to the magkongs ›orm of punishment.

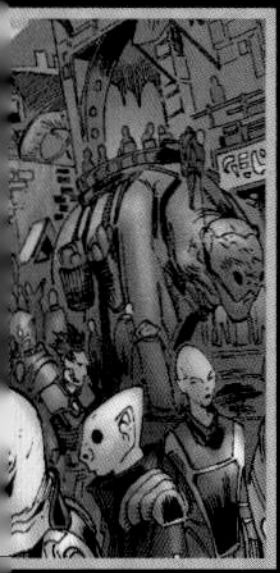

ARQUINDAE
(Arquinnius magnus)

One of the largest land animals native to Sakaar, the arquindae measure approximately 4.5 meters at the hips, with males reaching weights of up to 40 tons. In the wild, arquindae live in small family groups led by older females, although most adult males live in bachelor herds apart from the females and young. Native to the Twisted Wood and the smaller forested regions within the Vandro and Torkaw river valleys, arquindae consume massive amounts of vegetation on a daily basis, migrating seasonally according to the availability of food and water.

Arquindae were first domesticated by the Imperials in approximately 1000 Pre. Used primarily for farming at first, arquindae soon came to be viewed primarily as military beasts. Outfitted with metal armor and back-mounted howdahs capable of carrying up to 40 Imperial soldiers, arquindae were led into battle by specially-trained Imperials who had spent years conditioning the great beasts for battle. Arquindae were instrumental in the dominance of the Imperial armies over the Native Hive Kingdoms and were later prevalent when the Imperial kingdoms began warring against each other. Today, the arquindae are still used by the Empire in its war against the Fillians. While drammoths are usually preferred for transportation in the high mountain elevations, arquindae are used for troop movements across the plains and forests.

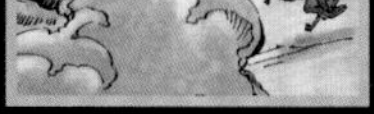

TRIZELLE
(Grazaorus lopos)

Admired for their grace and beauty but hunted for their succulent meat, the trizelle live in herds of 20-75 in the arid semi-desert regions of Wukar and the forested river valleys of Okini and Lower Vandro. Often seen grazing in massive groupings of multiple herds, the trizelle are 3-legged creatures, using their massive hind leg to bound away to safety at the first sight of danger. Trizelles can clear more than 10 meters per bound and can reach sprint speeds of up to 70 miles an hour.

Since ancient times, trizelle have been hunted for food by both the Natives and Imperials. Ancient Native and Imperial civilizations relied nearly exclusively on the trizelle as a food source before learning agricultural techniques, also using the animal's bones to carve primitive tools. Even today, trizelle meat remains a delicacy among Imperial oligarchs and is the served as the featured course at high-society events.

SAKAAR:
WILDEBOTS

*I*n the year 542 Post, a technologically-advanced interstellar spaceship exited the Great Portal and crash landed in Upper Vandro Province. This ship was manned by two Autocrons, a race of iron-based, non-organic lifeforms originating from the planet Cron in the Betelguise Star System of the Milky Way Galaxy. These two particular Autocrons, designated Ten-Twentiwon and Ten-Thirtiate, were Holocaust Specialists, tasked with the mission of eradicating organic life on other planets so that their own people could be summoned to repopulate the lifeless planetoids.

When the Autocron ship first arrived, provincial officials dispatched a small battalion to apprehend the newly arrived offlanders so that they could be reprogrammed to serve as slaves. But the Autocrons resisted and fled into the nearby Twisted Wood, using the scrap technology from their downed spaceship to construct a makeshift encampment deep in the heart of the Twisted Wood. The Autocrons, who were used to living in a civilization where synthetic lifeforms ruled over organic life, were appalled by the state of affairs on Sakaar, where nearly all robots and mechanical constructs were enslaved and assigned the most dangerous of military missions and the most menial of household chores. Determined to liberate Sakaar's enslaved robot masses, the Autocrons began a series of high-profile raids upon Imperial storage depots and reverse engineering plants, abducting their robotic brethren and using their advanced aptitude for engineering and programming to rewire other robots for "independent thought" (in reality creating extremely complex sets of algorithms that enabled the liberated robots' artificial intelligence to simulate independent thought). Spare parts obtained in the raids were used by the Autocrons to repair themselves and their growing robot army when they were damaged in battle.

In 548 Post, the Autocrons decided it was time they liberated their most sought after targets, the Death's Head units that faithfully served the Father Emperor. The Autocrons calculated that reprogramming the Death's Heads to serve on their side would give them the power needed to overthrow the Emperor

and usher in an era dominated by synthetics. Realizing the [...] of their mission, the Autocrons led their entire robot arm[y] surprise attack against the Imperial Crown City in an at[tempt] to gain access to the city's four Death's Heads Barrack[s] after breaching the city's walls, the robots were met with [...] resistance from a large contingent of the Imperial Guar[d] the Death's Head Warguard. Since the Autocrons had p[roven] impervious to energy weapons in past encounters, the Em[pire] engineers had used offlander technology to develop pow[erful] sonic canons specifically designed to counter the Auto[crons] Pelted with blasts of concussive force generated from am[plified] sound which caused their vital systems to crash, the Auto[crons] did not survive the attack. Leaderless and without a ch[ain of] command, the surviving robots retreated back into the Tw[isted] Wood, where their once organized society soon devolved [into] a series of wild tribes in the absence of the Autocrons' u[se] of their artificial intelligence systems.

Now known as "wildebots," [the] increasingly erratic and feral [robots] still pose a great threat to the Em[pire's] citizens. Although they seem to ha[ve lost] their ambition to overthrow the Em[pire] after the death of the Autocrons — [they] are too unorganized to pose a legit[imate] threat to the Empire even if they w[anted] to — the wildebots still terroriz[e the] many Imperial villages and N[ative] hives that surround the Twisted Wood. As such, althoug[h the] Empire once provided the villages protection from wil[debot] attacks, the Red King has since decreed that the wildebo[ts are] a local problem best resolved by local authorities rather t[han the] responsibility of the federal military. Thus, villagers have [been] forced to deal with the wildebots themselves, many v[illages] digging moats around their perimeters to take advanta[ge of] the wildebots well-known aversion to water, although [many] suspect that the wildebots' artificial intelligence system[s are] gradually adapting to rid them of this exploited wea[kness.] While many of these wildebots are capable of reprogram[ming] and repairing each other, their skills do not approac[h the] expertise demonstrated years earlier by the Autocrons.

THE IMPERIALS:
HISTORY, CULTURE & SOCIETY

lthough legend has it that the nomadic Shadow People arrived on Sakaar from another planet countless millennia ago, there are conflicting stories concerning rigins of the Imperials. One leading theory is that the rial race evolved from a single tribe of Shadow People chose to abandon their traditional way of life in Sakaar's ntains and deserts and live along the Great Desert's more erate eastern border. After a few millennia, this wayward became increasingly isolated from the rest of civilization egan to develop different physical characteristics than Shadow People, including smaller, less muscular bodies; on-hued skin; and tendril-like protrusions emanating the chins of males. Sociologists who support this theory late that this is the origin of the current system of racial cteristic preferences we see in modern-day Imperial y: those Imperials with darker-hued skin and more ils are deemed socially superior to those Imperials with r skin and fewer tendrils because they are further along evolutionary process.

Empire does not officially recognize this theory of tion, however, because it feels that the Imperial race and, rticular, the royal bloodline of the Emperor, are unique uperior to the Shadow People or any other group on the t. According to the Empire's scientists and historians, the rials share no common ancestry with the Shadow People oever. Rather, the Empire's scientists speculate that the rials are a distinct race who arrived on Sakaar from off- t on their own accord years after the Shadow People first ot on the planet.

ite this ongoing debate, what is for certain is that the first ded appearance of an Imperial occurred in the year 1713 long the outskirts of the Great Desert. No longer able ithstand the extreme temperatures of the Great Desert he Shadow Mountains, the Imperials gradually began ating eastward into the plains and fertile river valleys of the Maga Mountains. These early Imperials were adic hunters and gathers, never settling in one location onstantly following the movements of the massive trizelle that populated the region.

s not until the year 1150 Pre that the Imperials learned agricultural techniques from the Native hives, who had been farming their own land for nearly 1,000 years. No longer dependent on following the trizelle herds for food, the Imperials began settling in small city-states along the Vandro River. Assignment of the highly coveted leadership roles in these fledgling Imperial societies was determined through a series of gladiator matches, with the last man standing appointed as the city-state's "Prime Lord."

The most crucial date in the modern-day Imperial calendar system coincides with the birth of the earliest known member of the royal bloodline in the year 0. Born in the ancient Imperial city-state of Andav along the Vandro River, this earliest known royal ancestor led a failed coup against Andav's Prime Lord at age 23. His grab for power thwarted, he and his followers were forced to flee Andav to avoid execution and travel southward where they founded the city-state of Umegus west of the Torkaw River later that year.

As these agricultural city-states flourished, the Imperial population on Sakaar grew exponentially. Due to overcrowding and social unrest in the established Imperial city-states, many Imperial warrior-clans began migrating into the north and further east in search of new land to colonize, leading to hostile competition between Imperials and Natives over land and natural resources as the Imperials began outnumbering the Natives, who had dominated the planet up until this point in history. As the Imperials slowly rose to dominance, an alliance of powerful Imperial warlords joined forces to consolidate power north of the Chaleen Plains in 133 Post, establishing Fillia, the first known Imperial kingdom. In the decades that followed, similar Imperial kingdoms were established in Okini, Tego, Vandro, Umegus, Wukar, and Kumar. In these new kingdoms, leadership was no longer determined through gladiatorial combat; rather, leadership was passed down through familial bloodlines. But the gladiator battles, or the "Great Games" as they had come to be known, remained a central form of entertainment in Imperial society, with retired soldiers, unemployed youths, and convicted criminals hoping for pardon now competing as gladiators for sport. In the year 181 Post, silver squares were established as the primary form of currency throughout many of the Imperial kingdoms, and the discovery of large silver deposits in the northwest region of

15

THE IMPERIALS:
HISTORY, CULTURE & SOCIETY

the Maga Mountains led to the Kingdom of Vandro's political and military dominance for centuries.

With the rise of a wealthy and educated Imperial noble class, the Kingdoms of Umegus and Vandro began operating as parliamentary systems, their kings reduced to mere figureheads and senators taking over the duties of governance. Although the practice of succession through familial bloodlines was formally abolished at this time, in reality, the same rich, land-owning families still retained political power over the generations while the poor masses experienced little to no upward social mobility.

After years of minor border skirmishes between the Imperial kingdoms, full scale wars broke out among the various kingdoms in 199 Post as they competed for land and resources, leading to what is today known as the "Dark Ages" of Imperial history. With the kingdoms of Vandro and Fillia maintaining their dominance throughout this period, the Dark Ages were characterized by bloody invasions and political assassinations. This instability lasted for hundreds of years until the rise in 486 Post of Angmo, a noble army general from Umegus who led a brilliant yet bloody military campaign across Sakaar, annexing all other territories into Umegus. When his march of conquest was finally completed in 500 Post, Angmo named his new political entity the "First Sakaarian Empire" and named himself as its "Father Emperor."

The era of peace under the Father Emperor's reign was short-lived, however. Voracious, amorphous alien invaders known as the Spikes attacked Sakaar in 504 Post, starting a 36 year war that stretched Imperial civilization to its limits. Although a Spike victory seemed imminent for many years, in the end, the Father Emperor prevailed over the Spikes and relocated the capital of the Empire to the newly constructed Crown City in 542 Post. To commemorate his epic defeat of the Spikes, the Father Emperor reinstated the Great Games, which had been suspended for many years during the Spike War. Upon the Father Emperor's death as a result of a hunting accident in 552 Post, his son, Sakaar's Hero Protector, assumed the throne, becoming the "Red King." In 560 Post, he declared a war against the Fillians, who he claimed were responsible for shooting down a Pleasure Cruiser and killing all on board.

Most recently, the Red King's authority has been chall[...] by a faction of rogue gladiators and slaves who broke free[...] their obedience slugs after a recent Great Games compe[...] at the Great Arena and fled the Crown City. Although [...] commentators were fearful that these escapees would[...] forces with the Fillian rebels, the Red King's advisors [...] assured the public that the Imperial Guard and Death [...] Warguard are on the verge of recapturing the runaways.

Imperial society is a highly militarized culture wherein [...] of the politicians are also generals in the Imperial G[...] although many are simply military strategists who rare[...] actual combat. A large number of soldiers are needed to[...] the slaves in order. As such, the Empire maintains a very [...] standing army, comprised of both the traditional Im[...] Guard and the more recent addition of the Death's [...] Warguard, a battalion of cybernetic war machines that a[...] on the planet decades ago and have since served the Em[...] Enlistment in the Imperial Guard was traditionally viewe[...] way for lower class Imperials to climb the rigid Imperial [...] ladder. However, in recent years, the Red King has increa[...] relied on the Death's Head Warguard and thus margina[...] the role of the Imperial Guard, much to the dismay of [...] poor Imperial youths who now see the Great Games as [...] only avenue for improving their social standing.

Imperial society functions as an oligarchy, wherein the [...] number of patricians who are members of the Im[...] Senate make all decisions of any importance, subject t[...] approval of the Emperor. Although, in theory, the Em[...] has the authority to make most decisions on his own, he [...] seeks the approval of the Senators (many of whom are [...] acquaintances) to give his policies a greater sense of legitir[...] In practice, the Emperor rarely hears any dissent from[...] Senate, as most Senators are his political cronies or we[...] oligarchs who remain largely unaffected by the vast ma[...] of his policies, which tend to have more a disproportie[...] negative impact on the lower classes.

THE IMPERIALS:
THE EMPEROR

NAME: Angmo II

SES: The Red King, the Hero Protector

UPATION: Emperor of the First Sakaarian Empire

ZENSHIP: Citizen of the Empire

CE OF BIRTH: Crown City, Imperia Province (formerly
 City, Tego Province), Planet Sakaar

OWN RELATIVES: Angmo (the Father Emperor, father,
sed), Enka (mother. presumed deceased)

UP AFFILIATION: Imperial Senate (head)

CATION: Tego Secondary Forums

TORY: To fully appreciate the exploits of the Red King,
must first be familiar with his esteemed father, the Father
eror. The Father Emperor of Sakaar is the Imperial soldier
ed warlord whose exploits united the nations of Imperia
ng the Wars of Empire and saved the planet from alien
sion during the Spike War. Much of the early history of
Father Emperor of Sakaar is shrouded in mystery — most
e official documents and records recording his early days
destroyed during the Wars of Empire and the Spike War.
mber of legends and stories regarding the Father Emperor's
circulate among survivors and veterans of those early wars.
he New Encyclopedia and the official history of Imperial
ar agree on the salient points of the following:

Father Emperor of Sakaar was born as the son of a Senator
the most privileged class of the city-state of Umegus in
ear 466 Post. The boy, named Angmo, grew up in the
sions of Congress, where the rich and influential enjoyed
e luxuries Umegus could provide. But while his peers
ed law and politics with the intention of inheriting their
rs' offices, Angmo spent his days sneaking past the walls
ounding the Mansions of Congress to play with the gangs
reet children who lived in the Umegan slums. He later
d the army under an assumed name, rising swiftly to the
of Captain. When the city was attacked by invaders from
Kingdom of Okini who had destroyed the bulk of the
 in an ambush, Angmo saved the day by arming the street
s of the slums and leading them against the invaders.
n the military leadership of the city decimated, Angmo
led his true identity and became a General. He promptly
uctured the army, admitting any person regardless of social

class. Any slave willing to fight was granted his or her freedom
and allowed to join. Angmo then led his troops against the
neighboring Kingdom of Okini in what became the start of
the Wars of Empire in 486 Post, making Okini's ruling class
pay for the death of his father with their blood following a
year-long siege of the capital city of T'msar. After Okini fell
to Angmo, he annexed it into a new political entity known
as Greater Umegus. Joined by the Kingdom of Wukar, which
voluntarily became part of Greater Umegus, General Angmo
then launched his famed march across Sakaar, demanding
the allegiance of all other kingdoms. Any who resisted were
attacked and conquered — with their noble classes slaughtered
and their slaves and oppressed lower classes granted all the
rights of the citizens of Greater Umegus. Over the next fifteen
years, Angmo's Wars of Empire led to the creation of a grand
coalition of states, which even included Native hives. After

THE IMPERIALS:
THE EMPEROR

the defeat of the Kingdom of Fillia, the final Imperial state to resist General Angmo's dominance, in 500 Post, General Angmo officially established the First Sakkarian empire and took the title of the Father Emperor of Sakaar. But with the external enemy defeated, some politicians from recently conquered member states of the Empire began to chafe under the Father Emperor's rule, claiming that that the Imperial Senate and Regional Community Congresses which Angmo had established were merely for show and that the people had no voice in the Father Emperor's new world order.

But before the grumbling could turn to action, the alien invaders known as the Spikes arrived on the planet and began their horrifying attack. All the Empire's member states united under the military leadership of the Father Emperor. Even the Shadow People, who had thus far resisted any allegiance with the Empire, entered into the Shadow Treaty with the Empire in 535 Post in order to fight the invaders. But even this combined might could not stop the Spikes. Struggling to find a way to defeat the Spikes and save his world, the Father Emperor walked into the barren expanses of the Northern Steppes for seven days of fasting and prayer. On his seventh day in the Steppes, the Great Portal emerged for the first time and a flagship full of cybernetic Death's Head units fell to the planet's surface. The Father Emperor and his troops were the first on the scene, and the Death's Head units kneeled at his feet after he used his Shadowforge blade to fell the lead unit of the Death's Heads. With his new legion of the Death's Head Warguard, the Father Emperor eventually defeated the Spikes in 540 Post, exiling them on Sakaar's broken moon of Sabyr after ordering a bombing raid that obliterated the Spikes' base of operations on Sakaar, which also happened to be the Father Emperor's hometown.

Following the Spike War, the Father Emperor ruled for many years, although tensions remained between him and the various Regional Community Congresses that he established. But, aside from the robot rebellions that occurred in the decade after the war, Sakaar knew peace for the rest of his days. The Father Emperor died in 552 Post while hunting on the plains of Upper Vandro, leaving his Empire to his son, Angmo II, the Hero Protector and Crown Prince of Sakaar. Upon ascending to the throne, he took the name "Red King."

The Red King's exploits predate his ascension to the Imp[erial] throne by decades. Born in 519 Post, just before the midp[oint] of the Spike War, the Crown Prince grew up in Geot City [(later] renamed Crown City), since the Spikes had already cap[tured] the First Imperial Capital City four years prior to his b[irth.] Although even oligarchs made sacrifices during these [years] of the war, the Crown Prince led a relatively pampered [life,] attending Tego's Secondary Forums and constantly yearni[ng to] enter the battle against the Spikes. Upon reaching age 1[0, the] impetuous young Crown Prince ran away from home, ord[ering] a young team of Imperial Guard trainees to accompany [him] on a mission to destroy the Spikes. Against all odds, the C[rown] Prince's team traveled all the way to the outskirts of the [Great] Desert where they found a young Shadow girl by the nam[e of] Caiera the Oldstrong, who appeared to be the sole surviv[or of] a Spike attack on her Shadow community. Although one [year] younger than the Crown Prince, Caiera was already taller [and] stronger than anyone of his soldiers due to her unique Sha[dow] physiology, and the Prince decided to recruit her into his ra[nks.] As the Crown Prince and his young troops ventured a[cross] Sakaar slaying Spikes, he became known as the Empire's [Hero] Protector. When the Father Emperor entered into the Sha[dow] Treaty with the Shadow People, Caiera became warboun[d to] the Crown Prince by treaty.

Since ascending to the Imperial throne in 552 Post, the F[ather] Emperor's ruling style has been criticized by rebels and [other] malcontents. His most controversial move in recent [years] was to initiate a war against the Fillians in 560 Post and [to] increase standard provincial tributes to help pay for his wa[r.]

HEIGHT: 5'10"
WEIGHT: 166 lbs.
EYES: Crimson
HAIR: None

ABILITIES/ACCESSORIES: The Red King is a bril[liant] military strategist and hand-to-hand combatant. Althoug[h he] possesses no superhuman powers of his own, the Red [King] does possesses the body of the original Death's Head [unit] that was permanently deactivated by his father, which he [uses] as a warsuit to increase his physical strength and spee[d to] superhuman levels.

THE IMPERIALS: RONAN KAIFI

NAME: Ronan Kaifi

SES: None

UPATION: Representative of the Fifth Community
gress

ZENSHIP: Slave of the Empire, former citizen of the
re

CE OF BIRTH: Rundi, Okini Province, Planet Sakaar

WN RELATIVES: Elloe Kaifi (daughter)

UP AFFILIATION: Fifth Community Congress

CATION: Rundi Secondary Forums; privately tutored

ORY: Born in the year 509 Post, Ronan Kaifi belonged
upper middle class family with a long history of public
ce and political activity in Okini. His grandfather was a
cilor to the King of Okini until he was slaughtered along
many others associated with the ruling family when
ral Angmo of neighboring Umegus conquered Okini in
Post at the start of the Wars of Empire. Ronan's father,
resented the Father Emperor as the man responsible for
wn father's death, was eventually elected to the position of
esentative in the local Community Congress, a political
ution with no real power established by the Father
eror in all provinces merely to give the conquered masses
e sense of participation in government. Real political
r in the provinces was held by the governors, who were
nally appointed to their positions by the Emperor himself
as a result, consisted entirely of his cronies and political

n his father's death, Ronan Kaifi was popularly elected
s vacant seat on the Fifth Community Congress in 538
Although Ronan advocated the Empire's existence as a
to provide much needed services to the less fortunate,
ventually concluded that the Empire's increasing greed
corruption were causing it to neglect its subjects. After
pleas for the Empire to protect his constituents against
ncreasingly frequent wildebot attacks went unanswered,
n began to speak out publically against the Empire's greed
corruption, joining a growing movement of upper middle
Imperials who were opposed to the Red King's policies.
ver, when several other critics of the Empire, such as
d Community Congress Representative Vesta Kaito of

Lower Vandro and Sixth Community Chancellor Emvo Kairee of Kumar, were either killed or kidnapped, Ronan Kaifi began to fear for his own safety and the safety of his family. As such, he hired former Imperial Guard Captain Lavin Skee to serve as his bodyguard and retainer. After surviving several planned assassinations thanks to Skee's intervention, Ronan Kaifi began secret meetings with rebel groups who planned to overthrow the Empire and continued to

vehemently protest the recent increase in tribute necessitated by the Emperor's war against the Fillians. Soon after, Ronan, along with his daughter Elloe and Captain Skee, were abducted from their home by a strike force of Death's Head units. Without formal charges leveled against them, the three were arrested and taken to the Maw as slaves. When Ronan spoke out against his unjust imprisonment and demanded to know what law he was charged with breaking, Primus Vand, the famed gladiator trainer, sent a terminal feedback charge through Ronan's obedience disk, vaporizing his body within seconds.

HEIGHT: 5'8"
WEIGHT: 153 lbs.
EYES: Black
HAIR: None

ABILITIES/ACCESSORIES: Having been extensively tutored by private scholars well into his adult years, Ronan Kaifi was a brilliant politician, having been elected to four seven-year terms in the Okini's Fifth Community Congress. An idealist whose faith in the in legal system never wavered, even under the Red King's rule, Ronan was a strong advocate for provincial rights and a harsh critic of the Emperor's policies. Not physically adept, he often relied on the muscle of his bodyguard, Lavin Skee.

THE IMPERIALS: PRIMUS VAND

REAL NAME: Primus Vand
ALIASES: Kumarson, the Kumarian Killer
OCCUPATION: Gladiator trainer / Imperial League promoter
CITIZENSHIP: Citizen of the Empire
PLACE OF BIRTH: Kumaria, Kumar Province, Planet Sakaar, Tayo Star System, Fornax Galaxy
KNOWN RELATIVES: Omegus Vand (father, deceased)
GROUP AFFILIATION: Imperial League
EDUCATION: Years of gladiatorial training

HISTORY: Born in the year 510 Post in Kumar Province, Primus Vand was the only son of Omegus Vand, once a high-ranking advisor to the King of Kumar. By the time of Primus' birth, however, his father no longer held political power and had been forced into a life of slavery after nearly all of Kumar's royal family had been killed during the Wars of Empire. Shortly after the Father Emperor ordered the construction of the Great Arena in 515 Post, Omegus and his family were forcibly relocated to Tego Province's Geot City where they were among the first group of slaves to start work on the Great Arena Project in 517 Post. Primus, only seven years old at the time, was also put to work on the project, carrying small slabs of marble to and from the construction site. After nine years of working on the Great Arena, Omegus and his wife were among the many slaves killed when a Spike attack caused part of the arena to collapse on them.

Primus, now an orphan at age 16, was spared from his parents' fate and continued to work on the Great Arena for nearly twenty years. Primus' hostility toward the Empire, which he blamed

for his parents' deaths, prompted his reassignment to the re-established gladiator training school at the Maw when i converted into a gladiatorial training facility. Through force of will, Primus managed to survive the hellish condi of the Maw (although losing his left eye in the process eventually graduated to competition in the Imperial Lea Great Games. After scoring several decisive victories in Great Arena that he helped build, the charismatic Pr became Sakaar's most beloved slave-warrior and, event was granted citizenship in the Empire by the Father Emp himself in 551 Post. Thrust into the limelight, Primus' h for the Empire was gradually replaced with his devotio the Great Games. Retiring from combat after four undef seasons, Vand found himself unable to leave the busines soon became both a promoter for the Imperial League a gladiator trainer at the Maw. Currently, Primus is invo in all aspects of the Great Games, from analyzing view ratings to gladiator recruitment. Although Primus tolerate presence of the current Emperor, his true allegiance is to spirit and tradition of the Great Games.

HEIGHT: 6'1"
WEIGHT: 203 lbs.
EYES: Crimson
HAIR: None

ABILITIES/ACCESSORIES: Primus Vand is an experie gladiatorial warrior, with years of training in various form armed and unarmed combat. Although no longer in the p of his fighting career, he commands respect from his gladiat pupils through the use of obedience disk technology.

THE IMPERIALS: GOVERNOR OF WUKAR

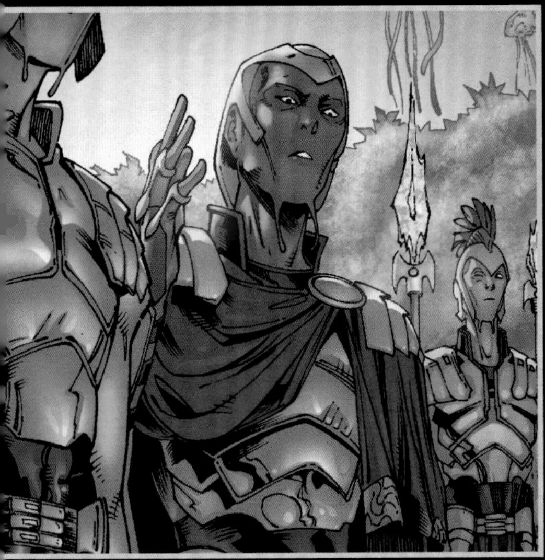

L NAME: Denebo Aruc III
ASES: Governor, the Red King's Queen
CUPATION: Governor of Wukar Province
IZENSHIP: Citizen of the Empire
CE OF BIRTH: Arcos City, Wukar Province, Planet ar, Tayo Star System, Fornax Galaxy
OWN RELATIVES: Denebo Aruc II (father, deceased), ebo Aruc I (grandfather, deceased)
OUP AFFILIATION: The Empire's Inner Circle
JCATION: Privately tutored

TORY: Denebo Aruc III was born in 538 Post, the first of e sons of Denebo Aruc II, the Steward of the Kingdom of car. Decades before Denebo III's birth, the King of Wukar assassinated by agents from the neighboring Kingdom of ni in 485 Post. Thus, Denebo II, as the kingdom's steward, ediately became the kingdom's political leader since the ous king had sired no male heirs. The Kingdom of Wukar, its small land area and meager natural resources, had orically been the weakest of Sakaar's Imperial kingdoms often relied on alliances with its larger neighbors to d being conquered by other kingdoms. So it came as no rise when, in the year 487 Post, Denebo II signed a treaty General Angmo of Umegus and contributed Wukarian forces to Umegus' year-long siege of the Okinian capital city of T'msar. After Okini finally fell to the combined might of Umegus and Wukar, Denebo II wholeheartedly supported Wukar's inclusion in Angmo's new "Greater Umegus," so long as it meant that Wukar could share in Greater Umegus' fortune. So devoted was his support that Denebo II, whose title officially changed to "Governor of Wukar," was the only provincial leader not replaced by one of the Father Emperor's political cronies during the Wars of Empire.

Upon Denebo II's death in 558 Post, his position of Governor of Wukar was inherited by his first son, Denebo III. Though many political observers thought it impossible, Denebo III was even more subservient to the Red King (the Father Emperor's son and current Emperor) than Denobo II was to the original Father Emperor. Always flanked by a contingent of Imperial Guards, Denebo III is often seen patrolling Wukar Province in search of rare detritus that has arrived through the Great Portal which he can present to the Red King to curry favor. A huge aficionado of the Great Games, he also enjoys staging gladiator competitions in honor of the Emperor. The Red King, fully aware of Denebo's unwavering loyalty to the Empire, often sends the Governor on missions outside of Wukar to serve as his personal representative. As such, Denebo III is often criticized and ridiculed as being the Emperor's personal lapdog. To compensate for this, he often goes out of his way to prove his individual worth and swaggers around with a false sense of bravado.

HEIGHT: 5'7"
WEIGHT: 159 lbs.
EYES: Crimson
HAIR: None

ABILITIES/ACCESSORIES: Although hand-to-hand combat is not his strength, the Governor has shown a natural affinity for the technology that falls through the Great Portal, often able to determine the use for technological gadgetry within hours. The Governor is much more comfortable with a blaster pistol than with a sword. Like the Lieutenant, he is a formidable military commander and well-versed in the War Book, an Imperial military treatise.

THE IMPERIALS: CROWN CITY

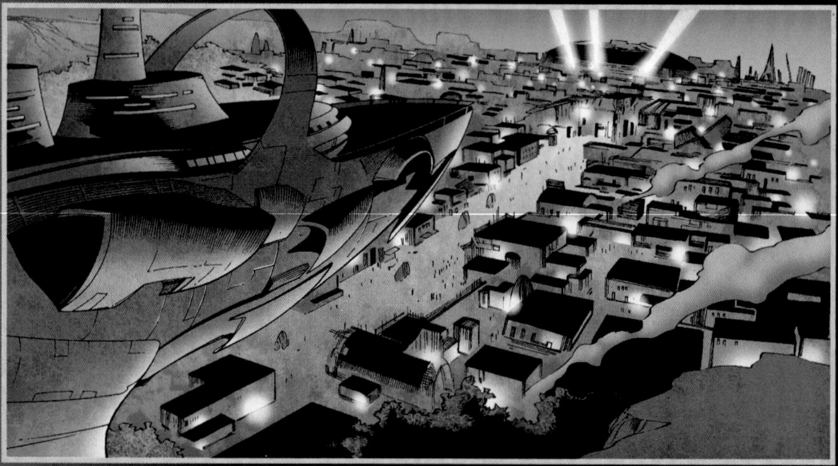

What is today the Imperial Crown City was once the City of Geot, capital of Tego Province. Geot was originally founded by Imperial settlers in the year 98 Post who established a flourishing logging industry in the area thanks to the village's close proximity to the Twisted Wood. As the years passed, Geot's population rapidly increased, and the city was named as the capital of Tego Kingdom when it was established in 151 Post. Geot continued to exist as Tego's capital even after it was annexed by the Father Empire in 495 Post and renamed "Tego Province." But when the Imperial Capital City in Umegus Province was overrun by the Spikes in 515 Post, the Father Empire realized that his Empire needed a new capital city, one that would be a fitting tribute to his glorious reign. Temporarily relocating his base of operations to the Mawkaw Mountains for the remainder of the Spike War, the Father Emperor secretly ordered that Geot be transformed into the new capital of the Empire – Crown City.

During the waning years of the Spike War, Empire slaves not suited for battle were put to work rebuilding Geot on a greatly enlarged pattern and a grander scale. Finally, in the year 542 Post, two years the Father Emperor's triu over the Spikes and 27 y after reconstruction of the first began, the foundation were performed and Geot officially renamed Crown capital of the First Sakaa Empire. Similarly, Tego renamed "Imperia" in hc of being the capital city's province.

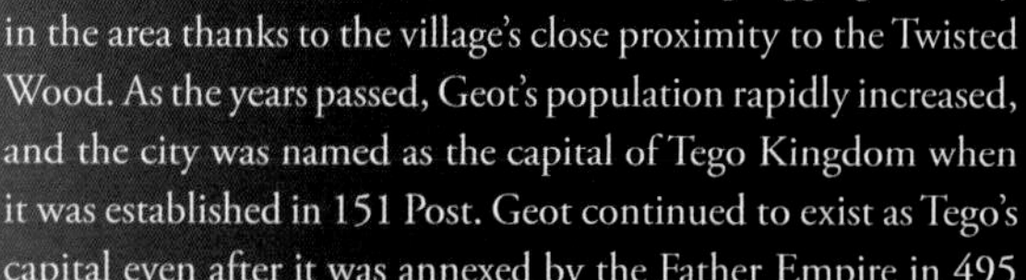

From its inception, the Cr City has been a municipali many dualities. As the home to many of the Empire's influential oligarchs and the center of government pow was a city of vast wealth and beauty — yet the majori the city consisted of poor slums to house its many slaves lower-class citizens. It was common to see ancient tools architecture being used side-by-side with the most moder alien technologies.

Today, the skyline of the Crown City is dominated by buildings: the Imperial Palace and the Great Arena. Imperial Palace, existing in the center of the city and ser as the main residence of the Red King, towers above all o buildings. The Imperial Palace is actually constructed from massive flagship once used by the Death's Head Warguar travel to Sakaar. The Great Arena, situated in the Crown C southwestern quadrant, is the city's largest single building serves as the central gathering place for all members of soc both poor and wealthy.

The Crown City is bisected by the Imperial Boulevard far the widest avenue in the city. Lined with statutes monuments honoring the Empire and its leaders, the Imp Boulevard serves as the location for lavish, state-spons parades which are frequently held to exhibit the Emp wealth and power. In addition to housing the Great Ar the southwestern quadrant of the city also contains the A District, a largely residential zone of sub-standard hou where many poorer Imperial citizens live. In the southeas

THE IMPERIALS: CROWN CITY

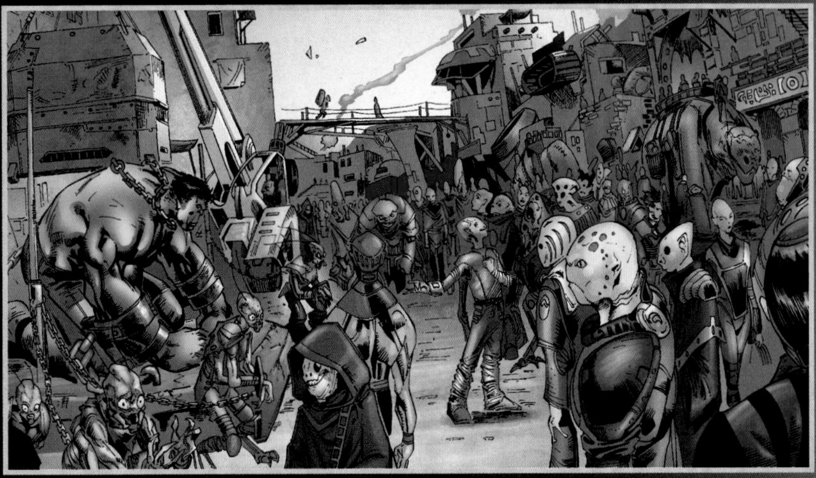

rant of the Crown City lies
ɔustling Public Square and
ketplace, where merchants
ı across Sakaar come to trade
ls and services. Adjacent to
Public Square are the Slave
ion Blocks, where slaves
claimed by the Empire are
ght and sold by private
es. The southeastern quarter
so home to the Outer Slums,
area teeming with cheaply-
tructed patchwork shelters
e many slaves and poor off-
ders reside.

tark contrast to the dreary southeastern quadrant is the
ent northwestern quadrant, a neighborhood consisting
ɔrawling manors, luxury shops, and immaculate public
s. This quadrant houses high-ranking Imperial oligarchs
wealthy merchants, though the vast majority of society's
archs choose to live outside city limits in the palatial

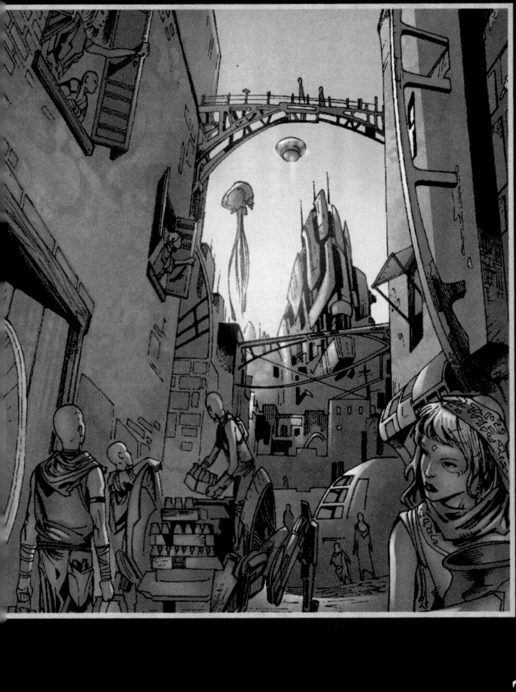

estates of the surrounding countryside. Although all quadrants of the Crown City contain a Death's Head Barracks, it is the Death's Head Barracks in the northwestern quadrant that works hardest to ensure that poorer citizens and slaves do not intrude into the more wealthy neighborhoods, going as far as to establish a protective security perimeter to separate the rich from the destitute. The northwestern quadrant also hosts several government buildings, such as the Imperial Senate, Judicial Rotunda, and Office of Imperial Administration.

Finally, the northeastern quadrant houses many of the Crown City's industrial complexes. Although most reverse-engineering takes place in the smog-filled factory parks of Okini Province, many duplicate factories are maintained in the Crown City in case the supply lines from Okini are ever interrupted. The Industrial District of the neighborhood is a largely residential zone which houses the lower-middle class Imperial citizens who toil in the factories and airfields. The northeastern quadrant also houses the headquarters of the Imperial Guard, although the Guard has become less important in recent years as the Red King has relied more on the Death's Head Warguard to carry out his military campaigns. Finally, the northeastern quadrant contains the Viewbox Transmission Center, which telecasts live feeds from the Great Games into public common areas as well as the private residences of the wealthiest of oligarchs.

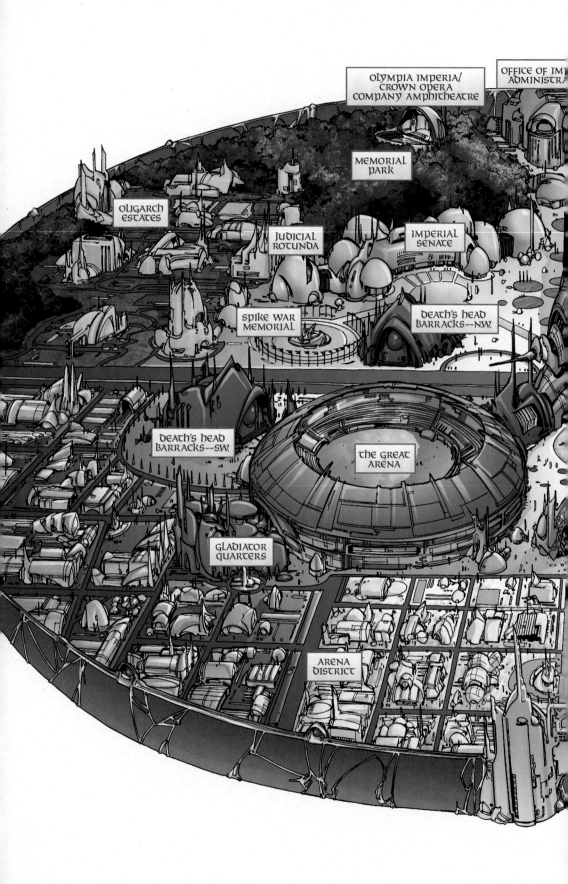

OLYMPIA IMPERIA/
CROWN OPERA
COMPANY AMPHITHEATRE

OFFICE OF IM[
ADMINISTRA

MEMORIAL
PARK

OLIGARCH
ESTATES

JUDICIAL
ROTUNDA

IMPERIAL
SENATE

SPIKE WAR
MEMORIAL

DEATH'S HEAD
BARRACKS--NW.

DEATH'S HEAD
BARRACKS--SW.

THE GREAT
ARENA

GLADIATOR
QUARTERS

ARENA
DISTRICT

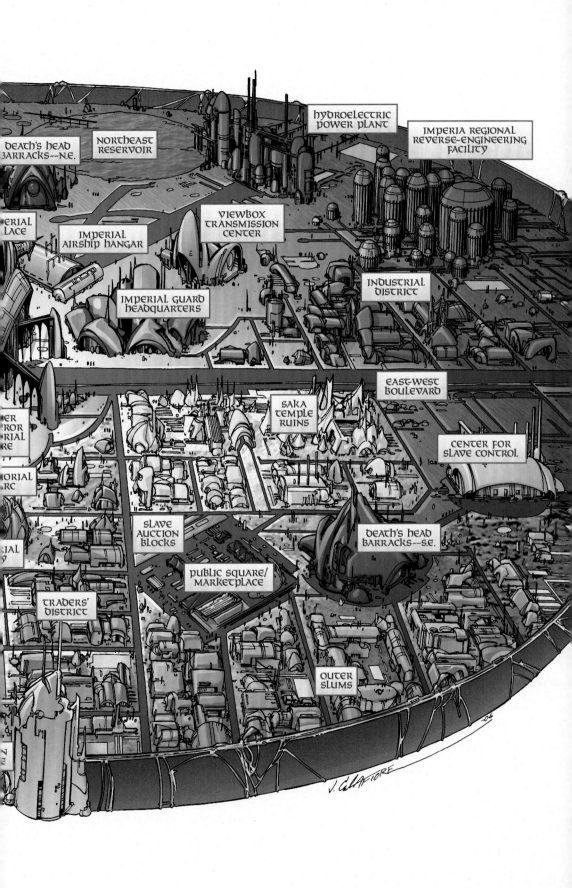

DEATH'S HEAD
BARRACKS--N.E.

NORTHEAST
RESERVOIR

HYDROELECTRIC
POWER PLANT

IMPERIA REGIONAL
REVERSE-ENGINEERING
FACILITY

ERIAL
LACE

IMPERIAL
AIRSHIP HANGAR

VIEWBOX
TRANSMISSION
CENTER

IMPERIAL GUARD
HEADQUARTERS

INDUSTRIAL
DISTRICT

ER
ROR
RIAL
RE

SAKA
TEMPLE
RUINS

EAST-WEST
BOULEVARD

CENTER FOR
SLAVE CONTROL

ORIAL
RC

SLAVE
AUCTION
BLOCKS

DEATH'S HEAD
BARRACKS--S.E.

IAL
Y

PUBLIC SQUARE/
MARKETPLACE

TRADERS'
DISTRICT

OUTER
SLUMS

-06

J. CALAFIORE

IMPERIAL TECHNOLOGY: DEATH'S HEAD UNIT

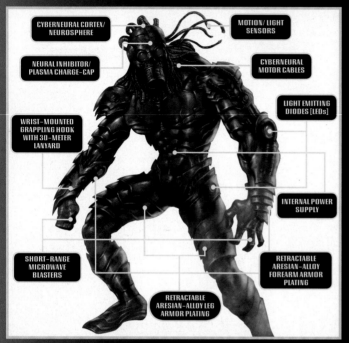

CYBERNEURAL CORTEX/ NEUROSPHERE

MOTION/ LIGHT SENSORS

NEURAL INHIBITOR/ PLASMA CHARGE-CAP

CYBERNEURAL MOTOR CABLES

LIGHT EMITTING DIODES [LEDs]

WRIST-MOUNTED GRAPPLING HOOK WITH 30-METER LANYARD

INTERNAL POWER SUPPLY

SHORT-RANGE MICROWAVE BLASTERS

RETRACTABLE ARESIAN-ALLOY FOREARM ARMOR PLATING

RETRACTABLE ARESIAN-ALLOY LEG ARMOR PLATING

the Death's Heads were still operational, cyberneural cortexes were apparently reb as a result of their journey through the Portal, causing them to wander aimlessly wi a set of programmed protocols to follow. Fe threatened by the presence of these cyber killing machines, the Father Emperor dest what he believed to be the Death's Heads unit. Immediately after the Father Emperor the unit, the remaining Death's Heads knee his feet, their malfunctioning artificial intellig telling them that he was their new lead unit.

While the destroyed Death's Head unit an disabled flagship were taken to Okini Pro to be studied by Empire's engineers, the F Emperor immediately put the remaining D Head units to use in the war against the Sp Supplementing the traditional Imperial G the Emperor's new "Death's Head Wargu proved especially adept at finding and k

*T*he year 536 Post was a dark period for the Empire. It was the height of the Spike War and the military alliance that the Father Emperor forged with the Shadow People one year earlier was proving insufficient to defeat the Spike invaders. Increasingly desperate for a way to end the war, the Father Emperor led a small contingent of troops into the Great Desert to pray and fast for seven days upon Prophet's Rock. On the seventh day, the Great Portal opened for the first time, emitting a surge of energy that rocked the entire planet to its core. Following this surge of energy through the Portal came a damaged alien flagship, which crash landed in the on the outskirts of the Great Desert. The Father Emperor and his troops were the first to approach the flagship, discovering that it contained approximately 300 cybernetic warriors known as "Death's Heads." Although

Spikes, their success attributable to the fact that their me bodies were immune to the Spikes' ability to infect consume organic material. Becoming increasingly relia the loyal and untiring Death's Heads, the Father Emper a series of successful military campaigns against the Spike the course of the next three years.

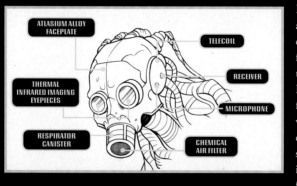

ATLASIUM ALLOY FACEPLATE

TELECOIL

RECEIVER

THERMAL INFRARED IMAGING EYEPIECES

MICROPHONE

RESPIRATOR CANISTER

CHEMICAL AIR FILTER

Finally, in the year 540 after six years of rev engineering the Death's flagship and unlockin technological secrets, Empire's engineers finally able to activat vessel's main propu engines and navigat systems. The Father Em immediately ordered flagship to conduc destructive bombing raid over the Spike stronghold in Un Province, after which the Father Emperor himself (outfitt a grandiose mechanized war suit constructed from the

IMPERIAL TECHNOLOGY: DEATH'S HEAD UNIT

...e defeated Death's Head lead unit) led the Death's Head ...guard in a ground assault that forced the devastated Spikes ...treat into one of their invading ships. Unknown to the ...s, this ship had been reprogrammed with new coordinates ...mperial engineers and launched back into space, sending ...urviving Spikes to permanent exile on the broken moon ...byr.

...e years following the war, the Death's Head units were ...ned to keep the peace in the outlying provinces and ...d with special government assignments, such as the ...mission to eradicate the great devil corkers which ...ed the inhabitants of Upper Vandro Province. However, ...the death of the Father Emperor and the ascension of ...Red King, many of the Death's Heads were recalled to ...mperial Crown City to serve as the Red King's personal ...ctors. Growing increasingly suspicious of the traditional ...rial Guard, which the paranoid Red King feared had been ...ated by Fillian sympathizers, the Red King began phasing ...ne duties of the Imperial Guard and replacing them with ...'s Heads units.

...ough Imperial engineers have been unsuccessful in their ...npts to create Death's Heads units of their own due to ...inability to understand the complexities of artificial ...igence, they have been able to repair damaged units ...ng as their cyberneural cortex and neurosphere are still ...e. Thus, there is an ever-dwindling number of Death's ...units on Sakaar, especially after enemies of the Empire ...ed tactics specifically aimed at destroying the irreparable ...osphere so the units can not be salvaged. Although the

current number of functional Death's Heads is uncertain, it is believed to be far less than the 300 that originally arrived on Sakaar 30 years ago.

Death's Heads contain a complex, brain-like artificial intelligence system housed in their cyberneural cortex and neurosphere. The Empire has also installed each unit with a neural inhibitor and plasma charge cap that is set to explode if anyone attempts to tamper with the unit's set protocols. Shielded by a nearly indestructible alien metal of unknown origin, the units' forearms and legs are outfitted with retractable shielding that expands at a moment's notice to protect the units from explosions and small arms fire. The units' hands are equipped with microwave emitters that can use radio waves to excite atoms within nearby matter, causing the matter to reach extremely high temperatures within seconds. The units are also equipped with motion and light sensors as well as light-emitting diodes that assist the units with global positioning. Although often issued mission-specific gear and weapons, all Death's Head units carry a standard-issue laser cannon for long-range assaults and a small arsenal of plasma grenades.

IMPERIAL TECHNOLOGY: IMPERIAL DREADNOUGHT

ORIGIN PLANET: Various
LENGTH: 1,137 meters
HEIGHT: 690 meters
WEAPONS:

2 Kree Disintegrator Cannons
24 Luphomoid twin Energy Blasters
10 Mobian Energy Harpoons
8 Xandarian Orienta-type Air-to-Surface Missiles
8 Deathfire Bombs

The most fearsome airship in the Empire's growing armada, the Imperial Dreadnought is a true testament to the resourcefulness and ingenuity of the Empire's engineers. After the Father Emperor ordered the Death's Head flagship to conduct the Deathfire Bomb attack on the old Imperial Capital City that signaled the end of the Spike War, he decreed that the flagship be retired and transported to the new Crown City to serve as his Imperial Palace — a monument to his epic defeat of the Spike invaders. As such, it fell on the shoulders of the Empire's engineers to construct a new heavy-artillery airship to serve as a symbol of the Empire's military superiority. Unfortunately, the Great Portal had a tendency to damage all space travel technology which passed through it beyond repair, forcing the engineers to cobble together a ship out of the component parts of several other ships. The first significant component of the Dreadnought came through the portal in 549 Post when a small fleet of Kree Imperial Battle Cruisers where drawn into the Great Portal while patrolling Kree System 114 in the Greater Magellanic Cloud, along the Skrull-controlled region of the Andromeda Galaxy. Although the engines and propulsion systems of the Imperial Battle Cruisers were destroyed, the hulls of the fallen ships served as a crucial staring point to the construction of the Dreadnoughts. Later, following the destruction of Tarnax IV, the Skrull Throneworld, by the world-devourer Galactus, various Skrull warlords began fighting each other for control of the Skrull Empire and a number of their

battle-damaged Skrull Command Cruisers and Star-[Shuttles were pulled through the Portal, proving very u to Sakaarian engineers who were looking for engines pow enough to lift the massive hulls of the Kree Imperial Cru off the ground. Finally, the Empire's engineers made se alterations of their own, adding several weapons systems various other vessels that came through the Portal over decade.

Dubbed the "Imperial Warnought," construction on Empire's new fleet of heavy artillery air-vessels was comp in the year 557 Post, just in time for the start of the Empe war against the Fillians. The Imperial Dreadnoughts pr to be extremely useful in the early days of the Emperor's as the Fillians did not have an air vessel powerful enoug counter the massive Dreadnoughts. But after the Dreadnou obliterated several towns and cities along the southern F border in a series bombing campaigns, the Fillians develop anti-aircraft defense system that prevented the Dreadnou from flying too deep into Fillian territory. Thus the Emp War fell into its current stalemate. Most recently, for the time in history, an Imperial Dreadnought was flown int Crown City and used to bomb a team of gladiators in the C Arena. Although it was first suspected that the Emperor hir ordered the attack, the Emperor's advisors have since as the concerned public that the bombing raid was the wo rogue Fillian-sympathizers within the Imperial Guard.

Due to the limited resources with which the Empire engi had to work, no two Imperial Dreadnoughts are exactly a However, all vessels are equipped with several standard feat In addition, each Imperial Dreadnought contains one int bomb bay capable of carrying a payload of up to 8 Dea Bombs or 64 conventional bombs. Imperial engineers made several modifications to the 350 ton Deathfire B since first discovered aboard the Death's Head flagship can be outfitted with chemical and biological warhead maximum damage (as was the case when the Father Em ordered the bombing of the Spikes in 540 Post) or they ca modified into precision strike weapons able to take out city blocks with focused explosions which only inflict mir damage upon the surrounding untargeted area.

IMPERIAL TECHNOLOGY: PLEASURE CRUISER

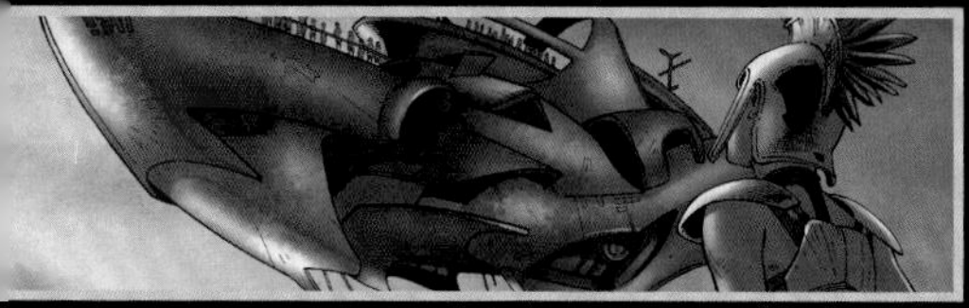

NET OF ORIGIN: Sirus X, Milky Way Galaxy
GTH: 345 meters
GHT: 169.5 meters
PONS: None

ps the planet's most well-known symbols of aristocratic r and excess are the Imperial Pleasure Cruisers. Despite importance in the social lives of Imperial oligarchs, the ure Cruisers only arrived on Sakaar via the Great Portal years ago, in Sakaar calendar year 558 Post. The Cruisers' og entries reveal that they were constructed on Sirus X in ilky Way Galaxy, a planet known as a haven for gambling ebauchery, and manufactured at the behest of Pro-Boscis rocurer, an intergalactic brothel owner and procurer of l pleasures. However, the seven Pleasure Cruisers were oped by the Great Portal while en route from Sirus X eir intended destination in the orbit of nearby planet vinkle and crash landed on Sakaar before Pro-Boscis ever is newly-constructed ships.

n acquired by Imperial engineers, the Cruisers were still in singly good condition. Only their ion propulsion engines destroyed by the Portal, forcing engineers to replace them substitute engines that were not powerful enough to ve orbit. When the prospect of transforming the Cruisers nilitary vessels by outfitting them with weapons and armor eemed too costly, the Emperor decided to use them for urpose for which they were created: entertainment. Today, mpire's fleet of six Pleasure Cruisers are constantly seen ting across Sakaar's skies at low altitudes. Used primarily ntertaining the Emperor's cronies as well as high-ranking nment oligarchs and their families, Pleasure Cruiser s are also available to the wealthy Imperial merchants can afford them. Pleasure Cruisers are usually flown to e, unsettled regions of Sakaar where their passengers can ve exotic wildlife unblemished by modern civilization, ney are more often than not flown to the locations of

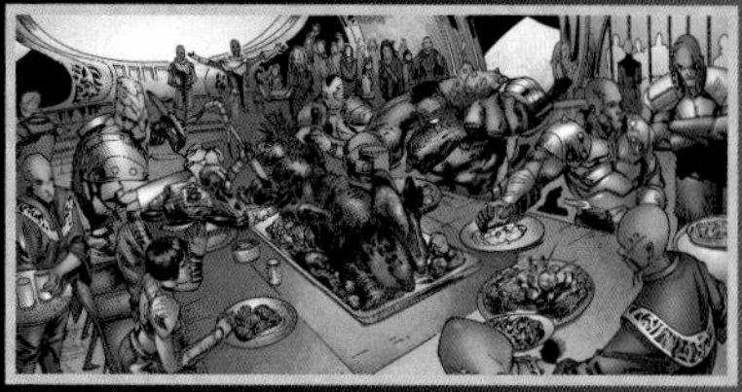

gladiator battles fought outside the walls of the Crown City, after which the Cruiser's captain often invites the victorious gladiators on board to mingle with his passengers. Although the Empire's fleet originally contained seven Pleasure Cruisers, one Pleasure Cruiser was shot down near the southern Fillian border in the year 560 Post, killing all passengers on board. Eyewitnesses claimed that it was a pack of Wildebots that had shot down the Pleasure Cruiser, but the Emperor insisted that the attack was perpetrated by Fillian terrorists and convinced the Imperial Senate to declare war upon the Fillians within weeks.

Each Pleasure Cruiser is equipped with every luxury and innovation that an Imperial could want. Staffed by a large workforce of domestic slaves and servbots, the crew attends to the passengers' every need. On the cruiser's lowest deck is a grand casino equipped with wall-to-wall viewboxes where the wealthiest of the Imperial upper-class wager large sums of silver squares on the results of gladiator matches and sometimes even on the outcomes of battles in the Emperor's War. Featuring a large portal window on each side, the Cruiser's largest room is the Main Banquet Hall, located on decks 9 through 11, where bountiful feasts are served to dignitaries and other esteemed guests of honor. Decks 14 and 15 house a wide array of luxury shops and spas. Decks 8, 12, and 13 feature elaborate, multi-layered, outdoor observation decks adorned by a cascade of balconies. The remaining decks consist primarily of broad hallways lined with the curtain-covered, circular entrances to the Cruiser's many private rooms.

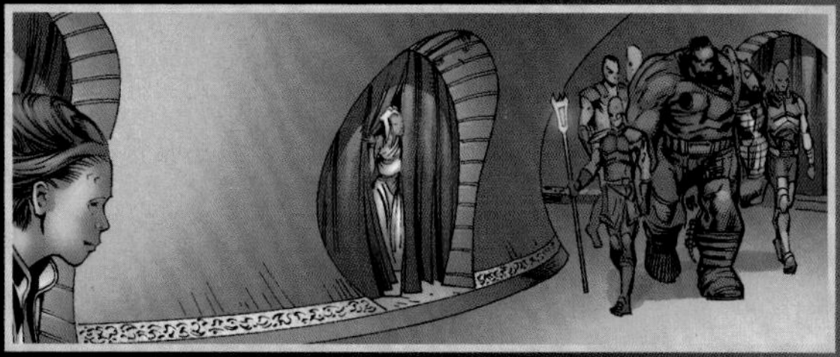

IMPERIAL TECHNOLOGY: MISCELLANEOUS TECH

OBEDIENCE DISKS

The Great Portal brought a Kree Starstealth-class Assault Vessel, which was departing a Kree Space Station Web located in the Milky Way Galaxy's Duggil Star System, to Sakaar in 551 Post. In addition to several hundred Kree Uni-Blaster weapons, the Empire found a small arsenal of Kree Neuro-Lances, staff-like weapons which could shock a victim's central nervous system to the point of death.

The Empire's engineers not only replicated the Kree technology, but vastly improved upon it. While the original design of the Neuro-Lance (or "Obedience Staff," as it is also called) required the user to be in close proximity to his intended victim, the Empire's engineers created disk-like receptors that allowed the Neuro-Lance's user to debilitate victims from a safe distance. These "obedience slugs" or "control disks," as they are also called, are attached to a protruding spike that is plunged directly into the victim's nervous system. The Neuro-Lance user can then use his weapon to send an extremely powerful electrical current through the disk-wearer's nervous system, compelling them to obey his commands. Those who resist the Neuro-Lance's control for an extended period are either killed or rendered brain dead. Today, the Obedience Disk/ Neuro-Lance technology is used primarily to prevent slaves and gladiators from rebelling. The technology has also proven effective against beings without traditional nervous systems, such as robots, due to its ability to interfere with and override their sensory and motor functions.

TRANSPORT PLATFORMS

In Sakaar calendar year 558 Post, the wreckage of a massive Star Cruiser landed in Wukar Province via the Great Portal. The Star Cruiser, which had apparently been destroyed before even entering the Portal, contained only a few robot survivors who revealed that they had served as pilot-droids for Commander Gormagga Kraal, a notorious intergalactic warlord who had escaped the ship's destruction

via his personal Solo-Cruiser. The ship's functional h platforms were promptly salvaged and transported to Empire's reverse-engineering facilities in Okini Provinc further study. The Empire's engineers quickly reconstr the off-world technology and, by 559 Post, used it to c "transport platforms," a revolutionary new technology transformed Sakaarian transportation forever. Equipped anti-gravity engines that push against the planet's fiel gravity, the transport platforms offered a fuel-efficient r of transportation which could reach locations inaccessib larger vessels. Today, use of transport platforms is widesp through the Empire. Many large Imperial vessels, such a massive Warnoughts, house multiple transport platform their hangars for troop transport.

VIEWBOXES

The technology that gave rise to Empire's current viewbox broadca system first arrived on Sakaar in the h a Thulcan-class Cargo Cruiser belon to the Federation of Matriculo technologically-advanced, cosmopc planet of the Verge Galaxy inhabited by commercial formers, alchemists, and communications specia Matriculon's communications specialists had devel technology that allowed them to receive and tran information anywhere is the known universe. The C Cruiser was en route to one of the Federation's cust planets when it was pulled through the Great Porta crashed on Sakaar. The Empire scientists quickly ada the technology to a form where it could be used on Sa Although not able to send or receive off-planet transmis the Viewbox Transmission Center constructed in the C City beams signal feeds to all of the Empire's prov where they are received by individual viewbox units. T personal viewboxes are usually only found in the homes o wealthiest Imperial oligarchs – all other citizens are rele to watching the giant viewbox screens constructed b Empire in its cities' public squares. In addition to broadca the Emperor's public addresses, viewbox feeds also simu the ever-popular Gladiator Games.

THE NATIVES:
HISTORY, CULTURE & SOCIETY

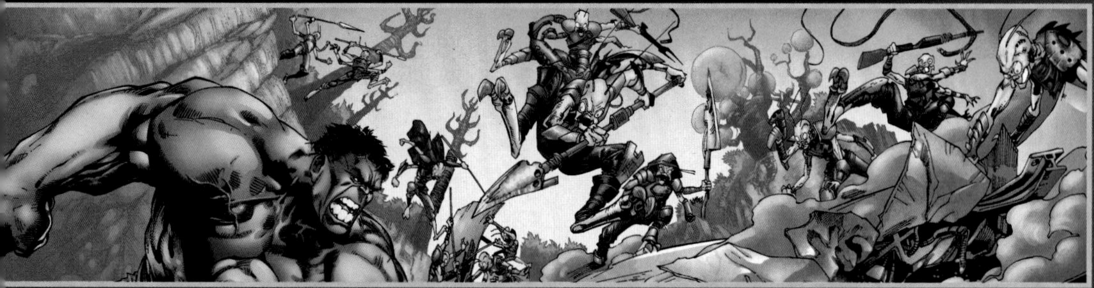

ɿnodern-day Native species is believed to have first evolved . the ancient insect colonies that inhabited the Chaleen ıs over 200 million years ago. Having the distinction of ȝ Sakaar's only native sentient species, Native civilization loped largely uninterrupted by outside influences, the threat to their security being the predatory great devil ers that relied on Natives as their primary food source. ɔproximately 2100 Pre, the Natives, who were up until ɔoint primarily hunters and gatherers, began developing ultural techniques and domesticating small animals such as ɔwly jackworm, which they used as a source of food. With dvent of agriculture, Native civilization began to develop ly, ushering in the Age of the Great Hive Kingdoms of een. Although not technically political entities in the true of the word, these massive familial groupings, which ıally contained anywhere between 100-200 Natives per were each ruled by a hive king and housed in towering, stic hive spires constructed from hardened mud and . As Native civilization flourished, the various hives began nding into other regions of Sakaar and different Native species eventually began to emerge.

the peaceful coexistence between the Native hive loms and the other sentient races of Sakaar was not ned to last. In approximately 1150 Pre, the Imperials, a of crimson-skinned humanoids who had first appeared e outskirts of the Great Desert nearly 600 years earlier, n expanding westward along the Vandro River. At first, Natives welcomed these strange, nomadic newcomers and ıt them various agricultural techniques. In exchange, Natives began learning the Imperial language, although tructure of their chitinous mouth and mandibles, while ctly suited to produce various clicks and chirps, made unciation of many Imperial words difficult. But as the erial population began to proliferate and their small s began to swell into expansive city-states, the Imperials Natives began to compete for resources. The first major clash between the Native and Imperial civilizations occurred in the year 28 Post when Imperial warlords razed an ancient Native spire in modern-day Upper Vandro Province. Without a centralized government or an organized military, the Natives gradually began losing ground to the Imperials, leading to the decline of the Age of the Great Hive Kingdoms around the year 100 Post.

In the year 500 Post, when various independent Imperial kingdoms organized into the First Sakaarian Empire, Native society remained largely unaware of this significant political development. It was not until 509 Post, when the Father Emperor sent delegates to the various Native hives with the offer of an alliance, that the Natives finally took notice of the Empire. The Father Emperor's offer was simple: if the Natives agreed to fight alongside the Imperial Guard in the Spike Wars, the Father Emperor would grant them the land they inhabited by royal decree. Many of the Hive kings, weary from years of skirmishes with Imperials, readily accepted the offer and enlisted their hives. Although not technically members of the Imperial Guard, these special Native units (referred to by the Imperials as "Bug Brigades") were instrumental in several key battles, culminating in the Spikes' ultimate defeat in the year 540 Post.

Although the Father Emperor detested the Natives, whom he considered to be an inferior species, he nonetheless respected their service in the war and honored his deal with them for the most part. In the year 541 Post, the Father Emperor decreed that all detritus which exited through the Great Portal shall go to its first finders, even if those finders happened to be Natives. It was not until the Father Emperor's death in 552 Post, and his son's subsequent ascension to the Empire's throne, that Natives began to feel a change in the Empire's policies toward them. The Red King began implementing new policies which some critics claim are secretly designed to lead to the gradual genocide of the Native population.

THE NATIVES:
HISTORY, CULTURE & SOCIETY

SOCIETY

Native society is entirely centered around the patriarchal hive. Although the Native hives of today are considerably smaller than the great hives that existed during height of Native civilization, the basic social structure of the hive has remained unaltered. The hierarchy of hive life is relatively simple: the hive's king is the dominant authority figure and key decision maker while all of his "sons" live to work for the betterment of the hive. Within a well-functioning hive, the brothers live in peace with their father, though there are isolated incidents where ambitious sons have conspired to overthrow their king.

Only male Natives inhabit the hives. Ever since the Natives first evolved from lesser insectoid species, Native females (or "queens") are rumored to have lived in distant, densely forested regions of Sakaar where the protective foliage protects their sensitive flesh from the deleterious rays of the sun. Although Imperial scientists have yet to see a Native queen, Native slaves have described them as giant, solitary creatures barely able to move under their own power. In order to reproduce, a Native king must make a sojourn into these mythical forests in search of a queen. After an ancient mating ritual, the queen lays eggs on the king's carapace, keeping the few female eggs produced from their union to be raised separately in the forests. The king and queen then part ways, typically never to see each other again. Carrying the fertilized male eggs on his carapace, the king nurtures them and cares for them until he eventually creates a hive where the eggs are stored until they hatch. Only a select number of eggs hatch every year, allowing for diversity in the ages of the hive members.

Upon hatching, each Native larvae becomes "chem-bonded" with his hive, able to communicate via chemical pheromones with all its brothers, a phenomenon known as "chemming." Most Imperials regard the Natives as "bugs" with no real sense of individuality. Some scientists, however, claim that each Native is an individual with his own personality, hopes, dreams, and fears, but that it is the chem-bond with the hive which creates a feeling of acceptance, security, and purpose that is almost impossible for non-Natives to understand. The sense of community that the chem-bond instills is so powerful that a Native's greatest fear is not his own individual death, but rather his hive's death. Thus, a Native will typically be willing to die for his hive without any complaint.

Natives who are separated from their hives nearly always die within one to two years. However, there have been instances where unhived Natives have been known to su for decades, particularly when the Native is still young a time of separation. But unhived Natives (often deroga referred to "unhivers") are usually looked upon with scorn loathing by hived Natives, who view them as unclean out and forced to lead solitary existences shunned by both Im and Native alike.

Today, approximately 65 percent of Sakaar's Native popula serve as slaves to the Empire. Individual Natives usuall for a single silver square a piece under normal conditions when sold in groups that are both chem-bonded (to pro their lifespan) and neutered (to prevent metamorphosis king form), the price per Native can reach three to five squares.

PHYSIOLOGY

Imperial scientists have long r that a typical native lifespan consi four main phases, although a selec enter into a fifth stage. All Nativ begins with the translucent egg, up hundred of which are laid at one during the course of a mating between a Native king and queen king then departs with the male to establish a hive of his own, si handedly digging a large tunnel w serves as his new hive's nursery or suitable location is found. Once tunnel is dug, the male eggs are carefully implanted withi tunnel's walls to gestate. It is then the king's sole duty to g and nourish the eggs until the brood hatches. After the b hatches and matures into their adult stage, they are tasked expanding the hive beyond its original nursery tunnel.

Once the Native eggs hatch, the young are in their larval stage, worm-like grubs concerned with nothing more than satisfying their enormous appetites. Virtually defenseless in this stage, and with only limited chem-bonding ability, the Native larvae are confined to the dark safety of the nursery tunnels where they are tended to by adult members of the hive who bring

THE NATIVES: PHYSIOLOGY

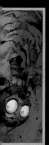

large amounts of vegetation for nourishment. When first ıed, Native larvae basically consist of large mandibles and llae for eating, an elongated thorax and abdomen, and ɪrdeveloped sensory organs such as antennae and eyes. The stage typically lasts for four to six months.

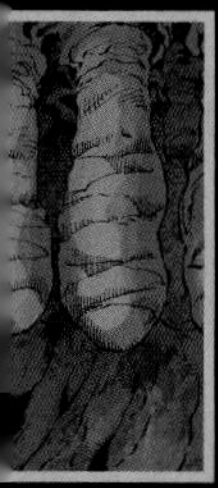

At the end of the Native larval stage, glands located in the Native brain begin to secrete a steroid that prompts the larvae to enter the pupae stage. Climbing to the top of the nursery tunnel, the Native larvae use decaying wood and dead plant matter, chewing it while mixing with saliva, to construct water resistant cocoons that suspend them upside down from the tunnel's ceiling. This pupae stage lasts ɔximately six months, during which many of the larvae's change their function.

At the end of the six month pupae stage, young Native adults emerge from their cocoons in their adult stage. These "nymphs" are anatomically identical to their older Native brethren, only on a smaller scale. Each adult nymph possesses two fully formed antennae, two compound eyes, six limbs, and postpharyngeal glands necessary for the chemical communication that is central to hive society. The nymphs are almost immediately put to work foraging ocal area for food and picking the hive's crops. Most ves become full grown within three years. The chitinous tivorid shells of Native adults contain high numbers of ent-rich melanophore cells that allow Natives to adapt e color of their surroundings over a period of time. This esulted in the various Native "races" that have evolved ıghout Sakaar.

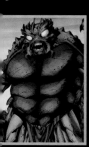

Although this adult stage is the final stage in life for the vast majority of Native males, a select few advance to a fifth stage in life – the king stage. Each Native hive contains one king. In a normally functioning hive, upon a king's death, one of his sons enters into a second pupae stage (although significantly shorter than the first) creating a protective cocoon that houses his body as his cells undergo another extreme change in function. The glands within the transforming adult's brain begin to produce steroids on a much larger scale as he develops a spiky, armor-like chitinous carapace, longer mandibles, clawed phalanges, and a much greater overall body mass. When he emerges from the cocoon, he is automatically recognized as the hive's new king. Scientists have not yet determined exactly what triggers the transformation, although most agree that the Native's chem-bonding capabilities must play a significant role.

ANTENNAE
POSTPHARYNGEAL GLAND
COMPOUND EYE
HUMERUS
RADIUS/ ULNA
MANDIBLES
OPPOSABLE THUMB
PHALANGES
FEMUR
TIBIA
TARSUS

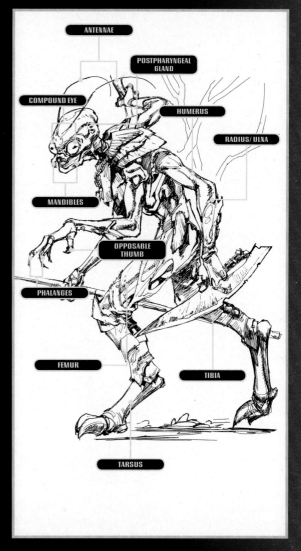

THE SHADOW PEOPLE:
HISTORY, CULTURE & SOCIETY

The Shadow People of Sakaar are a nomadic race of gray-skinned giants who have roamed throughout the planet's deserts and steppes since the beginning of recorded history. Despite their ancient origins, very little is known about the Shadow People's ways or culture. Only a few Shadow People — primarily those warbound to the Emperor — have spent any extended time among the citizens of the Empire. And no Imperial has ever been allowed to document the daily lives of Shadow People. What little we know of the lives and history of the Shadow People comes from the bits of information gleaned from individual Shadow People and often chance observations from afar made by travelers and soldiers in field.

THE SPIKE WAR AND THE SHADOW TREATY

Living the deserts and steppes in which the Empire had little interest, the Shadow People were largely unaffected by the wars between the Imperials and the rise of the Empire. But with the arrival of the alien invaders known as the Spikes, the Shadow People faced a threat which could not be denied. The Shadow People united their military forces under the leadership of the great warrior and strategist Hiroim the Shamed, who saved his people from destruction on numerous occasions. But eventually the Shadow recognized the need for the help of the Father Emperor in wiping the Spikes from their lands. The Shadow Treaty represents the first formal agreement ever made between Shadow People and Imperials. It guaranteed the political independence of the Shadow People and the assistance of the Empire in wiping out the Spikes in exchange for a certain number of Warbound Shadow dedicated to service to the Empire. The Father Emperor chose Hiroim to be his Warbound Shadow; the Father Emperor's son, later to become Emperor himself, chose a young Shadow warrior known as Caiera the Oldstrong, who still serves as his first lieutenant and personal bodyguard.

The Shadow People live in nomadic tribes, most no larger than a hundred members. The tribes form loose coalitions and pool military resources and leadership in times of crisis. Tribes are nomadic and live in camps which can be moved at an instant's notice. A tribe's location on any given day is nearly impossible for an outsider to guess, but the general patterns of movement seem to be linked to the seasons and the migration of the trizelle herds which provide the Shadow People with much of their food.

The survival of a Shadow tribe depends upon its success in hunting, so from childhood, every Shadow Person is trained to be a warrior. Traditional Shadow weapons include the javelin and a seven-foot-long staff with blades running along its entire length. Both men and women are hunters and warriors — the Shadow do not cultivate any crops, only occasio harvesting wild roots and vegetables to supplement their

Very few Shadow People make use of any of the adva technology that has fallen from the Great Portal ove past two generations. And given their nomadic lifestyle Shadow People undertake very little original manufactu of their own. But using techniques not yet understoo Imperial engineers, the Shadow People produce a lir number of forged items of incredible hardness and dural These "Shadowforge" products include virtually unbreal chains, armor, and weaponry that are among the most p possessions in the Empire. Imperial engineers have determ that the materials may actually be an alloy of stone and r but have been unable to identify the individual componer reproduce the process by which they were combined.

Ancient documents describe a great Shadow City somev in the Northern Steppes, but no traces of such a city hav been found. The only known permanent outposts cr by Shadow People are the Saka temples they have E usually along the highest and most inaccessible ridges mountaintops of the Steppes and deserts. A small numb Shadow People trained as Saka priests live in these ten and minister to the pilgrims who visit them. Most trib Shadow People also contain at least one Saka priest who n a pilgrimage to a Saka temple at least once a year.

Newly born Shadow People are much more developed than their Imperial counterparts — standing at least two feet tall, a Shadow infant finds its feet within minutes and can run within hours of birth. Development is rapid, with the average six-year-old Shadow Person having the height and build of the average thirteen-year-old Imperial. But once reaching adulthood, Shadow People are much longer-lived than Imperials.

THE SHADOW PEOPLE: THE LIEUTENANT

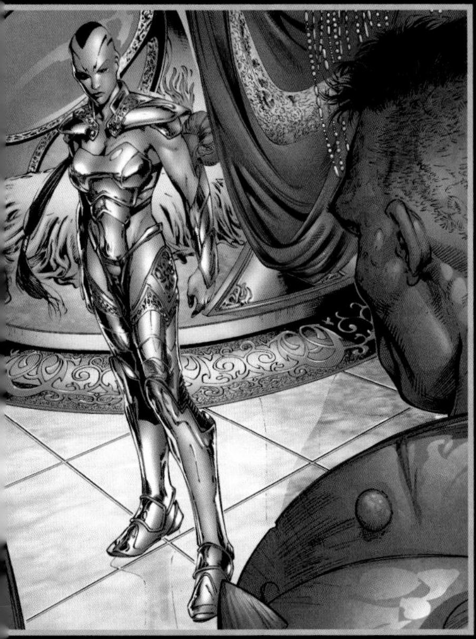

NAME: Caiera
SES: Caiera the Oldstrong, the Emperor's Shadow
UPATION: First Lieutenant of the Imperial Guard; nal bodyguard to the Red King
ZENSHIP: Citizen of the Empire
E OF BIRTH: The Great Desert, Planet Sakaar, Tayo System, Fornax Galaxy
WN RELATIVES: Parents (names unknown, presumed sed)
UP AFFILIATION: Imperial Guard
CATION: Tutored by Imperial military strategists since 3; trained by Shadow Elders until age 13

KGROUND: Caiera the Oldstrong is a Shadow Person serves as the personal bodyguard of the Emperor of ır. Her position is mandated by the Shadow Treaty, which des the Empire with a number of Warbound Shadow ors in exchange for the political independence of the ow People.

into a small tribe of Shadow People in the Steppes in Post, Caiera exhibited great strength and dexterity from a very young age. Village elders determined that she was an "Oldstrong," one of a very few Shadow People born in each generation with augmented physical powers. The elders began to train Caiera, helping her to discover, understand, and control her abilities, but before her training was complete, the alien invaders known as the Spikes attacked the tribe. The details of the skirmish have never been fully revealed, but most accounts assert that Caiera was her tribe's sole survivor and was rescued by the arrival of the Red King himself, then still just a Prince of Sakaar at the time.

Young Caiera was taken into Imperial custody and eventually entered the service of the Prince, receiving the rank of Lieutenant and leading his troops into war in their sorties against the Spikes. She swiftly developed a reputation for physical prowess, brilliant strategy, and an almost eerie coolness in even the most horrifying of battles. With the ratification of the Shadow Treaty in 535, Caiera was formally named the Prince's Shadow. She has remained with his troops ever since, never returning to the tribes or lands of the Shadow People. Suspicions were raised about her loyalty after the Father Emperor's Shadow, Hiroim the Shamed, broke his oath and left the service. But Caiera has remained with the Prince through his succession to the title of Emperor. Most recently, she defended the Emperor from the attack of the Green Scar in the Great Arena. She is currently deployed in the field, hunting down the Green Scar and his army of escaped slaves and gladiators.

HEIGHT: 7'0"
WEIGHT: 270 lbs.
EYES: Black
HAIR: Green

ABILITIES/ACCESSORIES: The exact nature of Caiera's "Oldstrong" powers have never been fully revealed or proven to the outside world, but her physical strength and dexterity are undeniable. She is widely considered to be one of the greatest hand-to-hand combatants on the planet, surpassed only, perhaps, by the Emperor himself in his Death's Head warsuit. Her strength levels have never been formally measured, but she has been seen in battle moving debris weighing more than a ton.

THE SPIKES:
HISTORY & PHYSIOLOGY

An extraterrestrial race of unknown origin, the history of the Spikes prior to their arrival on Sakaar remains a mystery. The voracious Spikes seem to be driven solely by an instinctive need to eat, grow, and reproduce. But to do so, they require massive amounts of organic material. It is speculated that decades ago, the Spikes ingested all of the organic material on their home planet, forcing them to develop space travel technology so they could venture to other planets in an attempt to satisfy their insatiable hunger. While other star-faring species were driven to space travel by the thrill of exploration or desire for conquest, the Spikes were interested only in feeding.

The Spikes are an intelligent species with their own language, culture, traditions, and history, but they are so different physiologically from the essentially humanoid inhabitants of Sakaar that Imperial scientists have been unable to decipher how to communicate with them. But although Spikes possess highly evolved nucleus-brains and are capable of rapid adaptation and construction of advanced technology when it suits them, their physiology remains relatively primitive. Their bodies consist primarily of an amorphous ball of cytoplasm protected by a thin outer plasma wall. Spikes have few internal organs, the most important being their complex, brain-like nucleus. Although they seem to lack a central nervous system, the Spikes exhibit total control over their cytoplasm, able to create tentacle-like extensions for mobility and manipulation of tools. If necessary, Spikes can pull themselves into shapes approximating the forms of other creatures in order to operate weapons or vehicles created for other species, although it is very stressful for them to hold these shapes for extended periods of time. Plus they have proven unable to fully mimic the appearance of another species since their bodies remain translucent and semi-liquid.

Spikes envelop and consume any organic matter with which they come into contact. When in the vicinity of a suitable biological host organism, a Spike extends a dagger-like psuedopod used to infect its victim. Once one of these pseudopods pierces the host organism's skin, Spike DNA is introduced into the victim's body. In a process that can take place in mere seconds, the host organism exhibits uncharacteristic behavior, slurred speech, and joint deformity as the Spike DNA integrates into the DNA

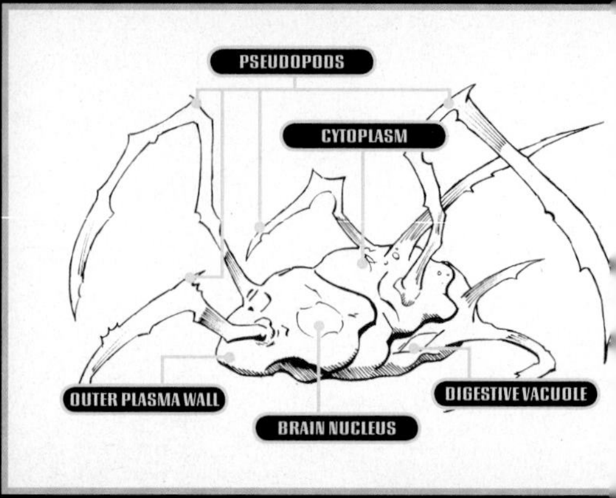

of the host cell chromosomes. The victim suffers from cord breakdown and/or other severe neurological dis as the fully-integrated Spike DNA replicates along wi host organism's cell genome. Ultimately, the host organ rendered brain dead, its body becoming completely gela as bones and cartilage are dissolved into the Spike cyto At this point, the Spike DNA has taken over complete c of the host organism's nervous system and bodily functic

The Spikes first arrived on Sakaar in the year 504 Post. their armada of enormous, spike-shaped vessels first dar the skies above Kumar Province and launched a devas attack upon the province's outlying cities, the Imperials opposed to the Father Emperor immediately toned dowr anti-Empire rhetoric and looked to their leader for guida this time of crisis. It soon became apparent that these st new aliens arrived on Sakaar to eat, and tended to rega humanoids on the planet as food rather than sentient orgar The Father Emperor promptly declared war on these "Sp named for the shape of their terrifying vehicles and the d like pseudopods with which they infected their victims minor skirmishes erupted across the Empire as new armadas entered Sakaar's atmosphere everyday. After a decades-long war, the Father Emperor eventually forc few Spike survivors to enter one of their own warships, Imperial scientists had reconfigured to take the Spikes permanent exile on Sabyr, Sakaar's broken moon. With ships and technology destroyed, it is assumed that the have been stranded on Sabyr ever since.

THE GREAT GAMES

The most time-honored of Imperial traditions, the Great Games trace their origins back to the early days of Imperial civilization. Around the year [?] Pre, when the early Imperials gave up their lives as [n]adic hunters and gatherers and began forming permanent [c]ultural-based societies, gladiator combat emerged as the [?] prevalent method of determining political leadership in [th]e fledgling city-states. Imperial men who expressed their [desir]e to rule were outfitted with crude weapons and armor [and s]et against each other in the confines of an enclosed circle. [The] last Imperial standing was awarded the title of "Prime [Lord]," the undisputed ruler of the city-state.

[As ti]me passed, these gladiator battles to determine leadership [deve]loped into civic social events eagerly attended by both [you]ng and old. The popularity of gladiator combat became [so g]reat among the masses that city-states began hosting the [figh]ts more frequently, allowing young warriors to test their [skill]s against one another even when political leadership was [no]t at stake. Gladiatorial combat even helped foster diplomacy [amo]ng the rival Imperial city-states as an event called the ["Gr]eat Games" was held once every ten years, pitting the [bigg]est gladiators from each city-state against each other to [crow]n the world's best warrior.

[Eve]ntually, with the rise of the Imperial kingdoms between [?] and 165 Post, leadership became hereditary – determined [thro]ugh familial bloodlines rather than hand-to-hand combat. [None]theless, gladiatorial combat remained the most popular [form] of entertainment in Imperial culture. While retired [sold]iers and unemployed youths became gladiators in hopes [of o]ne day being recognized in the Great Games, convicted [crim]inals were forced into less glamorous underground [figh]ting venues.

[The] games remained prevalent even during the Wars of [Emp]ire, with enemy prisoners of war being forced into combat [agai]nst each other to entertain the troops. It was only during [the] decades-long Spike War that the Great Games and nearly [all a]ssociated gladiatorial combat came to a total halt. With most of the Empire's money being spent on war efforts and most able-bodied Imperials being drafted into service, the resources were simply not available. Forcing the Imperials to give up one of their most beloved pastimes amounted to a tremendous psychological victory for the Spikes, and Imperial morale plummeted in the years that followed.

The Father Emperor noticed the psychological change in his subjects during this hiatus and knew that the Great Games needed to return once the Spike War was won. To this end, he ordered that the dilapidated Tego Arena be converted into a larger, more modern facility when Geot City was being converted into the new Imperial Crown City. In the year 542 Post, when the Crown City was officially named as the Empire's new capital following the defeat of the Spikes, the Great Arena was unveiled to the public and the Great Games and associated combat entertainment were reinstated by Imperial decree. The Father Emperor simultaneously established the Imperial League to handle the marketing and promotion of the Great Games and other associated forms of combat entertainment. In this current era of the Games, while most gladiators are convicted criminals, rebellious slaves, or captured enemy combatants or offlanders forced into the ring, some retired soldiers and unemployed youths still voluntarily become gladiators in hopes of one day making it to the Great Games and winning the adulation of the oligarchs.

Today, the Great Games are held on special occasions and anniversaries, such as commemorating the birthdays or death days of great Imperial heroes. Specifically, this year's Great Games celebrate what would have been the Father Emperor's centennial birthday celebration were he still alive today. There are currently several different attractions within the months' long Great Games program. The opening act usually features untrained slaves and criminals being hunted by animals of some kind, usually great devil corkers or rabid arfounds. The main attraction, the Great Games proper, involves trained teams of gladiators fighting either monsters or each other. Other special shows may include reenactments of famous battles in Imperial history or audience participation rounds in which lucky audience members get to hurl spears or daggers at animals or slaves in the arena. Non-violent entertainment,

THE GREAT GAMES

like singing or brief plays, has also been featured in the past, although this kind of programming has become less frequent after several divas from the Crown Opera Company were torn to pieces by a pair of escaped great devil corkers.

There are not many formal rules in today's Great Games. Fighting is typically to the death. Although, traditionally, slave-gladiators are awarded citizenship upon winning three consecutive matches in the Games, the Emperor always has the final decision as to whether to pardon or condemn. The only rule that has remained in force throughout the Games' centuries of existence is that fighting is generally hand-to-hand, without any of the technologically-advanced weaponry that has fallen through the Great Portal in recent decades. It is because of this adherence to traditional fighting techniques that the appearance of an Imperial Warnought and Death's Head Warguard at a recent Great Games match came as such a shock to spectators.

In addition to the Great Games and Imperial League, many underground gladiatorial venues exist in abandoned buildings and even within the Crown City's elaborate sewer system.

THE GREAT ARENA

The year 515 Post was disastrous for the Empire. The Spike invaders has just sacked the Imperial Capital City and killed tens of thousands. With the Great Games suspended due to the ongoing war and with few victories to celebrate, morale was at an all time low among Imperial Guard soldiers. Even in the Imperial cities not directly affected by the fighting, there was a growing consensus that it was only a matter of time before the Spikes prevailed. But the stoic Father Emperor did not lose heart. Regrouping and temporarily transferring his base of operations to a remote volcanic crater in the Mawkaw Mountains, he secretly ordered his generals in Tego Province to begin the city-wide expansion project that would eventually transform the city of Geot into the Imperial Crown City.

But the Father Emperor knew he needed more than a capital city to raise the spirits of his subjects. So, as the Gove of Tego and his advisors assembled a massive workforc slave laborers who were either too old or too infirm to into battle against the Spikes, the Father Emperor orc that Geot's ancient Tego Arena be rebuilt into a new spacious and modern facility that would serve as the cent the new capital's entertainment and social life. Constru on the "Great Arena Project" began in 517 Post as Imp architects began breaking down segments of the Tego Ar marble facade to expand the facility. Thousands of slaves shipped in from around the Empire, many dying in tran a result of getting caught in the crossfire between the S and Imperials. Actual construction of the Great Arena wa safer, as hundreds of slaves died from exhaustion or inj sustained on the job. Twenty-man teams of slaves were into the quarries of the southern Maga Mountains to ob the marble needed to expand the facility, taking years to the massive chunks of rock over the hostile terrain separa the quarries from the city. Shortly after the Great P opened in 536 Post, teams of male slaves were sent into surrounding countryside to obtain enormous shards of s metal that had fallen from the Portal, which were then use form the building's exterior walls. Female slaves were us left behind to cut and weld the enormous chunks of met they arrived.

THE GREAT GAMES

struction was finally completed in 548 Post, eight years the end of the Spike War and twenty-nine years after truction of the massive structure began. Today, the Great a exists exactly how the Father Emperor envisioned it, as a er of social life for both the Crown City's richest and poorest bitants. Standing nearly 70 meters high, the Great Arena fs all other structures in the Crown City's Arena District. osed by a 10-meter tall stone wall, the wide, elliptical a floor is covered in sand and carefully maintained by a of slaves before and after gladiator matches. A labyrinth nderground stone tunnels runs beneath the arena floor, ining immense cages where the fierce animal competitors kept prior to combat. An underground tunnel also ects the Great Arena to the nearby Gladiator Quarters, e the various slave-warriors are housed prior to their hes. Seating, now constructed mostly of metal, is divided different sections according to social status. The first level ating is reserved for the box seats of Imperial oligarchs, watch the matches while attended by teams of domestic ts, and also features the Emperor's private metal, open-air ox. Above the oligarch level is the middle tier of seating, pied by wealthy merchants and other members of upper- dle class society. The third and final level, located along op edge of the arena, is left for the poorest citizens and estic slaves, constantly patrolled by a legion of Imperial rdsman wielding Neuro-Lances.

E MAW

ed for its location in the northern expanse of the kaw Mountains, the Maw Gladiatorial Training Facility is lly located inside the largest known volcanic crater in the ntain range. The Maw first came to prominence during the e War, shortly after the Spikes launched their devastating ilt on the First Imperial Capital City in Umegus. The er Emperor and his army, who survived the attack, began ching for a new temporary base of operations. In 515 Post, e crossing the Mawkaw Mountains in retreat from a Spike nsive in Kumar Province, the Father Emperor discovered Maw. Soon realizing that the intense heat generated from Maw's magma rivers prevented Spike tracking devices pinpointing their location, the Father Emperor decided

to make the Maw his temporary headquarters until his new capital was constructed in Crown City.

Following the defeat of the Spikes, the Father Emperor reinstated the Great Games and associated gladiatorial combat events. But, unlike the games of old, these new games were to feature predominantly criminals, slaves, and captured enemy combatants. As such, it was felt that a harsh, prison-like training environment was needed to sculpt these unwilling participants into suitable gladiators – and the Father Emperor decided that the Maw was perfectly suited for such a role. Already equipped with metal guard towers from its time as an Imperial fortress during the Spike War, the Maw was outfitted with cages to house its trainees and elevated, air-conditioned facilities to house its trainers. The Maw soon earned a reputation as the Empire's most lethal gladiator training school.

Trainees are ferried up the Mawkaw mountainside in giant cages strapped to the backs of drammoth and, upon arrival, are immediately forced to battle against an assortment of vicious animals in the volcano's sweltering heat. In order to narrow the number of trainees down to more manageable levels, elimination matches are held in which twenty-two combatants are forced into combat against each other, with only the last seven living able to advance to the next rounds. Those few fortunate enough to survive the Maw's many challenges find themselves one step closer to every gladiator's dream: competition at the Great Games.

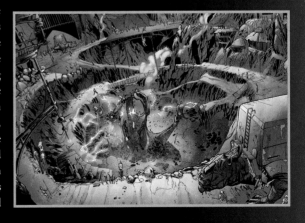

THE GREAT GAMES: BROOD CREATURE 2 OF 6 — BROOD

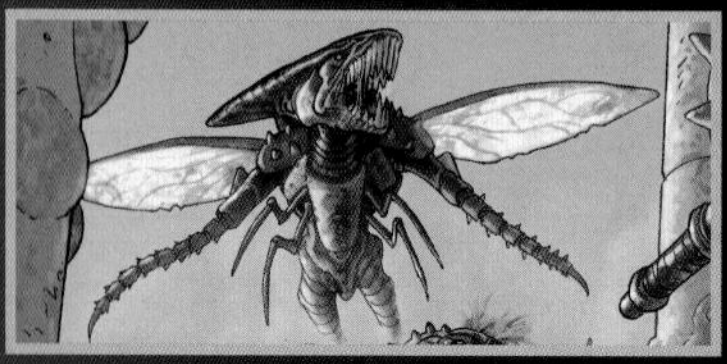

REAL NAME: Inapplicable
ALIASES: No-Name
PLACE OF BIRTH: Warrior-Prime Birthing Chambers, Throne City
CITIZENSHIP: Slave of the Empire; formerly member of the Brood Collective
PLANET: Broodworld
STAR SYSTEM: Unrevealed
GALAXY: Brood G
LENGTH: 8'0"
WEIGHT: 272 lbs.
HAIR: None
EYES: Yellow
VIEWBOX RATING: 5 of 10

BACKGROUND: The Brood Creature first arrived on Sakaar in the remains of a crystallized beast, severely weakened from the combined effects of starvation and the Great Portal. Although the hostile Brood refused to cooperate, we have learned about their race from other off-worlders and feedback data generated from their obedience disks.

The Brood are a savage insectoid alien race terrified of the possibility of extinction and instinctively driven to feed and procreate. The Brood are parasitic creatures who view other species merely as living incubators for their young. The Brood Queens implant their eggs in other living organisms, allowing the Brood embryos to slowly metamorphosize the host body until they hatch. Once hatched, the Brood fledglings fully consume the host body, effectively converting them into members of the Brood Collective who retain each hosts' knowledge and abilities.

Brood society operates with a collective intelligence under a matriarchal hive structure, ruled by a single Empress ("the Mother of All Mothers") who is guarded by an elite group of Brood known as the Firstborn, her direct descendants. The Empress is a being of great psionic ability and, under normal conditions, maintains a mind link with every individual Brood throughout the universe, controlling the complete loyalty of all her subjects. From among the many Brood Queens, the Empress selects one to act as Imperiatrix ("the Great Mother") and serve as her off-world representative in dealings with alien races.

Under the Firstborn and Queens rank the Warriors-Prime, an assemblage of Broodworld's most deadly female warriors who personally carry out the bidding of the Empress and her highest ranking Queens. The Warriors-Prime were most often dispatched to dispose of uninvited off-world visitors. Usually male, Drones serve as the expendable foot soldiers and laborers of at the bottom of Brood society.

Despite their savage appearance, the Brood are highly advanced in the field of bioengineering. Early in their history, they developed a mind-virus to enslave the Acanti, an ancient, peaceful, space-faring race of massive cetacean creatures which possessed the natural ability to fly faster than light. Using the Acanti as both a food source and living starships, the Brood captured the Prophet-Singer, the Acanti's leader and the caretaker of the race's collective "soul." The Prophet-Singer was taken to Broodworld where he eventually died in captivity; but instead of his body being burned in a star (as was customary in Acanti society since the collective soul would not pass to the next Prophet-Singer until the body of the current holder was completely destroyed), the Brood turned his rotting corpse into the foundation of their Throne City on Broodworld, with the Acanti's soul still trapped within. Without a soul to guide them, the Acanti quickly succumbed to the Brood mind-virus and served as their slaves for centuries.

With the Acanti and Star Sharks to serve as their transportation, the Brood quickly expanded into other galaxies, eventually coming into conflict with both the Shi'ar Empire of the Shi'ar Galaxy and the Kree Empire of the Greater Magellanic Cloud. The Brood eventually ventured as far as the Milky Way Galaxy and arrived on Earth, where they were opposed by a team of Terran mutants known as the X-Men, the first of many encounters between the Brood and Earth's mutant population. Later, when the Brood Imperiatrix captured the X-Men and brought them back to Broodworld, the X-Men were rescued by a baby Acanti (destined to be the next Prophet-Singer) and agreed to free the Acanti from enslavement by freeing their racial soul.

Brood Creature 2 of 6 was among Warriors-Prime dispatched to follow X-Men into the catacombs beneath T City and kill the intruders. But pri catching their prey, the Warriors-Prime swallowed whole by one of the giant cre native to the Broodworld catacombs. F the Brood could be digested alive, t Men released the Acanti's racial soul w in a blinding flash of light, judged all presence, transforming all beings it de unworthy into crystal, including the mo that consumed the Warriors-Prime. Tra in the belly of the crystallized beast, th living Warriors-Prime were safely hu into space as Broodworld exploded, dr for years before finally being drawn int Great Portal.

On Sakaar, the six Brood Creatures were from their crystal prison and sent to the After several deadly preliminary ma Brood Creature 2 of 6 was the only sur Brood left. With her psionic link to her and the Brood Empress severed, the B Creature was not expected to survive, after uncharacteristically forming an all with several other non-Brood gladi the Brood Creature has lasted longer most anticipated. Slowly gaining a not individuality, the Brood Creature has recently taken to referring to herself as Name."

ABILITIES AND TECHNIQUES: Li members of the Brood Warrior-Prime Brood Creature 2 of 6 possesses six legs, of wings, an armor-like chitin exoskel dagger-like teeth, and a long tail that d into two large stingers. In the arena, B Creature relies on her inherent physical to slaughter her opponents, although sh infrequently used her tentacle-like forel manipulate weaponry.

THE GREAT GAMES:
GREEN SCAR — TERRAN

_ NAME: Robert Bruce Banner
.SES: Hulk, the Green One, the Eye of Rage, the World Breaker, Harkanon, Haarg, Holku
CE OF BIRTH: Dayton, Ohio, United States of America
ZENSHIP: Slave of the Empire; formerly citizen of United States of America
NET: Earth   STAR SYSTEM: Sol   GALAXY: Milky Way
GHT: 7'6"   WEIGHT: 1,150 lbs.
R: Green   EYES: Green
VBOX RATING: 10 of 10

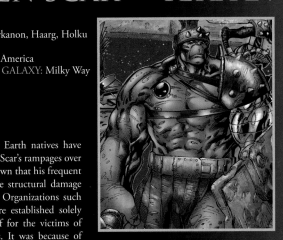

KGROUND: Arriving through the t Portal mere weeks ago in a space shuttle ked "S.H.I.E.L.D.," the Green Scar proven to be an accomplished warrior a most unique individual both inside outside of the arena. The Empire's top nicians have analyzed the feedback data ved from Green Scar's obedience disk have been unable to make sense of the n Scar's mind as of yet. Most agree this ue to the Green Scar's fractured psyche, ndition diagnosed on his homeworld Dissociative Identity Disorder." The full fications of the Green Scar's disorder are ear, but the Empire's engineers have been to piece together details of the Green s life by hacking into the databanks of pace shuttle that served as his transport kaar. Although the engineers have only able to access a small fraction of the banks' contents thus far, their progress s promising.

rding to the databanks, Green Scar me the creature he is today approximately arth years ago after being irradiated with ly charged radioactive particles at the site for a "gamma bomb" experiment ucted by one of Earth's governments. The lent altered Green Scar's cellular structure unleashed aspects of his personality that laid dormant for years. Now prone to of intense rage, the Green Scar would iently go on destructive rampages and regarded as a menace by Earth society, tantly hunted by the military of his home et. His mental state in a constant state of the Green Scar experienced periods of lucidity during which he joined forces other super-powered Earth natives and even regarded as a hero by his people at s, but these periods would never last and Green Scar would inevitably find himself he run from authorities again. Although

it is unclear how many Earth natives have been killed in the Green Scar's rampages over the years, if any, it is known that his frequent outbursts caused massive structural damage across his home planet. Organizations such as the Green Cross were established solely to provide disaster relief for the victims of the Green Scar's melees. It was because of this uncontrollable destructive nature that a secret cadre of super-powered Earth natives finally decided to banish the Green Scar from their planet. Luring him into space on a bogus mission to repair a satellite, the Earth natives secretly programmed the autopilot on Green Scar's shuttle on a direct course for an uninhabited planet where he could live in peace. But the Earth natives did not account for the Great Portal, which intercepted the shuttle and brought it to Sakaar. While most beings are immediately rendered unconscious by the strength-sapping properties of the Great Portal upon arrival on Sakaar, the Green Scar proved to be highly resilient. Landing in the desert region of Wukar Province, the Green Scar fended off an attack from a local Native hive immediately after making landfall and then refused to submit to the Governor of Wukar Province, who promptly incapacitated the Green Scar with a neuro-dart and immediately declared him property of the Empire.

The unconscious Green Scar was confined in Shadowforge chains and taken to the Imperial Crown City where he was auctioned off as a slave to Primus Vand, trainer of gladiators and promoter of the Great Games. After winning his opening match against a great devil corker and scarring the Emperor's face during an impromptu duel, the Green Scar was transported to the Maw for further training. He has since earned impressive victories over the notorious wildebot Eggbreaker and even his former ally the Silver Savage. Although

the Green Scar has since escaped from the Empire's custody, Empire officials assure us it is only a matter of time before the Green Scar is recaptured and sent back into the arena.

ABILITIES/TECHNIQUES: The Green Scar possesses incredible strength, estimated to be able to press in excess of 100 tons (although the upper limits of his strength remain a mystery). Additionally, his strength level increases in direct proportion to his anger, most likely caused by the escalation of his adrenaline levels during times of fear, rage, or stress. His leg muscles, in particular, are strong enough to leap 3 Earth miles in a single bound (and he is also reported to have nearly achieved orbit once while leaping into Earth's upper atmosphere). The gamma radiation that served as the catalyst for his current state fortified his cellular structure, endowing him with a high degree of resistance to injury, pain, and disease. The shuttle's databanks reveal that the Green Scar can withstand great heat without blistering, great cold without freezing, and great impacts. He can regenerate body tissue within seconds to minutes, although the effects of the Great Portal seem to have temporarily diluted many of these characteristics.

In the arena, the Green Scar relies primarily on his brute strength to win battles, although he has learned many new fighting techniques from both his opponents and allies since his initial battle. He has taken to using a battle axe in combat.

THE GREAT GAMES:
KAIFI, ELLOE — IMPERIAL

REAL NAME: Elloe Kaifi   ALIASES: None
PLACE OF BIRTH: Rundi, Okini Province
CITIZENSHIP: Slave of the Empire; formerly citizen of the Empire
PLANET: Sakaar   STAR SYSTEM: Tayo   GALAX
HEIGHT: 5'4"   WEIGHT: 120 lbs.
HAIR: Black   EYES: Crimson
VIEWBOX RATING: 1 of 10

BACKGROUND: Elloe Kaifi is a young Imperial woman born into the aristocratic classes as the daughter of Fifth Regional Community Congress Representative Ronan Kaifi. Born years after the end of the Spike War, Elloe's early childhood was relatively carefree. She enjoyed most of the privileges of the Imperial upper classes, including a classical education in the Secondary Forums, weekend summer trips aboard Imperial Pleasure Cruisers, and spacious living quarters in the gated mansions far from the squalor of the slave quarters of downtown Rundi. Elloe's greatest personal distinctions came from her participation in the Olympia Imperia, an annual series of competitive displays of physical beauty and prowess through which young aristocratic women debut into Imperial society. Elloe's grace and skill in various competitions during her debut year earned her great acclaim and the attention of numerous prospective suitors. But shortly after her appearances, wildebot problems among her father's constituency began to increase, prompting him to speak out against the Empire's policies more

than ever before. In 560 Post, when the tributes owed to the Empire by his constituents were increased twofold to help pay for the Emperor's War against the Fillians, Ronan Kaifi addressed a series of petitions to the Emperor, all of which were ignored. Investigating the situation, Ronan Kaifi learned of the true extent of the neglect of his people by the Empire, leading him to begin talks with the growing rebel movement in Fillia. But the more critical Ronan became, the more his family began to be ostracized by Imperial society, eventually culminating in a series of assassination attempts which Kaifi believed were sponsored by the Red King himself. Earlier this year, Kaifi was finally arrested, along with Elloe and his retainer and bodyguard Lavin Skee. Sent to the Maw, Ronan was killed before his daughter's eyes.

Elloe became part of the Green Scar's crew of gladiators and survived the horrors of the Maw, partly due to the help of Skee and partly due to her own rage — she became committed to the destruction of the Empire and the Emperor and, during Skee's temporary absence, was the only member of the Green Scar's team to side with insurgent rebels when given the chance aboard the Pleasure Cruiser. Elloe was imprisoned for her allegiance to the rebels while Skee went with the Green Scar's crew to fight in the Great Games.

Although Skee was killed in battle, the Green Scar and his crew defeated the Silver Savage the very next day, thus fulfilling the terms required to claim

their freedom. But Lieutenar the Oldstrong, the Emperor's revealed one final test for th would have to kill the captive order to gain their freedom. T Scar and the others instead rebel against the Empire, t hole in the wall of the Gre and escaping into the Twiste Rejoining the Green Scar, Ello one of his crew's angriest r always agitating for the course that will lead to direct conflict forces of the Empire.

ABILITIES AND TECHN
Elloe has no superhuman p abilities. Due to her training Olympia Imperia, Elloe the physical conditioning, dexterity, and agility of a top Elloe's hand-to-hand combat above average due to her trai gladiator and improve with e she spends in the field.

42

NAME: Korg
SES: None
CE OF BIRTH: Unrevealed
ZENSHIP: Slave of the Empire; formerly citizen of Kronan Empire

NET: Ria   STAR SYSTEM: Krona   GALAXY: Milky Way
GHT: 8'1"   WEIGHT: 2,045 lbs
R: None   EYES: Hazel
BOX RATING: 7 of 10

BACKGROUND: Korg and his fellow Krons first arrived on Sakaar two years ago. Although their Rian Class II Starship was badly damaged in the crash and unable to provide Imperial engineers with much useful data, several of the Kronans succumbed to the Empire's obedience disks, leading to the revelations about Korg and the history of his people.

Native to the planet Ria, the Kronans are a highly-advanced race who developed space-travel technology thousands of years ago shortly after creating the Gravitron, a device installed upon all Kronan starships that allows them to defy the laws of gravity). Having achieved space-travel capability, the Kronans soon set out to conquer other worlds, using their giant Mechano-class and Mechanoid-class robot drones to subjugate less-advanced civilizations. Approximately 1000 years ago, the Kronans attempted an invasion of Earth. Landing in the city-state of Babylon in a region designated Mesopotamia, the Kronan invasion force was confronted by King Gilgamesh, ruler of the nearby city-state of Uruk. Gilgamesh, with the assistance of a time-traveling warrior from Earth's future named Captain America, forced the ill-prepared Kronans to retreat to their starship and leave Earth.

After having millennia to contemplate the tactical errors made in their first Earth invasion, the Kronans staged another attempted invasion of the planet approximately 10 million years ago. Staging an attack from a secret base on Iapetus, a moon orbiting the nearby planet of Saturn, the Kronans amassed a much larger invasion force in the region of Norway on Earth's Scandinavian Peninsula. The brothers Korg and Margus, inexperienced young bricks at the time, were among the Kronans assembled for the attack. Anxious to conquer, the invasion force pursued a native bystander, Dr. Donald Blake, into a nearby cave where he uncovered

Mjolnir, the hammer of Thor, one of Earth's various thunder gods. Meanwhile, the Kronans proceded to attack Earth's military forces, using their illusion-casting technology to scare them into retreat. Eventually Blake, who had been transformed into Thor by Mjolnir's magic properties, confronted the Kronans and used his godly powers to defend against every attack the invaders initiated. Finally, the Kronans unleashed one of their Mechano-Monster units against the god, but Thor destroyed it with one swing of Mjolnir. Badly beaten and terrified at Thor's power levels, the Kronan invasion force once again fled to their starships and retreated, only to learn much later that not all Earth natives possessed Thor's godly powers.

In their hasty retreat, one of the Kronan starships crashed on an asteroid and became separated from the rest of the fleet. When Thor and a group of his fellow Earth gods happened upon the asteroid, the Kronans attacked in an attempt to steal the starship of the gods. Unable to match the power of the gods, the Kronans salvaged the Gravitron from their disabled vessel and modified it into a weapon to counter Thor. But Thor once again prevailed over the Kronans, destroying the vessel and setting off a chain reaction that destroyed the entire asteroid.

Meanwhile, the fleet of Korg and Margus faced similar hardships as they spent years skipping from asteroid to planetoid, trying to repair their ships' warp drives and eventually find their way home. After years of searching for the technology they needed, they finally conquered a small Kree settlement where they obtained the warp drive and navigational technology needed for a flight back to Ria. But soon after they set a new course for Ria, their vessel, at the front of the refurbished Kronan fleet, was sucked into the Great Portal, stranding the would-be conquerors on Sakaar in late 464 Post. Only six members of the Kronan crew, including

Korg and Margus, survived the horrific crash as their starship plunged into the side of the Maga Mountains. Although Korg was tossed far enough from the wreckage of the ship that he was not found by the Imperials when they captured his brothers, the five other survivors were immediately taken to the Maw where they were separated and outfitted with obedience disks. All of the Kronans resisted the obedience disks until they were rendered brain dead, transformed into mindless pawns of the Empire. Meanwhile, Korg, who thought his brothers had been killed in the crash, spent the next year avoiding capture by hiding in the Maga Mountains. Eventually captured by the Death's Head Warguard and brought to the Maw, Korg performed well in his first trial matches and survived the Maw's lethal tests, eventually forming an alliance with seven of his fellow gladiators. But when Korg was forced to battle the mind-controlled Margus and his fellow Kronans, whom he believed had perished in the crash, he nearly succumbed to grief. It was only through the encouragement of the Green Scar that Korg was able to destroy his Kronan brethren and advance to the next round of battles.

ABILITIES AND TECHNIQUES: Like all Kronans, Korg possesses a body made of a durable, silicon-based substance that grants him protection against nearly all forms of physical harm and gives him a rock-like appearance. In oxygen-rich atmospheres, Kronans possesses superhuman strength, able to press approximately 100 tons.

In the arena, Korg relies on nothing but his nearly impenetrable hide as a living weapon. An experienced military strategist, Korg is the consummate pragmatist and is constantly assessing his environment so he can tell what actions are necessary for his continued survival.

THE GREAT GAMES:
MIEK — NATIVE

REAL NAME: Miek
ALIASES: Miek the Unhived
PLACE OF BIRTH: Native Hive CP-23 (Imperial designation), Upper Vandro Province
CITIZENSHIP: Slave of the Empire
PLANET: Sakaar
STAR SYSTEM: Tayo
GALAXY: Fo
HEIGHT: 5'4"
WEIGHT: 120 lbs.
HAIR: None
EYES: Black
VIEWBOX RATING: 2 of 10

BACKGROUND: Miek is a member of the six-limbed, insectivorid race known as the Natives. While most Natives live in hives, where they communicate with their hive-mates through a process known as "chemming," Miek is alone or "unhived," an unusual and difficult status for a Native. Miek's hive was wiped out when he was an infant during a period of Imperial reclamation of post-war lands. Miek escaped the slaughter only to be caught by Imperial soldiers and sold into slavery. No one knows exactly what happened to Miek during the ensuing years, but like other captured Native nymphs, he may have been kept as a pet by Imperial aristocrats, used as slave labor by Imperial farmers, or forced to fight in the underground "Little Games," gladiatorial combat shows (unsanctioned by the Imperial League) conducted in the sewers of the Crown City by small-time promoters. All that is known for certain is that Miek eventually escaped slavery and lived as a runaway in the alleys and tunnels of Crown City for a time, developing a dark grey pigmentation as a result, before being recaptured and sold to the Great Games promoter/trainer Primus Vand. Vand included Miek in the group of slaves sent to be devoured by the great devil corkers in the opening act to the Spring Games of 566 Post. But among that group of gladiators was the Green Scar, who destroyed the great devil corkers and attacked the Emperor. Miek has since become a key member of the Green Scar's crew.

ABILITIES AND TECHNIQUES: Miek is a smaller-than-average Native with less-than-average strength. Fueled by an unending desire to survive, he is a ferocious six-limbed fighter who has more success in battle than his diminutive size seems to warrant. His chitinous insectivorid shell gives him minimal protection from ph harm.

In the arena, Miek survives by hi limbed fighting skills, often wie four weapons at a time to keep opponents off-balance.

THE GREAT GAMES:
HIROIM — SHADOW PERSON

NAME: Hiroim
ES: Hiroim the Shamed
E OF BIRTH: The Northern Steppes
ZENSHIP: Slave of the Empire; formerly citizen of the Empire
ET: Sakaar STAR SYSTEM: Tayo GALAXY: Fornax
HT: 7'2" WEIGHT: 430 lbs
: Black EYES: Black
BOX RATING: 8 of 10

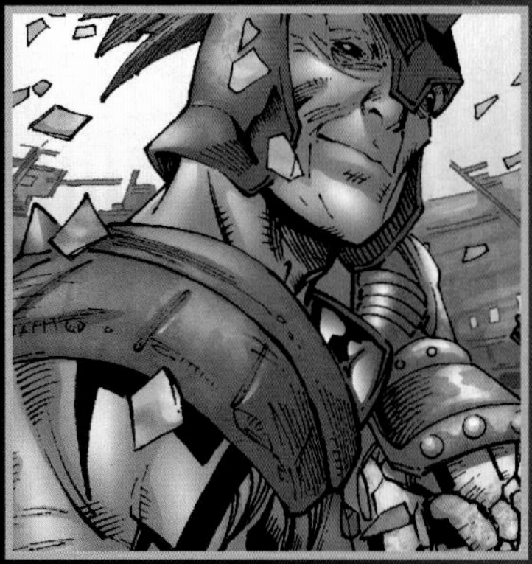

KGROUND: Hiroim the Shamed Shadow Warrior of the Shadow e of Sakaar. His parents were Saka s supposedly sworn to celibacy; after Hiroim was born in 485 both of his parents mysteriously peared from their mountain le in the unchartered regions of Northern Steppes. They have never seen since. Despite his illegitimate age, Hiroim was embraced by the ning Saka priests and raised within emple to be a priest himself. But m's true nature seemed to be more al than spiritual. When submitted ne ritual provocations associated the ceremony of initiation into priesthood, Hiroim was unable to ol his anger as a true Saka priest d — he lashed out, breaking naster's nose and earning his title im the Shamed."

m left the temple for southern nses of the Northern Steppes. He there among various tribes of ering Shadow People for a number ears, learning his people's martial ions and, despite his disgraced , providing the spiritual guidance ould based on his training for the priesthood.

n the alien invaders known as Spikes began their assault on the nern Steppes, Hiroim came into wn and found his true calling as rrior, displaying a sharp eye for gy and logistics. He became the military leader of an army of warriors from a coalition of Shadow tribes and was credited by many for saving the lives of thousands. But the Spikes were relentless, and when the Father Emperor proposed an alliance, the Shadow elders accepted. With the signing of the Shadow Treaty, the Father Emperor became entitled to claim the Warbound service of a Shadow Warrior. He picked Hiroim.

For many years, Hiroim served as the Shadow Guard of the Father Emperor of Sakaar. Shortly after the end of the Spike War, Hiroim left the service under mysterious circumstances. Since he had broken his Warbond to the Emperor, Hiroim was no longer welcome among the Shadow People. And he certainly had no place in the Empire. He spent years in the deserts, a lone hermit, studying the rites and rituals of the Saka Priests. But his life was still forfeit. And when he was captured by Imperial forces, he was sold to the gladiator promoter Primus Vand and brought to the Maw for training. He is now a key member of the Green Scar's crew, providing the team with strategic focus and spiritual perspective.

ABILITIES AND TECHNIQUES: Hiroim has the enormous strength of a trained Shadow Warrior and can lift up to a ton. His skills in hand-to-hand combat rank him as one of the planet's top warriors while his strategic abilities make him one of Sakaar's most formidable field commanders.

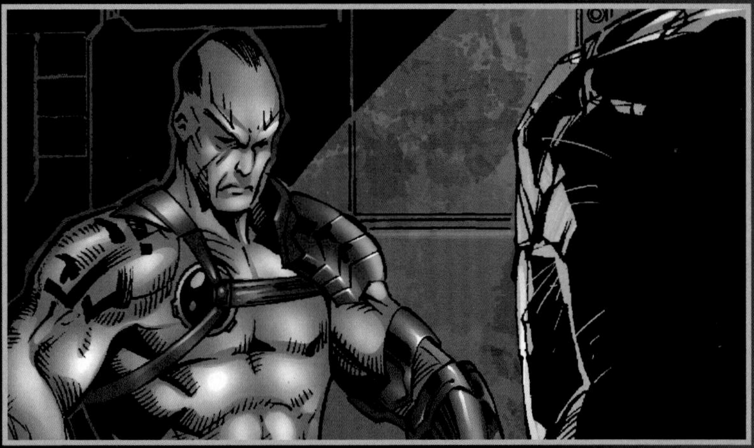

THE GREAT GAMES:
SILVER SAVAGE — ZENN-LAVIAN

REAL NAME: Norrin Radd   ALIASES: Silver Surfer
PLACE OF BIRTH: Unrevealed
CITIZENSHIP: Slave of the Empire; formerly citizen of Zenn-La
PLANET: Zenn-La   STAR SYSTEM: Deneb   GALAXY: Milky
HEIGHT: 6'4"   WEIGHT: 225 lbs.
HAIR: None   EYES: Silver
VIEWBOX RATING: 10 of 10

BACKGROUND: Arriving through the Great Portal only days ago on nothing except a silver board, the Silver Savage was found severely weakened in Okini Province. In his weakened state, he proved especially susceptible to the influence of the Empire's obedience disks and has since revealed much biographical data about himself.

The Silver Savage was born Norrin Radd on the planet Zenn-La, a utopian civilization of long-lived and technologically-advanced humanoids who had vanquished war, crime, disease, hunger, and poverty from their luxurious paradise. Encouraged by his father to avoid the aimless hedonism which had come to plague his world's society, Radd matured into a young man who immersed himself in stories of Zenn-La's adventurous history and longed for the age when his people strove for survival and enlightenment. But Radd's life was forever altered the day that the spacecraft of Galactus, the Devourer of Worlds, entered into Zenn-Lavian space, intending to consume the defenseless planet's life energies. Convincing Zenn-La's scientists to allow him to take a spaceship to confront Galactus, the adventurous Radd offered to become Galactus' herald and seek out new planets for him to consume in exchange for Galactus sparing Zenn-La. Galactus agreed, bestowing a small fraction of his vast store of cosmic power upon Radd and transforming him into the Silver Savage.

The Savage served as Galactus' faithful herald for years, finding his master energy-rich planets void of sentient life upon which to feed while exploring the wonders of the universe. But as time passed, it became increasingly difficult for the Savage to find planets uninhabited by sentient life that were capable of satiating Galactus' hunger. Unknown to

the Savage, Galactus started altering his mind so that he would lead his master to inhabited planets. But upon leading Galactus to the planet Earth, Savage's repressed nobility and humanity was rekindled, causing him to turn against Galactus and help save Earth from certain doom. In response, Galactus erected an energy barrier around Earth uniquely attuned to trap the Savage on the planet.

During his exile on Earth, the Savage formed an uneasy alliance with the Green Scar and several other super-powered Earth natives, which came to be known as "the Defenders." The Savage eventually made amends with Galactus after rescuing his current herald from the Skrull Empire, causing Galactus to finally end the Savage's exile on Earth. The Savage has been on countless cosmic adventures since then and was traversing the spaceways when he felt the presence of the Great Portal. Believing the Portal was calling to him, the Savage willingly entered, only to be rendered unconscious as he landed on Sakaar's surface in Okini Province where he was captured by a legion of the Death's Head Warguard and confined in Shadowforge shackles. Vastly weakened by the Great Portal, the Savage was vulnerable as never before; his normally impenetrable silver skin was pierced by the Empire's obedience disks, which prevented him from utilizing his power cosmic. With his very will now under Empire control, the Savage was forced into gladiatorial combat in the dank underground arenas of Okini Province. Even in his weakened physical state, the Savage easily defeated his opponents and soon came to the attention of Empire officials, who were looking for a formidable opponent for the Green Scar in the Great Games. The match between the Savage and the Green Scar, which was held in the Crown City's Great Arena, was touted as the of gladiator event of the century. By the time they clashed, both the Savage and the Green Scar had regained some of the power

they lost to the Great Portal, but it wa teamwork of Green Scar's allies that led Savage's defeat. At the end of the match severely beaten Savage, whose own obec disk had been destroyed during the cour the battle, used his cosmic power to s the obedience disks of everyone in the a allowing the gladiators and slaves to e into the surrounding countryside. believed that the Savage left Sakaar sh afterwards to fully replenish the powe lost due to the Great Portal.

ABILITIES/TECHNIQUES: The "p cosmic" bestowed upon the Savag Galactus enables him to absorb manipulate the universe's ambient c energies for a variety of effects. He augment his physical strength to incalcu levels and the hard, silvery coating o body is nearly indestructible under n conditions. He can navigate space an enter hyperspace when he exceeds the of light. The Savage is sustained entire the power cosmic and does not require water, air, or sleep to survive. He has demonstrated the ability to alter the s matter, cast illusions, fire energy blasts, and manipulate energy constructs, a and discharge most forms of energy phase through solid matter. His board, is composed of the same silvery, imper cosmic-powered material that coats his responds to his thoughts, even when not in physical contact with it. Upo arrival on Sakaar, many of these abilitie greatly reduced due to the effects of the Portal.

In the arena, the Savage has proven to aggressive hand-to-hand fighter, relyir vicious offensive tactics in the absence cosmic power. He has used his cosmic as a long shield in combat and has ad both a spiked mace and double-ha sword as his offensive weapons.

THE GREAT GAMES:
SKEE, CAPTAIN LAVIN — IMPERIAL

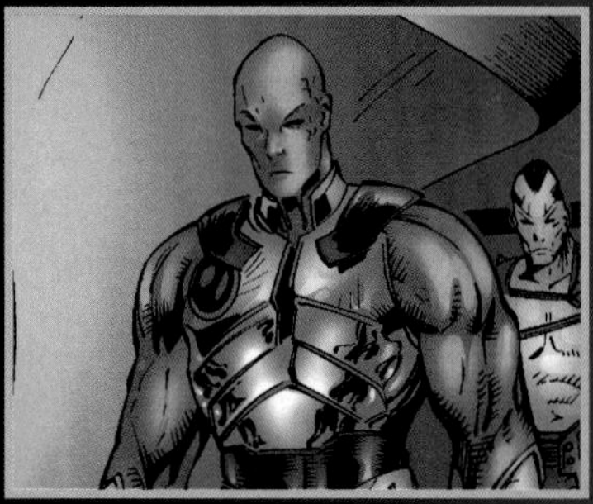

_ NAME: Lavin Skee
SES: The Captain, Scourge of the Spikes
CE OF BIRTH: T'msar, Okini Province
ZENSHIP: Slave of the Empire; formerly citizen of the Empire
NET: Sakaar STAR SYSTEM: Tayo GALAXY: Fornax
GHT: 7'1" WEIGHT: 437 lbs
R: None EYES: Black
VBOX RATING: 9 of 10

KGROUND: Etmo Skee, the paternal father of Lavin Skee, was a destitute g street merchant in T'msar, the capital f the Kingdom of Okini until 487 Post, the armies of General Angmo of the boring Kingdom of Umegus layed siege e city. Offered the chance to make more s life, Umegus was among many poor ians who willingly turned against their family and assisted General Angmo in ıering the kingdom. In return, Etmo was allowed to join General Angmo's y growing army and assisted Angmo as l the march across Sakaar, conquering Imperial kingdom in his path. Given a g of empowerment by his new role in ıo's army and his new status as a citizen, taught his children to honor the newly ished Imperial Guard above all other ations when the First Sakaarian Empire ounded in 500 Post.

reverence for the Imperial Guard was ıally passed down to Lavin Skee, the son of Etmo's eldest son. Lavin dreamed e day becoming a career soldier in the rial Guard like his father and his father's , both who served as highly decorated rial Captains during the decades-long War. Although, born in 531 Post, Lavin oo young to serve in the Spike War, he realized his dream when, in 546 Post, age of fifteen, he joined the Imperial d's 17th Okini Division. As a result own bravery in the Imperial Guard's aigns against the Autocron-led robot ions combined with the reputation of refathers, Lavin quickly rose through ilitary's hierarchy and achieved the rank ptain by 552 Post. After leading several ssful campaigns against wildebot raiders, was among several distinguished ins to be promoted to the Emperor's ıal guard in the Crown City.

But by the year 561 Post, the Red King, who had since ascended to the Imperial throne, became increasingly paranoid at the thought of Fillian sympathizers within the Imperial Guard, prompting him to remove all Imperial Guard captains from his personal guard and replace them with Death's Head units, whose programmed loyalty he trusted, led by his Shadow Lieutenant. The Imperial Guard captains were reassigned to menial civil order duty, leading hourly patrols of the Crown City's slums to ensure that all slaves were properly outfitted with obedience disks.

Captain Lavin Skee, who was already disturbed by the new Emperor's policies, was outraged at this perceived "demotion" and retired from the Guard at the first opportunity. Returning to his native province of Okini, Lavin hired himself out as a mercenary soldier until he was hired by Fifth Regional Community Congress Representative Ronan Kaifi. Kaifi, who had become a vocal critic of the Empire's policies since the end of the Spike War, feared for his life and the life of his family after a number of outspoken local community leaders who criticized the Empire were either killed or kidnapped by unknown parties, although many of these critics believed the wave of assassinations and abductions were orchestrated by the Red King himself. Thus, Kaifi hired Lavin to serve as his personal bodyguard, tasked with shadowing Kaifi and his family wherever they traveled. During this time, Lavin developed a close, sibling-like relationship with Elloe, Kaifi's only daughter. In the years that followed, Kaifi's fears proved very well founded, as Skee preempted several attempts on the politician's life. When a team of three Epsiloni mercenaries were hired to murder Kaifi, it was Lavin who caught wind of the planned assassination and preemptively killed the Epsiloni while they were en route to Kaifi's home. Although Kaifi suspected the Empire's involvement in the assassination attempts, he was not silenced and continued to protest against the injustice he perceived in the Empire's policies, such as the increase in tribute to support the Emperor's war against the Fillians.

But in early 566 Post, a contingent of ten Death's Heads stormed into the Kaifi residence, abducting Kaifi, Elloe, and Lavin, who were held without charges and transported to the Maw. After Kaifi was vaporized by the Maw trainer, Lavin and Elloe joined forces with a team of gladiators led by the Kronan Korg and the Terran Hulk. When Elloe was imprisoned after showing support for a group of Fillian terrorists on board a Pleasure Cruiser, Lavin blamed himself for not being there to protect her. Shortly after, while competing in a gladiator match, Lavin was mortally wounded when an Imperial Dreadnought dropped a Deathfire Bomb on the arena. Refusing to go down without a fight, Lavin grabbed the hilt of his sword one final time and charged into battle against a battalion of Death's Head units. Although Lavin did not survive, his death forged an even stronger bond between his teammates.

ABILITIES/TECHNIQUES: As a former captain in the Imperial Guard with many years of experience, Lavin Skee was trained in several forms of hand-to-hand combat and was an excellent military strategist. His only drawback was his pride, often opting to fight until the bitter end rather than retreating to fight another day.

In the arena, Lavin relied primarily on his military combat training to deftly outmaneuver opponents. He hurled spears in long-range combat but preferred his broadsword in hand-to-hand battles.

EMERGENCY ADDRESS: THE GREEN SCAR

The Red King's Address to the Emergency Session of the Imperial Senate, 566 Post:

"Friends, senators, governors, and trusted advisors,

I have called an Emergency Session of the Imperial Senate on this 370th day of the year 566 Post to address a very important crisis facing our beloved Empire – the beast known as the Green Scar. In his short time on our planet, this uncivilized offlander has caused nothing but trouble for our society. Unlike the wildebot pests or the great devil corkers which only target isolated populations, the Green Scar threatens to unravel the very fabric of our great Imperial civilization."

"To deal with this problem, I have dispatched Caiera the Oldstrong, my personal Warbound Shadow and First Lieutenant of the Imperial Guard, as well as Denobo Aruc III, the esteemed Governor of Wukar Province, into the field. Together, they will lead an elite coalition of the Imperial Guard and the Death's Head Warguard who are tasked with hunting down the Green Scar and capturing him so that he can be brought back to the Great Arena where he belongs, performing for our amusement."

"But, since the silver squares of the Imperial Treasury have already been earmarked to pay for the cost of our offensives against the Fillian terrorists, I regret to inform you that the Empire once again has no other choice but to assess increased tributes to finance our ongoing hunt for the Green Scar and his alliance of wayward slaves. A brief review of the Green Scar's activities on Sakaar clearly demonstrate the necessity of the tribute increase which will ensure his timely capture:"

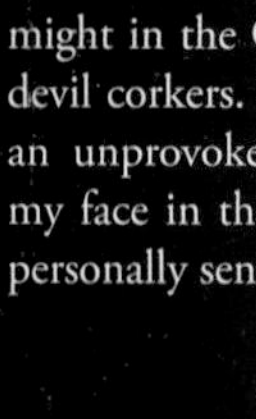

"Seconds after first setting foot on our planet, the brutish Green Scar immediately attacked a helpless hive of Natives. Luckily, the Governor of Wukar was on hand to defend the innocent Natives from the rampaging man-beast with a well-placed Neuro-Dart. The Green Scar was then sold to Imperial League promoter Primus Vand, who tested his otherworldly might in the Great Arena against a pair of ill-tempered great devil corkers. But after the man-beast prevailed, he launched an unprovoked attack against me, the Red King, scarring my face in the process. For his crimes against the Empire, I personally sentenced the Green Scar to the Maw."

"Unfortunately, the Green Scar survive[d] time in the Maw and joined forces with a [number] of his fellow slave-warrior survivors. Toge[ther] they were flown to the Chaleen Plains w[here] they defeated the notorious Egg-Breaker [and] his pack of wildebots before they were in[vited] on board one of the Empire's Pleasure Cru[isers] and confronted by a cell of Fillian terr[orists] who sought to recruit the Green Scar into their cause."

"The Green Scar and his allies again [saw] combat in the Great Arena, where they [were] attacked by an Imperial Warnought! Bu[t the] team survived the attack and assaulted a l[egion] of our finest Death's Heads units immed[iately] afterward. Although one of their number [was] killed in the melee, the Green Scar an[d his] allies formed an even closer bond as a res[ult]."

"In the main event of the Spring Games[, the] Green Scar's team was to battle the Imp[erial] League's newest gladiatorial sensation – [the] Silver Savage. But as soon as the battle sta[rted] the Green Scar's team demonstrated [their] cowardice by engaging in five-on-one ta[ctics] against their cosmic-powered competitor[.] Silver Savage eventually succumbed to [the] Green Scar's dirty tactics and was inadvertently freed [from] his obedience disk, which led him to use his cosmic pow[er to] destroy the obedience disks of all other slaves in his proxi[mity.] In the chaos that ensued, the Green Scar and his allies man[aged] to breach the Great Arena's walls, escape the Crown City [and] flee into the Twisted Wood where they have remained fugi[tives] ever since."

"Who knows what the Green Scar dr[eams] of in his slumber? I am willing to bet h[e has] nightmares of his impending defeat by [the] Empire!"